MULTIPARTY DEMOCRACY

This book adapts a formal model of elections and legislative politics to study party politics in Israel, Italy, the Netherlands, Britain, and the United States. The approach uses the idea of valence—that is, the party leader's nonpolicy electoral popularity—and employs survey data to model these elections. The analysis explains why small parties in Israel and Italy keep to the electoral periphery. In the Netherlands, Britain, and the United States, the electoral model is extended to include the behavior of activists. In the case of Britain, it is shown that there will be contests between activists for the two main parties over who controls policy. Regarding the recent 2005 election, it is argued that the losses of the Labour Party were due to Blair's falling valence. For the United States, the model gives an account of the rotation of the locations of the two major parties over the last century.

Norman Schofield is the William Taussig Professor in Political Economy at Washington University in St. Louis. He served as Fulbright Distinguished Professor of American Studies at Humboldt University Berlin in 2003–4 and held a Fellowship at the Center for Advanced Study in the Behavioral Sciences at Stanford in 1988–9. Professor Schofield is the author of *Architects of Political Change* (Cambridge University Press, 2006), *Mathematical Methods in Economics and Social Choice* (2003), *Multiparty Government* (coauthored with Michael Laver, 1990), and *Social Choice and Democracy* (1985). He received the William Riker Prize in 2002 for contributions to political theory and was co-recipient with Gary Miller of the Jack L. Walker Prize for the best article on political organizations and parties in the *American Political Science Review* for 2002–4.

Itai Sened is professor and chair of the Department of Political Science at Washington University in St. Louis. He is also the director of the Center for New Institutional Social Sciences there since 2000 and formerly taught at Tel Aviv University. Professor Sened is coauthor (with Gideon Doron) of *Political Bargaining: Theory, Practice, and Process* (2001), author of *The Political Institution of Private Property* (Cambridge University Press, 1997), and coeditor (with Jack Knight) of *Explaining Social Institutions* (1995). His research has been published in leading journals such as the *American Journal of Political Science*, *Journal of Politics*, *Journal of Theoretical Politics*, *British Journal of Political Science*, and the *European Journal of Political Research*.

POLITICAL ECONOMY OF INSTITUTIONS AND DECISIONS

Series Editor

Stephen Ansolabehere, Massachusetts Institute of Technology

Founding Editors

James E. Alt, Harvard University
Douglass C. North, Washington University, St. Louis

Other Books in the Series

Alberto Alesina and Howard Rosenthal, *Partisan Politics, Divided Government, and the Economy*

Lee J. Alston, Thráinn Eggertsson, and Douglass C. North, eds., *Empirical Studies in Institutional Change*

Lee J. Alston and Joseph P. Ferrie, *Southern Paternalism and the Rise of the American Welfare State: Economics, Politics, and Institutions, 1865–1965*

James E. Alt and Kenneth Shepsle, eds., *Perspectives on Positive Political Economy*

Josephine T. Andrews, *When Majorities Fail: The Russian Parliament, 1990–1993*

Jeffrey S. Banks and Eric A. Hanushek, eds., *Modern Political Economy: Old Topics, New Directions*

Yoram Barzel, *Economic Analysis of Property Rights*, 2nd edition

Yoram Barzel, *A Theory of the State: Economic Rights, Legal Rights, and the Scope of the State*

Robert Bates, *Beyond the Miracle of the Market: The Political Economy of Agrarian Development in Kenya*, 2nd edition

Charles M. Cameron, *Veto Bargaining: Presidents and the Politics of Negative Power*

Kelly H. Chang, *Appointing Central Bankers: The Politics of Monetary Policy in the United States and the European Monetary Union*

Peter Cowhey and Mathew McCubbins, eds., *Structure and Policy in Japan and the United States: An Institutionalist Approach*

Gary W. Cox, *The Efficient Secret: The Cabinet and the Development of Political Parties in Victorian England*

Continued on page following Index

MULTIPARTY DEMOCRACY

Elections and Legislative Politics

NORMAN SCHOFIELD AND ITAI SENED

Washington University in St. Louis

CAMBRIDGE
UNIVERSITY PRESS

CAMBRIDGE UNIVERSITY PRESS
Cambridge, New York, Melbourne, Madrid, Cape Town, Singapore, São Paulo

Cambridge University Press
32 Avenue of the Americas, New York, NY 10013-2473, USA

www.cambridge.org
Information on this title: www.cambridge.org/9780521450355

First published 2006

Printed in the United States of America

A catalog record for this publication is available from the British Library.

Library of Congress Cataloging in Publication Data

Schofield, Norman, 1944–
Multiparty democracy : elections and legislative politics / Norman Schofield and
Itai Sened.
    p.   cm. – (Political economy of institutions and decisions)
Includes bibliographical references and index.
ISBN-13:   978-0-521-45035-5 (hardback)
ISBN-10:   0-521-45035-7 (hardback)
ISBN-13:   978-0-521-45658-6 (pbk.)
ISBN-10:   0-521-45658-4 (pbk.)
    1. Political parties.   2. Democracy.   3. Elections.
I. Sened, Itai.   II. Title.   III. Series.
JF2051.S283   2006
324.9–dc22   2006005639

ISBN-13:   978-0-521-45035-5   hardback
ISBN-10:   0-521-45035-7   hardback

ISBN-13:   978-0-521-45658-6   paperback
ISBN-10:   0-521-45658-4   paperback

For Elizabeth and Sarit

Contents

ix

Contents

Contents

List of Tables and Figures

TABLES

FIGURES

List of Tables and Figures

xv

Preface

This book closes a phase of a research program that has kept us busy for more than ten years. It sets out a theory of multiparty electoral politics and evaluates this theory with data from Israel, Italy, the Netherlands, Britain, and the United States.

Four decades ago, our teacher and mentor, William H. Riker, started this effort with *The Theory of Political Coalitions* (1962). What is perhaps not remembered now is that Riker's motivation in writing this book came from a question that he had raised in his much earlier book, *Democracy in the United States* (1953): Why did political competition in the United States seem to result in roughly equally sized political coalitions of disparate interests? His answer was that minimal-winning coalitions were efficient means of dividing the political spoil. This answer was, of course, not complete, because it left out elections—the method by which parties gain political power in a democracy. His later book, *Positive Political Theory* (1973), with Peter Ordeshook, summed up the theory available at that time, on two-party elections. The main conclusion was that parties would tend to converge to an electoral center—either the median or mean of the electoral distribution. Within a few years, this convenient theoretical conclusion was shown to be dependent on assumptions about the low dimension of the policy space. The chaos results that came in the 1970s were, however, only applicable to two-party elections where there was no voter uncertainty. With voter uncertainty, it was still presumed that the mean voter theorem would be valid. The chaos theorem did indicate that in parliaments where the dimension was low and where parties varied in strength, stability would occur, particularly if there were a large centrally located or dominant party. Indirectly, this led to a reawakening of interest in completing Riker's coalition program. Now, the task was to examine the post-election situation in Parliament, taking party positions and strengths as given, and to use variants of rational choice theory to determine what government would form. While a number of useful attempts were made in this endeavor, they still provided only a partial solution, since elections themselves lay outside the theory. One impediment to combining a theory of election with a theory of coalition was that the dominant model of election predicted that parties would be indistinguishable—all located at the electoral mean, and all of equal size.

A key theoretical argument of this book is that this mean voter theorem is invalid when voters judge parties on the basis of evaluation of competence rather than just proposed policy. Developing this new theorem came about because of an apparent paradox resulting from work with our colleagues Daniela Giannetti, Andrew Martin, Gary Miller, David Nixon, Robert Parks, Kevin Quinn, and Andrew Whitford. On the basis of logit and probit models of the Netherlands, it was found by simulation that parties could have increased their vote by moving to the center. However, when the same simulation was performed using an empirical model for Israel in 1988, no such convergence was observed. Some later work on the United States then brought home the significance of Madison's remark in *Federalist 10* about "the probability of a fit choice." The party constants in the estimations could be viewed as valences, modelling the judgments made of the parties by the electorate. These judgments varied widely in the case of Israel, somewhat less so in Italy and Britain, and even less so in the Netherlands. The electoral theorem presented in Chapter 3 shows that if electoral uncertainty is not too high and electoral judgments are sufficiently varied, parties will, in equilibrium, locate themselves in different political "niches," some of which will be far from the electoral center. Immediately we have an explanation both for the occurrence of radical parties and for Duverger's (1954) hypothesis about the empty electoral center.

This book attempts to combine the resulting theory of elections with a theory of government formation, applicable both to polities with electoral systems based on proportional representation (or PR), such as Israel, Italy, and the Netherlands, but also to polities such as Britain and the United States with electoral systems based on plurality or "first past the post." Essentially we propose that, under PR, pure vote maximization is tempered by the beliefs of party leaders about the logic of coalition formation. Under the plurality electoral mechanism, party coalitions must typically occur before the election, and this induces competition between the activists within each party. Naturally, this model raises many new topics of theoretical concern, particularly since we combine notions of both non-cooperative game theory and social choice theory. Because the theoretical model presented here is quite abstract and technically demanding, we suggest that only the first section of Chapter 3 is covered on first reading. The formal sections of this chapter on electoral uncertainty and on the heart can be left for reading after the more substantive chapters have been examined.

Over the years, we have been fortunate to receive a number of National Science Foundation awards, most recently grant SES 0241732. Schofield wishes to express his appreciation for this support and for further support from the Fulbright Foundation, from Humboldt University, and from Washington University during his sabbatical leave from 2002 to 2003. We are also very grateful to the Weidenbaum Center at Washington University for research support. We thank Martin Battle and Dganit Ofek for research collaboration, and Alexandra Shankster, Cherie Moore, and Ben Klemens for help in preparing the manuscript. John Duggan made a number of perceptive remarks on the proof of the electoral theorem. Jeff Banks was always ready with insights about our earlier efforts to develop the formal model. Jim Adams and Michael Laver shared our enthusiasm for modelling the political world.

Our one regret is that Jeffrey Banks, Richard McKelvey, and William Riker are not here to see the results of our efforts. They would all have enjoyed the theory, and Bill, especially, would have appreciated our desire to use theory in an attempt to understand the real world. This book is dedicated to the memory of our friends.

Norman Schofield and Itai Sened.
St. Louis, Missouri, April 14, 2006

I

Multiparty Democracy

When Parliament first appeared as an innovative political institution, it was to solve a simple bargaining problem: Rich constituents would bargain with the King to determine how much they wished to pay for services granted them by the King, such as fighting wars and providing some assurances for the safety of their travel and property rights.

In the modern polity, governments have greatly expanded their size and the range and sphere of their services, while constituents have come to pay more taxes to cover the ever-growing price tag of these services. Consequently, parliamentary systems and parliamentary political processes have become more complex, involving more constituents and making policy recommendations and decisions that reach far beyond decisions of war and peace and basic property rights. But the center of the entire bargaining process in democratic parliamentary systems is still Parliament.

Globalization trends in politics and economics do not bypass, but pass *through* local governments. They do not diminish but increase pressure and demands put on national governments. These governments that used to be sovereign in their territories and decision spheres are now constantly feeling globalization pressures in every aspect of their decision-making processes. Some of these governments can deal with the extra pressures while others are struggling. A majority of these governments are coalition governments in parliamentary systems. Unlike the U.S. presidential system, parliamentary systems are not based on checks and balances but on a more literal interpretation of representation. Turnouts are much higher in elections, more parties represent more shades of individual preferences, and the polity is much more politicized in paying daily attention to daily politics. But in the end, the coalition government is endowed with remarkable power to make decisions about allocations of scarce resources that are rarely challenged by any other serious political player in the polity. In short, the future of globalization depends on a very specific set of rules in predominantly parliamentary systems that govern most of the national constituents of the emerging new global order (Przeworski et al., 2000). These sets of rules that constrain and determine how the voice of the people is translated to economic allocations of scarce resources are the subject of our book.

Over the last four decades, inspired by the seminal work of the late William H. Riker—*The Theory of Political Coalitions* (1962)—much theoretical work has been done that leads to a fair amount of accumulated knowledge on the subject. This book is aimed at three parallel goals. First, we enhance this fairly developed body of theory with new theoretical insights. Second, we confront our theoretical results with empirical evidence we have been collecting and analyzing with students and colleagues in the past decade, introducing, in the process, the new Bayesian statistical approach of empirical research to the field of study of parliamentary systems. Finally, we want to make what we know, in regards to both theory and empirical analysis, available to those who study the new democracies in Eastern Europe, South America, Africa, and Asia.

Since the collapse of the Soviet Union in the early 1990s, many countries in Eastern Europe, and even Russia itself, have become democratic. Most of these newcomers to the family of democratic regimes have fashioned their government structures after the model of Western European multiparty parliamentary systems. In doing so, they hoped to emulate the success of their western brethren. However, recent events suggest that even those more mature democratic polities can be prone to radicalism, as indicated by the recent surprising success of Le Pen in France, or the popularity of radical right parties in Austria (led by Haider) and Netherlands (led by Fortuyn).

In Eastern Europe, the use of proportional representative electoral systems has often made it difficult for centrist parties to cooperate and succeed in government. Proportional representation (PR) has also led to difficulties in countries with relatively long-established democratic systems. In Turkey, for example, a fairly radical fundamentalist party gained control of the government. In Israel, PR led to a degree of parliamentary fragmentation and government instability. These problems have greatly contributed to the particular difficulties presently facing any attempt at peace negotiations between Israelis and Palestinians.

In Russia, the fragmentation of political support in the Duma is a consequence of the peculiar mixed PR electoral system in use. Finally, in Argentina, and possibly Mexico, a multiparty system and presidential power may have contributed to populist politics and economic collapse in the former and disorder in the latter.

In all of the above cases, the interplay of electoral politics and the complexities of coalitional bargaining have induced puzzling outcomes. In general, scholars study these different countries under the rubric of "comparative" politics. In fact, however, there is very little that is truly "comparative," in the sense of being based on generalized inductive or deductive reasoning.

Starting in the early 1970s, scholars used Riker's theoretical insights in an empirical context, focusing mostly on West European coalition governments. This early mix of empirical and theoretical work on Europe by Browne and Franklin (1973), Laver and Taylor (1973), and Schofield (1976) provided some insights into political coalition governments. However, by the early 1980s it became clear that, to succeed, this research program needed to be extended to incorporate both empirical work on elections and more sophisticated work on political bargaining (Schofield and Laver, 1985).

The considerable amount of work done during the last few decades on election analysis, party identification, and institutional analysis has tended to focus on the United States, a unique two-party, presidential system. Unfortunately, most of this research has not been integrated with a theoretical framework that is applicable to multiparty systems. In two-party systems such as the United States, if the "policy space" comprises a single dimension, then a standard result known as the *median voter* theorem indicates that parties will converge to the median, centrist voter ideal point. It can be shown that even when there are more than two parties, then as long as politics is "unidimensional," then all candidates will converge to the median (Feddersen, Sened, and Wright, 1990). It is well known, however, that in multiparty proportional-rule electoral systems, parties do not converge to the political center (Cox, 1990). Part of the explanation for this difference may come from the fact that a standard assumption of models of two-party elections is that the parties or candidates adopt policies to maximize votes (or seats). In multiparty proportional-rule elections (that is, with three or more parties), it is not obvious that a party should rationally try to maximize votes. Indeed, small parties that are centrally located may be assured of joining government. In fact, in multiparty systems another phenomenon occurs. Small parties often adopt radical positions, ensure enough votes to gain parliamentary representation, and bargain aggressively in an attempt to affect government policy from the sidelines (Schofield and Sened, 2002). Thus, many of the assumptions of theorists that appear plausible in a two-party context, are implausible in a multiparty context.

In 1987, the National Science Foundation (under Grant SES 8521151) funded a conference with 18 participants at the European University Institute in Fiesole near Florence. The purpose of the conference was to bring together rational choice theorists and scholars with an empirical focus, in an effort to make clear to theorists that their models, while applicable to two-party situations, needed generalization to multiparty situations. At the same time, it was hoped that new theoretical ideas would be of use to the empirical scholars in their attempt to understand the complexities of West European multiparty politics. This was in anticipation of, but prior to, the collapse of the communist regimes in Eastern Europe. A book edited by Budge, Robertson, and Hearl (1987) analyzed party manifestos in West European polities and these data provided the raw material for discussion among the participants in the Fiesole Conference. The conference led to a number of original theoretical papers (Austen-Smith and Banks, 1988, 1990; Baron and Ferejohn, 1989; Schofield, Grofman and Feld, 1989; Laver and Shepsle, 1990; Schofield, 1993; Sened, 1995, 1996), three books (Laver and Schofield, 1990; Shepsle, 1990; Laver and Shepsle, 1996) and several edited volumes (Laver and Budge, 1992; Barnett, Hinich and Schofield, 1993; Laver and Shepsle, 1994; Barnett et al., 1995; Schofield, 1996).

Just as these works were being published in the mid-1990s, new statistical techniques began to revolutionize the field of empirical research in political science. This school of *Bayesian* statistics allows for the construction of a new generation of much more refined statistical models of electoral competition (Schofield et al., 1998; Quinn, Martin, and Whitford, 1999). These new techniques, and much-improved computer hardware and software, allowed, in turn, the study of more refined theoretical models (Schofield, Sened, and Nixon, 1998; Schofield and Sened, 2002). We are only in the beginning of this new era of the study of multiparty political systems.

The collapse of the Soviet Union and its satellite communist regimes and democratization trends in South America, Eastern Europe, and Africa create an urgency and a wealth of new cases and data to feed this research program with new challenges of immediate and obvious practical relevance. In particular, the domain of empirical concerns has grown considerably to cover new substantive areas including:

1. The rise of radical parties in Western Europe;
2. Cooperation and coalition formation in East European politics;
3. Fragmentation in politics in the Middle East and Russia;
4. Presidentialism and multiparty politics in Latin America; and
5. Policy implications of parliamentary and coalition politics.

Our book is motivated and guided by the vision of the late William H. Riker who believed that the process of forming coalitions was at the core of all politics, whether in presidential systems, such as in the United States, or in the multiparty systems common in Europe. In his writings, he argued that it was possible to create a theoretically sound, deductively structured, and empirically relevant science of politics. We hope this book will carry forward the research program Riker (1953) first envisioned more than fifty years ago.

On the practical side, we want our work to help developed and developing countries to better structure their institutions to benefit the communities they serve. In the end, stable democracies, even more so in a global order, are a necessary condition for popular benefits. And it is quite astonishing how directly relevant and how important is the set of rules that govern the conduct of government in democratic systems. It is this set of rules that will be at the center of attention in this book.

The particular cases we study are established democratic systems in Israel, Italy, the Netherlands, Britain, and the United States. This focus has allowed us to obtain electoral information and interpret it in a historical context. Given the theoretical framework developed in Chapter 3, we believe that our findings also apply to the new members of the family of democratic systems and can be used in these new environments. Only such new tests can genuinely establish the validity of our theoretical claims and empirical observations.

In pure parliamentary systems, parties run for elections, citizens elect members of these parties to fill seats in Parliaments, members of the Parliament form coalition governments, and these governments make the decisions on the distribution of resource allocations and the implementation of alternative policies. Even in the United States, there is the necessity for coordination or coalition between members of Congress and the President.

Once a government is in power, constituents have little, if any, influence on the allocation of scarce resources. Thus, much of the bargaining process takes place prior to and during the electoral campaign. Candidates who run for office promise to implement different policies. Voters supposedly guard against electing candidates unless they have promised policy positions to their liking. When candidates fail to deliver, voters have the next election to reconstruct the bargain with the same or new candidates.

Preferences are not easily aggregated from the individual level to the collective level of Parliament and transformed into social choices. There exists no mechanism that can aggregate individual preferences into well-behaved social preference orders without violating one or another well-established requirements of democratic choice mechanisms (Arrow, 1951). Individuals' preferences are present mostly inasmuch as they motivate social agents to act in the bargaining game set up by the institutional constraints and rules that define the parliamentary system. Members of Parliament or of Congress take the preferences of their constituents into account if they want to be elected or re-elected. Government thus consists of parliamentary or congressional members who are bound by their pre-electoral commitment to their voters.

The difficulty in detecting a clear relationship between promises made to voters and actual distributions of national resources is a result of the complexity of the process. At each level, agents are engaged in a bargaining process that yields results that are then carried to the next stage. Each layer of the bargaining process is, in large degree, obscure to us, and the interconnections between the multiple layers makes the outcome even more difficult to understand.

In this book we study the mechanism that requires government officials to take into account the preferences of their constituents in the political process. Democracy is representative inasmuch as it is based on institutions that make elected officials accountable to their constituents and responsible for their actions in the public domain. This accountability and responsibility are routinely tested in every electoral campaign. The purpose of this book is to clarify how voter preferences come to matter in a democracy-through the bargaining that takes place before and after each electoral campaign, then during the formation of government, and then within the tenure of each Parliament.

According to common wisdom, the essence of democracy is embedded in legislators representing the preferences of their constituents when

Table 1.1. *Political Systems Determined by the Electoral Rule and Party Discipline.*

Party Discipline		Electoral Rule	
		Proportional Rule	Plurality Rule
	Strong	West European Parliamentary Systems	English Westminster
	Weak	Factional	U.S. Presidential

making decisions over how to allocate scarce resources. Schofield et al. (1998: 257) distinguish four generic democratic systems based on two defining features: the electoral rule used and the culture of party discipline. Their observations are summarized in Table 1.1.

The two most common of these four types are the U.S. presidential and the West European parliamentary systems. Our book gives an analysis of the multiparty parliamentary systems of Israel, Italy, and the Netherlands based on PR. We also examine the "plurality" parliamentary system of Britain and the presidential system of the United States. The remarkable quality of studies in this field notwithstanding, our contribution is intended mainly to provide a comprehensive theoretical framework for organizing current and future research in this field.

Austen-Smith and Banks (1988, 2005) have suggested that the essence of a multiparty representative system (MP) is that it is characterized by a social choice mechanism intended to aggregate individual preferences into social choices in four consecutive stages:

1. The pre-electoral stage: Parties position themselves in the relevant policy space by choosing a leader and declaring a manifesto.
2. The election game: Voters choose whether and for whom to vote.
3. Coalition formation: Several parties may need to reach a contract as to how to participate in coalition government.
4. The legislative stage: Policy is implemented as the social choice outcome.

A comprehensive model of an MP game must include all four stages. A good way to think about it is to use the notion of backward induction: To study the outcome of a game with multiple sequential stages we start the analysis at the last stage. We figure out what contingencies may be favored at the last stage of the game and then go back to the previous stage to see if agents can choose their strategies at that earlier stage of the game to obtain a more favorable outcome at the following stage. In the context of the four-stage MP game, to play the coalition bargaining game, parties must have relatively clear expectations about what will happen at the legislative stage. To vote, voters must have expectations about the coalition formation game and the policy outcome of the coalition bargaining game. Finally, to position themselves so as to maximize their expected utility, parties must have clear expectations about voting behavior.

1.2 THE STRUCTURE OF THE BOOK

Chapter 2 introduces the basic concepts of the spatial theory of electoral competition. This is the theoretical framework that we utilize throughout the book. The chapter goes on to characterize the last stage of the MP game or the process by which Parliament determines future policies to implement by offering instances of how party leaders' beliefs about the electoral process and the nature of coalition bargaining will influence the policy choices prior to the election. We provide a nontechnical illustration of the logic of coalition bargaining in Section 2.8. Sections 2.9 and 2.10 provide an outline of the various electoral models we use.

Chapter 3 gives the technical details of the theoretical model we deploy. Unfortunately, the formal aspects of the model are quite daunting. Since the essence of the model is described in Chapter 2, we suggest that the reader pass over Chapter 3 in first reading, perhaps checking back on occasion to get the gist of the principal theorem.

The first part of the chapter gives the formal theory of vote maximization under differing stochastic assumptions. For the various models, the *electoral* theorem shows that there are differing conditions on the parameters of the model which are necessary and sufficient for convergence to the electoral mean. We essentially update Madison's perspective from *Federalist 10,* in which he argues that elections involve judgment, rather than just interests or preferences. We model these electoral judgments by a stochastic variable that we term *valence*. When the electorally perceived valences vary sufficiently among the parties, then low-valence parties have an electoral incentive to adopt radical policy positions. The electoral calculus in the model is then extended to a more general case in which party "principals," or decision makers, have policy preferences.

Chapter 4 begins the empirical modelling of the interaction of parties and voters. We provide an empirical estimation of the elections in 1988, 1992, and 1996 in Israel. The electoral theorem is used to determine where the vote-maximizing equilibria are located. It is shown that the location of the major parties, Labour and Likud, closely match the theoretical prediction of the theorem. We use the mismatch between the theory and estimated location of the low-valence parties to argue that they positioned themselves to gain advantage in coalition negotiation.

In Chapters 5, 6, and 7, we discuss in more detail elections in Italy, the Netherlands, and Britain. In Italy, we observe that the collapse of the political system after 1992 led to the destruction of the "core" location of the dominant Christian Democrat Party. The electoral model effectively predicts party positions, except possibly for the Northern League. In the Netherlands and Britain, the electoral theorem suggests that all parties should have converged to the electoral center. We propose an extension of the electoral theorem to include the effect of activists on electoral judgments. In Britain in particular, the model suggests that the effect of the "exogenous" valence is "centripetal," tending to pull the two major parties toward the electoral center. In contrast, we argue that the effect of party activists on the party's valence generates a "centrifugal" tendency toward the electoral periphery.

Chapter 8 considers the 1964 and 1980 elections in the United States to give a theoretical account, based on activist support, of the transformation that has been observed in the locations of the Republican and Democratic Parties. We suggest that this is an aspect of a *dynamic equilibrium* that has continually affected U.S. politics.

Throughout the book we draw conclusions from the empirical evidence to show how the basic electoral model can be extended to include coalition bargaining and activist support. These empirical chapters are based on work undertaken with our colleagues over the last ten years. The theoretical argument in Chapter 3 is drawn from Schofield and Sened (2002) and Schofield (2004, 2006b). Chapter 4 is adapted from Schofield and Sened (2005a) as well as earlier work in Schofield, Sened, and Nixon (1998). The analysis of Italy in Chapter 5 is based on Giannetti and Sened (2004). The study of elections in the Netherlands, given in Chapter 6, is based on Schofield et al. (1998), Quinn, Martin, and Whitford (1999), and Schofield and Sened (2005b). The work on the British election of 1979 in Chapter 7 uses the data and probit analysis of Quinn, Martin, and Whitford (1999), and the analysis of the 1992 and 1997 elections comes from Schofield (2005a,b). Chapter 8 discusses U.S. elections using a model introduced in Miller and Schofield (2003) and Schofield, Miller, and Martin (2003). In a companion volume, Schofield (2006a) presents a more detailed narrative of these events in U.S. political history.

1.3 ACKNOWLEDGMENTS

Material in this volume is reprinted with permission from the following sources:

D. Giannetti and I. Sened. 2004. "Party Competition and Coalition Formation: Italy 1994–1996." *The Journal of Theoretical Politics* 16:483–515. (Sage Publications)

G. Miller and N. Schofield. 2003."Activists and Partisan Realignment." *The American Political Science Review* 97:245–260. (Cambridge University Press)

N. Schofield. 1997. "Multiparty Electoral Politics." In D. Mueller [Ed.]. *Perspectives on Public Choice.* (Cambridge University Press)

N. Schofield. 2002. "Representative Democracy as Social Choice." In K. Arrow, A. Sen, and K. Suzumura [Eds.]. *The Handbook of Social Choice and Welfare.* New York: North Holland. (Elsevier Science)

N. Schofield. 2003. "Valence Competition in the Spatial Stochastic Model." *The Journal of Theoretical Politics* 15:371–383. (Sage Publications)

N. Schofield. 2004. "Equilibrium in the Spatial Valence Model of Politics." *The Journal of Theoretical Politics* 16:447–481. (Sage Publications)

N. Schofield. 2005a. "Local Political Equilibria." In D. Austen-Smith and J. Duggan [Eds.]. *Social Choice and Strategic Decisions: Essays in Honor of Jeffrey S. Banks.* (Kluwer Academic Publishers and Springer Science and Business Media)

N. Schofield. 2005b. "A Valence Model of Political Competition in Britain: 1992–1997." *Electoral Studies* 24:347–370. (Elsevier Science)

N. Schofield, A. Martin, K. Quinn, and A. Whitford. 1998. "Multiparty Electoral Competition in the Netherlands and Germany: A Model Based on Multinomial Probit." *Public Choice* 97:257–293. (Kluwer Academic Publishers and Springer Science and Business Media)

N. Schofield, G. Miller, and A. Martin. 2003. "Critical Elections and Political Realignment in the U.S.: 1860–2000." *Political Studies* 51:217–240. (Blackwell Publishers)

N. Schofield and I. Sened. 2002. "Local Nash Equilibrium in Multiparty Politics." *Annals of Operations Research* 109:193–210. (Kluwer Academic Publishers and Springer Science and Business Media)

N. Schofield and I. Sened. 2005a. "Modelling the Interaction of Parties, Activists and Voters: Why is the Political Center So Empty?" *European Journal of Political Research* 44:355–390. (Blackwell Publishers)

N. Schofield and I. Sened. 2005b. "Multiparty Competition in Israel: 1988–1996." *British Journal of Political Science* 35:635–663. (Cambridge University Press)

2

Elections and Democracy

2.1 ELECTORAL COMPETITION

[I]t may be concluded that a pure democracy, by which I mean a society, consisting of a small number of citizens, who assemble and administer the government in person, can admit of no cure for the mischiefs of faction.... Hence it is that such democracies have ever been spectacles of turbulence and contention; have ever been found incompatible with personal security...and have in general been as short in their lives as they have been violent in their deaths.

A republic, by which I mean a government in which the scheme of representation takes place, opens a different prospect....

[I]f the proportion of fit characters be not less in the large than in the small republic, the former will present a greater option, and consequently a greater probability of a fit choice. (Madison, 1787).

It was James Madison's hope that the voters in the Republic would base their choices on judgments about the fitness of the Chief Magistrate. Madison's argument to this effect in *Federalist 10* may very well have been influenced by a book published by Condorcet in Paris in 1785, extracts of which were sent by Jefferson from France with other materials to help Madison in his deliberation about the proper form of government. While Madison and Hamilton agreed about the necessity of leadership in the Republic, there was also reason to fear the exercise of tyranny by the Chief Magistrate as well as the turbulence or mutability of decision making both in a direct democracy and in the legislature. Although passions and interests may sway the electorate, and operate against fit choices, Madison argued that the heterogeneity of the large electorate would cause judgment to be the basis of elections. The form of the electoral college as the method of choosing the Chief Magistrate led to a system of representation that we may label "first past the post" by majority choice. It is intuitively obvious that such a method tends to oblige the various groups in the Republic to form electoral coalitions, usually resulting in two opposed presidential candidates. Of course, many elections have been highly contentious, with three or four contenders. The election of 1800, for example, had Jefferson, Burr, John Adams, and Pinckney in competition. In 1824, John Quincy Adams won the election against Andrew Jackson, William Crawford, and Henry Clay by the majority decision of Congress. In that election, Jackson had the greatest number (a plurality) of electoral college votes (99 out of 261) and a plurality of the popular vote, but not a majority. Perhaps the most contentious of elections was in 1860, when Lincoln won with 40 percent of the popular vote, and 180 electoral college votes out of 303, against Steven Douglas, Breckinridge, and Bell. See Schofield (2006a) for a discussion of this election.

Even though the use of this electoral method for the choice of President may be unsatisfactory from the point of view of direct democracy, it does appear, in general, to "force" a choice on the electorate. Proportional representation (PR), on the other hand, is a very different method rule. In such an electoral method, there is usually a high correlation between the share of the popular vote that a party receives and its representation in Parliament. Depending on the precise nature of the electoral method, there may be little incentive for parliamentary groups to form pre-election political coalitions. As a result, it is usually the case that no party gains a majority of the seats, so that post-election governmental coalitions are necessary. A consequence of this may be a high degree of governmental instability.

Although formal models of elections have been available for many decades, most of them were concerned with constructing a theoretical framework applicable to the United States. The models naturally concentrated on two-party competition, where the assumed motivation of each of the contenders was to gain a majority of the votes. As the remarks just made suggest, even such a framework is unable to deal with a number of the most interesting elections in U.S. history, where there are more than two candidates, and "winning" is not the same as vote maximization. More importantly, from our perspective, these models did not easily generalize to the situation of PR, where no party could expect to win.

The work presented here is an attempt to present an integrated theory of multiparty competition that can be applied, at least in principle, to polities with differing electoral systems.

2.2 TWO-PARTY COMPETITION UNDER PLURALITY RULE

The early formal models of two-party competition leave much to be desired. It seems self-evident that presidential candidates offer very different policies to the electorate. Although the members of Congress of the same party differ widely in the policies they individually espouse, there is an obvious difference in the general policy characteristics of the two parties. The Republican Party Manifesto that was intended to herald a new era of Republican dominance in 1994 could not be mistaken for the declaration of the Democrat Party. The variety of results known as the *median voter* theorem (Hotelling, 1929; Downs, 1957; Black, 1958; Riker and Ordeshook, 1973) were all based on the "deterministic" assumption that each voter picked the party with the nearest policy position. Assuming that policies necessarily resided in a single dimension, the effort by each contender to win a majority would oblige them to choose the policy position of the median voter. Such a voter's preferred policy is characterized by the feature that half the voters lie on the left of the position, and half on the right. This result can be generalized to the case with multiple candidates and costly campaigns (Fedderson, Sened, and Wright, 1990) or uncertainty in party location (McKelvey and Ordeshook, 1985), but it is crucial to the argument that there be only one dimension.

A corrective to this formal result was what became known as the *chaos* theorem. This was the conclusion of a long research effort from Plott (1967) to Saari (1996) and Austen-Smith and Banks (1999). An illustration of this theorem is given below. It was valid for two-party competition only, and assumed that the motivation of candidates was to gain a majority of the popular vote. Whether or not candidates had intrinsic policy preferences, these were assumed irrelevant to the desire to win. One variety of the theorem showed that in two dimensions, it was generally the case that no matter what position the first candidate took, there was a position available to the second that was winning. One way of expressing this is that there would be no two-party equilibrium, or so-called *core* (Schofield, 1983). As a consequence, candidates could, in principle, adopt indeterminate positions (McKelvey, 1976). In three dimensions, candidate positions could end up at the electoral periphery (McKelvey and Schofield, 1987).

Figure 2.1 gives an illustration with just three voters and preferred positions A, B, and C. The sequence of positions $\{x, a, b, c, d, e, f, g, h, y,\}$ is a majority trajectory, from x to y, with y beating h beating g, etc., and a beating x.

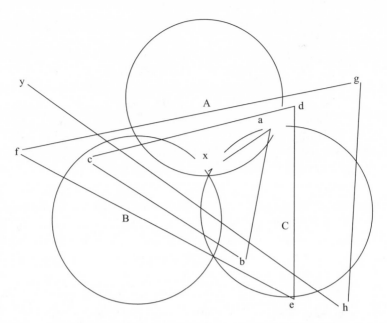

Figure 2.1. An illustration of instabiliy under deterministic voting with three voters with preferred points A, B, and C.

A third class of results assumed that candidates deal with this chaos through ambiguity in their policies, by "mixing" their declarations. The results by Kramer (1978) and Banks, Duggan, and Le Breton (2002) suggest again that candidate policies will lie close to the electoral center.

Yet another set of results weakened the assumption that voters were "deterministic" and instead allowed for a *stochastic* component in voter choice (Hinich, 1977). The recent work by McKelvey and Patty (2005) and Banks and Duggan (2005) has formalized the model of voter choice in two-party elections, where each candidate attempts to maximize expected plurality (the difference between the candidate's expected share and the opposition's) and has shown, essentially that the equilibrium is one where both candidates converge to the mean of the voter distribution.

Although Madison may have feared for the incoherence of voter choice, and his fears are, in essence reflected in the chaos theorem, there seems little evidence of the strong conclusion that may be drawn, that "anything can happen in politics" (Riker, 1980, 1982a). What does appear to be true, however, is that policy is mutable: One party wins and tries to implement its declared policy, and then later the opposition party wins, tries to undo the previous policies, and implement its own. If this is at all close to the nature of politics, then neither the median voter theorem, nor its stochastic variant has much to say about real politics.

2.3 MULTIPARTY REPRESENTATIVE DEMOCRACY

We consider that the aforementioned formal results, purporting to show the predominance of a centripetal tendency toward the electoral center in representative democracy, are fundamentally flawed. The reason is that they do not pay heed to Madison's belief that elections involve judgments as well as interests. We show by empirical studies of elections from five polities that judgments *do* form part of the utility calculus of voters. The weight given to judgment, rather than to preference in the stochastic vote model, we call *valence*. The studies show that adding valence to the empirical model enhances the statistical significance, as indicated by the so-called Bayes' factor. When these valence terms are included in the formal model, then convergence to the electoral mean depends on an easily computed "convergence coefficient." When the necessary conditions, given in our Theorems 3.1 and 3.2, are violated, then not all parties will locate at the electoral center. In fact, low-valence parties will find that their vote-maximizing positions are at the electoral periphery. We show that this prediction from the formal model accords quite well with the actual positioning of parties in Israel and Italy. We draw from this our main hypothesis.

Hypothesis 2.1: *A primary objective of all parties in a representative democracy is to adopt policy positions that maximize electoral support.*

We can test this hypothesis by using the parameter estimates of the empirical models to determine whether the actual locations of parties accord with the estimated equilibrium positions as indicated by the formal model. Our analyses indicate that for Israel and Italy there is a degree of concordance between empirical and formal analyses. The formal analysis indicates that the high-valence parties in Israel—Labour and Likud—should adopt positions relatively close to, but not precisely at, the electoral mean, but that the low-valence parties, such as Shas, should position themselves at the electoral periphery. The concordance is close, but not exact. The model we propose to account for the discrepancy between theory and fact in multiparty polities takes account of the policy preferences of parties in the sense that they are concerned to position themselves in the pre-election situation, so as to better their chances of membership in governing coalition.

> **Hypothesis 2.2:** *Any discrepancy between the estimated equilibrium positions of parties obtained from the application of Hypothesis 2.1 in polities based on proportional electoral methods arises because of the requirement of party leaders to consider post-election coalition negotiation.*

To evaluate this hypothesis in a formal fashion it is necessary to attempt to model how party leaders form beliefs about the effect their policy declarations have on the formation of post-election coalition government.

Obviously, considerations about coalition negotiation cannot be used to account for discrepancies between the theory derived from Hypothesis 2.1 and the location of parties in plurality polities such as Britain and the United States, if only because coalition formation, if it occurs, would be a pre-election phenomenon.

One way to adapt Hypothesis 2.1 is to extend the idea of valence, so that it is not exogenously determined, but is, instead, the consequence of the actions of activists who contribute time and resources to enhance the perceived valence of the party, or party candidate, in the electorate. This gives us our third hypothesis.

> **Hypothesis 2.3:** *Any discrepancy between the estimated equilibrium positions of parties obtained from the application of Hypothesis 2.1 in polities based on plurality electoral systems arises because the valence of each party is a function of activist support. When the model is transformed to account for activist valence, then the positions of parties should be in equilibrium with respect to vote maximization.*

Because of our ambition to present a unified theory of political choice, we are obliged to construct a theory for an arbitrary number, p, of parties (where p may be 2 or more) competing in a policy space X of dimension w. We hope to relate the theory that we present to empirical analyses drawn from five polities. Two of these (Israel and the Netherlands) use electoral systems for the Parliament that are based on PR. Israel in particular has a large number of parties. In addition, it used a plurality method for the selection of the Prime Minister in 1996. A third polity, Italy, used PR until 1992, but then adopted a mixed PR/plurality electoral method. The fourth polity, Britain, uses plurality rule, but has more than two parties.

The last polity we consider is the United States, but we start the discussion with the four-candidate election of 1860.

We suppose that the set of parties $P = \{1, \ldots, j, \ldots, p\}$ is exogenously determined. In fact, the number of parties competing with each other can vary from election to election. In principle, it should be possible to model the formation of new parties from activist groups. Our discussion of the United States in Chapter 8 suggests how this might be done.

Similarly, we use $N = \{1, \ldots, i, \ldots, n\}$ to denote the set of voters. Obviously, the set of voters varies from election to election so we should perhaps use a suffix to denote the various elections. As above, we assume that the policy space, X, has dimension w. We do not restrict w in an a priori fashion. There are many ways to determine the nature of X, but our preference is for a methodology based on some large-number electoral sample, by which we can ascertain the basic beliefs or concerns of the members of the voting public. The empirical analyses that we use suggest that only two dimensions are sufficient in each polity to obtain statistically significant models of voter choice.

Because we consider that Hypothesis 2.1 will not be entirely adequate, we shall work back from the post-election legislative phase to the election, and then consider the pre-election selection of party leader and the formation of party policy.

2.4   THE LEGISLATIVE STAGE

In this phase, the party positions are given by an array

$$\mathbb{Z} = (z_1, \ldots, z_j, \ldots, z_p),$$

where each z_j is a policy position in X that is representative of the party. The election that has just occurred has given a vector $V = (V_1, \ldots, V_p)$ of vote shares that has been turned by the electoral system into a vector $S = (S_1, \ldots, S_p)$ of parliamentary seat shares. This vector generates a family $\mathcal{D}$ of winning or decisive coalitions. It is usual, but not absolutely necessary, that $\mathcal{D}$ comprises the family of subsets of P that control at least half the parliamentary seats. Given the set P of parties, and all possible vectors of seat shares we let $\mathbb{D} = \{\mathcal{D}_t : t = 1, \ldots, T\}$ be the set of all possible families of winning coalitions. We regard $\mathbb{D}$ as one way to represent the set of possible election outcomes. We are generally most interested in the situation where *multiparty* refers to the feature that there are at least three parties, so that, in general, each $\mathcal{D}$ will consist of a number of disjoint coalitions. However, we can use some aspects of the model we propose to examine two-party competition. This suggests the following categorization:

2.4.1 *Two-Party Competition with Weakly Disciplined Parties*

This is essentially the situation in the U.S. Congress. From this perspective, every member of the House and Senate could be regarded as a single party, with a policy position representative in some fashion of the member's district or state. Similarly, the President's policy position would be some position made known in the course of the election. The decisive coalition structure, $\mathcal{D}$, is the set of possible decisive coalitions, involving the veto capacity of the President against Congress, and Congress's counterveto capacity (Hammond and Miller, 1987). Analyzing the legislative behavior of Congress is the basis for an extensive literature, but this is not our concern here. However, some aspects of the model we present here may be relevant to the selection of the President through the method of the electoral college. Instead of supposing that every member of Congress is a single party, it could also be supposed that members coalesced into factions, based on policy similarities. Coalition formation involving relatively disciplined factions could then be examined in the context of our model.

2.4.2 *Party Competition under Plurality Rule*

It is well known that plurality rule, or "first past the post," induces a distortion in the translation of vote shares to seat shares, sufficient usually to guarantee that one party or the other gains a majority of the seats. In this case, the decisive coalition, $\mathcal{D}$, can be assumed to be a single party. Under this assumption, the family of all possible government coalitions may be taken to be $\mathbb{D} = \{\mathcal{D}_j : j = 1, \ldots, p\}$, where each $\mathcal{D}_j$ comprises a single party, j. However, even in the case of the British Parliament it is in principle possible for no party to gain a majority. Thus, a more general formulation would be to allow $\mathbb{D}$ to include possible coalitions of parties. In the simpler models of legislative behavior in such a Parliament it is presumed that the majority party leader can control government policy making, with the cooperation of the Cabinet, and through the operation of the Whip. If party j controls a majority, and the policy position of the party leader is z_j, the policy outcome could be assumed to be z_j. However, there will always be some uncertainty in the willingness of the parliamentary members to support a particular position. Consequently, a more general formulation is to suppose that the post-election policy outcome is a "lottery," $\tilde{g}_t$, across various policy positions of different activist groups for the party. We characterize the various activist groups as being led by *party principals*. Chapter 7 on Britain develops this notion.

2.4.3 *Party Competition under Proportional Representation*

It is usual that no party controls a majority of the seats. In such a situation it is natural to assume that bargaining between the parties will be determined by the particular set, $\mathcal{D}_t$, of decisive coalitions that is created by the election. Assuming that the parties are strongly disciplined, so that each party, j, is represented by the policy position, z_j, of its leader, then the policy outcome will also be a lottery—that is, some combination of $\{z_j\}$ and probabilities. In this case, however, the precise lottery will depend on the positions of all parties. Moreover, this lottery will depend on the seat shares of the parties, and thus ultimately on the particular decisive structure, $\mathcal{D}_t$, holding after the election. Since $\mathcal{D}_t$ depends on the election result, and this depends on the vector $\mathbf{z}$ of party positions, we can show this dependence by writing $\tilde{g}_t(\mathbf{z})$ for this lottery.

2.4.4 *Coalition Bargaining*

Sened (1995, 1996) and Banks and Duggan (2000) have modeled bargaining between parties in the post-election phase and have shown that there are essentially two different situations. One situation is where a party, absent a majority, is nonetheless in such a commanding position because of its central position and seat share that it can essentially control policy. In this case, the dominant party, j, is termed a *core party*. The lottery can then be identified with z_j. The second situation is when there is no core party. In this case, bargaining theory suggests that any one of a number of possible coalition governments can come into being. As indicated by the notation, the policy positions and the probabilities associated with each of the governments will depend on $\mathcal{D}_t$ and z. We say *coalitional risk* is associated with the formation of government. In addition there will be bargaining over nonpolicy governmental perquisites. Empirical analyses of portfolio distribution have shown a relation between seat proportions in governing coalitions and portfolio shares (Browne and Franklin, 1973; Laver and Schofield, 1990). If we extend the idea of a post-election lottery to include government perquisites (such as cabinet positions), we can also denote this lottery by $\tilde{g}_t^\alpha(\mathbf{z})$, where α denotes a parameter that governs the tradeoff between policy preferences and perquisites. Obviously, party discipline may be only partial, and the uncertainty associated with the ability of party leaders to control their members will affect the lottery $\tilde{g}_t^\alpha(\mathbf{z})$. We therefore use this symbol to refer to the political agents' beliefs about the outcomes of coalition bargaining when political strength is given by the structure $\mathcal{D}_t$ and party locations are given by $\mathbf{z}$.

2.5 THE ELECTION

We use $\mathbf{L} = (L_1, \ldots, L_j, \ldots, L_p)$ to denote the set of leaders of the various parties at election time. An important component of the electoral models that we consider is that they incorporate the effect of valence.

Stokes (1963, 1992) first introduced this concept many years ago. Valence relates to voters' judgments about positively or negatively evaluated conditions that they associate with particular parties or candidates. These judgments could refer to party leaders' competence, integrity, moral stance, or "charisma" over issues such as the ability to deal with the economy, foreign threat, and so forth. The important point to note is that these individual judgments are independent of the positions of the voter and the party. Estimates of these judgments can be obtained from survey data (see, for example, the work on Britain by Clarke, Stewart, and Whiteley, 1995, 1997, 1998; and Clarke et al., 2004). However, from such surveys it is difficult to determine the "weight" an individual voter attaches to the judgment in comparison to the weight of the policy difference between the voter and the party. As a consequence, the empirical models usually estimate valence for a party or party leader as a constant or intercept term in the voter-utility function. The party valence variate can then be assumed to be distributed throughout the electorate in some appropriate fashion. This stochastic variation is expressed in terms of a vector of disturbances, which, in the most general model, is assumed to be distributed multivariate normal with covariance matrix, Ω. This formal assumption parallels that of multinomial probit (MNP) estimation. The more common assumption is that the errors satisfy a "Type I extreme value distribution," and this induces multinomial logit (MNL) estimation. To model the election in this way requires knowledge of the set of preferred points of voters $\{x_i\}$ together with the vector $(z_1, \ldots, z_j, \ldots, z_p)$ of party positions. In addition, the effects of sociodemographic characteristics of voters can be incorporated into the model. The model then assumes that the implicit utility of voter i for party j is increasing in the valence λ_j, of party j, and decreasing in the weighted quadratic distance between the voter's position and that of the party. In addition, it is possible to incorporate the influence that the sociodemographic characteristics η_i of voter i may have on the voter's political choice. The model is stochastic because of the implicit assumption that the valence λ_{ij} that voter i assigns to j is a combination of the expectation λ_j and a random disturbance ε_j, with appropriate distribution. Formal definitions of the various models are set out at the end of this chapter. Because voter utility is stochastic, it is impossible to assert with precision which party a voter will choose. However, it is possible in empirical models to estimate the probability matrix $[\rho_{ij}^*(\mathbf{z})]$. Here we use $\rho_{ij}^*(\mathbf{z})$ to denote the probability that voter i chooses party j. Note that because of uncertainty in estimation, $\rho_{ij}^*(\mathbf{z})$ will also be a stochastic variable with expectation $\bar{\rho}_{ij}(\mathbf{z})$. Taking the mean value gives the expected vote share, $\mathcal{E}_j(\mathbf{z})$, of party j. For the baseline formal model we use $V_j(\mathbf{z})$ to denote the expected vote share.

The results of empirical estimation give rise to estimates for the valences, represented by $\lambda = (\lambda_1, \ldots, \lambda_j, \ldots, \lambda_p)$. Obviously these valence values will depend on the characteristics $L = (L_1, \ldots, L_j, \ldots, L_p)$ of the various leaders.

In this formulation, given the choice of leaders

$$\mathbf{L} = (L_1, \ldots, L_j, \ldots, L_p)$$

and policy positions $\mathbf{z} = (z_1, \ldots, z_j, \ldots, z_p)$ then the "outcome" of the election is a stochastic variable, which we represent by the symbol $\Pi(\mathbf{z})$. By this we mean to emphasize that $\Pi(\mathbf{z})$ describes the common beliefs, or estimated probabilities, associated with all possible relevant features of the election that will occur as result of the set of declarations given by $\mathbf{z}$.

The "electoral game" revolves around the decision of each party to select a policy position or "manifesto" to declare to the electorate at the time of the election. There are a number of possible modelling strategies that ignore the uncertainty inherent in the election and focus on electoral expectations.

2.6 EXPECTED VOTE MAXIMIZATION

2.6.1 *Exogenous Valence*

In this formulation, the valence terms of the parties are fixed, or *exogenous*, and the leader and the other members of the party are agreed that the party's policy position should be one which maximizes the party's vote share. Since party share depends on other party positions, it is natural to deploy the Nash equilibrium concept (Nash, 1950a,b, 1951). In this case, a vector of party positions z^* is a pure Nash equilibrium (PNE) if no party may unilaterally change z_j so as to increase its vote share. In our analyses of Israel and Italy, we compare the formal model of voting, with exogenous valence, with empirical models based on MNL estimation to determine the degree of fit between the models. The results of the formal model presented in Chapter 3 make it evident that the conditions for existence of PNE are very restrictive. Instead, we focus on what we call a "local Nash equilibrium," denoted LNE. The conditions for existence of LNE can be computed from the parameters obtained by the estimation. Theorems 3.1 and 3.2 show that the necessary and sufficient conditions for convergence to the electoral mean for both logit (MNL) and probit (MNP) models depends on a *convergence coefficient*, c, given essentially by the expression

$$c = 2Av^2.$$

Here v^2 is the total electoral variance while A is a function of the parameters (β, λ) and is increasing in β and in the difference in valence between high- and low-valence parties. For the multinomial probit model based on the normal distribution, c is decreasing in the measure of total error variance. In two dimensions, the necessary condition is that $c \leq 2$. This result has a clear interpretation. If the "spatial effect," βv^2, is large, then a party with a low enough valence, λ_1, say, will find that its vote share increases as the party vacates the electoral mean. This immediately implies that the LNE will consist of party positions strung along a principal electoral axis. This necessary condition is violated in Israel, and we therefore obtain a theoretical reason why convergence does not occur. Because of a discrepancy between the prediction of the formal model and the estimated party positions, we deploy Hypothesis 2.2.

2.6.2 Activist Valence

Since parties require activist support, for resources of time and money, and this support will depend on the actual position adopted by the party, we may modify the voter utility equation to be dependent on the valence, $\mu_j(z_j)$, of the party and attributable to the contributions of the party members. This is intended to model the additional valence induced by the availability of activist resources which are used to carry the party message to the electorate. Although activists respond to the declared position, and thus indirectly affect the party choice, they do not directly control policy. The party leader must still choose a policy position to maximize the expected vote share, $\mathcal{E}_j(\mathbf{z})$. Notice however, that the party's choice of leader will affect the valence, or electoral perception, of the party. To keep distinct the leader's position and that of representative members of the party, we assume that the preferences of the members of the party are represented by an agent whom we call the *party principal*. The application of the formal model to empirical estimations for elections in Britain in 1979, 1992, and 1997, in Chapter 7, indicates that, under the exogenous valence model, the high-valence Labour and Conservative parties should have converged to the electoral mean. Simulation of an empirical model for the Netherlands for electoral data from 1979 also indicate that vote-maximizing parties should have converged to the center. Nonconvergence in these two polities leads us to a model of activist valence.

2.6.3 *Activist Influence on Policy*

Under the two earlier formulations, the leader's role is simply to implement the policy position chosen by the party principal. If the leader has no interest in the policy position, then it is obvious that there will be no credible commitment to the declared policy, except possibly because of the threat of activist revolt. In our analysis in Chapter 6 of the Netherlands in the elections of 1977 and 1981, we essentially suppose that each party position is chosen by the party principal.

A more general model includes the policy concerns of activists as well as party members in the formulation of the party manifesto.

2.7 SELECTION OF THE PARTY LEADER

The party comprises parliamentary members, party members, and activists. In principle, all members are interested in the policy proposed by the party and in the final governmental outcome. We can represent a delegate's utility by an additive expression involving perquisites and the quadratic loss given by the distance between the government's chosen policy and the delegate's preferred point.

Assume now that the leaders of each of the parties have been chosen, so that the valences are known. If the vector of positions of the other parties is also known, then a delegate of party j can, in principle, compute the stochastic result of the election to follow. That is to say, for any policy position, z_j, chosen by the party, we assume that the delegate has consistent beliefs about the nature of the electoral response. We represent these beliefs by the "belief operator" Π. Thus, when parties have chosen their strategies, $\mathbf{z}$, we assume they hold common beliefs, $\Pi(\mathbf{z})$, about the election. In particular, $\Pi(\mathbf{z})$ encodes information on the probability, $\pi_t(\mathbf{z})$, that the coalition structure, $\mathcal{D}_t$, occurs after the election. We have argued that when the coalition structure, $\mathcal{D}_t$, occurs, then the consequences of interparty bargaining can be represented by the lottery $\tilde{g}_t^\alpha(\mathbf{z})$. By taking expectations across all possible coalition structures, the delegate can compute the expected utility from a choice, z_j, and can therefore determine which choice of party position is the best response to the positions, $\mathbf{z}_{-j} = (\ldots z_{j-1}, z_{j+1}, \ldots)$, of the other parties.

The delegates may very well disagree in their computation of their party's best response. We have suggested that one way to overcome this intraparty conflict is for the party to choose a principal for the party, who in some fashion has typical policy preferences of the party elite. There are a number of obvious strategies for modelling the choice of the party manifesto.

(i) The principal computes the best response to the other party principals' choices, and writes the party manifesto, based on personal policy preferences. The leader of the party then presents the manifesto to the electorate.

(ii) The principal attempts to find a party leader whose own known policy preferences are a compromise between the heterogeneous preferences of the various activist and delegate subgroups within the party. Picking a party leader whose sincere policy position the party can endorse as its strategic policy declaration thus solves the problem of the credible commitment of the party leader to the declared policy of the party (Banks, 1990). Notice that this choice of the party leader may be one of extreme complexity, since it involves a long chain of reasoning, including guessing at the leader's likely electoral valence, the effect on the stochastic electoral operator, and the effect of the election outcome on coalition bargaining.

(iii) It is obviously an oversimplification to assume that the choice of party leader can be left to a party principal. The degree of policy conflict may be so extreme that different subgroups within the party elect their own principals to compete with each other over the choice of party leader. Miller and Schofield (2003) suggest that this is likely to be a characteristic of plurality electoral systems such as the United States and Britain. As a consequence, one can expect severely contested leadership elections after a party has performed poorly at the election. However, if the party succeeds at the election, then we can assume that the party leader will stay in power after the election, and can be credibly expected to implement his or her position.

The choice of the set of party leaders' policy positions, or party manifestos, can be expressed as an equilibrium to the very complex game just presented. While the usual equilibrium concept utilized to examine such games is Pure Nash equilibrium (PNE), the conditions known to be sufficient for existence of this equilibrium are unlikely to hold. We therefore use what we have called a "local Nash equilibrium" (LNE). The conditions for existence for an LNE are much less stringent than those for a PNE. Indeed, a PNE by definition must be an LNE, so that if an LNE of a particular kind fails to exist, then the PNE will also fail to exist. This local equilibrium concept essentially supposes that political protagonists consider "small" changes in strategy, rather than the "global" changes envisaged in the Nash equilibrium notion. Most importantly we give reasons to believe that the set of LNE is nonempty. Determining conditions for existence of LNE at the electoral mean is accomplished in Theorems 3.1 and 3.2, but the determination of this set analytically for general electoral models is very difficult. Nonetheless, once an empirical model has been constructed, then it is possible to estimate the set of LNE by simulation.

2.8 EXAMPLE: ISRAEL

To illustrate the framework just presented, we borrow some of our empirical findings from Chapter 4, in which we discuss in detail the case of Israel. We return to this illustration in Section 3.5. Table 2.1 gives the election results between 1988 and 2003, while Figure 2.2 presents our estimates of the party positions in 1992. The background to this figure is an estimate of the electoral distribution of voter ideal points, derived from Arian and Shamir (1995). We discuss estimation techniques and data in Chapter 4, where more details on the two policy dimensions are given. As in all our electoral figures, the outer contour line contains 95 percent of the voter ideal points, whereas the inner contours contain 75 percent, 50 percent, and 10 percent of the ideal points. We assume Euclidean loss functions based on the party points given in Figure 2.2, and ignore the additional complexity induced by governmental perquisites. (See Section 2.9 for a sketch of this electoral model.) We can show that Labour was a "core party" after the election of 1992. To see this, consider the obvious coalition based on the leadership of Likud. A coalition of Likud

Table 2.1. *Elections in Israel, 1998–2003.*

	Party	Knesset Seats				
		1988	1992	1996	1999	2003
Left	Labour (LAB)	39	44	34	28	19[a]
	Democrat (ADL)	1	2	4	5	2[a]
	Meretz (MRZ)	–	12	9	10	6
	CRM, MPM, PLP	9	–	–	–	3
	Communist (HS)	4	3	5	3	3
	Balad	–	–	–	2	3
Subtotal		53	61	52	48	36
Center	Olim	–	–	7	6	2[b]
	III Way	–	–	4	–	–
	Center	–	–	–	6	–
	Shinui (S)	2	–	–	6	15
Subtotal		2		11	18	17[b]
Right	Likud (LIK)	40	32	30	19	38[b]
	Gesher	–	–	2	–	–
	Tzomet (TZ)	2	8	–	–	–
	Israel beiteinu	–	–	–	4	7
Subtotal		42	40	32	23	45
Religious	Shas (SHAS)	6	6	10	17	11
	Yahadut (AI, DH)	7	4	4	5	5
	Mafdal (NRP)	5	6	9	5	6
	Moledet (MO)	2	3	2	4	–
	Techiya, Thia (TY)	3	–	–	–	–
Subtotal		23	19	25	31	22
TOTAL		120	120	120	120	120

[a] Am Ehad or ADL, under Peretz, combined with Labour, to give the party $19 + 2 = 21$ seats.
[b] Olim joined Likud to form one party giving Likud $38 + 2 = 40$ seats, and the right $40 + 7 = 47$ seats.

with Tzomet and the four religious parties controls only 59 seats out of 120. To be decisive, this coalition needs 61 seats and so must add either Meretz or Labour. If Meretz is added to the coalition, then the set of policies that this decisive coalition can implement can be identified with the convex hull of the points associated with the members of the coalition. However, the policy point representing Labour lies within this set. Consequently, if Labour proposes its ideal point, then no decisive coalition can propose another that it prefers. Thus, the Labour position cannot be defeated by another policy position supported by a decisive coalition. As

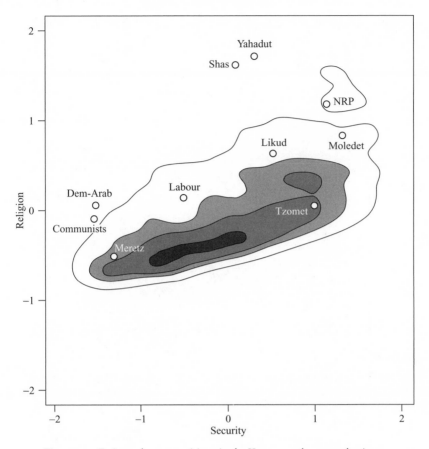

Figure 2.2. Estimated party positions in the Knesset at the 1992 election.

a consequence, we call this point the *core* of the coalition game, given the set of winning coalitions, $\mathcal{D}_{1992}$. Another way to show that Labour is at the core is to construct the median lines in the figure, where a median line through two party positions cuts the policy space in two, so that coalition majorities lie on either side of the line. For example, in Figure 2.3, the line through Shas and Labour (with 50 seats) has more than 10 seats on either side, thus demonstrating that it is a median. Three different median lines are drawn in Figure 2.3, all intersecting in the Labour position. The intersection of these lines guarantees that the Labour position is a core. This technique involving medians is one method of determining whether a party position is a core (see also McKelvey and Schofield, 1987).

All versions of coalition bargaining theory suggest that the core point will be the outcome (Sened, 1996; Banks and Duggan, 2000). Note also

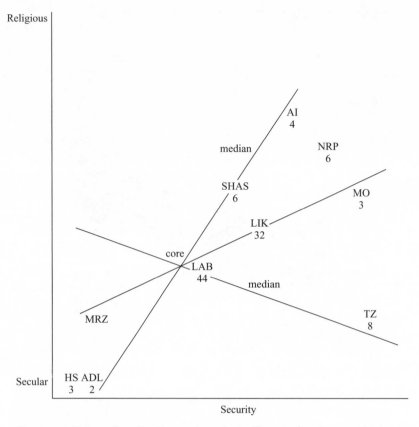

Figure 2.3. Estimated median lines and core in the Knesset after the 1992 election.

that this core point is "structurally stable," in the sense that a small perturbation of the preferred policy point of the parties does not change the core property. We denote the structurally stable core by $\mathbb{SC}_1(\mathbf{z})$. Notice that this concept depends on both the vector of party positions and the particular set of winning coalitions, $\mathcal{D}_{1992}$. We call $\mathcal{D}_{1992}$ the *decisive structure*. Since the core outcome is associated with a single party, even though that party lacks a majority of the seats, we expect the Labour Party to form a minority government (Laver and Schofield, 1990; Sened, 1996). As we discuss in Chapter 4, this is precisely what happened. We use the notation, $\mathbb{D}_1$, for the family of decisive structures, including $\mathcal{D}_{1992}$, under which Labour could be located at the core. We also say that this decisive structure implies that Labour is the strongest party and that its position implies that it is also *dominant*. Since Labour appears to have

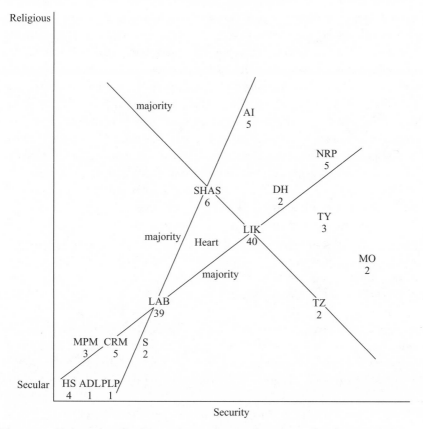

Figure 2.4. Estimated median lines and empty core in the Knesset after the 1988 election.

occupied the core position in 1992 we also say, for the post-election environment determined by $\mathbb{D}_1$ and z, that Labour was the *core party*.

However, for the coalition structure, $\mathcal{D}_{1988}$, that occurred in 1988, the coalition of the religious parties (with 23 seats) and Likud (with 40 seats) controlled 63 seats altogether. This gave the coalition a majority, even without Meretz or Labour. More generally, in this Parliament, there was no core policy. To see this, consider the Likud preferred point in Figure 2.4. Since Labour, the left, and Shinui together with Shas control 61 seats (a majority of the seats), they could potentially form a government coalition. Moreover, the declared position of Likud does not belong to the convex hull of the positions of this new potential coalition. Thus, the coalition can in principle agree to a policy point that each member prefers to the Likud policy, and on the basis of this new policy force through a vote of no confidence against the Likud-led government. Even if Likud agreed to a different policy point that Shas would find acceptable, there would always be a position that the new coalition can offer to Shas to overturn the government policy point. Clearly, the Likud position cannot be a core point. To form a government, whether based on the leadership of Labour or Likud, it is necessary to include other parties. The obvious party to include is Shas, which can be regarded as pivotal between coalitions based on Likud or Labour. Bargaining over government formation will then involve, at the least, Likud, Shas, and Labour. We suggest that the policy positions that can occur as a result of bargaining in the absence of a core party lie inside a subset of policies known as the *heart*. The formal definition of this set is provided in Chapter 3, but we can provide an informal definition using Figure 2.4. The median lines in this figure do not intersect, demonstrating that the core is empty. The results of McKelvey and Schofield (1987) show that, with the decisive structure, $\mathcal{D}_{1988}$, voting cycles can occur inside the set bounded by the positions of Likud, Labour, and Shas. Indeed, bargaining between the parties over policy will lead them into this set.

Figure 2.5 shows the estimated positions of the parties at the election of 1996. Precisely, as in 1988, and using Table 2.1 to compute $\mathcal{D}_{1996}$, we can assert that the core for 1996 is empty. A schematic representaion of the Knesset, together with the location of the heart after the election of 2003, is also given in Figure 2.6. We return to these figures in the following chapters.

We denote the family of coalition structures, including $\mathcal{D}_{1988}$, $\mathcal{D}_{1996}$, and $\mathcal{D}_{2003}$, with an empty core, by the symbol $\mathbb{D}_0$. Here 0 is taken to mean that the core is empty. Since the heart depends both on the location of the parties, $\mathbf{z}$, as well as the decisive structure, we use the symbol $\mathcal{H}_0(\mathbf{z})$ for the heart associated with $\mathbb{D}_0$.

The formal bargaining model proposed by Banks and Duggan (2000) gives a lottery or randomization across the convex set generated by the ideal points of all parties. The heart instead is based on the idea that the protagonists believe that, in the situation given by this election, there will be no minority government, but that a limited set of possible coalitions can occur. Although Labour was the strongest party (with 34 seats) under the decisive structure, $\mathcal{D}_{1996}$, it was no longer *dominant*. The key idea underlying the notion of the heart is that in the 1988 and 1996 situations, there are essentially three different possible governments: Likud, Shas, and parties on the "right"; Labour, Shas, and parties on the "left"; and the Labour, Likud coalition. From 1996 to the present, one or other of the first two coalition governments have been the norm, but Sharon and

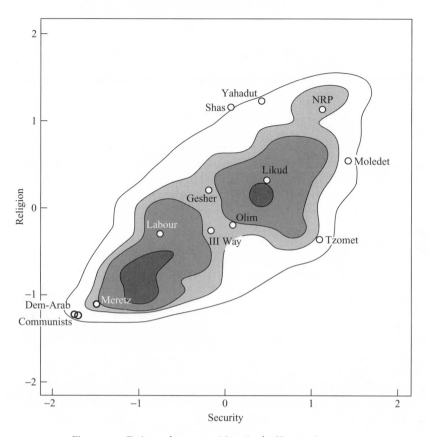

Figure 2.5. Estimated party positions in the Knesset in 1996.

Peres, leaders of Likud and Labour respectively, agreed to form this third coalition in January 2005. We regard the difference between the $\mathbb{D}_0$ structure holding in 1988 and 1996 and the $\mathbb{D}_1$ structure holding in 1992 to be crucial in understanding coalition bargaining. Because Labour benefits substantially when it is a core party, we expect Labour to adopt a position that increases the probability that $\mathbb{D}_1$ occurs. Conversely, Likud should attempt to maximize the probability that $\mathbb{D}_0$ occurs. Since these probabilities will depend on the beliefs of the party principals about the electoral outcome, and these beliefs depend on the vector of party positions, we can write

$$\pi_0(\mathbf{z}) = \Pr[\mathbb{D}_0 \text{ occurs at } \mathbf{z}] \text{ and } \pi_1(\mathbf{z}) = \Pr[\mathbb{D}_1 \text{ occurs at } \mathbf{z}].$$

In principle, these probabilities can be derived from the "belief operator" Π.

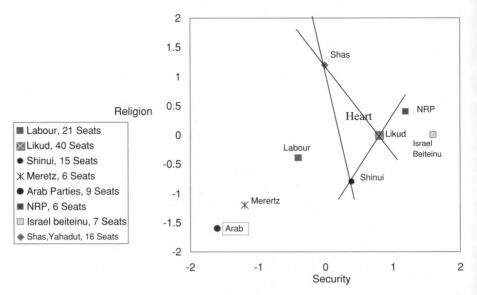

Figure 2.6. A schematic representation of the configuration of parties in the Knesset after 2003.

Thus, we can restate the conclusion of this argument.

Hypothesis 2.4: *Any potential core party, j, should adopt a position in an attempt to maximize the probability, $\pi_j(z)$, associated with the coalition structure $\mathbb{D}_j$, which allows j to be at a core position.*

In the example from Israel, this hypothesis would indicate that since Likud cannot expect to be a core party, then it should attempt to minimize $\pi_1(\mathbf{z})$, or alternatively, to maximize $\pi_0(\mathbf{z})$.

2.9 ELECTORAL MODELS WITH VALENCE

The spatial model with exogenous valence:

The empirical model assumes that the implicit utility of voter i for party j has the form

$$u_{ij}(x_i, z_j) = \lambda_{ij} - \beta \|x_i - z_j\|^2 + \theta_j^{\mathrm{T}} \eta_i. \tag{2.1}$$

Here $\theta_j^{\mathrm{T}} \eta_i$ models the effect of the sociodemographic characteristics η_i of voter i in making a political choice. That is, θ_j is a k-vector specifying how the various sociodemographic variables appear to influence the choice for party j. The term $\beta \|x_i - z_j\|^2$ is the Euclidean quadratic loss associated with the difference between the declared policy of party j and preferred position x_i of voter i. The model is stochastic because of the implicit assumption that $\lambda_{ij} = \lambda_j + \varepsilon_j$, where the disturbances $\{\varepsilon_j : j = 1, \ldots, p\}$ have some multivariate distribution Ψ. The definition of voter probability is

$$\rho_{ij}(\mathbf{z}) = \Pr[[u_{ij}(x_i, z_j) > u_{il}(x_i, z_l)], \text{ for all } l \neq j]$$

$$= \Pr[\epsilon_l - \epsilon_j < u_{ij}^*(x_i, z_j) - u_{il}^*(x_i, z_j), \text{ for all } l \neq j],$$

where

$$u_{ij}^*(x_i, z_j) = \lambda_j - \beta \|x_i - z_j\|^2 + \theta_j^{\mathrm{T}} \eta_i \tag{2.2}$$

is the observable component of utility. Particular assumptions on the distribution of the disturbances then allows estimation of the voter probabilities. Because the various parameters are estimated, we use $\rho_{ij}^*(\mathbf{z})$ to denote the stochastic variable, with expectation

$$\mathcal{E}xp(\rho_{ij}^*(\mathbf{z})) = \bar{\rho}_{ij}(\mathbf{z}). \tag{2.3}$$

Taking the mean value gives the empirical expected vote share,

$$\mathcal{E}_j(\mathbf{z}) = \frac{1}{n} \sum_i \bar{\rho}_{ij}(\mathbf{z}). \tag{2.4}$$

The baseline formal model is based on the parallel assumption that

$$u_{ij}(x_i, z_j) = \lambda_j - \beta \|x_i - z_j\|^2 + \varepsilon_j. \tag{2.5}$$

Here again $\{\varepsilon_j : j = 1, \ldots, p\}$ is distributed by Ψ. The probability $\rho_{ij}(\mathbf{z})$ is then defined in analogous fashion and the formal vote share is defined by

$$V_j(\mathbf{z}) = \frac{1}{n} \sum_{i=1}^{n} \rho_{ij}(\mathbf{z}). \tag{2.6}$$

Notice that we differentiate between the vote share $\mathcal{E}_j(\mathbf{z})$ for the empirical model and $V_j(\mathbf{z})$ for the baseline formal model. In particular, the formal model does not incorporate sociodemographic variables. Since the sociodemographic component of the empirical model is assumed not to be dependent on party position, the PNE and the LNE of the two models should coincide (when the parameters of the model coincide). We say the two models are compatible. The simplest distribution assumption to use is that Ψ is the Type I extreme value distribution. This parallels what is known as *multinomial condition logit* (MNL) estimation (Dow and Endersby, 2004).

When the valences are given by the vector $\lambda = (\lambda_1, \ldots, \lambda_j, \ldots, \lambda_p)$ and ranked $\lambda_1 \leq \ldots \lambda_j \leq \ldots \leq \lambda_p$, and the extreme value distribution is used, then the convergence coefficient is given by the expression

$$c = 2\beta[1 - 2\rho_1]v^2 = 2Av^2. \qquad (2.7)$$

Here ρ_1 is the common probability that a voter will choose the lowest valence party when all parties are at the electoral mean.

The spatial model with activist valence: In this case, the valence is partly a function of party position and is written $\mu_j(z_j)$ so that voter utility is given by the expression

$$u_{ij}(x_i, z_j) = \lambda_j + \mu_j(z_j) - \beta\|x_i - z_j\|^2 + \varepsilon_j. \qquad (2.8)$$

Electoral models based on exogenous valence and activist valence provide the basis for estimation of the electoral operator Π.

2.10 THE GENERAL MODEL OF MULTIPARTY POLITICS

2.10.1 *Policy Preferences of Party Principals*

In this model, principals are "policy motivated" but also benefit from government perquisites.

Consider a party delegate of party j who has a most-preferred policy point x_j. If the party joins a governing coalition after the election, and receives perquisites of office, denoted δ_j, then we can represent that delegate's utility by the expression

$$U_j((x_j, \alpha_j) : (y, \delta_j)) = U_j^*(y, \delta_j) = -\|y - x_j\|^2 + \alpha_j\delta_j, \qquad (2.9)$$

where y is the policy implemented by government, and again

$$-\|y - x_j\|^2$$

is a measure of the quadratic loss associated with the difference between the delegate's preferred point and y. The coefficient α_j gives the relative value of policy over perquisite.

2.10.2 *Coalition and Electoral Risk*

(i) We now consider the set of all possible decisive structures, say, $\{\mathbb{D}_0, \mathbb{D}_1, \mathbb{D}_t, \ldots, \mathbb{D}_p\}$, where $\mathbb{D}_t$, for $t = 1, \ldots, p$, is a possible coalition structure where party t can be a core party, and $\mathbb{D}_0$ is the family of coalition structures lacking a core. We let $\mathcal{H}_t(\mathbf{z})$ be the heart defined by $\mathbb{D}_t$ and the vector $\mathbf{z}$. We let Π denote the stochastic electoral operator, which defines *inter alia* the probabilities $\{\pi_t(\mathbf{z}) : t = 0, \dots, p\}$. These probability functions model the *electoral risk* associated with the polity. We implicitly assume that the operator Π is compatible with, and can be deduced from, the above electoral models.

(ii) Given a post-election coalition structure $\mathbb{D}_t$, and the vector of party positions $\mathbf{z}$, the beliefs of the parties regarding policy outcomes in the legislative stage can be expressed as a lottery $\tilde{g}_t(\mathbf{z})$ defined over the set of policy outcomes in the heart $\mathcal{H}_t(\mathbf{z})$. In particular, if the structurally stable core, $\mathbb{SC}_t(\mathbf{z})$, is nonempty at $\mathbf{z}$, then $\mathbb{SC}_t(\mathbf{z}) = \mathcal{H}_t(\mathbf{z})$ and so $\tilde{g}_t(\mathbf{z}) = \mathbb{SC}_t(\mathbf{z})$. These lottery or coalition functions model the *coalition risk* associated with the polity.

(iii) Given Π, then the beliefs of the party principals can be described by the *game form* $\tilde{g}(\mathbf{z}) = \{(\tilde{g}_t(\mathbf{z}), \pi_t(\mathbf{z})); t = 0, \dots, p\}$.

(iv) Each principal for party j attempts to maximize the expected utility function

$$U_j(\mathbf{z}) = \sum_{t=0}^{p} \pi_t(\mathbf{z}) U_j(\tilde{g}_t(\mathbf{z})). \qquad (2.10)$$

Here $U_j(\tilde{g}_t(\mathbf{z}))$ is the expected utility derived from the lottery $\tilde{g}_t(\mathbf{z})$ and determined by the policy preferences held by the principal of party j.

Hypothesis 2.5: *The outcome of the political game is a local equilibrium for the game given by the utility profile* $U = (U_1, \dots, U_p)$.

Comment: It follows from this hypothesis that any party j that has a reasonable expectation of locating at the core position will also be obliged to attempt to maximize π_j, the probability associated with the coalition structure through which it may be the core party. Calculation of π_j may be difficult, but a proxy for maximizing π_j for a party like Labour, in the example above, may be to maximize its expected vote share $\mathcal{E}_j$. In our analyses of Israel and Italy in Chapters 4 and 5, we find that there is a close correspondence between the estimated location of high-valence parties, and the positions computed to be local equilibria of the vote-maximizing game. This suggests that the unknown utility functions in Hypothesis 2.5 for at least some of the parties can be approximated by vote-share functions. Moreover, discrepancies found between the estimated positions and the equilibrium positions under vote maximization for the low-valence parties may be explained by the more general theory underlying Hypothesis 2.5. Combining the model of vote maximization with that of coalition bargaining is the topic of the next chapter.

3

A Theory of Political Competition

The spatial model of politics initially focused on the analysis of two agents, j and k, competing in a policy space X for electoral votes. The two agents (whether candidates or party leaders) are assumed to pick policy positions z_j, z_k, both in X, which they present as manifestos to a large electorate. Suppose that each member of the electorate votes for the agent that the voter truly prefers. When X involves two or more dimensions, then under conditions developed by Plott (1967), Kramer (1973), McKelvey (1976, 1979), Schofield (1978, 1983, 1985), and many others,[*] there will generically exist no Condorcet or *core* point unbeaten under majority rule. That is to say, whatever position, z_j, is picked by j there always exists a point z_k that will give agent k a majority over agent j.

However, the existence of a Condorcet point has been established in those situations where the policy space is one-dimensional. In this case, the agents can be expected to converge to the position of the median voter (Downs, 1957). When X has two or more dimensions, it is known that a Condorcet point exists when electoral preferences are represented by a spherically symmetric distribution of voter ideal points. Even when the distribution is not spherically symmetric, a Condorcet point can be guaranteed as long as the decision rule requires a sufficiently large majority (Caplin and Nalebuff, 1988). Although a PNE generically fails to exist in competition between two agents under majority rule, there will exist mixed strategy equilibria whose support lies within a central electoral domain called the *uncovered set*.[†]

---

[*] See also Cohen and Matthews (1980), McKelvey and Schofield (1986, 1987), Banks (1995), Saari (1996), and Austen-Smith and Banks (1999).
[†] See (Kramer, 1978; Miller, 1980; McKelvey, 1986; Cox, 1987a; Banks et al., 2002; Bianco and Sened, 2003; Bianco et al., 2006).

One problem with the application of these two types of models, in real-world politics, has been the extreme nature of the predictions. The instability results seem to suggest that the outcome of two-party political competition is dependent essentially on random events. The results for mixed strategy equilibria suggest a strong form of convergence in the positions of political agents. Attempts to extend these deterministic models to the situation with more than two parties have also shown instability, or nonexistence of pure strategy vote-maximizing equilibria (Eaton and Lipsey, 1975) or have had to impose additional conditions to deal with discontinuities in the pay-off functions of the agents (Dasgupta and Maskin, 1986).

A way of avoiding the intrinsic failure of continuity in the pay-off functions of agents in these deterministic models is to allow for a stochastic component in voter choice. Hinich (1977) argued that vote-maximizing candidates would adopt a position at the mean of the voter distribution when they faced a stochastic electorate. His argument for two-party competition has been extended by Enelow and Hinich (1982, 1984, 1989), Coughlin (1992), and most recently by McKelvey and Patty (2005) and Banks and Duggan (2005). Lin, Enelow, and Dorussen (1999) have also obtained a *mean voter* theorem for the general case of many candidates.

Applying a stochastic model of voting is the standard technique for estimating voter response in empirical analyses (Alvarez and Nagler, 1998; Alvarez, Nagler, and Bowler, 2000). In an early application it was noted by Poole and Rosenthal (1984) that there was no evidence of convergence to the electoral mean in U.S. presidential elections. As acknowledged in Chapter 1, we earlier completed stochastic models of elections with our collaborators for Britain, Germany, the Netherlands, Israel, Italy, and the United States. Simulation of these models has led to contradictory results. Sometimes the simulation resulted in convergence to the electoral mean (Netherlands and Britain) and sometimes divergence (Israel and Italy). In all cases however, there was no indication that the parties did indeed converge. In later chapters we review these empirical models.

These earlier models entailed the addition of heterogeneous intercept terms for each party. One interpretation of these intercept or constant terms is that they are valences or party biases. As we noted above, valence refers to voters' judgments about positively or negatively evaluated aspects of candidates, or party leaders, which cannot be ascribed to the policy choice of the party or candidate (Stokes, 1992). One may conceive of the valence that a voter ascribes to a candidate as a judgment of the candidate's quality or competence. This idea of valence has been utilized in a number of recent formal models of voting (Ansolabehere and Snyder, 2000; Groseclose, 2001; Aragones and Palfrey, 2002). To date, a full characterization of the effect of valence on the stochastic model has not been obtained for the case with an arbitrary number of parties.

The next section of this chapter presents such a characterization in terms of the Hessian of the vote-share function of the party leader or candidate who has the lowest valence. The empirical models typically assume that the stochastic component of the model is multinomial logit, derived from the Type I extreme value distribution on the errors. Theorem 3.1 makes this assumption, and shows that there exists a convergence coefficient, which is a function of all the parameters of the model and which classifies the model in the following sense: when the policy space is of dimension w, then the necessary condition for existence of a PNE at the electoral mean, and thus for the validity of the mean voter theorem, is that the coefficient is bounded above by w. Theorem 3.1 also shows that a weaker condition, that the convergence coefficient be bounded above by 1, is sufficient for an LNE at the mean. In the two-dimensional case, the eigenvalues of the Hessian can be readily computed. It is shown that the convergence coefficient is (i) an increasing function of the maximum valence difference, (ii) an increasing function of the number of parties or candidates, and (iii) an increasing function of the electoral variance of the voter-preferred points. In the more complex case, when the stochastic errors are multivariate normal, and therefore covariate, Theorem 3.2 asserts that a different convergence coefficient also classifies the model in precisely the same sense.

When the necessary convergence condition fails, then the origin will be a saddlepoint or minimum of the vote-share function for the lowest valence party. By changing position in the major electoral axis (or eigenspace of the vote function) this party can increase its vote share. It follows that in equilibrium, all parties will adopt positions on this principal axis, with the lowest-valence parties the furthest from the origin. No party will adopt a position at the electoral mean. Chapter 4 presents empirical electoral models for the elections of 1988, 1992, and 1996 in Israel. Chapter 5 follows with an analysis of the 1996 election in Italy. The results indicate that the necessary condition failed. Simulation of the empirical model for Israel found that the vote-maximizing positions of the parties were indeed not at the electoral mean. Our results show that there was a close correspondence between the estimated actual positions of the parties and the equilibrium positions obtained by simulation.

Both these stochastic models (based on the Type I extreme value distribution) assume that the party leaders are motivated simply to maximize vote shares in order to gain office. Moreover, because the model focuses on expected vote share, it ignores the possibility of uncertainty in electoral response. One way to introduce uncertainty, at least in two-party models, is to focus instead on the "probability of victory." Implicitly, such a model acknowledges that the vote-share functions are stochastic variables. To extend such a model to the multiparty case (where there are three or more parties) requires a modification of the notion of the "probability of winning." An obvious extension is to model electoral uncertainty in terms of the probabilities associated with different collections of decisive coalitions. The natural way to construct such a model is to allow party policy decisions to be made by party principals who have policy preferences. In the later part of this chapter, we model such policy-motivated choices using concepts from social choice theory.

3.1 LOCAL EQUILIBRIA IN THE STOCHASTIC MODEL

The purpose of this section is to construct a model of positioning of parties in electoral competition so as to account for the generally observed phenomenon of nonconvergence. The model adopted is an extension of the multiparty stochastic model of Lin, Enelow, and Dorussen (1999), constructed by inducing asymmetries in terms of valence. The basis for this extension is the extensive empirical evidence that valence is a significant component of the judgments made by voters of party leaders. There are a number of possible choices for the appropriate game form for multiparty competition. The simplest one, which is used here, is that the utility function for agent j is proportional to the vote share, V_j, of the agent. With this assumption, we can examine the conditions on the parameters of the stochastic model that are necessary for the existence of a PNE for this particular game form. Because the vote-share functions are differentiable, we use calculus techniques to estimate optimal positions. As usual with this form of analysis, we can obtain sufficient conditions for the existence of local optima, or LNE. Clearly, any PNE will be an LNE, but not conversely. Additional conditions of concavity or quasi-concavity are sufficient to guarantee existence of PNE. However, in the models we consider, it is evident that these sufficient conditions will fail, leading to the inference that PNE are typically nonexistent. Existence of mixed-strategy Nash equilibria is an open question in such games. It is of course true that the true utility functions of party leaders are unknown.

However, comparison of LNE, obtained by simulation of empirical models, with the estimated positions of parties in the various polities that have been studied can provide insight into the true nature of the game form of political competition.

The key idea underlying the formal model is that party leaders attempt to estimate the electoral effects of party declarations, or manifestos, and choose their own positions as best responses to other party declarations in order to maximize their own vote share. The stochastic model essentially assumes that party leaders cannot predict vote response precisely. In the model with exogenous valence, the stochastic element is associated with the weight given by each voter, i, to the average perceived quality or valence of the party leader.

Definition 3.1 *The Formal Stochastic Vote Model*

The data of the spatial model is a distribution, $\{x_i \in X\}_{i \in N}$, of voter ideal points for the members of the electorate, N, of size n. As usual, we assume that X is a compact convex subset of Euclidean space, $\mathbb{R}^w$, with w finite. Each of the parties, or agents, in the set $P = \{1, \ldots, j, \ldots, p\}$ chooses a policy, $z_j \in X$, to declare. Let $\mathbf{z} = (z_1, \ldots, z_p) \in X^p$ be a typical vector of agent policy positions. Given $\mathbf{z}$, each voter i is described by a vector $\mathbf{u}_i(x_i, \mathbf{z}) = (u_{i1}(x_i, z_1), \ldots, u_{ip}(x_i, z_p))$, where

$$u_{ij}(x_i, z_j) = \lambda_j - \beta \|x_i - z_j\|^2 + \epsilon_j = u_{ij}^*(x_i, z_j) + \epsilon_j.$$

Here $u_{ij}^*(x_i, z_j)$ is the observable component of utility. The term λ_j is the exogenous valence of agent j, β is a positive constant and $\|\cdot\|$ is the usual Euclidean norm on X. The terms $\{\epsilon_j\}$ are the stochastic errors, whose cumulative distribution will be denoted by Ψ.

We consider various distribution functions. The most common assumption in empirical analyses is that Ψ is the "Type I extreme value distribution" (sometimes called *log Weibull*). Our principal theorem is based on this assumption. However, we also consider the situation where the errors are independently and identically distributed by the normal distribution (iind), with zero expectation, each with stochastic variance σ^2. A more general assumption is that the stochastic error vector $\epsilon = (\epsilon_1, \ldots, \epsilon_p)$ is multivariate normal with general variance/covariance matrix Ω.

It is natural to suppose that the valence of party j as perceived by voter i is the stochastic variate $\lambda_{ij} = \lambda_j + \epsilon_j$, where λ_j is simply the expectation $\mathcal{E}xp(\lambda_{ij})$ of λ_{ij}. We assume in this chapter that the valence vector

$\lambda = (\lambda_1, \lambda_2, \ldots, \lambda_p)$ satisfies $\lambda_p \geq \lambda_{p-1} \geq \ldots \geq \lambda_2 \geq \lambda_1$.

Because of the stochastic assumption, voter behavior is modelled by a probability vector. The probability that a voter i chooses party j is

$$\rho_{ij}(\mathbf{z}) = \Pr[[u_{ij}(x_i, z_j) > u_{il}(x_i, z_l)], \text{ for all } l \neq j]$$
$$= \Pr[\epsilon_l - \epsilon_j < u_{ij}^*(x_i, z_j) - u_{il}^*(x_i, z_j), \text{ for all } l \neq j].$$

Here Pr stands for the probability operator generated by the distribution assumption on ϵ. The *expected vote share* of agent j is

$$V_j(\mathbf{z}) = \frac{1}{n} \sum_{i \in N} \rho_{ij}(\mathbf{z}). \tag{3.1}$$

We shall use the notation $V : X^p \to \mathbb{R}^p$ and call V the *party profile function*. In the vote model it is assumed that each agent j chooses z_j to maximize V_j, conditional on $\mathbf{z}_{-j} = (z_1, \ldots, z_{j-1}, z_{j+1}, \ldots, z_p)$.

Because of the differentiability of the cumulative distribution function, the individual probability functions $\{\rho_{ij}\}$ are C^2-differentiable in the strategies $\{z_j\}$. Thus, the vote share functions will also be C^2-differentiable. Let $x^* = (1/n)\Sigma_i x_i$. Then the mean voter theorem for the stochastic model asserts that the "joint mean vector" $\mathbf{z}_0 = (x^*, \ldots, x^*)$ is a PNE. Lin, Enelow, and Dorussen (1999) used C^2-differentiability of the expected vote-share functions, in the situation with zero valence, to show that the validity of the theorem depended on the concavity of the vote-share functions. They asserted that a sufficient condition for this was that the variance, σ^2, of each error term was "sufficiently large." Because concavity cannot in general be assured, we utilize a weaker equilibrium concept, that of "local strict Nash equilibrium" (LSNE). A strategy vector $\mathbf{z}^*$ is an LSNE if, for each j, z_j^* is a critical point of the vote function $V_j(z_1^*, \ldots, z_{j-1}^*, z_j, \ldots, z_{j+1}^*, \ldots, z_p^*)$ and the eigenvalues of the Hessian of this function (with respect to z_j) are negative. Definition 3.2 gives the various definitions of the equilibrium concepts used throughout this book.

Definition 3.2 *Equilibrium Concepts for the Formal Model*

(i) A strategy vector $\mathbf{z}^* = (z_1^*, \ldots, z_{j-1}^*, z_j^*, z_{j+1}^*, \ldots, z_p^*) \in X^p$ is a *local strict Nash equilibrium* (LSNE) for the profile function $V : X^p \to \mathbb{R}^p$ iff, for each agent $j \in P$, there exists a neighborhood X_j of z_j^* in

X such that

$$V_j(z_1^*, \ldots, z_{j-1}^*, z_j^*, z_{j+1}^*, \ldots, z_p^*) > V_j(z_1^*, \ldots, z_j, \ldots, z_p^*)$$

for all $z_j \in X_j - \{z_j^*\}$.

(ii) A strategy vector $\mathbf{z}^* = (z_1^*, \ldots, z_{j-1}^*, z_j^*, z_{j+1}^*, \ldots, z_p^*)$ is a *local weak Nash equilibrium* (LNE) iff, for each agent j, there exists a neighborhood X_j of z_j^* in X such that

$$V_j(z_1^*, \ldots, z_{j-1}^*, z_j^*, z_{j+1}^*, \ldots, z_p^*) \geq V_j(z_1^*, \ldots, z_j, \ldots, z_p^*)$$

for all $z_j \in X_j$.

(iii) A strategy vector $\mathbf{z}^* = (z_1^*, \ldots, z_{j-1}^*, z_j^*, z_{j+1}^*, \ldots, z_p^*)$ is a *strict*, respectively, *weak, pure strategy Nash equilibrium* (PSNE, respectively, PNE) iff X_j can be replaced by X in (i), (ii), respectively.

(iv) The strategy z_j^* is termed a *local strict best response*, a *local weak best response*, a *global strict best response*, a *global weak best response*, respectively, to $\mathbf{z}_{-j}^* = (z_1^*, \ldots, z_{j-1}^*, z_{j+1}^*, \ldots, z_p^*)$, depending on whether z_j^* locally or globally, strictly or weakly, maximizes V_j at $\mathbf{z}_{-j}^*$.

Obviously if $\mathbf{z}^*$ is an LSNE or a PNE, it must be an LNE, while if it is a PSNE, then it must be an LSNE. We use the notion of LSNE to avoid problems with the degenerate situation when there is a zero eigenvalue to the Hessian. The weaker requirement of LNE allows us to obtain a necessary condition for $\mathbf{z}_0^* = (x^*, \ldots, x^*)$ to be an LNE and thus a PNE, without having to invoke concavity. Theorem 3.1, below, also gives a sufficient condition for the joint mean vector $\mathbf{z}_0^*$ to be an LSNE. A corollary of the theorem shows, in situations where the valences differ, that the necessary condition is likely to fail. In dimension w, the theorem can be used to show that for $\mathbf{z}_0^*$ to be an LSNE, the necessary condition is that a convergence coefficient, defined in terms of the parameters of the model, must be strictly bounded above by w. Similarly, for $\mathbf{z}_0^*$ to be an LNE, then the convergence coefficient must be weakly bounded above by w. When this condition fails, then the joint mean vector $\mathbf{z}_0^*$ cannot be an LNE and therefore cannot be a PNE. Of course, even if the sufficient condition is satisfied, and $\mathbf{z}_0^* = (x^*, \ldots, x^*)$ is an LSNE, it need not be a PNE.

To state the theorem, we first transform coordinates so that in the new coordinates, $x^* = 0$. We refer to $\mathbf{z}_0 = (0, \ldots, 0)$ as the *joint origin* in this new coordinate system. Whether the joint origin is an equilibrium depends on the distribution of voter ideal points. These are encoded in the voter covariation matrix. We first define this and then use it to characterize the vote-share Hessians.

Definition 3.3 *The Voter Covariance Matrix, $\frac{1}{n}\nabla$*

To characterize the variation in voter preferences, we represent in a simple form the covariation matrix (or data matrix), ∇, given by the distribution of voter ideal points. Let X have dimension w and be endowed with a system of coordinate axes $(1, \ldots, r, s, \ldots, w)$. For each coordinate axis let $\xi_r = (x_{1r}, x_{2r}, \ldots, x_{nr})$ be the vector of the rth coordinates of the set of n voter ideal points. We use (ξ_r, ξ_s) to denote scalar product.

The symmetric $w \times w$ voter covariation matrix ∇ is then defined to be

$$\nabla = \begin{pmatrix} (\xi_1, \xi_1) & \cdot & \cdot & (\xi_1, \xi_w) \\ \cdot & (\xi_r, \xi_r) & \cdot & \cdot \\ \cdot & \cdot & (\xi_s, \xi_s) & \cdot \\ (\xi_w, \xi_1) & \cdot & \cdot & (\xi_w, \xi_w) \end{pmatrix}.$$

The covariance matrix is defined to be $\frac{1}{n}\nabla$.

We write $v_s^2 = \frac{1}{n}(\xi_s, \xi_s)$ for the electoral variance on the sth axis and

$$v^2 = \sum_{r=1}^{w} v_r^2 = \frac{1}{n}\sum_{r=1}^{w}(\xi_r, \xi_r) = trace\left(\frac{1}{n}\nabla\right)$$

for the total electoral variance. Here $trace(\frac{1}{n}\nabla)$ is the sum of diagonal terms in $\frac{1}{n}\nabla$. The electoral covariance between the rth and s^{th} axes is $(v_r, v_s) = \frac{1}{n}(\xi_r, \xi_s)$.

Definition 3.4 *The Extreme Value Distribution, Ψ*

(i) The cumulative distribution has the closed form

$$\Psi(h) = \exp[-\exp[-h]],$$

with probability density function

$$\Psi(h) = \exp[-h]\exp[-\exp[-h]],$$

and variance $\frac{1}{6}\pi^2$.

A Theory of Political Competition

(ii) With this distribution it follows from Definition 3.1 for each voter i, and party j, that

$$\rho_{ij}(\mathbf{z}) = \frac{\exp[u_{ij}^*(x_i, z_j)]}{\sum_{k=1}^{p} \exp u_{ik}^*(x_i, z_k)}. \tag{3.2}$$

Note that (ii) implies that the model satisfies the independence of irrelevant alternative property (IIA): For each individual i, and each pair, j, k, the ratio

$$\frac{\rho_{ij}(\mathbf{z})}{\rho_{ik}(\mathbf{z})}$$

is independent of a third party l (See Train, 2003: 79).

While this distribution assumption facilitates estimation, the IIA property may be violated. In the empirical work on the Netherlands given in Chapter 6 we consider the case of covariant errors, thus allowing for violation of IIA.

The formal model just presented, and based on Ψ is denoted $M(\lambda, \beta; \Psi)$.

Definition 3.5 *The Convergence Coefficient of the Model* $M(\lambda, \beta; \Psi)$

(i) At the vector $\mathbf{z}_0 = (0, \ldots, 0)$ the probability $\rho_{ij}(\mathbf{z}_0)$ that i votes for party j is

$$\rho_j = \left[1 + \sum_{k \neq j} \exp\left[\lambda_k - \lambda_j\right]\right]^{-1}. \tag{3.3}$$

(ii) The coefficient A_j for party j is

$$A_j = \beta(1 - 2\rho_j).$$

(iii) The Hessian for party j at $\mathbf{z}_0$ is

$$C_j = \left[2[A_j]\left(\frac{1}{n}\nabla\right) - I\right], \tag{3.4}$$

where I is the w by w identity matrix.

(iv) The *convergence coefficient of the model* $M(\lambda, \beta; \Psi)$ is

$$c(\lambda, \beta; \Psi) = 2\beta[1 - 2\rho_1]v^2 = 2A_1 v^2. \tag{3.5}$$

The definition of ρ_j follows directly from the definition of the extreme value distribution. Obviously if all valences are identical, then $\rho_1 = \frac{1}{p}$, as expected. The effect of increasing λ_j, for $j \neq 1$, is clearly to decrease ρ_1, and therefore to increase A_1, and thus $c(\lambda, \beta; \Psi)$.

Theorem 3.1 *The condition for the joint origin to be an LSNE in the model $M(\lambda, \beta; \Psi)$ is that the Hessian*

$$C_1 = \left[2[A_1] \left(\frac{1}{n} \nabla \right) - I \right]$$

of the party 1, with lowest valence, has negative eigenvalues.

Comment on the Theorem. The proof of Theorem 3.1 is given in the Appendix to this chapter. It depends on considering the first- and second-order conditions at z_0 for each vote-share function. The first-order condition is obtained by setting $dV_j/dz_j = 0$ where we use this notation for full differentiation, keeping $\{z_k : k \neq j\}$ constant. This allows us to show that z_0 satisfies the first-order condition. The second-order condition is that the Hessian $d^2 V_j/dz_j^2$ be negative definite at the joint origin. (A presentation of these standard results is given in Schofield, 2003b). If this holds for all j at z_0, then z_0 is an LSNE. However, we need only examine this condition for the vote function V_1 for the lowest-valence party. As we shall show, this condition on the Hessian of V_1 is equivalent to the condition on C_1, and if the condition holds for V_1, then the Hessians for $V_2, \ldots, V_p$ are all negative definite at z_0. As usual, conditions on C_1 for the eigenvalues to be negative depend on the trace, trace(C_1), and determinant, $\det(C_1)$, of C_1. These depend on the value of A_1 and on the electoral variance/covariance matrix, $\frac{1}{n} \nabla$. Using the determinant of C_1, we can show that $2 A_1 v^2 < 1$ is a sufficient condition for the eigenvalues to be negative. In terms of the convergence coefficient $c(\lambda, \beta; \Psi)$ we can write this as $c(\lambda, \beta; \Psi) < 1$. In a policy space of dimension w, the necessary condition on C_1, induced from the condition on the Hessian of V_1, is that $c(\lambda, \beta; \Psi) \leq w$. This condition is obtained from examining the trace of C_1. If this necessary condition for V_1 fails, then z_0 can be neither an LNE nor an LSNE.

Ceteris paribus, an LNE at the joint origin is "less likely" the greater are the parameters β, $\lambda_p - \lambda_1$, $\lambda_{p-1} - \lambda_1, \ldots, \lambda_2 - \lambda_1$ and v^2.

Note that for a general spatial model with an arbitrary, non-Euclidean but differentiable metric $d(x_i, z_j) = ||x_i - z_j||$, a similar expression for A_1 can be obtained, but in this case the covariance term $\frac{1}{n}V$ will not have such a ready interpretation. Note also that if the nondifferentiable Cartesian metric $d(x_i, z_j) = \Sigma_{k=1}^{w}|x_{ik} - z_{jk}|$ were used, then the first-order condition would be satisfied at the median rather than at the mean.

Even when the sufficient condition is satisfied, so the joint origin is an LSNE, the concavity condition (equivalent to the negative semi-definiteness of all Hessians *everywhere*) is so strong that there is no good reason to expect it to hold. The empirical analyses of Israel and of Italy, presented in Chapters 4 and 5, show that the necessary condition fails. In these polities, a PNE, even if it exists, will generally not occur at the origin.

The theorem immediately gives the following corollaries.

Corollary 3.1 *Assume X is two-dimensional. Then, in the model $M = M(\lambda, \beta; \Psi)$, the sufficient condition for the joint origin to be an LSNE is that $c(\lambda, \beta; \Psi)$ be strictly less than 1. The necessary condition for the joint origin to be an LNE is that $c(\lambda, \beta; \Psi)$ be no greater than 2.*

Proof. The condition that both eigenvalues of C_1 be negative is equivalent to the condition that $\det(C_1)$ is positive and $\text{trace}(C_1)$ is negative. Now

$$\det(C_1) = (2A_1)^2 \left[(v_1, v_1) \cdot (v_2, v_2) - (v_1, v_2)^2 \right]$$
$$+ 1 - (2A_1) \left[(v_1, v_1) + (v_2, v_2) \right].$$

By the triangle inequality, the term $\left[(v_1, v_1) \cdot (v_2, v_2) - (v_1, v_2)^2 \right]$ is non-negative. Thus, $\det(C_1)$ is positive if

$$2\beta[1 - 2\rho_1]v^2 < 1.$$

This gives the sufficient condition that $c(\lambda, \beta; \Psi) < 1$ for an LSNE at the joint origin, z_0^*.

The necessary condition for z_0^* to be an LNE is that the eigenvalues be nonpositive. Since $\text{trace}(C_1)$ equals the sum of the eigenvalues, we can use the fact that $\text{trace}(C_1) = (2A_1)[(v_1, v_1) + (v_2, v_2)] - 2$, to obtain the necessary condition

$$2\beta[1 - 2\rho_1]v^2 - 2 \leq 0 \text{ or } c(\lambda, \beta; \Psi) \leq 2.$$

Thus, $c(\lambda, \beta; \Psi) \leq 2$ gives the necessary condition. $\qquad\square$

Corollary 3.2 *In the two-dimensional case, the two eigenvalues of C_1, for the model $M(\lambda, \beta; \Psi)$, are*

$$a_1 = A_1\{[v_1^2 + v_2^2] + [[v_1^2 - v_2^2]^2 + 4(v_1, v_2)^2]^{\frac{1}{2}}\} - 1$$

$$a_2 = A_1\{[v_1^2 + v_2^2] - [[v_1^2 - v_2^2]^2 + 4(v_1, v_2)^2]^{\frac{1}{2}}\} - 1.$$

Proof. This follows immediately from the fact that $a_1 + a_2 = \text{trace}(C_1) = c(\lambda, \beta; \Psi) - 2$. $\qquad\square$

Corollary 3.3 *In the case that X is w-dimensional, then the sufficient condition for the joint origin to be an LSNE for the model $M(\lambda, \beta; \Psi)$ is that $c(\lambda, \beta; \Psi) < 1$, while the necessary condition for the joint origin to be an LNE is that $c(\lambda, \beta; \Psi) \leq w$.*

Proof. This follows immediately by the same proof technique as Corollary 3.1. $\qquad\square$

We now consider the model $M(\lambda, \beta; \sigma^2 I, \varphi)$ where the errors are independently and identically, normally distributed (iind), given by a covariance matrix $\sigma^2 I$, and with probability density function (pdf)

$$\varphi(h) = \frac{1}{\sigma\sqrt{2\pi}} \exp\left[-\frac{1}{2}\left[\frac{h}{\sigma}\right]^2\right].$$

Definition 3.6 *The Convergence Coefficient of the Model $M(\lambda, \beta; \sigma^2 I, \varphi)$.*

(i) For each agent j, define

$$\lambda_{av(j)} = \frac{1}{p-1} \sum_{k \in P-\{j\}} \lambda_k.$$

(ii) Define the coefficient A_j for the contest of agent j against the competing agents to be

$$A_j(\varphi) = \left[\frac{(p-1)\beta}{p\sigma^2}\right]\left[\lambda_{av(j)} - \lambda_j\right].$$

(iii) The Hessian matrix C_j associated with agent j is defined to be

$$C_j(\varphi) = \left[2A_j \left(\frac{1}{n}\nabla \right) - I \right].$$

(iv) The convergence coefficient of the model $M(\lambda, \beta; \sigma^2 I, \varphi)$ is given by

$$c(\lambda, \beta; \sigma^2 I, \varphi) = 2A_1(\varphi)v^2. \tag{3.6}$$

We now state the result on the model $M(\lambda, \beta; \sigma^2 I, \varphi)$.

Theorem 3.2 *The necessary and sufficient condition for the joint origin to be an LSNE for the model $M = M(\lambda, \beta; \sigma^2 I, \varphi)$ is that the eigenvalues of the Hessian matrix $C_1(\varphi)$ all be negative.*

The proof of this theorem is given in Schofield (2004) and follows in similar fashion to the proof of Theorem 3.1. As a corollary, necessary and sufficient conditions for convergence can be obtained for the model based on the normal distribution.

Note that the case $\lambda_p = \lambda_1$ was studied by Lin, Enelow, and Dorussen (1999). In this case, the convergence coefficient $c(\lambda, \beta; \sigma^2 I, \varphi)$ is zero so the joint origin, z_0, is an LSNE. Theorem 3.2 makes clear why Lin et al. argued that if σ^2 were sufficiently large, then a PNE would occur at the joint origin.

Train (2003: 39) comments that the "difference between extreme value and independent normal errors is indistinguishable empirically." For this reason, in examining whether convergence can be expected in the empirical logit model, we use the result for the formal model, $M(\lambda, \beta; \Psi)$. Corollary 3.2 and the obvious extension can be used to determine the eigenvalues of the appropriate Hessians in dimension n.

Recent work by Banks and Duggan (2005) has examined two-party competition for the probabilistic vote model. Instead of vote maximization, they assume each party j attempts to maximize the *plurality function* $U_j(z_j, z_k) = V_j(z_j, z_k) - V_k(z_j, z_k)$. To demonstrate that the joint mean (x^*, x^*) is a PNE of the plurality maximization game they use the concavity of the plurality vote functions. It is obvious, however, that if the eigenvalues of the Hessians just considered are not all nonpositive, then concavity will fail. Obviously analogues of Theorems 3.1 and 3.2 can be developed to obtain necessary conditions for existence of LNE and PNE in the plurality two-party game, depending on the distribution assumptions on the errors.

3.2 LOCAL EQUILIBRIA UNDER ELECTORAL UNCERTAINTY

Using the expected vote-share functions as the maxim and for the electoral game has its attraction. As we have seen, the expected vote-share functions can be readily computed because they are linear functions of the entries in the voter probability matrix $(\rho_{ij}(\mathbf{z}))$. At least for two-party competition, more natural payoff functions to use are the parties' *probability of victory*. To develop this idea, we can introduce the idea of the stochastic vote-share functions $\{V_j^*(\mathbf{z}) : j = 1, \ldots, p\}$. Then the expected vote-share functions used above are simply the expectations $\{\mathcal{E}xp(V_j^*(\mathbf{z}))\}$ of these stochastic variables. In the two-party case, the probability of victory for agents 1 and 2 can be written

$$\pi_1(\mathbf{z}) = \Pr[V_1^*(\mathbf{z}) > V_2^*(\mathbf{z})] \text{ and } \pi_2(\mathbf{z}) = \Pr[V_2^*(\mathbf{z}) > V_1^*(\mathbf{z})].$$

As Patty (2006) has commented, an agent's probability of victory is a complicated nonlinear expression of the voters' behavior as described by the vote matrix $(\rho_{ij}(\mathbf{z}))$. Just as we can define LNE and PNE for the game given by the profile function $V : X^p \to \mathbb{R}^p$, we can also define LNE and PNE for the two-party profile function $\pi = (\pi_1, \pi_2) : X^2 \to \mathbb{R}^2$. Duggan (2000, 2006), Duggan and Fey (2006), and Patty (2001, 2005) have explored those conditions under which equilibria for expected vote-share functions and probability of victory are identical. As might be expected these equilibria are generically different (Patty, 2006).

We now develop a model based on electoral uncertainty, which we consider to be a generalization of the Duggan/Patty models of two-party competition. To do this we introduce the idea of a party principal.

The strategy, z_j, of party j corresponds to the position of the party leader and is chosen by the party principal, j, whose preferred position is x_j. We first develop the model with only two parties. If party j wins the election with a leader at position $z_j \in X$, while party j receives a nonpolicy perquisite δ_j, then the payoff to the principal, j, is

$$U_j((x_j, \alpha_j) : (z_j, \delta_j)) = U_j^*(z_j, \delta_j) = -\|z_j - x_j\|^2 + \alpha_j \delta_j.$$

Thus, the profile function $U = (U_1, U_2) : X^2 \to \mathbb{R}^2$ can be taken to be given by the expected payoffs

$$U_1(z_1, z_2) = \pi_1(z_1, z_2)U_1^*(z_1, \delta_1) + \pi_2(z_1, z_2)U_1^*(z_2, 0)$$

$$U_2(z_1, z_2) = \pi_2(z_1, z_2)U_2^*(z_2, \delta_2) + \pi_1(z_1, z_2)U_2^*(z_1, 0).$$

This expression ignores the probability of a draw. In the case of a draw, the outcome can be assumed to be lottery between the party positions

z_1 and z_2. The multiparty model we propose is a natural extension of the two-party model and is built as follows. As before, we can examine conditions sufficient for existence of LNE or PNE for such a two-party profile function (see Cox, 1984, 1997 for an example). To extend this to a model of *multiparty* competition with $p \geq 3$, we must deal with the fact that it is possible that no party gains a majority of the parliamentary seats (or in the case of U.S. presidential elections, a majority of the electoral college). We argue that in multiparty competition the possible outcomes of the election correspond to the family of all decisive coalition structures

$$\mathbb{D} = \{\mathcal{D}_0, \mathcal{D}_1, \ldots, \mathcal{D}_t, \ldots, \mathcal{D}_T\},$$

which can be obtained from the set P of parties. For convenience, we may assume that the subfamily $\{\mathcal{D}_1, \ldots, \mathcal{D}_p\}$, with $p < T$, corresponds to the subfamily of coalition structures where the parties $\{1, \ldots, p\}$, respectively, win the election with a majority of the seats in the Parliament. Notice that the outcomes $\{\mathcal{D}_1, \ldots, \mathcal{D}_T\}$ are defined in terms of the distribution of seat shares $(S_1, S_2, \ldots, S_p)$ in the Parliament, and not simply vote shares. The more interesting cases are given by $t > p$, and for convenience we can assume that for such a t, the coalition structure $\mathcal{D}_t = \{M \subset N : \Sigma_{j \in M} S_j > 1/2\}$. Decisive coalition structures can of course be defined in more complex ways. Since there is an intrinsic uncertainty in the way votes are translated into seats, it makes sense to focus on the probabilities associated with these decisive structures. At a vector $\mathbf{z}$ of positions of party leaders, the probability that $\mathcal{D}_t$ occurs is denoted $\pi_t(\mathbf{z})$. We also assume that the vector

$$\pi(\mathbf{z}) = (\pi_1(\mathbf{z}), \ldots, \pi_p(\mathbf{z}))$$

corresponds to the probabilities that parties $1, \ldots, p$, respectively, win the election. This vector is generated by the belief operator Π introduced earlier. When party j wins then the outcome, of course, is the situation $(z_j, 1)$. That is, party j implements the position z_j of its party leader and takes a share 1 of nonpolicy perquisites. When no party wins, but a decisive coalition $\mathcal{D}_t$ occurs, for $t \geq p + 1$, then the outcome is a lottery that we denote by $\tilde{g}_t^\alpha(\mathbf{z})$. We assume

$$\tilde{g}_t^\alpha(\mathbf{z}) \in \tilde{W} = Bor(X \times \Delta_P).$$

Here Δ_P is the set of possible distributions of government perquisites among the parties, and $W = (X \times \Delta_P)$ while $Bor(X \times \Delta_P)$ is the space of Borel probability measures over $X \times \Delta_P$ endowed with the weak topology (Parthasathy, 1967). Thus, $\tilde{g}_t^\alpha(\mathbf{z})$ specifies a finite lottery of points in X

coupled with a lottery of distributions of perquisites among the parties belonging to the decisive structure $\mathcal{D}_t$ (see Banks and Duggan, 2000, for a method of deriving this lottery). We implicitly assume that the utility function of the principal of party j, given by the expression U_j^* above, defines the function

$$U_j : (X \times \Delta_P) \to \mathbb{R},$$

where

$$U_j(z, (\delta_1, \ldots, \delta_p)) = U_j^*(z, \delta_j) = -\|z - x_j\|^2 + \alpha_j \delta_j.$$

Further, we assume each U_j be extended to a function

$$U_j : (Bor(X \times \Delta_P)) \to \mathbb{R},$$

measurable with respect to the sigma-algebra on $Bor(X \times \Delta_P)$. Note that if $g \in \tilde{W}$, then it is a measure on the Borel sigma-algebra of W. Since $U_j : W \to \mathbb{R}$ is assumed measurable, the integral $\int U_j dg$ is well defined and can be identified with $U_j(g) \in \mathbb{R}$. Note, also, that in the weak topology, a sequence $\{g_k\}$ of measures converges to g if and only if $\int U dg_k$ converges to $\int U dg$ for *every* bounded, continuous utility function U with domain W. We further assume that $\tilde{g}_t^\alpha : X^P \to \tilde{W}$ is C^2-differentiable as well as continuous. This means that for all j the induced function $U_j^t : X^P \to \mathbb{R}$, given by $U_j^t(\mathbf{z}) = U_j \tilde{g}_t^\alpha(\mathbf{z})$, is also C^2-differentiable, so its Hessian with respect to z_j is everywhere defined and continuous. Observe that $\tilde{g}_t^\alpha$ is used to model the common beliefs of the principals concerning the outcome of political bargaining in the post-election situation given by $\mathcal{D}_t$. The common beliefs of the principals concerning electoral outcomes are given by a C^2-differentiable function $\pi : X^p \to \Delta_T$ from X^p to the simplex Δ_T (of dimension T-1) where T is the cardinality of the set of all possible coalition structures. At a vector $\mathbf{z}$ of positions of party leaders, the probability is $\pi_t(\mathbf{z})$ that the distribution of parliamentary seats among the parties gives the decisive structure $\mathcal{D}_t$. The *electoral probability function* π, induced from Π, models the uncertainty associated with the election. Note that this uncertainty also includes the uncertainty over the valences of the various party leaders. We now provide the formal definitions for the multiparty political game.

Definition 3.7 *The Game Form with Policy Preferences*

(i) The *electoral probability function* $\pi = (\pi_1, \ldots, \pi_T) : X^p \to \Delta_T$ is a smooth function from X^p to the simplex Δ_T (of dimension T-1), where $\mathbb{D} = \{\mathcal{D}_1, \ldots, \mathcal{D}_T\}$ is the set of all possible decisive coalition structures. This function captures the notion of *electoral risk*.

(ii) For fixed $\mathcal{D}_t$, the outcome of bargaining at the parameter $\alpha = (\alpha_1, \ldots, \alpha_p)$ and at the strategy vector $\mathbf{z}$ is a lottery

$$\tilde{g}_t^{\alpha}(\mathbf{z}) \in (Bor(X \times \Delta_P)).$$

This captures the notion of *coalition risk at* $\mathcal{D}_t$.

(iii) At the fixed decisive structure $\mathcal{D}_t$ and strategy vector $\mathbf{z}$, the payoff to the principal of party j is

$$U_j^t(\mathbf{z}) = \mathbf{U}_j(\tilde{g}_t^{\alpha}(\mathbf{z})).$$

(iv) The *game form* $\{\tilde{g}_t^{\alpha}, \pi_t\}$ at the parameter α is denoted $\tilde{g}^{\alpha}$. At the strategy vector $\mathbf{z}$, the payoff to the principal j is given by the von Neumann-Morgenstern utility function

$$U_j^g(\mathbf{z}) = \mathbf{U}_j(\tilde{g}^{\alpha}(\mathbf{z})) = \sum_{t=1,\ldots,T} \pi_t(\mathbf{z}) U_j^t(\mathbf{z}). \qquad (3.7)$$

(v) The *game profile* derived from the game form $\tilde{g}^{\alpha}$ at the utility profile $\{U_j\}$ is denoted

$$U^g = (\mathbf{U}_1 \circ \tilde{g}^{\alpha}, \ldots, \mathbf{U}_p \circ \tilde{g}^{\alpha}) = (..U_j^g..) : X^p \to \mathbb{R}^p.$$

(vi) The game form $\tilde{g}^{\alpha}$ is *smooth* iff the function $U^g : X^p \to \mathbb{R}^p$ is C^2-differentiable. Let $\mathbb{U}(X^p, \mathbb{R}^p)$ be the set of C^2-differentiable utility profiles $\{U : X^p \to \mathbb{R}^p\}$ endowed with the C^2 topology. (Roughly speaking, two profiles are close in this topology if all values and first and second derivatives of each U_j are close).

(vii) A *generic property in* $\mathbb{U}(X^p, \mathbb{R}^p)$ is one that is true for a set of profiles that is open dense in the C^2 topology. (See Hirsch, 1976 and Schofield, 2003a for the definition of the C^2-topology and the notion of generic property.)

(viii) For the fixed smooth game form $\tilde{g}^{\alpha}$, let $\{U : X^p \to \mathbb{R}^p\} \subset \mathbb{U}(X^p, \mathbb{R}^p)$ be the set of utility profiles induced as the parameters of voter ideal points and electoral beliefs are allowed to vary.

(ix) Let $\mathbb{G}$ be the set of smooth game forms. The transformation $\tilde{g} \to U^g : \mathbb{G} \to \mathbb{U}(X^p, \mathbb{R}^p)$ induces a topology on the set $\mathbb{G}$, where this topology is obtained by taking the coarsest topology such that this transformation is continuous.

(x) The vector $\mathbf{z}^* = (z_1^*, \ldots, z_{j-1}^*, \quad z_j^*, \quad z_{j+1}^*, \ldots, z_p^*) \in X^p$ is an LSNE for the profile $U \in \mathbb{U}(X^p, \mathbb{R}^p)$ iff for each j there is a neighborhood X_j of z_j^* in X, with the property that

$$U_j(z_1^*, \ldots, z_j^*, z_{j+1}^*, \ldots, z_p^*) > U_j(z_1^*, \ldots, z_j, z_{i+1}^*, \ldots, z_p^*)$$

for all $z_j \in X_j - \{z_j^*\}$.

(xi) $\mathbf{z}^* \in X^p$ is a *critical Nash equilibrium* (CNE) for the profile U iff, for each j, the first order condition $\frac{dU_j}{dz_j} = 0$ is satisfied at $\mathbf{z}^*$.

(xii) A PSNE for U is an LSNE for U with the additional requirement that each X_j is in fact X.

(xiii) For a fixed profile $x \in X^n$ of voter ideal points, fixed electoral beliefs π, and fixed game form g, the vector $\mathbf{z}^*$ is called the LSNE, PSNE, or CNE if it satisfies the appropriate condition for the game profile $U^g : X^p \to \mathbb{R}^p$.

(xiv) An LSNE $\mathbf{z}^* \in X^p$ for the profile U is *locally isolated* iff there is a neighborhood Z^* of $\mathbf{z}^*$ in X^p that contains no LSNE for U other than $\mathbf{z}^*$.

Schofield (2001) and Schofield and Sened (2002) have shown that, for each parameter, α, there is an open dense set of smooth game forms, with the property that each form $\tilde{g}^\alpha$ in the set exhibits a locally isolated LSNE. In principle, this result suggests that if the electoral function is smooth, and if the outcome of coalition bargaining is differentiable in the location of parties, then there will exist local equilibria that can be used to deduce party positions. Of course, this model is very much more complex than the vote maximizing version presented in the previous section.

For the Theorem to be valid, we require that the strategy space X^p is a compact, convex subset of a finite dimensional topological vector space. We shall call such a space a *Fan space* (Fan, 1964). We also require the following boundary condition on the profile. Say a profile $U \in \mathbb{U}(X^p, \mathbb{R}^p)$ satisfies the *boundary condition* if for every point $\mathbf{z}$ on the boundary of the Fan space, X^p, the induced gradient $(\frac{dU_1}{dz_1}, \ldots, \frac{dU_p}{dz_p})$ points toward the interior of X^p. Let $\mathbb{U}_b(X^p, \mathbb{R}^p)$ be the subspace of profiles satisfying the boundary condition.

Theorem 3.3 *Assume X is a Fan space and p is finite. Then the property that the LSNE exists and is locally isolated is generic in the topological space $\mathbb{U}_b(X^p, \mathbb{R}^p)$.*

Sketch of Proof. For each j, consider the set $T_j = \{\mathbf{z} \in X^p : \frac{dU_j}{dz_j} = 0\}$. By the inverse function theorem, T_j is generically a smooth manifold of dimension $(p-1)\dim(X)$. By transversality theory, the intersection $\cap_{j \in P} T_j$

is of codimension $p \dim(X)$ in X^p. But X^p has dimension $p \dim(X) = pw$. Since the set of CNE $\equiv \cap_{j \in P} T_j$, this shows that there is an open dense set $\mathbb{U}_b^*(X^p, \mathbb{R}^p)$ such that for each $U \in \mathbb{U}_b^*(X^p, \mathbb{R}^p)$, the set of CNE of U is of dimension 0; that is, it consists of locally isolated points. Now for each such U, construct a gradient field $\mu(U)$ on X^p whose zeros consist precisely of the CNE of U (see Schofield, 2001, for this construction). Since X is assumed to be compact, convex, it is homeomorphic to the ball. Because of the boundary assumption on profiles, the field $\mu(U)$ points inward on the boundary of X^p. The Morse inequalities (Milnor, 1963; Dierker, 1976) imply that there must be at least one critical point z^* of $\mu(U)$ whose index is maximal. Thus, the Hessian of each U_j at z^* must be negative definite, and z^* corresponds to a locally isolated LSNE of the profile U. $\qquad\square$

This theorem suggests that if we consider any fixed game form $\tilde{g}$, then existence of locally isolated LSNE is a generic property in the space U : $X^p \to \mathbb{R}^p\} \subset \mathbb{U}(X^p, \mathbb{R}^p)$. Moreover, if the transformation $\mathbb{G} \to \mathbb{U}(X^p, \mathbb{R}^p)$ is well behaved, in the sense that open sets are transformed to open sets, then continuity of the transformation would imply that existence of LSNE is a generic property in the space $\mathbb{G}$.

3.3   THE CORE AND THE HEART

In the previous section we assumed that the outcome of bargaining between the party leaders could be described by a lottery $\tilde{g}_t^\alpha(z)$, determined by the vector z of positions of party leaders. The analysis of Banks and Duggan indicated that in general this outcome would coincide with the *core* of the coalition game determined by the post-election decisive structure $\mathcal{D}_t$ and the vector z. To develop this idea further we now give the formal definitions of the core and other solution concepts based on social choice theory.

Definition 3.8 *Concepts of Social Choice Theory*

(i) A (strict) *preference* Q on a set, or space, W is a correspondence $Q: W \to 2(W)$, where $2(W)$ stands for the family of all subsets of W (including the empty set ϕ). Again, we assume W is a *Fan space*.

(ii) Let $Q : W \to 2(W)$ be a preference correspondence on the space W. The *choice* of Q is

$$\mathbb{C}(Q) = \{x \in W : Q(x) = \phi\}.$$

(iii) The covering correspondence Q^* of Q is defined by $y \in Q^*(x)$ iff $y \in Q(x)$ and $Q(y) \subset Q(x)$. Say y *covers* x. The *uncovered set*, $\mathbb{C}^*(Q)$ of Q, is

$$\mathbb{C}^*(Q) = \mathbb{C}(Q^*) = \{x \in W : Q^*(x) = \phi\}.$$

(iv) If W is a topological space, then $x \in W$ is *locally covered* (under Q) iff for any neighborhood Y of x in W, there exists $y \in Y$ such that

$$y \in Q(x) \text{ and } Y \cap Q(y) \subset Y \cap Q(x).$$

If x is not locally covered, then write $Q^{**}(x) = \phi$.

(v) The *heart* of Q, written $\mathcal{H}(Q)$, is defined by

$$\mathcal{H}(Q) = \{x \in W : Q^{**}(x) = \phi\}.$$

A preference Q is *convex* iff for all x, the preferred set $Q(x)$ of x is strictly convex. In general, if $\mathbb{C}(Q)$ is nonempty, then it is contained in both $\mathbb{C}^*(Q)$ and $\mathcal{H}(Q)$. It can be shown that if $\mathbb{C}(Q) \neq \phi$ and $Q' \to Q$ in an appropriate topological sense, then it is possible to find a sequence $\{z^s \in \mathcal{H}(Q')\}$ such that $\{z^s\}$ converges to some point in the core, $\mathbb{C}(Q)$.

Now let $CON(W)^P$ stand for all "smooth" convex preference profiles for the set of political agents $P = \{1, \ldots, p\}$. Thus $q \in CON(W)^P$ means $q = (q_1, \ldots, q_p)$, where each $q_j : W \to 2(W)$ is a convex preference whose indifference surfaces are smooth. In particular, this means we can represent the preference profile q by a C^2-utility profile $U \in \mathbb{U}(W, \mathbb{R}^p)$. Let rep: $CON(W)^P \to \mathbb{U}(X, \mathbb{R}^p)$ be the representation map.

Definition 3.9 *The Heart and the Uncovered Set*

(i) Let $\mathcal{D}$ be a fixed set of decisive coalitions and W be a Fan space. Let $q \in CON(W)^P$ be a smooth preference profile. Define

$$\sigma_\mathcal{D}(q) = \cup_{M \in \mathcal{D}} \{\cap_{i \in M} q_i\} : W \to 2(W)$$

to be the preference correspondence induced by $\mathcal{D}$ at the profile q. The *core* of the political game given by $\mathcal{D}$ at q, written $\mathbb{C}_\mathcal{D}(q)$, is $\mathbb{C}(\sigma_\mathcal{D}(q))$.

(ii) The *heart* of $\mathcal{D}$ at q, written $\mathcal{H}_\mathcal{D}(q)$, is defined to be $\mathcal{H}(\sigma_\mathcal{D}(q))$. The *uncovered set* of $\mathcal{D}$ at q, written $\mathbb{C}^*_\mathcal{D}(q)$, is $\mathbb{C}^*(\sigma_\mathcal{D}(q))$.

(iii) The *Pareto set* of the profile q is $\mathbb{C}_P(q) = \mathbb{C}(\sigma_P(q))$, where

$$\sigma_P(q) : \{\cap_{i \in P} q_i\} : W \to 2(W)$$

is the Pareto, or strict unanimity, preference correspondence.

(iv) A correspondence $Q: W \to Z$ is *lower hemi continuous* (lhc) with respect to topologies on W, Z iff for any open set $Y \subset Z$ the set

$$\{x \in W : Q(x) \cap Y \neq \phi\}$$

is open in W.

(v) A *continuous selection* g for Q is a function $g : W \to Z$, continuous with respect to the topologies on W, Z such that $g(x) \in Q(x), \forall x \in W$, whenever $Q(x) \neq \phi$.

(vi) A correspondence $\mathcal{H} : CON(W)^P \to 2(W)$ is called C^2-*lower hemi continuous* (C^2-lhc) if the map

$$\mathcal{H} \circ rep^{-1} : \mathbb{U}(X, \mathbb{R}^p) \to CON(W)^P \to 2(W)$$

is also lhc with respect to the C^2-topology on $\mathbb{U}(X, \mathbb{R}^p)$.

Schofield (1996, 1998, 1999a,b) has shown that the heart is nonempty, Paretian, and C^2-lhc. The heart correspondence can then be shown to admit a continuous selection (Michael, 1956).

Theorem 3.4 summarizes the technical properties of the heart correspondence.

Theorem 3.4 *Let W be a Fan space, and $\mathcal{D}$ any voting rule. Then $H_D : CON(W)^P \to 2(W)$ is C^2-lhc. Moreover, for any $q \in CON(W)^P$, the set $H_D(q)$ is closed, nonempty, and is a subset of the Pareto set $C_P(q)$. Moreover, H_D admits a continuous selection $g_D : CON(W)^P \to W$ such that $g_D(q) \in \mathbb{C}(\sigma_D(q))$ whenever $C(\sigma_D(q))$ is nonempty. Indeed, g_D can be factored to give a C^2-differentiable map*

$$g_D \circ rep^{-1} : \mathbb{U}(X, \mathbb{R}^p) \to CON(W)^P \to W.$$

This last property means that if U is a C^2-differentiable profile then the induced profile $U \circ g_D$ is also C^2-differentiable.

For convenience, we say g_D is a smooth *Paretian selection which converges to the core.*

To use Theorem 3.4 to model coalition bargaining, we assume as before that the preferred position of the *leader* (or *agent*) for party j determines the declaration z_j of the party. We assume that the outcome of bargaining is an element of $W = (X \times \Delta_P)$, namely a policy choice x and a distribution $(\delta_1, \ldots, \delta_p)$ of the total perquisites. Thus, the leader of party j receives utility

$$U_j((z_j, \alpha_j) : (x, (\delta_1, \ldots, \delta_p))) = U_j^*(x, \delta_j) = - \| z_j - x \|^2 + \alpha_j \delta_j.$$

This implies that the leader can be described by a smooth, strictly convex preference correspondence $q_j^{\alpha_j}(z_i) : X \times \Delta_P \to X \times \Delta_P$. Let $\alpha = (\alpha_1, \ldots, \alpha_p), \mathbf{z} = (z_1, \ldots, z_p)$, and $q^{\alpha}(\mathbf{z})$ denote the profile of leader preferences. The Pareto set $\mathbb{C}_P(q^{\alpha}(\mathbf{z}))$ in $X \times \Delta_P$ is the unanimity choice of this preference profile. As in the previous section, we now consider a family $\mathbb{D} = \{\mathcal{D}_1, \ldots, \mathcal{D}_t, \ldots, \mathcal{D}_T\}$ of decisive coalitions. We call each set $\mathcal{D}_t$ the *voting rule induced by the election.* For each $\mathcal{D}_t$, we can define the heart of the voting rule on the space $W = X \times \Delta_P$ as $\mathcal{H}_{\mathcal{D}_t}(q^{\alpha}(\mathbf{z}))$. This set we write as $\mathcal{H}_t^{\alpha}(\mathbf{z})$. We write the core $\mathbb{C}(\sigma_{\mathcal{D}_t}(q^{\alpha}(\mathbf{z})))$ as $\mathbb{C}_t^{\alpha}(\mathbf{z})$. Theorem 3.4 can then be applied to show that each correspondence $\mathcal{H}_t^{\alpha}$ is C^2-lhc and admits a C^2-selection which converges to the core $\mathbb{C}_t^{\alpha}(\mathbf{z})$. The family of correspondences $\{\mathcal{H}_t^{\alpha}\}$ we write as $\mathcal{H}_{\mathbb{D}}^{\alpha}$.

To extend these concepts to the situation where the electoral outcome is a lottery, we again use the definition of $\tilde{W} = Bor(X \times \Delta_P)$, the set of all lotteries over $X \times \Delta_P$, endowed with the weak topology. Now let $\tilde{\mathcal{H}}_t^{\alpha} : X^p \to 2(\tilde{W})$ be the extension of the heart correspondence to this space, so $\tilde{\mathcal{H}}_t^{\alpha}(\mathbf{z})$ is the set of lotteries over the set $\mathcal{H}_t^{\alpha}(\mathbf{z})$ with the induced topology. Then lhc of $\mathcal{H}_t^{\alpha}$ implies lhc of $\tilde{\mathcal{H}}_t^{\alpha}$ (Schofield, 1999a,b).

Theorem 3.5 *For a fixed voting rule, $\mathcal{D}_t$, there exists a smooth selection $\tilde{g}_t^{\alpha} : X^p \to \tilde{W}$ of the correspondence $\tilde{\mathcal{H}}_t^{\alpha} : X^p \to 2(\tilde{W})$, which converges to the core.*

As in the previous section, $\tilde{g}_t^{\alpha}$ is meant to capture the notion of *coalition risk* at the vector $\mathbf{z}$ of party positions and at the decisive structure $\mathcal{D}_t$. Convergence to the core is intended to capture the following logic. If the core $\mathbb{C}_t^{\alpha}(\mathbf{z})$ is nonempty, then the selection $\tilde{g}_t^{\alpha}(\mathbf{z})$ must put all probability weight on this set, guaranteeing that this is the outcome. In such a situation there is no coalition risk.

We can now repeat the analysis of the previous section for the case of a game form $\tilde{g}^{\alpha} = \{\tilde{g}_t^{\alpha}, \pi_t\}$ obtained as a selection from the heart correspondence. First, let K be some compact convex subset of $\mathbb{R}^p$ for the parameters α, and let $\tilde{g}$ be a general game form that specifies the game form $\tilde{g}^{\alpha} = \tilde{g}_t^{\alpha}, \pi_t\}$ for each $\alpha \in K$.

Definition 3.10 *The game form $\tilde{g}$, which specifies $\{\tilde{g}_t^{\alpha}, \pi_t\}$ at $\alpha \in K$ is* heart compatible over K *iff each component $\tilde{g}_t^{\alpha} : X^p \to \tilde{W}$ is a smooth selection of the heart correspondence $\tilde{\mathcal{H}}_t^{\alpha} : X^p \to 2(\tilde{W})$.*

Theorem 3.6 *There exists a game form $\tilde{g}$ which is heart compatible and has the following property: If the induced utility profiles are given by $\{U^g : X^p \to R^p\}$ then there is an open dense set in*

$$\{U^g : X^p \to \mathbb{R}^p\} \cap \mathbb{U}_b(X^p, \mathbb{R}^p)$$

such that each profile in this set exhibits a locally isolated LSNE.

In applying this Theorem, it will prove useful to consider the notion of a *structurally stable core* for the particular case when nonpolicy perquisites are zero.

Definition 3.11 *Consider the case $\alpha = (\alpha_1, \ldots, \alpha_p) = (0, \ldots, 0)$. If the core $\mathbb{C}_t^0(z)$ at z and $\mathcal{D}_t$ is nonempty then it is said to be structurally stable if, for any $x \in \mathbb{C}_t^0(z)$, there exists a neighborhood Z^* of z in X^p and a neighborhood X^* of x in X such that $X^* \cap \mathbb{C}_t^0(z^*) \neq \phi$ for all $z^* \in Z^*$.*

When the core at z and $\mathcal{D}_t$ is structurally stable then it is denoted $\mathbb{SC}_t^0(z)$.

In other words, the *policy core* $\mathbb{C}_t^0(\mathbf{z})$ is structurally stable if a small arbitrary perturbation of the profile $\mathbf{z}$ simply perturbs the location of the core. The symmetry conditions developed by McKelvey and Schofield (1986, 1987) allow us to determine when a policy core is structurally stable. In general, these symmetry conditions are easiest to use when the policy core coincides with the position of a party.

Definition 3.12 *A party j is said to be a core party at the profile $\mathbf{z} = (z_1, \ldots, z_p)$ and with the decisive structure $\mathcal{D}_t$ iff it is the case that $\mathbb{C}_t^0(\mathbf{z}) = z_j$ and there exists a neighborhood Z^* of $\mathbf{z}$ in X^p such that $\mathbb{C}_t^0(\mathbf{z}^*) = z_j^*$ for all $\mathbf{z}^* \in Z^*$.*

Notice that if j is a core party, then the core at z_j must also be structurally stable. Laver and Schofield (1990) argue that if j is a (nonmajority) core party at $\mathbf{z}$ and $\mathcal{D}_t$, then the party should be able to implement the policy position z_j by constructing a minority coalition government including party j, but not necessarily comprising a majority coalition. This follows because no majority coalition $M \in \mathcal{D}_t$ can propose some counter policy $z \in X$ that all parties in the coalition M prefer to z_j.

We earlier defined the decisive structures $\{\mathcal{D}_1, \ldots, \mathcal{D}_p\}$ to be those where party $1, \ldots, p$ respectively obtains a majority of the seats. Obviously a party with a majority can implement its position, so it must also be a core party. But this is also true for a nonmajority core party in the case that $\mathbb{SC}_t^0(\mathbf{z}) = z_j$. This allows us to partition $\mathbb{D}$ into equivalence classes. First, we use the term *feasible profile* to refer to a profile $\mathbf{z}$ that belongs to a subset X_0^p of profiles that are considered by the party principals. The following definitions depend on this restriction to such a subset of the joint strategy space.

> **Definition 3.13** *For each $j \in P$, let $\mathbb{D}_j$ denote the subfamily of $\mathbb{D}$ with the property that for each $\mathcal{D}_t \in \mathbb{D}_j$, two conditions hold: (i) there exists a feasible profile $\mathbf{z} = (z_1, \ldots, z_p)$ such that j is a core party at $\mathbf{z}$ and $\mathcal{D}_t$, and (ii) there is no feasible profile $\mathbf{z}'$ such that party $k \neq j$ is a core party at $\mathbf{z}'$ and $\mathcal{D}_t$.*

Note that party j will have a majority in the structure $\mathcal{D}_j$ so necessarily it will be the unique core party for any profile. As a result, $\mathcal{D}_j \in \mathbb{D}_j$. As Schofield (1995) has shown, for j to be a core party it is necessary that the vector of seat shares satisfies certain restrictions. The $\frac{3}{4}$ case where each of the four parties has exactly $\frac{1}{4}$ of the seat share is "exceptional" because then each of the parties is a core party in two dimensions. The restrictions that characterize $\mathbb{D}_j$ require that the jth seat share necessarily satisfies the condition $S_j > S_k$, for $k \neq j$. In the elections we examine below in Britain and in the United States, it is typical that one party k, say, gains a majority seat share so $S_k > \frac{1}{2}$. However, in the multiparty systems in Israel, Italy, and the Netherlands, based on variants of proportional electoral laws, no party gains a majority seat share. We argue that the crucial characteristic of the election is whether there exists a core party. For empirical applications we somewhat modify the definition of $\mathbb{D}_0$, made previously in Section 2.8.

Definition 3.14

(i) Let $\mathbb{D}_0$ denote the subfamily of $\mathbb{D} - \cup_{j=1}^{p} \{\mathbb{D}_j\}$ such that for each $\mathcal{D}_t \in \mathbb{D}_0$ and any feasible profile $\mathbf{z} = (z_1, \ldots, z_p)$ the policy core $\mathbb{C}_t^0(\mathbf{z})$ is either empty or not structurally stable.

(ii) Let Δ_{p+1} be the simplex of dimension p. Then the *modified electoral probability function* $\pi^* = (\pi_0^*, \ldots, \pi_p^*) : X^p \to \Delta_{\mathrm{pH}}$ is defined by

$$\pi_0^*(\mathbf{z}) = \Pr[\mathbb{D}_0 \text{ occurs at } \mathbf{z}].$$

$$\text{For } j = 1, \ldots, p, \pi_j^*(\mathbf{z}) = \Pr[\mathbb{D}_j \text{ occurs at } \mathbf{z}].$$

$$\pi_{p+1}^*(\mathbf{z}) = \Pr[\text{not } \mathbb{D}_0 \text{ or not } \cup_{j=1}^{p} \{\mathbb{D}_j\} \text{ occurs at } \mathbf{z}].$$

The $(p + 2)$ different states distinguished in this definition provide a qualitative characterization of the electoral outcomes.

3.4 EXAMPLE: THE NETHERLANDS

To illustrate the idea of the heart and coalition risk, consider the following example for the Netherlands.

Chapter 6 examines the elections of 1977 and 1981 in the Netherlands. There are four main parties: Labour (PvdA), Christain Democratic Appeal (CDA), Liberals (VVD), and Democrats (D'66), with approximately 40 percent, 35 percent, 20 percent, and 5 percent of the popular vote. Given uncertainty about the elections, there are two relevant coalition structures:

$$\mathbb{D}_0 = \{PvdA,CDA\},\{PvdA,VVD\},\{CDA,VVD\}$$

$$\mathbb{D}_{PvdA} = \{PvdA,CDA\},\{PvdA,VVD, D'66\},\{CDA,VVD,D'66\}.$$

The second structure is denoted $\mathbb{D}_{PvdA}$ because it is evident that a structurally stable policy core can occur at a profile

$$\mathbf{z} = (z_{PvdA}, z_{CDA}, z_{VVD}, z_{D'66})$$

whenever z_{PvdA} lies in the interior of the convex hull of the three positions $z_{CDA}, z_{VVD}, z_{D'66}$. To see this, note that although $\{CDA,VVD, D'66\}$ is a decisive coalition, its members cannot agree over a policy position that they all prefer to z_{PvdA}. It is also the case that this situation is insensitive to small perturbations of party positions, and so the core at z_{PvdA} is structurally stable. Thus, with this configuration PvdA is a core party.

On the other hand, with the decisive structure $\mathbb{D}_0$ there is no vector of party positions that gives a structurally stable core outcome. This situation is typical of the multiparty situations that we examine in Israel, Italy, and the Netherlands. Table 3.1 gives the election results for 1977 and 1981 in the Netherlands. It is immediately obvious that the coalition $\{CDA,VVD\}$ had 77 seats in 1977, and thus comprised a majority. Consequently, the coalition structure $\mathbb{D}_0$ was in place. However, in 1981, this coalition won only 74 seats, so the coalition structure was $\mathbb{D}_{PvdA}$ or $\mathbb{D}_1$. Figure 3.1 shows the electoral distribution together with the estimated party positions, based on survey data for 1979. These estimates are discussed in Chapter 6. We wish to emphasize here that optimal party positioning for the 1981 election depends on party estimates of the functions $\pi_0^*(\mathbf{z})$ and $\pi_1^*(\mathbf{z})$.

Table 3.1. *Election Results in the Netherlands, 1977–1981.*

Party (acronym)	1977	1981
	(Seats)	
Labour (PvdA)	53	44
Democrats '66 (D'66)	8	17
Liberals (VVD)	28	26
Christian Dem Appeal (CDA)	49	48
	(138)	(135)
Communists (CPN)	2	3
Dem '70 (D'70)	1	0
Radicals (PPR)	3	3
Pacific Socialists (PSP)	–	3
Reform Federation (RPF)	–	2
Reform Pol Ass (GDV)	1	1
Farmers Party (BP)	1	0
State Reform Party (SGP)	3	3
	(11)	(15)
Total	149	150

To apply the model presented above, consider the question of optimal position for the CDA prior to the 1981 election. To simplify the analysis, let us concentrate on the situation where the CDA expects the coalition structure $\mathbb{D}_0$. Thus, we may suppose that $\pi_1^*(\mathbf{z}) = 0$ for all feasible vectors $\mathbf{z}$. In a situation where perquisites are zero (so $\alpha = 0$), consider $\{g_0^0, \pi_0\}$ with $\pi_0 = 1$. Since D'66 plays no role under this coalition structure, we may ignore it, and suppose that the sincere positions of the principals of the three parties {PvdA,CDA,VVD} are given, as in Figure 3.2, by

$$\mathbf{z}_{prin} = (z_{PvdA}, z_{VVD}, z_{CDA}) = (-\sqrt{3}, 0), (\sqrt{3}, 0), (0, 1).$$

The heart $\mathcal{H}_0^0(\mathbf{z})$ associated with any vector $\mathbf{z}$ of party positions and the coalition structure $\mathbb{D}_0$ can easily be seen to be the convex hull of the party positions. For purposes of illustration, for any profile $\mathbf{z}$, let $\tilde{g}_0^0(\mathbf{z})$ be the lottery that specifies the uniform distribution across $\mathcal{H}_0^0(\mathbf{z})$. Obviously $\tilde{g}_0^0$ is a smooth selection of the heart correspondence. To illustrate the best response of the CDA, suppose the positions of PvdA and VVD are given by (z_{PvdA}, z_{VVD}) as in the figure and let us compare the utilities for the CDA at the positions $z_{CDA}^* = (0, 3)$ and $z_{CDA} = (0, 1)$. From the symmetry of the figure it follows that the von Neumann-Morgenstern utility function

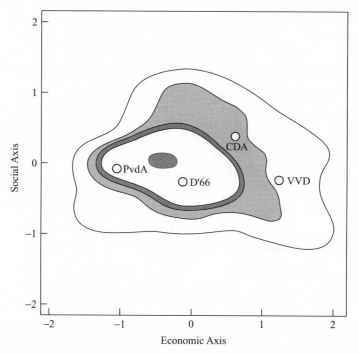

Figure 3.1. Estimated party positions in the Netherlands, based on 1979 data.

U_{CDA} satisfies the equation

$$U_{CDA}\big(\tilde{g}_0^0(z_{PvdA}, z_{CDA}^*, z_{VVD})\big) = \frac{1}{3} U_{CDA}\big(\tilde{g}_0^0(z_{PvdA}, z_{CDA}, z_{VVD})\big)$$

$$+ \frac{1}{3} U_{CDA}\big(\tilde{g}_0^0(z_{PvdA}, z_{CDA}, z_{CDA}^*)\big)$$

$$+ \frac{1}{3} U_{CDA}\big(\tilde{g}_0^0(z_{CDA}^*, z_{CDA}, z_{VVD})\big)$$

$$= U_{CDA}\big(\tilde{g}_0^0(z_{PvdA}, z_{CDA}, z_{VVD})\big).$$

By continuity, there is a position denoted y_{CDA} on the arc $[(0,1),(0,3)]$ which gives the best response of the CDA to (z_{PvdA}, z_{VVD}). The analysis of the example is developed further in Schofield and Parks (2000), where they show that there exist LSNE for this fixed coalition structure such that some parties adopt "radical" positions.

This example suggests that party principals may choose more radical positions for their leaders in order to influence coalition bargaining in their favor. We may call this phenomenon *the centrifugal effect of coalition risk.*

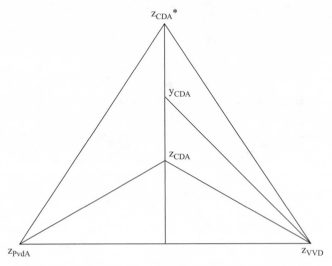

Figure 3.2. Coalition risk in the Netherlands at the 1981 election.

3.5 EXAMPLE: ISRAEL

To further illustrate the theory, consider again the Israeli case briefly discussed in Chapter 2. Figure 3.3 reproduces Figure 2.3 to show the estimated positions of the parties at the time of the 1992 election. Table 2.1 in Chapter 2 shows that, after this election in 1992, the coalition $M_1 = \{$Labour, Meretz, ADL, HS$\}$ controlled 61 seats while the coalition M_2 of the religious parties and the right, including Likud, controlled only 59 seats out of 120. Thus, the 1992 decisive structure may be written $\mathcal{D}_{1992}$ and has the form

$$\{M_1, M_2 \cup Labour, M_2 \cup Meretz\}$$

Since the Labour position z_{labour} in Figure 3.3 obviously lies inside the convex hull of the positions of parties in any winning coalition, we observe that $z_{labour} = \mathbb{SC}^0_{1992}(\mathbf{z})$ is the structurally stable core. Now it is possible to find a profile z with z_{likud} lying inside the convex hull of the positions of the parties in M_1. Such a profile we regard as empirically infeasible. It therefore follows that Labour would be the uniquely feasible core party under $\mathcal{D}_{1992}$. Thus, $\mathcal{D}_{1992} \in \mathbb{D}_{labour}$. Moreover, Labour is *dominant* under $\mathcal{D}_{1992}$ with the party positions similar to those given in Figure 3.3. As above we refer to this family of coalition structures as $\mathbb{D}_1$.

Again, using Table 2.1, we note that after the 1988 election, the coalition M_2 controlled 65 seats and so belonged to $\mathcal{D}_{1988}$. Clearly, there is a

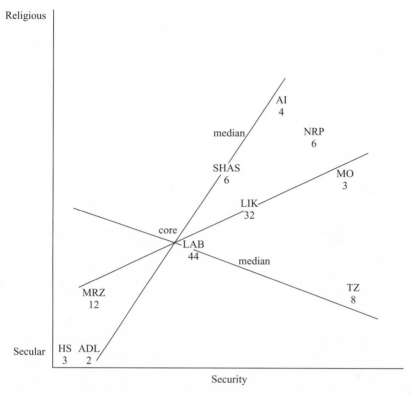

Figure 3.3. Estimated party positions and core in the Knesset after the 1992 election.

profile **z** with z_{labour} lying inside the convex hull of the positions of the parties in M_2, but again this can be regarded as infeasible. We can therefore assert that there is no feasible **z** such that $\mathbb{SC}^0_{1988}(\mathbf{z})$ is nonempty, which leads us to infer that $\mathcal{D}_{1988} \in \mathbb{D}_0$. Again, Figure 3.4 shows the heart $\mathcal{H}^0_0(\mathbf{z})$ given by the decisive structure $\mathbb{D}_0$ and profile **z** as given in the figure.

Prior to the 1996 election, there are therefore two qualitatively distinct possible outcomes, namely $\{\mathbb{D}_0, \mathbb{D}_1\}$. To examine optimal party positions prior to the election of 1996, first consider the outcomes under the assumption that $\mathbb{D}_1$ occurs. Without perquisites, the outcome will be $\mathbb{SC}^0_1(\mathbf{z}) = z_{labour}$. Since we assume party principals have policy preferences, the principal of Likud should choose a position to minimize $\pi^*_1(\mathbf{z}) = \Pr[\mathbb{D}_1]$. One obvious way to do this is to choose z_{likud} as a best response in order to maximize its expected vote share. In contrast, Labour should attempt to maximize $\pi^*_1(\mathbf{z}) = \Pr[\mathbb{D}_1]$. The principal of Shas cannot affect policy outcomes under this eventuality.

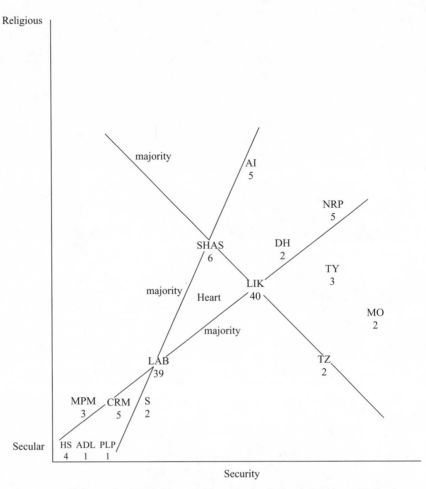

Figure 3.4. Estimated party positions and heart in the Knesset after the 1988 election.

Now consider the situation under $\mathbb{D}_0$. As indicated in Figure 3.4, the heart will be a subset of the convex hull of the positions in the coalition $M_3 = \{$Likud, Labour, Shas$\}$. As in the previous example, this suggests that Shas should adopt a "radical" position in order to influence coalition outcomes.

To summarize: Labour should adopt a position as a best response in order to maximize $\pi_1^*(\mathbf{z})$ while Likud should minimize $\pi_1^*(\mathbf{z})$. As a first approximation, these strategies can be interpreted as maximizing the vote-share functions V_{labour}, V_{likud}, respectively. For Shas, and other small religious parties, optimal strategies will depend on their estimates of π_0^* and π_1^*. Since these probabilities will be little affected by the Shas position,

66

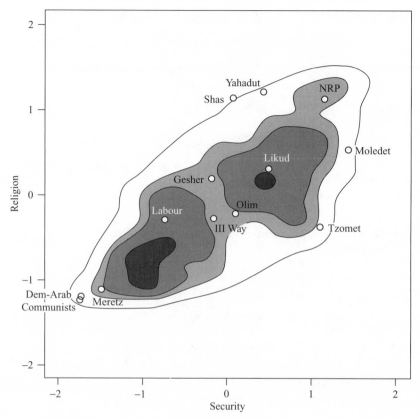

Figure 3.5. Estimated party positions in the Knesset after the 1996 election.

we can assert that the larger is the estimate of $\pi_0^*(\mathbf{z})$, then the further will the optimal Shas position be from the axis drawn between the Labour and Likud. Figure 3.5 shows the estimated positions of the parties at the election of 1996.

As we show in the next chapter, the position adopted by Shas in this figure is compatible with this interpretation of the motivations of the party principals.

3.6 APPENDIX: PROOF OF THEOREM 3.1

Proof of the Theorem   (See Schofield, 2006b).

At $\mathbf{z}_{-1} = (0, \ldots, 0)$, let $\rho_{i1}(z_1)$ be the probability that i votes for 1. Then

$$\rho_{i1}(z_1) = \Pr[[\lambda_1 - \beta||x_i - z_1||^2 - \lambda_j + \beta||x_i - z_j||^2 > \epsilon_j - \epsilon_1], \ j \neq 1].$$

Using Definition 3.4 for the extreme value distribution Ψ we obtain

$$\rho_{i1}(\mathbf{z}) = \frac{\exp[\lambda_1 - \beta||x_i - z_1||^2]}{\sum\limits_{j=1}^{p} \exp[\lambda_j - \beta||x_i - z_j||^2]}.$$

Thus,

$$\rho_{i1}(z_1) = [1 + \Sigma_{j=2}[\exp(f_j)]]^{-1},$$

$$\text{where } f_j = \lambda_j - \lambda_1 + \beta||x_i - z_1||^2 - \beta||x_i||^2,$$

$$\text{and } \frac{d\rho_{i1}}{dz_1} = 2(\beta(z_1 - x_i)[\rho_{i1}^2 - \rho_{i1}].$$

At $z_1 = 0$, $\rho_{i1} = \rho_1$ is independent of i, so we obtain

$$\frac{d\rho_{i1}}{dz_1} = 2(\beta(z_1 - x_i)[\rho_1^2 - \rho_1]$$

$$\text{and } \frac{dV_1}{dz_1} = \frac{1}{n} \sum_i \frac{d\rho_{i1}}{dz_1} = 0 \text{ at } z_1 = \frac{1}{n} \sum_i x_i.$$

This gives the first-order condition $z_1 = 0$. Obviously, the condition $\frac{dV_j}{dz_j} = 0$ is satisfied at $z_1 = \frac{1}{n} \sum_i x_i = 0$. Thus, $\mathbf{z}_0 = (0, \ldots, 0)$ satisfies the first-order condition.

At $z_{-1} = (0, \ldots, 0)$, the Hessian of ρ_{i1} is

$$\frac{d^2\rho_{i1}}{dz_1^2} = \{\rho_{i1} - \rho_{i1}^2\}\{[1 - 2\rho_{i1}][\nabla_{i1}(z_1)] - 2\beta I\}.$$

Here $[\nabla_{i1}(z_1)] = 4\beta^2[(x_i - z_1)(x_i - z_1)^{\mathrm{T}}$ is the w by w matrix of cross-product terms. Now $\sum_i[\nabla_{i1}(0)] = 4\beta^2 \nabla$, where ∇ is the electoral covariation matrix given in Definition 3.3. Then, the Hessian of V_1 at $z_1 = 0$ is given by

$$\frac{1}{n} \sum_i \frac{d^2\rho_i}{dz_1^2} = \{\rho_1 - \rho_1^2\} \left\{ [1 - 2\rho_1][4\beta^2] \left[\frac{1}{n}\nabla \right] - 2\beta I \right\}.$$

Because the first term $\{\rho_1 - \rho_1^2\}$ is positive, the eigenvalues of this matrix will be determined by the eigenvalues of

$$C_1 = \left[2[A_1] \left(\frac{1}{n}\nabla \right) - I \right],$$

$$\text{where } A_1 = \beta[1 - 2\rho_1],$$

as required. Moreover,

$$\lambda_p \geq \lambda_{p-1} \geq \ldots \geq \lambda_2 \geq \lambda_1$$

implies that $\rho_p \geq \rho_{p-1} \geq \ldots \geq \rho_2 \geq \rho_1$

so that $A_1 \geq A_2 \geq \ldots \geq A_p$.

This implies that $trace(C_1) \geq trace(C_2) \geq \ldots \geq trace(C_p)$

and $\det(C_1) \geq \det(C_2) \geq \ldots \geq \det(C_p)$.

Thus, if C_1 has negative eigenvalues, then so do $C_2, \ldots, C_p$, and this implies that $z_1 = z_2 = \ldots = z_p = 0$ will all be mutual local strict best responses. This shows that the stated condition is sufficient for $\mathbf{z}_0 = (0, \ldots, 0)$ to be an LSNE.

Conversely, if C_1 does not have negative eigenvalues, then $\mathbf{z}_0$ cannot be an LSNE. This gives the necessary condition. $\square$

4

Elections in Israel, 1988–1996

As discussed in Chapter 3, formal models of voting usually make the assumption that political agents, whether parties or candidates, attempt to maximize expected vote shares. Stochastic models typically derive the mean voter theorem—that each agent will adopt a convergent policy strategy at the mean of the electoral distribution. This conclusion, however, is contradicted by some of the empirical evidence.

In this chapter we emphasize the competitive dynamics of the electoral process in order to examine the inconsistency between theory and evidence. In particular, we argue that to fully elucidate vote motivations of the parties, it is necessary to incorporate valence terms in the statistical model and, therefore, in the theoretical model as well.

The *valence* of each party derives from the average weight given, by members of the electorate, to the overall competence of the particular party leader. In empirical models, a party's valence is independent of current policy declarations, and can be shown to be statistically significant in the estimation. As Theorem 3.1 has shown, when valence terms are incorporated in the formal model, then the convergent vote-maximizing equilibrium can fail to exist. We contend that the empirical evidence is consistent with a formal stochastic model of voting in which valence terms are included. *Low-valence parties,* in equilibrium, will tend to adopt positions at the electoral periphery. *High-valence parties* will contest the electoral center, but will not, in fact, occupy the electoral mean. We use evidence from the Israeli case to support and illustrate our theoretical argument.

Empirical and theoretical models of representative democracy typically have two distinct components. At the microlevel, individual voting behavior is modelled as a function of the preferences, or beliefs, of the voters and the policy positions or declarations of political candidates (or agents). It is commonly assumed that agents adopt strategies to maximize a utility function defined in terms of the overall vote share of the agent. Other possibilities include maximizing seat share, or some combination of policy consequences with seat or vote share, or probability of winning a majority (Duggan, 2000; Patty, 2005, 2006).

The natural formal concept to use in examining political agent strategies is that of *Nash equilibrium*—the vector of agent strategies with the property that no agent may deviate from the Nash equilibrium strategy and gain anything by doing so. Almost all formal models of agent strategy suggest that political agents, in equilibrium, will adopt convergent strategies; that is, they will adopt strategies that are located in some central domain of the space, as defined by voter preferences or beliefs (Calvert, 1985; Banks, Duggan, and Le Breton, 2002).

Arguments and evidence that parties do not adopt centrist strategies have been commonplace for decades (Duverger, 1954; Robertson, 1976; Daalder, 1984; Budge, et al., 1987). Theoretical models have been devised to account for policy divergence. These include theories based on activist support, (Aldrich, 1983a,b; 1995; Aldrich and McGinnis, 1989), directional voting (Adams and Merrill III, 1999; Merrill III and Grofman, 1999; Merrill III, Grofman, and Feld, 1999; Adams, 2001; Warwick, 2004; Adams, Merrill, and Grofman, 2005 and valence (Stokes, 1963, 1992).

Incorporating valence, or the perception in the electorate of a candidate's competence, is a plausible way to modify the usual vote models. Recent models incorporating valence have concentrated on adopting the basic Downsian model (Downs, 1957), where the voters "know with certainty" the location of the candidates (Ansolabehere and Snyder, 2000). Empirical models of voting make the implicit assumption that there is a degree of uncertainty (or more properly, risk) in the individual voter choice (Poole and Rosenthal, 1984). Therefore, it is appropriate to use, as a benchmark for such empirical studies, a formal model of voting that also incorporates risk.

The stochastic or probabilistic formal vote model has been developed to extend the early work of Hinich (1977). Initially focusing on two-candidate competition (Cahoon, Hinich, and Ordeshook, 1978; Enelow and Hinich, 1984; Coughlin, 1992), it has recently been extended to the case of multiparty competition with three or more candidates (Adams, 1999a,b; Lin, Enelow, and Dorussen, 1999). This work has indicated that parties will adopt convergent strategies at the mean of the electoral distribution. This conclusion is subject to a constraint that the stochastic component is "sufficiently" important. To date, the relevance of this result to empirical analysis of voting behavior has not been evaluated because the constraint has not been formulated in a precise enough fashion to be applied to empirical work. This chapter provides a re-evaluation of voting behavior in multiparty elections, in the light of Theorem 3.1 in the previous chapter.

For the discussion and analysis of the case of Israel we combine available and original survey data for Israel for 1988 to 1996 that allows us to construct an empirical model of voter choice in Knesset elections. We use expert evaluations to estimate party positions and then construct an empirical vote model that we show is statistically significant. Using the parameter estimates of this model, we developed a "hill-climbing" algorithm to determine the empirical equilibria of the vote-maximizing political game. Contrary to the conclusions of the formal stochastic vote model, the "mean voter" equilibrium (where all parties adopt the same position at the electoral mean) did not appear as one of the simulated equilibria. Since the voter model that we developed predicts voter choice in a statistically significant fashion, we infer that the assumptions of the formal stochastic vote model are compatible with actual voter choice. Moreover, equilibria determined by the simulation were "close" to the estimated configuration of party positions for the three elections of 1988, 1992, and 1996. We infer from this that the assumption of vote-share maximization on the part of parties is a realistic assumption to make about party motivation.

The usual assumption to make to ensure existence of a Nash equilibrium at the mean voter position depends on showing that all party vote-share functions are *concave* in some domain of the party strategy spaces (Banks and Duggan, 2005). Concavity of these functions depends on the parameters of the model. Because the appropriate empirical model for Israel incorporated valence parameters, these were part of the concavity condition for the baseline formal model. Concavity is a global property of the vote-share functions, and is generally difficult to empirically test. As in the formal analysis in the previous chapter, we focus on a weaker property known as *local concavity*, given by appropriate conditions on the second derivative (the Hessian) of the vote-share functions. If local concavity fails, then so must concavity. The constraints required for local concavity in the formal vote model are shown to be violated by the estimated values of the parameters in the empirical model. Consequently, our empirical model of vote-maximizing parties could not lead us to expect convergent strategies at the mean electoral position.

The formal result presented in Chapter 3 is valid in a policy space of unrestricted dimension, but has a particularly simple expression in the two-dimensional case.

Theorem 3.1 allows us to determine whether a low-valence party would in fact maximize its vote shares at the electoral mean. More precisely, we can determine whether the mean voter position is a best response for a low-valence party when all other parties are at the mean. In the empirical model, we estimate that low-valence parties would, in fact, minimize their vote share if they chose the mean electoral position. This inference leads us to the following conclusions: (i) some of the low-valence parties, in maximizing vote shares, should adopt positions at the periphery of the electoral distribution; (ii) if this does occur, then the first-order conditions for equilibrium, associated with high-valence parties at the mean, will be violated. Consequently, for the sequence of elections in Israel, we should expect that it is a nongeneric property for any party to occupy the electoral mean in any vote-maximizing equilibrium (Schofield and Sened, 2005b).

There may be constraints on policy choice because of activist party members, and ideological commitment by party elite. However, vote and seat shares are measures of party success, and are an obvious basis for party motivation. A formal model that does not give this due regard is unlikely to be particularly relevant. As we further elaborate in the next chapter, we infer from our results that vote maximization is the key factor in party policy choice. Clearly, optimal party location depends on the valence by which the electorate, on average, judges party competence.

Our simulations suggest that if a single party has a significantly high valence, for whatever reason, then it has the opportunity to locate itself near the electoral center. On the other hand, if two parties have high but comparable valences, then our simulation suggests that neither will closely contest the center. We observe that the estimated positions of the two high-valence parties, Labour and Likud, are almost precisely identical to the simulated positions under expected vote maximization. The positions of the low-valence parties are, as predicted, close to the periphery of the electoral distribution. However, they are not identical to simulated vote-maximizing positions. This suggests that the perturbation away from vote-maximizing equilibria is either due to policy preferences on the part of party principals or to the effect of party activists (Aldrich, 1983a,b; Miller and Schofield, 2003). We argue that this perturbation is best accounted for in terms of coalitional risk, as discussed in Chapter 3.

The formal and empirical analyses presented here are applicable to any polity using an electoral system based on PR. The underlying formal model is compatible with a wide variety of different theoretical political equilibria. The theory is also compatible with the considerable variation of party political configurations in multiparty systems (Laver and Schofield, 1990).

As in our discussion in the previous chapter, our analysis of the formal vote model emphasizes the notion of a *local* Nash equilibrium in contrast to the notion of a *global* Nash equilibrium usually employed in the technical literature. One reason for this emphasis is that we deploy the tools of calculus and simulation via hill-climbing algorithms to locate equilibria. As in calculus, the set of LNE must include the set of PNE. Sufficient conditions for existence of a PNE are therefore more stringent than for a LNE. In fact, the necessary and sufficient condition for LNE at the electoral center, in the vote-maximizing game with valence, is so stringent that we regard it to be unlikely to obtain in polities with numerous parties and varied valences. We therefore infer that existence of a PNE at the electoral center is very unlikely in such polities. In contrast, the sufficient condition for a local, noncentrist equilibrium is much less stringent. Indeed, in each polity there may well be multiple LNE. This suggests that the particular configuration of party positions in any polity can be a matter of historical contingency.

4.1 AN EMPIRICAL VOTE MODEL

As discussed in Chapter 3, we assume that the political preferences (or beliefs) of voter i can be described by a "latent" utility vector of the form

$$\mathbf{u}_i(x_i, \mathbf{z}) = (u_{i1}(x_i, z_1), \ldots, u_{ip}(x_i, z_p)) \in \mathbb{R}^p. \qquad (4.1)$$

Here $\mathbf{z} = (z_1, \ldots, z_p)$ is the vector of strategies of the set, P, of political agents (candidates, parties, etc.). The point z_j is a vector in a policy space X that we use to characterize party j. (For the formal theory, it is convenient to assume X is a compact, convex subset of Euclidean space of dimension w, but this is not an absolutely necessary assumption. We make no prior assumption that $w = 1$.) Each voter, i, is also described by a vector x_i, in the same space X, where x_i is used to denote the beliefs or "ideal point" of the voter. We assume

$$u_{ij}(x_i, z_j) = \lambda_j - A_{ij}(x_i, z_j) + \theta_j^\mathrm{T} \eta_i + \varepsilon_j. \qquad (4.2)$$

We use $A_{ij}(x_i, z_j)$ to denote some measure of the distance between the vectors x_i and z_j. In the usual Euclidean model presented in Chapter 3 it is assumed that $A_{ij}(x_i, z_j) = \beta \|x_i - z_j\|^2$, where $\| \ \|$ is the Euclidean norm on X and β is a positive constant. It is also possible to use an ellipsoidal distance function for A_{ij}, which we do later in Chapters 7 and 8. The term λ_j is called *valence* and was introduced earlier. The k-vector θ_j represents the effect of the k different sociodemographic parameters (class, domicile, education, income, etc.) on voting for the party j while η_i is a k-vector denoting the ith individual's relevant sociodemographic characteristics. We use θ_j^T to denote the transpose of θ_j so $\theta_j^T \eta_i$ is a scalar. The abbreviation SD is used throughout to refer to models involving sociodemographic characteristics. The vector ε_j is a stochastic error term, associated with the jth party. Early models of this kind assume that the elements of the random vector $\varepsilon = (\varepsilon_1, \ldots, \varepsilon_j, \ldots, \varepsilon_p)$ are independently distributed so the covariance matrix Ω of the error vector is diagonal. In the case the errors are also identically distributed, with variance σ^2, then the covariance matrix of ε is $I\sigma^2$, where I is the identity matrix.

In their study of U.S. presidential elections, Poole and Rosenthal (1984) assumed $\{e_j\}$ to be multivariate normal and pair-wise independent. More recent empirical analyses have been based on Markov Chain Monte Carlo (MCMC) methods, allowing for estimation when the errors are covariant (Chib and Greenberg, 1996). Assuming that the errors are independent and identically distributed via the Type I extreme value (or log-Weibull distribution) gives a *multinomial logit* (MNL) model, whereas assuming that the errors are distributed multivariate normal, and thus covariant, gives the *multinomial probit* (MNP) model. MNP models are generally preferable because they do not require the restrictive assumption of "independence of irrelevant alternatives" (Alvarez and Nagler, 1998). However, a comparison of MNP and MNL models suggests that the results are broadly comparable (Quinn, Martin, and Whitford, 1999). We use an MNL model in this chapter because comparison of MNL and MNP models suggest that the simpler MNL model gives an adequate account of voter choice. It is also much easier to use the MNL empirical model to simulate parties' vote-maximizing strategies (Quinn and Martin, 2002).

A variety of methods have been used to measure the distance or "policy" component $A_{ij}(x_i, z_j)$. Alvarez, Nagler, and Bowler (2000) used a National Election Survey for Britain to locate each voter (in a sample N, of size n) with regard to preferred positions on a large number of policy issues. Each voter was asked to locate the parties and the average across the survey population was used to estimate the position, on this large number of issues, of each party. This method has the virtue that data were not lost, but had the disadvantage that no representation of policy issues was possible.

In their study of U.S. presidential elections, Poole and Rosenthal (1984) used factor analysis to estimate the distribution of voter bliss points in a two-dimensional policy space, X, and also located presidential candidate positions in the same space. In their analysis, the second noneconomic dimension "capture[ed] the traditional identification of southern conservatives with the Democratic party" (Poole and Rosenthal, 1984: 287). For the election of 1968, they estimated identical λ-valence terms and β-coefficients for Humphrey and Nixon and found a much higher λ-valence term and β-coefficient for Wallace. They also noted that there was no evidence that candidates tended to converge to the electoral mean (cf. Hinich, 1977), but gave no explanation for this phenomenon.

There are many possible explanations for nonconvergence of candidate positions. For example, primaries may lead to the choice of more radical candidates for each party. In this chapter we make use of the formal model presented in Chapter 3.

Figures 4.1 and 4.2 are reproduced from Chapter 2, and show the "smoothed" distributions of voter ideal points for 1996 and 1992, while Figure 4.3 gives the distribution for 1988. (The outer contour line in each figure contains 95 percent of the voter ideal points).

All three figures were obtained by factor analysis of the surveys conducted by Arian and Shamir (1990, 1995, and 1999) for these three elections. Party positions were estimated by expert analysis of party manifestos, using the same survey questionnaires. (Earlier work on these estimations can be found in Schofield, Sened, and Nixon, 1998; and Ofek, Quinn, and Sened, 1998).

Each respondent for the survey is characterized by a point in the resulting two-dimensional policy space, X. Thus, the smoothed electoral distribution can be taken as an estimation of the underlying probability density function for the voter ideal points.

Table A4.1 (in the appendix to this chapter) presents the factor loadings for the 1996 analysis of the survey questions. "Security" refers to attitudes toward peace initiatives. "Religion" refers to the significance of religious considerations in government policy. The axes of the figures are oriented so that "left" on the security axis can be interpreted as supportive of negotiations with the PLO, while "north" on the vertical or religious axis is indicative of support for the importance of the Jewish faith in Israel. Comparing Figure 4.3 for 1988 with Figure 4.1 for 1996 suggests that the covariance between the two factors has declined over time.

Since the competition between the two major parties, Labour and Likud, is pronounced, it is surprising that these parties do not move to the

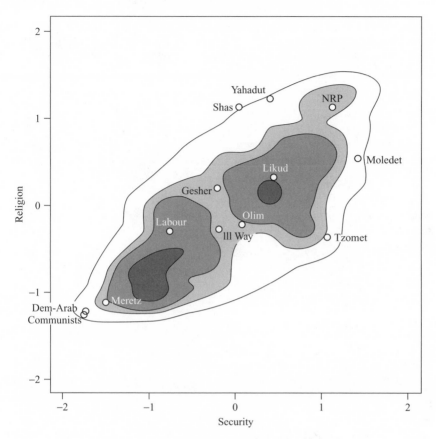

Figure 4.1. Party positions and electoral distribution (at the 95%, 75%, 50%, and 10% levels) in the Knesset at the election of 1996.

electoral mean (as suggested by the formal vote model) in order to increase vote and seat shares. The data on seats in the Knesset given in Chapter 2 (Table 2.1) suggests the vote share of the small Sephardic orthodox party, Shas, increased significantly between 1992 and 1996. As Figures 4.1 and 4.2 illustrate, however, there was no significant move by Shas to the electoral center. Our inference is that the shifts of electoral support are the result of changes in party valence. To be more explicit, we contend that prior to an election each voter i forms a judgment about the relative capability of each party leader. Let λ_{ij} denote the weight given by voter i to party j in the voter's utility calculation. The voter utility is then given by the expression:

$$u_{ij}(x_i, z_j) = \lambda_{ij} - \beta \|x_i - z_j\|^2 + \theta_j^{\mathrm{T}} \eta_i. \qquad (4.3)$$

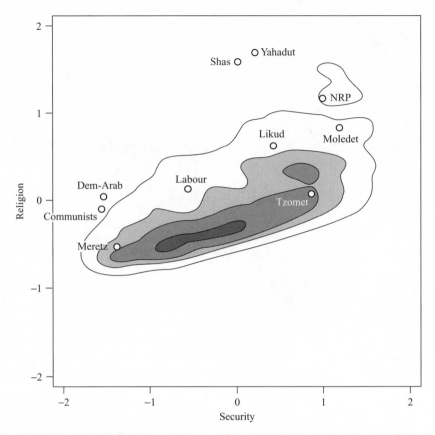

Figure 4.2. Party positions and electoral distribution (at the 95%, 75%, 50%, and 10% levels) in the Knesset at the election of 1992.

However, these weights are subjective, and may well be influenced by idiosyncratic characteristics of voters and parties. For empirical analysis, we shall assume $\lambda_{ij} = \lambda_j + \Delta_{ij}$, where Δ_{ij} is drawn at random from a Type I extreme value distribution. The expected value $\mathcal{E}xp(\lambda_{ij})$, of λ_{ij} is λ_j, and so we write $\lambda_{ij} = \lambda_j + \varepsilon_j$, giving (4.2). Since in this chapter we are mainly concerned with the voter's choice, we shall assume here that λ_j is exogenously determined. We relax this assumption in Chapter 6, where we focus on party behavior. Full details of the estimations of (4.3) for the parameters β and $\{\lambda_j$ for $j = 1, \dots, p\}$, and for the k by p matrix θ for the three elections are given in the appendix to this chapter.

Estimating the voter model given by (4.2) requires information about sample voter behavior. It is assumed that data is available about voter intentions; this information is encoded, for each sample voter i by the

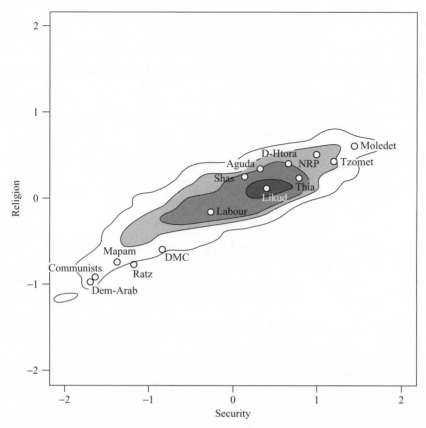

Figure 4.3. Party positions and electoral distribution (at the 95%, 75%, 50%, and 10% levels) in the Knesset at the election of 1988.

vector $c_i = (c_{i1}, \ldots, c_{ip})$, where $c_{ij} = 1$ if and only if j intends to vote (or did indeed vote) for agent j. Given the data set $\{x_i, \eta_i, c_i\}_N$ for the sample N (of size n) and $\{z_j\}_P$, for the political agents, a set $\{\rho_i^*\}_N$ of stochastic variables is estimated. The first moment of ρ_i^* is the probability vector $\rho_i = (\rho_{i1}, \ldots, \rho_{ip})$. Here ρ_{ij} is the probability that voter i chooses agent j.

There are standard procedures for estimating the model given by (4.2). The technique is to choose estimators for the coefficients so that the estimated probability takes the form:

$$\bar{\rho}_{ij}(\mathbf{z}) = \Pr[\,\bar{u}_{ij}(x_i, z_j) > \bar{u}_{il}(x_i, z_l) \text{ for all } l \in P \setminus \{j\}]. \qquad (4.4)$$

Here, $\bar{u}_{ij}$ is the jth component of the estimated latent utility function for i. The estimator for the choice is $\bar{c}_{ij} = 1$ if and only if $\bar{\rho}_{ij} > \bar{\rho}_{il}$ for all

$l \in P\backslash\{j\}$. The procedure minimizes the errors between the n by p matrix $[c]$ and the n by p estimated matrix $[\bar{c}]$. The vote share, $V_j^*(\mathbf{z})$, of agent i, given the vector z of strategies, is defined to be:

$$V_j^*(\mathbf{z}) = \frac{1}{n} \sum_i \rho_{ij}^*(\mathbf{z}). \tag{4.5}$$

Note that, since $V_j^*(\mathbf{z})$ is a stochastic variable, it is characterized by its first moment (its expectation), as well as higher moments (its standard variance, etc.). We follow the theory presented in Chapter 3 and focus on the expectation $\mathcal{E}xp(V_j^*(\mathbf{z}))$. As in the formal analysis, the estimate of this expectation, denoted $\mathcal{E}_j(\mathbf{z})$, is given by:

$$\mathcal{E}_j(\mathbf{z}) = \frac{1}{n} \sum_i \bar{\rho}_{ij}(\mathbf{z}). \tag{4.6}$$

A virtue of using the general voting model (4.3) is that the Bayes' factor, B_{st} (differences in log likelihoods associated with the comparison of model s against model t) can be used to determine which of various possible models is statistically superior (Kass and Raftery, 1995; Quinn, Martin, and Whitford, 1999).

We compared a variety of different MNL models against a pure MNP model for each election. The models were:

(i) MNP: a pure spatial multinomial probit model with $\beta \neq 0$ but $\theta \equiv 0$ and $\lambda = 0$
(ii) MNLSD: a pure logit sociodemographic (SD) model, with $\beta = 0$, involving the component θ, based on respondent age, education, religious observance, and origin (whether Sephardic, etc.)
(iii) MNL1: a pure multinomial logit spatial model with $\beta \neq 0$, but $\theta \equiv 0$ and $\lambda = 0$
(iv) MNL2: a multinomial logit model with $\beta \neq 0$, $\theta \neq 0$, and $\lambda = 0$
(v) Joint MNL: a multinomial logit model with $\beta \neq 0$, $\theta \neq 0$, and $\lambda \neq 0$

The pure sociodemographic model MNLSD gave poor results and this model was not considered further.

Full details of the joint MNL models are given in Tables A4.2, A4.3, and A4.4 in the appendix to this chapter.

For comparison of the models, Table 4.1 gives standard interpretations of the Bayes' factors of model comparisons, while Tables 4.2 to 4.4 give the comparisons for MNP, MNL1, MNL2, and Joint MNL for the three elections. Note that the MNP model had no valence terms. Observe from Table 4.4 that, for the 1996 election, the Bayes' factor for the comparison

Table 4.1. *Interpretation of Evidence Provided by the Bayes Factor B_{st}.*

$\ln(B_{st})$	B_{st}	Evidence in favor of M_s against M_t
0 to 1	1 to 3	Insignificant
1 to 3	3 to 20	Positive
3 to 5	20 to 150	Strong
>5	>150	Very strong

Table 4.2. *Bayes Factor B_{st} for M_s against M_t for the 1988 Election.*

	M_t	Spatial MNP	Spatial MNL1	Spatial MNL2	Joint MNL
	Spatial MNP	n.a.	278***	−38	−73
M_s	Spatial MNL1	−278	n.a.	−316	−352
	Spatial MNL2	38***	316***	n.a.	−35
	Joint MNL	73***	352***	35***	n.a.

*** = very strong support for M_s.

Table 4.3. *Bayes Factor B_{st} for M_s against M_t for the 1992 Election.*

	M_t	Spatial MNP	Spatial MNL1	Spatial MNL2	Joint MNL
	Spatial MNP	n.a.	50***	−24	−71
M_s	Spatial MNL1	−50	n.a.	−74	−121
	Spatial MNL2	24***	74***	n.a.	−47
	Joint MNL	71***	121***	47***	n.a.

*** = very strong support for M_s.

Table 4.4. *Bayes Factor B_{st} for M_s against M_t for the 1996 Election.*

	M_t	Spatial MNP	Spatial MNL1	Spatial MNL2	Joint MNL
	Spatial MNP	n.a.	239***	−17	−49
M_s	Spatial MNL1	−239	n.a.	−255	−288
	Spatial MNL2	17***	255***	n.a.	−33
	Joint MNL	49***	288***	33***	n.a.

*** = very strong support for M_s.

Table 4.5. *National and Sample Vote-Shares and Valence Coefficients for Israel, 1988–1996.*

	1988 National	1988 Sample	1992 National	1992 Sample	1996 National	1996 Sample	1988 λ^*	1992 λ^*	1996 λ^*
Labour	30.7	28.5	36.0	35.8	27.5	44.0	0.30	0.91	4.15
Meretz, Ratz	4.4	8.3	10.0	11.9	7.6	6.0	0.00	0.00	0.00
Dem, Arab	1.0	–	1.6	–	3.0	–	–	–	–
Communist	2.8	–	2.5	–	4.3	–	–	–	–
Olim	–	–	–	–	5.8	–	–	–	–
Third Way	–	–	–	–	3.2	1.8	–	–	−2.34
Likud	31.8	49.7	26.2	30.2	25.8	43.0	2.84	2.73	3.14
Tzomet	2.0	2.5	6.7	9.6	–	–	−0.75	−0.37	–
Shas	4.8	3.6	5.2	3.6	8.7	2.0	−5.78	−4.67	−2.96
Yahadut	–	–	3.3	–	3.3	–	–	–	–
NRP	4.0	2.9	5.2	4.6	8.0	5.1	−3.00	−0.44	−4.52
Moledet	1.5	–	2.5	4.4	2.4	1.8	–	0.38	−0.89
Techiya, Thia	3.2	4.4	–	–	–	–	0.39	–	–
Others	8.0	–	0.8	–	0.4	–	–	–	–
β coefficients							1.32	1.25	1.12
Log marginal likelihoods							−597	−834	−465
n							505	781	794
Vote % correctly predicted							52%	46%	64%

* Normalized with respect to a zero valence for Meretz.

of the Joint MNL model with MNL1 was of order 288, so clearly sociodemographic variables add to predictive power. However, the valence constants add further to the power of the model. The spatial distance, as expected, exerts a very strong negative effect on the propensity of a voter to choose a given party. To illustrate, Table 4.5 shows that, in 1996, the β coefficient was estimated to be approximately 1.12. In short, Israeli voters cast ballots, to a very large extent, on the basis of the issue positions of the parties. This is true even after taking the demographic and religious factors into account. The coefficients on "religious observation" for Shas and the NRP (both religious parties) were estimated to be 3.022 and 2.161, respectively. Consequently, a voter who is observant has a high probability of voting for one of these parties, but this probability appears to fall off rapidly the further the voter's ideal position is from the party position.

In each election, factors such as age, education, and religious observance play a role in determining voter choice. Obviously, this suggests that some parties are more successful among some groups in the electorate than would be implied by a simple estimation based only on policy positions.

Tables 4.2 through 4.4 indicate that, in all three elections, the best model is the joint MNL that includes valence and the sociodemographic factors along with the spatial coefficient β. In particular, there is strong support, in all three elections, for the inclusion of valence. This model provides the best estimates of the vote shares of parties and predicts the vote choices of the individual voters remarkably well. Therefore, this is clearly the model of choice to use as our best estimator for what we refer to as the *stochastic electoral response function*. Adding valence to the MNL model makes it superior to both MNL and MNP models without valence. Adding the sociological factors increases the statistical validity of the model. Table 4.5 provides a summary of the estimation results for the three elections. Note that the 1996 estimation correctly predicts 64 percent of the vote choice and 72 percent and 71 percent of survey participants who voted Labour and Likud, respectively. This success rate is particularly impressive in light of the number of parties that participated in this electoral campaign.

It is possible that an MNP valence model of these elections would have been statistically superior. However, such a model with seven parties would have been difficult to estimate. Moreover, comparison of MNP and MNL models for the Netherlands reported by Quinn, Martin, and Whitford (1999) and discussed in Chapter 6, suggests that the two classes of models are broadly comparable. Dow and Endersby (2004: 111) also suggest that "researchers are justified in using MNL specifications." Since our purpose in constructing the empirical model was to examine the mean voter theorem, as given by Theorem 3.1, it was appropriate to adopt the MNL assumption of independent errors with a Type I extreme value distribution.

Throughout our analyses, we assume that because the sociodemographic components of the model are independent of party strategies, we are able to use the estimated parameters of the model to simulate party movement in order to increase the expected vote share of each party. Hill-climbing algorithms were used for this purpose. Such algorithms involve small changes in party position, and are therefore only capable of obtaining local optima for each party. Consequently, a vector

$\mathbf{z}^* = (z_1^*, \dots, z_p^*)$ of party positions that results from such a search is what we have called a *local Nash equilibrium* or LNE. We now repeat the definition of an LNE as given in Chapter 3 for the context of the empirical vote-maximizing game defined by $\mathcal{E} : X^p \to \mathbb{R}^p$.

Definition 4.1 *Equilibrium Concepts for the Empirical Model*

(i) A strategy vector $\mathbf{z}^* = (z_1^*, \dots, z_{j-1}^*, z_j^*, z_{j+1}^*, \dots, z_p^*) \in X^p$ is a *local strict Nash equilibrium* (LSNE) for the profile function $\mathcal{E} : X^p \to \mathbb{R}^p$ iff for each agent $j \in P$, there exists a neighborhood X_j of z_j^* in X such that

$$\mathcal{E}_j(z_1^*, \dots, z_{j-1}^*, z_j^*, z_{j+1}^*, \dots, z_p^*) > \mathcal{E}_j(z_1^*, \dots, z_j, \dots, z_p^*)$$

for all $z_j \in X_j - \{z_j^*\}$.

(ii) A strategy vector $\mathbf{z}^* = (z_1^*, \dots, z_{j-1}^*, z_j^*, z_{j+1}^*, \dots, z_p^*)$ is a *local weak Nash equilibrium* (LNE) for $\mathcal{E}$ iff for each agent j there exists a neighborhood X_j of z_j^* in X such that

$$\mathcal{E}_j(z_1^*, \dots, z_{j-1}^*, z_j^*, z_{j+1}^*, \dots, z_p^*) \geq \mathcal{E}_j(z_1^*, \dots, z_j, \dots, z_p^*)$$

for all $z_j \in X_j$.

(iii) A strategy vector $\mathbf{z}^* = (z_1^*, \dots, z_{j-1}^*, z_j^*, z_{j+1}^*, \dots, z_p^*)$ is a *strict*, respectively, *weak, pure strategy Nash equilibrium* (PSNE, respectively, PNE) for $\mathcal{E}$ iff X_j can be replaced by X in (i), (ii), respectively.

(iv) The strategy z_j^* is termed a *local strict best response*, a *local weak best response*, a *global weak best response*, a *global strict best response*, respectively, to $\mathbf{z}_{-j}^* = (z_1^*, \dots, z_{j-1}^*, z_{j+1}^*, \dots, z_p^*)$.

As noted previously, in these definitions *weak* refers to the condition that z_j^* is no worse than any other strategy. While LSNE are easier to use in the formal analysis, we focus on LNE for empirical anlysis. Clearly, a PNE must be an LNE, but not conversely. As we have emphasized, above, a condition that is sufficient to guarantee that an LNE is a PNE for the electoral game is *concavity* of the vote functions.

Definition 4.2 *The profile $\mathcal{E} : X^p \to \mathbb{R}^p$ is concave iff for each j, and any real α and $x, y \in X$, then*

$$\mathcal{E}_j(\alpha x + (1 - \alpha)y) \geq \alpha \mathcal{E}_j(x) + (1 - \alpha)\mathcal{E}_j(y).$$

Concavity of the payoff functions $\{\mathcal{E}_j\}$ in the jth strategy z_j, together with continuity in z_j and compactness and convexity of X is sufficient for existence of a PNE (Banks and Duggan, 2005).

In the following section we discuss the relevance of mean voter theorem for empirical analysis. As previously mentioned, this theorem asserts that the vector $\mathbf{z}^* = (x^*, \ldots, x^*)$ (where x^* is the mean of the distribution of voter ideal points) is a PNE for the vote-maximizing electoral game (Hinich, 1977; Enelow and Hinich, 1984; Lin et al., 1999). As in the formal discussion, we call $(x^*, \ldots, x^*)$ the *joint electoral mean*. Since the electoral distribution can be readily normalized, so $x^* = 0$, we also use the term *joint electoral origin*. We used a hill-climbing algorithm to determine the LNE of the empirical vote models for the three elections.

Our simulation of the empirical models found five distinct LNE for the 1996 election in Israel. A representative LNE is given in Figure 4.4.

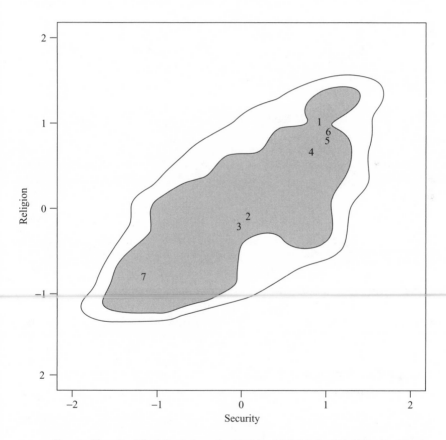

Key: 1= Shas, 2 = Likud, 3 = Labour, 4 = NRP, 5 = Moledet, 6 = Third Way, 7 = Meretz

Figure 4.4. A representative local Nash equilibrium of the vote-maximizing game in the Knesset for the 1996 election.

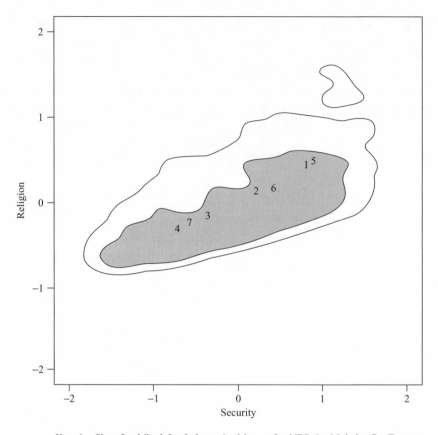

Key: 1 = Shas, 2 = Likud, 3 = Labour, 4 = Meretz, 5 = NRP, 6 = Moledet, 7 = Tzomet

Figure 4.5. A representative local Nash equilibrium of the vote-maximizing game in the Knesset for the 1992 election.

Notice that the locations of the two high-valence parties, Labour and Likud, in Figure 4.1 closely match their simulated positions in Figure 4.4. Obviously, none of the estimated equilibrium vectors in Figure 4.4 correspond to the convergent situation at the electoral mean. Figures 4.5 and 4.6 give representative LNE for 1992 and 1988. The close match with the Labour and Likud positions was observed in all simulated LNE.

It has been noted many times before that parties do not converge to an electoral mean. Various theoretical models have been offered to account for this phenomenon. Our analysis in this chapter is meant as a further contribution to this literature. Before we begin our discussion of

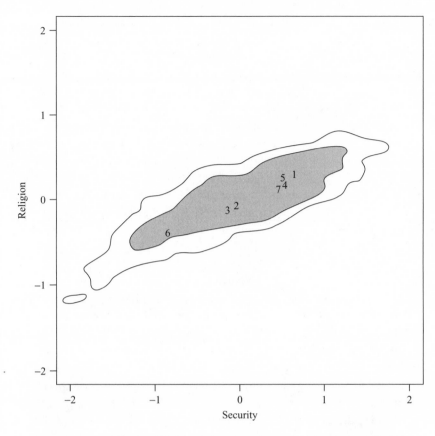

Key: 1 = Shas, 2 = Likud, 3 = Labour, 4 = Tzomet, 5 = NRP, 6 = Ratz, 7 = Thia

Figure 4.6. A representative local Nash equilibrium of the vote-maximizing game in the Knesset for the 1988 election.

the results just presented, several preliminary conclusions appear to be of interest.

1) First, the empirical MNL model and the formal model based on the extreme value distribution Ψ (as discussed in Chapter 3) are mutually compatible.
2) Second, the set of LNE obtained by simulation of the empirical model must contain any PNE for this model (if any exist). Since no LNE was found at the joint mean position, it follows that the mean voter theorem is invalid, given the estimated parameter values of the empirical model. This conclusion is not susceptible to any counter-argument that the parties may have utilized evaluation functions other than

expected vote shares, because only vote-share maximization was allowed to count in the hill-climbing algorithm used to generate the LSNE.

3) A comparison of Figures 4.1, 4.2, and 4.3 with the simulation Figures 4.4, 4.5, and 4.6 makes it clear that there are marked similarities between estimated and simulated positions. This is most obvious for the high-valence parties, Labour and Likud, but also for the low-valence party Meretz. This suggests that the set of expected vote-share functions $\{\mathcal{E}_j\}$ is a close proxy to the actual, but unknown, utility functions $\{U_j\}$, deployed by the party leaders.

4) Although the equilibrium notion of LNE that we deploy is not utilized in the game theoretic literature, it has a number of virtues. In particular, Theorem 3.3 shows that an LSNE, and thus an LNE, will exist, for "almost all" party utility profiles $\{\mathcal{E}_j\}$, as long as these profiles are differentiable in the strategy variables and satisfy the "boundary condition" on the set X_o^p of feasible strategy profiles. Clearly, X_o^p can be chosen sufficiently extensive so that all gradients point toward its interior. Moreover, the definition of $\{\mathcal{E}_j\}$ makes it obvious that it is differentiable. On the other hand, existence for PNE is problematic when concavity fails.

5) Although the local equilibrium concept is indeed "local," there is no formal reason why each of the various LNE that we obtain should be, in fact, "close" to one another. It is noticeable in Figures 4.4, 4.5, and 4.6 that the LNE for each election are approximate permutations of one another, with low-valence parties strung along what we call the *electoral principal axis*.

In the following section, we examine the formal vote model in order to determine why the mean voter theorem appears to be invalid for the estimated model of Israel. The formal result will explain why low-valence parties in the simulations are far from the electoral mean, and why all parties lie on a single electoral axis.

4.2 COMPARING THE FORMAL AND EMPIRICAL MODELS

The point of this section is to use the Israeli example to present a case in which the necessary condition of Theorem 3.1 is not satisfied. This failure has significant consequences for the behavior of political parties in this electoral competition. As we demonstrate here, in such an electoral environment, some parties have a clear incentive to formulate divergent policy positions rather than converge at an LNE at the origin of the distribution of the voters' ideal points. We first note that the expected vote-share functions $\{\mathcal{E}_j\}$ of the empirical model just discussed are not exactly the same as the formal vote functions presented in Chapter 3. The principal difference is that the empirical model incorporates sociodemographic characteristics. In the simulation, these characteristics were held fixed, because by definition they are unaffected by party policy choices. We should expect that when the values of the empirical parameters are utilized in the formal model, then the equilibrium characteristics of the model should mirror the results of simulation. In fact, we find an exact parallel between the model and simulation.

In 1996, the lowest-valence party is the NRP with valence -4.52. The spatial coefficient is $\beta = 1.12$. As Table A4.1 shows, the electoral variances are 1.0 and 0.732 with covariance 0.591. We can use Theorem 3.1 to compute

$$\rho_{NRP} \simeq \frac{1}{1 + e^{4.15+4.52} + e^{3.14+4.52}} \simeq 0.$$

Thus $A_{NRP} = \beta = 1.12$.

Hence $C_{NRP} = 2(1.12) \begin{pmatrix} 1.0 & 0.591 \\ 0.591 & 0.732 \end{pmatrix} - I = \begin{pmatrix} 1.24 & 1.32 \\ 1.32 & 0.64 \end{pmatrix}$

and $c(\Psi) = 3.88$.

Then the eigenvalues for the NRP are 2.28 and -0.40, giving a saddlepoint, and a value for the convergence coefficient of 3.88. The major eigenvector for the NRP is $(1.0, 0.8)$, and along this axis the NRP vote-share function increases as the party moves away from the origin. The minor, perpendicular axis is given by the vector $(1, -1.25)$ and on this axis the NRP vote-share decreases. Figure 4.4 gives one of the local equilibria in 1996, obtained by simulation of the model. The figure makes it clear that the vote-maximizing positions lie on the principal electoral axis through the origin and the point $(1.0, 0.8)$. As we noted, five different LNE were located; in all cases, the two high-valence parties, Labour and Likud, were located at almost precisely the same positions. The only difference between the various equilibria were that the positions of the low-valence parties were perturbations of one another. Compare this analysis with Figure 4.4.

We next analyze the situation for 1992, by computing the eigenvalues using Theorem 3.1 again. From the empirical model we obtain $\lambda_{shas} = -4.67$, $\lambda_{likud} = 2.73$, $\lambda_{labour} = 0.91$, $\beta = 1.25$. When all parties are at the origin, then the probability that a voter chooses Shas is

$$\rho_{shas} \simeq \frac{1}{1 + e^{2.73+4.67} + e^{0.91+4.67}} \simeq 0.$$

Thus $A_{shas} = \beta = 1.25$.

$$C_{shas} = 2(1.25)\begin{pmatrix} 1.0 & 0.453 \\ 0.453 & 0.435 \end{pmatrix} - I = \begin{pmatrix} 1.5 & 1.13 \\ 1.13 & 0.08 \end{pmatrix}$$

$$c(\Psi) = 3.6.$$

Then the two eigenvalues for Shas can be calculated to be $+2.12$ and -0.52 with a convergence coefficient for the model of 3.6. Thus we find that the origin is a saddlepoint for the Shas Hessian. The eigenvector for the large, positive eigenvalue is the vector $(1.0, 0.55)$. Again, this vector coincides with the principal electoral axis. The eigenvector for the negative eigenvalue is perpendicular to the principal axis. To maximize vote share, Shas should adjust its position—but only on the principal axis. This is exactly what the simulation found. Notice that the probability of voting for Labour is $[1 + e^{1.82}]^{-1} = 0.14$, and $A_{labour} = 0.9$, so even Labour will have a positive eigenvalue at the origin. Figure 4.5 gives one of the two different LNE obtained from simulation of the empirical model. Again, the prediction obtained from the formal model and the simulation are consistent.

Calculation for the model for 1988 gives eigenvalues for Shas of $+2.0$ and -0.83 with a convergence coefficient of 3.16, and a principal axis through $(1.0, 0.5)$. Again, vote-maximizing behavior by Shas should oblige it to stay strictly to the principal electoral axis. The three simulated vote-maximizing local equilibrium positions indicated that there was no deviation by parties off the principal axis or eigenspace associated with the positive eigenvalue. Again, compare the prediction with the representative LNE given in Figure 4.6.

Thus the simulations for all three elections were compatible with the predictions of the formal model based on the extreme value distribution. All parties were able to increase vote shares by moving away from the origin, along the principal axis, as determined by the large, positive principal eigenvalue. In particular, the simulation confirms the logic of the above analysis. Low-valence parties, such as the NRP and Shas, in order to maximize vote shares must move far from the electoral center. Their optimal positions will lie either in the "northeast" quadrant or the "southwest" quadrant. The vote-maximizing model, without any additional information, cannot determine which way the low-valence parties should move.

As noted above, the simulations of the empirical models found multiple LNE essentially differing only in permutations of the low-valence party positions.

In contrast, since the valence difference between Labour and Likud was relatively low in all three elections, their optimal positions would be relatively close to, but not identical to, the electoral mean. The simulation figures for all three elections are also compatible with this theoretical inference. It is clear that once the low-valence parties vacate the origin, then high-valence parties, like Likud and Labour, will position themselves almost symmetrically about the origin, and along the major axis. It should be noted that the positions of Labour and Likud, particularly, closely match their positions in the simulated vote-maximizing equilibria.

The correlation between the two electoral axes was much higher in 1988 ($r^2 = 0.70$) than in 1992 or 1996 (when $r^2 \simeq 0.47$). It is worth observing that as r^2 falls from 1988 to 1996, a counter-clockwise rotation of the principal axis can be observed. This can be seen in the change from the eigenvalue (1.0, 0.5) in 1988 to (1.0, 0.55) in 1992 and then to (1.0, 0.8) in 1996. Notice also that the total electoral variance increased from 1988 to 1992 and again to 1996. Indeed, Figure 4.1 indicates that there is evidence of bifurcation in the electoral distribution in 1996.

In comparing Figure 4.1, of the estimated party positions, and Figure 4.4, of simulated equilibrium positions, there is a notable disparity particularly in the position of Shas. In 1996, Shas was pivotal between Labour and Likud, in the sense that to form a winning coalition government, either of the two larger parties required the support of Shas. It is obvious that the location of Shas in Figure 4.1 suggests that it was able to bargain effectively over policy, and presumably perquisites. Indeed, it is plausible that the leader of Shas was aware of this situation, and incorporated this awareness in the utility function of the party.

The relationship between the empirical work and the formal model, together with the possibility of strategic reasoning of this kind, suggests the following conclusion.

Conjecture 4.1 The close correspondence between the simulated LNE based on the empirical analysis and the estimated actual political configuration suggests that the true utility function for each party j has the form $U_j(\mathbf{z}) = \mathcal{E}_j(\mathbf{z}) + \delta_j(\mathbf{z})$, where $\delta_j(\mathbf{z})$ may depend on the beliefs of party leaders about the post-election coalition possibilities, as well as the effect of activist support for the party.

Developing a formal model based on this conjecture could be used to show that the LNE for $\{U_j\}$ would be close to the LNE for $\{\mathcal{E}_j\}$.

If this were true as a general conjecture, it would be possible to use a combination of multinomial logit electoral models, simulations of these models, and the formal electoral model based on exogenous valence to study general equilibrium characteristics of multiparty democracies. In the next section we offer one way of constructing this more complex formal model.

4.3   COALITION BARGAINING

In this section we discuss the formation of coalition government in order to provide a tentative account for the discrepancy we have noted between vote-maximizing positions, as obtained from simulation and predicted by the formal model, and estimated party positions.

Six coalition governments formed during the period covered in Table 2.1. Following the 1988 election, Likud and Labour formed a national unity coalition. Figure 4.3 shows that Likud and Labour were the closest and therefore the most likely coalition partners. The coalition that formed in 1988, however, was clearly oversized. It included Labour, Likud, Shas, NRP, Aguda, and Degel HaTora for a total of 92 seats, which is more than three quarters of the 120 seats in the Knesset.

Three points are noteworthy. First, at this point in time, the riots in the occupied territories, the so-called First Intifada, reached new peaks of violence. Riker (1962) gave one reason for oversized coalitions: national crisis in terms of external threat. Second, the national unity government formed after both major parties failed to form minimal winning coalitions on their own. (As before, we use the standard term *minimal winning*, MW, for a coalition that is winning but may lose no member and still win). The left block had 55 seats, including 2 independent Arab Nationalists (Progress and Democratic Arab) and 4 Communist delegates. The right had 65, including 2 from Tzomet, 3 from Techiya, and 2 from Moledet. These were all regarded as too extreme right-wing parties to be admitted into the coalition at that time. Finally, a common interpretation of the situation suggests that while neither Labour nor Likud could form coalitions on their own, they both wanted to include the religious parties in order to keep future options open.

However, this coalition did not last. Eighteen months after it was sworn in it collapsed and Likud formed the second, slightly oversized, coalition including Likud, Shas, NRP, Yahadut, and the three extremist parties of Moledet, Tzomet, and Thia. This coalition formally controlled 65 of the 120 seats, but Moledet and Tzomet constantly complained about the "soft" policy of the government toward the Arabs in the occupied territories and the willingness of Likud to endorse the conference for peace that was held in Madrid in 1991. When the conference started, both Tzomet and Moledet left the government, leaving behind a strictly minimum winning coalition. As Figure 4.3 shows, this was a natural coalition in terms of ideological proximity. The coalition lasted until the election of 1992.

The first coalition to form after the 1992 election was a minimal winning coalition of Shas, Labour, and Meretz, controlling 62 seats. Observers soon realized two basic facts about the newly elected Knesset and the new government. First, Labour was at the structurally stable core position, $\mathbb{SC}_1^0(z)$, given the post-election decisive structure. Chapter 2 and the example in Chapter 3 both discuss this characteristic of the configuration of party positions. Second, Meretz and Shas were unlikely partners in the same coalition (Sened, 1996). Seventeen months after its conception, Shas left the coalition, leaving Rabin at the head of a minority coalition of 56 seats. This minority government proved to be not only remarkably stable—it lasted 31 months and longer than any coalition in the last two decades—but remarkably effective in pursuing an audacious policy toward a peace agreement with the PLO and Jordan and introducing major reforms in the public sector.

Sened (1996) gives a lengthy account of how this coalition came to be and how effective it was in legislation and in pursuing its peace initiative in spite of its minority status. One important aspect of this account is what led Shas to abandon the 1992 coalition. As the coalition agreement was signed, Prime Minister Itzhak Rabin promised Shas that he would delay the passage of several basic laws in the Knesset. In Israel, basic laws serve as substitutes for the constitution. They have special status, as they require special majorities in order to be amended or discontinued. In 1992, Shas was particularly concerned about two such basic laws:

(1) Freedom and Human Dignity, and
(2) Freedom of Occupation.

Both laws were appropriately interpreted by the spiritual leadership of the ultra orthodox Shas party as serious constraints on the ability of the religious establishment in Israel to intervene in the private choices of Israeli citizens. Rabin was unable to keep his promise, the laws passed, and Shas resigned (Sened, 1996: 366). The lesson of this important political event is three fold.

First, the laws coincided with the core policy position of the Labour party. While a Prime Minister gave his word to a coalition partner to delay the passage of the law he could not keep his promise because it was the Knesset that passed the laws. As we argue throughout this book, it is Parliament and not any particular coalition that passes legislation. Moreover, it is the structure of Parliament, and not the composition of any particular coalition, that determines the final legislative outcome.

Second, while Rabin promised repeatedly to enlarge his coalition, he never bothered to do so. This coalition remained unbeaten until the 1996 election, surviving the controversy over its policies that eventually brought about the assassination of Prime Minister Rabin in November of 1995.

Finally, this coalition was the "cheapest" coalition to occur in Israeli politics, in the sense that Labour kept almost all the important portfolios to itself (Nachmias and Sened, 1999).

The first coalition to form after the 1996 elections was again slightly oversized. It included all the parties of the upper right quadrant of Figure 4.1 (except Moledet) as well as Gesher and III Way. Together the 8 parties in this coalition controlled 66 of 120 Knesset seats. Figure 4.1 illustrates remarkable spread of the ideological positions of the coalition members and the inflated number of coalition members. The bargaining model that we introduce below would predict that partners in this coalition should be able to extract significant government perquisites out of the formateur (Likud). Nachmias and Sened (1999) have tested this hypothesis. They show that the first Netanyahu government ranked 4th among 34 coalition governments in terms of government perquisite allocated per seat held by a coalition partner other than Likud. On average, each such seat earned the Knesset member approximately 3.5 times more government perquisites than a seat held by a Likud member. (We measure perquisites in terms of the percentage of the annual government budget controlled by the coalition member divided by the number of seats this party has in the Knesset). A seat held by a coalition partner other than Likud was worth 2.3 percent of the annual budget, while a seat held by a Likud member was worth 0.65 percent. This difference was statistically significant, and substantially higher than the average percentage calculated across the 33 previous coalitions. Netanyahu, the leader of Likud, eventually refused to allocate additional resources to Gesher, and this led Gesher to leave the coalition. Netanyahu remained at the head of a strictly minimal winning coalition government that stayed in power until the 1999 election.

The most important lesson to draw from these results is that parties may position themselves away from simple vote-maximizing positions if in doing so they become more attractive coalition partners. There are at least three reasons why a party may move away from its vote-maximizing position.

First, a central party may try to capture the core of the polity in order to obtain more of the government perquisites through its position as a dominant party. We conjecture that this was the strategy of Labour in 1992. The estimated position of Labour in Figure 4.2 is somewhat "north" and "west" of the simulated vote-maximizing position given in Figure 4.5.

A second incentive suggests itself on the basis of the bargaining model outlined in Section 3.3. If the party believes that there will be no core party after the election, and it is able to guess at the location of the heart, then it may be able to adjust its position to take advantage of this estimate.

A third incentive, particularly relevant to a pivotal party like Shas, is to be closer to both potential coalition formateurs.

Schofield, Sened, and Nixon (1998) suggest that a combination of these two last incentives explains the position of Shas in Figure 4.1. Obviously, the Shas position is at the center of the security dimension and very far "north" on the religious dimension. This position is far from a simple vote-maximizing position on the basis of the electoral model based on fixed, or exogenous, valences.

It is interesting to note in this respect how Shas seems to have behaved in an increasingly sophisticated fashion. We suggest that at the time of the 1992 election, Shas may have calculated that the coalition structure $\mathbb{D}_0$ was most likely. As the example in Chapter 3 indicated, this would lead Shas to adopt a fairly radical position in order to extract perquisites from government. Labour ended up capturing the structurally stable core in the Knesset and Shas ended up too far away to be an attractive coalition member. In 1996, the loss of votes for Labour meant that the $\mathbb{D}_0$ coalition structure did occur. Shas adjusted its position by moving "south" on the religious axis and was able to bargain its way into lucrative membership in both of Netanyahu's coalitions (Nachmias and Sened, 1999). Since then, Shas has remained pivotal between Labour coalitions, led by Barak, and Likud coalitions led by Sharon. We discuss in Chapter 9 the recent changes in the political configuration of the Knesset.

4.4 CONCLUSION: ELECTIONS AND LEGISLATIVE BARGAINING

In a very simple sense, legislative bargaining models often assume that the composition of the coalition government determines the nature of legislation and policy implementation. In contrast, the previous section suggests that it is necessary to tie the pre-election party positioning to the expected final coalitional outcome. As we have discussed in Chapters 2 and 3, under the post-election coalition structures given by $\mathbb{D}_1$, the structurally stable core $\mathbb{SC}_1^0(\mathbf{z})$ at the vector $\mathbf{z}$ is nonempty, and the heart $\mathcal{H}_1^0(\mathbf{z})$ collapses to $\mathbb{SC}_1^0(\mathbf{z})$. The discussion of the 1992 election suggests that the policy position of Labour meant that it was not only the *strongest* party, in terms of seat shares, but the configuration of party positions meant that it was also *dominant*, in the sense that its position could be expected to be implemented with certainty. We can then expect a minority government, as did occur under Rabin's leadership. In contrast, under a coalition structure belonging to $\mathbb{D}_0$, the core is empty, and the vector of party positions $\mathbf{z}$, together with the distribution of seat shares, defines the heart $\mathcal{H}_0^0(\mathbf{z})$ of the legislature. In such a situation, one expects one of a number of possible coalition governments. Indeed, all such governments must command the support of at least a majority of the seats in the Parliament. If they do not, then a majority counter-coalition will be able to engineer a vote of no confidence. Although this argument is clearest when nonpolicy perquisites are irrelevant, we argue that a similar argument holds when perquisites are incorporated. This observation about the fundamental difference between the core situation $\mathcal{H}_1$ and the noncore situation $\mathcal{H}_0$ is crucial, we believe, to an understanding of the sharp qualitative shift that can occur in legislative bargaining.

As the Israel examples in Chapter 2 and 3 illustrate, the potentially dominant party, Labour, should attempt to maximize the probability π_1 that the election outcome $\mathbb{D}_1$ occurs. In contrast, since Likud had available no feasible position, prior to 2003, that would allow it to be dominant, then it should attempt to maximize the probability π_0 that $\mathbb{D}_0$ occurs. As a first approximation, we may assume that $U_j(\mathbf{z}) = \mathcal{E}_j(\mathbf{z})$ for $j =$ Labour or Likud. This provides an explanation of why the positions of Labour and Likud are close to their estimated vote-maximizing positions in the elections of 1988, 1992, and 1996.

The parties with low valence may have more complex incentives depending on their beliefs concerning the game form $\tilde{g}^\alpha = \{\tilde{g}_t^\alpha, \pi_t\}$. The vote-maximizing model suggests that they will adopt positions on the periphery of the voter distribution, but their precise location may be off the principal electoral axis if they believe that such a position can be advantageous in coalition bargaining.

We return to this analysis in Chapter 9.

It should be possible to test this model against other hypotheses that point to the composition of the coalition as the main determinant of final policy outcomes in multiparty parliaments (see, for example, Laver and Shepsle, 1990, 1994, 1996).

4.5 APPENDIX

Table A4.1. *Factor Analysis Results for Israel for the Election of 1996.*

Issue Question	Factor weights*	
	Security	Religion
Chance for peace	0.494 (0.024)	–
Land for peace	0.867 (0.013)	–
Religious law vs. democracy	0.287 (0.038)	0.613 (0.054)
Must stop peace process	−0.656 (0.020)	–
Agreement with Oslo accord	−0.843 (0.012)	–
Oslo accord contributed to safety	−0.798 (0.016)	–
Personal safety after Oslo	−0.761 (0.020)	–
Israel should talk with PLO	−0.853 (0.016)	–
Opinion of settlers	0.885 (0.015)	–
Agree that Palestinians want peace	−0.745 (0.016)	–
Peace agreement will end Arab-Israeli conflict	−0.748 (0.018)	–
Agreement with Palestinian state	−0.789 (0.016)	–
Should encourage Arabs to emigrate	0.618 (0.022)	–
What must Israel do to prevent war?	−0.843 (0.019)	–
Settlements 1	0.712 (0.014)	–
Settlements 2	0.856 (0.014)	–
National security	0.552 (0.023)	–
Equal rights for Arabs and Jews in Israel	−0.766 (0.018)	–
More government spending toward religious institutions	–	0.890 (0.035)
More government spending toward security	0.528 (0.049)	0.214 (0.065)
More government spending on immigrant absorption	0.342 (0.052)	0.470 (0.065)
More government spending on settlements	0.597 (0.040)	0.234 (0.055)
More government spending in Arab sector	−0.680 (0.019)	–
Public life should be in accordance with Jewish tradition	–	1.000 (constant)
Views toward an Arab minister	−0.747 (0.019)	–
Var (Security)	1.000 (constant)	
Var (Religion)	0.732	
Covar (Security, Religion)	0.591	

* Standard errors in parenthesis.

Table A4.2. *Multinomial Logit Analysis of the 1996 Election in Israel (normalized with respect to Meretz).*

		Posterior	95% Confidence Interval	
	Party	Mean	Lower Bound	Upper Bound
Spatial Distance	β	1.117	0.974	1.278
Constant λ coefficients	Shas	−2.960	−7.736	1.018
	Likud	3.140	0.709	5.800
	Labour	4.153	1.972	6.640
	NRP	−4.519	−8.132	−1.062
	Moledet	−0.893	−4.284	2.706
	Third Way	−2.340	−4.998	0.411
Ashkenazi	Shas	0.066	−1.831	1.678
	Likud	−0.625	−1.510	0.271
	Labour	−0.219	−0.938	0.492
	NRP	1.055	−0.206	2.242
	Moledet	0.819	−0.560	2.185
	Third Way	−0.283	−1.594	1.134
Age	Shas	0.014	−0.058	0.086
	Likud	−0.024	−0.063	0.008
	Labour	−0.040	−0.077	−0.012
	NRP	−0.064	−0.111	−0.020
	Moledet	−0.026	−0.088	0.026
	Third Way	0.014	−0.034	0.063
Education	Shas	−0.377	−0.693	−0.063
	Likud	−0.032	−0.180	0.115
	Labour	0.011	−0.099	0.120
	NRP	0.386	0.180	0.599
	Moledet	0.049	−0.219	0.305
	Third Way	−0.067	−0.298	0.150
Religious Observation	Shas	3.022	1.737	4.308
	Likud	0.930	0.270	1.629
	Labour	0.645	0.077	1.272
	NRP	2.161	1.299	3.103
	Moledet	0.897	−0.051	1.827
	Third Way	0.954	0.031	1.869
Correctly Predicted	Shas	0.309	0.210	0.414
	Likud	0.707	0.672	0.740
	Labour	0.717	0.681	0.752
	NRP	0.408	0.324	0.493
	Moledet	0.078	0.046	0.115
	Third Way	0.029	0.017	0.043
	Meretz	0.286	0.226	0.349
	Entire Model	0.638	0.623	0.654
$n = 794$		Log marginal likelihood = −465.		

Table A4.3. *Multinomial Logit Analysis of the 1992 Election in Israel (normalized with respect to Meretz).*

	Posterior		95% Confidence Interval	
	Party	Mean	Lower Bound	Upper Bound
Spatial Distance	β	1.253	1.098	1.408
Constant λ coefficients	Shas	−4.671	−7.993	−1.539
	Likud	2.725	1.100	4.304
	Labour	0.914	−0.627	2.560
	NRP	−0.442	−2.291	1.247
	Tzomet	−0.369	−1.653	0.905
	Moledet	0.380	−1.348	2.108
Ashkenazi	Shas	0.453	−0.907	2.106
	Likud	−0.881	−1.463	−0.283
	Labour	−0.727	−1.360	−0.125
	NRP	−0.083	−1.020	0.815
	Tzomet	−0.559	−1.385	0.200
	Moledet	−0.918	−1.772	−0.854
Age	Shas	0.011	−0.028	0.053
	Likud	0.019	−0.006	0.047
	Labour	0.042	0.013	0.069
	NRP	0.018	−0.014	0.054
	Tzomet	0.010	−0.025	0.044
	Moledet	−0.020	−0.052	0.012
Education	Shas	0.077	−0.087	0.228
	Likud	−0.193	−0.305	−0.089
	Labour	−0.069	−0.088	0.028
	NRP	−0.138	−0.267	−0.015
	Tzomet	−0.027	−0.136	0.079
	Moledet	0.032	−0.078	0.142
Religious Observation	Shas	2.024	1.394	2.791
	Likud	0.658	0.320	0.977
	Labour	0.141	−0.255	0.536
	NRP	1.595	1.081	2.203
	Tzomet	0.526	0.022	0.983
	Moledet	0.446	−0.166	01058
Correctly Predicted	Shas	0.405	0.315	0.504
	Likud	0.503	0.463	0.545
	Labour	0.595	0.552	0.633
	NRP	0.234	0.176	0.299
	Tzomet	0.253	0.207	0.303
	Meretz	0.470	0.415	0.530
	Moledet	0.114	0.080	0.149
	Entire Model	0.475	0.460	0.490
$n = 781$	Log marginal likelihood $= -834.$			

Table A4.4. *Multinomial Logit Analysis of the 1988 Election in Israel (normalized with respect to Meretz).*

	Party	Posterior Mean	95% Confidence Interval Lower Bound	95% Confidence Interval Upper Bound
Spatial Distance	β	1.315	1.083	1.569
Constant λ coefficients	Shas	−5.777	−10.092	−2.324
	Likud	2.839	0.325	5.047
	Labour	0.297	−2.547	3.011
	NRP	−2.989	−6.874	0.333
	Tzomet	−0.745	−4.480	2.570
	Thia	0.388	−3.247	4.023
Ashkenazi	Shas	−1.108	−2.326	0.075
	Likud	−2.384	−3.171	−1.731
	Labour	−1.461	−2.320	−0.594
	NRP	−1.485	−2.300	−0.674
	Tzomet	−1.760	−2.797	−0.696
	Thia	−1.418	−2.549	−0.287
Age	Shas	0.031	−0.024	0.091
	Likud	0.017	−0.024	0.066
	Labour	0.034	−0.466	0.988
	NRP	−0.059	−0.144	0.013
	Tzomet	−0.017	−0.078	0.045
	Thia	−0.042	−0.094	0.010
Education	Shas	−0.169	−0.443	0.094
	Likud	−0.183	−0.369	0.006
	Labour	−0.069	−0.272	0.126
	NRP	−0.063	−0.360	0.179
	Tzomet	−0.045	−0.274	0.215
	Thia	−0.042	−0.305	0.221
Religious Observation	Shas	3.163	2.133	4.141
	Likud	0.650	0.094	1.261
	Labour	0.235	−0.375	0.924
	NRP	2.856	1.936	3.997
	Tzomet	0.716	−0.113	1.683
	Thia	0.807	0.009	1.605
Correctly Predicted	Shas	0.261	0.157	0.371
	Likud	0.648	0.605	0.688
	Labour	0.504	0.454	0.552
	NRP	0.219	0.136	0.331
	Tzomet	0.046	0.023	0.076
	Meretz	0.449	0.373	0.515
	Thia	0.112	0.074	0.163
	Entire Model	0.525	0.506	0.544
$n = 505$		Log marginal likelihood = −597		

5

Elections in Italy, 1992–1996

5.1 INTRODUCTION

Understanding Italian politics in terms of coalition theory has proved very difficult. From the office-seeking perspective, the common occurrence of both minority and surplus coalitions during the 1970s and the 1980s seemed puzzling (Axelrod, 1980; Laver and Schofield, 1990; Strom, 1990). Other writers have been intrigued by the apparent instability of Italian coalition governments during this same period (Sartori, 1976; Pridham, 1987). The theoretical challenge has become even harder after the institutional upheaval of the early 1990s. So much has changed in terms of electoral rule, party alignment, and party composition that it has been hard to follow, let alone explain.

Recently, Mershon (1996a,b, 2002) has made a significant contribution to the study of Italian politics by combining a theoretical approach with careful data analysis. Our own theoretical model of multiparty politics is offered as an extension of Mershon's earlier work.

Different sources of data are used in this chapter. For party policy positions before 1996 we rely on the most updated version of the Comparative Manifesto Project (CMP) (Budge et al., 2001). The methodological status of the CMP data set, obtained via content analysis of party platforms, has been challenged on various grounds. First, the CMP research strategy is meant to ascertain salience of issues rather than party positions on those issues (Laver, 2001). Second, party positions derived from the content analysis of party platforms do not necessarily coincide with voter perceptions of these positions. We use the CMP analyses only to give an approximate indication of party positions prior to 1996. For the 1996 election, we use original data obtained by Giannetti and Sened (2004). These include mass and expert surveys. We believe that this methodological strategy is better suited to determine parties' policy positions since it is based on expert judgments and voter perceptions, both of which can be represented by locations in the same policy space. As in Chapter 4, we use a visual approach to the data to make the complexities of Italian politics more readily explicable. This facilitates examination of the Italian political system with simple policy diagrams.

In Section 5.2, we give a systematic account of Italian electoral and coalition politics before 1992. In Section 5.3, we discuss the institutional revolution of the 1990s. Sections 5.4 and 5.5 interpret election and coalition formation following the 1994 and 1996 campaigns, respectively.

One preliminary remark immediately illustrates the advantage of our theoretical approach and will prove very useful for the discussion that follows. As in the case of Israel, our distinction between the two generic coalition structures is very helpful in modelling the transition from the "old" Italian politics that persisted until the early 1990s to the recent "new" Italian politics. The latter is characterized by a $\mathbb{D}_0$ coalition structure, where the core is empty, whereas the former was characterized by a $\mathbb{D}_1$ structure with a structurally stable core at the position of the dominant Christian Democrat (DC) Party. As we demonstrate in the sections that follow, this observation allows us to make sense of this transformation in Italian politics. We use this framework to illustrate the usefulness of the model in understanding such political transformations.

5.2 ITALIAN POLITICS BEFORE 1992

Governments in Italy both change and remain the same. The Christian Democratic Party (DC) always held governing power. But almost no government stayed in office more than a few years, and many governments collapsed after only a few months. How can instability coexist with stability in this way? (Mershon, 1996a: 534)

[T]he core Christian Democrat Party leads a dance with three or four partners often forming new governments after less than a year. The 1992 election and the appearance of the Lombardy/Northern League [NL] may have resulted in a major transformation in Italy, with the destruction of the core. (Schofield, 1993: 9)

The first question posed by Mershon (1996a) provides a central motivation for her work on politics in Italy for the period 1947 to 1987 (Mershon, 1996b, 2002). While the Christian Democrats (DC) headed every cabinet between 1946 and 1981 and was always in government until the election of 1992, government coalitions were typically unstable.

The average duration of minimum winning and surplus coalitions was 17 months and 9 months for minority coalitions, for the period from 1945 to 1987 (Laver and Schofield, 1990).

The model presented in Chapter 3 provides a straightforward solution to this puzzle. Laver and Schofield (1990) were the first to suggest that the DC simply occupied the core position from 1945 to 1987. They proposed a one-dimensional model, in which the core always exists and coincides with the party that controls the median legislator. Schofield (1995) then extended the model to a two-dimensional one where the structurally stable core coincides with the position of the largest party located at a central position. He called such a party *dominant*. The second quotation from Schofield (1993) reflects his observation that the changes in party strengths, and particularly the emergence of the Northern League (NL) in 1992, destroyed the dominance of the DC.

The following hypothesis is derived by Schofield (1995) and Sened (1996) based on an earlier version of the general coalition model presented in Chapter 3 above, and developed by Schofield and Sened (2002) and Giannetti and Sened (2004).

Hypothesis 5.1: *If the structurally stable core of the political game is nonempty and coincides with the position of the largest party, then this dominant party will always be a member of the government coalition.*

Figure 5.1 represents the estimates of party positions in 1987, based on the CMP data and using the technique given in Laver (2001). The two dimensions are an economic left–right dimension and a (vertical) liberal–conservative social dimension (partially based on religious attitudes).

In Figure 5.1, the "median" lines are given by the arcs such as

$$\{DC - PCI, \; DC - PSDI, \; DC - PRI, \; DC - PLI\}.$$

As mentioned before, a median line bisects the policy space, so that coalition majorities lie on either side of the line. These medians all intersect at the policy position of the DC. This property is a sufficient condition for DC to be located at the core position. Another way to see this is to consider the convex compromise sets associated with winning coalitions. The DC position in Figure 5.1 belongs to the convex compromise set associated with the winning coalition

$$\{PCI, PSI, PSDI, PRI, PLI\}$$

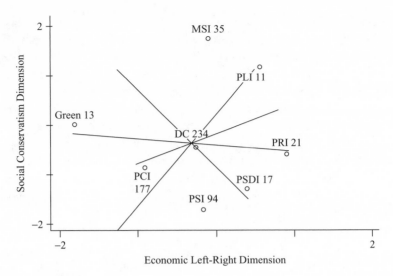

Figure 5.1. Party policy positions (based on the manifesto data set) and party seat strength in Italy in 1987.

If the DC position lay outside this set, then this large, though somewhat unlikely coalition, could theoretically agree to a policy position different from that of the DC. Assuming the DC position did indeed belong to the larger coalition compromise set, then it follows that bargaining between the parties will result in the DC obtaining the policy position that it had chosen (Schofield, 1995; Sened, 1996; Banks and Duggan, 2000). Moreover, this conclusion is not affected by small perturbations of party positions. Thus DC can be seen to be a core party, located at the structurally stable core position (Giannetti and Sened, 2004).

If the results obtained for 1987 could be generalized, it is plausible to argue that a fundamental underlying $\mathbb{D}_1$ coalition structure characterized Italian politics until 1992. It is our understanding that the $\mathbb{D}_1$ structure, illustrated in Figure 5.1, was typical of Italian politics during the entire period between 1946 and 1992. This explains the otherwise puzzling apparent coalition instability combined with outcome stability noted by Mershon (1996a,b, 2002).

The model does not explain the phenomenon of short-lived coalition governments in Italy. To date, no comprehensive model of government termination has been elaborated in the formal literature (Laver, 2003). In her study of coalition politics in Italy, Mershon (2002) offers the low costs of "making and breaking governments" by Italian political parties as a plausible explanation for constant government turnover. We suggest that because the DC was positioned at the core, it was able to implement its policy, even through minority government when it so chose. On occasion it would form minimal winning or surplus coalitions in order to placate other parties in the Chamber of Deputies with nonpolicy perquisites. The dominance of the DC disappeared in the election of 1992.

5.3   THE NEW INSTITUTIONAL DIMENSION: 1991–1996

In the early 1990s, Italian politics experienced a dramatic change. Corruption scandals shook the Italian political elites. A political crisis resulted and a major institutional revolution followed, changing the entire electoral system after almost 40 years of PR. This marked the beginning of what has been called the "Second Italian Republic." This prompted an extensive literature on the "Italian transition." (See for instance, Bartolini and D'Alimonte, 1995; D'Alimonte and Bartolini, 1997).

The first and most notable change affected the identity and the set of relevant actors. Old parties either disappeared or went through major transformations in ideologies and electoral strategies. New parties emerged or split off from old parties. The main changes in parties' identities between 1991 and 1996 are discussed below.

The Communist Party (PCI) transformed into the Democratic Party of the Left (PDS), splitting off from the "far left" RC.

On January 18, 1994, the last National Assembly of the DC was held. The party renamed itself Partito Popolare Italiano (PPI). A right-wing faction, Centro Cristiano-Democratico (CCD), split off. Between 1994 and 1996, the Socialist Party (PSI) and other center parties

$$\{PSDI, PRI, PLI\}$$

(that had systematically formed the pentapartito coalition governments with DC in the 1980s) dissolved. The PSI dropped from a vote share of 13.6 percent in 1992 to a vote share of 2.2 percent in 1994.

In January 1994, Forza Italia (FI) led by the media magnate Silvio Berlusconi formed, just a few months before the elections. In January 1995, the fascist party, the Movimento Social Italian (or MSI) transformed into Alleanza Nazionale (MSI-AN), generating a splinter party, MSFT, on its right. Figure 5.2 provides a simplified, graphic presentation of this major party realignment that is but one aspect of this major transformation of the Italian political landscape in the late 1980s and early 1990s.

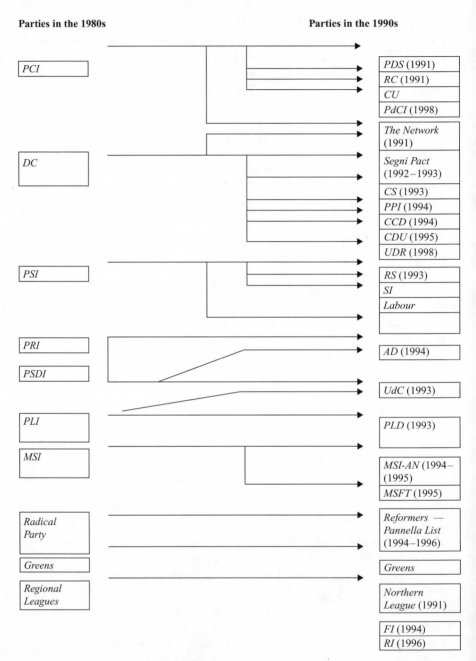

Figure 5.2. Changes in the political party landscape between the 1980s and 1990s.

Table 5.1. *Italian Elections: Votes/Seats in the Chamber of Deputies, 1987–1996.**

Parties	1987 Vote share %	Seats	1992 Vote share %	Seats	1994 Vote share %	Seats	1996 Vote share %	Seats
DP	1.7	8	–	–	–	–	–	–
RC	–	–	5.6	35	6.0	39	8.6	35
Greens	2.5	13	2.8	16	2.7	11	2.5	14
PCI-PDS	26.6	177	16.1	107	20.4	125	21.1	175
Network	–	–	1.9	12	1.9	6	–	–
PSI	14.3	94	13.6	92	2.2	14	–	–
PSDI	2.9	17	2.7	16	–	–	–	–
PRI	3.7	21	4.4	27	–	–	–	–
AD	–	–	–	–	1.2	18	–	–
DC-PPI	34.3	234	29.7	206	11.1	33	6.8	70
Segni Pact	–	–	–	–	4.7	13	–	–
PLI	2.1	11	2.9	17	–	–	–	–
RI	–	–	–	–	–	–	4.3	26
PR-Pannella List	2.6	13	1.2	7	3.5	–	1.9	0
Northern League (NL)	0.5	1	8.7	55	8.4	117	10.1	59
CCD	–	–	–	–	–	29	5.8	19
CDU	–	–	–	–	–	–		11
FI	–	–	–	–	21.0	111	20.6	123
MSI-AN	5.9	35	5.4	34	13.5	109	15.7	93
Others	2.9	6	5.0	6	3.4	5	2.7	5
Total	100	630	100	630	100	630	100	630

* *Note.* In order to compare electoral results before and after electoral reform in 1993, the results given for 1994 and 1996 refer to PR contests only.

Table 5.1 shows the vote shares of the main party lists and their respective seat weights in the chamber between 1987 and 1996. The 1992 election gave the first indication of the coming transformation. The popular vote for the DC fell below 30 percent and the main beneficiary of shifting voter choice was the Northern League (NL), a federation of regionalist groups that won 8.7 percent of the national vote and 55 seats. NL became the second most popular party in Northern Italy (with 20.5 percent compared with 25.5 percent for the DC).

We can illustrate the effect of this election with Figure 5.3, which develops the idea about the destruction of the core proposed by Schofield

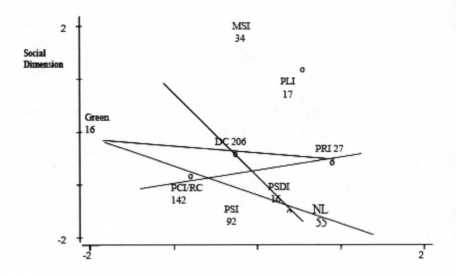

Economic left-right dimension

Figure 5.3. Hypothetical party policy positions and seats in Italy in 1992.

(1993). Assuming the traditional parties were positioned as they were in 1987, and the NL was positioned in the southwest of the figure, then the coalition {PCI/RC,PSI,PSDI,PRI,NL} obtained a majority of 332 seats. (In the figure, the position marked PCI is taken to represent both PCI, with 107 seats, and the RC with 35 seats.) More importantly, the compromise set of this coalition no longer contained the DC position. Another way of showing this is that there is a new median line from the PRI to the PCI that does not intersect the DC position. Thus, the DC was no longer at a core position, and was therefore no longer a dominant party. This suggestion is of course somewhat hypothetical, but it accords with the changes that were to come.

These changes were accompanied by a transformation in the perceptions of the defining features of Italian politics. The emergence of a North–South dimension, partially overlapping with the issue of corruption, is central. This *institutional dimension,* as we refer to it here, is really a compound one, composed of demands for federal reforms led by the Northern League and the reactive proposals by the establishment parties for electoral reforms. These competing calls for reform evolved in an environment pervaded by judicial investigations of political corruption.

In a "heresthetic move" (Riker, 1986), Umberto Bossi, leader of the NL, put the North–South issue on the political agenda in the late 1980s.

A socioeconomic North–South divide had preceded the formation of the unitary state (Putnam, 1993). The strategy of the Northern League reversed the traditional *questione meridionale* ("the Southern issue") into a Northern issue, putting the demand for federal reform at the center of the political agenda. This strategy is central in four of the Northern League's electoral campaign issues in the early 1990s. First, there was the fight against disproportionate party power (*partitocrazia*), which was regarded as the source of patronage, clientelism, and corruption. Second, the League's anti-southern stand was tied to the common perception of the inefficiency of public services in Southern Italy. Third, the League's anti-immigrant stance was related to the influx of third-world illegal immigrants from the South. Finally, the *partitocrazia* was portrayed by the League as ineffective in dealing with the mafia, following accusations that the party establishment relied on the mafia to govern the South (Leonardi and Kovacks, 1993).

The Northern League's recreation of the North–South dimension can be seen as an example of the transformation of policy dimensions. In the same way, the issue of race and civil rights in the United States has the capacity to alter "the political environment within which [it] originated and evolved ... replacing one dominant alignment with another and transforming the character of the parties themselves" (Carmines and Stimson, 1989: 11; Miller and Schofield, 2003).

As a reaction to the reemergence of the North–South tensions, leaders of the winning majority attempted to bring about more accountable democratic institutions. The Christian Democrat leader Mario Segni championed a referendum on reducing the number of preferential votes in parliamentary elections, allegedly associated with corrupt vote trading in the South. (The electoral law allowed voters to express up to four preferential votes for candidates in the party lists.)

On June 9, 1991, the multiple-preference vote procedure was discontinued by an overwhelming majority of 95.6 percent. After the success of the 1991 referendum, a new referendum committee was set up to abolish clauses of the existing electoral law for the Senate. On April 18 1993, 82.7 percent of voters cast their ballot for change. On August 1993, a Parliament still dominated by the old political elite, approved a new electoral law at the national level. Italy switched from an almost pure PR system to a mixed system that allocated 75 percent of the seats by plurality and only the remaining 25 percent by PR.

Thus, the North–South tension reintroduced by Bossi and the Northern League was transformed into a new dimension of institutional change that reshaped political competition and brought about new party alignments. The general issue of reform was central in that a strong demand for change determined a transformation of the rules of political competition, which then contributed to the reshaping of the entire party system.

On these grounds, our a priori assumption that the institutional dimension is most relevant for understanding Italian politics from the early to mid-1990s seems justified.

In the next two sections we return to a close examination of the theory in the context of the two electoral campaigns that followed. A central theme in this elaboration is Schofield's (1993) notion of the "evaporation of the core" of Italian politics. We contend that this transformation has similarities to the changes in Israel described in the Chapter 4. The transition was from a $\mathbb{D}_1$ coalition structure, with the dominant or core DC party at its center, so characteristic of Italian politics from 1945 to 1987, to a $\mathbb{D}_0$ structure, with an empty core. This has had a profound effect on the nature and dynamics of Italian politics in the 1990s. Our analysis of the 1994 and 1996 elections illustrates this observation.

5.4 THE 1994 ELECTION

The introduction of a new dimension to the issue space of Italian politics, coupled with the demise of old parties and the emergence of new ones, led to a significant transformation of Italian politics to a parliamentary system characterized by a $\mathbb{D}_0$ structure, where the core is empty. Our theory suggests that the expected set of outcomes is typically characterized by the policy heart of the Parliament. This means less stability in the outcome space and a very different type of political game. We no longer expect "policy stability" through the exercise of power by the dominant DC party. Instead we expect policy instability as each governing coalition is replaced with one of a very different composition. Indeed, we might expect a degree of political chaos, reminiscent of the formal results on voting.

5.4.1 *The Pre-Election Stage*

In March 1994 Italy had its first election under the new electoral system. (A discussion of this election, and the one following in 1996 can be found in Corbetta and Parisi, 1997). The plurality part of the new electoral law sets up a coalition-formation phase before, rather than after, the election. Parties form pre-electoral coalitions, declare common policy packages to be implemented once in government, and bargain over the allocation of

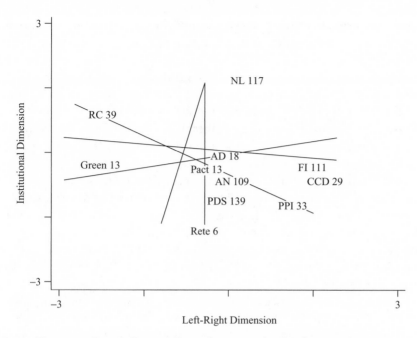

Figure 5.4. Party policy positions and seats in Italy after the 1994 election.

seats. But the PR tier still gives parties a strong incentive to maintain separate policy positions.

The parties' positions in Figure 5.4 for 1994 were estimated from CMP data. A left–right scale was constructed from parties' scores on economic and social issues. (Party positions may appear at variance with common perceptions as far as the AN is concerned. The "low" score of this party on the left–right dimension may be partially explained by the fact that the MSI has always been more of a populist than a "Thatcherite" right-wing party. While expert and mass surveys data commonly agree on placing the party at the extreme right of the scale, estimates obtained from content analysis of party manifestos between 1946 and 1996 suggest that our estimate of the party location may be quite accurate.)

We operationalized the "institutional dimension" as party scores on issues of decentralization. The NL scored the highest on this dimension. Notice that the vertical dimensions is Figures 5.1 and 5.4 are quite different.

In 1994, four pre-electoral coalitions, Progressisti on the left, Patto per l'Italia at the center, and Polo delle Libertà and Polo del Buon Governo on the right, contested the plurality component. They are best seen as mere electoral alliances. Parties agreed on the presentation of common candidates in the districts but did not campaign on a common policy platform.

Progressisti was composed of Partito Democratico della Sinistra (PDS), Regio Calabria (RC), Greens, La Rete (The Network), various factions of the PSI, minor left parties, and the new movement of moderate left, Democratic Alliance (AD). The members of the Progressisti alliance issued a brief joint document. The campaign revealed clear differences between their policy positions.

DC was divided in three: the Popolari per la Riforma, founded by Segni, the Partito Popolare Italiano (PPI), and the right-wing faction, Centro Cristiano Democratico (CCD). The Northern League explored the possibility of reaching an agreement with Segni. The failure of this agreement on January 24, 1994, marks the end of the attempts to unite the center political forces. Eventually, PPI and Segni formed the electoral alliance Patto per l'Italia.

On January 24, Berlusconi launched the new political movement, Forza Italia (FI) on a liberal right program, advocating lower taxes, fiscal federalism, and direct election of the head of the state. Berlusconi formed two electoral alliances: one with the Northern League in the North (Polo delle Libertà), and the other with the MSI-AN in the South (Polo del Buon Governo). In the North, AN contested the elections on its own. The Northern League (NL) did not run in the South. The NL managed to stress its policy differences with FI. Bossi was confident that NL would defeat FI on the PR ballot and could dictate institutional reforms to the new government. In Southern Italy, FI allied with AN, while MSI-AN downgraded its policy differences with FI. Despite the project of a radical renovation launched by secretary Fini in January 1994, the AN was still very conservative on the institutional dimension, positioning itself as a radical party, supporting national unity, and against federalism, though still stressing its antiestablishment stance.

5.4.2   *The Electoral Stage*

The elections resulted in a major transformation of the political scene. Most striking was the success of FI, a party that did not exist just months before the election. FI became the leading national party with 21 percent of the vote, which translated into 15.7 percent of the seats. The NL kept its vote share close to its 1992 share. Thanks to the pre-electoral agreement that gave 63.4 percent of single-member districts in Northern and Central

Italy to the NL candidates, the NL became the largest parliamentary party, with 18.6 percent of the seats in the Chamber but only 8.4 percent of the vote. AN more than doubled the electoral strength of the former MSI (from 5.4 percent to 13.5 percent). The splinter factions of the former CD ended up with roughly half of the vote (15.8 percent) that they had in 1992. The translation of votes into seats further penalized the centrist alliance, which ended up with only 7.3 percent of the seats despite having a PR vote share of 15.8 percent. Table 5.2 displays the result of the 1994 elections. For the sake of the discussion we divided parties into three blocks: Progressisti (left), Patto per l'Italia (center) and Polo (right). We also give seat subtotals for the PDS and FI groups.

We do not have a good data set to model voter choice for this election. We present the results of the election in Table 5.2 for the sake of completeness and without further interpretation.

5.4.3   The Coalition Bargaining Game

Following the 1994 election, FI, AN, NL, and CCD formed a winning coalition controlling 366 seats: 111 for FI, 117 for NL, 109 for AN, and 29 for CCD. Again, a coalition is *minimal winning* (MW) if it is winning but cannot lose a coalition member and remain winning. Thus this coalition is MW if the CCD, which contested the election under the FI label, is counted as part of FI. CCD formed a parliamentary group after the election. If we count CCD as a distinct party the coalition is not MW.

In the Senate, the coalition was short of a majority, controlling 156 seats out of 315. It passed the investiture vote due to the defection of four PPI deputies who voted in its favor.

Figure 5.4 shows the fundamental change that took place in the structure of the Italian Parliament: The core is now empty. The intrinsic instability of this structure sheds some light on the puzzling question of why Bossi decided to withdraw his support from the Berlusconi government after only 8 months, although NL was overrepresented in Parliament and controlled five ministers, including Budget and Constitutional Reform. From a pure office-seeking perspective, it is possible to argue that the legislative weights' distribution, which made the NL a pivotal party, and the actual allocation of ministerial positions, gave the party a strong incentive to defect (Giannetti and Laver, 2001).

An alternative explanation of the NL strategy relies on future electoral concerns. The European elections, held under the PR electoral system on June 12, 1994, can be regarded as an important event that provided

Table 5.2. *The 1994 Election Results in Italy: Chamber and Senate.**

Party Blocks	Parties	Chamber				Senate		
		PR Vote Share%	Plurality Vote Share%	Seats	Seats%	Vote Share%	Seats	Seats%
	RC	6.0	–	39	6.2	–	18	5.7
	PDS	20.4	–	109	17.3	–	60	19.0
	PSI	2.2	–	14	2.2	–	12	3.8
	Ind Left	–	–	10	1.6	–	4	1.3
	CS	–	–	5	0.8	–	4	1.3
	RS	–	–	1	0.2	–	1	0.3
	Total PDS	–	–	139	22.1	–	81	25.7
	AD	1.2	–	18	2.9	–	10	3.2
	Greens	2.7	–	11	1.7	–	7	2.2
	Network	1.9	–	6	1.0	–	6	1.9
Progressi (Left)	Total	34.4	32.8	213	33.8	32.9	122	38.7
	PPI	11.1	–	33	5.2	–	30	9.5
	Segni/Pact	4.7	–	13	2.1	–	1	0.3
Patto (Center)	Total	15.8	15.6	46	7.3	16.7	31	9.8
	FI	21.0	–	99	15.7	–	32	10.2
	UdC	–	–	4	0.6	–	3	1.0
	PLD	–	–	2	0.3	–	–	–
	Reformers	–	–	6	1.0	–	1	0.3
	Total FI	–	–	111	17.6	–	36	11.5
	Northern League	8.4	–	117	18.6	–	60	19.0
	AN	13.5	–	109	17.3	–	47	14.9
	CCD	–	–	29	4.6	–	12	3.8
	Pannella	3.5	–	–	–	–	1	0.3
Polo (Right)	Total	46.4	46.2	366	58.1	42.7	156	49.6
	SVP	0.6	–	3	0.5	0.7	3	1.0
	PvdA		–	1	0.2	0.1	1	0.3
	LdAM	0.2	–	1	0.2	–	–	–
	Others	2.6	4.3	–	–	6.9	2	0.6
Total All		100.0	98.9	630	100.0	100.0	315	100.0

* *Source*: Data derived from Ministry of Interior and political parties.

Note: These results differ slightly from those of Bartolini and D'Alimonte (1995) due to different aggregation procedures being used.

parties critical information about shifting voter choice. The NL's support fell to 6.6 percent of the national vote compared with FI's 30.6 percent. The NL faced the serious prospect of being absorbed by FI, which created a strong incentive for the NL to ask for earlier national elections.

From our theoretical perspective, the plausible explanation to Bossi's move is that, following his defeat in the European elections, he realized that the policy implemented by the FI-led government was too far from the declared position of NL. The office-related perquisites were no longer enough to compensate for the deviation from the NL ideal point. This also explains why NL adopted a more radical stance inside the government, and eventually, on December 17, advanced a motion of no confidence against the government; this motion was also signed by the PPI. Berlusconi's attempts at keeping a parliamentary majority failed. On December 22, 1994, Berlusconi resigned. The head of the state entrusted Dini, former Treasury Minister in Berlusconi's cabinet, with the formation of a new government. Dini's cabinet was non-partisan. All ministers were professionals with no parliamentary affiliation, including the Prime Minister himself. But the government was supported by a parliamentary majority that included center-left parties plus the NL. On January 25, 1995 the Dini cabinet carried the vote of confidence: 302 voted in favour (PDS, PPI, NL), 39 opposed (RC), and 270 abstained (FI, AN, CCD, plus 5 deputies of the NL). Then on February 1, Dini carried the confidence vote in the Senate: 191 voted in favour (PDS, PPI, NL), 17 opposed (RC), and 2 abstained (1 NL and 1 AN). The senators of the Polo (FI, AN, CCD) did not take part in the vote as a sign of protest.

The Dini cabinet lasted about a year. Facing 13 no-confidence votes and resorting quite often to restrictive procedures such as emergency decrees, Dini eventually resigned in January 1996.

According to the theory offered in Chapter 3, the transformation to a $\mathbb{D}_0$ coalition structure with empty core results in a set of policy outcomes – the heart of the Parliament. Since possible outcomes are associated with lotteries over this set, one can expect coalition instability. Indeed, two coalitions lasted less than a year each. This was not uncommon in Italian politics, even prior to 1992. What is new, and what we can attribute to the shift to a $\mathbb{D}_0$ structure, is that the consecutive coalitions were different in composition and in policy goals.

Just as the $\mathbb{D}_1$ structure typified Italian politics up until 1987, so does it appear that the more unstable $\mathbb{D}_0$ structure will characterize politics in the future. Certainly, it appears unlikely that the PDS or FI will receive sufficient electoral support to become dominant parties.

Our analysis of the 1996 election in the next section shows that no party became a dominant, core party. Indeed, the analysis indicates that, in this election, the centrifugal forces associated with factionalized vote maximizing became even more important.

5.5 THE 1996 ELECTION

For the 1996 election we obtained survey data from attitudinal questions. Just as in Chapter 3, the data were analyzed using exploratory and then confirmatory factor analysis. The analysis yielded two underlying factors. One factor is related to questions on the future institutional design of Italy. The other is the common left–right dimension (but with the commonly observed new twist, in Europe, of issues related to foreign workers and postmodernist moral values). Just as in the analysis of Israel, the questions that related to these two factors were given to experts on Italian politics, who were asked to answer the questions as the party leaders would. The responses allowed us to locate the parties in the same policy space used to represent voters' opinions. Figure 5.5 displays the distribution of the Italian electorate and the positions of the parties.

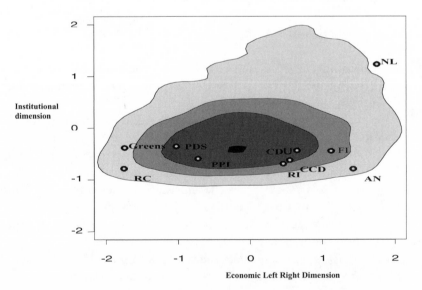

Figure 5.5. Distribution of Italian voter ideal points and party positions in 1996. The contours give the 95%, 75%, 50%, and 10% highest density regions of the distribution.

5.5.1 The Pre-Election Stage

The 1996 election saw significant changes in the formation of pre-electoral coalitions. In line with Duverger's (1954) famous prediction, only two pre-electoral coalitions formed: center left and center right. More importantly, parties that formed electoral coalitions did not issue their own electoral platforms but subscribed to joint platforms. But parties were still the most important actors in the pre-electoral and post-electoral legislative game.

The center-left coalition, Ulivo, consisted of PDS, PPI, Greens, center, socialist, and local parties. RC was no longer a member of the left alliance but made electoral agreements to avoid contesting some plurality seats. RC supported candidates of the Ulivo except in two districts; the Ulivo supported candidates of RC in 27 single-member districts for the election of the Chamber and 17 single-member districts for the election of the Senate. RC ran the elections with its own electoral platform and declared that it would not take part in the future government in the event of a victory of the left. On the other hand, the Ulivo claimed that the electoral agreement with RC would make it easier to gain a "self-sufficient" parliamentary majority.

Before the election, a new party, RI, led by Dini, joined the Ulivo coalition. The political debate about the meaning of the Ulivo coalition highlights political actors' electoral strategies, given the incentives set up by the new electoral law.

Trying to position the PDS at the center of the policy space, the new secretary D'Alema made clear that the PDS could aspire to rule Italy only if it detached itself from the neocommunists and joined forces with the PPI. On the other hand, according to prospective Prime Minister, Prodi, and other prominent political leaders, the Ulivo was to be seen as the first step in the process of federating center-left political groups, leading eventually to a unified party. Once in government, Prodi declared:

The government that today is going to ask the investiture vote is aware that this Parliament is profoundly different from the previous ones. For the first time, the electoral competition has not been dominated by distinct parties or mere electoral alliances but by two coalitions, that campaigned on their own distinct platforms in order to rule the country. . . . This government will be bound to the program that was submitted to the electorate. . . . It is not incidental that the head of the state wanted to point out the political novelty of the electoral competition receiving not parties' delegations but the two coalitions' delegations. (*Atti Parlamentari*: May, 22, 1996).

We may interpret this as an attempt to recreate a dominant party.

Following a similar strategic plan, Dini, the leader of RI, attempted to position himself at the median position on the relevant dimensions. Eventually Dini allied with the left. Dini's party ended up pivotal to the coalition of the left. As Table 5.3 shows, the left coalition, if combined with RI, attained a majority. If RI joined the right, the coalition of the right would still have remained a minority. It is plausible that Dini joined the left for this reason. As he himself declared: "Without us the Ulivo will not win. Prodi may capture those voters who sympathize with the PDS already. It is RI that will capture the center electorate. We are the surplus value of the coalition" (quoted in Giannetti and Sened, 2004).

On the right, FI and AN consolidated the 1994 alliance forming Polo della Libertà, which for the first time ran candidates nationwide. MSI-AN renamed itself AN in 1995 and for the first time declared its commitment to decentralization and privatization. The fact that AN moved toward the center can be inferred also from the birth of a splinter on its right, MSFT. The AN position on both dimensions was closer to FI than in 1994. This must have helped consolidate the Polo coalition. The other two members of the Polo coalition were CCD and CDU, both splinters of the PPI.

The NL refused any alliance and contested the elections separately. According to Diamanti (1997), "The 1996 election is a turning point in the Northern League political strategy." The key word was no longer "federalism" but "secession." The leader, Bossi, presented the 1996 election as a referendum on the "independence of Northern Italy," claiming that the NL was the only force capable of fighting against the resurgent *partitocrazia* and of defending the interests of the North. The creation of the "Parliament of the North" and the organization of mass demonstrations in favor of the "independence of Padania" highlight this strategic change. As Figure 5.5 illustrates, the NL positioned itself at an extreme pro-federalist position on the institutional dimension.

We speculate that it may have positioned itself hoping to be pivotal between a center-left and a center-right coalition. Given the complexities of the electoral system, a tie between the two coalitions was probable. If this is correct interpretation of the NL position, then it parallels our inference about the strategic maneuvering of Shas in the case of the 1992 and 1996 elections in Israel. As Table A5.1, shows, the NL had the lowest valence of all the parties. With Ulivo and Polo positioned near the electoral center, and both coalitions led by high-valence parties, the NL would be at a vote-minimizing position anywhere near these parties. We suggest that its strategy was to attempt to achieve two goals. First, by adopting a position to the "north" in Figure 5.5, it affected the location

Table 5.3. *The 1996 Election Results in Italy: Chamber and Senate.**

Party Blocks	Parties	Chamber PR Vote Share%	Chamber Plurality Vote Share%	Chamber Seats	Chamber Seats%	Senate Vote Share%	Senate Seats	Senate Seats%
RC		8.6	2.6	35	5.6	2.9	11	3.5
Ulivo	PDS	–	–	139	–	–	–	–
	Ind. Left	–	–	12	–	–	–	–
	CU	–	–	8	–	–	–	–
	Labour	–	–	6	–	–	–	–
	CS	–	–	5	–	–	–	–
	Network	–	–	5	–	–	–	–
	Total PDS	21.1	–	175	27.8	–	98	31.1
	PPI	–	–	61	–	–	–	–
	UD	–	–	6	–	–	–	–
	PRI	–	–	2	–	–	–	–
	UL	–	–	1	–	–	–	–
	Total PPI	6.8	–	70	11.1	–	32	10.2
	RI-Dini List	–	–	10	–	–	–	–
	Segni Pact	–	–	9	–	–	–	–
	SI	–	–	7	–	–	–	–
	Total RI	4.3	–	26	4.1	–	11	3.5
	Greens	2.5	–	14	2.2	–	14	4.4
	PsdA	0.1	–	–	–	–	1	0.3
Ulivo	Total	34.8	42.2	285	45.2	41.2	156	49.5
Local	SVP	–	0.4	3	0.5	0.5	2	0.6
	PvdA	–	0.1	1	0.2	0.1	1	0.3
	Total Local Parties		0.5	4	0.7	0.6	3	0.9
Left: Ulivo+ RC	Total	43.4	45.3	324	51.4	41.8	170	53.9
	CCD	5.8	–	19	3.0	–	16	5.1
	CDU	–	–	11	1.7	–	9	2.9
	FI	20.6	–	123	19.8	–	47	14.9
	AN	15.7	–	93	14.6	–	44	14.0
Polo	Total	42.1	40.3	246	39.0	37.3	116	36.8
Right	LdAM	0.2	0.2	1	0.2	0.2	–	–
	MSFT	0.9	1.7	–	–	2.3	1	0.3
	Pannella List	1.9	0.2	–	–	1.6	1	0.3
Polo+ Right	Total	45.1	42.4	247	39.2	41.4	118	37.4
	NL	10.1	10.8	59	9.4	10.4	27	8.6
	Other Lists	1.4	1.5	–	–	3.5	–	–
Total		100.0	100.0	630	100.0	100.0	315	100.0

* *Source*: Data derived from Ministry of Interior and political parties.
Note: Note that these electoral results differ slightly from thse of Bartolini and D'Alimonte (1997) due to different aggregation procedures being used.

of the heart of the Italian polity, moving it further north in the literal sense of the words. Second, it may have chosen this extreme position in order to affect its expected reward from coalition government. In the illustration of our theoretical model in Chapter 3, we attributed similar motives designed to extract more office-related perquisites by the orthodox religious party Shas in the 1992 and 1996 elections in Israel. We believe that this model provides a general explanation for the puzzling, but recurrent, phenomenon of extremist parties in coalitional polities adopting positions that are more radical than those their voters actually support.

5.5.2 The Electoral Stage

Italian politics remains very factionalized, and the new-found institutional structures will take time to mature. The electoral centers of the two coalitions, Ulivo and Polo, are not sufficiently powerful to create strong centripetal forces in the system. Our interpretation of the 1996 electoral results is that the high-valence pre-electoral bi-coalitional struggle at the center provided the motivation for low-valence parties to head to the periphery of the electoral distribution. This phenomenon, which we can call the *centrifugal tendency* is clearly illustrated in Figures 5.5 and 5.6. It is also apparent in the electoral results themselves.

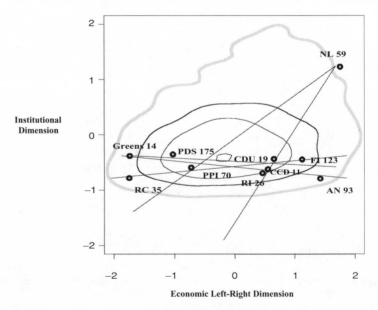

Figure 5.6. Party policy positions and the empty core following the 1996 election in Italy.

Table 5.3 reports the electoral results for the 1996 election in Italy, both for the Chamber and the Senate. In the Chamber, Ulivo took 42.2 percent of the vote on the plurality ballot and 34.8 percent on the proportional ballot. This vote share translated to 285 seats (45.2 percent). RC got 8.6 percent of the vote on the proportional ballot and 35 seats (5.6 percent). With several minor local parties, the center-left coalition controlled a total of 324 seats (51.4 percent).

The Polo coalition obtained 40.3 percent of the vote on the plurality ballot and 42.1 percent on the proportional ballot. This vote share translated into a total of 246 seats (39 percent). The NL actually raised its vote share to 10.8 percent of the national vote on the plurality part and 10.1 percent on the PR component (from the 8.4 percent PR it had in 1994). This electoral success translated into a total of only 59 seats (9.4 percent). Thus, in spite of its electoral success, the NL was unable to play a pivotal role between left and right in the coalition bargaining game that followed. Similar to the mistake made by Shas in the elections of 1992, the NL may have gone too far with its strategy of secession, allowing the center-left coalition to obtain enough seats to form a coalition without it. By refusing to form pre-electoral coalitions with any of the two major pre-electoral coalitions, it paid a heavy price in getting very little out of the by-now dominant share of the seats obtained by plurality.

The results of an MNL estimation for the election are shown in Table A5.1 in the appendix. As in the analysis for Israel, the empirical model includes sociodemographic (SD) parameters. The effects for age and education that have so greatly preoccupied previous studies of vote choices in Italy (e.g., Ricolfi, 1993; Corbetta and Parisi, 1997) appear insignificant. (Significance is based on the 95 percent confidence intervals reported in the two columns on the right of the table. Because zero belongs to this confidence interval for the age and education coefficients, for all parties, we cannot reject, at the 95 percent level, the hypothesis that these parameters are indeed zero.) This does not imply that these variables do not have a causal effect. As in our analysis of the Netherlands in Chapter 6, we infer that the voter sociodemographic variables partially influence beliefs, but the beliefs (or voter ideal points) are predominant in characterizing voter choice.

Three important aspects of the voter choice in Italy come out very clearly from Table A5.1. First, as in our other tests of the model, party policy positions were the most important factor in explaining vote choice in Italy in the 1996 election. This can be seen from the confidence interval on the spatial coefficient, β. Second, the party constants, interpreted throughout the book as measures of party valence, are all significantly different from zero. The fact that they all have negative signs is easy to interpret. These constants are all relative to the valence score of the RC, which is normalized to be zero. In terms of the formal model, the important comparison is between the lowest valence (namely that of NL) and the valence of RC. This difference is clearly statistically significant. It is also relevant that the estimated valence of NL is not contained in the confidence intervals for the valences of the PDS and FI. This lends support to our theoretical argument that low-valance parties will position themselves at the electoral extreme, in any vote-maximizing equilibrium. In other words, a party such as the NL should rationally avoid competition with the high-valance parties. Here, as in Israel, these parties eventually counter the centripetal forces of the electoral system by leading the more centrist parties to move away from the center to better compete with parties at the periphery. In light of the political discussion in Italy prior to the 1996 election over the importance of capturing the center and creating a dominant party, it is interesting that low-valance parties like the Greens, the NL, and the AN exert strong centrifugal pressure on the entire political system, forcing even the parties regarded as centrist to move away from the center. In this respect it is worthwhile to compare the party policy positions maps of 1994 and 1996. These two maps are not directly comparable because of the different methods of estimation. But general trends can be observed. The AN appears to have moved out to the right while the declared intentions of the PDS and FI to move to the center were checked by the AN on the right, the Greens and RC on the left, and the NL to the north.

The pull of the NL toward the north seems so much more powerful once one observes the remarkable relative advantage of the NL in Italy's northeast, northwest and central geographic regions. These are demonstrated by the very large positive estimates for these SD parameters for the NL (see Table A5.1 for these regions). While the 95 percent confidence intervals include zero, the parameters are significant at the 90 percent level.

The fact that the model does not seem to predict the vote choice of individual voters is not particularly significant. To expect a statistical model to predict the vote choice of the Italian voter among nine different parties is a little too much to ask. The relative success of the model in predicting the vote choice for the PDS, FI, and NL suggest that the problem stems from the complexity of the computation and estimation effort required rather than any misspecification of the model itself.

Before considering the coalition game we first note that vote maximizing should lead to convergence in Italy for the election in 1996, at least on the basis of exogenous valence as developed in Theorem 3.1. The high valence difference between the lowest valence party, NL, and RC was 20.1 for the election. With all parties at the electoral mean, the probability of voting for NL is zero. Since the spatial coefficient $\beta = 0.21$ and the total electoral variance is 1.50, with negligible electoral covariance, we obtain a value for the convergence coefficient of $c = 0.6$, well below the sufficient bound of 1.0. On the other hand, the very high SD coefficients for the NL in the nothern regions of Italy suggest that the party should adopt a vote maximizing position that was radical on the institutional axis. By doing so, it will increase its vote share from zero. Although this does not follow directly from Theorem 3.1, it would be consistent with a formal model that estimated differing party valences in different subsets of the population. Thus, we can infer that NL should move away from the origin on both axes. Obviously this inference is mirrored in the position of NL in Figure 5.5.

Once NL moves from the origin, then so will the other parties. However, since the electoral variance on the institutional axis is much smaller than on the economic axis, the eigenvalue on the institutional axis will generally be negative. In other words, it appears that the origin will be a saddlepoint for the other parties. We therefore have an explanation of why all parties other than the NL are positioned on this axis. As in the case of Israel, we may refer to the economic axis as the principal electoral axis. Notice also that no party has a valence very much higher than the other, although the RC has the highest valence ($\lambda_{RC} = 0$). From the formal theory we would expect no party to be located near the electoral origin. This prediction is clearly substantiated. Theory thus indicates that the positions of the parties in Figure 5.5 are close to a local equilibrium of the vote-maximizing game. As we found in Israel, there are indications that the NL position was chosen not simply to maximize votes, but to affect coalition bargaining. It should also be mentioned that the significant role of the regional SD parameters in the NL vote share indicate that activists are important in influencing the NL policy position. We take up this possibility in the next chapter in the discussion of politics in the Netherlands.

5.5.3 *The Coalition Bargaining Game*

Figure 5.6 clearly shows that the core of the 1996 Chamber is empty, since the median lines of NL–RI, NL–RC, PDS–FI, PDS–AN, and FI–PPI do not intersect. The relevant coalition structure of the Italian Parliament remained $\mathbb{D}_0$ after 1996. Following the elections, Prodi formed a center-left minority coalition comprising the Ulivo (PDS, PPI, RI, Greens) and small local parties (the SVP with three seats and the PvdA with one). The coalition controlled 285 seats and relied on the external support of RC (35 seats) to pass the majority threshold (of 316) in the Chamber. In the Senate, Ulivo controlled 155 seats (98 of PDS, 32 of PPI, 11 of RI, 14 of Greens), together with the support of RC (11 seats) and the 4 seats of local parties (1 PSdA, 2 SVP, 1 PVdA) giving it 170.

The Prodi government just managed to survive for two years. Eventually, on October 9, 1998, it fell after the leader of RC refused to support the annual budget bill. The coalition government was defeated on a vote of no confidence by one vote (312 yes, 313 no).

After the 1996 election the strategy of the NL changed substantially. Prodi succeeded in bringing Italy into the first round of the European monetary union (or EMU) in May 1998. This deprived the NL of a powerful weapon to use against the government. NL suffered substantial losses in the local elections of June 1998. Bossi perhaps realized that he had gone too far with his policy declaration preceding the 1996 election. In August 1998, Bossi declared that the NL had given up its goal of secession. The "Parliament of the North" was dissolved as well. Bossi, the principal of the NL, seems to have made the same mistake that Shas had made in 1992. In 1992, the leader of Labour, Rabin, in Israel, preferred to form a minority government rather than acquiesce to the demands of Shas over policy and government perquisites (Sened, 1996). In the same way, Prodi in Italy preferred to lead a coalition with a shaky minuscule majority rather than coalesce with Bossi (Giannetti and Sened, 2004). This miscalculation cost Bossi and his party dearly.

5.6 CONCLUSION

The analysis conducted so far clearly illustrates the importance of the post-election coalition structure in Parliament together with the trade-off between vote-maximizing positions and party positioning focused on coalition risk. A $\mathbb{D}_1$ structure, with a nonempty core, guarantees some stability. Though this need not enhance government duration, it does appear to affect policy coherence. An empty core or $\mathbb{D}_0$ structure tends to lead to constantly shifting government coalitions. As for the two pressures that decide the positioning of the party, a particular position may be appropriate in terms of a party's vote share but detrimental to its bargaining position in the coalition bargaining stage of the game. Taking a risk in positioning with the coalition bargaining game in mind may lead to loss of electoral support, or to being outmaneuvered by a clever party leader. For both the Shas in Israel and the NL in Italy, this electoral effect may take time to make itself felt. This explains why parties may be willing to bet on such a risky strategy. The hope, presumably, is that the party's inclusion in the government coalition will enable them to repay voters for its deviation from the voters' perceived interests. It is also possible that the party can be hijacked by activists.

The stochastic nature of the electoral response function adds yet another level of uncertainty to the party positioning strategy prior to each election. Not just the risk involved, but the need to constantly balance vote-maximizing strategies with the resource availability, when resources depend so much on activists who may push agendas that are not necessarily vote maximizing, makes the calculus of party positioning difficult both for party principals and modelers. To maintain a high valence so as to be able to compete at the center of the voter distribution, a party needs activist resources. The next two chapters will discuss the tension between obtaining activist support and adopting an electorally advantageous position.

One purpose of this chapter was to show how the formal model applied to multiparty competition under a roughly proportional electoral rule captured some intriguing aspects of political change in Italy in the last three decades. A stable coalition structure characterized the system until 1987. The emergence of a new dimension, together with the electoral success of the NL in 1992, brought about the destruction of the prevailing decisive structure and opened up a new era in coalition politics. Governments that formed after the two elections held under the new electoral system found themselves struggling to survive. This kind of coalitional instability is different from the situation prior to 1992. Under the $\mathbb{D}_1$ structure, governments appeared to change regularly but the DC remained dominant. After 1992 and the emergence of the new, $\mathbb{D}_0$, empty core structure, consecutive coalitions are more likely to be different both in composition and in policy goals. The confusing Italian election of April, 2006, suggests that Italian coalition politics will remain unstable for some time to come.

We also hope to have shown the usefulness of the spatial model in establishing the empirical relevance of formal theory in the study of politics. Logit models of elections are commonly used to estimate voter response, but the theory of how party principals respond to the electorate is less developed. The formal vote model developed in Chapter 3 can be applied to this substantive question. The difference between the theoretically predicted positions and those determined by the empirical model then allows us to extend the theory to include other party motivations. In this chapter, and the previous one on Israel, we hope to have shown that some of the discrepancy can be accommodated by developing the cooperative theory of the core and the heart. In the next three chapters we turn our attention to more complex electoral models.

5.7 APPENDIX

Table A5.1 *Logit Analysis for the 1996 Election in Italy (normalized with respect to RC).*

Parameter	Party	Posterior Mean	95% Confidence	
			Lower	Upper
Spatial Distance β		0.206	0.024	0.388
Constant λ	PDS	−1.353	−2.501	−0.205
	Greens	−2.533	−4.649	−0.417
	PPI	−2.374	−4.538	−0.210
	RI	−7.490	−14.714	−0.266
	NL	−20.110	−39.350	−0.870
	CCD	−5.866	−11.331	−0.401
	FI	−1.845	−3.532	−0.158
	AN	−1.133	−2.152	−0.114
Age	PDS	0.039	−0.009	0.086
	Greens	0.005	−0.012	0.022
	PPI	0.051	−0.010	0.113
	RI	0.074	−0.013	0.160
	NL	0.009	−0.011	0.028
	CCD	0.054	−0.012	0.119
	FI	0.035	−0.011	0.082
	AN	0.028	−0.010	0.065
Education	PDS	0.196	−0.081	0.474
	Greens	0.481	−0.178	1.139
	PPI	0.035	−0.098	0.168
	RI	0.805	−0.252	1.861
	NL	0.092	−0.093	0.276
	CCD	0.705	−0.148	1.558
	FI	0.357	−0.084	0.798
	AN	0.343	−0.100	0.785

Elections in Italy, 1992–1996

Parameter	Party	Posterior Mean	95% Confidence Lower	95% Confidence Upper
Northwest region	PDS	−0.393	−0.672	−0.115
	Greens	−0.416	−0.641	−0.191
	PPI	−0.123	−0.179	−0.067
	RI	−0.456	−0.800	−0.111
	NL	20.410	−0.630	41.450
	CCD	−0.616	−0.914	−0.318
	FI	−0.313	−0.409	−0.216
	AN	−1.244	−2.385	−0.103
Northeast region	PDS	0.430	−0.101	0.960
	Greens	0.382	−0.151	0.915
	PPI	0.635	−0.105	1.374
	RI	0.521	−0.217	1.258
	NL	20.880	−0.640	42.400
	CCD	0.110	−0.127	0.346
	FI	0.020	−0.254	0.294
	AN	−0.363	−0.569	−0.157
Center region	PDS	−0.236	−0.340	−0.131
	Greens	−0.178	−0.189	−0.168
	PPI	−0.380	−0.527	−0.234
	RI	0.115	−0.180	0.409
	NL	17.760	−0.660	36.180
	CCD	−0.026	−0.198	0.147
	FI	−0.710	−1.016	−0.404
	AN	−0.838	−1.548	−0.128
Correctly Predicted	PDS	0.287		
	Greens	0.071		
	PPI	0.135		
	RI	0.054		
	NL	0.302		
	CCD	0.044		
	FI	0.214		
	AN	0.189		
	RC	0.130		
	Model	0.208		
$n = 1367$				

6

Elections in the Netherlands, 1979–1981

6.1 THE SPATIAL MODEL WITH ACTIVISTS

As our discussion of Israel in Chapter 4 illustrated, government in multiparty polities, based on proportional electoral methods, requires the cooperation of several parties. The model of coalition bargaining indicates that a large, centrally located party, at a core position, will be dominant. Such a core party can, if it chooses, form a minority government by itself and control policy outcomes.* If party leaders are aware of the fact that they can control policy from the core, then this centripetal tendency should lead parties to position themselves at the center.

Yet, contrary to this intuition there is ample empirical evidence that party leaders or political contenders do not necessarily adopt centrist positions. For example, Budge et al. (1987) and Laver and Budge (1992), in their study of European party manifestos, found no evidence of a strong centripetal tendency. The electoral models for Israel and Italy presented in the previous two chapters estimated party positions in various ways, and concluded that there is no indication of policy convergence by parties. Theorem 3.1 indicates why convergence does not occur in these two polities. In this chapter, we re-examine the earlier empirical analyses for the Netherlands (Schofield et al., 1998; Quinn, Martin, and Whitford, 1999; Quinn and Martin, 2002) to determine if the nonconvergence noted previously can be accounted for by the electoral theorem.

Contrary to the results of Chapter 4, we show that the valence terms, while relevant, are insufficiently different in the Netherlands for the elections of 1979 and 1981 so that convergence to the electoral center is

---

* See Schofield, Grofman, and Feld (1989), Laver and Schofield (1990), Schofield (1993, 1995), Sened (1995, 1996), Banks and Duggan (2000), Schofield and Sened (2002).

indeed predicted for the vote-maximizing electoral model. The conflict between theory and evidence suggests that the models be modified to provide a better explanation of party policy choice (Riker, 1965). This can be done either by changing the model of voter choice (e.g., Adams, 1999a,b, 2001; Merrill III and Grofman, 1999) or by considering more complex versions of the rational calculations of politicians.

In this chapter, we use a variety of empirical analyses to estimate the degree of centripetal tendency in the Netherlands. As far as electoral models are concerned, we develop the idea of valence, introduced in the previous chapters. We examine party positioning strategies in the Netherlands to show why these terms are required. We use Theorems 3.1 and 3.2 from Chapter 3 to examine whether local Nash equilibrium can occur at the electoral origin. We conduct additional empirical analysis to determine whether convergence should be expected on theoretical grounds at various electoral competitions.

While using the same theoretical model as in the previous chapter, our preoccupation in this chapter is with party's strategic behavior and not with voters' choice. Therefore, it is of great interest to us that our estimations for the election in the Netherlands suggest that the valence terms of the leaders of the major parties were quite similar. Under the assumption that these valence terms were exogenously determined, the mean voter theorem should have been valid and convergence to the mean should have occurred. Since there is no evidence of convergence by the major parties, we consider, instead, a more general valence model based on activist support for the parties (Aldrich and McGinnis, 1989). This activist valence model (Schofield, 2005a) presupposes that party activists donate time and other resources to their party. Such resources allow parties to present themselves more effectively to the electorate, increasing their valence. Thus, choosing an optimal position for the party becomes a difficult choice between the more radical preferences of activists and electoral considerations.

In the model of voting that we introduced in Chapter 3 and applied in Chapters 4 and 5, we have shown that many local equilibria exist, all of which can be found by simulation. Since this set of LNE contains all PNE, it is possible, in principle, to examine these LNE to see if any one of them would qualify as a PNE. The usual sufficient condition for existence of PNE is concavity of the party utility functions. Theorem 3.1 shows that the local version of this property, namely *local concavity* at the origin typically fails in these electoral games. This immediately implies that concavity fails. The failure of a sufficient condition for existence of equilibrium does not, of course, imply nonexistence. Nonetheless, it suggests that PNE are unlikely to exist in the vote-maximization game. In the absence of a PNE and in the presence of multiple LNE, party leaders may be unable to coordinate on which particular local equilibrium to adopt. Thus, every local equilibrium of the model is a potential outcome of the political situation.

In the previous empirical analyses, valence terms, associated with each party, were crucial for the validity of the electoral model. Such valence terms were assumed be an exogenous feature of the election, characterizing each party by an average electoral evaluation of the competence of the party leader. We now consider the possibility that these terms are determined by party position.

By representing a coalition of activists, the party obtains resources. These contributions allow it to advertise its effectiveness, and thus gain electoral support (Aldrich and McGinnis, 1989). Since activist coalitions tend to be more radical than the average voter, parties are faced with a dilemma. By accommodating the political demands of activists, a party gains resources that it can use to enhance its valence; but by adopting radical policies to accommodate the demands of activists, it may lose electoral support due to the policy effect on voters. In this more general framework the party must balance the electoral effect, determined by its position, against the activist valence effect. One crucial difference emerges when valence is interpreted in this more general fashion. In the model where valence is fixed, our results indicate that concavity fails, casting doubt on the existence of PNE. However, when valence is affected by activist support, then it will naturally exhibit "decreasing returns to scale" (i.e., concavity). Consequently, when concavity of activists' valence is sufficiently, pronounced, then a PNE will exist but it will most assuredly not coincide with the electoral mean. In some polities, activists' valence is pronounced and so only one PNE exists. To determine whether such a PNE exists is extremely difficult, since the model requires data not just on voter-preferred positions but also a detailed examination of activist motivations. Nonetheless, the general model that we propose appears to be compatible with the rich diversity of party systems that we survey.

In this chapter, we study the elections in the Netherlands in 1977 and 1981 to illustrate the interaction among activists, the valance effect, policy preferences of voters at large, and the vote-maximizing motivations of party leaders. We use party delegate positions to construct an electoral model based on the implicit assumption that activists control party position. It turns out that the parameters of the multinomial logit (MNL) and multinomial probit (MNP) models, with and without sociodemographic components, suggest that parties should have converged to the electoral center. Thus, in contrast to the empirical analysis of Israel, there is indirect evidence that activists did influence the policy positions of the parties.

6.2 MODELS OF ELECTIONS WITH ACTIVISTS IN THE NETHERLANDS

In Chapter 3, we introduced a formal model where each voter i, when presented with a choice between p different parties whose policy positions are described by the vector $z = (z_1, \ldots, z_p)$, then chooses party $j \in P$ with some probability ρ_{ij}.

Recall that in this model, each party j is identified with a policy point, z_j, in a policy space X of dimension w. Each voter i is similarly identified with an ideal policy point x_i, together with individual characteristics, η_i. Let x denote the $(n \times w)$ matrix representing the voter ideal points. The variate $c_i = (\ldots c_{ij} \ldots)$ describes i's choice. If voter i actually chooses party j, then $c_{ij} = 1$; otherwise, $c_{ij} = 0$. As before, we concentrate on the probability ρ_{ij} that $c_{ij} = 1$, noting that $\Sigma_{i \in P} \rho_{ij} = 1$. Since c_{ij} is a binary variable, the expectation $\mathcal{E}xp(c_{ij})$ is ρ_{ij}. The expectation $\mathcal{E}_j(z)$ at the vector z of the stochastic vote share V_j^* of party j, can be estimated by taking the average of the estimations $\{\bar{\rho}_{ij}(z)\}$ across the sample. Thus,

$$\mathcal{E}_j(z) = \frac{1}{n} \sum_i \bar{\rho}_{ij}(z). \qquad (6.1)$$

In general, the empirical variance of V_i^* will be significant. This is illustrated by Figure A6.1 in the appendix to this chapter, which shows the estimated stochastic vote share functions for the electoral model of the Netherlands. (This figure is taken from Schofield et al., 1998)

We now modify the earlier notation and write

$$\rho(x : z) = \rho(x : z_1, \ldots, z_p) = (\rho_{ij}) \qquad (6.2)$$

to denote that this is an n by p matrix which depends on both x and z. The formal stochastic model introduced in Chapter 3 assumes that this matrix is derived from the $(n \times p)$ matrix of distances $(\delta_{ij}) = (||x_j - z_i||)$ where, as before, $|| \; ||$ is the Euclidean norm on X. Again, we assume the error vector $\varepsilon = (\varepsilon_1, \ldots, \varepsilon_p)$ has a cumulative distribution function Ψ. The probability function ρ_{ij} depends on the assumption made on Ψ, and is given by

$$\rho_{ij}(\mathbf{z}) = \Pr\left[\varepsilon_j - \beta\delta_{ij}^2 + \lambda_j + \theta_j^{\mathrm{T}}\eta_i > \varepsilon_k - \beta\delta_{ik}^2 \right.$$
$$\left. + \lambda_k + \theta_k^{\mathrm{T}}\eta_i : k \neq j\right]. \tag{6.3}$$

As before, β is the positive spatial coefficient, λ_j is the valence of party j, $\theta_j^{\mathrm{T}}\eta_i$ gives the effect of sociodemographic influence on i's vote, and Pr stands for the probability operator derived from the cumulative distribution.

Computation of this probability obviously depends on the distribution assumption made on the errors. Most formal voting models with stochastic voters assume that voter choice is pairwise statistically independent. The analogous empirical MNL model already discussed in Chapters 3 and 4 assumes "Independence of Irrelevant Alternatives" (IIA). That is, for any two parties, j, k, the ratio

$$\frac{\rho_{ij}(\mathbf{z})}{\rho_{ik}(\mathbf{z})} = \frac{\exp[-\beta\delta_{ij}^2 + \lambda_j + \theta_j^{\mathrm{T}}\eta_i]}{\exp[-\beta\delta_{ik}^2 + \lambda_k + \theta_k^{\mathrm{T}}\eta_i]} \tag{6.4}$$

is independent of $\rho_{il}(\mathbf{z})$ for a third party l. It has generally been inferred that assuming the Type I extreme value distribution (or log Weibull) and thus IIA would result in existence of equilibrium at the electoral mean (Adams, 2001). The simulation of the MNL model for Israel given in Chapter 4 has already shown this to be incorrect. The IIA assumption is not satisfied by the more general stochastic MNP model. Such a model does not require the assumption of independent errors. A Markov Chain Monte Carlo (MCMC) technique due to Chib and Greenberg (1996) was used by Schofield et al. (1998) and Quinn, Martin, and Whitford (1999) to model elections in the Netherlands, Germany, and Britain. Here we re-examine these earlier analyses for the Netherlands for 1977 to 1981 in the light of the new formal results reported in Chapter 3.

In the MNP model, with constant valence terms $\{\ldots, \lambda_j, \ldots\}$, the probability matrix (ρ_{ij}) is determined by the $(p-1)$ dimensional vector of error differences $e_j = (\varepsilon_p - \varepsilon_j, \ldots, \varepsilon_{j-1} - \varepsilon_j, \ldots, \varepsilon_1 - \varepsilon_j)$. If the covariance matrix of ε is known to be Ω, then, the covariance of e_j is given by the matrix

$$\sum_j(\Omega) = \begin{pmatrix} \mathcal{E}xp(\epsilon_p - \epsilon_j, \epsilon_p - \epsilon_j) & \cdot & & \cdot \\ \mathcal{E}xp(\epsilon_p - \epsilon_j, \epsilon_{p-1} - \epsilon_j) & & & \cdot \\ \mathcal{E}xp(\epsilon_p - \epsilon_j, \epsilon_1 - \epsilon_j). & \cdot & \mathcal{E}xp(\epsilon_1 - \epsilon_j, \epsilon_1 - \epsilon_j) \end{pmatrix}.$$

Once this is estimated then we obtain the multivariate probability density function, φ of the $(p-1)$ variate. In parallel to the proof of Theorem 3.2 we use

$$g_{ij}(\mathbf{z}) = \left(\ldots, \beta\delta_{ik}^2 - \beta\delta_{ij}^2 - \lambda_k + \lambda_j - \theta_k^T\eta_i + \theta_j^T\eta_i, \ldots\right) \quad (6.5)$$

to denote the $(p-1)$ comparison vector, by which we model the calculation made by voter i of the choice between party j with the other parties $k \in \{1, \ldots, j-1, j+1, \ldots, p\}$.

By definition, $\rho_{ij}(\mathbf{z})$ is given by $\int \varphi(e_j)de_j$, with bounds from $-\infty$ to $g_{ij}(\mathbf{z})$.

Theorem 3.1 assumed that the distribution function Ψ of the errors was the Type I extreme value distribution. Here we examine empirical estimation carried out under the more general assumption that the errors are multivariate normal, with nondiagonal covariance matrix Ω and error difference covariance matrices.

To estimate voter ideal points in the two elections in the Netherlands, Schofield et al. (1998) and Quinn, Martin, and Whitford (1999) used survey data for 1979, collected for a number of European countries by Rabier and Inglehart (1981). We use these data and the previous exploratory factor analysis based on the voter response profile to estimate the nature of the underlying policy space X. In the Netherlands, two dimensions were significant: the usual left–right dimension and a second concerned with scope of government. (Table A6.1 in the appendix to this chapter reports the weights associated with the two policy dimensions.) The response of voter i to the survey gave the location of the individual's ideal point in the policy space. For each party j, the data set (ISEIUM, 1983) was used to estimate the ideal points of the elite members (or delegates) of that party, namely $\{x_l^j : l \in N_j\}$, where N_j, represents the elite of party j. Since the estimated policy space was two-dimensional, the position $z_j \in X$ of party j was obtained by taking the two-dimensional median of the delegate positions. This position was taken to represent the "sincere" ideal point of party j. The representative delegate of party j whose ideal point is z_j we call the *principal* of party j.

Figure 6.1 gives the resulting estimation of the distribution of voter ideal points, together with the estimated positions of the party principal positions of the four parties. Labor (PvdA), Christian Democratic Appeal (CDA), Liberals (VVD), and Democrats 66 (D'66). Table 6.1 gives the election results for 1977 and 1981.

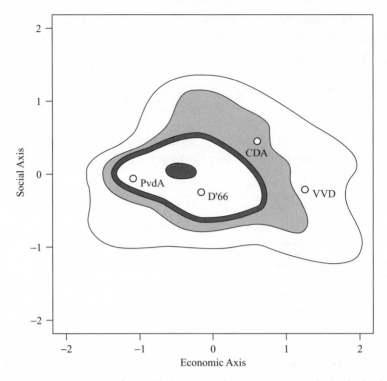

Figure 6.1. Distribution of voter ideal points and party positions in the Netherlands.

For the electoral estimations we adopt the following hypothesis.

Hypothesis 6.1: *The positions of the party principals can be used as proxies for the electorally perceived positions of the parties.*

On the basis of this hypothesis, a number of separate estimations using these data were carried out. The results are given in Table 6.2.

The first MNP model is discussed in Schofield et al. (1998). In this model, all valence terms were set to zero. It included a comparison of the "pure" spatial model, based on $\rho(\mathbf{x}, \mathbf{z})$; a sociodemographic model (SD), based on $\rho(\eta)$, where η represents the vector of such individual characteristics; and a joint model $\rho(\eta, \mathbf{x}, \mathbf{z})$, using the spatial component as well as η. As expected, sociodemographic characteristics were significant in predicting voter choice. For example, status as a manual worker would be expected to increase the probability of voting for the PvdA. Table 6.2 gives the national vote shares in the two elections of 1977 and 1981, as well as the sample vote shares, calculated for these four parties. The

Table 6.1. *Election Results in the Netherlands, 1977–1981.*

	1977	1981
Party (acronym)	(Seats)	
Labour (PvdA)	53	44
Democrats '66 (D'66)	8	17
Liberals (VVD)	28	26
Christian Dem Appeal (CDA)	49	48
	(138)	(135)
Communists (CPN)	2	3
Dem '70 (D70)	1	0
Radicals (PPR)	3	3
Pacific Socialists (PSP)	–	3
Reform Federation (RPF)	–	2
Reform Pol Ass (GDV)	1	1
Farmers Party (BP)	1	0
State Reform Party (SGP)	3	3
	(11)	(15)
Total	149	150

survey sample vote shares in Table 6.2 can be compared with the party seat distributions given in Table 6.1. Note that the national vote share of the Labour Party (PvdA) declined from 38 percent in 1977 to 32.4 percent in 1981. Its sample share was 36.9 percent in 1979 and the estimated

Table 6.2. *Vote-Shares, Valences, and Spatial Coefficients for Empirical Models in the Elections in the Netherlands, 1977–1981.*

Party	National Vote, 1977 %	National Vote, 1981 %	Sample Vote, %	Esatimated Share[a] %	Confidence Interval of Vote Share[b] %	Valences in MNL[c]	Valences in MNP[d]
D'66	6.1	12.6	10.4	10.6	(6.1, 16.1)	0	0
PvdA	38.0	32.4	36.9	35.3	(30.6, 38.9)	1.596	0.622
CDA	35.9	35.2	33.8	29.9	(30.1, 40.1)	1.403	0.655
VVD	20.0	19.8	18.9	24.2	(14.9, 24.6)	1.015	0.334
β			0.456	0.499	0.737	0.420

[a] Estimated by an MNP spatial model without valence or SD.
[b] Estimated by an MNP spatial model without valence but with SD.
[c] Estimated by an MNL model with valence without SD.
[d] Estimated by an MNP model with valence without SD.

expectation from the MNP model, without the SD terms, was 35.3 percent with a 95 percent confidence interval of (30.9, 39.7).

We have emphasized that the vote-share functions are stochastic variables, with significant variance. This can be illustrated by Figure A6.1 in the appendix to this chapter. The estimated shares based on the MNP model without SD or valence are fairly close to the sample shares, though the VVD estimation was poor. The log marginal likelihood (LML) was calculated to be -626. Adding sociodemographic characteristics to the MNP model improved the prediction, as the 95 percent confidence intervals in Table 6.2 indicate. The LML changed to -596, so the Bayes' factor (Kass and Raftery, 1995) or the difference between log likelihoods of the MNP spatial model with SD and without was 30 ($= 626 - 596$), suggesting that the joint SD model was statistically superior to the pure spatial model.

Simulation of these two models found that each of the parties could have increased vote share by moving away from their locations in Figure 6.1 toward the electoral mean. We shall show below that this inference is consistent with Theorem 3.2 when applied to empirical models including valence. Schofield et al. (1998) raised the question: If the positions given in Figure 6.1 are indeed the party positions, then why do the parties not approach the electoral center to increase vote share?

To study this question further, an MNL model based on Hypothesis 6.1 was estimated to include valence (λ), but without SD. The estimated valences are also reported in Table 6.2. Notice that in the model with $\lambda \neq 0$, the valences are normalized by setting the valence of D'66 to zero. Comparing this MNL valence model with the MNL model without valence gave a very significant Bayes' factor of 75, corresponding to a chi-square of 149. Even comparing it to the above MNP model with SD but without valence, gave a Bayes' factor of 64 ($= 596 - 532$). Clearly, the valence terms increase the statistical likelihood of the voter model.

It should be pointed out that the coefficients, β and λ, are not directly comparable between the MNL and MNP models. The MNL models are based on the (iid) extreme value distribution with error variance $\sigma^2 = \frac{1}{6}\pi^2 = 1.6449$, while the MNP models are based on some appropriate normalization for the error difference variances.

Although probit models have theoretical advantages, it would appear from the above that the MNL and MNP models give comparable results in terms of predictions about party vote shares. To more fully examine the effect of valence, Tables A6.2 and A6.3 in the appendix present the result of MNP and MNL estimation for models involving both SD and

Table 6.3. *Log Likelihoods and Eigenvalues in the Dutch Electoral Model.*

Spatial Models	Convergence Coefficient	Eigenvalue First	Second	LML[a]
MNL no valence or SD[b]	na	na	na	−606
MNL no valence, with SD[b]	na	na	na	−565
MNL with valence, no SD[c]	1.19	−0.18	−0.64	−532
MNL with valence and SD[c]	1.38	−0.04	−0.58	−465
MNP without valence or SD[d]	na	na	na	−626
MNP without valence, with SD[d]	na	na	na	−596
MNP with valence, no SD[c]	0.75	−0.48	−0.77	−545
MNP with valence and SD[c]	1.55	+0.05	−0.50	−427
Non-Spatial, MNP pure SD[c]				−596

[a] LML = log marginal likelihood.
[b] Based on Schofield and Sened (2005b), using extreme value distribution.
[c] Based on Quinn, Martin, and Whitford (1999).
[d] Based on Schofield, Martin, Quinn, and Whitford (1998).

valence. Quinn et al. (1999) previously computed the Bayes' factors for the various models and found the joint spatial MNP and MNL models, $\rho(\eta, \mathbf{x}, \mathbf{z})$, with valence superior to the pure MNP and MNL sociodemographic models $\rho(\eta)$ without a spatial component. This suggests that the appropriate causal model is one in which SD characteristics (η_i) influence beliefs (x_i) which in turn affect the probability vector of voter choice (ρ_i). Table 6.3 reports the log marginal likelihoods of the eight different models.

An important inference for our argument here is that, as in the case of Israel, the explanatory power of each empirical model is much increased by adding in the valence terms (Stokes, 1963, 1992). Indeed, pairwise comparison of a model with valence, but without SD, against one without valence, but with SD, suggests that the valence terms, to some degree, substitute for using the individual characteristics of voters. We draw three conclusions from the log likelihoods presented in Table 6.3.

Conclusion 6.1

(i) There is strong justification for Hypothesis 6.1. The log marginal likelihoods of all spatial models, when compared with the pure SD models, indicate that these estimated party positions provide a useful basis for modelling electoral choice. Indeed, the 95 percent confidence intervals of the β coefficients in Tables A6.2 and A6.3 allow us to reject the hypothesis that the spatial coefficients are zero.

(ii) The valence terms are all significant. More importantly, the confidence interval on the high-valence party, the PvdA, excludes 0, so we can infer that there is a significant valence difference.

(iii) Although the sociodemographic terms are important, their effect can to some extent be captured by valence.

(iv) The valence differences are reduced when SD terms are included. As a consequence, when examining the models to determine whether convergence is to be expected, it is important to include SD.

Given that there is evidence for the statistical significance of the estimation, we can examine the question of convergence.

It is obvious that if the valence of party j is increased, then the probability that a voter chooses the party also increases. As we have observed, it is not the absolute values of the valences that are relevant but the pairwise differences in the valences. For estimation purposes we set the lowest valence of one party to zero. For example, in the MNL model presented in Table A6.2, the valence of D'66 was normalized to be zero. In the MNP model with SD however it turns out that the religious sociodemographic variable affects the vote choice. The result is that the CDA is estimated to have the lowest valence for this model. We now utilize the results of the formal model given in Chapter 3 on the basis of the following hypothesis.

Hypothesis 6.2: *The results of the formal model given in Chapter 3 are applicable to the analysis of empirical models.*

These empirical models are not directly comparable to the formal electoral model presented in Chapter 3. In particular, the sociodemographic components are not included in the formal model. In computing the coefficients and eigenvalues for the MNL models we used the results given in Theorem 3.1 for the extreme value distribution, Ψ. For the MNP models it is necessary to modify the definition of the Hessians to account for error covariance. First, we note that the electoral variance on the first axis is 0.658, whereas on the second it is 0.289. The reason these are both different from 1.0, is that the normalization was done with respect to the variance of the delegate points on the first axis.

Table 6.3 also presents the results of the computation of the eigenvalues of the Hessians at the origin for the lowest-valence party. These computations are presented in a technical appendix to this chapter. Tables A6.1

and A6.2 in the appendix give the estimation results, including the valences for the various parties as well as the sociodemographic coefficients
for the MNL and MNP models. According to the results of Chapter 3, if
the convergence coefficient is bounded above by 1.0, then we may argue
that the origin will, for sure, be a local equilibrium. It is evident that the
convergence coefficients of three of the four baseline formal models satisfy
this condition. We regard this as strong evidence that the earlier inference
made by Schofield et al. (1998) about convergence to the electoral origin
is generally unaffected by the addition of valence to the models. An additional simulation by Quinn and Martin (2002) provides further support
for the convergence result.

As we have noted, adding sociodemographic terms tends to reduce the
valence coefficients, because these explain less of the voter choice. This has
the effect of reducing valence difference between high- and low-valence
parties, thus changing the estimated convergence coefficients. However,
as Table 6.3 indicates, the effect on the MNL models is trivial. The only
model that gives a noncentrist equilibrium is the MNP model with valence and SD. Because the correlation between the two electoral axes is
negligible, we can treat the two axes separately. Table 6.3 shows that
for this model, the eigenvalue of the CDA Hessian on the second axis
is negative. This implies that, in local equilibrium, all parties should be
at the zero position on the second axis. Because the eigenvalue for the
CDA on the economic axis is positive (albeit small), then it is possible
that its vote-maximizing position will be away from the origin. We cannot predict whether it should move to the right or the left. We can infer,
however, that all parties, in equilibrium in this model, should be strung
along the economic axis. It is also the case that the vote-share functions
of the parties were "close" to concave. This can be seen from examining
the vote probability functions presented in Figures A6.2 and A6.3 (in the
appendix to this chapter), based on the positions of the parties given in
Figure 6.1. The inference is that the parties should adopt positions on the
economic axis, but very close to the electoral origin. Note also that, for
three of the four models, because the eigenvalues are typically negative,
and "large" in magnitude with respect to the parameters of the various
models, then the origin is not only likely to be a local equilibrium with
respect to vote-maximizing, but also the unique Nash equilibrium. Comparing Figure 6.1 with the predictions of the formal model we therefore
infer that it is very unlikely that the CDA position is a component of a
vote-maximizing equilibrium. Although the positions of the PvdA, VVD,

and D'66 are not in obvious contradiction to the formal interpretation of the MNP/SD empirical model, there is evidence that these parties could have increased vote share by moving from their presumed positions in Figure 6.1 toward the electoral center. On the basis of Hypothesis 6.2 we are led to the following conclusion.

Conclusion 6.2 *It is unlikely that the estimated positions given in Figure 6.1 can belong to a local equilibrium on the basis of an electoral model with fixed exogenous valences.*

It is possible that the CDA position is one chosen in response to coalition risk, as discussed in Section 3.1 in Chapter 3, as well as in the empirical illustrations from Israel and Italy in Chapters 4 and 5. There are two distinct coalition structures relevant to politics in the Netherlands:

$$\mathbb{D}_0 = \{PvdA,CDA\}, \{PvdA,VVD\}, \{CDA,VVD\}, \text{ and}$$

$$\mathbb{D}_{PvdA} = \{PvdA,CDA\}, \{PvdA,VVD,D'66\}, \{CDA,VVD,D'66\}.$$

After the May 1977 election, structure $\mathbb{D}_0$ can be taken to represent the electoral outcome since the {CDA,VVD} coalition had 77 seats out of 149, and was therefore winning. This coalition did indeed form a government, but only after 6 months of negotiation. After the 1981 election, this coalition controlled only 74 seats (out of 150) so we can represent the outcome by $\mathbb{D}_{PvdA}$. A {PvdA,D'66,CDA} coalition government with 109 seats first formed and then collapsed to a minority {D'66,CDA} government. A new election had to be called in September 1982. Although the post-1981 election situation is designated a $\mathbb{D}_{PvdA}$ coalition structure, the PvdA could only be at a core position if it adopted a position inside the convex hull of the {CDA,VVD,D'66} positions. In fact, the heart, given the positions in Figure 6.1, together with the seat strengths in 1981, is the convex hull of the three positions {PvdA,D'66, CDA}. Thus, the minority coalition government that did indeed form is compatible with the notion of the heart. Moreover, as Section 3.4 illustrated, the CDA may gain advantage in coalition bargaining if it adopts a radical strategic position on the second axis.

Notice that the model suggests that there is strong centripetal pressure on the PvdA, in terms of adopting a centrist position to both gain seats and possibly control the core policy position. The coefficient for the PVdA for manual labor given in Appendix Table A6.3, is high and significant, suggesting that activists had a centrifugal influence on the policy preferences of the party. This influence appears to have overcome the centripetal tendency generated by the formal model with fixed exogenous valences.

It is also noticeable from the tables that the sociodemographic coefficient associated with religion was highly significant for the CDA, in both MNL and MNP models. This also suggests that activists concerned about policy on this axis were influential in determining the CDA position. We are therefore led to the conclusion that activists for both these parties generated centrifugal forces within each party and that these countered the centripetal effect our analysis has shown to be associated with the model of vote maximizing.

Instead of supposing that valence is exogenously determined at the time of the election, we now consider the more general hypothesis that valence is determined by the effect of activists on party support and that these valence *functions* affect the local Nash equilibrium positions that parties adopt. By contributing support, the party elite enhances the popularity of the party. We conjecture that the activist valence terms will not, in fact, be constant, but will be maximized at the center of the distribution of the positions of the elite or delegates of the parties. This follows because at this position the contributions of the party activists will be maximized. Consequently, it is plausible that the valence functions will be concave in the positions adopted by the parties. We conjecture that noncentrist LNE may exist, and that they may indeed be PNE of this more complex electoral game.

Our analysis of these elections in the Netherlands suggests the following conclusion concerning the interplay of electoral and coalition risk in the strategic calculations of policy-motivated party activists.

Conclusion 6.3 *Because the coalition structure $\mathbb{D}_{PvdA}$ is advantageous to the PvdA, this party should attempt to maximize the probability π_{Pvda} that this is the election outcome, and a proxy for this is to maximize the expected vote-share function $\mathcal{E}_{PvdA}$. On the other hand, while the CDA should attempt to maximize the probability π_0 that the coalition structure $\mathbb{D}_0$ occurs, it can be rational for the party to consider the consequences of coalition risk, and choose a position that allows it to bargain effectively with its probable coalition partners.*

As mentioned above, the estimates for party locations in Figure 6.1 were derived from the ISEIUM delegate surveys. It is a reasonable assumption that each delegate of a party has a preferred position to offer to the electorate. Obviously, there is a calculus involved as delegates optimize between their own preferences and the desire to gain votes. The empirical analysis of the Netherlands is based on the assumption that the principal's position for each party is the one that is offered to the electorate by the party. In fact, the positions given in Figure 6.1 closely correspond to the positions estimated by De Vries (1999) using an entirely different methodology based on policy choices of the parties. These chosen positions then generate activist support and the estimated valences. Conclusion 6.3 is compatible with the more complex model, articulated in Chapter 3, in which the party principal chooses a party leader with a different position because of the realization that the chosen position not only affects vote share, but independently influences the probability that the party will join in coalition government. These observations suggest the following general hypothesis on the nature of the centipetal and centrifugal tendencies.

Hypothesis 6.3: *The centripetal tendency associated with simple vote maximization in the model with exogenous valence is balanced by:*

(i) the motivation of concerned party principals to affect the final coalition government policy, and

(ii) the requirement to gain support from activists, thus indirectly increasing overall electoral support for the party.

We have suggested in this chapter that there is some evidence that both influences can affect party position. It is difficult to determine which of these two effects is more important. However, one way to examine the influence of activists is to consider a polity where the coalition effect can be disregarded. The next two chapters will examine the activist hypothesis in the context of empirical models of elections in Britain and the United States.

6.3 TECHNICAL APPENDIX: COMPUTATION OF EIGENVALUES

Here we show how the coefficients and eigenvalues given in Table 6.3 can be computed. As Figure 6.1 indicates, the electoral variance on the first economic axis is $v_1^2 = 0.658$, whereas on the second it is $v_2^2 = 0.289$. The covariance is negligible.

We can calculate the various coefficients and eigenvalues for the four models with valence.

(i) As an illustration of Theorem 3.1, for the extreme value formal model $M(\Psi)$ without SD we find $\lambda_{d'66} = 0$, $\lambda_{Pvda} = 1.596$, $\lambda_{cda} = 1.1403$, $\lambda_{vvd} = 1.015$, and $\beta = 0.737$. At the joint origin the probability of voting for D'66 is

$$\rho_{d'66} = \frac{1}{1 + e^{1.596} + e^{1.403} + e^{1.015}} = 0.074.$$

Thus, $A_{d'66} = 0.737(0.852) = 0.627$.

$$C_{d'66} = (1.25)\begin{pmatrix} 0.658 & 0 \\ 0 & 0.289 \end{pmatrix} - I = \begin{pmatrix} -0.18 & 0 \\ 0 & -0.64 \end{pmatrix}$$

$$c(\Psi) = 2A_{d66}(0.658 + 0.289) = 1.187$$

Since the eigenvalues are -0.18 and -0.64, both negative, it is obvious that the model based on the extreme value distribution gives an LSNE at the joint origin.

(ii) When sociodemographic variables are added to the MNL model (Quinn, Martin, and Whitford, 1999) the valence differences are changed and we find that the CDA is the lowest-valence party, $\lambda_{cda} = -0.784$. The other valences are now $\lambda_{vvd} = 0.313$, $\lambda_{Pvda} = 2.112$ and $\lambda_{d'66} = 0$. Using the model Ψ we find $\beta = 0.665$. Thus,

$$\rho_{cda} = \frac{1}{1 + e^{2.896} + e^{1.097} + e^{0.784}} = 0.04.$$

Hence, $A_{cda} = 0.0665(0.99) = 0.664$.

$$C_{cda} = (1.33)\begin{pmatrix} 0.658 & 0 \\ 0 & 0.289 \end{pmatrix} - I = \begin{pmatrix} -0.12 & 0 \\ 0 & -0.61 \end{pmatrix}$$

$$c(\Psi, SD) = 1.25.$$

Again, both eigenvalues are negative and the necessary condition is satisfied. Note the large negative eigenvalue on the second axis in contrast to the small eigenvalue on the first axis.

(iii) With the probit model (without SD), we find $\lambda_{d'66} = 0$, $\lambda_{cda} = 0.655$, $\lambda_{Pvda} = 0.622$, $\lambda_{vvd} = 0.334$, and $\beta = 0.420$. Thus, the average valence excluding D'66 is $\lambda_{av(d'66)} = 0.537$.

Because the errors have nondiagonal covariance matrix Ω, we now compute the covariance matrix of the difference vector,
$e_{d'66} = (\epsilon_{cda} - \epsilon_{d'66}, \epsilon_{Pvda} - \epsilon_{d'66}, \cdots, \epsilon_{vvd} - \epsilon_{d'66})$. This will be the symmetric matrix

$\Sigma_{d'66}(\Omega)$

$$= \begin{pmatrix} \mathcal{E}xp(\epsilon_{cda} - \epsilon_{d'66}, \epsilon_{cda} - \epsilon_{d'66}) & \cdot & & \cdot \\ \mathcal{E}xp(\epsilon_{cda} - \epsilon_{d'66}, \epsilon_{Pvda} - \epsilon_{d'66}) & & \cdot & \\ \mathcal{E}xp(\epsilon_{cda} - \epsilon_{d'66}, \epsilon_{vvd} - \epsilon_{d'66}) & \cdot & \cdot & \mathcal{E}xp(\epsilon_{vvd} - \epsilon_{d'66}, \epsilon_{vvd} - \epsilon_{d'66}) \end{pmatrix}.$$

Here $\mathcal{E}xp$ denotes expectation. Normalization gives the following matrix:

$$\Sigma_{d'66}(\Omega) = \begin{pmatrix} 1.0 & -0.06 & 1.258 \\ -0.06 & 0.186 & 0.558 \\ 1.258 & 0.558 & 0.454 \end{pmatrix}$$

The sum of the terms in this matrix is $var(\Sigma_{d'66}(\Omega)) = 5.15$.

From Theorem 3.2, we find that the Hessian matrix $C_{d'66}$ associated with the D'66 is given by

$$C_{d'66}(\Omega) = \left[2 A_{d'66} \left(\frac{\nabla}{n} \right) - I \right],$$

where $\frac{\nabla}{n}$ is the electoral covariance matrix and

$$A_{d'66} = \left[\frac{(p-1)^2 \beta}{var(\Sigma_{d'66})} \right] \left[\lambda_{av(d'66)} - \lambda_{d'66} \right] = 0.39.$$

Since the number of parties $p = 4$, we find

$$C_{d'66}(\Omega) = (0.78) \begin{pmatrix} 0.658 & 0 \\ 0 & 0.289 \end{pmatrix} - I$$

$$= \begin{pmatrix} -0.48 & 0 \\ 0 & -0.77 \end{pmatrix}$$

so again the eigenvalues are negative. The convergence coefficient is given by

$$c(\Omega) = 2 A_{d'66}(0.658 + 0.289) = 0.75.$$

(iv) Finally, for the MNP model with SD we find $\lambda_{cda} = -0.408$, $\lambda_{av(cda)} = 0.443$, and $\beta = 0.455$. The error difference covariance matrix is

$$\Sigma_{cda} = \begin{pmatrix} 1.0 & -0.141 & 0.170 \\ -0.141 & 1.383 & 0.489 \\ 0.170 & 0.489 & 0.936 \end{pmatrix}$$

so $var(\Sigma_{cda}) = 4.355$. Thus,

$$A_{cda}(\Omega) = 0.8 \text{ and } C_{cda} = \begin{pmatrix} 0.05 & 0 \\ 0 & -0.5 \end{pmatrix}.$$

The coefficient $c(\Omega, SD) = 1.55$. Obviously the sufficient condition fails, and one of the eigenvalues is positive. Although the necessary condition does not fail, it is clear that the origin is now a saddlepoint for the CDA for this model. Thus, under a pure vote-maximizing model, incorporating sociodemographic characteristics of the voters, the CDA may well move away from the origin, along the first, high-variance economic axis so as to gain votes. However, because this eigenvalue on the economic axis is small in modulus (at least in comparison to the eigenvalue on the second axis) in equilibrium we expect the PvdA, D'66 and VVD to be close to the origin on the second axis. That is, in the equilibrium for the MNP model with SD, all parties should be located on the economic axis.

Naturally there is uncertainty about the correct model. However, the analyses indicate that it is unlikely that the positions in Figure 6.1 can constitute a local equilibrium under the assumption of exogeneous valence.

6.4   EMPIRICAL APPENDIX

Appendix Table A6.1. *Factor Weights for the Policy Space in the Netherlands.*

Issue	Dimension 1	Dimension 2
Income distribution	+0.510 (10.86)	−0.148 (1.92)
Terrorism	−0.232 (4.28)	−0.253 (2.51)
Nuclear energy	−0.297 (6.74)	–
Enterprises	+0.526 (12.0)	–
Environment	+0.306 (7.46)	–
MNC	+0.612 (12.6)	−0.229 (2.42)
Abortion	+0.327 (5.56)	+0.390 (2.45)

Chi-square over d.o.f. = 1.76; Sample size (n) = 529.

Appendix Table A6.2. *Probit Analysis of the 1979 Dutch Survey Data (normalized with respect to D'66).*

Model Variable	Party	Mean	95% Confidence Interval	
			Lower Bound	Upper Bound
β (MNP)		0.455	0.341	0.571
Valence	PvdA	1.298	0.165	2.433
	VVD	0.031	−1.116	1.175
	CDA	−0.408	−3.530	2.640
Manual Labour	PvdA	0.865	0.377	1.408
	VVD	−0.522	−1.350	0.268
	CDA	0.537	0.023	1.151
Religion	PvdA	−0.082	−0.295	0.124
	VVD	−0.012	−0.271	0.242
	CDA	0.736	0.427	1.108
Income	PvdA	−0.043	−0.089	0.002
	VVD	0.059	0.005	0.116
	CDA	0.021	−0.029	0.068
Town Size	PvdA	0.162	−0.073	0.407
	VVD	0.017	−0.283	0.321
	CDA	−0.236	−0.015	0.517
Education	PvdA	−0.113	−0.170	−0.054
	VVD	−0.002	−0.074	0.073
	CDA	−0.062	−0.128	0.000
Correctly Predicted %	PvdA	61.2		
	VVD	49.5		
	CDA	62.3		
	D66	20.4		
	MNP Model	56.4		
Sample Size = 529				

Source: Quinn, Martin, and Whitford (1999) and Schofield, Martin, Quinn, and Whitford (1998).

Elections in the Netherlands, 1979–1981

Appendix Table A6.3. *Multinomial Logit Analysis of the 1979 Dutch Survey Data (normalized with respect to D'66).*

Model Variable	Party	Mean	95% Confidence Interval	
			Lower Bound	Upper Bound
β (MNL)		0.665	0.557	0.785
Valence	PvdA	2.112	1.276	2.927
	VVD	0.313	−0.920	1.273
	CDA	−0.784	−1.206	−0.265
Manual Labour	PvdA	1.406	0.444	2.508
	VVD	−0.547	−1.996	0.937
	CDA	1.064	0.012	2.330
Religion	PvdA	0.080	−0.234	0.408
	VVD	0.080	−0.236	0.434
	CDA	1.382	1.070	1.757
Income	PvdA	−0.056	−0.141	0.038
	VVD	0.095	0.004	0.201
	CDA	0.019	−0.065	0.115
Town Size	PvdA	0.373	−0.055	0.878
	VVD	0.221	−0.271	0.774
	CDA	0.517	0.058	1.044
Education	PvdA	−0.203	−0.311	−0.086
	VVD	−0.056	−0.173	0.078
	CDA	−0.148	−0.266	−0.033
Correctly Predicted %	PvdA	62.5		
	VVD	49.9		
	CDA	62.2		
	D66	19.3		
	MNL Model	55.5		

Sample Size = 529

Source: Quinn, Martin, and Whitford (1999) and Schofield, Martin, Quinn, and Whitford (1998).

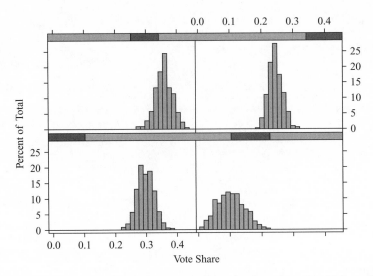

Figure A6.1. Estimated stochastic vote-share functions for the Pvda, VVD, CDA, and D'66 (based on 1979 data and the party positions given in Figure 6.1). (Source: Schofield, Martin, Quinn, and Whitford, 1998.)

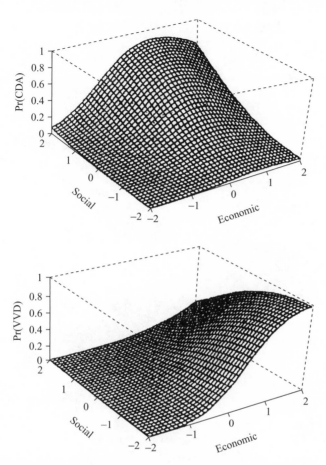

Figure A6.2. Estimated probability functions for voting for the CDA and VVD. (Source: Schofield, Martin, Quinn, and Whitford, 1998.)

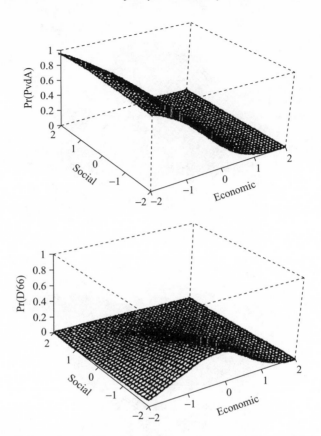

Figure A6.3. Estimated probability functions for voting for the Pvda and D'66. (Source: Schofield, Martin, Quinn, and Whitford, 1998.)

7

Elections in Britain, 1979–2005

The previous chapters on the proportional electoral systems of Israel, Italy, and the Netherlands have considered the hypothesis that the policy positions of parties were chosen not simply to maximize vote-shares, but incorporated strategic concerns over the effect of position on the probability of joining a government coalition. However, this coalition consideration is generally not present in the plurality electoral system of Britain. (For convenience we use the term Britain for the United Kingdom). We can therefore use our electoral model for this polity to determine the degree to which simple vote-maximization characterizes policy choices. We first discuss the MNP model used by Quinn, Martin, and Whitford (1999) to study the election of 1979 in Britain, and then extend the analysis to MNL models of the 1992 and 1997 elections. In all three cases the estimated parameters give low convergence coefficients. Theorem 3.1 then implies that convergence to the electoral center should have occurred under vote-share maximization.

Since there is no evidence of convergence by the major parties in Britain (Alvarez, Nagler, and Bowler, 2000) we develop the activist valence model mentioned in the previous chapter. We now allow the contributions of activists to indirectly enhance the valence of the party leader. The principal result we offer shows that there is a tradeoff to be made between the leader's "exogenous" valence and this "indirect" valence induced by the activists for the party.

We suggest that the valence of the Labour Party, under Tony Blair, increased in the period up to 1997. As a consequence of the relative decline of the Conservative Party leader's valence, the Conservative Party was obliged to depend increasingly on activist support, forcing it to adopt a more radical position. Conversely, Blair's high valence weakened

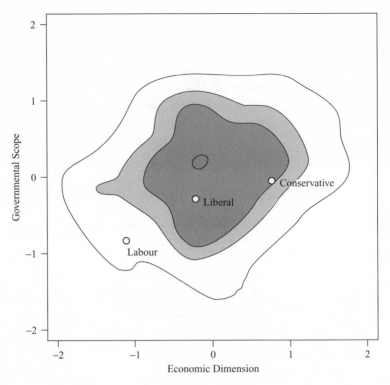

Figure 7.1. Distribution of voter ideal points and party positions in Britain in the 1979 election, for a two-dimensional model, showing the highest density contours of the sample voter distribution at the 95%, 75%, 50%, and 10% levels.

his dependence on activists and allowed him to adopt a more centrist, election-winning position.

We propose the following hypothesis:

Hypothesis 7.1: *If policy choices in a plurality electoral system appear to conflict with vote-maximization in the simple exogenous valence model, then this is due to the influence of activists for the party.*

7.1   THE ELECTIONS OF 1979, 1992, AND 1997

We now examine this indirect role played by activists in determining the policy decisions of parties in Britain. To set the scene, Figure 7.1 presents the estimated positions of the party principals of the three major parties at the election of 1979, in a two-dimensional policy space.

Just as in the case of the Netherlands, the estimation used the middle level Elites Study (ISEIUM, 1983) coupled with the Rabier-Inglehart (1981) Eurobarometer study (see Quinn, Martin, and Whitford, 1999, and Schofield, 2005b for further details.) The electoral variances were 0.605 on the first axis and 0.37 on the second, giving a total variance of 0.975. For the MNL model incorporating sociodemographic characteristics, the spatial coefficient was $\beta = 0.27$ and the convergence coefficient

Table 7.1. *Elections in Britain in 2005, 2001, 1997, and 1992.*

2005	Seats	Seats %	Vote %
Party			
Labour Party (LAB)	356	55.2	35.3
Conservative Party (CON)	198	30.7	32.3
Liberal Democrats Party (LIB)	62	9.6	22.1
Total: major parties	615	95.2	89.7
Scottish National Party (SNP)	6	1.0	1.5
Plaid Cymru (PC)	3	0.5	0.6
Independent, Respect, KHHC	3	0.5	0.3
Northern Ireland in total, comprising:	18	2.8	2.5
Ulster Unionists (UU)	1		0.5
Democratic Union	9		0.9
SDLP	3		0.5
Sinn Fein	5		0.6
Total	646		

2001	Seats	Seats %	Vote %
Party			
Labour Party (LAB)	412	62.6	40.1
Conservative Party (CON)	166	25.1	31.7
Liberal Democrats Party (LIB)	52	7.8	18.6
Total: major parties	630	97.5	90.4
Scottish National Party (SNP)	5	0.8	1.8
Plaid Cymru (PC)	4	0.6	0.7
Independent	1		
Northern Ireland in total, comprising:	18	2.8	
Ulster Unionists (UU)	6		
Democratic Union	5		
SDLP	3		
Sinn Fein	4		

(continued)

Table 7.1. *(continued)*

1997	Seats	Seats %	Vote %
Party			
Labour Party (LAB)	419	63.6	44.4
Conservative Party (CONS)	165	25.0	31.4
Liberal Democrats Party (LIB)	46	6.9	17.2
Total: major parties	630	95.5	93.0
Scottish National Party (SNP)	6	0.9	2.0
Plaid Cymru (PC)	4	0.6	0.5
Independent	1		
Northern Ireland in total, comprising:	18	2.7	
Ulster Unionists (UU)	10		
UK Unionists	1		
Democratic Union	2		
SDLP	3		
Sinn Fein	2		

1992	Seats	Seats %	Vote %
Party			
Labour Party (LAB)	271	41.6	34.5
Conservative Party (CON)	336	51.6	41.9
Liberal Democrats Party (LIB)	20	3.1	17.9
Total: major parties	627		94.3
Scottish National Party (SNP)	3	0.5	1.9
Plaid Cymru (PC)	4	0.6	0.5
Northern Ireland	17	2.6	3.3

was calculated to be 0.26. The eigenvalues of the Hessians of all parties at the origin were then negative. With the MNP model the coefficient was even smaller—0.08—and the eigenvalues of all parties close to -1.0. As in the previous example from the Netherlands, the origin was an LSNE. Indeed, the estimation suggests that the origin was a PSNE. This inference conflicts with the estimated positions of the parties given in Figure 7.1.

To pursue this contradiction further, we now consider more recent elections. Table 7.1 gives details on the elections of 1992, 1997, 2001, and 2005 in Britain. As usual with plurality electoral rules, small gains in vote-share lead to large gains in seat share. British National Election Surveys (British Election Studies, 1992, 1997) were used to construct a single-factor model of the voter distribution (see Table 7.3 for the survey questions). We shall call this factor the *economic dimension*. Note that

Table 7.2. *Factor weights from the British National Election Survey for 1997.*

Britain (without Scotland), 1997

Issue		Factor weights
1.	Unemployment and Inflation	0.265
2.	Taxation and Services	0.223
3.	Nationalization	0.225
4.	Redistribution	0.318
5.	European Community	0.087
6.	Women's Rights	0.149

Scotland, 1997

Issue		Factor weights
1.	Unemployment and Inflation	0.127
2.	Taxation and Services	0.104
3.	Nationalization	0.156
4.	Redistribution	0.580
5.	European Community	0.008
6.	Women's Rights	0.137
7.	Scottish Nationalism	0.101

Table 7.3. *Question Wordings for the British National Election Surveys for 1997.*

1. Do you feel that the government's top priority should be getting people back to work, keeping prices down, or somewhere in between?
2. Do you feel the government should raise taxes and spend more money on health and social services, or do you feel they should cut taxes and spend less on these services?
3. Do you feel the government should nationalize or privatize more industries?
4. Do you feel the government should be more concerned with equalizing people's incomes, or less concerned?
5. Do you feel Britain should unite with the European Union or protect its independence from the European Union?
6. Do you feel women should share an equal role in business, industry, and government, or do you feel a woman's place is in the home?
7. Do you feel Scotland should a) become independent, separate from the UK and the European Union, b) become independent, separate from the UK, but a part of the European Union, c) remain part of the UK, with its own elected assembly, with taxation and spending powers, or d) remain as it is?

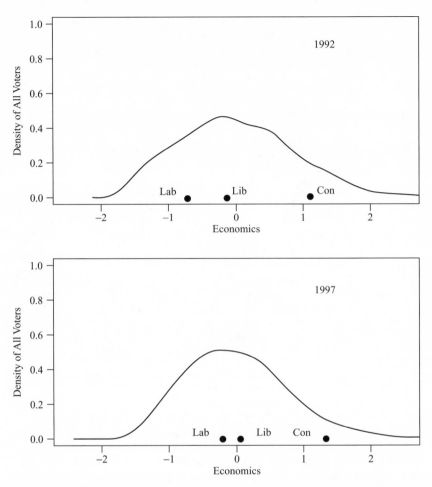

Figure 7.2. Estimated party positions in the British Parliament in 1992 and 1997, for a one-dimensional model (based on the National Election Survey and voter perceptions) showing the estimated density function (of all voters outside Scotland).

Scottish Nationalism is, of course, an issue in Scotland but not in the rest of the country.

Table 7.2 gives the factor weights for 1997 for Britain (subdivided into Britain without Scotland, and Scotland alone). The 1992 weights were very similar. Figure 7.2 presents the estimated distribution of voter ideal points (for voters outside Scotland), on the basis of this single economic dimension. The voter distribution in Scotland was somewhat similar, though less symmetric, and skewed to the left. The party positions for the Labour Party (Lab), Liberal Democrat Party (Lib), Conservative

Table 7.4. *Sample and Estimation Data for Elections in Britain, 1992–1997.*

1992	Sample %	Coefficients	Confidence interval	Correct prediction %
UK without Scotland		$\beta = 0.56$	[0.50, 0.63]	50.0
Conservative	49.3	$\lambda = 1.58$	[1.38, 1.75]	62.9
Labour	32.4	$\lambda = 0.58$	[0.40, 0.76]	47.4
Liberals	18.2	$\lambda = 0.00$		19.7
Scotland		$\beta = 0.50$	[0.31, 0.67]	35.6
Conservative	30.2	$\lambda = 1.68$	[1.18, 2.21]	48.6
Labour	31.4	$\lambda = 0.91$	[0.38, 1.51]	37.2
SNP	25.9	$\lambda = 0.77$	[0.26, 1.30]	29.5
Liberals	12.3	$\lambda = 0.00$		12.8

1997	Sample %	Coefficients	Confidence interval	Correct prediction %
UK without Scotland		$\beta = 0.50$	[0.44, 0.56]	45.7
Conservative	31.9	$\lambda = 1.24$	[1.03, 1.44]	45.2
Labour	49.6	$\lambda = 0.97$	[0.85, 1.07]	56.1
Liberals	18.5	$\lambda = 0.00$		19.0
Scotland		$\beta = 0.50$	[0.40, 0.64]	40.5
Conservative	14.2	$\lambda = 0.92$	[0.58, 1.24]	33.7
Labour	52.7	$\lambda = 1.33$	[1.10, 1.57]	56.3
SNP	20.4	$\lambda = 0.42$	[0.16, 0.72]	21.5
Liberals	12.5	$\lambda = 0.00$		12.8

Party (Con), and Scottish National Party (SNP) were inferred by taking average voter perceptions of the locations of these parties.

The positions Lab, Lib, and Con in the two election years (for voters outside Scotland) were given by the vectors

$$\mathbf{z}_{92} = (z_{lab}, z_{lib}, z_{con}) = (-0.65, -0.11, +1.12) \tag{7.1}$$

$$\mathbf{z}_{97} = (-0.2, +0.06, +1.33). \tag{7.2}$$

See Figure 7.2.

In 1992 the SNP position was perceived to be $z_{snp} = -0.3$, and in 1997 it was $+0.14$.

Using these data, MNL models were constructed for the four cases in 1992 and 1997, for Scotland and the rest of the country. These models allowed us to estimate the exogenous valence terms, as in Table 7.4.

The estimated coefficients in the two elections were

$$(\lambda_{con}, \lambda_{lab}, \lambda_{lib}, \beta)_{1997} = (+1.24, 0.97, 0.0, 0.5) \qquad (7.3)$$

$$(\lambda_{con}, \lambda_{lab}, \lambda_{lib}, \beta)_{1992} = (+1.58, 0.58, 0.0, 0.56) \qquad (7.4)$$

These estimates are compatible with extensive survey research which demonstrates the relationship between positive attitudes to party leaders and voting intentions (King, 2002; Clarke et al., 2004). Notice that the Conservative Party valence fell, while that of the Labour Party rose. These changes in valences are presumed to be independent of the apparent *perceived move away from the electoral center* by the Conservative Party, and the *perceived move toward the electoral center* by the Labour Party.

The empirical model was relatively successful, in the sense that the model prediction success rate was approximately 50 percent. As Table 7.4 indicates, the 95 percent confidence intervals for the valences of the Labour Party and Conservative Party exclude zero. We infer that the valence differences between the Liberal Democrats and both Labour and the Conservatives are non-zero. The log marginal likelihood of the 1997 MNL model with valence was -531, giving a Bayes' factor of 75 over the MNL model without valence. For Britain without Scotland in 1997 we can use the results of Chapter 3 to compute the convergence coefficient for these two elections. Because the model is MNL we use the formal model based on the Type I extreme value distribution. Since the model is one-dimensional, the electoral variance on the single axis is normalized to be 1.0. Because the valence of Lib is normalized to be zero, we find that for 1997 the eigenvalue of the Hessian of the Liberal Democrat Party at the joint origin is -0.28. A similar value of -0.18 was obtained for 1992.

The results of Chapter 3 thus imply convergence for the formal model. Even using the upper estimated bound of the parameters, we obtain similar estimates for the eigenvalues. Thus, on the basis of the formal model, we can assert with a high degree of certainty that the low-valence party, the Liberal Democrats, can be located at an LNE at the origin if all other parties also locate there. According to the model, the vote-share of the Liberal Democrat Party would have been 13 percent in 1992, or 14 percent in 1997, had the other two parties located at the origin in these elections. Because the two major parties did not locate at the origin, the actual vote-share of 17 percent to 18 percent for the Liberals is compatible with these estimates.

Thus, under the assumptions of fixed or exogenous valence, vote-maximization, and unidimensionality, a version of the mean voter theorem should have been valid for the British elections of 1992 and 1997. Although Figure 7.2 indicates that a position close to the center was adopted (or seen to be adopted) by the Liberal Democrats in 1992 and 1997, this was not so obvious for the Labour Party, and was clearly false for the Conservative Party. Indeed, for both subsets of the electorate (within Scotland and outside), the Labour Party was perceived to approach closer to the center between 1992 and 1997, but the Conservative Party was perceived to become more radical.

7.2 ESTIMATING THE INFLUENCE OF ACTIVISTS

In an attempt to account for the obvious disparity between the conclusions of the vote-maximization model and party location, we considered the hypothesis that party location was determined by party elites. As we proposed in the discussion of the Netherlands, the location of the delegates or elite positions can be used to determine the position of maximum activist support for each party. This, in turn, will determine the precise equilibrium location of each party. While activists contribute time and money and affect overall political support for the party, the activist locations will tend to be more radical than the average voter. This presents the party leader with a complex "optimization problem." We use the activist valence argument to offer a conjecture about how party leaders deal with this problem by choosing differing policy positions to present to the electorate (Robertson, 1976).

Figure 7.3 gives the estimated voter distribution in the British election of 1997, based on the British National Election Survey but using the two dimensions obtained from factor analysis. (See Table 7.2 for the factor weight associated with this second "European" dimension.) Positions of MPs of each party were estimated on the basis of an MP sample response to the British National Election questionnaire. For each party, the average of the party MP positions was used as an estimate of the position of each party "principal." The estimated positions of individual MPs in the survey are given in Figure 7.4.

A considerable difference among ideal points of MPs within parties can be observed. The second, "vertical," axis in Figure 7.3 is determined by "pro-Europe" versus "pro-British" (or "anti-Europe") attitudes. The party principal positions of Labour (LAB) and Conservatives (CONS) are separated on both axes, but more so on the Europe axis. The small number of Ulster Unionists (UU) appeared to be similar to other Conservatives, but more extreme on the pro-British axis. The single sampled MP

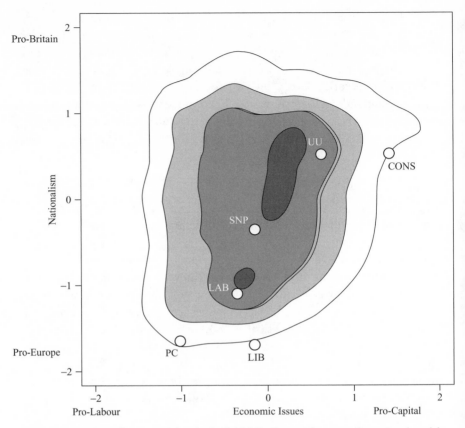

Figure 7.3. Estimated party positions in the British Parliament for a two-dimensional model for 1997 (based on MP survey data and the National Election Survey) showing highest density contours of the voter sample distribution at the 95%, 75%, 50%, and 10% levels.

for Plaid Cymru (PC, from Wales) was similar to other left, pro-Europe Labour MPs, while the single sampled member of the SNP (from Scotland) also resembled other Labour MPs who were less pro-Europe. The fifteen sampled Liberal Democrats (with principal position denoted LIB) were all somewhat left of center, and very pro-Europe.

The empirical estimates presented above, and those based on the one-dimensional model, suggest that the Labour valence had increased from 1992 to 1997. In terms of this empirical model, this increase was independent of the greater voter support induced by the party moving closer to the electoral center under Tony Blair. We now consider the following hypothesis.

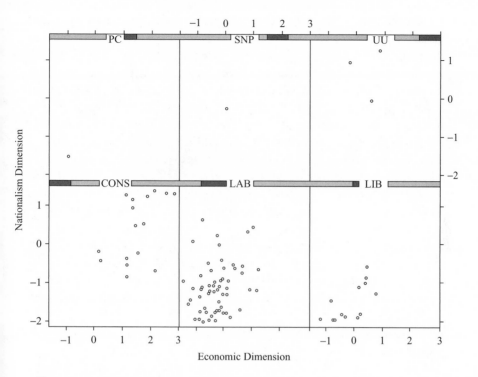

Figure 7.4. Estimated MP positions in the British Parliament in 1997, based on MP survey data and a two-dimensional factor model derived from the National Election Survey.

Key

PC:	**Plaid Cymru (Welsh Nationalist Party)**
SNP:	**Scottish Nationalist Party**
UU:	**Ulster Unionists**
CONS:	**Conservative Party**
LAB:	**Labour Party**
LIB:	**Liberal Democrat Party**

Hypothesis 7.2: *The apparent move by the Labour Party toward the electoral center between 1992 and 1997 was a consequence of the increase of the valence of the leader of the party, rather than a cause of this increase.*

To develop this hypothesis, we shall assume that the party principal positions given in Figure 7.3 do indeed represent in some sense the average location of party activists. We then attempt to model the influence of activists on optimal party position.

Note first that the positions perceived by the electorate in 1997 and given by the vector $z_{97} = (-0.2, +0.06, +1.33)$ are very close indeed to the projections of the positions of the party principals onto the economic axis in Figure 7.3. This leads us to infer that the party principal positions do influence perceived party positions. Just as we did in Chapter 6, we can examine whether the party principal positions can be a local equilibrium to a simple vote-maximizing game. The Technical Appendix to this chapter shows that when we include the second European axis then the Liberal Party eigenvalue on this axis is positive. This calculation is based on zero electoral covariance between the two axes, and the greater electoral variance on the second "Europe" axis. In other words, if all three parties were at the electoral center, then the positive eigenvalue of the Hessian on the second dimension would give the Liberal Democrat Party leader an incentive to change position, but only on the second axis. We may infer that the average preferred position of the party MPs would induce the party leader to adopt a pro-Europe position. If the Liberal Party were to adopt a pro-Europe position as indicated by its principal's position, then the logic of vote-maximization would induce the Labour Party leader to make a similar move. Thus, the positions LAB and LIB are compatible with the simple vote-model with exogenous valence.

This conclusion still leaves unexplained the perceived location of the Conservative Party (CONS).

Under the assumptions of the fixed valence model, the Conservative Party should have adopted a vote-maximizing position closer to the origin than did the Labour Party. We suggest that the Conservative Party did not converge on the mean because of the subtle interrelationship between exogenous valence and activist valence. Blair's increasing valence in the period up to 1997 resulted in a decrease in the importance of the activists in the party (Seyd and Whiteley, 2002). This led to a more centrist vote-maximizing strategy by Labour, associated with a larger "electoral sphere of influence." In contrast, decreasing Conservative leader valence led to an increase in the importance of activists. To maintain grassroots support, the Conservatives were forced to adopt quite radical positions, both on the question of Europe and on economic issues.

Schofield (2003b, 2004, 2005a,b) presents a formal analysis of these differing valence effects. It is consistent with this more general model that all parties at the election of 1997 were at vote-maximizing positions. We now turn to this extension.

In essence, the model we propose suggests that if the leader of one party benefits from increasing valence, then the party's optimal strategy will be to move toward the political center in order to take advantage of the electoral benefits. In contrast, a party, such as the Liberal Democrat Party, whose leader is unable to take advantage of high valence, cannot expect to gain commanding electoral support, even when the party adopts a centrist position.

In the following section, we present the underlying formal electoral model that we use, and state the constraint on the model parameters, which is sufficient for concavity and thus for existence of a noncentrist pure strategy Nash equilibrium. Indeed we show that the joint vote-maximizing positions will generally not be at the voter mean. We briefly discuss the optimality condition when both "exogenous" valence and "activist" valence are involved, and indicate why activists become more relevant when leader valence falls.

7.3   A FORMAL MODEL OF VOTE-MAXIMIZING WITH ACTIVISTS

We return briefly to the model we introduced in Chapter 3 so that we can extend it here to account for noncentrist political choice in the case of Britain.

In the model with valence, the stochastic element is associated with the weight given by each voter i to the perceived valence of the party leader. We now allow valence to be indirectly affected by party position.

Definition 7.1 *The formal model* $M(\lambda, A, \mu; \Psi)$

In the general valence model, let $z = (z_1, \ldots, z_p) \in X^p$ be a typical vector of policy positions. Given z, each voter i is described by a vector $u_i(x_i, z) = (u_{i1}(x_i, z_1), \ldots, u_{ip}(x_i, z_p))$, where the utility of voter i, at the party declaration vector z, is given by

$$u_{ij}(x_i, z_j) = \lambda_j + \mu_j(z_j) - A_{ij}(x_i, z_j) + \varepsilon_j. \qquad (7.5)$$

The term $A_{ij}(x_i, z_j)$ is derived from a general metric. The errors $\{\varepsilon_j\}$ are again assumed to be distributed by the Type I extreme value distribution, Ψ. For party j, the vote-share $\mathcal{E}_j$ is the expectation

$$\frac{1}{n} \sum_i \rho_{ij}.$$

For convenience, in terminology below we shall refer to the effect of candidate strategies on the expected vote-share function $\mathcal{E}_j$, through change in $\mu_j(z_j)$, as the *valence* component of the vote. Change in $\mathcal{E}_j$ through the effect on the policy distance measure $A_{ij}(x_i, z_j)$ we shall refer to as the *nonvalence*, or *policy* component. We discuss this activist model below. One important modification of the pure spatial model that we make is that the salience of different policy dimensions may vary among the electorate. More precisely, we assume that

$$A_{ij}(x_i, z_j) = ||x_i - z_j||_i^2 \tag{7.6}$$

may vary with different i.

The term $\mu_j(z_j)$ is called the *activist valence* of the party. Notice that activist valence is now a function of the leader position z_j. To distinguish the two forms of valence, we call λ_j the *exogenous valence*.

We propose an extension of the model presented in Chapter 3 to include activist valence. In this new model the first-order condition for vote-share maximization is not satisfied at the mean. We now briefly sketch the procedure for determining the first-order condition. The choice of voter i now depends on the comparison *vector*

$$g_{ij}(\mathbf{z}) = (..., \delta_{ik}^2 - \delta_{ij}^2 - \lambda_k + \lambda_j - \mu_k(z_k) + \mu_j(z_j), ...) : \text{for all } k \neq j), \tag{7.7}$$

where $\delta_{ij}^2 = ||x_i - z_j||_i^2$, etc.

Section 7.6.2 in the appendix to this chapter shows that the first-order solution z_j^* is given by the balance equation

$$z_j^* = \frac{1}{2}\frac{d\mu_j}{dz_j} + \sum_{i=1}^n \alpha_{ij} x_i. \tag{7.8}$$

In this equation, the coefficients α_{ij} depend on $\{\lambda_k, \lambda_j, \mu_k(z_k), \mu_j(z_j)\}$ and are increasing in $\{\lambda_j, \mu_j(z_j)\}$ and decreasing in $\{\lambda_k, \mu_k(z_k) : k \neq j\}$. The actual coefficients will depend on the distribution assumption made on the errors. For convenience let us write

$$\sum_i \alpha_{ij} x_i = \frac{d\mathcal{E}_j^*}{dz_j}. \tag{7.9}$$

Then we can rewrite the balance equation as

$$\left[\frac{d\mathcal{E}_j^*}{dz_j} - z_j^*\right] + \frac{1}{2}\frac{d\mu_j}{dz_j} = 0. \tag{7.10}$$

The bracketed term on the left of this expression is the *marginal electoral pull* and is a gradient vector pointing toward the *weighted electoral mean*. This weighted electoral mean is simply that point at which the electoral pull is zero. In the case $\mu_j = 0$ for all j, then for each party j, it is obvious that all α_{ij} are identical, so $z_j^* = \frac{1}{n}\Sigma x_i$. This gives, as in the proof of Theorem 3.1, the point where the marginal electoral pull is zero.

The vector $\frac{d\mu_j}{dz_j}$ "points toward" the position at which the party's activist valence is maximized. We may term this vector the *(marginal) activist pull*. When this marginal or gradient vector $\frac{d\mu_j}{dz_j}$ is increased, then the equilibrium is pulled away from the weighted electoral mean, and we can say the "activist effect" is increased. On the other hand, if the activist valence functions are fixed, but λ_j is increased, or the terms $\{\lambda_k : k \neq j\}$ are decreased, then the vector $\frac{d\mathcal{E}_j^*}{dz_j}$ increases in magnitude, the equilibrium is pulled toward the weighted electoral mean, and we can say the "electoral effect" is increased.

When the first-order condition is satisfied for all parties at the vector z* then say z* is a *balance solution* or satisfies *the balance condition*.

Moreover, if the activist effect is concave, then the second-order condition (or the negative definiteness of the Hessian of the "activist pull") will guarantee that a vector z* that satisfies the balance condition will be an LSNE. Schofield (2003b) proved this result for iind errors. These observations then give the following theorem.

Theorem 7.1 *Consider the vote-maximization model*
M(λ, A, μ; Ψ) based on a disturbance distribution Ψ and including both exogenous and activist valences. The first-order condition for z to be an equilibrium is that it satisfies the balance condition. Other things being equal, the equilibrium position z_j^* will be closer to a weighted electoral mean the greater is the party's exogenous valence, λ_j. Conversely, if the activist valence function μ_j is increased, due to the greater willingness of activists to contribute to the party, the nearer will z_j^* be to the activist-preferred position. If all activist valence functions are highly concave, in the sense of having negative eigenvalues of sufficiently great magnitude, then the balance solution will be a PNE.*

The proof of this result is given in Section 7.6.2 in the Technical Appendix.

Figure 7.5 illustrates this result, in a two-dimensional policy space derived from the data as presented in Figure 7.3. We have observed that overall Conservative valence dropped from 1.58 in 1992 to 1.24 in 1997, while the Labour valence increased from 0.58 to 0.97. These estimated valences include both exogenous valence terms for the parties and the activist component. Nonetheless, the data presented in Clarke et al., (1998,

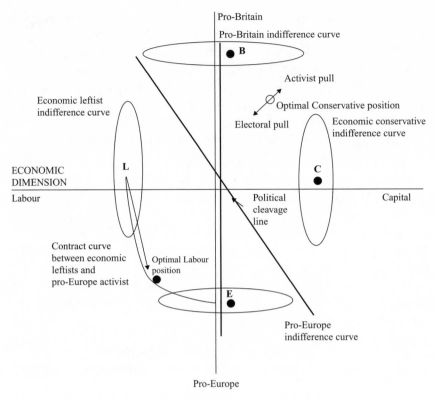

Figure 7.5. Illustration of vote-maximizing party positions of the Conservative and Labour leaders for a two-dimensional model.

2004) suggest that the Labour exogenous valence λ_{lab}, due to Blair, rose in this period. Conversely, the relative exogenous term λ_{con} for the Conservatives fell. Since the coefficients in the equation for the electoral pull for the Conservative Party depend on $\lambda_{con} - \lambda_{lab}$, the effect would be to increase the marginal effect of activism for the Conservative Party, and pull the optimal position away from the party's weighted electoral mean.

Indeed, it is possible to include the effect of two potential activist groups for the Conservative Party: one "pro-British," centered at the position marked B in Figure 7.5 and one "pro-Capital," marked C in the figure. The optimal Conservative position will be determined by a version of the balance equation, but one that equates the "electoral pull" against the two "activist pulls." Since the electoral pull fell between the elections, the optimal position z_{con}^* will be one that is "closer" to the locus of points that generates the greatest activist support. This locus is where the joint marginal activist pull is zero. This locus of points can be called the *activist contract curve* for the Conservative Party.

Note that in Figure 7.5, the indifference curves of representative activists for the parties are described by ellipses. This is meant to indicate that preferences of different activists on the two dimensions may accord different saliences to the policy axes. The activist contract curve given in the figure, for Labour, say, is the locus of points satisfying the activist equation $\frac{d\mu_{lab}}{dz_{lab}} = 0$. This curve represents the balance of power between Labour supporters most interested in economic issues concerning labour (centered at L in the figure) and those more interested in Europe (centered at E). The optimal positions for the two parties will be at appropriate positions that satisfy the balance condition. In other words, each optimal position will lie on a locus generated by the respective activist contract curves and the party's weighted electoral mean point where the electoral pull is zero. As the theorem states, because the coefficients of the weighted electoral mean for Labour depend on $\lambda_{lab} - \lambda_{con}$, we would expect a rise in this difference to pull the party "nearer" the electoral origin.

In Chapter 8 we apply this model and show that the equation for this contract curve from the preferred pro-European point (s_E, t_E) to the pro-labour point (s_L, t_L) is given by the equation

$$\frac{(y - t_E)}{(x - s_E)} = S\frac{(y - t_L)}{(x - s_L)} \tag{7.11}$$

where

$$S = \frac{b^2}{a^2} \cdot \frac{e^2}{f^2}. \tag{7.12}$$

Here, $\frac{b}{a} > 1$ measures the degree to which activists for the Labour Party are more concerned with economics rather than with Europe, while $\frac{e}{f} > 1$ measures the opposite ratio for Europe activists. Obviously, with identical saliences, $S = 1$, and the contract curve is linear.

The "political cleavage line" in the figure is a representation of the electoral dividing line if there were only the two parties in the election. The weighted electoral mean should lie on the intersection of the political cleavage line and the line connecting the two party positions.

As Theorem 7.1 indicates, when the relative exogenous valence for a party falls, then the optimal party position will approach the activist contract curve. Moreover, the optimal position on this contract curve will depend on the relative intensity of political preferences of the activists of each party. For example, if grassroots "pro-British" Conservative Party activists have intense preferences on this dimension, then this feature will be reflected in the activist contract curve and thus in the optimal Conservative position.

For the Labour Party, it seems clear that two effects are present. Blair's high exogenous valence gave an optimal Labour Party position that was closer to the electoral center than the optimal position of the Conservative Party. Moreover, this affected the balance between pro-Labour or "old left" activists in the party and "New Labour" activists, concerned with modernizing the party through a European style "social democratic" perspective. This inference, based on our theoretical model, is compatible with Blair's successful attempts to bring "New Labour" members into the party (See Seyd and Whiteley, 2002, for documentation). To relate this analysis to the idea of a party principal offered in earlier chapters, we may say that the both parties are characterized by competition between opposed party principals, located at L and E for Labour, and at C and B for the Conservative Party.

7.4 ACTIVIST AND EXOGENOUS VALENCE

Our purpose in introducing the notions of "exogenous valence" and "activist valence" has been to explore the possibility that the relationship between the party and the potential party activists will be affected by the exogenous valence of the leader. Party leaders can either exploit changes in their valence, or become victims of such changes. The theoretical framework that we have offered is intended to provide an explanation for the seemingly radical policy choices of the Labour Party during the period of Conservative government from 1979 until about 1992. By *radical* we mean simply that the party adopted positions that appeared to be far from the electoral center. In recent years, the Conservative Party appears to have adopted policy choices that are radical, but on the European axis. According to the model just presented, these policy choices are perfectly rational in that they are designed to maximize votes. A similar argument will be applied in the next chapter to apparently radical policy choices in the Republican–Democrat electoral competition in the United States.

Although the elections of the 1980s are not examined here, we conjecture that, during this period, the electorate, in general, viewed Margaret Thatcher as more competent than her rival Neil Kinnock. In the model that we have proposed, Thatcher's perceived degree of competence, or exogenous popularity valence, was relatively independent of the particular policies that she put forward for the party. It is, of course, a simplification to assume that the perception of her competence was independent of the policy preferences, or the sociodemographic characteristics, of individual voters. In principle it would be possible to refine the above model by examining optimal party positions with respect to these variables.

The simple model presented above suggests that the low average perception of Kinnock's competence, in comparison to Thatcher's, obliged him to pay great weight to the activists within the Labour Party. As a consequence, both Labour and Conservative Parties adopted vote-maximizing, but relatively radical, positions far from the electoral center. Even though the Liberal or Liberal Democrat Party adopted a centrist position, its low exogenous valence kept it in the third party position.

It is possible that Thatcher was deposed from the leadership of the Conservative Party precisely because her falling personal valence led to greater electoral weight for powerful activist elements in her party. Indeed, the party mandarins may have understood the nature of the balance condition, although Thatcher probably denied it. We have, somewhat simplistically, characterized the optimal activist intraparty balance in terms of a contract curve. In fact, the process by which the party leader is selected by the competing party principals can be expected to be highly contentious.

During Major's tenure as leader of the Conservative Party, the debacle over the value of sterling and the change to John Smith as the Labour Party leader led to a transformation in the relative exogenous valences of the two parties. Clarke, Stewart, and Whiteley (1998) note the rapid change in voter intentions in favor of Labour when John Smith took over from Kinnock, in July of 1992, and again when Blair took over the leadership of the party in July of 1994. Time-series analyses of voter intentions show quite clearly how these are determined by perceptions of government competence in dealing with economic problems (see also Seyd and Whiteley, 1992; Clarke et al., 1995, 1997, 1998; Clarke, Sanders et al., 2004).

In addition, however, voting intentions will be affected by judgments about the presumed "fitness" of the party leaders. Our estimates of these average electoral judgments suggest that Tony Blair was perceived to be much more fit than earlier Labour Party leaders to head the government. By themselves, however these changes in electoral judgments would not have given the Labour Party such a clear majority in 1997. The model that we propose suggests that Blair's enhanced valence made it possible for him to persuade the "Old Labour" activists of the party that it was in the best interests of the party to move to a much more centrist policy position. This transformation of the party was electorally credible, and led to the overwhelming Labour Party victory in 1997.

Up until 2003, the Conservative Party leaders, William Hague and Iain Duncan Smith, seemed to have been deemed by the electorate to have low exogenous valence. One way to estimate exogenous valence of a leader is to take as a proxy the difference between the proportion of the electorate who are satisfied with the leader and those who are not. The valence proxy for Blair in 1997 was about 0.5, whereas the valence proxy for Hague was about −0.2. In 2002, the valence proxy for Duncan Smith was about −0.1. Consistent with our model and with the estimations given above, Conservative Party activists have exerted their power to move the party further from the electoral origin. This led, first of all, to the Conservative Party defeat in 2001, and to the struggle inside the party over which activist group would construct the party policy in the future. The leadership contest was won by Michael Howard in October 2003. By the election of 2005, the proxies of both Howard, the Conservative Party leader, and Blair, were similar at about −0.2.

Recent international events, and Blair's responses to them, appear to have decreased his personal valence. As Table 7.1 indicates, in May 2005 the Labour Party lost nearly sixty seats that it had won in 2001. The drop of nearly 6 percent of the popular vote would appear to be entirely due to the increased electoral mistrust caused by Blair's handling of the Iraq situation. There has been a move to force Blair to resign in favor of Gordon Brown, but at the time of writing, it is fairly subdued.

While the number of seats for the Conservatives increased by thirty over the 2001 figure, the popular vote-share hardly increased over the levels for 1997 and 2001. This was obviously the reason that Howard announced his resignation "sooner rather than later" from the party leadership immediately after the election. In December, 2005, the party chose a new leader, David Cameron. It remains to be seen whether the electorate will judge him to be a competent leader.

The model proposed here suggests that this change in Blair's valence from 2001 to 2005 may induce conflict inside the Labour Party, between economic activists, on the one hand, and pro-Europe social democrats on the other. Indeed, a third axis of political choice, concerned with the Middle East, may have come into existence recently.

7.5 CONCLUSION

We have presented the electoral model for Britain in order to contrast the political configurations of party positions that are possible in a polity whose electoral system is based on plurality rule with those in polities such as Israel, Italy, and the Netherlands, based on proportional representation.

We contend that the result on the formal model presented in Theorems 3.1 and 7.1, together with the empirical analysis, indicate that the vote-maximizing principle (with valence), together with the simple structure of the stochastic vote-model, accounts for party divergence in particular and party behavior more generally. The analysis also suggests that party activism is an essential component of any electoral model.

It has been argued that proportional rule and plurality lead to very different political patterns (Riker, 1953, 1982; Duverger, 1954; Taagepera and Shugart, 1989). Although Theorem 7.1 of this chapter (together with Theorem 3.1) is based on the simple assumption of vote-maximization it should be possible to extend it to deal with seat maximization, under different electoral rules. This could provide a theoretical explanation for different configurations observed in multiparty polities.

The various spatial maps that we presented here and in the chapters on Israel, Italy, and the Netherlands, demonstrate considerable variety. One conclusion that can be drawn from the two electoral theorems is that centrifugal and centripetal forces will both be relevant. This follows because activist coalitions will typically occur on the electoral periphery. An argument to this effect can be seen as the basis for Duverger's contention that the "centre does not exist in politics" (Duverger, 1954: 215; Daalder, 1984). In line with this assertion, Theorems 3.1 and 7.1 suggest, contrary to the mean voter theorem, that a crowded political center is highly unlikely.

Under plurality rule, the two principal parties, if their valences are sufficiently close, will compete over the center, but in such a way that their "spheres of influence" are disjoint. In addition, activists will tend to pull parties to the periphery, as suggested by Figure 7.5.

Under proportional representation, as our discussion of Israel illustrated, high-valence parties such as Labour and Likud may position themselves close to the electoral center. In the absence of a core party, coalition formation requires the assistance of smaller, low-valence parties. These parties will tend to locate at the periphery, either because of the logic of vote-maximization, or again, because of the influence of party activists.

Theorem 7.1 does not necessarily imply that all parties will avoid the electoral center. Our analysis has shown that there are centrist parties in Israel, Italy, the Netherlands, and Britain. However, though their policy positions would suggest that they should be candidates for government leadership, their low valence may make this difficult.

At a more general level, the spatial theory offered here could be used to construct a theory of party formation. The exogenous valences may be assumed to be random initially. High-valence parties will jockey at the electoral center as described above. Severe competition will generate nonconcavities in voter response and force some parties to retreat from the electoral center. Small, low-valence parties may emerge at the periphery and activist coalitions will form to generate support for their chosen policies. As these activist coalitions become more efficient, the party vote-functions may become increasingly concave (as the eigenvalues of the relevant Hessians become large and negative). This has the effect of stabilizing party positions. This suggests to us why it is that there is, on the one hand, such great variation in party configurations, and on the other, considerable stability within each political system.

7.6 TECHNICAL APPENDIX

7.6.1 *Computation of Eigenvalues*

(i) The one-dimensional model for 1992, with $\beta = 0.56$ gives:

$$\rho_{lib} = \frac{e^0}{e^0 + e^{1.58} + e^{0.58}} = \frac{1}{7.36} = 0.13$$

$$A_{lib} = \beta(1 - 2\rho) = 0.41$$

$$C_{lib} = 0.82 - 1 = -0.18.$$

(ii) The one-dimensional model for 1997, with $\beta = 0.5$ gives:

$$\rho_{lib} = \frac{e^0}{e^0 + e^{1.24} + e^{0.97}} = \frac{1}{7.08} = 0.14$$

$$A_{lib} = \beta(1 - 2\rho) = 0.36$$

$$C_{lib} = 0.72 - 1 = -0.28.$$

(iii) The two-dimensional model for 1997 gives:

$$C_{lib} = (0.72) \begin{pmatrix} 1.0 & 0 \\ 0 & 1.5 \end{pmatrix} - I = \begin{pmatrix} -0.28 & 0 \\ 0 & +0.8 \end{pmatrix}.$$

7.6.2 *Proof of Theorem 7.1*

To simplify the proof, we consider the case with $A_{ij}(x_i, z_j) = ||x_i - z_j||^2$. For the extreme value distribution Ψ we have

$$\rho_{i1}(x_i, z_1) = \left[1 + \Sigma_{j=2}[\exp(f_j)]\right]^{-1},$$

$$\text{where } f_j = \lambda_j + \mu_j(z_j) - \lambda_1 - \mu_1(z_1) + ||x_i - z_1||^2 - ||x_i - z_j||^2$$

is the comparison function used by i in evaluating party j in contrast to party 1. We then obtain

$$\frac{d}{dz_1}[\rho_{i1}] = -\left[2(z_1 - x_i) - \frac{d\mu_1}{dz_1}\right]\left[1 + \sum_{j=2}\exp(f_j)\right]^{-2}\left[\sum_{j=2}\exp(f_j)\right]$$

$$= \left[2(x_i - z_1) + \frac{d\mu_1}{dz_1}\right][\rho_{i1}][1 - \rho_{i1}].$$

Thus

$$\sum_i \frac{d}{dz_1}[\rho_{i1}] = \sum_i \left[2(x_i - z_1) + \frac{d\mu_1}{dz_1}\right][\rho_{i1}][1 - \rho_{i1}] = 0,$$

or

$$\left[2z_1 - \frac{d\mu_1}{dz_1}\right]\sum_i[\rho_{i1}][1 - \rho_{i1}] = \sum_i 2x_i[\rho_{i1}][1 - \rho_{i1}],$$

so

$$z_1 - \frac{1}{2}\frac{d\mu_1}{dz_1} = \sum_i \alpha_{i1}x_i,$$

where

$$\alpha_{i1} = \frac{[\rho_{i1}][1 - \rho_{i1}]}{\Sigma_i[\rho_{i1}][1 - \rho_{i1}]}.$$

Clearly the coefficient α_{i1} is increasing in μ_1 and λ_1, and decreasing in λ_j, μ_j for $j \neq 1$. An identical argument holds for each party j giving an equilibrium at a weighted electoral mean satisfying, for all j, the balance equation:

$$\left[\frac{d\mathcal{E}_j^*}{dz_j} - z_j^*\right] + \frac{1}{2}\frac{d\mu_j}{dz_j} = 0. \tag{7.13}$$

To examine the second-order condition, note that now the Hessian of party 1 is given by

$$\frac{1}{n}\sum_i \frac{d^2\rho_{i1}}{dz_1^2} = \frac{1}{n}\sum_i [\rho_{i1} - \rho_{i1}^2]\left[4[1 - 2\rho_{i1}][\nabla_i^*] + \left[\frac{d^2\mu_1}{dz_1^2} - 2I\right]\right].$$

Here, $[\nabla^*] = \frac{1}{n}\Sigma_i [\nabla_i^*]$ is the total electoral covariance matrix taken about the point $z_1 - \frac{1}{2}\frac{d\mu_1}{dz_1}$. Even though the matrix term involving ∇^* may have positive eigenvalues, if the eigenvalues of $\frac{d^2\mu_1}{dz_1^2}$ are negative, and of sufficiently large modulus, then the Hessian will also have negative eigenvalues.

Obviously, this can give a PSNE. $\qquad\qquad\qquad\qquad\qquad\square$

Note that for a general spatial model with $A_{ij}(x_i, z_j) = ||x_i - z_j||_i^2$ involving different coefficients in different dimensions, the only change will be in the definition of the weighted electoral mean. It is also worth mentioning that the model can be developed with the Cartesian norm:

$$A_{ij}(x_i, z_j) = \sum_{r=1}^{w} |x_{ir} - z_{jr}|.$$

Instead of a weighted *electoral mean* the first-order condition will give a weighted *electoral median*.

8

Political Realignments in the United States

8.1 CRITICAL ELECTIONS IN 1860 AND 1964

This chapter will develop the idea of activist influence in elections presented in the previous chapter, but will apply the model to the transformation of electoral politics that has seemed to occur in recent elections in the United States. Indeed we shall use the model to suggest that a slow transformation has occurred in the locations of Republican and Democrat presidential candidates, and as a consequence, pattern of majorities for the two parties in the States of the Union have shifted. In our account, this is because the most important policy axes have slowly rotated. We ascribe this to the shifting balance of power between different activist groups in the polity.

Just to illustrate the idea, Table 8.1 shows the shift in state majorities for the two-party candidates between 1896 and 2000, whereas Table 8.2 shows the similarity between the two elections. It is clear that there is a strong tendency for states that voted Republican in 1896 to vote Democrat in 2000, and vice versa. Aside from the fact that a number of states had been formed out of the territories in the period from 1860 to 1896, there is little substantive difference between the pattern of Democrat and Republican states in 1860 and 1896. However, as Table 8.1 suggests, the states that voted Republican for Lincoln in 1860, or for McKinley in 1896, tended to vote Democrat in 2000.

Prior to 1856 of course, there was good reason to believe that the Democrat Party had almost become the permanent majority, by controlling almost all southern and western states. Schofield (2006) argues that the Democrat Party was intersectional, with support in both North and South. Riker (1980, 1982) had suggested that this predominance of the

Table 8.1. *Presidential State Votes, 1896 and 2000.*

	DEM 1896	REP 1896		
DEM 2000	*Washington*		Connecticut	*California*
			Delaware	*Iowa*
			Illinois	*Maine*
			Maryland	*Oregon*
			Massachusetts	*Vermont*
			Michigan	*Wisconsin*
			Minnesota	
			N. Jersey	
			N. York	
			Pennsylvania	
			Rhode Island	
REP 2000	*Colorado*	**Alabama**	W. Virginia	*Indiana*
	Florida	**Arkansas**		*N. Hampshire*
	Idaho	**Georgia**		*N. Dakota*
	Kansas	**Louisiana**		*Ohio*
	Kentucky	**Mississippi***		
	Montana	**Missouri**		
	Nebraska	**Nevada**		
	S. Dakota	**N. Carolina**		
	Tennessee	**S. Carolina**		
	Utah	**Texas**		
	Virginia			
	Wyoming			

Italicized states are those that were Republican in 1960.
Bold states are those that were Democratic in 1960.
* Although Kennedy outpolled Nixon in Mississippi (31% to 25%), a plurality voted for
  electors who cast their electoral votes for segregationist Harry Byrd.

Democrat Party was broken by Lincoln in the election of 1860, as a result
of his ability to bring the issue of slavery to the forefront.

To seek the causes of this recent electoral realignment we can start
with the election of 1860. In that election, Abraham Lincoln, the Republican contender, won the presidential election by capturing a majority
of the popular vote in fifteen northern and western states. The Whig or
"Conservative Union" candidate, Bell, only won three states (Virginia,
Kentucky, and Tennessee), while the two Democrat candidates, Douglas
and Breckinridge, took the ten states of the South. (See Schofield, 2006a:
Table 5.2)

From 1836 to 1852, Democrat and Whig vote shares had been roughly
comparable (Ransom, 1989), with neither party gaining an overwhelming

Table 8.2. *Simple Regression Results between the Elections of 1896,
1960, and 2000, by State.*

Dependent Variable	% Democrat vote 1960	% Democrat vote 2000	% Democrat vote 2000
Independent Variable	% Democrat vote 1896	% Democrat vote 1960	% Democrat vote 1896
coef. (st. error)	−0.049 (0.046)	0.762 (0.198)	−0.266 (0.053)
t statistic	−1.06	3.84	−4.98
r^2	0.02	0.23	0.37

preponderance in the North or South. However, in 1852, the Democrat Pierce won 51 percent of the popular vote, but because of its distribution, the plurality nature of the electoral college gave him 254 electoral college seats out of 296. Similarly, in 1856, the Democrat, Buchanan, won 45 percent of the popular vote, and took 174 electoral college seats out of 296. Fremont, the candidate for the Republican Party, did well in the northern and western states, but still lost 62 electoral college votes in these states to Buchanan. The Whig, Fillmore, only won 8 electoral college votes in the border states.

Thus, between 1852 and 1860, the American political system was transformed by a fundamental "realignment" of electoral support. (See Schofield, 2006a: Table 5.1)

The sequence of presidential elections between 1964 and 1972 also has features of a political transformation, where race and civil rights again played a fundamental role. Except for President Eisenhower, Democrats had held the presidency since 1932. The 1964 election, in particular, had been a landslide in favor of Lyndon Johnson. By 1972, this imbalance in favor of the Democrats was completely transformed. The Republican candidate, Nixon, took 60 percent of the popular vote, while his Democrat opponent, McGovern, only won the electoral college votes of Massachusetts and Washington, D.C.

In between, of course, was the three-way election of 1968, between Humphrey, Nixon, and Wallace. In some respects, this election parallels the 1856 election between Buchanan, Fremont, and Fillmore. Nixon won about 56 percent of the vote in 1968, but Humphrey had pluralities in seven of the northern "core" states, as well as Washington D.C., Hawaii, and West Virginia. The Southern Democrat, Wallace, with only about 9 percent of the popular vote, won six of the states of the old Confederacy. (See Schofield, 2006a: 197–199, for the results of the elections of 1964 to 1972).

It is intuitively obvious that, in some sense, Humphrey and McGovern can be likened to Fremont and Lincoln, at least in terms of the "civil rights" policies that they represented, while Wallace and Goldwater resemble Breckinridge. It is equally clear that the elections of 1968 and 1972 were critical in some sense since they heralded a dramatic transformation of electoral politics that mirrored the changes from 1856 to 1860. In both cases, parties increasingly differentiated themselves on the basis of a civil rights dimension, rather than the economic dimension. This raises the question about why Republican policy concerns circa 1860 should be similar to Democrat positions circa 1972.

When Schattschneider (1960) first discussed the issue of electoral realignments, he framed it in terms of strategic calculations by party elites. For example, in discussing the election of 1896, Schattschneider argued that the Populist, William Jennings Bryan, instigated a radical agrarian movement which, in economic terms, could be interpreted as anti-capital. To counter this, the Republican Party became aggressively pro-capital. Because conservative Democrat interests feared populism, they revived the sectional cleavage of the Civil War era, and implicitly accepted the Republican dominance of the North. According to Schattschneider, this "system of 1896" contributed to the dominance of the Republican Party until the later transformation of politics brought about in the midst of the Depression by F. D. Roosevelt.

Recently, Mayhew (2000, 2002), has questioned the validity of the concepts of a "critical election" and of "electoral realignment" as presented by Schattschneider (1960) and other writers (Key, 1955; Burnham, 1970; Sundquist, 1973; Brady, 1988; Abramowitz and Saunders, 1998; etc.). Indeed, it is true that one fundamental difficulty with this literature on realignment is that its principal analytical mode has been macropolitical, depending on empirical analysis of shifting electoral preferences. In general, the literature has not provided a theoretical basis for understanding the changes in political preferences. Electoral choices are, after all, derived from perceptions of party positions. Schattschneider implied that these party, or candidate, positions are, themselves, strategically chosen in response to perceptions of the party elite of the social and economic beliefs of the electorate.

Formally speaking, this implies that politics is a "game." Individual voters have underlying preferences that can be defined in terms of policies, and they perceive parties in terms of these policies. Party strategists receive information of a general kind, and form conjectures about the nature of aggregate electoral response to policy messages. Finally, given the utilities that strategists have concerning the importance of policy, and of electoral success, they advise their candidates how best to construct "utility maximizing" strategies for the candidates.

In the previous chapters of this book we have proposed that the "game" takes place in a policy space X, say, which is used to characterize individual voter preferences. Each candidate j offers a policy position z_j to the electorate, chosen so as to maximize the candidate's utility. Typically, this utility is a function of the "expected" vote share of the candidate. It is also usually assumed that all candidates have similar utilities, in that each one prefers to win. While there are many variants of this model, the conclusion asserted by the mean voter theorem, for example, is that all candidates will adopt identical, or almost identical, policy positions in a small domain of the policy space, centrally located with respect to the distribution of voter-preferred points.

Any such formal model has little to contribute to an interpretation of critical elections or of electoral realignment. From the point of view of this literature, change can only come about through the transformation of electoral preferences by some exogenous shock. Even allowing for such shocks, the divergence of party positions observed by Schattschneider can only occur if perceptions of party strategists are radically different. This seems implausible.

In this chapter, we develop the model proposed in Chapter 7, in which rational political candidates attempt to balance the need for resources with the need to take winning policy positions. Voters choose among candidates for both policy and nonpolicy reasons. The policy motivations of voters pull candidates toward the center. However, centrist policies do little to earn the support of party activists, who are more ideologically extreme than the median voter, and who supply vital electoral resources. Candidates realize that the resources obtained from party activists make them more attractive, independent of policy positions. This implies that candidates must balance the attractiveness of activists' resources against the centrist tug of voters.

During most elections, there is a stable pattern of partisan cleavages and alliances. In such an environment, candidates can adopt equilibrium vote-maximizing positions that allow them to appeal to one set of partisan activists or another. But in certain critical elections, candidates realize that they can improve their electoral prospects by appealing to party activists on a new ideological dimension of politics. In the next section, we present a sketch of the possible repositioning of presidential candidates in the critical elections of 1860, 1896, 1932, and 1964–1968. We then develop an overview of the model to focus on the nature of activists' choices. In the final two sections, we draw some further inferences with a view to providing a deeper understanding of recent political alignments.

8.2   A BRIEF POLITICAL HISTORY, 1860–2000

Before introducing the model, it will be useful to offer schematic representations of the "critical elections" between 1860 and 1968 in order to illustrate what it is we hope to explain.

For Schattschneider, the 1896 election was based on an attack by Bryan against the sectional cleavage of the Civil War and the Reconstruction. It is therefore consistent with this argument that the contest between the Republican, McKinley, and the Populist Democrat, Bryan, was characterized by policy differences on a "capital" dimension. It is also convenient to refer to this dimension as an "economic" dimension. McKinley clearly favoured pro-business policies, while Bryan made a case for soft-money (bimetallism) and easy credit, both attractive to hard-pressed agrarian groups of the time. The sectional conflict of the Civil War era had obviously been over civil rights, so we can describe this earlier conflict in terms of a "social" dimension. Another way of characterizing this dimension is in terms of labour, since policies that restricted the civil rights of southern blacks had significant consequences for the utilization of labour. To give a schematic representation of the election of 1860, we may thus situate Lincoln and Breckinridge in opposition on the social dimension, as in Figure 8.1. The Whig, Bell, may be interpreted as standing for the commercial interests, particularly of the northeast. In contrast, Douglas represented the agrarian interests of the West, and his support came primarily from states such as Iowa, Ohio, Indiana, Illinois, and so forth.

With two distinct dimensions and four candidates, it is immediately obvious that the policy space could be divided into four quadrants. Voters who had conservative preferences on both social and economic axes we may simply term *Conservatives*. In the 1860 election, such voters would have commercial interests and be pro-slavery. On the other hand, voters with commercial interests, but who felt strongly that slavery should be restricted we call *Cosmopolitans*. Voters opposed to both slavery and commercial interests, we call *Liberals*. (This term is clearly something of a misnomer in 1860 since such voters would, at the time, probably be "free soil" farmers in states such as Illinois, etc.). Agrarian, anticommercial interests who were conservative on the social axis, we term *Populists*. For

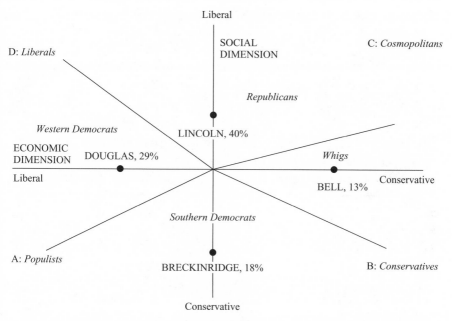

Figure 8.1. A schematic representation of the election of 1860 in a two-dimensional policy space.

convenience, we denote these four quadrants as A (Populists), B (Conservatives), C (Cosmopolitans), and D (Liberals).

The boundaries in Figure 8.1 indicate the division of the electorate into the supporters of the four presidential candidates in 1860. Figure 8.1 is intended to imply that each of the candidates in 1860 had to put together a coalition of divergent interests. Prior to 1852, the social or labour dimension played a relatively unimportant role, at least in presidential elections. How and why this dimension came into prominence in 1856 has been discussed at length elsewhere, using notions from social choice theory (Riker, 1982; Weingast, 1998; Schofield, 2006a). It is our contention that the economic and social dimensions are always relevant to some degree in U.S. political history. However, at various times, one or the other may become less important, for reasons we shall explore. After the Civil War, and the disappearance of the Whig Party (and of the distinct Western Democrat faction, represented by Douglas), political conflict between Republicans and Democrats focused on the social axis, as illustrated in Figure 8.2.

The horizontal "partisan cleavage line" is intended to separate the Republican and Democrat voters immediately after the Civil War. It is

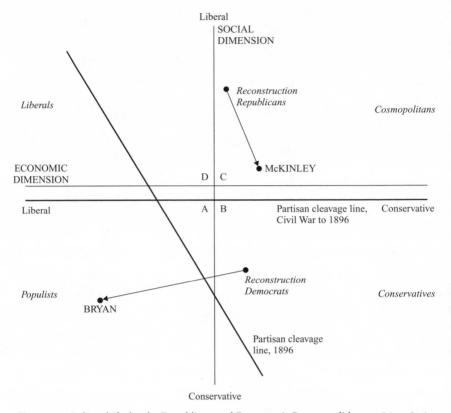

Figure 8.2. Policy shifts by the Republican and Democratic Party candidates, 1860–1896.

consistent with Schattschneider's interpretation of the election of 1896 that McKinley adopted a much more pro-business, or conservative, position on the economic axis, while Bryan took up a policy position in the populist quadrant (A). The 1896 partisan cleavage line in Figure 8.2 is used to distinguish between Republican and Populist Democrat voters. Figure 8.2 makes it intuitively clear why Bryan could not win the election. Moreover, support for conservative economic policies would lead to Republican predominance. As Schattschneider (1960: 85) observed, "the Democrat party carried only about an average of two states (outside of southern and border states) between 1896 and 1932." The increasing "degree of competition" between Democrat and Republican parties in 1932 can be represented by the positioning of F. D. Roosevelt and Hoover near the economic axis, as in Figure 8.3.

Note that the successful Roosevelt coalition comprised what we have called Populists and Liberals opposed to Conservatives and Cosmoplitans.

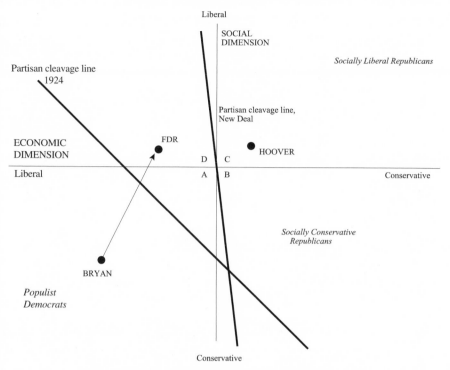

Figure 8.3. Policy shifts by the Democratic Party *circa* 1932.

The standard formal model (Downs, 1957) has tended to generalize from the location of party positions in the period from 1932 to 1960 and to infer that political competition is primarily based on the economic axis, and involves the coalition {A,D} against {B,C}. However, as Carmines and Stimson (1989) have analyzed in great detail, "race" (or "policy" on the social dimension) has become increasingly important since about 1960. Indeed, they present data to suggest that Republicans in the Senate tended to vote in a more liberal fashion on racial issues than Democrats prior to 1965.

Although L. B. Johnson may have had many of the characteristics of a Southern Democrat while he was Senate leader, he introduced, while President, the major policy transformation of the Great Society. Figure 8.4 presents a plausible policy position for Johnson in 1964, as well as presidential candidate positions for the period 1964 to 1980. The candidate positions for the elections of 1968 and 1976 are compatible with the empirical work of Poole and Rosenthal (1984: Figs 1, 3), while the positions

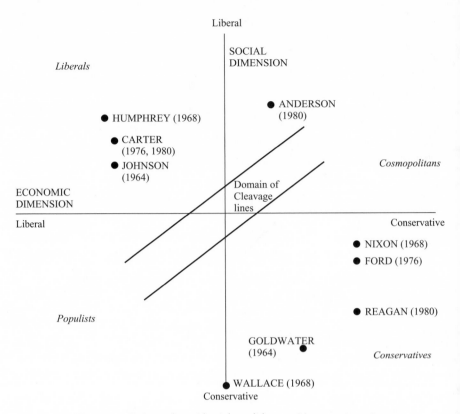

Figure 8.4. Estimated presidential candidate positions, 1964–1980.

for the elections of 1964 and 1980 are based on our analyses discussed below.

A number of comments are necessary to understand the significance of this figure. As in the previous two figures, a partisan cleavage line can be drawn in the policy space for each election, determined by the positions of the two principal presidential candidates. What we denote as the "Domain of Cleavage lines" in Figure 8.4 includes these partisan cleavage lines for the various elections. As our analysis (presented in Figure 8.5 below) suggests, the cleavage line for the 1964 election would fall below and to the right of the origin. Since the origin is at the mean of voter bliss points, this is meant to represent Johnson's successful candidacy for President.

The standard spatial model of candidate positioning implies that attempts by candidates to maximize votes draws them into the electoral center. It is apparent, however, that the estimates of candidate positions, presented in Figure 8.4, contradict this inference. Indeed, the positioning of Republican and Democrat candidates in Figure 8.4 suggests that voters who can be described as Cosmopolitan (with preferences in the policy domain C) or Populists (in domain A) may find it difficult to choose between the candidates.

In the next section, we examine the standard spatial model to determine the basis for this inference, and then consider in somewhat more detail how empirical analysis suggests how the standard spatial model may be adapted to better account for candidate behavior. The principal goal of our modified activist voter model of elections is to provide the foundation for a theory of dynamic electoral change that can provide a formal account of the inferred transformation or "rotation" in the policy space presented in Figures 8.1 through 8.4.

8.3   MODELS OF VOTING AND CANDIDATE STRATEGY

As we have discussed in the previous chapters, the formal model of voting assumes that voter utility is given by the expression

$$\mathbf{u}_i(x_i, \mathbf{z}) = (u_{i1}(x_i, z_1), \ldots, u_{ip}(x_i, z_p)) \in \mathbb{R}^p. \tag{8.1}$$

Here, $\mathbf{z} = (z_1, \ldots, z_p)$ is the vector of strategies of the set P of political agents (candidates, parties, etc.). The point z_j is the position of candidate j in the space X. Previously we assumed that

$$u_{ij}(x_i, z_j) = \lambda_j - A_{ij}(x_i, z_j) + \theta_j^{\mathrm{T}} \eta_i + \varepsilon_j, \tag{8.2}$$

where A_{ij} was the symmetric Euclidean metric and $\theta_j^{\mathrm{T}} \eta_i$ gave the effect of the sociodemographic characteristics of voter i on vote probabilities.

As we have seen, both the MNL and MNP models typically provide an excellent account of voter choice. For example, the MNL two-dimensional voter model of Poole and Rosenthal (1984) for the 1968 and 1976 elections had success rates for voter choice of over 60 percent. Their estimates of the 1968 and 1976 candidate locations closely correspond to the positions of candidates indicated in Figure 8.4. As Poole and Rosenthal (1984: 287) suggest, "the second dimension captures the traditional identification of southern conservatives with the Democratic party."

Our own analyses, presented in Figures 8.5 and 8.6, suggest that the second dimension is, in fact, a long-term factor in U.S. elections. Each circle in these figures represents the ideal point of a voter in a factor space derived from the National Election Surveys of 1964 and 1980, respectively.

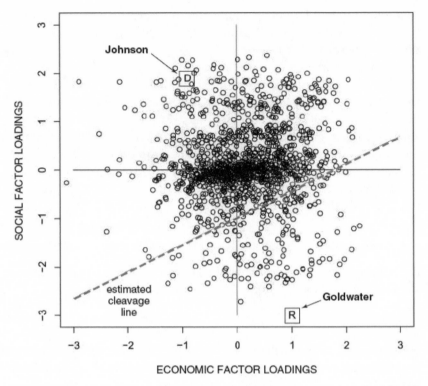

Figure 8.5. The two-dimensional factor space, with voter positions and Johnson's and Goldwater's respective policy positions in 1964, with linear estimated probability vote functions (log likelihood = −617).

A standard confirmatory factor analysis was used to estimate the factor space. Standard hypothesis tests suggest that a two-factor model was appropriate. A pure linear spatial probit model was used to estimate the probability $\rho_{i,dem}$ that a voter i would choose the Democratic candidate. Thus, instead of basing the model on voter utility based on Euclidean distance, as in earlier chapters, we assumed that

$$\rho_{i,dem} = \lambda_{dem} + ax_i + by_i, \qquad (8.3)$$

where (x_i, y_i) are the coordinates of the ideal point of voter i in the two dimensions.

The "estimated cleavage lines" in these two figures gives the boundary $\rho_{i,dem} = \frac{1}{2}$. (North of this line, the voters choose the Democratic candidate, and south they choose the Republican.) The cleavage lines were estimated using a probit model, with the factor scores on each dimension used as

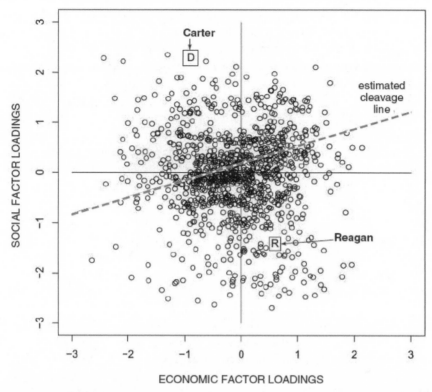

Figure 8.6. The two-dimensional factor space, with voter positions and Carter's and Reagan's respective policy positions in 1980, with linear estimated probability vote functions (log likelihood = −372).

covariates. In both the 1964 and 1980 models, the estimated coefficients were highly statistically significant ($p < 0.001$ in all cases). Both models classify reasonably well; the McKelvey and Zavoina R^2 for 1964 is 0.2000 and for 1980 is 0.465. (See Schofield, Miller and Martin, 2003, for further details.) Given the estimated probabilities, it is possible to infer the location of the two candidates. For example, for 1964, the symbol R is used to indicate our estimation of the position of Goldwater and D that of Johnson. Comparing the results for 1964 and 1980 suggests that Carter was just as "liberal" on economic issues as was Johnson, but slightly more liberal on social issues. Notice that in 1964, the cleavage line $\rho_{i,dem} = \frac{1}{2}$ passes "south" of the origin, so that a clear majority of the voter sample is assigned a probability greater than $\frac{1}{2}$ of voting for Johnson. In contrast, in 1980, the cleavage line passes "north" of the origin, giving Reagan the advantage.

In 1964, the total electoral variance on the two axes was 1.28, while in 1980 the variance was very similar at 1.365. Since the linear probability model is different from the one used in our previous analyses, we cannot use the convergence coefficient directly. In terms of the linear probit model, it is evident that Goldwater in 1964 and Carter in 1980 had lower exogenous valences than their respective competitors. The above analyses suggest that all candidates were indeed positioned some distance from the electoral origin.

Figures 8.5 and 8.6 buttress the remark made by Poole and Rosenthal (1984: 288) that their analysis "is at variance with simple spatial theories which hold that the candidates should converge to a point in the center of the [electoral] distribution" (namely, the origin in Figures 8.5 and 8.6). Poole and Rosenthal suggest that this "party stability," of divergent candidate locations, is the result of the need of candidates to appeal to a support group to be nominated. Our earlier results suggest that the divergent positions were consistent with vote maximization.

To see this, note that in their estimation of the vote function for 1968, the intercept, or valence λ for Humphrey and Nixon was 3.416, while for Wallace, it was 7.515. Moreover, the coefficient β was 5.260 for Humphrey and Nixon, but 7.842 for Wallace. In other words, the underlying valence, or innate attractiveness of Wallace was high, but voter support dropped rapidly as the distance between the voter ideal point and the Wallace position increased. In their analysis of the 1980 election, the β coefficient for the third independent, National Union candidate, John Anderson, was 1.541. Anderson took only 6.6 percent of the national vote, and this is reflected in his estimated λ coefficient of -0.19, in contrast to $\lambda = 3.907$ for Carter and Reagan.

We now develop the model proposed in Chapter 7, where valence comprises two components. For candidate j, there is an "innate" or exogenous valence whose distribution is characterized by the stochastic error term ε_j. As before, the expectation of the valence term for candidate j is identified with the average valence λ_j, of j in the electorate. The second component, μ_j, is affected by the money and time that activists make available to candidate j. Essentially, this means that this second valence component μ_j is a function of the policy choices of candidates. We can ignore the exogenous valence terms since they have been examined above. Concentrating on activist valence gives the following expression for voter utility:

$$u_{ij}(x_i, z_j) = \mu_j(z_j) - A_{ij}(x_i, z_j) + \varepsilon_j. \tag{8.4}$$

For convenience, in the discussion below we refer to the effect of candidate strategies on the expected vote-share function $\mathcal{E}_j$, through change in $\mu_j(z_j)$, as the *valence* component of the vote. Change in $\mathcal{E}_j$ through the effect on the policy distance measure $A_{ij}(x_i, z_j)$ we refer to as the *nonvalence*, or *policy* component. We discuss this "activist" model in the next section. One important modification of the pure spatial model that we make is that the salience of different policy dimensions varies among the electorate. More precisely, we assume that

$$A_{ij}(x_i, z_j) = ||x_i - z_j||_i^2. \tag{8.5}$$

Here, $||\cdots||_i$ is an "ellipsoidal" norm giving a metric whose coefficients depend on x_i. We make this assumption clearer in the following section, where we assume that activists, motivated primarily by one policy dimension or the other, may choose to donate resources that increase their candidate's valence. We argue that it is the candidate's attempt to position himself with respect to different types of activists that accounts for the partisan realignment.

8.4   A JOINT MODEL OF ACTIVISTS AND VOTERS

We adapt a model of activist support first offered by Aldrich (1983a,b) and introduced in the previous chapter.

Essentially the model is a dynamic one based on the willingness of voters to provide support to a candidate. Given current candidate strategies **z** let

$$C(\mathbf{z}) = (C_1(\mathbf{z}), \ldots, C_p(\mathbf{z})) \tag{8.6}$$

be the current level of support to the various candidates. The candidates deploy their resources, via television, and other media, and this has an effect on the vector $\mu(\mathbf{z}) = (\mu_1(z_1), \ldots, \mu_p(z_p))$ of candidate-dependent valences. We assume that each μ_j is in fact a function of $C_j(z_j)$.

At this point, a voter i may choose to add his own contribution c_{ij} to candidate j as long as

$$c_{ij} < \mu_j(z_j) - A_{ij}(x_i, z_j) + \varepsilon_j. \tag{8.7}$$

The total contributions to candidate j is then Σc_{ij}. Aldrich considered an equilibrium of this dynamic process between two candidates, 1 and 2, where the candidate's position, z_j, was defined to be the mean of the ideal points of all activists who supported this candidate. The existence

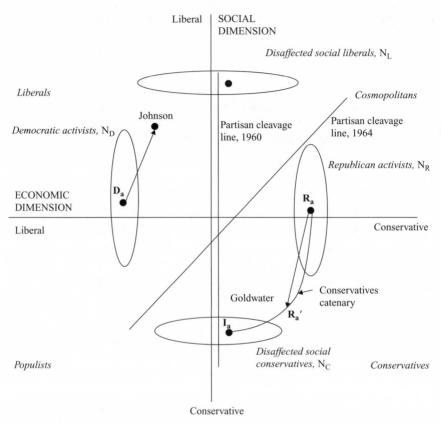

Figure 8.7. Illustration of vote-maximizing positions for a Republican presidential candidate (Goldwater) facing a Democratic candidate (Johnson).

of such a candidate equilibrium can be seen most easily with reference to Figure 8.7. (This figure is adapted from Miller and Schofield, 2003.)

Consider a group of Republican "economic" activists. The Republican candidate j is situated at the position $R_a = (x_j, y_j)$, while the activist has an ideal point (s_i, t_i). Then the activist's utility at a position (x, y) given by

$$u_{ij}((s_i, t_i), (x, y)) = \mu_j(z_j) - A_{ij}((s_i, t_i), (x, y)), \qquad (8.8)$$

where

$$A_{ij}((s_i, t_i), (x, y)) = \frac{(x - s_i)^2}{a^2} - \frac{(y - t_i)^2}{b^2} \qquad (8.9)$$

is induced from an ellipsoid metric. The activist contributes some amount, $c_{ij} < u_{ij}((s_i, t_i), (x_j, y_j))$, to the Republican candidate.

Because this activist is most concerned about economic issues, it is natural to assume that $a < b$. If the activist actually had an ideal point $(s_i, t_i) = R_a$, then his indifference curve would be given by the "ellipsoid" centered at R_a, say. Depending on various parameters, there will exist a domain N_R, say, in X, with the property that every voter whose ideal point (s_i, t_i) belongs to N_R is a contributor to the Republican candidate. For purposes of illustration, we may take N_R to be represented by the "ellipsoid" of ideal points centered on R_a, as in Figure 8.7. It is natural to assume that there is an opposing Democratic candidate, whose position is at D_a, say, and an opposing set N_D of Democratic activists whose ideal points belong to a similar set but are centered on D_a. Aldrich showed, essentially, that these conditions could be satisfied, such that R_a was given by the mean point of the set N_R, while D_a was the mean of the set N_D. It is obvious that for such an activist equilibrium to exist, it is necessary that each μ_j, regarded as a function of campaign contributions, is concave (or has diminishing returns) in contributions to candidate j. (A more refined model could naturally include voter income.)

As Figure 8.7 indicates, a typical socially conservative voter would regard Democrat and Republican candidates as equally unattractive, and tend to be indifferent. Let us now suppose that such a voter, g, has bliss point (s_g, t_g), say, near the position I_a, with utility function

$$u_{gj}((s_g, t_g), (x, y)) = \mu_j(z_j) - \left(\frac{(x - s_g)^2}{e^2} + \frac{(y - t_g)^2}{f^2} \right). \quad (8.10)$$

Let N_C be the set of such "disaffected" social conservatives who would be willing to contribute to a candidate as long as this candidate adopted a policy position close to $I_a = (x_k, y_k)$. We suggest that such social conservatives regard social policy to be of greater significance and so $e > f$ in this equation. Unlike Aldrich, we now suppose that the Republican candidate adopts a position, not at the position R_a, but at some compromise position R_a' between R_a and I_a. It is easy to demonstrate that the "contact curve" between the point (s_i, t_i) and the point (s_g, t_g) is given by the equation

$$\frac{(y - t_i)}{(x - s_i)} = S \frac{(y - t_g)}{(x - s_g)}, \quad (8.11)$$

where

$$S = \frac{b^2}{a^2} \frac{e^2}{f^2}. \quad (8.12)$$

This contract curve between Republican economic activists and disaffected social activists is labeled the "Conservatives catenary" in Figure 8.7. If the candidate moves on this catenary then the resulting number of activists will be of the order of $q N_R + (1 - q) N_C$, where q is some constant (<1) dependent on the position taken by the candidate. Because of the asymmetry involved, the total number of activists may increase, thus increasing overall contributions to the Republican candidate. Clearly, there are plausible conditions under which μ_{rep} increases as a result of such a move, thus potentially increasing the vote share of the Republican candidate.

Determination of existence of a candidate PNE in this modified model depends, as before, on continuity and concavity of the candidate utility (or vote-share) functions $\{U_j\}$. While each U_j will be a function of $\mathbf{z}$, its dependence on $\mathbf{z}$ will be more complex than the simple relationship implicit in the model we have studied above. It is important to note that this proposed model involves differing voter utility functions. To preserve continuity of voter response, it is necessary that the coefficients of voter policy loss vary continuously with the voter-preferred policy. With these assumptions, candidate vote-share functions $\{U_j\}$ will be continuous in candidate strategies. Concavity of the candidate utility functions and thus existence of PNE will then follow from assumptions about the concavity of the activist valence functions. It is worth emphasizing that the greater the relative saliencies, b/a and e/f, the greater will be S and thus, the more significant will be the attraction of using activist groups to enhance electoral support.

Chapter 3 has shown that LNE will generally exist, and will be locally isolated, for almost all games of the kind considered here, as long as the game is smooth. As we have seen in the chapter on Britain, this allows us to assume that equilibria do exist in these complex activist games.

Computation of LNE will generally depend on the factors we have specified: the elasticity of response of the disaffected, potential activists, and the effect of contributions on the valence functions $\{\mu_j\}$. If the contribution term is very significant, then adopting a position to maximize contributions is clearly rational. For example, let us use R and D to denote the positions adopted by the two candidates (as in Figure 8.7). Then it is, in principle, possible to estimate the contributions and thus the valence function. As the results of Chapter 7 indicated, a move by either candidate toward the origin will increase the *nonvalence* component of the electoral vote, but at the same time, decrease contributions, and thus decrease the *valence* component of the vote. It is the optimal balance of valence and nonvalence vote components that is encapsulated in the notion of LNE.

8.5 THE LOGIC OF VOTE MAXIMIZATION

The simple probabilistic voter model suggests that it is relatively easy for voters to identify attractive candidates, and for candidates to learn about voter response (McKelvey and Ordeshook, 1985). For candidates, the use of opinion polls can be used to indicate how small changes in policy objectives should affect support. The earlier theories of Hinich (1977) and Enelow and Hinich (1984) mentioned in Chapter 3 argued that candidates will gain most electoral support at the centre. The fact that candidates do not act in this way suggests that these theories need serious revision. One extreme response is to propose that voter support is independent of candidate declarations. As suggested before, this is equivalent to supposing that the spatial component of the model is irrelevant. Indeed, earlier sociological or psychological models (Berelson, Lazerfield, and McPhee, 1954; Campbell et al., 1960) essentially made this assumption. The sociological model regarded voter choice simply as a function of "party identification." It is clear enough that if one fundamental cleavage is dominant, and party candidates adopt fixed positions on this cleavage (as in Figure 8.7) then voters will find candidate choice relatively easy. Over a sequence of elections, it is plausible to believe that voters will tend to identify with one party or the other. From one election to another, voter saliencies will vary, and this will affect activist support, and thus candidate vote shares. It is this phenomenon that Aldrich's activist model analyzed (Aldrich, 1983a,b; Aldrich and McGinnis, 1989; Aldrich, 1995). If we are correct in our interpretation of U.S. electoral politics, then an optimal response by a Democrat candidate to the socially conservative Republican position is to adopt a more economically centrist position. It is possible that Clinton's successes in 1992 and 1996 were a results of such a strategy.

Over the years there will be slow transformations in the principal electoral cleavage, and it is the change from one cleavage, or electorally perceived dimension, to another that constitutes an electoral "realignment."

The beginning of the last transformation of the principal cleavage in U.S. politics from an economic dimension to a social, or civil rights, dimension is generally understood to have been triggered by the Civil Rights Act of 1964 (Huckfeldt and Kohfeld, 1989; Edsall and Edsall, 1991; Mann, 1996). This political event eventually brought about the electoral shifts that we described earlier. The evidence suggests that the degree of party identification dropped from 1964 to 1980 (from about 35 percent of the electorate to 20 percent: see Clarke and Stewart, 1998). During the period from 1960 to 1972, attitudes of Democrat and Republican activists became increasingly polarized over civil rights issues (Carmines and Stimson, 1989). There is therefore no doubt that both voter perceptions and activist attitudes began to change rapidly in the 1960s. The model presented in the previous section suggests that these changes were due to strategic calculations on the part of candidates. To amplify this inference, let us consider how such calculations can be made.

Unlike candidate choice in the simple spatial model, strategic calculation in the proposed activist model is dependent on uncertain outcomes. Consider the strategy of L. B. Johnson to push through the Civil Rights Act of 1964. Clearly, it appealed to those voters designated "disaffected social liberals" in Figure 8.7. The argument presented above suggests that the total number of Democrat activists could increase as a consequence of this policy initiative. The resources made available could, moreover, increase Johnson's overall valence. At the same time, voters, particularly in the Southern states, who traditionally identified with the Democrat party, would suffer a utility loss. Such disaffected social conservatives would then more readily switch to the Republican party. However, the tradeoff between the valence and policy components of voter response is intrinsically difficult to make. For L. B. Johnson, the calculation may well have been that the Democrat coalition of southern social conservatives and economic liberals was unstable. A second, but contradictory, possibility, apparent from 1957 onwards, was that the Republican Party could also move to attract social liberals and create a winning coalition. The actions undertaken by Johnson, first as leader of the Senate in the late 1950s, and then as President after J. F. Kennedy's assassination in 1963, all suggest that he was extremely shrewd in estimating electoral and congressional support, but also capable of extreme risktaking. In 1957, for example, he persuaded the Southern Democratic senators not to deploy their traditional filibuster, but to accept the Voting Rights Bill (Caro, 2002). Indeed, Johnson's maneuvers in the Senate can be characterized as "heresthetic" (to use the term invented by Riker [1982]).

After Kennedy was elected President in 1960 (by a very narrow margin of victory against Nixon), he delayed sending a Civil Rights Bill to Congress, precisely because of the possible effect on the South. To push through the Civil Rights Act in July 1964, Johnson effectively created, with Hubert Humphrey's support, an unstable coalition of liberal Northern

Democrats and moderate Republicans, with sufficient votes in the Senate to effect "cloture," to block the southern Democratic filibusters (Branch, 1998). This was the first time since Reconstruction that the southern veto was overwhelmed. The danger for Johnson in the election of 1964 was that a Republican candidate could make use of the fact of Republican Party support for civil rights to attract disaffected social liberals. Traditional Republican Party activists were thus in an electoral dilemma, but resolved it by choosing the southern social conservative, Goldwater.

Once L. B. Johnson initiated the policy transformation, the strategic calculation of Republican candidates, whether Nixon, Ford, Reagan, or Bush, became much easier. The knowledge of the existence of a set of disaffected social conservatives meant that such voters would appear increasingly attractive to Republican candidates. This in turn created an electoral dilemma for Democrats, as they attempted to maintain support of both economic and social liberals. As economic competition decreased in importance and class became less relevant as an indicator of voter choice, activist support for Democrat candidates from the remnant of the New Deal coalition would fall. One possible response for a Democrat would be to seek new potential activists among the Cosmopolitans—the economically conservative social liberals. Obviously, this would create conflict within the Democrat Party elite. A natural response by the Republican Party was to move their policy choices into quadrant A, the Populist domain. President G. W. Bush's initiatives in 2002, over protection for the steel industry and farm subsidies, indicate that this could, indeed, be his strategy. Support for G. W. Bush in the 2004 election would seem to support this hypothesis. (See also Fiorina, 2005.)

We suggest that the initial policy move by Johnson in 1964 had a basis in rational electoral calculation. Obviously the model proposed here ignores the element of attitude to risk, and this clearly must have been relevant to Johnson's motivation, so this feature is worth adding to the model. At a general level it does appear that the resulting moves and countermoves by Democrat and Republican candidates were in local equilibrium at each election, while the equilibria themselves appear to have slowly changed over the last forty years. We could say that the entire process of political realignment over this period was in "dynamic equilibrium."

8.6 DYNAMIC LOCAL EQUILIBRIA

Under plurality rule, or winner-takes-all electoral methods, it is obvious that presidential candidates, if they hope to win, must attempt to create majority coalitions of disparate interests (Schlesinger, 1994). The historical record suggests that stable equilibria can occur, but these will be based on one or the other of the two principal cleavages—economic and social—that characterize beliefs in the society. Any such equilibrium, by definition, will create two groups of disaffected, and opposed, voters. Either one of these groups of voters can become a political force once they realize their potential. This depends, of course, on their ability to successfully signal to a candidate, such as L. B. Johnson, that they would be willing to contribute time and money. Although we have suggested that an equilibrium will exist in this activist-voter model, we have not attempted an analysis of the complexities of the signaling game between possible presidential candidates and potential activists.

It should also be evident, from the structure of the activist model presented here, that the willingness of voters to become activists depend on the salience ratios (denoted by b/a and e/f for the economically and socially concerned voters, respectively). These ratios may change within the electorate as a result of exogenous shocks. In turn, this will affect the activist response to candidate positions and thus the positional valences of the candidates. The standard spatial model has principally depended on using data based on voter-preferred policies to estimate electoral support. To estimate the more complex activist model proposed here, it would be necessary to explore the variation of cleavage saliencies within the electorate.

Although we still view the political process as a "game" involving rational utility–maximizing voters and candidates, we suggest that this game is much more complex than previous models have suggested. We believe that the model proposed here can be developed so as to offer a more empirically relevant theory of electoral dynamics.

A task that still remains is to develop a macropolitical account of the long run transformations that can be observed in U.S. politics. We can only offer a very tentative outline of such a theory at present. We have suggested above that these electoral changes are based on new configurations of "factor" coalitions, where *factor* refers to the classic dimensions of capital, labor, and land power. In the 1896 election, the twenty-two states that voted for the Republican, McKinley, all had significant industrial working class populations. Because of the growth of the economic power of the United States, there existed a natural expansionist coalition based on capital and industrial labor (Rogowski, 1989). The hard-money policy of the Republicans naturally affected the agrarian interests (who tended to be indebted), as argued by Bardo and Rockoff (1996). This is an old theme in U.S. politics (Beard, 1913). The twenty-three states that voted for the Populist-Democrat, Bryan, were all basically agrarian but lacked sufficient population and electoral college votes to upset the capital–labor coalition.

In the 1930s, economic decline broke the capital–industrial labor coalition. By the 1960s, the Democrat coalition comprised half of Bryan's southern Populist states and half of McKinley's commercial Republican coalition. By the 2000 election, the transformation was complete. The remainder of Bryan's coalition became Republican, and the remainder of McKinley's became Democrat. The decline of agriculture and the growth of modern industries in the southern and western states gave them the population and electoral college votes just sufficient for a Republican presidential victory. Clearly, the knife-edge result of the 2000 election indicates that voters in states such as Wisconsin, Michigan, Minnesota, Pennsylvania, and Iowa could be persuaded by G. W. Bush's populist strategies to join the Republican activist coalition. Such continuing transformation maintains the dynamic equilibrium of U.S. politics.

8.7 APPENDICES

(i) The Civil Rights Act.
   Date: 02 JUL 64
   88th Congress, H. R. 7152
   An Act

To enforce the constitutional right to vote, to confer jurisdiction upon the district courts of the United States to provide injunctive relief against discrimination in public accommodations, to authorize the Attorney General to institute suits to protect constitutional rights in public facilities and public education, to extend the Commission on Civil Rights, to prevent discrimination in federally assisted programs, to establish a Commission on Equal Employment Opportunity, and for other purposes.

Be it enacted by the Senate and House of Representatives of the United States of America in Congress assembled, That this Act may be cited as the "Civil Rights Act of 1964."

(ii) Amendment XIV of the Constitution.

Section 1. All persons born or naturalized in the United States and subject to the jurisdiction thereof, are citizens of the United States and of the State wherein they reside. No State shall make or enforce any law which shall abridge the privileges or immunities of citizens of the United States; nor shall any State deprive any person of life, liberty, or property, without due process of law; nor deny to any person within its jurisdiction the equal protection of the laws.

Section 2. Representatives shall be apportioned among the several States according to their respective numbers, counting the whole number of persons in each State, excluding Indians not taxed. But when the right to vote at any election for the choice of electors for President and Vice President of the United States, Representatives in Congress, the Executive and Judicial officers of a State, or the members of the Legislature thereof, is denied to any of the male inhabitants of such State, being twenty-one years of age, and citizens of the United States, or in any way abridged, except for participation in rebellion, or other crime, the basis of representation therein shall be reduced in the proportion which the number of such male citizens shall bear to the whole number of male citizens twenty-one years of age in such State.

Section 3. No person shall be a Senator or Representative in Congress, or elector of President and Vice President, or hold any office, civil or military, under the United States, or under any State, who, having previously taken an oath, as a member of Congress, or as an officer of the United States, or as a member of any State legislature, or as an executive or judicial officer of any State, to support the Constitution of the United States, shall have engaged in insurrection or rebellion against the same, or given aid or comfort to the enemies thereof. But Congress may by a vote of two-thirds of each House, remove such disability.

Section 4. The validity of the public debt of the United States, authorized by law, including debts incurred for payment of pensions and bounties for services in suppressing insurrection or rebellion, shall not be questioned. But neither the United States nor any State shall assume or pay any debt or obligation incurred in aid of insurrection or rebellion against the United States, or any claim for the loss or emancipation of any slave; but all such debts, obligations and claims shall be held illegal and void.

Section 5. The Congress shall have power to enforce, by appropriate legislation, the provisions of this article.

The Fourteenth Amendment of the Constitution was passed by the House and Senate on the 8th of June and the 13th of June, 1866.

9

Concluding Remarks

9.1 ASSESSMENT OF THE MODEL

We briefly conclude with an assessment of the model presented in this book, together with some remarks on how the work can be extended.

The essence of democracy is that voters respond to the past acts and promises of party leaders. It has been traditional to use manifestos as measures of promises, and to gauge the distance between the preferred policy of the voter and the promise of the party leader as the "disutility" of the voter. In addition, of course, the voter may not trust the party leader. Valence is one very simple way to model the judgment of the voter about the degree to which the party leader can be trusted. This addition to the standard spatial model of voting changes one of the principal results of the model, namely the mean voter theorem. As the main theorem of Chapter 3 shows, it is no longer necessarily the case that all parties will converge to an electoral center. Instead, each election will be characterized by a convergence coefficient. Empirical analysis associated with the election can be used to give a list of valence coefficients for each of the party leaders. If the valences are similar, then the convergence coefficient will be low, and symmetry will induce all parties to converge to the center.

The formal model shows that this convergence coefficient is an increasing function of the valence differences, the electoral variance, and the spatial parameter. Moreover, with many parties with differing valences, the coefficient will tend to be high. When the coefficient exceeds the dimension of the policy space, then the lowest-valence party will vacate the electoral mean in order to increase its vote share. One way to interpret this finding is that in such a circumstance the low-valence party can guarantee itself more votes by seeking the electoral periphery rather than by competing directly with high-valence parties.

It is often thought that radical parties gain few votes because they are radical. The theory presented here suggests that when policy is important, and when electoral preferences are heterogeneous, then only parties that are generally trusted by the electorate can approach the electoral center. The movement away from the electoral center by a low-valence party will be determined by the principal component of the electoral distribution. Asymmetry in the nature of electoral preferences will result in a principal electoral dimension, and it is this dimension that is the "eigenspace" for a low-valence party. Once the lowest-valence party leaves the electoral mean, then so will others. In general, all parties will adopt positions on the principal component of the voter distribution, but higher-valence parties will choose positions nearer the mean.

This stochastic spatial model does not specify whether parties move up or down the principal electoral component. The theory assumes that the final vector of party positions is in "local equilibrium." Given a system of electoral parameters, there may be multiple local equilibria. Nonetheless, it is plausible that the particular local equilibrium that occurs is "path dependent." That is, the previous historical situation generates a set of political niches wherin parties typically reside. Notice that the differing local equilibria may be associated with very different political configurations. It may also be the case that small changes in the electoral parameters can dramatically transform the local political equilibrium, destroying political niches and leading to the creation of new parties and new niches.

9.2 PROPORTIONAL REPRESENTATION

When the electoral system is based on some form of proportional representation, it is generally impossible for one party to gain a majority. Because coalitions involve compromise over policy, rational party principals should nominate leaders for the party who are in a position to bargain effectively with other party leaders. For low-valence parties occupying niches far from the electoral center, this motivation may cause the party elite to consider party leaders who have preferred positions that are even more radical than the vote-maximizing position. For high-valence parties, whose niches are close to the electoral center, there is an added centripetal tendency. If the party can position itself centrally and gain enough seats to be dominant, then it can occupy the "structurally stable core" position, which will allow it, under some circumstances, to control government, and perhaps to construct a minority government. Small changes in electoral support can therefore make a big difference whether a party is dominant or not.

9.2.1 *The Election of September 2005 in Germany*

Though we have not considered a formal model of German elections, the recent election in Germany on September 18, 2005, can be used to illustrate some of the logic of coalition. The CDU/CSU (Christian Democrats, under Merkel) took 35.2 percent of the popular vote (and 225 seats in the 613-seat Bundestag). The SPD (Social Democrats, led by Schroeder) took 34.3 percent (and 222 seats) against 8.1 percent (and 51 seats) for the Greens, 8.7 percent (and 54 seats) for the Left Party, including PDS (Party for Democratic Socialism), and 9.8 percent (with 61 seats) for the FDP (Free Democrats). The previous SPD–Green coalition had 47.1 percent of the vote but 306 seats out of 603 in the Bundestag (slightly more than proportional because the PDS had failed to gain 5 percent of the vote). The CDU–CSU–FDP coalition thus had 286 seats (not a majority), while the SPD–Green coalition had 273 seats. Figure 9.1 suggests that the PDS lies on a separate axis (labelled East/West) from the other four parties. In which case it is obvious that the PDS (mostly excommunists from East Germany) would be crucial in creating a majority with either the SPD–Green or the CDU–CSU–FDP coalition. It may be able to select a coalition partner and effectively pivot in the coalition game. Notice that there are at least three very different coalitions that can come into being, and these together define the *heart* of the Bundestag, namely the convex hull of the party positions, as in Figure 9.1.

For multiparty polities in which there is no majority party, we have argued that there are essentially two qualitatively different post-election decisive structures. One is where Parliament is characterized by a structurally stable core, or, in more traditional terms, a central dominant party. The second is one in which no such dominant core party emerges and the core of the legislature is empty. In the case of a structurally stable core, the policy that Parliament is expected to implement is the policy position of the dominant party. If the core is empty, the policy that Parliament will adopt is bound to shift constantly but remain within what we termed the *heart* of Parliament. If Figure 9.1 gives an approximate estimate of party positions after the September 2005 election in Germany, then there is obviously no core party. In the full theory of coalition formation presented in Chapter 3, we suggest that, in the absense of a core, the *cheapest minimal winning* coalition will tend to form, where this term refers to the

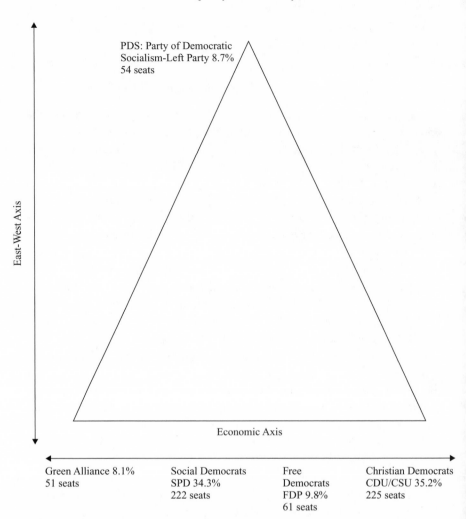

Figure 9.1. Schematic representation of party positions in the Bundestag in Germany, September 2005.

"smallest average policy distance" between the coalition members. The CDU-SPD coalition that finally formed in November, 2005, is an example of such a coalition.

9.2.2 *Recent Changes in the Israel Knesset*

We may also make some comments with regard to recent changes in Israel. Figure 9.2 provides a schematic representation of the 2003 Knesset

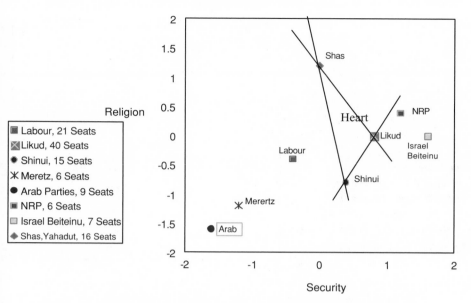

Figure 9.2. A schematic representation of the configuration of the Knesset in 2003.

based on the party positions estimated in Chapter 3 and seat allocations given in Table 2.1. The figure shows Labour with 21 seats, after Am Ehad, with 2 seats, joined Labour in 2003, while Likud has 40 seats after being joined by Olim, with 2 seats. Although Barak, of Labour, became Prime Minister in 1999, he was defeated by Ariel Sharon, of Likud, in the election for prime minister in 2000. The set denoted the heart in this figure represents the coalition possibilities open to Sharon after 2003.

The figure can be used to understand the consequences after Sharon seemingly changed his policy on the security issue in August, 2005, by pulling out of the Gaza Strip. First, the Likud party reacted strongly against this change in policy. In the first week of November, 2005, Amir Peretz, a union activist, and leader of Am Ehad, won the election for leader of the Labour Party. This event can be seen as an illustration of the argument in Chapters 7 and 8 above, where we suggest that a party that fails to attract voters because of a low relative valence will eventually be controlled by party activists. From this perspective, the low valence of Labour vis-à-vis Sharon was the reason the Labour members chose Peretz.

Many observers regarded the change in the leadership of Labour as a critical transformation in the political map of Israel. However, as Figure 9.3 suggests, the shift to the left by Labour under Peretz had no effect

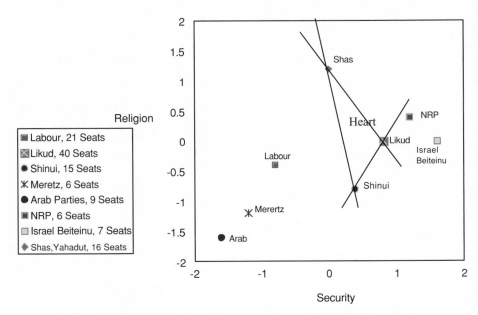

Figure 9.3. The configuration of the Knesset after Peretz becomes leader of Labour.

on the heart of the Knesset. According to our model, there would be no effect on party bargaining.

However, the move by Labour did have indirect consequence. In a highly publicized move, Sharon left the Likud Party and signaled a strong move to the left by allying with Shimon Peres, the former leader of Labour and the author of the Oslo accords. Together these two, with a number of other senior Labour Party members, formed the new party, *Kadima* ("Forward"). This move positioned Sharon at the origin of the electoral space at (0,0) as shown in Figure 9.4. In Chapter 3 the simulations of elections in Israel demonstrated that Likud was unable to "capture the core." By moving Labour to the left, Peretz created the opportunity for Sharon to out-maneuver him. Sharon could strategically move to a position that would increase the probability that he would control the core. Because Sharon's own party members would not support him in this move, he had to leave Likud and form Kadima.

However, Figure 9.4 suggests that the seat strengths were insufficient for Sharon to actually conrol the core in 2005. Indeed, the heart is bounded by the three median lines drawn in the figure. Since these lines do not intersect, the core is empty. Note however, that the new configuration

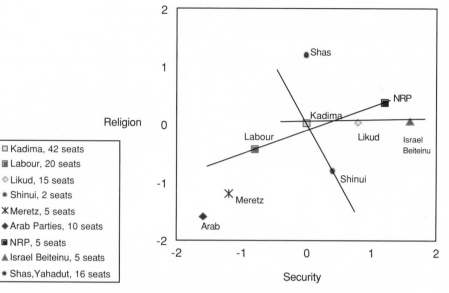

Figure 9.4. The effect of the creation of Kadima by Ariel Sharon on the configuration of the Knesset.

of the heart suggests a possible government coalition of Kadima with supporters from factions of either Likud or Labour.

In a less publicized move, Sharon took his political maneuvering a step further, obtaining the support of Uriel Reichman, founder of the Shinui party, for Kadima. On the face of it, this move seemed hard to explain. Although Reichman is a notable figure in Israel (currently the President of IDC, the largest and most successful private university in Israel), he has never held an elected office. In fact, Sharon promised Reichman the position of Minister of Education in a Kadima coalition government. The purpose of this contract is clear from Figure 9.5. By obtaining Reichman's support, Sharon made a small move "south" in the policy space towards the structurally stable core. Indeed this position is very close to the position previously held by the Labour Party, under the leadership of Rabin, at the 1992 election in Israel.

Figure 9.5 gives our estimates of party positions at the March 28, 2006, election to the Knesset. Because of Sharon's stroke in January, 2006, Ehud Olmert had taken over as leader of Kadima. Although his valence was presumably lower than that of Sharon, Kadima was still able to take 29 seats. Likud, together with religious parties, took 50 seats. One surprise of the

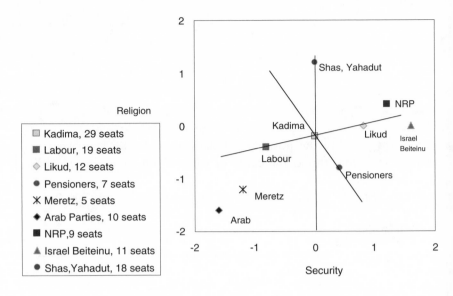

Figure 9.5. The configuration of the Knesset after the election of 28 March, 2006.

election was the appearance of a pensioners' party with 7 seats. However, this had no effect on coalition bargaining. Because a coalition between Labour and the religious parties is infeasible, we can infer that Kadima is located at the structurally stable core position (as indicated in Figure 9.5). It appears that Sharon's change of policy has led to a fundamental transformation in the political configuration, from the $\mathbb{D}_0$-coalition structure that had persisted since 1996, to a $\mathbb{D}_1$-structure associated with the new core party, Kadima.

9.3   PLURALITY RULE

Under plurality rule (in Britain or the United States, for example), we follow Miller and Schofield (2003) and suggest that coalition formation principally takes place inside the party rather than outside. In the United States, for example, parties are coalitions of disparate interests that are maintained only by bargaining between opposed activist groups. For Britain, we have refined this model, and have examined the effect on the "exogenous" valence of the party leader on the bargain made between the leader and the various activist support groups. Since exogenous valence is intrinsic to the party leader, calculating the marginal effects of *exogenous* valence and *activist* valence allows us to conclude that increasing leader valence reduces the radical effect of activists.

Although the theory is most readily applied to the situation where there are disciplined parties in the Parliament, it is also applicable to the more complex situation of weakly disciplined parties in the U.S. Congress, with a President able to implement a veto. For presidential elections, we argue that the changing composition of activist support has generated a slow transformation in the positions of the candidates for the two parties. We suggest that this is the cause of what is sometimes called *political realignment.*

Although we have not examined the relationship between President and Congress in the U.S. case, we might expect a core to exist (or at least a restricted heart) when the presidential party controls both House and Senate. In this case, computation of the heart will depend on the particular distribution of policy preferences in both houses of Congress as well as the policies to which the President is committed.

9.4 THEORY AND EMPIRICAL EVIDENCE

The theory that we have presented in this volume came about because of the apparent empirical refutation of the generally accepted theories of elections. In our earlier work with our collaborators on Britain, Israel, the Netherlands, the United States, and, later, Italy, we found no evidence of a significant centripetal tendency to an electoral center. Initially, we did not see the significance of the intercept or valence terms in the electoral models. The simulations that we performed for Israel, however, made it clear that these terms, though they appeared to be trivial, had the effect of completely changing the nature of the equilibria. The "first-order theory" with exogenous valence that we developed gave quite a good approximation to the major party positions in Israel. Moreover, the formal result was bolstered by the correspondence between the theoretical finding and the simulation of the electoral model.

The "second-order theory" involving the "structurally stable core" and coalition bargaining, gave us a qualitative explanation for the location of pivotal parties, such as Shas in Israel, off the principal electoral axis.

The analysis of Italy and the Netherlands made it obvious that party activists should be brought into the electoral equation. The empirical work on Britain, based on the MP survey data, suggested that activists for each party would be quite heterogeneous, and this reinforced the inference made by Miller and Schofield (2003) that a party is itself a coalition.

This suggested the tradeoff between activist support and leader valence. The importance of activists in the U.S. party system, together with the changing nature of the intraparty bargain then naturally led us to the idea of the transformation of party candidate positions and the phenomenon of political realignment.

This "third-order theory" of activists is only sketched here, but we believe it will prove a fertile source of ideas about party competition.

We hope that this nested set of theories will be used in the future to construct an empirically relevant theory of democracy.

References

Abramowitz, A., and K. Saunders. 1998. "Ideological Realignment in the U.S. Electorate." *The Journal of Politics* 60(4):634–652.

Adams, J. 1999a. "Multiparty Spatial Competition with Probabilistic Voting." *Public Choice* 99:259–274.

Adams, J. 1999b. "Policy Divergence in Multicandidate Probabilistic Spatial Voting." *Public Choice* 100:103–122.

Adams, J. 2001. *Party Competition and Responsible Party Government.* Ann Arbor: University of Michigan Press.

Adams, J., and S. Merrill, III. 1999. "Modeling Party Strategies and Policy Representation in Multiparty Elections: Why are Strategies So Extreme?" *American Journal of Political Science* 43:765–781.

Adams, J., S. Merrill, III, and B. Grofman. 2005. *A Unified Theory of Party Competition.* Cambridge: Cambridge University Press.

Aldrich, J. H. 1983a. "A Downsian Spatial Model with Party Activists." *American Political Science Review* 77(3):974–990.

Aldrich, J. H. 1983b. "A Spatial Model with Party Activists: Implications for Electoral Dynamics." *Public Choice* 41:63–100.

Aldrich, J. H. 1995. *Why Parties?* Chicago: Chicago University Press.

Aldrich, J. H., and M. McGinnis. 1989. "A Model of Party Constraints on Optimal Candidate Positions." *Mathematical and Computer Modelling* 12:437–450.

Aldrich J. H., G. J. Miller, C. W. Ostrom Jr., and D. Rohde. 1986. *American Government.* Boston: Houghton Mifflin.

Alvarez, M., and J. Nagler. 1998. "When Politics and Models Collide: Estimating Models of Multicandidate Elections." *American Journal of Political Science* 42:55–96.

Alvarez, M., J. Nagler, and S. Bowler. 2000. "Issues, Economics, and the Dynamics of Multiparty Elections: The British 1987 General Election." *American Political Science Review* 94:131–150.

Ansolabehere, S., and J. Snyder. 2000. "Valence Politics and Equilibrium in Spatial Election Models." *Public Choice* 103(2000):327–336.

Aragones, E., and T. Palfrey 2002. "Mixed Equilibrium in a Downsian Model with Favored Candidate." *Journal of Economic Theory* 103:131–161.

References

Arian, A., and M. Shamir. 1990. *The Election in Israel: 1988.* Albany: SUNY Press.

Arian, A., and M. Shamir. 1995. *The Election in Israel: 1992.* Albany: SUNY Press.

Arian, A., and M. Shamir. 1999. *The Election in Israel: 1996.* Albany: SUNY Press.

Arrow, K. 1951. *Social Choice and Individual Values.* New Haven: Yale University Press.

Austen-Smith, D., and J. S. Banks. 1988. "Elections, Coalitions and Legislative Outcomes." *American Political Science Review* 82:405–422.

Austen-Smith, D., and J. S. Banks. 1990. "Stable Portfolio Allocations." *American Political Science Review* 84:891–906.

Austen-Smith, D., and J. S. Banks. 1999. *Positive Political Theory I: Collective Preferences.* Ann Arbor: University of Michigan Press.

Austen-Smith, D., and J. S. Banks. 2005. *Positive Political Theory II: Strategy and Structure.* Ann Arbor: University of Michigan Press.

Austen-Smith, D., and J. R. Wright. 1992. "Competitive Lobbying for a Legislator's Vote." *Social Choice and Welfare* 19:229–257.

Axelrod, R. 1980. *Conflict of Interest.* Chicago: Markham.

Banks, J. S. 1990. "A Model of Electoral Competition with Incomplete Information." *Journal of Economic Theory* 50:309–325.

Banks, J. S. 1995. "Singularity Theory and Core Existence in the Spatial Model." *Journal Mathematical Economy* 24:523–536.

Banks, J. S., and J. Duggan. 2000. "A Bargaining Model of Collective Choice." *American Political Science Review* 94:73–88.

Banks, J. S., and J. Duggan. 2005. "The Theory of Probabilistic Voting in the Spatial Model of Elections." In D. Austen-Smith and J. Duggan [Eds.]. *Social Choice and Strategic Decisions.* Heidelberg: Springer.

Banks, J., J. Duggan, and M. Le Breton. 2002. "Bounds for Mixed Strategy Equilibria and the Spatial Model of Elections." *Journal of Economic Theory* 103:88–105.

Bardo, M., and H. Rockoff. 1996. "The Gold Standard as a Good Housekeeping Seal of Approval." *The Journal of Economic History* 56(2):389–428.

Barnett, W., M. Hinich, and N. Schofield [Eds.]. 1993. *Political Economy: Institutions, Competition and Representation.* New York: Cambridge University Press.

Barnett, W., H. Moulin, M. Salles, and N. Schofield [Eds.]. 1995. *Social Choice, Welfare and Ethics.* New York: Cambridge University Press.

Baron, D. P., and J. A. Ferejohn. 1989. "Bargaining in Legislatures." *American Political Science Review* 83:1181–1206.

Bartolini, S., and R. D'Alimonte [Eds.]. 1995. *Maggioritario non troppo.* Bologna: Il Mulino.

Beard, C. 1913. *An Economic Interpretation of the Constitution of the United States.* New York: Macmillan.

Berelson, B. R., P. R. Lazarfield, and W. N. McPhee. 1954. *Voting: A Study of Opinion Formation in a Presidential Campaign.* Chicago, IL: Chicago University Press.

Bianco, W. T., I. Jeliazkov, and I. Sened. 2006. "The Limits of Legislative Action: Determining the Set of Enactable Outcomes Given Legislators' Preferences." *Political Analysis,* in press.

Bianco, W. T., and I. Sened. 2003. *Uncovering Majority Party Influence in Legislatures.* Washington University in St. Louis: Typescript.

Bingham Powell, G. 2000. *Elections as Instruments of Democracy.* New Haven: Yale University Press.

Black, D. 1958. *The Theory of Committees and Elections.* Cambridge: Cambridge University Press.

Brady, D. 1988. *Critical Elections and Congressional Policy Making.* Stanford University Press.

Branch, T. 1998. *Pillar of Fire.* New York: Simon and Schuster.

British Election Study. 1992. *National Cross-Section Survey Dataset.* University of Essex: ESRC Data Archive.

British Election Study. 1997. *National Cross-Section Survey Dataset.* University of Essex: ESRC Data Archive.

Browne, E., and M. Franklin. 1973. "Aspects of Coalition Payoffs in European Parliamentary Democracies." *American Political Science Review* 67:453–469.

Budge, I., H.-D. Klingemann, A. Volkens, and J. Bara [Eds.]. 2001. *Mapping Policy Preferences—Estimates for Parties, Electors, and Governments 1945–1998.* Oxford: Oxford University Press.

Budge, I., D. Robertson, and D. Hearl [Eds.]. 1987. *Ideology, Strategy and Party Change: A Spatial Analysis of Post-War Election Programmes in Nineteen Democracies.* Cambridge: Cambridge University Press.

Burnham, W. 1970. *Critical Elections and the Mainsprings of American Politics.* New York: Norton.

Cahoon, L., M. J. Hinich, and P. Ordeshook. 1978. "A Statistical Multidimensional Scaling Method Based on the Spatial Theory of Voting." In P. C. Wang [Ed.]. *Graphical Representation of Multivariate Data.* New York: Academic Press.

Calvert, R. L. 1985. "Robustness of the Multidimensional Voting Model: Candidates, Motivations, Uncertainty and Convergence." *American Journal of Political Science* 29:69–85.

Campbell, A., P. E. Converse, W. E. Miller, and D. E. Stokes. 1960. *The American Voter.* New York: John Wiley.

Caplin, A., and B. Nalebuff. 1988. "On 64 Percent Majority Rule." *Econometrica* 56:787–814.

Carmines, E. G., and J. A. Stimson. 1989. *Issue Evolution, Race and the Transformation of American Politics.* Princeton: Princeton University Press.

Caro, R. A. 2002. *The Years of Lyndon Johnson: Master of the Senate.* New York: Knopf.

Chib, S., and E. Greenberg. 1996. "Markov Chain Monte Carlo Simulation Methods in Econometrics." *Econometric Theory* 12:409–431.

Clarke, H., D. Sanders, M. Stewart, and P. Whiteley. 2004. *Political Choice in Britain.* Oxford: Oxford University Press.

Clarke, H. D., and M. C. Stewart. 1998. "The Decline of Parties in the Minds of Citizens." *Annual Review of Political Science* 1:357–378.

References

Clarke, H., M. Stewart, and P. Whiteley. 1995. "Prime Ministerial Approval and Governing Party Support: Rival Models Reconsidered." *British Journal of Political Science* 25(4):597–622.

Clarke, H., M. Stewart, and P. Whiteley. 1997. "Tory Trends, Party Identification and the Dynamics of Conservative Support Since 1992."*British Journal of Political Science* 26:299–318.

Clarke, H., M. Stewart, and P. Whiteley. 1998. "New Models for New Labour: The Political Economy of Labour Support, January 1992–April 1997." *American Political Science Review* 92:559–575.

Cohen, L., and S. Matthews. 1980. "Constrained Plott Equilibria, Directional Equilibria and Global Cycling Sets." *Review of Economic Studies* 47:975–986.

Corbetta P., and A. Parisi [Eds.]. 1997. *A Domanda Risponde. Il Cambiamento del Voto Degli Italiani Nelle Elezioni del 1994 e del 1996.* Bologna: Il Mulino.

Coughlin, P. 1992. *Probabilistic Voting Theory.* Cambridge: Cambridge University Press.

Cox, G. 1984. "An Expected Utility Model of Electoral Competition." *Quality and Quantity* 18:337–349.

Cox, G. 1987a."The Uncovered Set and the Core." *American Journal of Political Science* 31:408–422.

Cox, G. 1987b. "Electoral Equilibrium under Alternative Voting Institutions." *American Journal of Political Science* 30:82–108.

Cox, G. 1990. "Centripetal and Centrifugal Incentives in Electoral Systems." *American Journal of Political Science* 34:903–935.

Cox, G. 1997. *Making Votes Count.* Cambridge: Cambridge University Press.

Daalder, H. 1984. "In Search of the Center of European Party Systems." *American Political Science Review* 78:92–109.

D'Alimonte R., and S. Bartolini [Eds.]. 1997. *Maggioritario per caso.* Bologna: Il Mulino.

Dasgupta, P., and Maskin E. 1986. "The Existence of Equilibrium in Discontinuous Economic Games, I: Theory, II: Applications." *Review of Economic Studies* 53:1–42.

De Vries, M. 1999. *Governing with Your Closest Neighbor.* Nijmegen: Ipskamp.

Diamanti, I. 1997. "La Lega: dal Federalismo alla Secessione." In R. D'Alimonte and D. Nelken [Eds.]. *Politica in Italia 1997.* Bologna: Il Mulino.

Dierker E. 1976. *Topological Methods in Walrasian Economics.* Heidelberg: Springer.

Dow, J. K., and J. Endersby 2004. "Multinomial Probit and Multinomial Logit: A Comparison of Choice Models for Voting Research." *Electoral Studies* 23:107–122.

Downs, A. 1957. *An Economic Theory of Democracy.* New York: Harper & Row.

Duggan, J. 2000. "Equilibrium Equivalence under Expected Plurality and Probability of Winning Maximization." University of Rochester: Typescript.

Duggan, J. 2006. "Candidate Objectives and Electoral Equilibrium." In B. Weingast and D. Wittman [Eds.]. *Oxford Handbook of Political Economy.* Oxford: Oxford University Press.

Duggan, J., and M. Fey. 2006. "Electoral Equilibrium with Policy Motivated Candidates."*Games and Economic Behavior*, in press.

References

Duggan, J., and A. Jarque-Llamazares. 2001. *Equilibrium Nonexistence in a Model of Democracy.* University of Rochester: Typescript.

Duverger, M. 1954. *Political Parties: Their Organization and Activity in the Modern State.* New York: Wiley.

Eaton, C., and R. Lipsey. 1975. "The Principle of Minimum Differentiation Reconsidered: Some New Developments in the Theory of Spatial Competition." *Review of Economic Studies* 42:27–50.

Edsall, J. B., and M. D. Edsall. 1991. *Chain Reaction.* New York: Norton.

Enelow, J., and M. J. Hinich. 1982. "Ideology, Issues, and the Spatial Theory of Elections." *American Political Science Review* 76:493–501.

Enelow, J., and M. J. Hinich. 1984. *The Spatial Theory of Voting.* Cambridge: Cambridge University Press.

Enelow, J., and M. J. Hinich. 1989. "The Location of American Presidential Candidates." *Mathematical and Computer Modelling* 12:461–470.

Fan, K. 1964. "A Generalization of Tychonoff's Fixed Point Theorem," *Math. Annalen* 42:305–310.

Feddersen, T. J., I. Sened, and S. G. Wright. 1990. "Sophisticated Voting and Candidate Entry under Plurality Rule." *American Journal of Political Science* 34:1005–1016.

Fiorina, M. 2005. *Culture War?* New York: Longman.

Giannetti, D., and M. Laver. 2001. "Party Systems Dynamics and the Making and Breaking of Italian Governments." *Electoral Studies* 20:529–553.

Giannetti, D., and I. Sened. 2004. "Party Competition and Coalition Formation: Italy 1994–1996." *The Journal of Theoretical Politics* 16:483–515.

Groseclose, T. 2001. "A Model of Candidate Location When One Candidate Has Valence Advantage." *American Journal of Political Science* 45:862–886.

Hammond, T. H., and G. Miller. 1987. "The Core of the Constitution." *American Political Science Review* 81:1155–1174.

Hinich, M. J. 1977. "Equilibrium in Spatial Voting: The Median Voter Theorem is an Artifact." *Journal of Economic Theory* 16:208–219.

Hirsch M. 1976. *Differential Topology.* Heidelberg: Springer.

Hotelling, H. 1929. "Stability in Competition." *Economic Journal* 39:41–57.

Huckfeldt, R., and C. Kohfeld. 1989. *Race and the Decline of Class in American Politics.* Urbana-Champaign: University of Illinois Press.

ISEIUM. 1983. *European Elections Study: European Political Parties' Middle Level Elites.* Mannheim: Europa Institut.

Kass, R., and A. Raftery. 1995. "Bayes Factors." *Journal of the American Statistical Association* 91:773–795.

Key, V. O. 1955. "A Theory of Critical Elections." *Journal of Politics* 17:3–18.

King, A. [Ed.] 2002. *Leaders' Personalities and the Outcomes of Democratic Elections.* Oxford: Oxford University Press.

Kramer, G. H. 1973. "On a Class of Equilibrium Conditions for Majority Rule." *Econometrica* 41:285–297.

Kramer, G. H. 1978. "Existence of Electoral Equilibrium." In P. Ordeshook [Ed.]. *Game Theory and Political Science.* New York: New York University Press.

Laver, M. 1998. "Models of Government Formation." *Annual Review of Political Science* 1:1–25.

Laver, M. [Ed.] 2001. *Estimating the Policy Positions of Political Actors*. London: Routledge.

Laver, M. 2003. "Government Termination." *Annual Review of Political Science* 6:23–40.

Laver, M., and I. Budge [Eds.]. 1992. *Party Policy and Government Coalitions*. London: Macmillan.

Laver, M., and W. B. Hunt. 1992. *Policy and Party Competition*. New York: Routledge.

Laver, M., and N. Schofield. 1990. *Multiparty Governments: The Politics of Coalition in Europe*. Oxford: Oxford University Press. Reprinted 1998. Ann Arbor: University of Michigan Press.

Laver, M., and K. A. Shepsle. 1990. "Coalitions and Cabinet Government." *American Political Science Review* 84:873–890.

Laver, M., and K. A. Shepsle [Eds.]. 1994. *Cabinet Ministers and Parliamentary Government*. Cambridge: Cambridge University Press.

Laver, M., and K. A. Shepsle. 1996. *Making and Breaking Governments*. Cambridge: Cambridge University Press.

Laver, M., and M. Taylor. 1973. "Government Coalitions in Western Europe," *European Journal of Political Research* 1:205–248.

Leonardi, R., and M. Kovacs. 1993. "L'irresistibile Ascesa della Lega Nord." In S. Hellman and E. G. Pasquino [Eds.]. *Politica in Italia. Edizione 93*. Bologna: Il Mulino, 123–141.

Lin, T., M. J. Enelow, and H. Dorussen. 1999. "Equilibrium in Multicandidate Probabilistic Spatial Voting." *Public Choice* 98:59–82.

Madison, J. 1787. "Federalist 10." In J. Rakove [Ed.] 1999. *Madison: Writings*. New York: Library Classics.

Mann, R. 1996. *The Walls of Jericho*. New York: Harcourt Brace.

Mayhew, D. 2000. "Electoral Realignments." *Annual Review of Political Science* 3:449–474.

Mayhew, D. 2002. *Electoral Realignments*. New Haven: Yale University Press.

McKelvey, R. D. 1976. "Intransitivities in Multidimensional Voting Models and Some Implications for Agenda Control." *Journal of Economic Theory* 12:472–482.

McKelvey, R. D. 1979. "General Conditions for Global Intransitivities in Formal Voting Models." *Econometrica* 47:1085–1112.

McKelvey, R. D. 1986. "Covering, Dominance and Institution Free Properties of Social Choice." *American Journal of Political Science* 30:283–314.

McKelvey, R. D., and P. Ordeshook. 1985. "Elections with Limited Information: A Fulfilled Expectations Model Using Contemporaneous Poll and Endorsement Data as Information Sources." *Journal of Economic Theory* 36:55–85.

McKelvey, R. D., and J. W. Patty. 2005. *A Theory of Voting in Large Elections*. Harvard University: Typescript.

McKelvey, R. D., and N. Schofield. 1986. "Structural Instability of the Core." *Journal of Mathematical Economics* 15:179–188.

McKelvey, R. D., and N. Schofield. 1987. "Generalized Symmetry Conditions at a Core Point." *Econometrica* 55:923–933.

References

Merrill III, S., and B. Grofman. 1999. *A Unified Theory of Voting*. Cambridge: Cambridge University Press.

Merrill III, S., B. Grofman, and S. Feld. 1999. "Nash Equilibrium Strategies in Directional Models of Two-Candidate Spatial Competition." *Public Choice* 98:369–383.

Mershon, C. 1996a. "The Costs of Coalition: Coalition Theories and Italian Governments." *American Political Science Review* 90:534–554.

Mershon, C. 1996b. "The Costs of Coalition: The Italian Anomaly." In N. Schofield [Ed.]. *Collective Decision Making: Social Choice and Political Economy*. Boston: Kluwer.

Mershon, C. 2002. *The Costs of Coalition*. Stanford: Stanford University Press.

Michael, E. 1956. "Continuous Selections I." *Annals of Mathematics* 63:361–382.

Miller, G., and N. Schofield. 2003. "Activists and Partisan Realignment in the U.S." *American Political Science Review* 97:245–260.

Miller, N. 1980. "A New Solution Set for Tournament and Majority Voting." *American Journal of Political Science* 24:68–96.

Milnor, J. 1963. *Morse Theory*. Princeton: Princeton University Press.

Nachmias, D., and I. Sened. 1999. "The Bias of Pluralism: The Redistributive Effects of the New Electoral Law in Israel's 1996 Election." In A. Arian and M. Shamir [Eds.]. *The Election in Israel, 1996*. Albany: SUNY Press.

Nash, J. 1950a. "The Bargaining Problem." *Econometrica* 18:155–162.

Nash, J. 1950b. "Equilibrium Points in N-Person Games." *Proceedings of the National Academy of Science, USA* 36:48–49.

Nash, J. 1951. "Non-Cooperative Games." *Annals of Mathematics* 54:286–295.

Nash, J. 1953. "Two Person Cooperative Games" *Econometrica* 21:128–140.

Ofek, D., K. Quinn, and I. Sened. 1998. *Voters, Parties and Coalition Formation in Israel: Theory and Evidence*. Washington University in St. Louis: Typescript.

Parthasathy, K. 1967. *Probability Measures on Metric Spaces*. New York: Academic Press.

Patty, J. W. 2001. "Plurality and Probability of Victory: Some Equivalence Results." *Public Choice* 112:151–166.

Patty, J. W. 2005. "Local Equilibrium Equivalence in Probabilistic Voting Models." *Games and Economic Behavior* 51:523–536.

Patty, J. W. 2006. "Generic Difference of Vote Share and Probability of Victory Maximization in Simple Plurality Elections with Probabilistic Voters." *Social Choice and Welfare*, in press.

Plott, C. R. 1967. "A Notion of Equilibrium and Its Possibility under Majority Rule." *American Economic Review* 57:787–806.

Poole, K., and H. Rosenthal. 1984. "U.S. Presidential Elections 1968–1980: A Spatial Analysis." *American Journal of Political Science* 28:283–312.

Pridham, G. 1987. *Political Parties and Coalition Behavior in Italy*. London: Routledge.

Przeworski, A., M. E. Alvarez, J. A. Cheibub, and F. Limongi. 2000. *Democracy and Development: Political Institutions and Well-Being in the World, 1950–1990*. Cambridge: Cambridge University Press.

Putnam, R. D. 1993. *Making Democracy Work: Civic Traditions in Modern Italy*. Princeton: Princeton University Press.

References

Quinn, K., and A. Martin. 2002. "An Integrated Computational Model of Multiparty Electoral Competition." *Statistical Science* 17:405–419.

Quinn, K., A. Martin, and A. Whitford. 1999. "Voter Choice in Multiparty Democracies." *American Journal of Political Science* 43:1231–1247.

Rabier, J., and R. Inglehart. 1981. *Eurobarometer II April 1979. The Year of the Child in Europe*. Ann Arbor: Inter-University Consortium for Political and Social Research.

Ransom, R. 1989. *Conflict and Compromise*. Cambridge, UK: Cambridge University Press.

Ricolfi, L. 1993. "La Geometria dello Spazio Elettorale in Italia." *Rivista Italiana di Scienza Politica* 23:433–474.

Riker, W. H. 1953. *Democracy in the United States*. New York: Macmillan.

Riker, W. H. 1962. *The Theory of Political Coalitions*. New Haven: Yale University Press.

Riker, W. H. 1965. "Theory and Science in the Study of Politics." *Journal of Conflict Resolution* 56:375–379.

Riker, W. H. 1980. "Implications From the Disequilibrium of Majority Rule For the Study of Institutions." *American Political Science Review* 74:432–446.

Riker, W. H. 1982a. *Liberalism against Populism*. San Francisco: Freeman.

Riker, W. H. 1982b. "The Two Party System and Duverger's Law: An Essay on the History of Political Science." *American Political Science Review* 76:753–766.

Riker, W. H. 1986. *The Art of Political Manipulation*. New Haven: Yale University Press.

Riker, W. H., and P. C. Ordeshook. 1973. *An Introduction to Positive Political Theory*. Englewood Cliffs, NJ: Prentice-Hall.

Robertson, D. 1976. *A Theory of Party Competition*. London: Wiley.

Rogowski, R. 1989. *Commerce and Coalitions*. Princeton, NJ: Princeton University Press.

Rosenthal, H., and E. Voeten. 2004. "Analyzing Roll Calls with Perfect Spatial Voting." *American Journal of Political Science* 48:620–632.

Saari, D. 1996. "The Generic Existence of a Core for q Rules." *Economic Theory* 9:219–260.

Sartori, G. 1976. *Parties and Party Systems: A Framework of Analysis*. Cambridge: Cambridge University Press.

Schattschneider, E. E. 1960. *The Semi-Sovereign People*. New York: Holt, Rinehart and Winston.

Schlesinger, J. A. 1994. *Political Parties and the Winning of Office*. Ann Arbor: University of Michigan Press.

Schofield, N. 1976. "Kernel and Payoffs in European Government Coalitions," *Public Choice* 26:29–49.

Schofield, N. 1978. "Instability of Simple Dynamic Games." *Review of Economic Studies* 45:575–594.

Schofield, N. 1983. "Generic Instability of Majority Rule." *Review of Economic Studies* 50:695–705.

Schofield, N. 1985. *Social Choice and Democracy*. Heidelberg: Springer.

Schofield, N. 1993. "Political Competition and Multiparty Coalition Governments." *European Journal of Political Research* 23:1–33.

References

Schofield, N. 1995. "Coalition Politics: A Formal Model and Empirical Analysis." *Journal of Theoretical Politics* 7:245–281.

Schofield, N. [Ed.]. 1996. *Collective Decision Making: Social Choice and Political Economy.* Boston: Kluwer.

Schofield, N. 1996. "The Heart of a Polity." In N. Schofield [Ed.]. *Collective Decision Making: Social Choice and Political Economy.* Boston: Kluwer.

Schofield, N. 1997. "Multiparty Electoral Politics." In D. Mueller [Ed.]. *Perspectives on Public Choice.* Cambridge: Cambridge University Press.

Schofield, N. 1998. "Aggregation of Smooth Preferences." *Social Choice and Welfare* 15:161–185.

Schofield, N. 1999a. "The C^1–topology on the Space of Smooth Preference Profiles." *Social Choice and Welfare* 16:347–373.

Schofield, N. 1999b. "The Heart and the Uncovered Set." *Journal of Economics* (Suppl.) 8:79–113.

Schofield, N. 2001. "Generic Existence of Local Political Equilibrium." In M. Lassonde. [Ed.]. *Approximation, Optimization and Mathematical Economics.* Heidelberg: Springer.

Schofield, N. 2002. "Representative Democracy as Social Choice." In K. Arrow, A. Sen, and K. Suzumura [Eds.]. *The Handbook of Social Choice and Welfare.* New York: North Holland.

Schofield, N. 2003a. *Mathematical Methods in Economics and Social Choice.* Berlin: Springer.

Schofield, N. 2003b. "Valence Competition in the Spatial Stochastic Model." *The Journal of Theoretical Politics* 15:371–383.

Schofield, N. 2004. "Equilibrium in the Spatial Valence Model of Politics." *The Journal of Theoretical Politics* 16:447–481.

Schofield, N. 2005a. "Local Political Equilibria." In D. Austen-Smith and J. Duggan [Eds.]. *Social Choice and Strategic Decisions: Essays in Honor of Jeffrey S. Banks.* Heidelberg: Springer.

Schofield, N. 2005b. "A Valence Model of Political Competition in Britain: 1992–1997" *Electoral Studies* 24:347–370.

Schofield, N. 2006a. *Architects of Political Change: Constitutional Quandaries and Social Choice.* Cambridge: Cambridge University Press.

Schofield, N. 2006b. "The Mean Voter Theorem: Necessary and Sufficient Conditions for Convergence." *Review of Economic Studies*, in press.

Schofield, N. 2006c. "Social Choice and Elections." In J. Alt, J. Aldrich, and A. Lupia [Eds.]. *A Positive Change in Political Science: The Legacy of Richard McKelvey's Writings.* Ann Arbor: University of Michigan Press.

Schofield, N., B. Grofman, and S. Feld. 1989. "The Core and Stability in Spatial Voting Games." *American Political Science Review* 82:195–211.

Schofield, N., and M. Laver 1985. "Bargaining Theory and Portfolio Payoffs in European Coalition Governments 1945–1983." *British Journal of Political Science* 15:143–164.

Schofield, N., A. Martin, K. Quinn, and A. Whitford. 1998. "Multiparty Electoral Competition in the Netherlands and Germany: A Model Based on Multinomial Probit." *Public Choice* 97:257–293.

References

Schofield, N., G. Miller, and A. Martin. 2003: "Critical Elections and Political Realignment in the U.S.: 1860–2000." *Political Studies* 51:217–240.

Schofield, N., and R. Parks. 2000. "Nash Equilibrium in a Spatial Model of Coalition Bargaining." *Mathematical Social Science* 39:133–174.

Schofield, N., and I. Sened. 2002. "Local Nash Equilibrium in Multiparty Politics." *Annals of Operations Research* 109:193–210.

Schofield, N., and I. Sened. 2005a. "Modelling the Interaction of Parties, Activists and Voters: Why Is the Political Center So Empty?" *European Journal of Political Research* 44:355–390.

Schofield, N., and I. Sened. 2005b. "Multiparty Competition in Israel: 1988–1996." *British Journal of Political Science* 35:635–663.

Schofield, N., I. Sened, and D. Nixon. 1998. "Nash Equilibria in Multiparty Competition with Stochastic Voters." *Annals of Operations Research* 84:3–27.

Sened, I. 1995. "Equilibria in Weighted Voting Games with Side-Payments." *Journal of Theoretical Politics* 7:283–300.

Sened, I. 1996. "A Model of Coalition Formation: Theory and Evidence." *Journal of Politics* 58:350–372.

Seyd, P., and P. Whiteley. 1992. *Labour's Grassroots*. Oxford: Clarendon Press.

Seyd, P., and P. Whiteley. 2002. *New Labour's Grassroots*. Basingstoke, UK: Macmillan.

Shepsle, K. A. 1990. *Models of Multiparty Competition*. Chur, Switzerland: Harwood Academic Press.

Stokes, D. 1963. "Spatial Models and Party Competition." *American Political Science Review* 57:368–377.

Stokes, D. 1992. "Valence Politics." In D. Kavanagh [Ed.]. *Electoral Politics*. Oxford: Clarendon Press.

Strom, K. 1990. *Minority Government and Majority Rule*. Cambridge: Cambridge University Press.

Sundquist, J. 1973. *Dynamics of the Party System*. Washington, DC: Brookings Institution.

Taagepera, R., and M. S. Shugart. 1989. *Seats and Voters: The Effects and Determinants of Electoral Systems*. New Haven: Yale University Press.

Train, K. 2003. *Discrete Choice Methods for Simulation*. Cambridge: Cambridge University Press.

Von Neumann, J., and O. Morgenstern. 1944. *The Theory of Games and Economic Behavior*. New York: Wiley.

Warwick, P. 2004. "Proximity, Directionality, and the Riddle of Relative Party Extremeness." *Journal of Theoretical Politics* 16:263–287.

Weingast, B. 1998. "Political Stability and Civil War: Institutions, Commitment, and American Democracy." In R. Bates, A. Greif, M. Levi, J. L. Rosenthal, and B. Weingast [Eds.]. *Analytic Narratives*. Princeton, NJ: Princeton University Press.

Index

PENGUIN ENGLISH LIBRARY

TUDOR INTERLUDES

Peter Happé read English at Cambridge, and
afterwards took a Ph.D at Birkbeck College,
London, with a thesis on Tudor drama. He is
now Deputy Head of Yateley Comprehensive
School.

✣ TUDOR ✣
INTERLUDES

Edited with an introduction and notes by
PETER HAPPÉ

PENGUIN BOOKS

Penguin Books Ltd, Harmondsworth, Middlesex, England
Penguin Books Inc., 7110 Ambassador Road, Baltimore, Maryland 21207, U.S.A.
Penguin Books Australia Ltd, Ringwood, Victoria, Australia

—

This collection published in the Penguin English Library 1972
Introduction and notes copyright © Peter Happé, 1972

—

Made and printed in Great Britain by
Hazell Watson & Viney Ltd
Aylesbury, Bucks
Set in Monotype Fournier

Contents

*Extracts

Introduction

This collection draws upon ten plays, some of which are given in full and some in extract. They have been chosen to represent some of the dramatic styles which have come to be associated with the term 'interlude'. In the hope of affording as full a sample as possible, two preliminary episodes are included from *The Pride of Life* (fourteenth century) and *Mankind* (fifteenth century), and the selection ends with part of the Elizabethan play *The Boke of Sir Thomas More*, which looks back upon the interlude from the viewpoint of the fully developed public theatre of the 1590s.

In this introduction I shall deal first with some general features of the interlude and its historical development. This will be followed by consideration of each of the plays in chronological order to show its relationship to other interludes of a similar type.

It must be admitted that no general consensus has emerged amongst scholars as to what 'interlude' really means. As Chambers points out[1], this is partly due to the imprecision with which the word was used in the Middle Ages, covering, as it did, a wide variety of dramatic presentations from the fourteenth to the sixteenth century. Its use in this book is largely a matter of editorial convenience, and I shall try to explain what I think the plays I have chosen have in common to justify it here.

First, we may try a negative approach: several important types of drama are not included. The full-scale morality play, which demands open-air production and the elaborate marshalling of many actors before a large audience, is one. Similarly the mystery cycles are omitted on grounds of size and the kind of performance they were given. The subject matter of the mystery cycles, the Christian story from Adam to Judgement Day, is also dissimilar to that of the interludes included here. Again, there is a very general type of dramatic entertainment of a festival nature which must be ruled out. For the most part, this material has not come down to us in the form of complete play texts, but we know that lavish entertain-

1. E. K. Chambers, *The Mediaeval Stage*, 1903, Vol. II, p. 181.

ments at court, often processional and allegorical, continued into
the reign of James I, and became one of the chief forerunners of the
highly successful court masque, which is a distinct literary form,
more lavish and more poetic than the interludes.

In saying this I have already begun to set up difficulties of classi-
fication, for the length of the interludes does vary considerably –
at least one play, Sir David Lyndsay's *Ane Satire of the Thrie
Estaitis* (1539–54), is far too long to be an interlude, and yet it
contains episodes which are distinctly typical in size and scope.
Some of the interludes do deal with scriptural subjects; and some
were intended for the court, made use of the resources of royal
patronage, and contained material from the folk festivals.

Likewise it is difficult to identify the general characteristics of the
plays included. This is, in part, due to the length of the period under
consideration. Since the plays did not follow a strict convention,
the historical change is enormous. Alfred Harbage in his *Annals of
English Drama, 975–1700* lists some ninety plays which might be
called interludes (not all of them survive by any means); and the
number of plays lost without any trace is problematic. We know
that there were 'interluders' at court from 1494 ('les pleyars of the
Kyngs enterluds'[2]), and clearly there must have been a sufficiently
varied repertoire for this company to draw upon in its task of
entertaining the court at the many festive occasions, some of which
were prolonged for several days.

As to the chronology of the interludes, there is a very early
fragment dating from 1290–1335, the *Interludium de Clerico et
Puella*, but the interlude really began with *Fulgens and Lucres*
(1494), and developed under popular and court influences of different kinds through the first half of the sixteenth century. Its most
vigorous period seems to have been after 1550, and it continued to
attract attention from writers and actors until about 1580. By this
time a new style of professional drama had been initiated at The
Theatre, which was opened in 1576, and this rapidly overtook the
interludes in public favour.

Let us now consider some general characteristics. The most
important are size and scope. It is not certain that the genre was
originally intended to be part of a banquet, but a tradition has

2. Chambers, op. cit., p. 187.

grown up that it was. *Fulgens and Lucres* was divided into two parts, the first of which was arranged to finish so that feasting might take place. Quite often the plays have about one thousand lines, which suggests that they would not be the sole reason for assembling the audience, and one looks for other reasons which might provide the chief motive, a feast perhaps, or other items of display, agility or music. The brevity of many interludes meant that the dramatic content must be simple, so that the great cosmic sweep of the mystery cycle and the morality play had to be cut down. The hero could still be tempted, but it was not so easy to bring on stage the World, the Flesh, and the Devil, as well as the Seven Deadly Sins. Nevertheless the action was often sufficiently complex to allow a mixture of comic and serious. The comedy might only be the mockery of a foolish or misguided hero, but there is a persistent concern to make the audience laugh, which suggests two things: an attempt to work out the serious effects of comedy, and the insistent demand that the audience be entertained.

Not a great deal is known about the circumstances of performance, but there is sufficient to enable us to see what kind of audiences were aimed at, and how this affected subject matter and structure. The interludes were bound to depend upon the social conditions and the aesthetic interests of Tudor society. There seem to have been two main types of performance. One is popular, represented here by *Youth*, and by the preliminary extracts from *The Pride of Life* and *Mankind*, which are included to show how effective the short popular play could be at the time when interludes were about to come into being. *Youth* can be performed by five players, and it has none of the aristocratic or intellectual pretensions of *Fulgens and Lucres*. The intellectual discipline is homiletic, and it deals with a simple moral doctrine, addressed to an audience which contained many ordinary people. Most likely it was performed by a small company of travelling players. It demands practically no properties or stage effects: the stocks could be found in almost any village – if indeed fixed stocks were used, for the text allows for chains and manacles to be brought on. That it is representative of a type of interlude is suggested by its sharing certain lines with *Hickscorner* (c. 1513) and its general similarity with *Mundus et Infans* (c. 1500–1522). It is also interesting that it was printed at least three times in the sixteenth century, suggesting that it was in some demand and sold well.

Most of the other plays included here were performed indoors in more aristocratic, not to say regal, surroundings. *Sir Thomas More* was written for the Elizabethan public stage of the 1590s, but the episode containing the preparations for an interlude throws valuable light upon what the Elizabethans thought were the circumstances of performance at the house of a great man. It draws attention to the closeness of the audience – More was supposed to have joined in to help a crisis in production – and shows some of the difficulties encountered by interluders in costume and doubling. Noticeably, four of the players in the episode are men. This seems perfectly credible for an aristocratic performance which was not at court. The court could offer men, as we have seen, but it also had at its disposal the boys of the choir schools in London. Most of our plays could have been performed by boys: in several of them internal evidence makes this certain. In *The Play of the Wether* the restriction normally imposed by doubling seems to have been ignored, for ten actors appear on the stage in the final scene. No doubt the large number of boys available made doubling unnecessary.

Nevertheless, doubling plays an important part in the structure of the interlude, for it tends to impose a pattern of alternating interest upon these plays. This is clearly seen in *Apius and Virginia*, where the serious story is kept distinct from the comic, and there is time for the actors to change costumes and parts. A feature of *Like Will to Like* is that its sixteen parts are divided for five actors in the printed text. The implications of this are that, whilst it may have been performed at court without doubling, the necessity of doing so was constantly in mind, and the printer could make this an advertising feature when he came to sell his copies. This adaptability of the texts is a pronounced characteristic of the interludes of whatever social type. There seems to be little doubt that it was intended that many of the plays should be performed in various places, outdoor and indoor, and before general audiences as well as before elite groups like scholars (school and university), lawyers, clergy, or municipal officials. *Like Will to Like* contains suggestions of a hall: one of the spectators is described as being 'in the angle', most probably a corner of the hall. Such a dining hall seems to have been a popular venue for dramatic performances, and the doors at the kitchen end of the hall could be conveniently adapted for the actors' entrances. However, if the performance was to be in a completely different place, the line could easily be omitted or adapted.

Some plays require a good deal of singing. In the elite plays like *Apius and Virginia* this would be quite appropriate for the choir boys. The songs are not particularly distinguished as lyrics, but they do have dramatic point, and are well placed in terms of plot as well as entertainment. In the common plays the musical tradition was probably established because of the presence of minstrels among the groups of professional actors. There is little doubt that the rise of the common actor occurred at roughly the same time as the disappearance of the itinerant minstrel. Notably, *Mankind* calls for minstrels, and the play is distinctive in its use of song.

The extraordinary thing about the two major types of interlude is the way in which items like doubling and song are in common. This is perhaps a reflection of the close social ties in Tudor society. England was still a very small country, and players of one social group would probably be well aware of the activities of another.

A general aspect of the interludes which must be considered is the allegorical and didactic nature of the subject matter. The chief inspiration of this was undoubtedly the morality plays of the fourteenth and fifteenth centuries. These plays derive from homiletic literature, and instruct the Christian in the doctrines necessary for his soul's health. The moralities present the fallibility of man, the ubiquitous success of temptation, and the divine grace which may redeem all. The steps in this process are presented by means of abstract characters representing the vices and virtues which, through man's choice, influence his life. Because the interlude worked with a more limited scope, the truths it presented became more specific. *Youth* deals with salvation, but not with the variety of temptations found in *The Castell of Perseverance* (1400–1425) or Medwall's *Nature* (c. 1490–1501). Some of this restriction is undoubtedly due to the limited number of actors available, and it is notable that in some plays vices and virtues are left out of the later stages of the plot simply because there was no one to take the parts.

But the social changes behind the development of the interludes also appear to have modified the didactic function. In some of Heywood's plays, intended for court entertainment in the 1520s and 1530s, the didacticism has almost disappeared. In *Wether*, whilst we have Mery Report, who is an abstraction, though not specifically a moral one, most of the characters stand for little more than themselves. At most we can say that the Water Miller speaks as a typical Water Miller. In general, however, didacticism remained a strong impulse, many of the plays being called 'moral interludes'. It often referred to a particular facet of social life, like Protestant controversy or the education of the young (the Prodigal Son became a familiar theme). The last of the interludes, written in the 1570s and 1580s, persist in making moral vices and virtues the motive forces in the action, and in seeing the misfortunes of their characters as the results of vices who appear as characters at crucial moments in the stories.

Thus the interludes owe a great deal to the morality play in moral purpose, and in the characterization which depended upon this. There are other debts in the social types like the gallant, the loose woman, or the rural clown, who figure repeatedly in the interludes throughout the sixteenth century. Moreover the moralities had focused attention upon the sufferings of man and the miseries which attended them. Often, as one would expect, the moralities had shown this misery as the result of sin, but that does not prevent the sorrow from being movingly presented –

> I bolne and bleyke in blody ble
> And as a flour fadyth my face.
> To helle I schal bothe fare and fle
> But God me graunte of hys grace.
> (*The Castell of Perseverance*, lines 2999–3002)

The later interludes often seem to be nearer to tragic drama; indeed the word 'tragedy' appears on title-pages as well as in texts, and lamentation, as that of Virginius for Virginia, becomes a set piece of the interludes. Similarly, comedy is present in the morality, and continues to be an important feature in the interlude. Whereas the comic episodes in the moralities often signified moral depravity, they are much more complex in the interludes. The comic roles are

12

expanded, and in some cases, especially in Heywood's plays, the comedy becomes a matter of verbal ingenuity rather than crude farce. This is no doubt the result of the influence of classical models, which was particularly strong after 1525. Nevertheless farce remained a mainstay of the interlude, and the lack of decorum which the fooling entailed was the cause of much critical distaste at the end of the sixteenth century. It also attracted adverse comment from theological controversialists who castigated the moral depravity of the stage.

Whilst the moral doctrines of the Old Church and the New are the main subject matter of the interludes, it is notable that a wider variety of material is also used for the plots. Sometimes they appear to be original, but there is frequent use of literary material currently available. Thus *Fulgens and Lucres* draws upon a translation of the *Controversia de Vera Nobilitate* (1481), and *Apius and Virginia* is probably derived from Chaucer's *Phisicien's Tale*. Increasingly, stories of classical origin found their way on to the stage, as in the case of Pikeryng's *Horestes* (1567), and use was made of other well-known tales like those of Griselda, Susanna, and Mary Magdalene. The importance of the use of such material in the development of English drama is very great, for it shows that writers of interludes were prepared to select stories which seemed to have inherent dramatic possibilities.

This broadening in the scope of the subject matter is related to the general evolution of the interludes in the sixteenth century. I have already spoken of the large number of plays which might be called interludes, and it is not surprising that in such a long period there should be considerable development of dramatic technique. There is not a uniform development, however, nor a development towards a particular end, and one hesitates to use the word 'refinement' to describe what happened. In some ways *Fulgens and Lucres*, the earliest interlude selected here, is the most advanced as a play. It shows considerable literary skill and a fine grasp of the intimate relationship between actors and audience. But social changes, the wide variety of public taste, and, most especially, developments in the capacities of the players and in their organization, all reflected upon the type of play that was written for the troupes.

The writers of interludes had to learn what could be done with the limited number of actors at their disposal, and they had to make their plays adaptable. They therefore became much more skilful and resourceful in the use they made of doubling. Gradually individual actors were expected to undertake more parts in each production, so that by 1561 Thomas Preston's *Cambises* was arranged for eight actors to take thirty-eight parts. This kind of complexity had important effects upon the plot. In the earlier interludes there is not usually a final scene in which all the characters meet. Since the same actors have to play parts from the good and the bad groups, there is only limited opportunity for direct encounters between the two sides. Comedy tends to be concentrated in a series of separate episodes, different in style and tone from the serious action. Many characters or groups of characters simply drop out of the plot. Time has to be allowed for actors to change their costumes, and in consequence there are elaborate songs and soliloquies. These technical problems, taken together, were a serious handicap, and there is no doubt that the development of the role of the 'Vice' was a significant step in overcoming them.

In discussing this character it is necessary to speak of '*the* Vice' to distinguish him from other characters who represent moral evils. He appears to have originated from among this number, and he almost always retains a homiletic function as the character who focuses the evil impulse in the plot and schemes for the downfall of the hero. The role develops gradually during the first half of the sixteenth century, and is not certainly identified by name until Avarice in *Respublica* (1553). (Some of Heywood's plays name a Vice, but these examples are not typical of the later role, and are better seen as contributing to its development.) The villains in the popular plays like *Youth* have a ruthless cynicism which foreshadows him, and they share a disposition to mock the virtuous. When the plots of the interludes become more complex, the schemes of the villains become more cunning. Naturally a leader emerges who prompts the evil in his companions, and this role, apparently after 1553, becomes an extensive one. The part is embellished with many kinds of verbal tricks, puns, proverbs, ambiguities, oaths, obscenities, and fanciful nonsense. The art of deception becomes more ingenious, and in the later interludes such as *Apius and Virginia* and *Like Will to Like* the Vice has become the chief part. In a number of plays his is the only part which cannot be doubled. He strives to make a quick rapport with the audience and was probably costumed so extravagantly (making great play with his ludicrous wooden dagger) as to have an immediate effect upon the audience, who would know how to respond to his tricks as soon as he appeared before them. Sometimes he kisses girls in the audience, and he frequently offers fraternal greeting to Cutpurse and Pickpurse busy among them.

His is also the main comic part. The name of the role appears in court records in 1551–2 in a way which suggests that the court fool was influential in his development. Later there is no limit to his fooling, and we find that in *Like Will to Like* the moral function has dwindled. The play seems to be a series of contrivances for revealing the comic virtuosity of the part. The Vice often rejoices in his ability to play many parts, but his true character is never obscured from the audience. He is irresponsible, weeps crocodile tears, triumphs over his victims, and even on the occasions when he is hanged (as in *Apius and Virginia*) he is quick to turn a comic phrase about it. More frequently, he escapes with a promise that he will return to plague other victims on some future occasion.

I have dwelt upon the Vice at some length because he seems to me to be one of the most important achievements of the interlude. He became so important after 1560 that he was virtually indispensable for many writers. He was generally accepted as a theatrical convention for about twenty years, and there are echoes of him in plays by Shakespeare and Ben Jonson. It cannot be said that he civilized the drama, but he certainly imparted a crude vitality to the interlude, and provided a high spot in the performances which many in the audiences remembered long after he had disappeared.

Until recent years, criticism of the interlude has been very caustic. Historians of the drama, anxious to push on to the Golden Age of the Elizabethans, have recorded the phases of the interlude with scant courtesy, choosing often to dwell upon banalities and inelegancies. Recent work by Craik, Bevington and Spivack[3], however, has shown that the makers of interludes were dramatic craftsmen, cobbling here and there perhaps, but grappling with problems of presentation, structure, characterization and mood. By

3. See the Note on Books, p. 37.

1576 these playwrights had shown that tragic and comic situations and the moral issues underlying them could be presented in dramatic form.

Two introductory episodes: 'The Pride of Life' and 'Mankind'

These plays belong to the medieval drama; but in certain aspects they foreshadow the interlude. Both illustrate the powerful influence of popular as distinct from court drama upon the interlude, and are forerunners of *Youth* in particular.

The Pride of Life embodies the medieval world picture. The moral allegory is pressed home by the tragedy of destruction and the imminence of death. The play has analogues with the Dance of Death, in which Death led men of all ranks to the grave. The action illustrates the sorrow of sin, and shows in moving terms how Man, here the King of Life, is incapable of appreciating his own folly, and is led to death. Of the characters who surround the King of Life, the Queen and the Bishop are concerned for his salvation and attempt to warn him against his own errors. The Messenger, Mirth, is a counter-influence. He is much loved and trusted by the King, and, whilst he does not offer temptation, he furthers the King's desires, and generally encourages the boasting and recklessness which are symptoms of the King's vulnerability. In this respect the play explores the relationship between the foolish hero and his tricky servant, who callously encourages disaster. The King seems unaware of the risks he is running: when these are pointed out to him by his wife and by the Bishop in the sermon, he deliberately discounts them and turns to Mirth. In the lost conclusion of the play, it seems that Death himself appeared and slew the King of Life, and that salvation could only be achieved by the intercession of the Virgin.

The author pursues a firm dramatic line. Though the characterization and the emotions are simple, the presentation of the plot is effective, and is striking in that it is an interrelated series of events, a genuine dramatic sequence: the play is in no sense a static debate. It has its dynamic in the character of the King and in the momentum of approaching disaster. Moreover, the author's language is impressive in its presentation of emotions, so that, as the plot develops, the feelings of the characters are modified: this process is essentially a drama. The play is consistently simple and direct, and this single-mindedness is important in the later interludes since it was always necessary to make effects quickly and directly. This necessity arose from the *ad hoc* methods of staging and from the short time available in the convention of the interludes.

The Prologue tells the story, and, in doing so, fulfils the function of the Banns which often preceded the early plays and acted as a kind of advertisement. They are associated with itinerant companies performing in the open air, as in *The Castell of Perseverance*. The action is arranged so that only three or four characters are on stage at one time, and it is likely that this was dictated by the number of players available. However, the absence of the concluding episodes makes it difficult to judge the exact size of the company.

The simplicity of the characterization suggests an unsophisticated audience, but it is important to note that in a brief play it is often necessary to rely upon easily recognizable characters. To some extent the boasting of the King is similar to the ranting tyrants of the mystery cycles.

Mankind, which was probably written over a century later, was also intended for a popular audience. It has a number of ingredients which *The Pride of Life* does not have, but it shares its immediacy and the adaptability necessary for touring. The extract chosen here contains references to a number of villages in East Anglia where it was probably performed. The rogues show a considerable advance upon Mirth. Under the leadership of Mischief, they plot with ingenuity, if somewhat ineffectually. The main stock-in-trade of these players consists of vigorously comic routines like the wailing of Newguise and Nowadays after Mankind has belaboured them. But the most successful villain is Titivillus, who is a kind of devil, a set piece whose entrance is carefully prepared. He is so important that the players take a collection before his arrival. It is he who produces the trick which overthrows Mankind, and when he has brought 'Mankynde to myscheff and to schame' he departs in satisfaction.

This group of villains is clearly one of the growing points for the interlude. It became a convention that the work of temptation be carried out by a group such as this. There would be four or five characters representing different named vices, and exhibiting both low cunning and stupidity. The descendants of the group in *Mankind* are found in *Youth*, in Skelton's *Magnyfycence* (c. 1515), and in *Respublica*. Later the leader emerges more strongly, and some playwrights found it possible to concentrate all the evil in one character, the Vice. The result of this development was that much of the comic villainy had to be communicated by soliloquy, or by the operation of the Vice in the sub-plot. But *Mankind*, or similar lost plays, must have established the vigorous comedy of crime before the interlude began to develop fully. This comedy, though crude, had a number of powerful ingredients, notably ignorance and folly, a disposition to mock the virtuous, a callous lack of sympathy for victims, obscenity, and indulgence in lechery, drunkenness, and petty theft. Perhaps these are common to low comedy in most cultures, but there is no doubt that they became an integral part of the interlude.

'Fulgens and Lucres'

This interlude is a very accomplished piece of work: its importance is to be measured by the innovations it contains and by the technical skill with which they are brought off. In speaking of innovations we must of course enter a proviso that we do not know how many plays of a similar nature are lost. The technical skill of the dramatist, Henry Medwall, suggests that he may have learned from other writers, and from other writings of his own. Probably the play owes much to folk plays and festivals, particularly in the comic wooing, which, as C. R. Baskervill has shown[4], has many affinities with the activities of the Lords of Misrule. Nevertheless a play which deals with human affairs in secular terms is very rare before the time of Shakespeare, and so too is a play in which a woman is one of the most important characters. This is also one of the earliest plays to give a clear idea of what could be achieved by the interlude in providing well informed, neatly arranged comic entertainment, with due respect for the time

4. 'Conventional Features of *Fulgens and Lucres*', *Modern Philology* xxiv (1927), pp. 419–42.

of dining. The first half of the play sets the problem – the nature of true nobility – and entertains the audience with the humorous wooing of Jone, the maid; the second part, after a further interval for feasting, presents the claims of the two suitors for Lucres, and resolves the conflict between them.

The central concern of the play, true nobility, is essentially a medieval topic, to be found, for example, in Chaucer's *Wife of Bath's Tale*, but the method of treating it is distinctly uncommon, as far as drama is concerned. There is no moral confrontation, and the action of the play does not depend upon temptation, corruption, and redemption, which are the almost universal pattern of moralities and interludes. The cast contains no moral abstractions, and the play does not have the irresistible impulse towards rewards and punishments which characterizes many other interludes. Indeed the plot itself is very thin, and the action of the play is almost entirely a debate in which the two suitors present their claims. In Bonaccorso's version, the ultimate source of the play, the debate is referred to the Senate for further consideration, and in the end it is left unresolved. Medwall, in an attempt to make the ending more dramatic, allows Lucres to make her choice, and he clearly thinks that it is a wise one. As a debate the play may be compared to Heywood's *Play of the Wether*, which also eschews moral abstractions and has a plot mainly concerned with presenting different points of view.

Medwall achieves much in the comic episodes of the play. The wooing of the maid in Part One is a comic statement of some aspects of the courtship of Lucres, and the by-play of the two Players, A and B, provides obscene comedy, humorous discussion with the audience, and, at the beginning of Part Two, a fairly serious discussion of the place of comedy in the play (II.21–46). This discussion is somewhat apologetic. That the comedy is 'impertinent' is recognized, and Player A makes the excuse that it is necessary to keep all the audience interested, even those who are chiefly diverted by 'tryfles and iapys'. No doubt Medwall means what he says, and the audience was as disparate as this implies, but the apology is an ingenious way of keeping the audience together and setting up a pervasive sense of comedy. The play's serious content can thus be seen in a comic framework, and there is no sense of a division between the doctrine and the fun. We may also feel that the importance attached to the position of women – something Medwall shares with the humanism of More – is a matter fit for comedy. It was a theme of Chaucer's poetic comedy, as well as of Shakespeare's plays. The paradox is that, in spite of the energetic pretensions of her suitors, Lucres appears the most noble. Medwall's achievement is not so novel as it might appear; the interplay of comic and serious in the Wakefield Second Shepherds' Play is equally subtle. The story of Mak is a comic counterpart to the story of the Nativity: as in *Fulgens and Lucres*, the comedy reinforces the main story. This is a line of development to which many of the writers of interludes paid scant attention, and the want of artistic unity which resulted was the occasion of much criticism for most of the sixteenth century.

The technical achievements of the play are even more remarkable than the comic spirit. Medwall was writing for an aristocratic audience, which was probably assembled in the hall of Morton's palace at Lambeth to honour the Flemish and Spanish ambassadors in 1497. The acting area was a cleared space, with the audience pressing close upon the actors. Medwall meets the difficulties of this proximity by making use of it. The actors, like characters in folk entertainments, emerge from among the spectators, complaining at one point of the press near the door. One, posing as a member of the audience, pretends to mistake his colleague, also apparently one of the audience, for one of the players. This is hotly denied, and the two players proceed to discuss the plot as though they knew about what was to come only as a result of gossiping with the 'real' actors. This is an extremely effective *tour de force* in that it consciously asserts the difference between the real world of the audience and the imaginary world of ancient Rome where the story is to take place. In the absence of formal methods of setting up the play by scenery and other technical aids, this is a remarkably successful device. The author seems to be conscious of the audience throughout; by means of nicely conceived asides and by making his characters address the audience directly, he maintains the sense that they are especially privileged onlookers. It is one of the chief characteristics of interludes to maintain this illusion, but Medwall does it with a sureness of touch which is nowhere surpassed. In other plays the Vice often tells the audience about himself and his schemes. This happens repeatedly in *Apius and Virginia* and *Like Will to Like*, but in *Fulgens and Lucres* the awareness of the nature of theatrical illusion is combined with an acute sense of the physical circumstances in which the play was performed.

To achieve all this Medwall must have been able to rely upon considerable professional competence in his actors. It seems likely that the play was performed by men, with the exception of the female parts, which might be taken by boys. The dances and songs might also require professional competence. We note that it was at this time that the interluders at court are first recorded, so that it seems likely that there were professional actors and performers working in London who could come to Medwall's assistance.

'Youth'

The author of *Youth* inherited the homiletic tradition from the fifteenth-century morality. The play is a dramatic sermon which urges the virtues of Charity and Humility against the vices of Riot, Pride and Lechery. The moral aim is vigorously pursued, and the play preserves in outline the structure which is common to the moralities and to many – though not all – later interludes: this is the pattern of foolish and short-sighted self-indulgence, typified by drunkenness, boasting and lechery, followed by repentance and a new start under the tutelage of wiser masters. However, in common with two contemporary plays, *Mundus et Infans* and *Hickscorner*, *Youth* shows an impulse towards simplicity and directness. The reason for this development is not at all clear, though one may suggest that it is related to the need for mobility and brevity, and to changes in theatrical conditions. This is not a completely satisfying explanation, but clearly there was a change of fashion in plays which led to the restriction of the imaginative world of the longer allegorical plays like *The Castell of Perseverance* and Medwall's *Nature*. There is not much evidence, however, that the essential premises about the weakness of human nature and the need for repentance suffered any change at all. Instead there occurred a greater concentration upon specific evils and their cure.

As the title indicates, the author concentrates upon youth, thus

heralding the major preoccupation with education found in many
later interludes. In his presentation of Youth, he picks the pervasive
medieval theme of human impermanence. Youth, in enjoying his
physical powers, likens himself to a tree which grows and flourishes,
and by this comparison suggests that he represents Spring. But
Charity warns him against decay and death:

> What shal it be whan thou shalt flyt
> Fro the wealth into the pyt?
> Therfore of it be not to boolde,
> Least thou forthink it whan thou art olde.
> Ye may be lykened to a tre:
> In youth, floryshyng with royalte,
> And in age it is cut downe,
> And to the fyre is throwne.

(lines 70–77)

Thus the author sets up the conflict between life and death which
fascinated many medieval writers, and which is one of the universal
themes of folk play and literature. But, for the medieval Christian
author, this antinomy could be dealt with only by reference to
moral doctrine, and so Charity offers the eternal virtues as the only
solution.

In the details of the moral exposition, the author followed many
of the conventions of the morality, and, by doing so, he presumably
assisted in their transmission to later playwrights (subsequent re-
printing of the play makes this the more likely; see p. 115). Thus
the play begins with a short sermon from Charity addressed solely
to the audience, and it ends with a prayer which also embraces
them. The villains speak the language of criminals, and show
conventional familiarity with gambling and taverns, and with
Newgate and Tyburn. Their leader is Riot, who is not himself a
specific sin so much as the embodiment of criminal tendencies and
the follies of Misrule. Aided by his companions he ridicules the
virtues and puts Charity in the stocks. When his plans are in ruins
he accepts defeat with a curse and goes on his way.

Youth's change of heart is symbolized by his 'newe araye'
(line 758), which is also a conventional feature. But the repentance
is the play's greatest dramatic weakness, since there is no reason

why his conversion should occur when it does. From a homiletic point of view, it may be desirable that such a change come suddenly, but the dramatist sacrifices too much in terms of credibility. This problem of unmotivated repentance is a persistent difficulty in the interludes, and may be accounted for by the need for brevity.

The play is not strictly divided into comic and serious. The virtues speak soberly, and so does Youth after his repentance; the vices speak and act with brash vulgarity, and their jokes, usually at the expense of the virtues, are coarse, so as to indicate unworthiness. Some of the action involves physical threats, and there was no doubt a good deal of jostling and molesting in the performances.

These features, together with the simplified moral doctrine and the general adaptability, suggest that the play was written for popular audiences. It was probably performed by five adults, Lechery being doubled with Humility. Such limited arrangements for doubling are typical of popular plays in the first two decades of the sixteenth century.

'The Play of the Wether'

Though the canon of John Heywood's work is still a matter for academic dispute, he was undoubtedly a skilful playwright, working within a pattern of court entertainment to which he made a substantial contribution. Medwall and John Rastell had shown that departures could be made from the morality idiom in subject matter and characterization. Heywood follows Medwall in writing about human beings, and in presenting moral ideas without using abstractions. Most of the characters in his plays are social types, and the centre of dramatic interest is usually the encounters between them. This means that his plays approximate to debates. *Wether* is typical in that all the suitors come to present their claims for the kind of weather most suited to their particular avocations. Weather in itself is a fairly trivial subject for dispute, and the upshot of the play is that Jupiter decides to persevere with the mixture which is already being provided. However, as D. M. Bevington suggested[5], this subject gives an opportunity to present the need for compro-

5. 'Is John Heywood's *Play of the Wether* really about the weather?', *Renaissance Drama* VII (1964), pp. 11–19.

mise and reconciliation in human affairs. Such an objective would be particularly apt in a time of national dissension, and it fits in with the humanistic thought of More, who was probably one of Heywood's supporters at court. The play is in no sense a criticism of the King – Jupiter remains a dignified figure throughout – but it does urge understanding and tolerance.

The debates within the play are a nice balance of conflicting claims, and at least two social pairs are made to confront one another, the two women and the two millers. In these episodes the types are clearly defined, and their opposing points of view are well matched and impartially presented. None of the eight suitors repeats the arguments of the others, and Heywood is clearly concerned to build up a set of mutually exclusive demands.

Mery Report acts as the porter, giving access to Jupiter only where the rank of the suitor demands it. Exercising the function of the licensed fool he comments briskly on each of the suitors, and, in most cases, he ridicules them. Though he is called a Vice – one of the earliest characters to be given the title – he is neither a moral abstraction nor an example of the later Vice role. He is dressed in 'light aray', which suggests a fool's costume, and may expect the reaction normally given to the fool – enjoyment of his ridicule, and appreciation of the truth which his apparently foolish comments contain.

The structure of the play is very simple: each suitor says his piece in turn, except for the two debates already mentioned. At the end, all the suitors are assembled – thus making it impossible for the parts to be doubled – and Jupiter descends to give his verdict. Except for this simplicity, *Wether* shows no great development in dramatic structure, but it is effective enough within its own limits, and is likely to have appealed to the aristocratic audience. The moral is offered obliquely, and with tact, and the ending is suitably pious.

The later development of the interlude does not, however, follow the line taken by Heywood in this play, perhaps because his achievement was very much circumscribed within narrow social and intellectual limits. Farce of this type could not, in fact, be expanded to take a wider view of human affairs and human character. The later interludes persisted in the morality tradition, and it was upon the development of this that their achievement and their influence were to depend.

'Wit and Science'

In our next play we find a return to the pre-eminence of allegory. Like *Wether* it is a court play, and relies upon boys for most of the important parts. Music is important in the play, and the probability is that it was performed by eight actors, four of whom were accomplished singers and instrumentalists. There were enough musicians to provide viols for the four-piece setting of 'Exceeding Measure' (lines 620, 629–42), as well as the six voices required for 'Welcome, Mine Own' (lines 989–1020), and the 'quere' for the last song. Probably men as well as boys were used in these musical episodes.

But the success of the music is overshadowed by the allegory. John Redford was Master of the Choristers at St Paul's choir school from 1531 to 1534, and his concern is chiefly educational, within the limits of Renaissance ideas. The play shows how Wit relies upon Reason to achieve his end of marrying Science, whom we should probably call Knowledge or Enlightenment. Wit, the virtue of Erasmus and More, must overcome the monster Tediousness, and journey to Mount Parnassus for inspiration. Reason, also beloved of More, helps him by giving self-awareness, represented as the glass of Reason, and by showing him how to make proper use of Instruction, Study, and Diligence. The traditional structure of moral allegory is adapted to the story of Wit's education, for, like Mankind, Wit falls into temptation and is endangered through his own stupidity. His first encounter with Tediousness is a disaster: ignoring his advisers, he rushes into a fight, and is killed. He is revived by Honest Recreation, Comfort, Quickness, and Strength, and then goes astray again by indulging too heartily in recreation. He falls into the power of Idleness, a female character who recalls Lechery in *Youth*. But the use of this traditional allegorical pattern does not preclude originality, for, in a well-sustained comic passage, Idleness changes Wit's clothes for those of the fool, Ignorance, and blackens his face while he is asleep. This leads to comic misunderstandings when Wit, dressed as the fool, again assays Science.

In this episode Wit displays foolish pride and boastfulness, but the allegorical significance of the play is never presented in the moral terms of the earlier morality plays. Redford keeps his mind firmly upon the virtues of scholarship, and he is entirely successful in creating an educational allegory for the benefit of his pupils. All the characters are fitted neatly into the allegorical scheme, and one feels that for this author allegory is neither prop nor decoration, but an end in itself. Though English writers have exhibited what might be called a chronic devotion to allegory, there have been few who have achieved so comprehensive and precise an effect as Redford does in this play.

Apart from the features of the morality we have noted, Redford adapts the *débat* technique in the slanging match between Idleness and Honest Recreation, a passage which recalls the argument between the Laundress and the Gentlewoman in *Wether*. There are medieval features in the ranting of Tediousness and in his allegiance to 'Mahound', a sign of his evil nature. However, the strongest dramatic analogue seems to be the folk play. Tediousness is a kind of giant, wearing a visor and carrying a club, and in these features he resembles the monster killed by St George in later versions of the folk play. The central episode of the folk play is the conflict between hero and monster, and in several versions the hero is killed and has to be brought to life again. This death and revival (usually called the 'renouveau') is often accompanied by a comic wooing. The fortunes of Wit are thus similar to those of the folk-play hero, but we must remember that the details of the folk play as they have been recorded in the twentieth century are not necessarily the same as they would have been in the sixteenth. Perhaps the jig of Idleness also suggests dances embodied in the folk play. The exact analogues here must remain conjectural, but it is certain that court entertainment often contained elements from folk festivals, and that the court as well as the peasantry was accustomed to celebrate the changing of the seasons.

But Redford's chief accomplishment lies in the restrained and persuasive tone of his play. Its good humour and discrimination suggest that it was possible to be learned without being pedantic.

'Respublica'

This is the most political of the plays in the present selection. The author was not the first in the field. He was preceded by Lyndsay in *Ane Satire of the Thrie Estaitis* and Bale in *King Johan* (1538), but his greatest debt is probably to *Magnyfycence*. In his picture of courtly corruption he shares with Skelton a sense of outrage at the abuses of political power. But the political situation which Skelton had before him was different from that faced by the author of *Respublica*, and each play naturally reflects the particular problems of its time. *Respublica*, as a political satire, attacks the abuses of the years just past, abuses perpetrated by the Protestant manipulators of Edward VI (1547–53), who feathered their own nests and who are represented here by Avarice. The play eschews the violence of religious controversy, there being no hint of theological or ecclesiastical changes which Mary may have been contemplating in 1553. Indeed it looks forward to the emergence of a new national prosperity under Mary, who is represented in the play by the goddess Nemesis.

However, the political allegory does not work by a series of specific identifications, or at least none (save that of Nemesis-Mary) is now apparent. Avarice may represent the Protestant fleecers, but there does not seem to be any individual profiteer in mind. Instead the evil significance of Avarice is conveyed firstly by his being one of the Seven Deadly Sins (this is a Catholic morality play), and then by the vigour of his activities. He is a comic miser with purses under his cloak; he mutters to himself and grumbles at his associates; he exhibits a comic concern for the security of his wealth; and generally he acts as an eccentric villain.

Beyond this, Avarice is significant as an early example of the Vice, the arch-intriguer common in the interludes of the 1560s and 1570s. Indeed he is perhaps the first who can be properly identified (leaving aside the characters whom Heywood had called Vices). The Vice was a comic role of the first importance, and already we can see in *Respublica* that Avarice dominates the action, is on stage for long periods, and makes the strongest impression upon the other characters and upon the audience. Like the later

27

Vices, he adopts an alias and a disguise, and displays a verbal facility, including a power of equivocation, which overshadows his assistants. This reminds the audience of the ingenuity of evil which is really, *sub specie aeternitatis*, only folly. Clearly the interludes of the thirty years after *Respublica* were largely sustained by the theatrical magnetism of characters like Avarice. The rising professional companies of adult players quickly took up the lead given them by the boys' companies.

Besides the characterization of Avarice, there are other technical features in *Respublica* which give evidence of growing theatrical expertise. The group of villains indulge in comic by-play which demands good timing and a capacity to manage the audience's response from climax to climax. Some of this is achieved by the clownish comedy of ignorance, and some by being quick on cues and giving pace to the lines. There are also well-managed scenes of rejoicing and of panic, and effective use is made of the conventions of alias and disguise whereby the villains nearly give themselves away through carelessness or stupidity.

The play continues the morality theme of retribution. This was the conventional method of restoring the fortunes of the virtuous, and here it is worked out by means of the four daughters of God, and the coming of Nemesis, a classical figure adapted to the needs of the political allegory. This impulse is important in the development of tragedy and the chronicle play later in the century.

'Apius and Virginia'

It may be felt that the literary achievements of R. B. hardly match his pretensions, but the latter are important in the history of the drama because they illustrate the direction in which taste was moving in the 1560s. The author had derived from his books a sense that drama could be impressive and deal with powerful emotions, and he chooses to achieve this by repeated references to classical figures who had the same feelings as his own characters. It is not a very effective method, but it is certainly a well-tried one. The books which influenced him were those which were available in the curriculum of sixteenth-century schools, particularly Ovid, who provided tales of a passionate and tragic nature. He probably used Chaucer's *Phisicien's Tale* as his direct source, but he embellished the story with many details from Seneca, who was an influence in early English tragedy. *Gorboduc*, which owes much to Seneca, had already appeared (1562), and other plays in the same mould soon followed, especially *Gismond of Salerne* (1566) and *Jocasta* (1566). Thomas Newton's *Seneca His Tenne Tragedies Translated into English* were in preparation at this time and appeared in 1581. R. B. finds inspiration for the tyrant Apius in the style of Seneca, and the monologues of Apius have a number of references to the fashionable horrors found in the tragedies. At the same time, we must not overlook the fame of Herod in the mystery cycles, whose ranting was still sensational when Shakespeare wrote *Hamlet* a generation later.

On the title-page the play is called a 'Tragicall Comedie'. Besides the ranting Apius, there are other elements which support the first word of this description. The most important is the attempt to create dilemmas for both Apius and Virginia. The problem for Apius is how to achieve his lustful objective without compromising the justice which his office enjoins upon him. But he does not resist for very long, and the persuasions of Haphazard soon encourage him to take a chance, to hazard on hap: by a cheap trick, he seeks to gain possession of the heroine, and in so doing he destroys himself and her. He is a picture of the corrupt judge, and as such he is condemned by the author. Virginia's dilemma is the difficulty of preserving her chastity. Carefully nurtured by a loving family, she is destined for wifely fidelity. The demands of Apius force her to choose between death and dishonour, and the author strives to make her request for death at the hands of her father pathetic and morally imposing. Although he elaborates this episode far beyond his source, he does not succeed: but his attempt to create a pathetic death scene is a notable ingredient in his conception of tragedy.

It may be that the play is to be seen as an early attempt at tragicomedy. Certainly the idea of comedy is interpreted, as far as the serious characters are concerned, as a means of vindicating the virtuous. Virginia dies, but her fame lives on, and she is presented as an example of virtuous chastity. Remote as it may be, this notion of comedy is found in the *Divine Comedy*. The difficulty for the modern reader is that, in the end, the concern with moral abstractions outweighs the human interest as the author struggles to make us believe that all is well.

Moreover he interprets comedy as clowning. Alongside the main story we are shown the fashionable buffoonery of the Vice, who adds to his success with Apius by corrupting the servants, persuading them to take a chance and to fall short in the execution of their duties. While the songs of Virginius and his family show high-minded virtue, the Vice's songs with the servants show his corrupting influence. Although there may be a theoretical connection between the Vice's influence upon the main and the secondary plots, there is little contact between the characters concerned in them. This may be due to the alternating structure imposed by doubling requirements, but we are justified in seeing in it a reflection of a fundamentally mechanical application of contemporary notions of tragedy and comedy.

The author is not able to free himself from the narrow interpretation of human conduct imposed by the ethical traditions of the moralities, and his approach to both comedy and tragedy is dominated by them. Thus the final denouement of the play is managed by the appearance of moral abstractions who bring punishment for Apius and the Vice, and recognition for the virtue of Virginia. R. B.'s moral position is closely allied to that taken by other authors of homiletic tragedy in the 1560s, notably Thomas Preston in *Cambises*, and John Pikeryng in *Horestes*. In both these plays, tragedy is approached and tragic situations are outlined, but the authors avoid the final implications of tragedy in favour of moral simplification.

Haphazard is one of the most fully developed of all the examples of the Vice in the interludes. He displays the heartless manipulation of his victims (he destroys Apius as well as Virginia) and the vigorous inventiveness which characterize the role elsewhere. He also has the verbal facility and the capacity to change his moods which make the Vice a lively element in the late interludes. His part is long enough and sufficiently complex to be played by the most experienced actor in the troupe. Without him, the various objectives of the author would simply fall apart. His moral significance is that he attacks ordered society, which should be supported

30

by justice, and which depends upon the blessings of domestic happiness and the virtues of loyalty, fidelity, honour, and love, which the family preserves. The emphasis placed upon the latter is probably to be explained by the auspices under which the play was produced: it is a subject most appropriate to the education of the young.

'Like Will to Like'

Although this play is provided with a description on the title-page which proclaims its didactic purpose, and although it is embellished with quotations from Cicero's ethical writings, the Bible, and other theological sources, it cannot be said that the author makes a great showing as a moralist. The moral of the play is that villains attract one another, and at the beginning Lucifer instructs Nichol Newfangle, the Vice, to bring together evil-doers of similar nature. Such a moral is really very commonplace – indeed it was already proverbial before Fulwell took it up – and the moral education which the play offers is scrappy. Newfangle does succeed in bringing together groups of sinners, and he actively pursues the objective of bringing three of them to the gallows; but the plot is so episodic that there is little sense of moral argument in it. The play is made to appear the more eclectic because it lacks the traditional hero who could be the victim of the Vice's scheming temptation, and consequently there is no central action. It is hardly surprising that the author has to rely on strident repetition of 'Like will to like, quoth the Devil to the Collier' in order to keep up a moral front.

An attempt is made to give a coherent structure by means of the two appearances of the Devil. These scenes are perhaps the most successful, because they have a visual effect, and they were striking enough to be remembered by playwrights for some years afterwards. Newfangle has served his apprenticeship in Hell, and the author draws attention to the Devil's incompetence by making him ridiculous. The Vice has nothing but contempt for his 'godfather', and although he does act as a wrecker in human affairs, he is quick to make fun of the Devil. Such inconsistencies are part of the traditions of Devils and Vices upon the stage, and they have the effect of differentiating these characters from human beings. This has comic possibilities as well as a moral advantage, in that it illustrates the irreducible nonsense of sin: sin is the greatest folly of all. At the end of the play Newfangle rides off to Hell on the Devil's back. This is a reward for satisfactory work, but one may ask what kind of reward a journey to Hell really is. As a piece of stage-craft it is very effective, and is comparable to the bridling of Lust in *The Triall of Treasure* as recalled in the extract from *Sir Thomas More*.

The intervening episodes show how successfully Newfangle brings like to like. He encourages the alliance between Tom Tosspot and Ralph Roister, both tavern figures given to gambling, as foreshadowed in medieval literature, and in the miscellaneous villains in *Mankind*, *Youth*, and *Hickscorner*. Indeed this group of popular interludes seems the main theatrical antecedent of *Like Will to Like*. What is notable is that Fulwell seems to have more theatrical resource than his predecessors. Newfangle also succeeds in bringing Haunce and Philip Fleming together as drunkards (following a convention that Flemings were heavy drinkers), and he unites Cutpurse and Pickpurse, two characters who emerge in earlier plays as the sparring partners of the Vice.

The Virtues in this play have little to do with the episodes dominated by the Vice. In one scene Virtuous Living demonstrates that he is not like Newfangle and finds his company unattractive, but this can only be regarded as paying superficial attention to the conflict of vices and virtues, and very little dramatic effect is made out of the scene. Newfangle, having been the instrument of corruption for Cutpurse and Pickpurse, turns upon them and acts as the servant of Severity, who comes to judge them.

There is no evidence that this play was ever performed, but the stage directions suggest that the author had a clear idea of certain dramatic effects. The writing of the Vice's part is particularly vigorous, and it seems likely that the play would appeal to a certain level of audience, though perhaps not the most sophisticated. The Vice's part contains a number of items designed to draw the audience into the action. The play must stand or fall by its theatrical potential, and serves as a useful indication of the kind of competence found among writers of interludes. If it survived alone, one might suspect that it was a barren exercise, but its similarity with other plays which take a proverb as their main theme suggests that it represents a distinctly popular type. One might instance the work of William Wager to support this; but Wager's plays (two of which have been published recently in an accessible form[6]) are more coherent from a moral point of view.

'Sir Thomas More'

Our last extract is a retrospect. *Sir Thomas More* was written by Elizabethan dramatists for the theatre of their time, some sixty or seventy years after the events contained in the story. A theatrical revolution had brought new conventions into being, and the history of the development of the interlude seems to have been telescoped for the dramatic purpose of this play. The interlude is supposed to have been performed in More's lifetime, which means before 1535, but it is more typical of interludes in the period following *Respublica*. Perhaps it draws upon Anthony Munday's own recollections from childhood and upon what his elders had told him. Whatever its source, the play is a fascinating compendium of many of the features of the interludes collected in this book. We find the allegory adapted for the education of the young and offering advice, as in the original *Wit and Science*, together with a good deal of detail concerning the Vice, who, as we have seen, comes after 1553. Inclination is clearly played by the leading actor (the spokesman for the group) and he uses his dagger as an indication of his role.

The extract covers most effectively the problems of producing an interlude. We are shown the tension which arises over the missing beard, and are given an insight into the considerable burdens of doubling and of costume change which the players had to endure. The company is small, and More is impressed by the list of parts undertaken by the boy. We also see the dependence upon patronage. The players offer their wares at the beginning; one of them consults More during the technical crisis; and the reward which follows the performance (or rather the abortive performance) is anxiously scrutinized. More's generosity and his hospitality are much ap-

6. W. Wager, *'The longer Thou Livest'* and *'Enough is as Good as a Feast'*, ed. R. Mark Benbow, Nebraska, 1967; London, 1968.

preciated by the players. The interlude is accepted by him as part of the entertainment for his guest, the Lord Mayor, who is dining at his home. It is hard to say whether the fact that the banquet is to take place in a different room from the performance is merely a stage convenience, or a reflection of a contemporary practice: evidence from elsewhere favours the former explanation.

Some anachronisms seem to have crept into Munday's view of the interlude. As far as we can tell, two of the plays mentioned, *Lusty Juventus* and *Impatient Poverty*, appeared after More's death. The list of plays on offer suggests remarkable versatility on the part of the players, which may not be surprising; but there is perhaps a hint or two of a theatrical London more developed and complex than the evidence suggests was possible in the first half of the century. Oagle, the costumier, seems to have been Munday's contemporary rather than More's.

But in spite of this, Munday appears sensitive to the interlude. Without adopting Ben Jonson's supercilious air, he suggests the simple dramatic effects of the interlude, and allows More to reveal some of the difficulties and shortcomings. The players are honest men, if somewhat hard-pressed. Munday's historical concern is a measure of the debt owed by Elizabethan playwrights and actors to their inheritance.

Editorial Note

In preparing the texts I have tried to preserve the character of the original language as far as possible. I have transliterated the obsolete letters '3' and 'þ', and, to avoid possible confusion, I have adopted the modern convention for distinguishing 'u' and 'v'. I have supplied punctuation throughout. Otherwise very little modernization has been attempted, and the many inconsistencies of spelling have been left undisturbed.

In determining the texts I have relied in the first instance upon the earliest manuscripts or printed books, or upon facsimiles of these. I owe a considerable debt to the work of modern editors, and I have made specific acknowledgement in a number of places. Each text has a brief preface giving bibliographical information.

Difficult words are explained at the foot of the page at their first appearance, and sometimes I have repeated the explanations. A list of these explanations, arranged alphabetically, is at the end of the volume. Fuller explanations of individual phrases and other notes are numbered and printed at the end of the book.

A Note on Books

In the following selective bibliography I have listed the most important works on the interlude. There is, regrettably, insufficient space for a full list of interludes. Details of editions of the plays in this volume will be found in the prefatory note to each play. Several of the works listed below contain detailed bibliographies, of which the most recent is that appended to F. P. Wilson's *The English Drama, 1485–1585* by G. K. Hunter.

The place of publication is London, unless otherwise specified.

1. *Bibliographical Works*

F. W. Bateson, *Cambridge Bibliography of English Literature*, 5 vols., 1940–57

W. W. Greg, *A Bibliography of English Printed Drama to the Restoration*, 4 vols., 1962

A. Harbage, *Annals of English Drama, 975–1700*, revised by S. Schoenbaum, 1962 (Supplements 1966 and 1970)

A. W. Pollard and G. R. Redgrave, *A Short Title Catalogue of Books Printed in England, 1475–1640*, 1926

C. J. Stratman, *A Bibliography of Mediaeval Drama*, Berkeley, 1954

2. *Collections and Series*

J. Q. Adams, *Chief Pre-Shakespearean Dramas*, Boston, 1924

W. Bang, *Materialien zur Kunde des alteren englischen Dramas*, Louvain, 1902–

A. Brandl, *Quellen des weltlichen Dramas in England vor Shakespeare*, Strassburg, 1898

R. Dodsley, *A Select Collection of Old English Plays*, Fourth Edition by W. C. Hazlitt, 15 vols., 1874–6

Early English Text Society (E.E.T.S.)

J. S. Farmer, *Tudor Facsimile Texts*, 143 vols., 1907–14
    'Lost' Tudor Plays, 1907
    Anonymous Plays, Four Series, 1905

C. M. Gayley, *Representative English Comedies*, 4 vols., New York, 1903–14

Malone Society Reprints and *Collections*, 1907–

J. M. Manly, *Specimens of the Pre-Shakespearean Drama*, 2 vols., 1897–8

3. *Critical Studies*

J. E. Bernard, *The Prosody of the Tudor Interlude*, New Haven, 1939

D. M. Bevington, *From 'Mankind' to Marlowe*, Cambridge, Mass., 1962

    Tudor Drama and Politics, Cambridge, Mass., 1968

F. S. Boas, *An Introduction to Tudor Drama*, Oxford, 1933

M. C. Bradbrook, *The Growth and Structure of Elizabethan Comedy*, 1955

    The Rise of the Common Player, 1962

C. F. T. Brooke, *The Tudor Drama*, Cambridge, Mass., 1911

E. K. Chambers, *The Mediaeval Stage*, 2 vols., Oxford, 1903

    The English Folk Play, Oxford, 1933

    English Literature at the Close of the Middle Ages, Oxford, 1945

M. P. Coogan, *An Interpretation of the Moral Play 'Mankind'*, Washington, D.C., 1947

L. A. Cormican, 'Morality Tradition and the Interludes', in *The Age of Chaucer*, ed. B. Ford (Penguin Books), 1954

H. Craig, *English Religious Drama of the Middle Ages*, Oxford, 1955

T. W. Craik, *The Tudor Interlude*, Leicester, 1958

L. W. Cushman, *The Devil and the Vice in the English Dramatic Literature before Shakespeare*, Halle, 1900

M. Doran, *Endeavors of Art*, Madison, 1954

W. Farnham, *The Mediaeval Heritage of Elizabethan Tragedy*, Berkeley, 1936, reprinted 1963

P. Hogrefe, *The Sir Thomas More Circle*, Urbana, 1959

G. R. Owst, *Literature and Pulpit in Mediaeval England*, second edition, Oxford, 1961

A. W. Reed, *Early Tudor Drama*, 1926

C. Ricks (ed.), *English Drama to 1710*, 1971

A. P. Rossiter, *English Drama from early times to the Elizabethans*, 1950

B. Spivack, *Shakespeare and the Allegory of Evil*, New York, 1958

E. J. Sweeting, *Early Tudor Criticism*, Oxford, 1940

R. J. E. Tiddy, *The Mummers' Play*, Oxford, 1923

M. P. Tilley, *A Dictionary of the Proverbs in England in the Sixteenth and Seventeenth Centuries*, Ann Arbor, 1950

B. J. Whiting, *Proverbs in the Earlier English Drama*, Cambridge, Mass., 1938

G. Wickham, *Early English Stages*, 2 vols., 1959–62

F. P. Wilson, *The English Drama, 1485–1585*, Oxford, 1969, with a
    bibliography by G. K. Hunter

O. E. Winslow, *Low Comedy as a Structural Element in English Drama*,
    Chicago, 1926

THE PRIDE OF LIFE

This play survived into modern times only as a fragment of 502 lines. The manuscript was probably written in the first quarter of the fifteenth century, and was found in the Account Roll of the Priory of the Holy Trinity, Dublin, for the years 1337–46. The text was the work of two scribes with differing dialects and hand-writing: scribe A copied lines 1–4, 33–82, 127–54, 327–438, and B lines 5–32, 83–126, 155–326, and 439–502. It was written out in four columns, interrupted by older material on the parchment. As the continuation of these columns was lost, there are two 'lacunae' in the text (at lines 126 and 326), and the end of the play is missing, though the Prologue gives some indications about the plot.

Recent work by Professor Norman Davis suggests that the date of composition may be as early as the middle of the fourteenth century.* This conclusion is based upon a consideration of linguistic forms in the text. He has also pointed out that the work has enough similarities with the Kildare Poems to suggest that the original is Anglo-Irish. Previously scholars had thought that the work originated in England.

Besides the problems raised by the work of the two scribes, and by the missing portions, the preparation of the text for the modern reader is made more difficult by the destruction of the manuscript by fire in 1922. The editor must rely upon the work of his five predecessors:

James Mills, *Account Roll of the Priory of the Holy Trinity, Dublin, 1337–1346*, Dublin, 1891. This contains a reproduction of some eighty lines of the manuscript. Mills suggested the title of the play

A. Brandl, *Quellen des weltlichen Dramas in England vor Shake-speare*, Strassburg, 1898

F. Holthausen, *Archiv* 108 (1902)

* I am grateful to Professor Davis for showing me the proofs of his Introduction before publication.

O. Waterhouse, *The Non-Cycle Mystery Plays*, 1909, Early English Text Society, Extra Series 104

N. Davis, *Non-Cycle Plays and Fragments*, 1970, Early English Text Society, Supplementary Text No. 1

It appears that the manuscript was slightly damaged on the left-hand edge, and difficult to read in a number of places. It has therefore been necessary to include some editorial conjectures, which are placed in brackets in this edition. These conjectures are chiefly those of Brandl and Holthausen.

I have attempted to preserve the character of the language of the period: most of the changes I have made are typographical. The old letters '3' and 'þ' have been changed to 'y' or 'gh' and to 'th'. The scribes themselves were confused by these letters, however, and a number of changes have been made here to regularize the position. Similarly 'f' and 'v' caused them some difficulty, and I have attempted to remove this obstacle. A particular problem arises with words (nouns, verbs, and adjectives) ending in '-h'. Scribe A, with almost complete consistency, leaves this letter out (line 3 *bet*; compare line 81 *deth*); B generally puts it in (line 5 *beth*), but he is less consistent than A (line 9 *stondit*). For the convenience of the modern reader, I have added '-h' where the sense demands it.

In general my text is based upon that of Mills, and I have listed below (pp. 384–5) his readings where mine differ significantly. Many inconsistencies of spelling remain. It would be a bold undertaking, and one beyond the scope of this edition, to attempt to eliminate the changes made by the scribes and to restore the author's original spelling.

The Pride of Life

PROLOGUS[1]
Pees[2] and horkynt[3], hal ifer,
[rich] and por, yong and hold,
men and wemen, that beth her,
both lerit and leut, stout and bold!

Lordinges and ladiis that beth hende,
herkenith al with mylde mode
[how ou]re gam schal gyn and ende:
lorde us wel spede that sched his blode!

Nou stondith stil and beth hende
[and pra]yith al for the weder[4]　　　　　　10
[and] ye schal or ye hennis wende
be glad that ye come hidir.

Her ye schullin here spelle
of mirth and eke of kare;
herkenith and I wol you telle
[how the proud[5]] schal ffare.

[Of the Kyng of] Lif I wol you telle;
[he stondith[6]] first bi-ffore
[al men that beth] of fflessch and ffel
[and of woman i-]bore.　　　　　　　　　20

[He is forsoth ful] stronge to stonde,
[and is] by-comin of kinge,
[giveth] lawis in eche a londe
[and nis] dradd of no thinge.

1 *Pees* peace　*horkynt* hearken　*hal* all　*ifer* together　2 *hold* old
3 *beth* are　*her* here　4 *lerit* learned　*leut* ignorant　5 *hende*
gracious　6 *mode* manner　7 *gam* play　9 *Nou* now　11 *or* before
hennis hence　*wende* go　13 *spelle* story　14 *eke* also　15 *wol* will
16 *ffare* make out　19 *ffel* skin　20 *i-bore* born　22 *by-comin*
descended　23 *eche a* every　*londe* land, kingdom　24 *nis* is not
dradd afraid

43

[In] pride and likinge his lif he ledith,
lordlich he lokith with eye;
[prin]ce and dukes, he seith, him dredith,
[he] dredith no deth ffor to deye.

[He] hath a lady lovelich al at likinge
ne may he of no mirth mene ne misse[7];   30
he seith in swetnisse he wol set his likinge
and bringe his bale boun in-to blisse[8].

Knyghtis he hath cumlich
in bred and in leinth;
not I nevir non such
of stotey ne off strynth.

Wat helpith to yilp mucil of his mit,
or bost to mucil of his blys?
[Ne] sorou may sit onis sit,
[and myrth may he] not miss.   40

[Her stant ek the] ladi of lond
[the faire]st a lord for to led;
[glad] may he be for to stond
[and b]ehold that blisful bled.

That ladi is lettrit in lor
as cumli becomith for a quen;
[and munith] hir mac evirmor,
as a dar, for dred him to ten[9].

---

25 *likinge* pleasure 26 *lordlich* lordly 28 *deye* die 29 *lovelich* lovely *at likinge* for his pleasure 30 *mene* complain 32 *bale* injury, evil *boun* bound 33 *cumlich* handsome 34 *bred* breadth *leinth* length (of stature) 35 *not* knew 36 *stotey* cunning *off* of *strynth* strength 37 *Wat helpith* what does it help? *yilp* boast *mucil* much *mit* might 39 *onis* in his *sit* sight 41 *Her* here *stant* stands *ek* also 42 *led* lead 44 *bled* flower, blossom 45 *lettrit* learned *lor* doctrine 46 *cumli* beautiful 47 *munith* has in mind *mac* mate 48 *a* she *dar* dares *ten* vex

Ho bid him bewar or he smert[10]
for in his lond Deth wol alond;   50
[as] ho levit him gostlich in hert
[ho b]it him bewar of his hend.

Ho begynit to charp of char
thes wordis wythout lesing:
'Deth doth not spar
knyghtis, cayser, ne kyng.

'Nou, lord, lev thy likyng
Whych bringith the soul gret bal.'
This answer ho had of the kyng:
'Ye[a], this [is] a womanis tal.'   60

The kyng hit ne toke not to hert,
for hit was a womanis spech:
[and y]et hit mad him to smert
[wh]an him mit help no lech.

The quen yit can hir undirstond
wat help thar mit be,
and sent aftir the bicop of the lond
for he chout mor than he.

He cham and prec[h]it al that he couthe
and warnit him hal of his hind;   70
[h]it savrit not in the kyngis mouth,
bot hom he bad him wynd.

49 *Ho* she *or* lest *smert* suffer   50 *wol alond* will go along
51 *levit* loved *gostlich* spiritually   52 *bit* bade *hend* end
53 *charp* talk *char* care   54 *lesing* lies   55 *spar* spare   56 *cayser*
emperor   57 *lev* leave   58 *bal* injury   60 *womanis* woman's *tal*
tale, speech   61 *hit* it   64 *lech* physician   65 *can* began
undirstond consider   66 *thar* there   68 *chout* knew   69 *cham* came
prechit preached *couthe* knew   70 *warnit* warned *hal* wholly,
fully *hind* end   71 *savrit* savoured   72 *hom* home *wynd* go

Wand the bicop is hom wend
fram that [sterne] stryf,
[to Deth a me]ssenger than send
[is by] the Kyng of Lif.

[The kyng] him wold do undirston[d]
[that al] he may del and dit
[he ne] wold cum into his ouin lond
on him to kyt his mit[11].   80

Deth comith[12] – he dremith a dredfful dreme –
welle aghte al carye![13] –
and slow ffader and moder and then heme:
he ne wold none sparye.

Sone affter hit be-fel that deth and life
beth togeder i-take[14],
and ginnith and strivith a sterne strife,
(the) King of Life to wrake.

With him drivith a-doun to grounde,
he dredith no thing his knightis,   90
and delith him depe dethis wounde,
and kith on him his mightis.

Qwhen the body is doun i-broght
the soule sorow a-wakith,
the bodyis pride is dere a-boght,
the soule the ffendis takith.

And throgh priere of Oure Lady mylde –
al godenisse scho wol qwyte –
scho wol prey her son so mylde
the soule and body schul dispyte.   100

---

73 *Wand* when *wend* gone 74 *stryf* contest 77 *do* make
78 *al* whatever *del* act *dit* do 80 *kyt* quit *mit* might
81 *dremith* dreams 82 *aghte* was bound *carye* to care 83 *slow*
slew *heme* uncle 84 *sparye* spare 86 *i-take* met 88 *wrake*
destroy 92 *kith* quits 93 *Qwhen* when 94 *soule* soul's 95 *a-boght* paid for 98 *qwyte* requite 100 *dispyte* pity

The cors that nere knewe of care
no more then stone in weye
schal [knowe] of sorow and sore care
[and lie] be-twene ham tweye.

The soule ther-on schal be weye
that the ffendes have i-kaghte[15]:
and Our Lady schal ther-for preye
so that with her he schal be lafte.

Nou beith in pes and beith hende
and distourbith noght oure place[16],   110
ffor this oure game schal gin and ende
throgh Ihesus Cristis swete grace[17].

REX VIVUS *incipi*[e]*t sic dicendum*[18]
Pes, now, ye princes of powere so prowde,
ye kinges, ye kempes, ye knightes i-korne,
ye barons bolde, that beith me o-bowte;
[do] schal yu my sawe, swaynis i-[s]worne.

Sqwieris stoute, stondith now stille,
and lestenith to my hestes I hote yu now her:
or [I] schal wirch yu wo with werkes of wil,
and doun schal ye drive, be ye never so dere.   120

King ich am, kinde of kinges i-korre,
al the worlde wide to welde at my wil:
Nas ther never no man of woman i-borre
o-gein me withstonde that I nold him spille.

---

101 *cors* body   *nere* never   102 *then* than (and so frequently)
weye road   105 *be weye* lament   106 *i-kaghte* grabbed   108 *lafte*
left   109 *pes* peace   111 *game* play   114 *kempes* champions
i-korne chosen   115 *o-bowte* about   116 *sawe* bidding   *swaynis*
men   *i-sworne* bound to me by oath   118 *hestes* instructions
hote give   *her* here   119 *wirch* exercise, impose upon   *werkes*
painful tasks   *wil* [my] whim, pleasure   121 *ich* I   *kinde* breed
i-korre chosen   122 *welde* wield, manipulate   123 *Nas* was not
i-borre born   124 *o-gein* against   *nold* would not   *spille* destroy

Lordis of lond, beith at my ledinge,
al men schal a-bow in hal and in bowr ...¹⁹

[REGINA]
Baldli thou art mi bot,
tristili and ful treu;
of al mi rast thou art rot,
I nil chong fer no new.   130

REX
Al in wel ich am bi-went,
may ne grisful thing me grou;
likyng is wyth me bi[-lent],
alyng is it mi behou.

Strenth and Hel, knyghtis kete,
Deth rift in ded,
lok that for no thing ye let
smartli to me sped.

Bringith wyth you brit brondis,
helmis brit and schend;   140
for ich am lord ofir al londis
and that is wel i-sen.

PRIMUS MILES, FORTITUDO
Lord, in truthe thou mit trist
fethfuli to stond:
thou mit liv as the[e] list
for wonschild is thu fond.

125 *ledinge* rule 126 *hal* hall 127 *Baldli* bravely *bot* remedy,
comfort 128 *tristili* trustworthily *treu* true 129 *rast* rest *rot*
root 130 *nil* will not *chong* change *fer* for 131 *wel* comfort
bi-went established 132 *grisful* wretched, sorrowful *grou* grieve
133 *likyng* pleasure *bi-lent* settled 134 *alyng* wholly, entirely
mi behou proper to me 135 *kete* brave 136 *rift* strikes *in ded*
in deed, certainly 137 *let* omit 138 *smartli* swiftly *sped* support
139 *brit* bright *brondis* swords 140 *helmis* helmets *schend*
shining 141 *ofir* over 142 *i-sen* seen 143 *trist* trust 144 *fethfuli*
faithfully 145 *list* please 146 *wonschild*(?) child of plenty
fond found

Ich am strenth, stif and strong;
neuar is such non
in al this world brod and long
i-mad of blod and bon.   150

Hav no dout of no thing
that evir may befal;
ich am Strenth thi derling
flour of knitis al.

SECUNDUS MILES, SANITAS
King of Lif that berist the croun
as hit is skil and righte:
I am Hele i-com to toun,
thi kinde curteyse[20] knighte.

Thou art lord of lim and life
and king with-outen ende;   160
stif and strong and sterne in strif
in londe qwher thou wende.

Thou nast no nede to sike sore
ffor no thing on lyve;
thou schal lyve ever more:
qwho dar with the strive?

REX
Strive? nay, to me qwho is so gode?[21]
hit were bot ffolye;
ther is no man that me dur bode
any vileynye.   170

147 *stif* valiant 148 *neuar* nowhere *such non* such a one 150
i-mad made *blod* blood *bon* bone 151 *dout* fear 154 *flour*
flower 155 *berist* bearest 156 *skil* fitting 157 *toun* town 158
curteyse courteous, possessing knightly virtues 159 *lim* limb
162 *londe* kingdom *qwher* where *wende* go 163 *nast no* hast
not any *sike* sigh 166 *qwho* who *the* thee 167 *gode* good
168 *bot* but 169 *dur* dare *bode* threaten

Qwher-of schuld I drede
qwhen I am King of Life?
fful evil schuld he spede
to me that werch strive.

I schal lyve ever mo
and croun ber as kinge;
I ne may never wit of wo,
I lyve at my likinge.

REGINA
Sire, thou saist as the liste,
thou livist at thi wille;   180
bot somthing thou miste,
and ther-ffor hold the stille.

Thinke thou haddist beginninge
qwhen thou were i-bore;
and bot thou mak god endinge
thi sowle is fforlore.

Love God and holy chirche,
and have of him som eye;
ffonde his werkes for to wirch
and thinke that thou schal deye.   190

REX
Douce dam, qwhi seistou so?
Thou spekis noght as the sleye;
I schal lyve ever mo
ffor bothe two thin eye[22].

171 *Qwher-of* of what   173 *spede* thrive, fare   174 *werch* threatens
176 *ber* bear   177 *wit* know   179 *the liste* you please   184 *i-bore*
born   185 *bot* unless   186 *fforlore* utterly lost   188 *eye* fear
189 *ffonde* try   *wirch* carry out   191 *Douce* sweet   *dam* lady
seistou sayest thou   192 *noght* not   *sleye* cunning, wise

Woldistou that I were dede
that thou might have a new?
Hore, the devil gird of thi hede,
bot that worde schal the rewe.

REGINA

Dede, sire? Nay, God wote my wil,
that ne kepte I noghte[23];   200
hit wolde like me fful ille
were hit thare-to broghte.

[Yet] thogh thou be kinge
nede schalt have ende;
deth ourecomith al thinge
hou-so-ever we wende.

REX

Ye, dam, thou hast wordis fale –
hit comith the of kinde;
this nis bot women tale
and that I wol the ffinde.   210

I ne schal never deye
ffor I am King of Life.
Deth is undir myne eye
and ther-ffor leve thi strife.

Thou dost bot mak myn hert sore
ffor hit nel noght helpe;
I prey the, spek of him no more,
qwhat wolte of him yelpe?

195 *Woldistou* do you wish   *dede* dead   197 *Hore* whore   *gird* smite   *of* off   198 *bot* unless   *the rewe* cause you regret   199 *wote* knows   200 *kepte* cared for   204 *nede shalt* needs must 206 *wende* turn about   207 *fale* many   208 *the* to thee   *of kinde* by nature   210 *the ffinde* reveal to you   211 *deye* die   214 *leve* leave 216 *nel* will not   218 *yelpe* boast

REGINA

Yilpe, sire? nay, so mot I the,
I sigge hit noght ther-ffore;   220
bot kinde techit bothe the and me,
ffirst qwhen we were bore,

for dowte of deth-is maistri
to wepe and make sorowe[24]:
holy writ and prophecye
ther-of I take to borowe.

Ther-ffor qwhile ye have mighte
and the worlde at wille,
I rede ye serve God almighte
bothe loude and stille[25].   230

This world is bot ffantasye
and fful of trechurye;
gode sire, for youre curteysye,
take this for no ffolye.

Ffor god [wot] wel the sothe,
I ne sey hit for no fabil:
Deth wol smyte to the;
in ffeith, loke thou be stabil.

REX

Qwhat prechistou of Dethis might
and of his maistrye?   240
He ne durst onis with me fight
for his bothe eye[26].

Streinth and Hele, qwhat sey ye,
my kinde, kornin knightes?
Schal Deth be lord over me
and reve me of mightes?

219 *so mot I the* as I may thrive 220 *sigge* say 221 *bot* but
kinde nature *techit* taught 224 *dowte* fear *maistri* authority
229 *rede* advise 235 *wot* knows *sothe* truth 238 *stabil* firm
239 *prechistou* do you preach 241 *onis* once 244 *kornin* chosen
246 *reve* deprive *mightes* powers

I MILES

Mi lord, so brouke I my bronde,
God that may ffor-bede
that Deth schold do the wronge
qwhile I am in thi thede.   250

I wol with-stonde him with strife,
and make his sidis blede,
and tel him that thou art King of Life
and lorde of londe and lede.

II MILES

May I him onis mete
with this longe launce
in ffelde other in strete
I wol him give mischaunce.

REX

Ye, thes be knightes of curteisye
and doghti men of dede;   260
of Deth ne of his maistrie
ne have I no drede.

Qwher is Mirth my messager,
swifte so lefe on lynde?
He is a nobil bachelere[27]
that rennis by the wynde.

Mirth and solas he can make
and ren so the ro;
lightly lepe oure the lake
qwher-so-ever he go.   270

247 *so* unless   *brouke* break   *bronde* sword   250 *thede* kingdom
252 *sidis* sides   254 *lede* people   257 *other* or   260 *doghti* brave
264 *so* as   *lynde* lime tree   266 *rennis* runs   268 *ren* run   *ro* roe-
deer   269 *lake* stream

53

Com and her my talente –
A-none and hy the blyve –
qwher any man as thou hast wente
dorst with me to strive?

NUNCIUS[28]
King of Lif and lord of londe,
as thou sittis on thi se
and florresschist with thi bright bronde
to the I sit on kne.

I am Mirth, wel thou wost,
thi mery messagere,   280
that wostou wel with-oute bost
ther nas never my pere,

doghtely to done a dede
that ye have ffor to done,
hen to Berewik o-pon Twede[29]
and com o-gein fful sone.

Ther is no thing the i-liche
in al this worlde wide
of gold and silver and robis riche
and hei hors on to ryde.   290

I have ben bothe fer and nere
in bataile and in strife.
Ocke, ther was never thy pere:
ffor thou art King of Life.

271 *her* hear   *talente* wish, desire   272 *A-none* at once   *hy* haste
blyve quickly   273 *qwher* whether   *wente* known   276 *se* throne
281 *wostou* you know   *bost* boast   282 *pere* equal   283 *doghtely*
bravely   284 *have ffor to done* require to be done   287 *the i-liche*
like you   290 *hei* proud   291 *ben* been   293 *Ocke* (exclamation)
oh!

REX

Aha Solas, now thou seist so
thou miriest me in my mode:
thou schal, boy, ar thou hennis go
be avaunsyd, bi the rode.

Thou schal have for thi gode wil
to thin avauncemente   300
the castel of Gailispire-on-the-Hil[30]
and the Erldom of Kente[31].

Draw the cord[32], sire Streynth,
rest I wol now take;
on erth in brede ne leynth
ne was nere yet my make.

> *Et tunc clausio tentorio dicet Regina*
> *secrete nuncio*[33]

REGINA

Messager, I pray the nowe,
ffor thi curteysye,
go to the bisschop for thi prowe
and byd him hydir to hye.   310

Bid him be-ware be-ffore,
sey him that he most preche;
my lord the king is ney lore
bot he wol be his leche.

Sey him that he wol leve noght
that ever he schal deye;
he is in siche errour broghte
of god stont him non eye[34].

---

295 *seist* sayest   296 *miriest* cheer   297 *ar* before   298 *avaunsyd*
advanced   *rode* rood, cross   306 *make* equal   309 *prowe* advantage   310 *hye* come   311 *be-ware* be aware   312 *sey* tell   313 *ney*
nearly   *lore* lost   314 *bot* unless   *leche* physician   315 *leve* believe
318 *stont* stands

NUNCIUS
Madam, I make no tarying
with softe wordis mo,   320
ffor I am Solas, I most singe
over al qwher I go.

      Et cantat[35]

Sire bisschop, thou sittist on thi se,
with thi mitir on thi hevede,
my lady the qwen preyith the
hit schold noght be bi-levyd[36].

     .   .   .   .

[EPISCOPUS[37]]
The world is nou so wo-lo-wo,
in such bal i-bound,
that dred of God is al ago
and treuth is go to ground.   330

Med is mad a demisman,
Streyint bet-ith the lau,
Geyl is mad a cepman,
and Truyth is don of dau.

Wyt is nou al trecri,
Othis fals and gret,
Play is nou vileni,
and Corteysi is let.

Lov is nou al lecuri,
cildrin beth onlerit,   340
halliday is glotuni:
thes lau-is beth irerit[38].

321 *most* must 324 *mitir* mitre *hevede* head 326 *bi-levyd*
believed 327 *wo-lo-wo* full of sorrow 328 *bal* pain 331 *Med*
Reward, Profit *demisman* judge 332 *Streyint* Strength *bet-ith*
beats *lau* law 333 *Geyl* Cunning *cepman* merchant 334 *don of
dau* done to death 335 *nou* now *trecri* treachery 336 *Othis*
oaths 338 *let* hindered 339 *lecuri* lechery 340 *cildrin* children
onlerit ignorant 342 *lau-is* laws *irerit* raised

Slet[39] men beth bleynd
and lokith al amis,
he bicomith onkynd
and that is reuth i-wis.

Frend may no man find
of fremit ne of sib;
the ded beth out of mind,
gret soru it is to lib. 350

Thes[e] ricmen beth reuthyles,
the por goth to ground;
and fals men beth schamles,
the soth ich hav i-found.

The rich kynyit it is wrong
al that the por doth,
for that is sen, day and nit,
wo-sa wol sig soth.

Paraventur men halt me a fol
to sig that soth tal; 360
thai farith as ficis in a pol —
the gret eteith the smal.

Rich men sparth for nothing
to do the por wrong,
thai thinkith not on her ending,
ne on Deth that is so strong.

Nothir thai lovith God, ne dredith
nothir him, no his lauis;
touart Hel fast ham drauth
ayeins har ending dauis. 370

343 *Slet* clever 345 *he* they 346 *reuth* pity *i-wis* indeed 348 *fremit* stranger *ne* nor *sib* relative 350 *lib* live 351 *reuthyles* merciless 354 *soth* truth 355 *kynyit* consider 357 *sen* seen 358 *wo-sa* whoever *sig* say 359 *Paraventur* perhaps *halt* consider 360 *tal* tale 361 *ficis* fish (pl.) *pol* pool 363 *sparth* spare 365 *her* their own 369 *touart* towards *Hel* Hell *ham drauth* they drag themselves 370 *har* their *dauis* days

Bot God of his godnis
gif ham gras to amend;
into the delful derknys
the[y] goth wythout hend.

Ther is dred and sorow
and wo withoutin wel;
no man may othir borow
be ther[e] nevir so fel.

Ther ne fallith no maynpris
ne supersidias[40],   380
thagh he be kyng or iustis
he passith not the p[l]as.

Lord that for his manhed
and also for his god,
that for lov and not for dred
deit oppon the rod,

Gif you gras your lif to led
that be your soulis to bot;
God of hevin for his godhed
lev that hit so mot. Amen.   390

Tunc dicet regi[41]

Schir kyng, thing oppon thin end
and hou that thou schalt dey,
wat uey that thou schalt wend
bot thou be bisey.

---

372 *gras* grace   373 *delful* (?) full of devils   374 *hend* end   377
othir other (fate)   *borow* get   378 *fel* terrible   379 *fallith* occurs
maynpris bail   380 *ne* nor   *supersidias* writ (staying legal proceedings) 382 *passith* leaves   384 *god* good   386 *deit* died   *rod*
rood   388 *bot* remedy   390 *lev* love [us]   *mot* may be   391,
399 *thing* think   393 *uey* way   394 *bot* unless   *bisey* careful

Eke that thou art lenust[42] man
and haddist bigyning,
and evirmor hav thout opon
thi dredful ending.

Thou schalt thing thanne
and mac the evir yar   400
that Deth is not the man
for no thing the wil spar[43].

Thou schalt do dedis of charite
and lern Crist-is lor,
and lib in hevin lit
to savy thi soul fre sor.

REX

Wat, bissop, byssop babler,
schold I of Deth hav dred?
Thou art bot a chagler —
go hom thi wey, I red.   410

Wat com thou therfor hidir
with Deth me to afer!
That thou and he both togidir
into the se i-got uer!

Go hom! God gif the sorow,
thou wreist me in mi mod[44];
war woltou prech tomorou?
Thou nost uer bi the rod.

Troust thou I nold be ded
in mi yyng lif;   420
thou lisst, screu, bolhed;
evil mot thou thrive.

397 *thout* thought   400 *yar* ready   404 *lor* teaching   405 *lit* light
406 *savy* save   *fre* from   *sor* sorrow   409 *chagler* cackler   410 *red*
advise.   412 *afer* frighten   414 *se* sea   *i-got* cast   *uer* were   416
wreist annoy   417 *war* where   *woltou* will you   418 *nost* knowest
uer where   419 *nold* do not wish to   420 *yyng* young   421 *lisst*
liest   *screu* shrew   *bolhed* blockhead   422 *mot* may

Wat schold I do at churg, wat?
Schir bisop, wostou, er?
Nay churc nis no wyl cot,
hit wol abid ther.

I wool let car away
and go on mi petying
to hontyng and to o[th]ir play
for al thi long prechyng.   430

I am kyng as thou mit se
and hav no ned to char
the w[h]yle the quen and [my mey]ne
about me beth yar.

EPISCOPUS
Thynk, schir king, one othir trist
that thyng [thou] misst son[45]:
thogh thou lev nou as the list
Deth wol cum rit son,

And give the dethis wounde
for thin outrage;   440
with-in a litil stounde
then artou but a page.

Qwhen thou art graven on grene
thy mete is fleys and molde[46];
then helpith litil, I wene,
thi gay croun of golde.

Sire kyng, have goday,
Crist I you be-teche.
REX
Ffare wel, bisschop, thi way,
and lerne bet to preche.   450

Hic adde[t][47]

423 *churg* church   424 *er* eh?   425 *wyl* wild   *cot* cat   428 *petying*
(?) desire   432 *char* care   433 *meyne* attendants   435 *trist*
consolation   437 *lev* live   441 *stounde* time   442 *artou* art thou
443 *graven* buried   444 *mete* meat, food   *fleys* flies   *molde* earth
449 *Ffare* go   450 *bet* better

Nou, maifay, hit schal be sene,
I trow yit to-daye,
qwher Deth me durst tene
and mete in the way.

Qwher artou, my messagere,
Solas bi thi name;
loke that thou go ffer and nere
as thou wolt have no blame,

My banis ffor to crye
by dayis and bi nighte: 460
and loke that thou aspye,
ye, bi al thi mighte,

Of Deth and of his maistrye
qwher he durst com in sighte
o-geynis me and my meyne
with fforce and armis to ffighte.

Loke that thou go both est and west
and com o-geyne on-one.
NUNCIUS
Lorde, to wende I am prest;
lo, now I am gone.   470

            Et eat platea[48]

Pes and listenith to my sawe[49]
bothe yonge and olde;
as ye wol noght ben aslawe
be ye never so bolde.

I am a messager, i-sente
ffrom the King of Life,
that ye schal ffulfil his [tal]ente
on peyne of lym and lif,

451 *maifay* by my faith   452 *yit to-daye* this very day   453, 464
qwher whether   453 *tene* annoy   455 *Qwher* where   457 *nere* near
459 *banis* banns, proclamation   468 *on-one* at once   469 *prest*
ready   471 *sawe* saying   473 *aslawe* slain   478 *lym* limb

His hestes to hold and his lawe
uche a man on honde   480
lest ye be henge and to-draw
or kast in hard bonde.

Ye wittin wel that he is king
and lord of al londis,
kepere and maister of al thing
with-in se and sondis.

I am sente ffor to enquer
o-boute ferre and nere,
if any man dar werre a-rere
a-gein suche a bachelere.   490

To wrother hele he was i-bore
that wold with him stryve;
be him sikir he is i-lore
as here in this lyve.

Thegh hit wer the King of Deth
and he so hardy were;
bot he ne hath might ne meth
the King of Lif to a-ffere.

Be he so hardy or so wode
in his londe to a-ryve,   500
he wol se his herte blode
and he with him stryve⁵⁰.

481 *to-draw* torn apart   482 *bonde* bonds   483 *wittin* know
486 *se* sea *sondis* sands   489 *werre* war *a-rere* raise up   490
bachelere warrior   491 *To wrother hele* to evil fortune *i-bore* born
493 *sikir* secure *i-lore* lost   497 *meth* power   498 *a-ffere* frighten
499 *wode* mad   502 *and* if

MANKIND

Mankind (composed 1465–70) is one of the three fifteenth-century *Macro Plays*, the others being *The Castell of Perseverance* (1400–1425) and *Wisdom* (1460–63). The manuscript is now in the Folger Shakespeare Library, Washington, D.C. It is written in the East Midlands dialect, and this is consistent with the references to a number of villages in Norfolk and Cambridgeshire where it was presumably performed. The original performances were probably given by a travelling company of six players who took the seven parts. The play is notable for its vigorous writing and the strong sense of the dramatic which the author showed in creating lively situations.

The play tells of the temptation of Mankind by a group of villains, Newguise, Nowadays, and Nought, who are led by Mischief. Mankind is so well advised by Mercy, who was probably represented as a priest, that he scorns the villains and beats them. They call upon Titivillus, a devil, and he succeeds in bringing Mankind to the point of suicide. Mercy intervenes, scourges the villains and brings salvation.

Editions

THE MACRO PLAYS

F. J. Furnivall and A. W. Pollard, 1904 and 1924, Early English Text Society, Extra Series 91

Mark Eccles, 1969, Early English Text Society, 262

MANKIND

J. M. Manly, *Specimens of the Pre-Shakespearean Drama*, Boston, 1897, Vol. 1

A. Brandl, *Quellen des weltlichen Dramas in England vor Shakespeare*, Strassburg, 1898

J. S. Farmer, *Tudor Facsimile Texts*, 1907

J. Q. Adams, *Chief Pre-Shakespearean Dramas*, 1924

The present extract, which corresponds to lines 348–604, is based upon Farmer's facsimile, collated with the edition by Eccles.

Mankind

[Mankind, having been mocked by Newguise, Nowadays and Nought, drives them away.]

MANKYNDE Hey yow hens, felouse, wyth bredynge;
　Leve yowur derysyone and yowur japynge.
　I must nedys labure, yt ys my lyvynge.

NOWADAYS What, ser? we came but lat hethyr.
　Xall all this corne grow here,
　That ye xall have the nexte yer?
　Yf yt be so, corne hade nede be dere;
　Ellys ye xall have a pore lyffe.

NOUGHT Alasse, goode fadere, this labor fretyth yow to the
　　　bone.
　But for yowur croppe I take grett mone:　　　　　　　　10
　Ye xall never spende yt alonne.
　I xall assay to geett yow a wyffe.
　How many acres suppose ye here by estymacyone?

NEWGYSE Ey, how ye turne the erth uppe and downe!
　I have be in my days in many goode towne,
　Yett saw I never such another tyllynge.

MANKYNDE Why stonde ye ydyll? Yt ys pety that ye were
　　　borne!

NOWADAYS We xall bargene wyth yow and nother moke
　　　nor scorne:
　Take a goode carte in hervest, and lode yt wyth yowur
　　　corne,
　And what xall we gyf yow for the levynge?　　　　　　20

NOUGHT He ys a goode starke laburrer, he wolde fayne do
　　　well.

---

1 *Hey* hurry *bredynge* reproach　2 *derysyone* scorn　*japynge*
jeering　4 *lat* late　5 *Xall* shall　9 *fretyth* wears　10 *mone* sorrow
12 *geett* get　17 *pety* pity　18 *bargene* bargain　*nother* neither
moke mock　20 *levynge* living (income)　21 *starke* vigorous
fayne willingly

He hath mett wyth the goode man Mercy[1] in a schroude
    sell:
For all this he may have many a hungry mele.
Yet woll ye se, he ys polytyke:
Here xall be goode corne, he may not mysse yt;
Yf he wyll have reyne, he may overpysse yt;
And yf he wyll have compasse, he may over-blysse yt
A lytyll wyth hys ars lyke[2].

MANKYNDE Go and do yowur labur, Gode lett yow never
    the!
Or with my spade I xall yow dynge, by the Holy Trinyte!   30
Have ye none other man to moke, but ever me?
Ye wolde have me of yowur sett;
Hye yow forth lyvely, for hens I wyll yow dryffe.
    [Beats them]

NEWGYSE Alas my jewellys, I xall be schent of my wyff.

NOWADAYS Alasse, and I am lyke never for to thryve;
    I have such a buffett.

MANKYNDE Hens, I sey, Newgyse, Nowadays, and Nowte!
Yt was seyde beforne: all the menys xull be sought
To perverte my condycions and brynge me to nought;
Hens, thevys, ye have made many a lesynge!   40

NOUGHT Marryde I was for colde[3], but now am I warme.
Ye are evyll avysyde, ser, for ye have done harme.
By cokkys body sakyrde, I have such a peyne in my arme;
I may not chonge a man a ferthynge.

MANKYNDE Now I thanke God, knelynge one my kne;
Blyssyde be hys name, he ys of hye degre!
By the subsyde of hys grace, that he hath sente me,
Three of myne enmys I have putt to flyght.
Yet this instrument, soverens, ys not made to defende.

---

22 *schroude* unfortunate   *sell* moment   24 *polytyke* wise   26 *reyne*
rain   27 *compasse* compost   29 *the* thrive   30 *dynge* strike   33
dryffe drive   34 *jewellys* testicles   *schent* scolded   38 *menys* means
xull (xuld) would   40 *lesynge* lie   41 *Marryde* destroyed
43 *cokkys* God's   *sakyrde* sacred   44 *chonge* change   49 *soverens*
masters (the audience)

Davide seyth: *Nec in hasta nec in Gladio salvat Dominus*[4].　　50

NOUGHT No, mary, I beschrew yow, yt ys in spadibus[5];

Therfor Crystys curse cum one yowur hedybus[5],

To sende yow lesse myght.

　　Exiant

MANKYNDE I promytt yow thes felouse wyll no more cum
　　　　here:

For summe of them, certenly, were summewhat to nere.

My fadyr Mercy avysyde me to be of a goode chere

Ande agayne my enmys manly for to fyght.

I xall convycte them, I hope, everychone.

Yet I say amysse, I do yt not alone:

Wyth the helpe of the grace of Gode I resyst my fone　　60

Ande ther malycyuse herte.

Wyth my spade I wyll departe, my worschyppull
　　　　soverence,

Ande lyve ever wyth labure to corecte my insolence.

I xall go fett corne for my londe, I prey yow of pacyence:

Ryght sone I xall reverte.

　　[*Exit*]

　　[*Myscheff enters*]

MYSCHEFF Alas, alasse, that ever I was wrought!

Alasse the whyll, I [am] wers the[n] nought!

Sythyne I was here – by hyme that me bought[6] –

I am utterly onedone.

I, Myscheff, was here at the begynnynge of the game[7]　　70

Ande arguyde wyth Mercy, Gode gyff hyme schame!

He hath taught Mankynde, wyll I have be vane,

To fyght manly ageyne hys fone:

For wyth hys spade that was hys wepyne

Newgyse, Nowadays, Nought hath all to-betene.

I have grett pyte to se them wepyn[g]e.

Wyll ye lyst? I here them crye.

　　Clamant[8]

---

54 *promytt* promise　58 *convycte* conquer　*everychone* every one
60 *fone* foes　63 *insolence* pride　65 *reverte* return　67 *then* than
68 *Sythyne* since　72 *wyll* while　*vane* absent　74 *wepyne* weapon
75 *to-betene* thrashed

Alasse, alasse! cum hether, I xall be yowur borow.
A-lac, a-lac, *vene, vene*[9], cum hether, wyth sorowe;
Pesse, fayer babys; ye xall have a nappyll to-morow.   80
Why grete ye so, why?

NEWGYSE Alasse, master, alasse, my privyte!

MYSCHEFF A, wher? alake, fayer babe, ba me;
Abyde; to sone I xall yt se.

NOWADAYS Here, here, se my hede, goode master!

MYSCHEFF Lady, helpe! sely darlynge, *vene, vene*;
I xall helpe the of thi peyne:
I xall smytt of thi hede and sett yt one agayne.

NOUGHT By owur lady, ser, a fayer playster.
Wyll ye of wyth hys hede? yt ys a schreude charme.   90
As for me, I have none harme.
I were loth to forbere myne arme.
Ye pley: *in nomine patris*[10] choppe!

NEWGYSE Ye xall not choppe my jewellys, and I may.

NOWADAYS Ye, Cristys crose, wyll ye smyght my hede
awey?
Ther, wher one and one[11]. Oute, ye xall not assay;
I myght well be callyde a foppe.

MYSCHEFF I kan choppe yt of and make yt agayne.

NEWGYSE I hade a schreude recumbentibus, but I fele no
peyne.

NOWADAYS Ande my hede ys all save and holl agayne.   100
Now, towchynge the mater of Mankynde,
Lett us have ane interleccyone, sythene ye be cum
hethere:
Yt were goode to have ane ende.

MYSCHEFF How, how, a mynstrell! know ye ony out?[12]

NOUGHT I kan pype in a Walsyngham Wystyll[13], I, Nought,
Nought.

---

78 *borow* protector 80 *fayer* fair *a nappyll* an apple 81 *grete* weep 82 *privyte* private parts 86 *sely* dear 89 *playster* plaster 90 *schreude* wicked 92 *forbere* lose 93 *pley* are joking 97 *foppe* fool 99 *recumbentibus* blow 100 *save* cured *holl* whole 102 *interleccyone* conference 104 *ony out* any at all

MYSCHEFF Blow apase, and thou xall brynge hyme in wyth
     a flewte.

TITIVILLUS [*off stage*] I come wyth my legges under me.

MYSCHEFF How, Newgyse, Nowadays, herke or I goo:

  When owur hedes were togethere I spake of *si dedero*.

NEWGYSE Ye[a], go thi wey, we xal gather mony one-to;   110

  Ellys ther xall no man hyme se.

  Now gostly to owur purpos, worschypfull soverence:

  We intende to gather mony, yf yt plesse yowur
     neclygence,

  For a man wyth a hede that [is] of grett omnipotens.

NOWADAYS Kepe yowur tayll, in goodness, I prey yow,
     goode brother.

  He[14] ys a worschyppull man, sers, savynge yowur
     reverens;

  He lovyth no grotys[15], nor pens or to-pens;

  Gyf us rede reyallys[16], yf ye wyll se hys abhomynabull
     presens!

NEWGYSE Not so; ye that mow not pay the tone pay the
     tother.

  At the goode man of this house fyrst we wyll assay.   120

  Gode blysse yow, master; ye say us yll, yet ye wyll not
     sey nay.

  Lett us go by and by and do them pay:

  Ye pay all a-lyke, well mu[s]t ye fare!

NOUGHT I sey, Newgyse, Nowadays, *Estis vos
     pecuniatus?*[17]

  I have cryede a fayer wyll, I beschrew yowur patus[18].

NOWADAYS *Ita vere, Magister*[19]; cumme forth now yowur
     gatus;

  He ys a goodly man, sers, make space and be ware!

    [*Enter Titivillus*]

---

106 *apase* quickly   *flewte* flute   108 *or* before   110 *one–to* for this
112 *gostly* in a holy way   115 *tayll* tally [of the takings]
117 *to-pens* twopenny pieces   118 *rede* red [gold] *abhomynabull*
unnatural, odious   119 *mow* may *the tone* the one *the tother*
the other   122 *do* cause to   125 *wyll* while *beschrew* curse

TITIVILLUS *Ego sum dominancium dominus*[20], and my name
       ys Titivillus.
  Ye that have goode hors, to yow I sey *Caveatis*[21];
  Here ys ane abyll felyschyppe to tryse hyme out at
       yowur gates.   130
      (*loquitur ad Newgyse*[22])
  Ego probo sic[23]: ser Newgyse, lende me a peny!
NEWGYSE I have a grett purse, ser, but I have no monay;
  By the masse I fayll two farthyngys of ane halpeny.
  Yet hade I ten pounds this nyght that was.
TITIVILLUS (*loquitur ad Nowadays*)
  What ys in thi purse? thou art a stout felow.
NOWADAYS The deull have [the] qwyll[24], I am a clene
       jentyllman.
  I prey Gode I be never wers storyde then I am.
  Yt xall be otherwyse, I hope, or this nyght passe.
TITIVILLUS (*loquitur ad Nought*)
  Herke now, I say: thou hast many a peny.
NOUGHT *Non nobis domine non nobis*[25]; by Sent Deny!   140
  The deull may daunce in my purse for ony peny;
  Yt ys as clene as a byrdes ars.
TITIVILLUS Now I say yet ageyne, *caveatis.*
  Her ys ane abyll felyschyppe to tryse hem out of
       yowur gatys.
  Now I sey, Newgyse, Nowadays, and Nought,
  Go and serche the contre, anone, that [yt] be soughte,
  Summe here, summe ther, what yf ye may cache oughte.
  Yf ye fayll of hors, take what ye may ellys.
NEWGYSE Then speke to Mankynde for the recumbentibus
       of my jewellys.
NOWADAYS Remembre my brokyne hede, in the
       worschyppe of the vii devylls[26].   150
NOUGHT Ye, goode ser, and the sytyca in my erme.

---

130 *tryse* snatch   133 *fayll* fall short of, lack   136 *deull* devil
qwyll while   137 *storyde* stored, provided   138 *or* before   146
soughte searched   147 *what yf* to see if   *oughte* anything
151 *sytyca* sciatica *erme* arm

TITIVILLUS I know full well what Mankynde dyde to yow;
    Myschyff hat informyde [me] of all the matere thorow.
    I xall venge yowur quarell, I make Gode a vow.
    Forth, and espye w[h]ere ye may do harme.
    Take W[illiam] Fyde, yf ye wyll have ony mo.
    I sey, Newgyse, wethere art thou avysyde to go?

NEWGYSE Fyrst I xall begyne at M[aster] Huntington of
        Saustone[27];
    Fro thens I xall go to Wylliam Thurlay of Haustone,
    And so forth to Pycharde of Trumpyngtone: 160
    I wyll kepe me to thes three.

NOWADAYS I xall goo to Wyllyham Bakere of Waltone,
    To Rycherde Bollman of Gaytone;
    I xall spare Master Woode of Fullburne:
    He ys a *noli me tangere*[28].

NOUGHT I xall goo to Wyllyam Patryke of Massyngham;
    I xall spare Master Alyngtone of Botysam
    And Hamonde of Soffeham.
    Felous, cum forth and go we hens togethyr,
    For drede of *in manus tuas*[29] qweke[30].   170
    Syth we xall go, lett us be well ware wethere[31].
    Yf we may be take, we come no more hethyr;
    Lett us con well owur neke-verse[32], that we have not a
        cheke.

TITIVILLUS Goo yowur wey, a deull wey, go yowur wey
        all;
    I blysse yow with my lyfte honde: foull yow befall!
    Come agayne – I werne – as sone as I yow call,
    And brynge yowur avantage into this place!
    To speke wyth Mankynde I wyll tary here this tyde
    Ande assay hys goode purpose for to sett asyde.
    The goode mane Mercy xall no lenger be hys gyde;   180
    I xall make hym to dawnce another trace.
    Ever I go invysybull, yt ys my jett;

157 *wethere* whither   171 *ware* careful   *wethere* whither   173 *con*
learn   *cheke* throttling   175 *lyfte* left   *honde* hand   177 *avantage*
booty   178 *tyde* occasion   180 *lenger* longer   181 *trace* dance
182 *jett* fashion

Ande be-for hys ey, thus, I wyll hange my nett[33],
To blench hys syght: I hope to have hys fote-mett.
To yrke hym of hys labur I xall make a frame:
Thys borde xall be hyde undur the erth prevely;
Hys spade xall entur – I hope – onredyly;
Be then he hath assayde, he xall be very angry
And lose hys pacyens, peyne of schame.
I xall menge hys corne wyth drawke and wyth durnell,   190
Yt xall not be lyke to sow nor to sell.
Yondyr he commyth – I prey of counsell;
He xall wene grace were wane.
MANKYNDE Now Gode of hys mercy sende us of hys sonde!
I have brought sede here to sow wyth my londe.
Qwyll I overdylew yt here yt xall stonde.
In nomine Patris, et Filii et Spiritus Sancti[34]: now I wyll
    begyn.
Thys londe ys so harde yt makyth wnelusty and yrke:
I xall sow my corne at wyntur and lett Gode werke.
Alasse, my corne ys lost, here ys a foull werke;   200
I se well by tyllynge lytyll xall I wyne.
Here I gyf uppe my spade for now and for ever.
    Here Titivillus goth out wyth the spade
To occupye my body I wyll not put me in dever.
I wyll here my evynsonge here, or I dyssever.
Thys place I assynge as for my kyrke;
Here in my kerke I knell on my kneys:
Pater noster, qui es in celis[35] –
    [*Titivillus re-enters*]
TITIVILLUS I promes yow I have no lede one my helys.

184 *blench* deceive *fote-mett* measure, size 185 *yrke* weary
frame device 186 *borde* board *prevely* secretly 187 *onredyly*
with difficulty 189 *peyne of* for fear of 190 *menge* mix *drawke*
weed *durnell* darnel 192 *of counsell* be secret 193 *wene* think
wane absent 194 *sonde* message 196 *Qwyll* while *overdylew* dig
over 198 *wnelusty* dull 201 *wyne* win 203 *dever* duty, obligation
204 *dyssever* depart 205 *assynge* establish 206 *knell* kneel *kneys*
knees 208 *lede* lead *helys* heels

I am here ageyne to make this felow yrke.
Qwyst, pesse! I xall go to hys ere and tytyll therin. 210
A schorte preyere thyrlyth hevyn; of thi preyere blyne!
Thou art holyer then ever was ony of thi kyn,
Aryse and avent thee; nature compellys.

MANKYNDE I wyll in to thi yerde, soverens, and cume
   ageyne sone.
For drede of the colyke and eke of the stone
I wyll go do that nedys must be done;
My bedys xall be here for who-summe-ever wyll cumme.
 Exit

TITIVILLUS Mankynde was besy in his prayere, yet I dyde
   hym aryse;
He ys conveyde – be Cryst – frome hys dyvyne
   servyce[36].
Wethere ys he? trow ye, I-wysse, I am wondur wyse: 220
I have sent hyme forth to schyte lesynges.
Yff ye have ony sylver, in happe pure brasse,
Take a lytyll power of Parysch[37] and cast over hys face
And evyne in the howll-flyght let hyme passe.
Titivillus kane lerne yow many praty thyngys.
I trow Mankynde wyll cume ageyne sone,
Or ellys – I fere me – evynsonge wyll be done.
Hys bedys xall be trysyde asyde, and that anone.
Ye xall [se] a goode sport yf ye wyll abyde.
Mankynde cummyth ageyne, well fare he! 230
I xall answere hyme *ad omnia quare*[38].
Ther xall be sett a-broche a clerycall mater;
I hope of hys purpose to sett hym asyde.

---

210 *Qwyst* hush *pesse* peace *ere* ear *tytyll* whisper 211 *thyrlyth* pierces *blyne* desist 213 *avent* relieve 217 *bedys* beads
(rosary) 218 *dyde* caused to 219 *conveyde* taken (craftily)
220 *I-wysse* indeed *wondur* wonderfully 221 *schyte* excrete
lesynges lies 222 *happe* chance 223 *power* powder 224 *evyne*
evening *howll-flyght* twilight 225 *kane* can 228 *trysyde*
snatched 232 *a-broche* open *clerycall* learned, priestly (ironical)

74

MANKYNDE Evynsonge hath be in the saynge, I trow, a
　　　　 fayer wyll;
　　I am yrke of yt, yt ys to longe be one myle.
　　Do wey, I wyll no more so oft over the chyrche-style.
　　Be as be may, I xall do another.
　　Of labure and preyer I am nere yrke of both.
　　I wyll no more of yt, thou[gh] Mercy be wroth.
　　My hede ys very hevy, I tell yow, for soth!　　　　　　240
　　I xall slepe full my bely and he wore my brother.
　　　[*He falls asleep*]

TITIVILLUS Ande ever ye dyde, for me kepe now yowur
　　　　 sylence!39
　　Not a worde, I charge yow, peyne of forty pens.
　　A praty game xall be scheude yow, or ye go hens.
　　Ye may here hyme snore, he ys sade a-slepe.
　　Qwyst, pesse! the Deull ys dede! I xall goo ronde in hys
　　　　 ere.
　　Alasse, Mankynde, alasse! Mercy stowne a mere:
　　He ys runn a-way fro hys master, ther wot no man
　　　　 where:
　　More over he stale both a hors and a nete.
　　But yet, I herde sey, he brake hys neke as he rode in
　　　　 Fraunce.　　　　　　　　　　　　　　　　　250
　　But I thynke he rydyth over the galouse to lerne for to
　　　　 daunce
　　By-cause of hys theft, that ys hys governance.
　　Trust no more on hym; he ys a marryde man.
　　Mekyll sorow wyth thi spade be-forne thou hast wrought;
　　Aryse and aske mercy of Newgyse, Nowadays and
　　　　 Nought.
　　Thei cun avyse the for the best; lett ther goode wyll be
　　　　 sought.

---

241 *and* if　*wore* were　244 *scheude* shown　*or* before　245 *sade*
heavily　246 *ronde* whisper　247 *stowne* has stolen　*mere* mare
248 *wot* knows　249 *stale* stole　*nete* ox, or cow　251 *galouse*
gallows　252 *governance* behaviour　253 *marryde* ruined　254
Mekyll great　256 *cun* know how to　*the* thee

Ande thi owne wyff brethell[40], and take a lemman.

Far-well, everychone, for I have done my game,
For I have brought Mankynde to myscheff and to schame.
   [*Exit*]

257 *lemman* mistress

¶Here is cõteyned a godely interlude of Fulgens
Cenatoure of Rome. Lucres his doughter. Gayus
flaminius. & Publi9. Cozneli9. of the disputacyon of
noblenes. & is deuyded in two ptyes / to be played at
ii.tymes. Cõppyled by mayster Henry medwall. late
chapelayne to þ ryght reuerent fader in god Johan
Mozton cardynall & Archebysshop of Caũterbury.

Facsimile of the title-page of the 1515 edition of Fulgens and Lucres
(by permission of the Huntington Library, San Marino, California)

The only known edition of the play was printed by John Rastell *c.* 1515, and is now in the Henry E. Huntington Library in California. The title-page reads:

> Here is conteyned a godely interlude of Fulgens Cenatoure of Rome. Lucres his doughter. Gayus flaminius. & Publius. Cornelius. of the disputacyon of noblenes. and is devyded in two partyes/to be played at ii. tymes. Compyled by mayster Henry medwall. late chapelayne to the ryght reverent fader in god Johan Morton cardynall & Archebysshop of Caunterbury.

Medwall served Morton, probably as schoolmaster as well as chaplain, from about 1490 until the latter's death in 1500. The play was written during this decade: it may have been intended to entertain the Spanish and Flemish ambassadors in 1497.

A copy of the play was known to seventeenth-century booksellers, but for a long period only two leaves were thought to exist. These are known as the Bagford fragments consisting of sig. e. iii and iv (II. 126–230), and are now in the British Museum (Harleian MS. 5919, f.20, No. 98). They have been reprinted twice:

> W. Bang and R. B. McKerrow, *Materialien zur Kunde des alteren englischen Dramas*, xii, Louvain, 1905
> W. W. Greg, *Malone Society Collections*, I, ii (1908), 1909

In 1919 the full text came to light in the Mostyn sale at Sotheby's, and three modern editions have resulted:

> Seymour de Ricci, New York, 1920 (facsimile)
> F. S. Boas and A. W. Reed, Oxford, 1926
> F. S. Boas in *Five Pre-Shakespearean Comedies*, 1934

The source of the play has been identified as John Tiptoft's translation of the *Controversia de Vera Nobilitate* by Bonaccorso of Pistoja, printed by Caxton in 1481. The play is the earliest secular

drama to have survived intact. The version which follows is based
upon the work of de Ricci and of Boas and Reed, and includes the
introductory section, which gives valuable indications of the circumstances of performance, and the whole of Part Two.

Fulgens and Lucres

PART ONE

Intrat A dicens[1]

A For goddis will
What meane ye, syrs, to stond so still?
Have not ye etyn & your fill,
And payd no thinge therfore?
I wys, syrs, thus dare I say,
He that shall for the shott pay
Vouchsaveth that ye largely assay
Suche mete as he hath in store.
I trowe your disshes be not bare
Nor yet ye do the wyne spare: 10
Therfore be mery as ye fare.
Ye ar welcom eche oon
Unto this house withoute faynynge.
But I mervayle moche of one thinge,
That after this mery drynkynge
And good recreacyon
There is no wordes amonge this presse,
Non sunt loquele neque sermones[2],
But as it were men in sadnes
Here ye stonde musynge   20
Where aboute I can not tell.
Or some els praty damesell
For to daunce and sprynge[3].
Tell me what calt[4], is it not so?
I am sure here shalbe somewhat ado,
And I wis, I will know it or I go
Withoute I be dryvyn hens.
    Intrat B

---

3 *etyn* eaten 6 *shott* reckoning 7 *largely* copiously 11 *fare*
proceed 13 *faynynge* deception 14 *mervayle* marvel *moche*
much 17 *presse* crowd 22 *praty* skilful 26 *or* before

[B] Nay, nay, hardely, man, I undertake
  No man wyll suche mastryes make,
  And it were but for the maner sake⁵.   30
  Thou maist tary by licence
  Among other men and see the pley.
  I warand no man wyll say the nay.
A I thinke it well evyn as ye say
  That no man wyll me greve.
  But I pray you, tell me that agayn,
  Shall here be a play?
B   Ye, for certeyn.
A By my trouth, therof am I glad and fayn.
  And ye will me beleve,
  Of all the worlde I love suche sport,   40
  It dothe me so myche plesure and comfort,
  And that causith me ever to resort
  Wher suche thing is to do.
  I trowe your owyn selfe be oon
  Of them⁶ that shall play.
B   Nay, I am none.
  I trowe thou spekyst in derision
  To lyke me therto.
A Nay, I mok not, wot ye well,
  For I thought verely by your apparell
  That ye had bene a player.
B   Nay, never a dell⁷.   50
A Than I cry you mercy,
  I was to blame, lo, therfor I say.
  Ther is so myche nyce aray
  Amonges these galandis nowaday
  That a man shall not lightly
  Know a player from another man.
  But now to the purpose wher I began,
  I see well here shalbe a play than.

28 *hardely* truly   31 *licence* permission   35 *greve* disappoint   38
fayn content   39 *And* if   47 *lyke* liken   51 *Than* then   53 *nyce*
extravagant   54 *galandis* gallants   55 *lightly* easily

B Ye, that ther shall doutles,
  And I trow ye shall like it well.   60
A It semeth than that ye can tell
  Sumwhat of the mater.
B   Ye, I am of counsell[8];
  One tolde me all the processe.
A And, I pray you, what shall it be?
B By my fayth, as it was tolde me
  More than ones or twyse,
  As fare as I can bere it awaye,
  All the substaunce of theyr play
  Shall procede this wyse.

[B describes the contents of the play, explaining that Lucres, the daughter of Fulgens, is to choose a husband from two suitors, Publius Cornelius, a nobleman, and Gaius Flamineus, who has risen from humble origins by his own merits. The choice is to fall on Flamineus, but A is doubtful whether this is the proper solution. The rest of the players arrive, and Part One is enacted.

The suitors make their pleas to Lucres, who promises to give her decision. A becomes the servant of Flamineus, and B serves Cornelius, each determined to advance the suit of his master. A and B are also rivals for the affection of Lucres' maid: she proves too clever, and makes fools of them. A announces that Lucres and Fulgens will hear the pleas of the suitors, but the audience must first be given time to finish dinner. This ends Part One.]

PART TWO

  Intrat A dicens
[A] Muche gode do it you everyche one,
  Ye wyll not beleve how fast I have gone,
  For fere that I sholde come to late.
  No forse[9] I have lost but a lytyll swete,
  That I have taken upon this hete,
  My colde corage to abate.

---

63 *processe* plot 67 *fare* far 1 *everyche* every 4 *swete* sweat
5 *hete·*heat

But now to the matter that I cam fore,
Ye know the cause therof before,
Your wittis be not so short.
Perde[10], my felowys and I were here   10
Today whan ye where at dyner[11]
And shewed you a lytyll disport
Of one Fulgens and his doughter Lucres,
And of two men that made grett besynes
Her husbonde for to be:
She answered to them bothe than
Loke whiche[12] was the more noble man
To hym she wolde agre.
This was the substance of the play
That was shewed here today,   20
All be it that there was
Dyvers toyes mengled yn the same
To styre folke to myrthe and game
And to do them solace:
The whiche tryfyllis be impertinent[13]
To the matter principall,
But never the lesse they be expedient
For to satisfye and content
Many a man withall.
For some there be that lokis and gapys   30
Only for suche tryfles and iapys,
And some there be amonge
That forceth lytyll of suche madnes,
But delytyth them in matter of sadnes,
Be it never so longe.
And every man must have hys mynde,
Ellis thay will many fautys fynde
And say the play was nought.
But no force I car not,
Let them say and spare not,   40

12 *disport* entertainment   14 *besynes* trouble   22 *toyes* jokes
25 *impertinent* irrelevant   30 *gapys* stares   31 *iapys* tricks   32 *amonge*
at this same time   33 *forceth* care   37 *fautys* faults

For God knoweth my thought:
It is the mynde and intent
Of me and my company to content
The leste that stondyth here,
And so I trust ye wyll it alowe —
By Godis mercy where am I now?
It were almys[14] to wrynge me by the eare
By cause I make suche degression
From the matter that I began
When I entred the halle.   50
For had I made a gode contynuaunce[15]
I shoulde have put you in remembraunce
And to your myndis call
How Lucres wyll come hyder agayne,
And her sayde lovers bothe twayne,
To dyffyne thys question
Whether of them ys the more noble man.
For theron all this matter began;
It is the chefe foundacyon
Of all thys proces both all and some.   60
And yf thes players where ons come
Of this matter will they speke:
I mervell gretely in my mynde
That thay tary so long behynde
Theyre howre for to breke.
But what, syrs, I pray you everychone,
Have pacyens, for thay come anone.
I am sure they wyll not fayle
But thay wyll mete in this place
As theyre promys and apoyntment wase,   70
And ellis I have merveyle.
Let me se what is now a cloke —
A, there commyth one, I here hym knoke,
He knokythe as he were wood.

54 *hyder* hither   56 *dyffyne* decide   57 *Whether* which (of the two)
60 *proces* action   63, 71, 81 *mervell, merveyle, marvell* marvel
70 *wase* was   72 *a cloke* o'clock   74 *wood* mad

One of you[16] go loke who it is.
    [*Enter B*]
B Nay, nay, all the meyny of them, I wis,
  Can not so moche gode.
  A man may rappe tyll his naylis ake
  Or ony of them wyll the labour take
  To gyve hym an answere[17].   80
A I have grete marvell on the
  That ever thou wylt take upon the
  To chyde ony man here.
  No man is so moche to blame as thow
  For longe taryinge.
B   Ye, God avow!
  Wyll ye play me that?
  Mary, that shall be amended anone;
  I am late comen, and I wyll sone be gone,
  Ellis I shrew my catt[18].
  Kockis body, syr, it is a fayre resone,   90
  I am com hedyr att this season
  Only at thy byddynge,
  And now thou makyst to me a quarell
  As though all the matter were in parell
  By my longe taryynge.
  Now God be with you, so mote I the,
  Ye shall play the knave alone for me.
A What? I am afrayde,
  I wis ye are but lewyde:
  Turne agayne, all be shrewyde![19]   100
  Now are you fayre prayde[20].
B Why than, is your angyr all do?
A Ye mary is it, lo!
B So is myne too.
  I have done clene.
  But now how goyth this matter forth
  Of this mariage?

76 *meyny* company   90 *Kockis body* by God's body   94 *parell* peril
99 *lewyde* ignorant

A By Saynt Iame, ryght nought worth,
  I wot nere what thay meane,
  For I can none other wise thinke   110
  But that some of them begyn to shrinke[21]
  By cause of ther longe tariage.
B Shrynke now, quoth a! Mary, that were mervele.
  But one thinge of surete I can the tell
  As touchynge this mariage:
  Cornelius my mayster apoyntyth hym[22] ther upone,
  And dowtles he wyll be here anone
  In payne of forty pens,
  In so muche that he hath devysyde
  Certayne straungers fresshly disgisyd   120
  Att his owne expens
  For to be here this nyght also.
A Straungers, quoth a! What to do?
B Mary, for to glade with all
  This gentylwoman at her hedyr comynge.
A A then, I se well we shall have a mummynge[23].
B Ye, surely, that we shall,
  And therfor never thinke it in thy mynde
  That my mayster wyll be behynde
  Nor slacke at this bargyn.   130
      [Enter Cornelius]
  Mary, here he commyth, I have hym aspyde.
  No more wordis, stonde thou asyde,
  For it is he playne.
COR. My frynde, where abowt goist thou all day?
B Mary, syr, I came heder to asay
  Whedyr these folke had ben here,
  And yet thay be not come,
  So helpe me God and holydome.
  Of that I have moche marvaile, that thay tary so.
COR. Mary, go thi way, and wit where thay wyll or no. 140
B Ye, God avow, shall I so?

120 *fresshly* gaily   124 *glade* please   140 *wit* find out   *where* whether

87

COR. Ye, mary, so I say.

B Yet in that poynt, as semyth me,
   Ye do not accordynge to your degre.

COR. I pray the, tell me why.

B Mary, it wolde becom them well inow
   To be here afore and to wayte upon you,
   And not you to tary
   For theyr laysyr and abyde them here
   As it were one that were ledde by the eare,   150
   For that I defy.
   By this mene you sholde be theyr druge,
   I tell you trought I,
   And yet the worst that greveth me
   Is that your adversary sholde in you se
   So notable a foly:
   Therfore witdraw you for a seasone.

COR. By Seynt Johan, thou sayst but reasone.

B Ye, do so hardely,
   And whan the tyme drawith upon   160
   That thay be com everychone
   And all thinge redy
   Than shall I come streyght away
   For to seche you withoute delay.

COR. Be it so hardely.
   But one thinge whyle I thinke therone;
   Remember this when I am gone;
   Yef hit happon so
   That Lucres come in fyrst alone
   Go in hand[24] with her anone,   170
   How so ever thou do,
   For to fele her mynde toward me,
   And by all meanis possyble to be
   Induce her ther unto.

B Than some token you must gyve me,

---

144 *accordynge* as is appropriate 146 *inow* enough 148 *tary*
cause to wait 149 *laysyr* leisure 152 *druge* drudge 153 *trought*
trust 164 *seche* seek

For ellis she wyll not beleve me
That I cam from you.

COR. Mary, that is evyn wysely spoken.
Commaunde me to her by the same token,
She knowyth it well inow,   180
That as she and I walkyde onis togedyr
In her garden hedyr and thedyr
There happonde a straunge case,
For at the last we dyd se
A byrd sittynge on a holow tre,
An ashe I trow it was,
Anone she prayde me for to assay
Yf I coude start the byrde away.

B And dyde ye so? Alas, alas!

COR. Why the devyll sayst thou so?   190

B By cokkis bonis, for it was a kocko,
And men say amonge
He that throwyth stone or stycke
At suche a byrde, he is lycke
To synge that byrdes songe.

COR. What the devyll recke I therfore?
Here what I say to the evermore,
And marke thine erand well.
Syr, I had no stone to throw with all,
And therfore she toke me her musc²⁵ ball,   200
And thus it befell,
I kyst it as strayght as ony pole
So that it lyghtyde evyn in the hole
Of the holow ashe.
Now, canst thou remember all this?

B By God, I wolde be loth to do amys
For some tyme I am full rashe.
Ye say that ye kyst it evyn in the hole
Of the holow ashe as strayte as a pole?

179 *Commaunde* commend   191 *By cokkis bonis* by God's bones
kocko cuckoo   192 *amonge* commonly   196 *recke* care   202 *kyst*
threw

89

Sayde ye not so? 210

COR. Yes.

B   Well then, let me alone,
As for this erande it shall be done
As sone as ye be go.

COR. Fare well then. I leve the here.
And remembyr well all this gere
How so ever thou do.
    Et exeat Cornelius

B Yes, hardely this erande shall be spoken.
But how say you, syrs, by this tokene,
Is it not a quaynt thinge?
I went he hade bene a sad man, 220
But I se well he is a made man
In this message doynge.
But what, chose he for me![26]
I am but as a messanger, perde;
The blame shall not be myne but his,
For I wyll his token reporte
Whether she take it in ernest or sporte,
I wyll not therof mys.
Be she wroth or well apayde
I wyll tell her evyn as he sayde. 230
    Intrat Lucres
God avow, here she is,
It is tyme for me to be wyse.
Now welcome, lady, floure of prise,
I have sought you twyse or thryse
Wythin this houre I wys.

LUC. Me, syr, have ye sought me?

B Ye, that I have, by God that bowght me.

LUC. To what intent?

B Mary, for I have thingis a few
The which I must to you shew 240
By my maysters commaundment.

---

215 *gere* matter   219 *quaynt* cunning   221 *made* mad   229 *apayde*
satisfied   233 *floure* flower   *prise* value

Publius Cornelius is hys name,
Your veray lover in payne of shame,
And yf ye love hym not ye be to blame.
For this dare I say,
And on a boke make it gode,
He lovyd you better than his one hart blode.

LUC. Hys harde bloode? Nay, nay,
Half that love wolde serve for me.

B Yet sithe he dyde you fyrst se   250
In the place where he dwellis
He had lovyd you so in hys hart
That he settyth not by hymself a fart
Nor by noo man ellis.
An by cause ye shulde gyve credence
Unto my sayng in hys absence,
And trust to that I say,
He tolde me tokyns two or three
Whiche I know well as he tolde me.

LUC. Tokyns, what be thay?   260

B Let me se; now I had nede to be wyse,
For one of his tokyns is very nyse,
As ever I harde tell.
He prayd you for to beleve me
By the same tokyn that ye and he
Walkyd togeder by a holow tre.

LUC. All that I know well.

B A, than I am yet in the ryght way,
But I have som other thyng to say
Towchyng my credence   270
Whiche as I thynke were best to be spared,
For happely ye wold not have it declared
Byfore all this audience.

LUC. Nay, nay, hardely spare not;
As for my dedis I care not
Yf all the worlde it harde.

243 *veray* true   248 *harde* heart   250 *sithe* since   262 *nyse* foolish
263 *harde* heard   270 *Towchyng* concerning   *credence* credit

91

B Mary, than shall I procede.
  He shewde me also in very dede
  How ther satt a byrde
  And than ye delyveryd hym your muskball   280
  For to throw at the byrd withall,
  And than, as he sayd, ye dyd no wors
  But evyn fayr kyst hym on the noke of the ars.
LUC. Nay, ther thow lyest falsely, by my fay.
B Trouth, it was on the hole of thars I shulde say,
  I wyst well it was one of the too,
  The noke or the hole.
LUC.   Nay, nor yet so.
B By my fayth, ye kyst hym or he kyst you
  On the hole of thars, chose you now;
  This he tolde me sure.   290
  How be it I speke it not in reprove,
  For it was done but for gode love
  And for no synfull pleasure.
LUC. Nay, nay, man, thou art farr amys.
  I know what thyn erande is
  Though thow be neclygent.
  Of thy foly thou mayst well abasshe,
  For thou shuldis have sayde the holow asshe,
  That hole thy mayster ment.
B By God avow, I trow it was.   300
  I crye you mercy, I have done you trespas.
  But I pray you take it in pacyence
  For I mystoke it by necligence,
  A myscheef com theron!
  He myght have sent you this gere in a letter,
  But I shall go lerne myn erande better,
  And cum ayen anon.
          Et exeat
LUC. Ye, so do hardely.
  Now, forsoth, this was a lewed message
  As ever I harde sith I was bore.   310

    283 noke corner   297 abasshe be ashamed   301 trespas wrong

And yf his mayster have therof knowlege
He wyll be angry with hym therfore.
How be it, I will speke therof no more,
For hyt hath ben my condiscyon alwey
No man to hender, but to helpe where I may.

    Intrat A

A Feyr maysters[27], lyketh it you to know
  That my mayster comaunde me to you?
LUC. Commaundeth you to me?
A Nay, commaundeth you to hym.
LUC. Wele amendyd, by Saynt Sym.   320
A Commaundeth he to you, I wolde say,
  Or ellis you to he, now chose ye may
  Whether lyketh you better.
  And here he sendyth you a letter —
  Godis mercy, I had it ryght now.
  Syrs, is there none there among you[28]
  That toke up suche a wrytyng?
  I pray you, syrs, let me have it agayne.
LUC. Ye ar a gode messanger for certeyne;
  But I pray you, syr, of one thyng,   330
  Who is your mayster? Tell me that.
A Maister, what call ye hym? Perde, ye wott
  Whome I mene well and fyne.
LUC. Yet I know not, so mot I go.
A What yes, perde, he that wolde have you so.
LUC. I suppose there be many of tho
  Yf I wolde enclyne.
  But yet know I not who ye mene.
  I holde best that ye go ageyene
  To lerne your maysters name.   340
A By my fayth and I holde it best,
  Ye may say I am a homely gest
  In ernest and in game.
LUC. Abyde, I shall go to you nere honde[29].
  What ys your owne name I wolde understonde:

<hr>

315 *hender* hinder   342 *gest* fellow

Tell me that or I go,
I trow thou canst not well tell.
A By my fayth not verely well
  By cause ye say so.
        Et scalpens caput post modicum intervallum dicat[30]
  By this lyght I have forgoten.   350
  How be it by that tyme I have spoken[31]
  With som of my company
  I shall be acerteyned of this gere.
  But shall I fynde you agayne here?
LUC. Ye, that thow shalt happely.
        Et exeat A [*Enter Cornelius*]
COR. Now, fayr Lucres, accordyng to thappoyntement[32]
  That ye made with me here this day
  By cause ye shall not fynde me there neclygent,
  Here I am come your wyll to obey,
  And redy am I for my selfe to sey   360
  That as towchyng the degre of noble condycion
  Betwyxt me and Gayus there may be no comparison:
  And that shall I shew you by apparent reason,
  Yf it shall lyke you that I now begynne.
LUC. Nay, ye shall spare it for a lytyll season
  Tyl suche tyme that Gayus your adversary come in,
  For I wyll gyve you therin none audience
  Tyll ye be both to-ge[d]er in presence.
  And in ony wyse kepe well your patience,
  Lyke as I have bound you both to the peace.   370
  I forbyde you utterly all manner of violence
  Durynge this matter, and also that ye seace
  Of all suche wordis as may gyve occasion
  Of brallynge or other ongodely condycion.
COR. There shal be in me no suche abusyon
  In worde nor dede, I you promyse.
  But now let me se, what occupation
  Or what maner of passe tyme wyll ye devyse

---

353 *acerteyned* informed   355 *happely* perhaps   372 *seace* cease
374 *brallynge* brawling   *ongodely* ungodly

Whyle that these folke dothe tary this wyse?
Wyll ye see a bace daunce[33] after the gyse   380
Of Spayne, whyle ye have nothynge to do?
All thynge have I purvaide that belongyth therto.

LUC. Syr, I shall gyve you the lokynge on[34].

COR. Wyll ye do so? I aske no more.
Go sone and bidde them come thens anone
And cause the mynystrelles to come in beffore.
            [*Enter Minstrels*]

B Mary, as for one of them his lippe is sore;
I trow he may not pype, he is so syke.
Spele up tamboryne, ik bide owe frelike[35].
            Et deinde corisabunt[36]

LUC. For sothe, this was a godely recreacyon.   390
But, I pray you, of what maner nation
Be these godely creatours?
Were they of Englonde or of Wales?

B Nay, they be wylde Irissh Portyngales[37]
That dyde all these pleasures.
How be it, it was for my maysters sake,
And he wyll deserve it, I undertake,
On the largest wyse.

COR. Go thy selfe; why stondis thou so?
And make them chere; let it be do   400
The best thou canst devyse.

B Yes, they shall have chere hevyn hye,
But one thing I promyse you faithfully,
They get no drynke therto.
            Exeat B
            [*Enter Gaius.*] *Dicat Lucres*[38]

[LUC.] Lo, here thys man ys come now.
Now may ye in your matter procede.
Ye remember both what I sayde to you
Touchynge myne answere; I trow it is no nede
Ony more to reherse it.

382 *purvaide* provided 385 *sone* soon 392 *creatours* creatures
409 *reherse* repeat

COR.   No, in veray dede,

For moche rehersall wolde let the spede   410
Of all this matter, it nedyth no more.
Let us roundely to the matter we come for.

LUC. Ye, that I pray you, as hartly as I can.
But fyrst me semyth it were expedient
That ye both name some indifferent man
For to gyve betwyxt you the forseyde iugement.

COR. Nay, as for that, by myne assent
No man shall have that office but ye.

GA. And I holde me well content that so it be.

LUC. Ye, but notwythstondyng that ye therto agre 420
That I sholde this question of nobles diffine,
It is a grete matter whiche, as semyth me,
Pertayneth to a philosopher or ellis a devyne.
How be it, sith the choyse of this matter is myne
I can be content under certayne protestacyon,
Whan that I have harde you, to say myne opinion.
Lo, this wyse I mene and thus I do intende,
That what so ever sentence I gyve betwyxt you two,
After myne owne fantasie it shall not extende
To ony other person; I wyll that it be so,   430
For why no man ellis hath theryn ado.
It may not be notyde for a generall precedent[39],
All be it that for your partis ye do therto assent.

GA. As touchyng that poynt we holde us well content.
Your sentence shall touche no man but us twayne,
And sith ye shall gyve it by our owne agrement
None other man ought to have thereat disdayne.
Wherfor all thys dout ye may well refrayne
And in the matter principall this tyme wolde be spent.

COR. Than wyll I begynne.

GA.   I holde me well content. 440

---

410 *let* prevent 412 *roundely* directly 415 *indifferent* impartial
416 *forseyde* aforesaid 421 *nobles* nobility 425 *protestacyon*
protest, reluctance 428 *sentence* judgement 429 *fantasie* inclination 438 *refrayne* restrain

COR. Syth ye have promysed, fayre Lucres, here to fore,
    That to the more noble man ye wyll enclyne,
    Vary not fro that worde and I aske no more.
    For than shall the victory of this cause be myne,
    As it shalbe be easy to iugge and diffyne.
    For every creature that ony reason hase,
    Me semyth I durst make hym self iugge in this case,
    Save that I fere me the beaute of your face
    Sholde therin blynde hym so that he ne myght
    Egally disserne the wronge fro the right.   450
    And if he were half so wyse a man in dede
    As he reputeth hym self for to be,
    Upon your saide answere he sholde not nede
    To gaynesay in this matter or travers with me.
    My noblenes is knowen thorow all the cyte;
    He knoweth hym selfe the noblenes of my kyn,
    And at that one poynt my proces I wyll begyne.

    Amonge all thistoryes of Romaynes that ye rede
    Where fynde ye ony blode of so gret noblenes
    As hath ben the Cornelys[40] wherof I am brede?   460
    And if so be that I wolde therin holde my pease,
    Yet all your cornecles beryth gode witnes
    That my progenytours and auncetours have be
    The chefe ayde and diffence of this noble cyte.

    How ofte have myne auncetours in tymes of necessitie
    Delyverd this cyte from dedely parell
    As well by theyr manhode as by theyr police!
    What ieopardi and paine they have suffred in the quarell
    Thempire[41] to encrece, and for the comune wele,
    It nedith not the specialities to reherse or name   470
    Sith every trew Romaine knoweth the same.

450 *Egally* equally   454 *travers with* cross with   457 *proces* argument   462 *cornecles* chronicles   463 *auncetours* ancestors *be* been   466 *parell* peril   468 *ieopardi* risk   470 *specialities* particulars

In every manys howse that histories be rife
And wrytten in bookes, as in some placis be
The gestis of Arthur, or of Alexandyrs life[42],
In the whiche stories ye may evidently se
And rede how Cartage that royall cyte
By Cipion[43] of Affrick my grete graunte sire
Subduede was and also ascribede to his empire.

And many other cyties that dyde conspire
Ayenst the noble senatoure makynge resistence,   480
As often as necessite did it require
They were reducyd unto due obedience
Eyther by the policy or by the violence
Of my sayde aunceters. Thistories be playne
And witnesse that I speke not these wordis in vayne.

My blode hath ever takyn such payne
To salvegarde the comune wele fro ruyn and decay
That by one advyse the Cenat dyde ordeyne
Them to be namyd the faders of the contray[44],
And so were myne auctours reputed alway   490
For in every nede they dyde upon them call
For helpe as the chylde doth on the fader naturall.

How be it to praye them it was no nede at all
For of their owne myndis they were redy alway.
In tokyn of the same, for a memoriall
Of theyr desertis, the cytie dyde edifye
Triumphall arches wheruppon ye may
To my grete honour se at this day
Thymages of myn auncetours evyn by and by
By cause that theyr noblenes sholde never dye.   500

In token also that they were worthy
Grete honour and prayse of all the contray,
It is commaunded and used generally

472 *rife* plentiful   478 *ascribede* subjected   *empire* rule   487 *salve-*
garde safeguard   489 *contray* country   490 *auctours* ancestors
496 *edifye* erect   499 *by and by* nearby

That every cytezen that passith that way
By the sayde images he must obey,
And to that fygures make a due reverence
And ellis to the lawes he dothe grete offence.

Sith it is so than that of convenience
Suche honoure and homage must nedis be do
To these dede ymagis, than muche more reverence   510
To me sholde be gevyn, I trow ye thinke so,
For I am theyr very ymage, and relyque to
Of theyr flesch and blode, and veray inherytoure
As well of theyr godes as of theyr sayde honoure.

To me they have left many a castell and toure
Whiche in theyr triumphes thay rightfully wan;
To me they have also left all theyr tresoure
In suche abundance that I trow no man
Within all Rome sith it fyrst began
Had half the store as I understonde   520
That I have evyn now at ons in my honde.

Lo in these thynges my noblenes doth stonde
Whiche in myne oppynyon suffiseth for this intent,
And I trow there is no man throwgh all this londe
Of Italy but if he were here present
He wolde to my sayng in this matter assent,
And gyve unto me the honoure and pre-eminence,
Rather than make agayne me resistence.

   [*To Gaius*]
I marvayle gretly what shulde thy mynde insence
To thinke that thy tytle therin sholde be gode.   530
Parde, thow canst not say for thy deffence
That ever there was gentilman of thy kyn or blode,
And if there were oone it wolde be understonde
Without it be thy self, whiche now of late
Among noble gentylmen playest check mate[45].

505 *obey* bow   508 *convenience* suitability   510 *dede* dead   515 *toure*
tower   516 *wan* won   528 *agayne* against

LUC. No more therof, I pray you; suche wordis I hate,
   And I dyde forbid you them at the begynnyng,
   To eschue thoccasyon of stryfe and debate.
GA. Nay, let hym alone, he spekyth after his lernyng,
   For I shall answer hym to every thyng   540
   Whan he hath all said, if ye woll here me,
   As I thinke ye wyll of your equyte.
COR. Abide, I must make an ende fyrst, perde.
   To you, swete Lucres, I wolde have said beffore
   That yf ye wyll to my desyre in this matter agre,
   Doubtles ye shall blesse the tyme that ever ye were bore,
   For riches shall ye have at your will ever more,
   Without care or study of laboriouse besynes,
   And spend all your dayes in ease and plesaunt idelnesse.

   About your owne apparell ye can do non excesse   550
   In my company that sholde displese my mynd;
   With me shall ye do non other maner of besynes
   But hunt for your solace at the hart and hynde,
   And some tyme where we convenient game fynde
   Oure hawkis shal be redy to shew you a flight
   Whiche shal be right plesaunt and chereful to your sight.

   And yf so be that in huntyng ye have no delyght,
   Than may ye daunce a whyle for your disport;
   Ye shall have at your pleasure both day and night
   All maner of mynstralsy to do you comfort.   560
   Do what thyng ye wyll, I have to support
   Our chargis, and over that I may susteyne
   At myne owne fyndyng an .L⁴⁶ or twayne.

   And as for hym I am certayn
   Hys auncetours were of full poore degre,
   All be it that now withyn a yere or twayne
   By cause that he wold a gentilman be

---

542 *equyte* impartiality   546 *bore* born

He hath hym goten both office and fee
Whiche after the rate of hys wrechyd sparyng
Suffiseth scarsely for hys bare lyvynge.   570

Wherfore, swete Lucres, it were not accordyng
For your grete beaute with hym to dwell,
For there sholde ye have a thredebare lyvynge
With wrechyd scarcenes, and I have herde tell
That maydens of your age love not ryght well
Suche maner of husbondis without it be thay
That forceth lytyll to cast themself away[47].

I mene specyally for suche of them as may
Spede better if they wyll, as ye be yn the case,
And therfore Lucres what so ever he wyll say   580
Hys title agaynst you to force and embrace,
Ye shall do your owen selfe to grete a trespas
Yf ye folow hys part and enclyne therto.
Now say what ye wyll, syr, for I have all doo.

[GA.[48]] With ryght gode will I shall go to,
So that ye will here me with as grete pacience
As I have harde you, reason wolde soo.
And what so ever I shall speke in this audience
Eyther of myn owne merites or of hys insolence,
Yet fyrst unto you all, syrs, I make this request,   590
That it wolde lyke you to construe it to the best.

For lothe wolde I be as ony creature
To boste of myne owne dedis; it was never my gyse:
On that other syde, loth I am to make ony reportur
Of this mans foly or hym to dispice,
But never the lesse this matter towchith me in such wise,
That what so ever ye thinke in me, I must procede
Unto the veray trouth therof, as the matter is in dede.

568 *fee* property   569 *sparyng* frugality   571 *accordyng* suitable
576 *maner* type   586 *So that* provided that   589 *insolence* presumption   593 *gyse* custom   594 *reportur* narration   595 *dispice* despise

To make a grete rehersall of that ye have saide
The tyme will not suffre, but never the lesse   600
Two thinges for your self in substaunce ye have layd
Whiche as ye suppose maketh for your nobles,
Upon the whiche thingis dependith all your processe.
Fyrst of your auncetours ye allege the noble gestis,
Secondly the substaunce that ye have of theyr bequestes.

In the whiche thingis onely by your owne confession
Standeth all your noblenes, this sayd ye beffore:
Where unto this I say, under the correction
Of Lucres oure iugge here, that ye ar never the more
Worthy in my oppynion to be callyd noble therfore,   610
And withoute ye have better causes to shew than these
Of reson ye must the victory of this matter lese.

To the fyrst parte, as touching your auncetours dedes,
Some of them were noble lyke as ye declare;
Thestoris bereth witnes, I must graunt them nedes,
But yet for all that some of them ware
Of contrary diposycion, like as ye are,
For they dyde no proffite, no more do ye,
To the comon wele of this noble cytie.

Yf ye wyll the title of noblenes wynne   620
Shew what have ye done yourself therfore.
Some of your owne meritis let se bryng in,
Yf ever ye dyde ony syth ye were bore;
But surely ye have no suche thyng in store
Of your owne merites wherby of right
Ye shulde appere noble to ony mannys sight.

But neverthelesse I wyll you not blame
Thowgh ye speke not of your owne dedes at all.
And to say the trowght ye may not for shame,
Your lyfe is so voluptuouse and so bestiall   630

604 *gestis* deeds   612 *lese* lose   615 *Thestoris* the histories   *nedes*
of necessity   629 *trowght* truth

In folowynge of every lust sensuall
That I marvaille no thynge in my mynde
Yf ye leve your owne dedis behynde.

[*To Lucres*]

He wenyth that by hys proude contenaunce
Of worde and dede with nyse aray,
Hys grete othys and open mayntenaunce
Of theftis and murdres every day,
Also hys ryotouse disportis and play,
Hys sloth, his cowardy and other excesse,
Hys mynde disposed to all unclennesse,   640
By these thyngis oonly he shall have noblenesse.

Nay, the title of noblenes wyll not ensue
A man that is all gevyn to suche insolence,
But it groweth of longe continued vertu,
As I trust, lady, that youre indifference
Can well diffyne by your sentence.
Hys auncetours were not of suche condicion
But all contrary to hys disposicyon.

And therfore they were noble withouten faile
And dyde grete honoure to all the contrey   650
But what can theyr sayde noblenes advayle
To hym that takyth a contrary way,
Of whome men spekith every day
So grete dishonoure that it is marvel
The contrey suffereth hym therin to dwelle?

And where he to wyteth⁴⁹ me of pore kyn
He doth me therin a wrongfull offence,
For no man shall thankis or praysyng wyn
By the gyftis that he hath of natures influence.
Lyke wyse I thinke by a contrary sense   660
That if a man be borne blynde or lame
Not he hymselfe but nature therin is to blame.

634 *contenaunce* style 635 *nyse* elaborate 636 *mayntenaunce*
illegal support 638 *disportis* pleasures 639 *cowardy* cowardice
646 *sentence* judgement 651 *advayle* avail

Therfor he doth not me therin repreve,
And as for that poynt, this I wott welle
That both he and I cam of Adam and Eve.
There is no difference that I can tell
Whiche makith oon man an other to excell
So moche as doth vertue and godely maner,
And therin I may well with hym compare.

How be it, I speke it not for myne one prayse,   670
But certeynly this hath ever be my condicion:
I have borne unto God all my daies
His laude and prayse with my due devocion;
And next that I bere all wayes
To all my neyghbours charitable affeccyon.
Incontynency and onclennes I have had in abhominacion,
Lovyng to my frende and faythfull with all,
And ever I have withstonde my lustis sensuall.

One tyme with study my tyme I spende
To eschew Idlenes, the causer of syn;   680
An other tyme my contrey manly I deffend,
And for the victoryes that I have done therin
Ye have sene your selfe, syr, that I have come in
To this noble cytee twyse or thryse
Crownyd with lawryel as it is the gyse.

By these wayes, lo I do aryse
Unto grete honoure fro low degre,
And yf myn heires will do like wyse
Thay shal be brought to nobles by me.
But, Cornely, it semyth by the   690
That the nobles of thyn auncetours everycheon
Shall utterly starve and die in the alone.

And where he to witeth me on that other syde
Of small possession and grete scaecenes,

663 *repreve* prove wrong   685 *lawryel* laurel   *gyse* custom
689 *nobles* nobility   692 *starve* perish   693 *witeth* alleges   694
scaecenes poverty

For all that, lady, if ye will with me abidde
I shall assure you of moderate richesse,
And that sufficient for us both doutles.
Ye shall have also a man accordyng
To youre owne condicions in every thing.

Now, Lucres, I have shewyd unto you a parte   700
Of my title that I clayme you by,
Besechynge you therfore with all my hart
To considre us both twayne indifferently,
Whiche of us twayne ye will rather alow
More worthy for nobles to marry with you.

LUC. Syrs, I have hard you both at large –
COR. Nay, abide, Lucres, I pray you hertly,
Sithe he leyeth many thynges to my charge,
Suffre that I may therunto repply.
LUC. I wis replication shall not be necessary   710
Withoute that ye have some other thing in store
To shew for your self than ye dyde beffore.
COR. Why, lady, what thing will ye desyre more
Than I have shewyd to make for noblenes?
LUC. Yes, som thyng ther ys that makyth therfore
Better than ye have shewid in your processe.
But now let me se what man of witnes
Or what other proves will ye forth bryng
By the whiche eyther of you may iustifie his sayng.
GA. As for my parte, I wyll stonde gladly   720
To the commune voyce of all the contrey.
LUC. And ye lyke wyse, syr?
COR.   Ye, certaynly,
I shall in no wyse your worde dissobey.
LUC. Than wyll I betwyxt you both take this way:
I shall go enquyre as faste as I may
What the commune fame wyll theryn reporte,
And whan I have therof a due evidence

698 *accordyng* suitable   699 *condicions* inclinations   703 *indifferently*
impartially   710 *replication* reply

Than shall I agayne to you resorte
To shew you thopynyon of my sentence[50]
Whome I wyll iugge to have the pre-emynence.   730

COR. Nay, fayre Lucres, I you requyre
Let me not now depart in vayne,
Not knowyng theffect of my desyre[51].

LUC. Syr, allthough it be to you a payne,
Yet must ye do so evyn both twayne.
Eche of you depart hens to hys owne place
And take no more labour or payne in this case;
For as towchyng theffect of my sentence[52]
I shall go write it by gode advysement
Sone after that I am departed fro hens;   740
And than to eyther of you both shalbe sent
A copy of the same to this intent
That of none other person it shall be sayn
Sith it concerneth but onely unto you twayne.

GA. This is a gode waye, as in my mynde.
Ar not ye, syr, content in lyke wyse?

COR. I wot nere yet[53]. I wyll prayse as I fynde
And as I have cause; that is evyr my gyse.

GA. Well, Lucres, will ye commaunde me ony servyce?

LUC. No servyce at all, syr; why say ye so?   750
Our lorde spede you both where so ever ye goo.

    Et exeant Publius Cornelius et Gaius Flaminius

Now som mayde happely, and she were in my case,
Wolde not take that way that I do intend,
For I am fully determyned with Godis grace
So that to Gaius I wyll condyscend,
For in this case I do hym commend
As the more noble man sith he thys wyse
By meane of hys vertue to honoure doth aryse.
And for all that I wyll not dispise
The blode of Cornelius, I pray you thinke not so.   760
God forbede that ye sholde note me that wyse,
For truely I shall honoure them where so ever I go

---

752 *happely* perhaps   755 *condyscend* agree   761 *note* consider

And all other that be of lyke blode also,
But unto the blode I wyll have lytyl respect
Where tho condicyons be synfull and abiect.
I pray you all, syrs, as meny as be here,
Take not my wordis by a sinistre way.
    [*Enter B*]

B Yes, by my trouth, I shall witnes bere,
Wheresoever I be com another day,
How suche a gentylwoman did opynly say   770
That by a chorles son she wolde set more
Than she wolde do by a gentylman bore.

LUC. Nay, syr, than ye report me amys.

B I pray you, tell me how sayd ye than?

LUC. For God, syr, the substaunce of my wordis was this:
I say evyn as I saide whan I began,
That for vertue excellent I will honoure a man
Rather than for hys blode, if it so fall,
That gentil condicyons agre not with all.

B Than I put case that a gentilman bore   780
Have godely maners to his birth accordyng.

LUC. I say of hym is to be set gret store,
Suche one is worthy more lawde and praysyng
Than many of them that hath their begynnyng
Of low kynred, ellis God forbede.
I wyll not afferme the contrary for my hede,
For in that case ther may be no comparyson.
But never the lesse, I said this before
That a man of excellent vertuouse condicions,
Allthough he be of a pore stoke bore,   790
Yet I wyll honour and commende hym more
Than one that is descendide of ryght noble kyn
Whose lyffe is all dissolute and rotyde in syn.
And therfore I have determyned utterly
That Gaius Flaminius shall have his intent;
To hym onely I shall my self apply

765 *condicyons* personal qualities   783 *lawde* laud   790 *stoke* stock
793 *rotyde* rotted

To use me in wedloke at his commaundement;
So that to Cornelyus I wyll never assent
All though he had as grete possession
As ony one man in Cristen region.   800
I shall in no wyse favour or love hys condicyon
How be it that his blode requyreth due reverence,
And that I shall gyve hym with all submyssion,
But yet shall he never have the pre-eminence
To speke of very nobles by my sentence.
Ye be hys servaunt, syr, go your way,
And report to your mayster evyn as I say.

    [Exit Lucres[54]*]*

B Shall I do that erand? Nay, let be,
By the rode, ye shall do it yourselfe for me![55]
I promyse you faythfully   810
I wolde my mayster had be in Scotland
Whan he dyd put this matter in her hand
To stond to her iugèment.
But for asmoche as it is so
That this wrong to hym is doo
By a woman, he must let it goo
And holde hym content.
But he is of suche disposycion
That whan he hereth of this conclusion
He wylbe starke madd,   820
Ye, by my trowth, as made as an hare[56]:
It shall make hym so full of care
That he wyll with hym self fare
Evyn as it were a lade.
And so wold not I, so mote I thee,
For this matter and I were as he,
It shulde never anger me:
But this wold I do,
I wolde let her go in the mare name[57].

    [Enter A]

A What now, syrs, how goth the game?   830

---

805 *very* true   811 *be* been   820 *starke* completely   824 *lade* lad

What, is this woman go?
B Ye, ye, man.
A   And what way hathe she takyn?
B By my fayth, my mayster is forsakyn
And nedis she wyll agre
Unto thy mayster, thus she saieth,
And many causes therfore she leyeth
Why it shulde so be.
A I marvayle gretely wherof that grue.
B By my fayth, she saide, I tell the true,
That she wolde nedis have hym for his vertue   840
And for none other thynge.
A Vertue, what the devyll is that?
And I can tell, I shrew my catt,
To myne understondynge.
B By my fayth, no more can I
But this she said here opynly,
All these folke can tell.
A How say ye, gode women, is it your gyse
To chose all your husbondis that wyse?
By my trought, than I marvaile.   850
B Nay, this is the fere, so mot I goo,
That men chise not theyr wyffes so
In placis where I have be,
For wiffes may well complayne and grone,
Al be it that cause have they none
That I can here or se.
But of weddyd men there be ryght fewe
That welle not say the best is a shrew;
Therin they all agree.
I warne you weddyd men everichone   860
That other remede have ye none
So moche for your ease,
And ye wold study tyll tomorow
But let them evyn alone with sorow

836 *leyeth* adduces   838 *grue* grew   852 *chise* choose   854 *grone* groan   861 *remede* remedy

Whan they do you displease.

A Tusshe, here is no man that settyth a blank[58]
  By thy counsell or konneth the thank[59],
  Speke therof no more:
  They know that remedy better than thow.
  But what shall we twayne do now?   870
  I care most therfore,
  Me thinketh that matter wolde be wist.

B Mary, we may goo hens whan we lyst,
  No man saith us nay.

A Why than, is the play all do?

B Ye, by my feyth, and we were ons go
  It were do streght wey.

A And I wolde have thought in vere dede
  That this matter sholde have procede
  To som other conclusion.   880

B Ye, thou art a maister mery man,
  Thou shall be wyse I wot nere whan[60].
  Is not the question
  Of noblenes now fully defynde,
  As it may be so by a womans mynde?
  What woldyst thow have more?
  Thow toldest me that other day
  That all the substaunce of this play
  Was done specially therfor
  Not onely to make folke myrth and game,   890
  But that suche as be gentilmen of name
  May be somwhat movyd
  By this example for to eschew
  The wey of vyce, and favour vertue.
  For syn is to be reprovyd
  More in them, for the degre,
  Than in other parsons such as be
  Of pour kyn and birth.
  This was the cause principall,
  And also for to do with all   900

881 *maister* pre-eminent   897 *parsons* persons

This company some myrth.
And though the matter that we have playde
Be not percase so wele conveyde,
And with so great reason
As thistory it self requyreth,
Yet the auctour therof desyrith
That for this season
At the lest ye will take it in pacience.
And yf therbe ony offence –
Show us where in or we go hence –   903 910
Done in the same,
It is onely for lacke of connynge,
And not he, but his wit runnynge[61]
Is there of to blame.
And glade wolde he be, and ryght fayne,
That some man of stabyll brayne
Wolde take on hym the labour and payne
This mater to amende.
And so he wyllyd me for to say,
And that done, of all this play   920
Shortely here we make an end.

903 *percase* by chance   912 *connynge* skill, craft

Thē̃terlude of youth.

Iℇſu that his armes dyd ſprede
And on a tree was done to dead
From all perils he you defende
I deſyꝛe audyence tyl I haue made an ende
Foꝛ am come from God aboue
To occupye his lawes to your behoue
And am named Charytye
There maye no man ſaued be
Wythout the helpe of me
Foꝛ he that Charytye doth refuſe
Other vertues thought he do vſe
            I.t.

Facsimile of the first page of the Lambeth fragment of Youth

The earliest known edition of *Youth* is the Lambeth fragment consisting of sig. A. i, ii, iii, iv (lines 1–246). This edition is undated, but it is unlikely to be earlier than 1528. There is no title-page, the heading being 'Thenterlude of youth'. Two other sixteenth-century editions have survived:

John Waley, B.M. C.34.b.24. Undated (?1557)
William Copland. B.M. C.34.e.15. Undated (?1562)

The best modern edition is by W. Bang and R. B. McKerrow, *Materialien zur Kunde des alteren englischen Dramas*, xii, Louvain, 1905. These editors conclude that none of the existing texts is printed directly from one of the others, and suppose that at least two other printed editions must have existed in order to account for the present state of the texts. If five editions appeared by 1562, the play must have been exceptionally popular.

The play, which is anonymous, was probably written as early as 1515, and shares some passages with *Hickscorner* (c. 1513). This edition follows Waley as far as possible, but I have accepted some minor changes from the Lambeth fragment and from Copland. There is one stage direction (line 387) in the original texts: the rest are modern.

Youth

    [*Enter Charity*]
[CHARITY] Iesu, that his armes dyd sprede
    And on a tree was done to dead,
    From all perils he you defende.
    I desyre audyence tyl I have made an ende,
    For I am come from God above

To occupye his lawes to your behove,
And am named Charytye.
There maye no man saved be
Wythout the helpe of me.
For he that Charytye doth refuse   10
Other vertues though he do use
Without Charitye it wyl not be.
For it is written in the faythe
Qui manet in charitate in deo manet[1];
I am the gate, I tell the,
Of heaven, that ioyful citye.
Ther maye no man thider come,
But of Charyty he must have some,
Or ye[2] may not come iwis
Unto heaven, the citie of blysse.   20
Therfore Charitie who wil hym take
A pure soule it wyl him make
Before the face of God.
In the *A.B.C.*[3] of bokes the least
Yt is written *deus charitas est.*
Lo, Charytie is a great thinge:
Of all vertues, it is the kynge.
Whan God in earth was here livinge
Of Charyti he found none endinge.
I was planted in his hart.   30
We two might not departe.
Out of hys harte I dyd sprynge
Throughe the myght of the heaven kinge.
And all prestes that be
Maye singe no masse[4] without Charitie.
And Charyte to them they do not take,
Thei may not receyve him that did them make,
And all thys worlde, of noughte.
        [*Enter Youth*]

6 *occupye* concern myself with   *behove* advantage   19 *iwis* indeed
31 *departe* separate   36 *And* if (and so frequently elsewhere)   38 *of*
noughte from nothing

YOUTHE Abacke[5], felowes, and gyve me roume,
  Or I shall make you to avoyde sone.   40
  I am goodle of persone.
  I am pereles where ever I come.
  My name is Youth, I tell the.
  I florysh as the vine tre.
  Who may be likened unto me
  In my youthe and iolytye?
  My hearte is royall and bushed thicke,
  My body plyaunt as a hasel styck,
  Mine armes be bothe bigge[6] and strong,
  My fingers be both faire and longe,   50
  My chest bigge as a tunne,
  My legges be full lighte for to runne,
  To hoppe and daunce and make mery.
  By the masse I recke not a chery
  What so ever I do.
  I am the heyre of my fathers lande:
  And it is come into my hande,
  I care for no more.
CHARITE Are you so disposed to doo,
  To folowe vyce and let vertue go?   60
YOUTHE Ye syr, even so.
  For nowe a dayes he is not set by
  Without he be unthryftye.
CHARITE You had nede to ask God mercye.
  Why do you so prase your body?
YOUTHE Why, knave, what is that to the?
  Wylt thou let me to prayse my body:
  Why shuld I not praise it and it be goodli?
  I wil not let for the.
CHARITE What shal it be whan thou shalt flyt   70
  Fro the wealth into the pyt?

---

40 *avoyde* go away *sone* soon 42 *pereles* without equal 47
bushed well grown 51 *tunne* (wine) barrel 54 *recke* care 62 *set
by* considered to be of importance 63 *Without* unless 67 *let* prevent, stop 71 *wealth* prosperity, well-being

Therfore of it be not to boolde,
Least thou forthink it whan thou art olde.
Ye may be lykened to a tre:
In youth, floryshyng with royalte,
And in age it is cut downe,
And to the fyre is throwne.
So shalt thou, but thou amende,
Be burned in hel without ende.

YOUTHE Ye horson, trowest thou so?   80
Beware leaste thou thyder go!
Hence, caytyfe, go thy way,
Or with my dagger I shal the slay.
Hens, knave, out of this place,
Or I shall lay the on the face.
Sayest thou that I shal go to hel
For evermore there to dwel?
I had lever thou had evyll fare.

CHARITE A yet, syr, do by my rede
And aske mercy for thy mysdede,   90
And you shalt be an herytoure of blysse
Where al ioye and myrthe is,
Where thou shal se a gloryus syght
Of aungeles singyng with saintes bright
Before the face of God.

YOUTHE What, syrs, above the sky?
I had nede of a ladder to climbe so hie.
But what and the ladder slyppe,
Than am I deceyved yet.
And if I fal, I catche a quecke.   100
I may fortune to breke my necke,
And that ioynte is yll to set.
Nay, nay, not so.

CHARITE O yet remember and cal to thy minde

73 *forthink* regret 78 *but* unless 85 *lay* strike 88 *lever* rather
fare luck 89 *rede* advice, opinion 91 *herytoure* heir, inheritor
99 *Than* then 100 *quecke* choke (from hanging)

The mercy of God passeth al thyng.
For it is wryten by noble clerkes
The mercye of God passeth all werkes.
That witnesseth holy scrypture saynge thus:
Miserationes domini super omnia opera eius[7].
Therfore doute not Goddes grace: 110
Therof is plenty in every place.

YOUTHE What, me thynke ye be clerkyshe,
For ye speake good gibbryshe.
Syr, I pray you, and you have any store,
Soyle me a question or ye cast out any more,
Least whan your connynge is all done
My question have no solucyon.
Syr, and it please you, thys:
Why do men eate mustarde with saltfysshe?[8]
Sir, I pray you, soile me thys question,   120
That I have put to your discrecyon.

CHARITE This question is but vanitie.
Yt longeth not to me
Suche questions to assoyle.

YOUTHE Sir, by God that me dere bought,
I se your connynge is littell or nought.
And I shuld folowe your scole
Sone ye wolde make me a fole.
Therfore crake no longer here,
Least I take you on the eare   130
And make your head to ake.

CHARITE Sir, it falleth not for me to fight
Nether by day ne by night.
Therfore do my counsayle, I saye,
Than to heven thou shalt have thy way.

YOUTHE No syr, I thynke ye wyll not fighte.
But to take a mannes purs in the night

105 *passeth* surpasses   112 *clerkyshe* like a learned priest, sanctimonious   115 *Soyle* answer (as a riddle)   *or* before   *cast* spew
123 *longeth* belongs   124 *assoyle* solve   129 *crake* chatter   130 *take* strike

Ye wyll not say nay.
For suche holy caitifes
Were wonte to be theves, 140
And such wolde be hanged as hye
As a man may se with his eye.
In faith this same is true.

CHARITE God save every christen body
From such evell destenye,
And sende us of his grace
In heven to have a place.

YOUTHE Nay, nay, I warrant the
He hathe no place for the.
Wenest thou he wyll have suche fooles 150
To syt on his gaie stooles?
Naye, I warrant the, naye.

[CHARITY⁹] Well, sir, I put me in Goddes wyll
Whether he wyll me save or spyll.
And sir, I pray you do so
And truste in God what so ever ye do.

YOUTHE Syr, I praye the holde thy peace,
And talke to me of no goodnes,
And soone loke thou go thy waye
Leste with my dagger I the slaye. 160
In faythe yf thou meve my harte,
Thou shalte be wearye of thy parte
Or thou and I have done.

CHARITE Thynke what God suffered for the:
His armes to be spred upon a tre,
A knight with a speare opened his side,
In his harte appeared a wounde wyde
That bought both you and me.

YOUTHE Goddes faste¹⁰, what is that to me?
Thow dawe, wylte thou rede me 170
In my youth to lose my ioylytie?
Hence, knave, and go thy waye,

150 *Wenest thou* do you think   154 *spyll* destroy   161 *meve* move
170 *dawe* dolt   *rede* counsel

Or wyth my dagger I shall the slaye.

CHARITE O syr, heare what I you tell,
And be ruled after my counsell,
That ye might syt in heven on hye
With God and his company.

YOUTHE A yet of God thou wilte not ceasse
Tyll I fyght in good earneste.
On my fayth I tell the true   180
Yf I fyght thou wylte it rue[11]
All the dayes of thy lyfe.

CHARITE Syr, I se it wyll none otherwise be.
I wyll go to my brother Humilitie,
And take good counsayle of hym,
Howe it is best to be do theryn.

YOUTHE Ye, mary, sire, I pray you of that.
Me thinke it were a good sight of your backe.
I wolde se your heles hither,
And your brother and you together   190
Fettred fine fast.
Iwys, and I had the kay,
Ye shulde singe *wel away*,
Or I let you lose.

CHARITE Farewell, my maysters, everychone[12].
I wyll come agayne anone
And tel you howe I have done.

YOUTHE And thou come hither agayne
I shall sende the hens, in the divels name.
      [*Charity goes out*]
What nowe, I maye have my space   200
To iet here in thys place.
Before I myght not stere
Whan the churle Charitie was here,
But nowe amonge al thys chere
I wold I had some company here.
Iwis my brother Riot wold helpe me
For to beate Charitye,

186 *do* done   192 *kay* key   201 *iet* show off   202 *stere* move

And his brother to.
   [*Enter Riot*[13]]

RYOT Huffa, huffa, who calleth after me?
  I am Riot, ful of iolyte.   210
  My heart is lyght as the wynde,
  And all on Riot is my mynde,
  Where so ever I go.
  But wote ye what I do here?
  To seke Youth my compere.
  Fayne of hym I wolde have a sight,
  But my lippes hange in my lyght[14].
  God spede, master Youth, by my faie.

YOUTHE Welcom, Riot, in the devels waye:
  Who brought the hither today?   220

RYOT That dyd my legges, I tell the.
  Me thought thou dyd call me,
  And I am come now here
  To make roiall chere,
  And tell the how I have done.

YOUTHE What, I wende thou hadst ben henged.
  But I se thou arte escaped.
  For it was tolde me heere
  You toke a man on the eare,
  That his purse in your bosome did flye,   230
  And so in Newgate[15] ye dyd lye.

RYOT So it was, I beshrewe your pate.
  I come lately from Newgate.
  But I am as readye to make chere
  As he that never came there.
  For and I have spendyng,
  I wyll make as mery as a kynge,
  And care not what I do.
  For I wyll not lye longe in prison,
  But wyll get forthe soone.   240
  For I have learned a pollycie

215 *compere* companion   218 *faie* faith   226 *wende* thought
229   *toke* struck   236 *and* if

That wyll lose me lyghtlye
And sone let me go.

YOUTHE I love well thy discretyon,
For thou arte all of one condicion.
Thou arte stable and stedfast of mynde
And not chaungable as the wynde.
But sir, I praye you, at the leaste,
Tell me more of that ieste
That thou tolde me ryght nowe.   250

RYOT Moreover I shall tell the
The mayre of London sent for me,
Forth of Newgate for to come,
For to preche at Tyborne[16].

YOUTHE By our Lady, he dyd promote the
To make the preche at the galowe tre.
But syr, how diddest thou scape?

RYOT Verely, syr, the rope brake,
And so I fell to the ground,
And ran away safe and sound.   260
By the way I met with a courtyers lad,
And twenty nobles of gold in hys purs he had.
I toke the ladde on the eare;
Besyde his horse I felled him there.
I toke his purs in my hande,
And twenty nobles therin I fande.
Lorde, howe I was mery.

YOUTHE Goddes fote, thou diddest ynoughe there
For to be made knight of the colere[17].

RYOT Ye, syr, I truste to God allmyght,   270
At the nexte cessions[18] to be dubbed a knight.

YOUTHE Now, syr, by thys lyght,
That wolde I fayne se,
And I plyght the, so God me save,
That a surer colere thou shalt have,
And because gold colers be so good chepe,

242 *lyghtlye* easily   261 *courtyers* courtier's   266 *fande* found
274 *plyght* promise

123

Unto the roper I shal speke
To make the one of a good pryce,
And that shalbe of warrantyse.

RYOT Youth, I pray the, have adoo[19],   280
And to the taverne let us go.
And we will drynke divers wine
And the cost shal be myne.
Thou shalt not pay one peny iwis,
Yet thou shalt have a wenche to kysse,
Whan so ever thou wilte.

YOUTHE Mary, Ryot, I thanke the
That thou wylt bestowe it on me,
And for thy pleasure, so be it.
I wold not Charity shuld us mete   290
And turne us agayne,
For right nowe he was with me
And said he wolde go to Humilitie
And come to me agayne.

RYOT Let him come if he will.
He were better to bide styll.
And he gyve the croked langage[20],
I wyll laye him on the visage.
And that thou shalt se sone
How lightly it shall be done.   300
And he wyll not be ruled with knockes,
We shall set him in the stockes
To heale his sore shinnes.

YOUTHE I shall helpe the if I can
To dryve awaye that hangman.
Herke, Riot, thou shalt understande
I am heyre of my fathers land,
And nowe they be come to my hand
Me thynke it were best therfore
That I had one man more   310
To wayte me upon.

RYOT I can spede the of a servaunte of pryce

279 *warrantyse* guarantee

That wil do the good service.
I se him go here beside.
Some men call him Mayster Pryde.
I sweare by God in Trinitie
I wyll go fetche him unto the,
And that even anone.

YOUTHE Hye the apace and come agayne,
And brynge with the that noble swayne.   320
    [*Riot goes to meet Pride and brings him back*]

RYOT Lo, Mayster Youth, here he is,
A pretty man and wise.
He wyl be glad to do you servyce[21]
In al that ever he may.

YOUTHE Welcome to me, good fellowe,
I pray the, whence commest thou?
And thou wylt my servaunt be,
I shall geve the golde and fee[22].

PRIDE Syr, I am content, iwis,
To do you any servis   330
That ever I can do.

YOUTHE By likelyhod thou shulde do well ynowe,
Thou art a lykely felowe.

PRIDE Yes, syr, I warrant you.
Yf ye wyll be rulde by me,
I shall you brynge to hye degre.

YOUTHE What shall I do, tell me,
And I wyll be ruled by the.

PRIDE Mary, I shall tell you:
Considre ye have good ynowe,   340
And think ye come of noble kinde,
Above all men exalte thy minde,
Put downe the poore and set nought bi them,
Be in company with gentle men,
Iette up and downe in the waye,
And your clothes loke they be gaye.
The pretye wenches wyll saye than

332 *ynowe* enough   347 *than* then

125

Yonder goeth a gentelman;
And pore felowe that goeth you by
Will do of his cap and make you curteisie.   350
In faith, this is true.
YOUTHE Sir, I thanke the, by the roode,
For thy counsell that is so good.
And I commit me even nowe
Under the techynge of Ryot and you.
RYOT Lo, Youth, I tolde you
That he was a lustye felowe.
YOUTHE Mary, syr, I thanke the,
That you wolde brynge hym unto me.
PRYDE Syr, it were expedyente that ye had a wife   360
To live with her all youre life.
RYOT A wyfe! Nay, nay, for God avowe,
He shall have fleshe inoughe.
For by God that me dere bought
Over muche of one thinge is nought.
The devyl sayd he had lever burne al his lyfe
Than ones for to take a wife.
Therfore I saye, so God me save,
He shall no wife have.
Thou haste a syster, fair and fre,   370
I knowe well hys lemman she wyll be.
Therfore I wolde she were here,
That we might go and make good chere
At the wine some where.
YOUTHE I pray you, hither thou do her brynge,
For she is to my likinge.
PRYDE Syr, I shall do my diligence
To bringe her to your presence.
YOUTHE Hye the apace, and come agayn.
To have a sight I wolde be faine   380
Of that lady fre.
        [*Pride goes out*]

350 *do of* take off   370 *fre* noble   371 *lemman* mistress   380
faine glad

RYOT Syr, in faith, I shall tell you true,
    She is a freshe and faire of hue,
    And verye propre of bodye.
    Men call her Lady Lechery.
YOUTHE My herte burneth, by God of myght,
    Till of that lady I have a syght.
        Intret Superbia cum Luxuria et dicat Superbia[23]
PRYDE Syr, I have fulfylled your entent,
    And have brought you in thys present
    That you have sent me fore.   390
YOUTHE Thou art a redy messengere.
    Come hither to me, my herte so dere.
    Ye be welcome to me as the hert in my body.
LECHERI Syr, I thanke you and at your pleasure I am.
    Ye be the same unto me.
YOUTHE Maisters, wyl ye to taverne walk.
    A worde with you there wyll I talke,
    And gyve you the wine.
LECHERI Gentle man, I thanke you verely.
    And I am all redye   400
    To waite you upon.
RYOT What, sister Lecherye,
    Ye be welcome to our companye.
LECHERI Well, wanton, well, fye for shame
    So sone ye do expresse my name.
    What if no man shuld have knowne?
    Iwis, I shal you bete, well, wanton, well.
RYOT A lytell pretye nyset![24]
    Ye be well nise, God wote.
    Ye be a lytell pretly pye[24], iwis ye go ful gingerlie.   410
LECHERI Wel I se your false eye
    Winketh on me full wantonly.
    Ye be full wanton, iwis.
YOUTHE Pryde, I thanke you of your laboure
    That you had to fetch thys fayre floure.

---

408 *nyset* foolish wench   409 *wote* knows   410 *pye* magpie (term
of affection)   *gingerlie* daintily   415 *floure* flower

127

PRYDE Lo, Youth, I tolde the
    That I wolde brynge her with me.
    Sir, I pray you tel me nowe
    Howe doth she lyke you?
YOUTHE Verely, wel she pleased me,   420
    For she is courteis, gentyll and fre.
    Howe do you, fayre Ladye:
    Howe fare you, tell me?
LECHERI Syr, if it please you, I do well ynowe,
    And the better that you wyl wite.
YOUTHE Riot, I wolde be at the taverne fayne,
    Least Charitie us mete and turne us agayne.
    Than wold I be sory because of thys farye[25] ladi.
RYOT Let us go agayne betyme,
    That we maye be at the wyne,   430
    Or ever that he come.
PRYDE Hie the apace, and go we hence,
    We wil let for none expence.
YOUTHE Now we wil fil the cup and make good chere.
    I trust I have a noble[26] here.
    Herke, sirs, for God almighte,
    Herest thou not howe they fight[27].
    In fayth we shal them part.
    Yf there be any wine to sell
    They shall no longer together dwell,   440
    No, than I beshrewe my herte.
RYOT No, syr, so mote I the[28].
    Let not thy servauntes fight within the.
    For it is a carefull lyfe
    Evermore to lyve in strife.
    Therefore yf ye wyll be ruled bi mi tale,
    We will go to the ale,
    And se howe we can do.
    I truste to God that sitteth on hye,
    To lese that lyttell companye   450

419 *lyke* please   425 *wite* know   429 *betyme* soon   431 *Or* before
433 *let* spare   444 *carefull* full of care   450 *lese* lose

Within an houre or two.

PRIDE Now let us goo, for Goddes sake,
And se howe merye we can make.

RYOT Now lette us go apace;
And I be last there, I beshrewe my face.

YOUTHE Nowe let us go, that we were there
To make this Ladye some chere.

LECHERI Verelye sir, I thanke the
That ye wyll bestowe it on me.
And whan it please you on me to call,   460
My heart is yours, bodye and all.

YOUTHE Faire Ladye, I thanke the,
On the same wyse ye shall have me,
Whan so ever ye please.

PRYDE Riot, we tarye very longe.

RYOT We wyl go even now, with a lusty songe.

PRYDE In fayth, I wyll be Rector Chorye²⁹.

YOUTHE Go to it then hardely, and let us be agate.
        [Enter Charity]

CHARITE Abide, felowe, a worde with the.
Whether go ye, tell me?   470
Abyde and here what I shall you tell,
And be ruled by my counsel.

PRYDE Naye, no felowe, ne yet mate.
I trowe thy felowe be in Newgate.
Shal we tell the whether we go?
Nay, iwis, good Iohn-a-Pepo³⁰.
Who learned the, thou mistaught man,
To speake so to a gentylman?
Thoughe his clothes be never so thinne
Yet he is come of noble kinne.   480
Thoughe thou gyve him suche a mocke,
Yet he is come of a noble stocke,
I let the well to wite.

RYOT What, syr Iohn³¹, what saye ye,

---

468 *agate* on the road   473 *mate* friend   483 *well* clearly   *wite*
understand

Wolde you be fetred nowe?
Thynke nat to long I pray you,
It maye fortune come sone ynowe.
Ye shall thynke it a lytell soone.

CHARITE Yet, syrs, let thys cease,
And let us talke of goodnes.   490

YOUTHE He turned his tale, he is aferde.
But faith he shalbe skerd.
He weneth by flatterynge to please us againe,
But he laboureth all in vayne.

CHARITE Syr, I pray you me not spare,
For nothinge I do care
That ye can doe to me.

RYOT No, horeson, sayst thou so?
Holde him, Pride, and let me go.
I shall fet a payre of rynges   500
That shall sit to his shinnes,
And that even anon.

PRIDE Hye the apace and come agayne,
And bringe with the a good chaine
To holde him here stil.
          [Riot goes out]

CHARITE Iesu, that was borne of Marye milde,
From all evyll he us shielde,
And sende you grace to amende,
Or oure lyfe be at an ende.
For I tell you trewlye,   510
That ye lyve full wickedlye.
I praye God it amende.
          [Enter Riot, with fetters]

RYOT32 Lo, syrs, loke what I bringe.
Is not thys a ioly ringinge?
By my trouth, I trowe it be.
I will go wyt of Charitie.
How sayest thou, Mayster Charitie,

---

485 *fetred* fettered   491 *aferde* afraid   492 *skerd* scared   500 *rynges*
fetters   516 *wyt* learn

Dothe this geare please the?

CHARITE They please me well in dede:
The more sorowe, the more mede.   520
For God saide whyle he was a man,
Beati qui persecutionem patiuntur propter iusticiam[33];
Unto his apostles he sayde so,
To teache them howe they shulde do.

PRIDE We shall se how they can please;
Sit downe, sir, and take your ease.
Me thinke these same were ful meete
To go about your fayre feete.

YOUTHE By my truthe, I you tell
They wolde become him very well.   530
Therfore hye that they were on,
Unto the taverne that we were gone.

RYOT That shall ye se anone,
Howe soone they shall be on.
And after we wyll not tary longe,
But go hence with a mery songe.

PRYDE Let us begyn all at once.

YOUTHE Nowe have at it, by cockes bones,
And soone let us goo.
    [*Youth, Riot and Pride put Charity in the stocks,
    and go out with Lechery*]

CHARITE Lo, maisters, here you maye see beforne   540
That the weede overgroweth the corne.
Nowe maie ye see all in this tide
How the vice is taken, and vertue set aside.
Yonder ye maye see Youth is not stable,
But evermore chaungeable;
And the nature of men is frayle,
That he wotteth not what may avayle
Vertue for to make.
O good Lorde, it is a pitifull case
Sith God hath lent man wyt and grace,   550

520 *mede* reward   527 *meete* suitable   538 *cockes* God's   542 *tide*
occasion

To chose of good and evyll,
That man shulde voluntarylye
To suche thynges himselfe applye,
That his soule shuld spyll.

[*Enter Humility*]

HUMILITYE Christ that was crucified and crowned with
        thorne,
And of a virgin for man was borne,
Some knowledge sende to me
Of my brother Charitye.

CHARITE Dere brother Humilitie,
Ye be welcome unto me. 560
Where have ye be so longe?

HUMILITYE I shall do you to understande
That I have sayd myne evensonge.
But sir, I praye you tel me nowe
Howe this case happened to you.

CHARITE I shall tell you anone.
The felowes that I tolde you on
Have me thus arayed.

HUMILITYE Sir, I shall undo the bandes
From your feete and your handes. 570

[*Releases him*]

Sir, I praye you tell me anone
Whether they be gone,
And when they come againe.

CHARITE Sir, to the taverne they be gone,
And they wyll come againe anone
And that shall you see.

HUMILITYE Then wyll we them exhorte
Unto vertue to resorte, and so forsake syn.

CHARITE I will helpe you that I can
To convert that wicked man. 580

[*Enter Youth, Riot and Pride*]

YOUTHE Abacke, galantes, and loke unto me,
And take me for your speciall[34].
For I am promoted to hye degree;
By ryght I am kinge eternal.

132

Neither duke, ne lorde, baron, ne knight
That may be lykened unto me.
They be subdued to me by ryght,
As servantes to their masters shulde be.

HUMILITYE Ye be welcome to thys place here.
We thinke ye labour all in vayne   590
Wherefore your braynes we wyll stere
And kele you a lytel agayne.

YOUTHE Saiest thou my braynes thou wylt stere,
I shall laye the on the eare.
Were thou borne in Trumpington[35]
And brought up at Hogges Norton?[36]
By my faith, it semeth so:
Well go, knave, go.

CHARITE Do by our counsell and our rede,
And aske mercye for thy mysdede,   600
And endever the for Goddes sake
For thy sinnes amendes to make,
Or ever that thou die.

RYOT Harke, Youth, for God avowe,
He wolde have the a sainte nowe.
But Youth, I shall you tell,
A yonge sainte, an olde devyll.
Therfore I holde the a foole,
And thou so folowe his scole.

YOUTHE I warrant thee, I wyll not do soo.   610
I wyll be ruled by you two.

PRYDE Then shall ye do well.
Yf ye be ruled by our counsell,
We wyll bringe you to hye degree,
And promote you to dignitee.

HUMILITYE Sir, it is a pitifull case
That you wolde forsake grace
And to vyce applye.

YOUTHE Whie, knave, dothe it greve thee?

---

591 *stere* stir, trouble   592 *kele* make less violent, assuage
599 *rede* advice   619 *Whie* why

Thou shalt not answer for me.   620
When my soule hangeth on the hedge once,
Then take thou and caste stones
As faste as thou wylte.

CHARITE Syr, if it please you to do thus,
Forsake them and do after us,
The better shall you do.

RYOT Syre, he shall do well inowe,
Thoughe he be ruled by neither of you.
Therfore crake no longer here,
Least you have on the eare,   630
And that a good knocke.

PRIDE Lyghtlye se thou avoyde the place,
Or I shall gyve the on the face.
Youth, I trowe that he wolde
Make you holy or ye be olde,
And I swere by the rode
It is tyme inoughe to be good
Whan that ye be olde.

YOUTHE Syr, by my truthe, I the say
I wyll make mery whiles I may,   640
I can not tell you howe long.

RYOT Ye sir, so mote I thryve,
Thou art not certayne of thy life.
Therfore thou were a starke foole
To leve myrthe and folowe their scole.

HUMILITYE Syr, I shall him exhorte
Unto us to resorte,
And you to forsake.

PRIDE Aske him if he wyll do so,
To forsake us and folowe you two: 650
Nay, I warrant you, nay.

HUMILITYE That shall you se even anone.
I wyll unto him gone,
And se what he will saye.

625 *do after us* follow our teaching   629 *crake* boast   642 *mote*
might   644 *starke* utter, complete

RYOT Hardeley go on thy waye;
  I know well he will say naye.

YOUTHE Ye, syr, by God that me dere bought,
  Me thinke ye laboure all for nought.
  Wenest thou that I wyll for the,
  Or thy brother Charytie,   660
  Forsake thys good companye?
  Nay, I warrant the.

PRIDE No, mayster, I praye you of that,
  For anye thynge forsake us nat;
  And all oure counsell rule you by,
  Ye may be Emperour or ye dye.

YOUTHE While I have life in my body,
  Shall I be ruled by Riot and the?

RYOT Sir, than shall ye do well
  For we be true as stele.   670
  Syr, I can teache you to play at the dice[37]
  At the quenes game, and at the Iryshe,
  The treygobet, and the hasarde also,
  And many other games mo.
  Also at the cardes I can teche you to play,
  At the triump, and one and thyrtye,
  Post, pinion, and also aumsace,
  And at an other they call dewsace.
  Yet I can tel you more, and ye wyll con me thanke[38];
  Pinke and drinke, and also at the blanke,   680
  And many sportes mo.

YOUTHE I thanke the, Riot, so mote I the,
  For the counsell thou haste geven me.
  I will folowe thy minde in every thinge,
  And guide me after thy learnynge.

CHARITE Youth, leve that counsell, for it is nought,
  And amende that thou hast myswrought
  That thou maist save that God hath boughte.

YOUTHE What saye ye, Mayster Charitie,
  What hath God bought for me?   690

655 *Hardeley* foolishly   687 *myswrought* done wrongly

By my trouth, I knowe not
Whether that he goeth in white or blacke.
He came never at the stues,
Nor in no place where I do use.
Iwis, he bought not my cap,
Nor yet my ioylie hat.
I wot not what he hath bought for me.
And he bought any thynge of myne,
I wyll geve hym a quarte of wyne,
The nexte tyme I hym meete.   700

CHARITE Sir, this he dyd for the:
When thou wast bonde, he made the free,
And bought the wyth his bloud.

YOUTHE Sire, I praye you, tell me
Howe may thys be[39],
That I knowe I was never bonde
Unto none in Englande?

CHARITE Sir, I shall tell you.
Whan Adam had done greate trespas,
And out of paradise exiled was,   710
Then all the soles as I can you tell
Were in the bondage of the devyll of hell,
Tyll the father of heaven of hys great mercie
Sent the seconde person in Trinitie
Us for to redeme.
And so with his precyous bloude,
He bought us on the roode,
And our soules dyd save.

YOUTHE Howe shulde I save it? Tell me nowe,
And I wyll be ruled after you my soule to save.   720

RYOT What, Youth, wyll you forsake me?
I wyll not forsake thee.

HUMILITYE I shall tell you shortely;
Knele downe and aske God mercye,
For that you have offended.

PRIDE Youth, wylte thou do so,

693 *stues* stews   701 *dyd* did   711 *soles* souls

136

Folowe them and let us go?
Marye, I trowe naye.
YOUTHE Here all sinne I forsake,
And to God I me betake.   730
Good Lorde, I praye the have no indignacion
That I a sinner shulde aske salvacyon.
CHARITE Nowe thou muste forsake Pryde,
And all Riot set aside.
PRIDE I wyll not him forsake,
Neither early ne late,
I wende he wolde not forsake me;
But if it wyll none otherwise bee
I wyll go my waye.
YOUTHE Sir, I praye God be your spede   740
And helpe you at your nede.
    [*Pride goes out*]
RYOT I am sure thou wilt not forsake me,
Nor I wyll not forsake thee.
YOUTHE I forsake you also,
And wyll not have with you to do.
RYOT And I forsake the utterlye.
Fye on the, caytife, fye!
Once a promise thou dyd me make
That thou wolde me never forsake.
But nowe I se it is harde   750
For to truste the wretched worlde.
Farewell, masters, everycheone.
    [*Riot goes out*]
HUMILITYE For your synne looke ye morne,
And evyll creatures loke ye tourne.
For your name who maketh inquisicion
Saye it is Good Contricion,
That for sinne doth morne.
CHARITE Here is a newe araye,
For to walke by the waye,
Your prayer for to saye.   760

    737 *wende* thought   754 *tourne* reject   755 *inquisicion* inquiry

HUMILITYE Here be bedes for your devocyon,
 And kepe you from all temptacyon.
 Let not vyce devoure.
 Whan ye se mysdoing men,
 Good counsell geve them,
 And teach them to amende.

YOUTHE For my synne I wyll morne,
 All creatures I wyll turne;
 And whan I see misdoinge men,
 Good counsell I shall geve them,   770
 And exorte them to amende.

CHARITE Then shall ye be an heritour of blysse,
 Where all ioye and myrth is.

YOUTHE To the whiche eternall
 God brynge the persons all
 Here beynge, Amen.

HUMILITYE Thus have we brought our matter to an ende
 Before the persons here present.
 Wolde every man be contente
 Leaste on other daye we be shente.   780

CHARITE We thanke all thys presente
 Of theyr meeke audyence.

HUMILITYE Iesu that sytteth in heaven so hye,
 Save all this faire companye,
 Men and women that here be:
 Amen, Amen, for Charitie.

❦ ❦ ❦

780 *shente* blamed

138

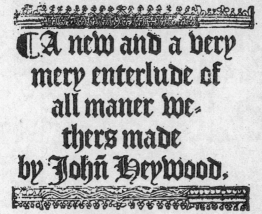

¶The play of the wether

¶A new and a very mery enterlude of all maner we- thers made by Johñ Heywood.

The players names.
Jupiter a god.
Mery reporte the vyce.
The gentylman.
The marchaunt.
The ranger
The water myller.
The wynde myller.
The gentylwoman.
The launder.
A boy the lest that can play.

Facsimile of the title-page of the first edition of The Play of the Wether *(1533) (by permission of the Master and Fellows of Magdalene College, Cambridge)*

The earliest edition was printed by William Rastell in 1533, a copy being preserved in the Pepys Collection at Magdalene College, Cambridge. The title-page reads:

> The play of the wether
>   A new and a very
>   mery enterlude of
>   all maner we-
>   thers made
> by John Heywood,

> The players names.
> Jupiter a god.
> Mery reporte the vyce.
> The gentylman.
> The marchaunt.
> The ranger.
> The water myller.
> The wynde myller.
> The gentylwoman.
> The launder.
> A boy the lest that can play.

This is clearly the best edition, probably printed from the author's manuscript, and is the basis of the present edition via J. S. Farmer, *Tudor Facsimile Text*, 1908. Other early editions by Wyer, Kytson (?1549–79), and Awdeley (?1559–75) have also survived.

There are three modern editions:

A. Brandl, *Quellen des weltlichen Dramas in England vor Shakespeare*, Strassburg, 1898
C. M. Gayley, *Representative English Comedies*, New York, 1903
J. Q. Adams, *Chief Pre-Shakespearean Dramas*, Boston, 1924

Heywood (1497–?1579) had a long life and a distinguished career. He was a musician at court from about 1515 to 1528. *Wether* was probably written in 1527, and the pension he was granted in 1528 may have been a reward for this. At least three plays are certainly his, and three others have been attributed to him. He continued to assist in the provision of entertainments until 1544, when he was exiled for conspiracy. His family relationships place him in the orbit of More. He married Elizabeth, sister of William Rastell who printed two of his plays. As their father, John Rastell, was More's brother-in-law, Heywood would be in close contact with the humanistic ideas of More, and the plays reflect this. The chief source of *Wether* has been shown to be Lucian's dialogue *Icaromenippus*, which was translated by More in 1505–6 and Erasmus in 1512.

The Play of the Wether

JUPITER
 Ryght farre to longe as now were to recyte
The auncyent estate wherin our-selfe hath reyned,
What honour, what laude, gyven us of very ryght,
What glory we have had, dewly unfayned,
Of eche creature, whych dewty hath constrayned;
For above all goddes, syns our fathers fale[1],
We, Iupiter, were ever pryncypale.

 If we so have ben, as treuth yt is in dede,
Beyond the compas of all comparyson,
Who coulde presume to shew for any mede,   10
So that yt myght appere to humayne reason,
The hye renowme we stande in at this season?
For syns that heven and erth were fyrste create,
Stode we never in suche tryumphaunt estate,

 As we now do wherof we woll reporte
Suche parte as we se mete for tyme present,
Chyefely concernynge your perpetuall conforte,
As the thynge selfe shall prove in experyment;
Whyche hyely shall bynde you, on knees lowly bent,
Soolly to honour our hyenes, day by day.   20
And now to the mater gyve eare, and we shall say.

   6 *syns* since 15 *woll* will 20 *Soolly* solely

Before our presens, in our hye parlyament,
Both goddes and goddeses of all degrees
Hath late assembled, by comen assent,
For the redres of certayne enormytees
Bred amonge them thorow extremytees,
Abusyd in eche to other of them all,
Namely, to purpose, in these moste specyall.

Our foresayd father Saturne, and Phebus,
Eolus and Phebe², these four by name,   30
Whose natures not onely so farre contraryous,
But also of malyce eche other to defame,
Have longe tyme abused ryght farre out of frame,
The dew course of all theyr constellacyons³,
To the great damage of all yerthly nacyons:

Whyche was debated in place sayde before.
And fyrste, as became our father moste auncyent,
Wyth berde whyte as snow, his lockes both cold and hore,
Hath entred such mater as served his entent⁴,
Laudynge his frosty mansyon in the fyrmament,   40
To ayre and yerth as thynge moste precyous,
Pourgynge all humours that are contagyous.

How be yt, he alledgeth that, of longe tyme past,
Lyttel hath prevayled his great dylygens;
Full oft uppon yerth his fayre frost he hath cast,
All thynges hurtfull to banysh out of presens.
But Phebus, entendynge to kepe hym in sylens,
When he hath labored all nyght in his powres,
His glarynge beamys maryth all in two howres.

Phebus to this made no maner answerynge.   50
Wheruppon they both then Phebe defyed,
Eche for his parte leyd in her reprovynge⁵
That by her showres superfluous they have tryed

25 *enormytees* irregularities   26 *thorow* through   35 *yerthly* earthly
40 *fyrmament* sky

143

In all that she may theyr powres be denyed:
Wherunto Phebe made answere no more
Then Phebus to Saturne hadde made before.

Anone uppon Eolus all these dyd fle,
Complaynynge theyr causes, eche one arow,
And sayd, to compare, none was so evyll as he;
For when he is dysposed his blastes to blow,   60
He suffereth neyther sone-shyne, rayne, nor snow.
They eche agaynste other, and he agaynste all thre —
Thus can these iiii in no maner agre.

Whyche sene in themselfe, and further consyderynge,
The same to redres was cause of theyr assemble;
And also that we, evermore beynge,
Besyde our puysaunt power of deite,
Of wysedome and nature so noble and so fre,
From all extremytees the meane devydynge,
To pease and plente eche thynge attemperynge,   70

They have, in conclusyon, holly surrendryd
Into our handes, as mych as concernynge
All maner wethers by them engendryd,
The full of theyr powrs, for terme everlastynge,
To set suche order as standyth wyth our pleasynge,
Whyche thynge, as of our parte, no parte requyred,
But of all theyr partys ryght humbly desyred

To take uppon us. Wherto we dyd assente.
And so in all thynges, wyth one voyce agreable,
We have clerely fynyshed our foresayd parleament,   80
To your great welth, whyche shall be fyrme and stable,
And to our honour farre inestymable.
For syns theyr powers, as ours, addyd to our owne,
Who can, we say, know us as we shulde be knowne?

56 *Then* than   58 *arow* in succession   70 *plente* plenty   *attemperynge* moderating   71 *holly* wholly

But now, for fyne, the reste of our entent,
Wherfore, as now, we hyther are dyscendyd,
Is onely to satysfye and content
All maner people whyche have ben offendyd
By any wether mete to be amendyd;
Uppon whose complayntes, declarynge theyr grefe,   90
We shall shape remedy for theyr relefe.

And to gyve knowledge for theyr hyther resorte
We wolde thys afore proclaymed to be,
To all our people, by some one of thys sorte
Whom we lyste to choyse here amongest all ye.
Wherfore eche man avaunce, and we shall se
Whyche of you is moste mete to be our cryer.

Here entreth Mery Reporte

M.R. Brother, holde up your torche a lytell hyer![6]
Now I beseche you, my lorde, loke on me furste.
I truste your lordshyp shall not fynde me the wurste.   100
IUP. Why, what arte thou that approchyst so ny?
M.R. Forsothe, and please your lordshyppe, it is I.
IUP. All that we knowe very well, but what I?
M.R. What I? Some saye I am I *per se* I.
But, what maner I so ever be I,
I assure your good lordshyp, I am I.
IUP. What maner man arte thou? Shewe quyckely!
M.R. By God, a poore gentylman dwellyth here by.
IUP. A gentylman? Thy-selfe bryngeth wytnes naye,
Bothe in thy lyght behavour and araye[7].   110
But what arte thou called, where thou dost resorte?
M.R. Forsoth, my lorde, Mayster Mery Reporte.
IUP. Thou arte no mete man in our bysynes,
For thyne apparence ys of to mych lyghtnes.
M.R. Why, can not your lordshyp lyke my maner,
Myne apparell, nor my name nother?
IUP. To nother of all we have devocyon.

---

85 *fyne* conclusion 89 *mete* suitable 94 *sorte* company (the audience) 102 *and* if 114 *lyghtnes* triviality 116 *nother* neither

M.R. A proper lycklyhod of promocyon!
    Well than, as wyse as ye seme to be,
    Yet can ye se no wysdome in me.   120
    But syns ye dysprayse me for so lyghte an elfe,
    I praye you geve me leve to prayse my selfe;
    And for the fyrste parte, I wyll begyn
    In my behavour at my commynge in,
    Wherin I thynke I have lytell offendyd,
    For, sewer, my curtesy coulde not be amendyd.
    And as for my sewt your servaunt to be,
    Myghte yll have bene myst for your honeste.
    For, as I be saved, yf I shall not lye,
    I saw no man sew for the offyce but I.   130
    Wherfore yf ye take me not or I go,
    Ye must anone, whether ye wyll or no.
    And syns your entent is but for the wethers,
    What skyls our apparell to be fryse[8] or fethers?
    I thynke it wysdome, syns no man forbad it,
    Wyth thys to spare a better, yf I had it.
    And for my name, reportyng alwaye trewly,
    What hurte to reporte a sad mater merely?
    As, by occasyon, for the same entent,
    To a sertayne wedow thys daye was I sent,   140
    Whose husbande departyd wythout her wyttynge,
    A specyall good lover, and she hys owne swettynge.
    To whome, at my commyng, I caste such a fygure,
    Mynglynge the mater accordynge to my nature,
    That when we departyd, above all other thynges
    She thanked me hartely for my mery tydynges.
    And yf I had not handled yt meryly,
    Perchaunce she myght have take yt hevely.
    But in suche facyon I coniured and bounde her,
    That I left her meryer then I founde her.   150
    What man may compare to shew the lyke comforte

---

121 *elfe* mischievous child 126 *sewer* sure 130 *sew* sue 134 *skyls*
matters 141 *wyttynge* knowledge 145 *departyd* separated 148
hevely gravely 149 *coniured* charmed, bewitched

That dayly is shewed by me, Mery Reporte?
And, for your purpose at this tyme ment,
For all wethers, I am so indyfferent,
Wythout affeccyon, standynge so upryght,
Son-lyght, mone-lyght, ster-lyght, twy-lyght, torch-lyght,
Cold, hote, moyst, drye, hayle, rayne, frost, snow,
    lightnyng, thunder,
Cloudy, mysty, wyndy, fayre, fowle above hed or under,
Temperate, or dystemperate, what ever yt be,
I promyse your lordshyp, all is one to me.   160

IUP.

    Well, sonne, consydrynge thyne indyfferency,
And partely the rest of thy declaracyon,
We make the our servaunte, and immedyately
We woll[9] thou departe and cause proclamacyon,
Publyshynge our pleasure to every nacyon.
Whyche thynge ons done, wyth all dylygens,
Make thy returne agayne to this presens,

    Here to receyve all sewtters of eche degre.
And suche as to the may seme moste metely,
We wyll thow brynge them before our maieste,   170
And for the reste, that be not so worthy[10],
Make thou reporte to us effectually,
So that we may heare eche maner sewte at large.
Thus se thow departe, and loke uppon thy charge.

M.R. Now, good my lorde god, Our Lady be wyth ye!
Frendes, a fellyshyppe[11], let me go by ye:
Thynke ye I may stand thrustyng amonge you there?
Nay, by god, I muste thrust about other gere.
    Mery Reporte goth out

IUP. Now, syns we have thus farre set forth our purpose,
A whyle we woll wythdraw our godly presens,   180
To enbold all such more playnely to dysclose,

---

154 *indyfferent* impartial   155 *affeccyon* emotion   156 *Son-lyght*
sunlight *ster* star   168 *sewtters* suitors   172 *effectually* with due
care

As here wyll attende, in our foresayde pretens.
And now, accordynge to your obedyens,
Reioyce ye in us, wyth ioy, most ioyfully,
And we ourselfe shall ioy in our owne glory.

At thende of this staf the god hath a song played in his
trone or Mery Report come in
Mery Report cometh in

M.R. Now, syrs, take hede, for here cometh goddes
      servaunt!
Avaunte, cartely keytyfs, avaunt!
Why, ye dronken horesons, wyll yt not be?
By your fayth, have ye nother cap nor kne?
Not one of you that wyll make curtsy   190
To me, that am squyre, for Goddes precyous body?
Regarde ye nothynge myne authoryte?
No 'Welcome home!' nor 'Where have ye be?'
How be yt, yf ye axyd, I coulde not well tell,
But suer I thynke a thousande myle from hell.
And on my fayth, I thynke, in my conscyens,
I have ben from hevyn as farre as heven is hens[12]:
At Lovyn, at London, and in Lombardy,
At Baldock, at Barfolde, and in Barbary,
At Canturbery, at Coventre, at Colchester,   200
At Wansworth, and Welbeck, at Westchester,
At Fullam, at Faleborne, and at Fenlow,
At Wallyngford, at Wakefield, and at Waltamstow,
At Tawnton, at Typtre, and at Totnam,
At Glouceter, at Gylford, and at Gotham,
At Hartforde, at Harwyche, at Harrow-on-the-Hyll,
At Sudbery, Suthampton, at Shoters Hyll,
At Walsyngham, at Wyttam, and at Werwycke,
At Boston, at Brystow, and at Berwycke,
At Gravelyn, at Gravesend, and at Glastynbery,   210
Ynge Gyngiang Iayberd, the paryshe of Butsbery[13].

---

182 *pretens* intention   185 *staf* verse   187 *cartely* boorish   *keytyfs*
wretches   194 *axyd* asked

The devyll hymselfe, wythout more leasure,
Coulde not have gone halfe thus myche, I am sure.
But now I have warned them, let them even chose;
For, in fayth, I care not who wynne or lose.
 Here the Gentylman before he cometh in bloweth his
 horne

M.R. Now, by my trouth, this was a goodly hearyng.
I went ye had ben the gentylwomens blowynge.
But yt is not so, as I now suppose,
For womens hornes[14] sounde more in a mannys nose.

GENTYLMAN Stande ye mery, my frendes, everychone.   220

M.R. Say that to me, and let the reste alone.
Syr, ye be welcome, and all your meyny.

GENT. Now, in good sooth, my frende, God a mercy,
And syns that I mete the here thus by chaunce,
I shall requyre the of further acqueyntaunce.
And brevely to shew the, this is the mater:
I come to sew to the great god Iupyter
For helpe of thynges concernynge my recreacyon,
Accordynge to his late proclamacyon.

M.R. Mary, and I am he that this must spede: 230
But fyrste tell me what be ye in dede.

GENT. Forsoth, good frende, I am a gentylman.

M.R. A goodly occupacyon, by Seynt Anne!
On my fayth, your mashyp hath a mery lyfe,
But who maketh al these hornes, yourself or your wife?
Nay, even in ernest, I aske you this questyon.

GENT. Now, by my trouth, thou art a mery one.

M.R. In fayth, of us both, I thynke never one sad,
For I am not so mery but ye seme as mad!
But stand ye styll and take a lyttell payne,   240
I wyll come to you, by and by, agayne.
Now, gracyous god, yf your wyll so be,
I pray ye, let me speke a worde wyth ye.

IUP. My sonne, say on, let us here thy mynde.

M.R. My lord, there standeth a sewter even here behynde:

***

217 *went* thought 222 *meyny* company 234 *mashyp* mastership

A gentylman in yonder corner,
And, as I thynke, his name is Mayster Horner.
> *Here he poynteth to the women*
A hunter he is, and comyth to make you sporte.
He wolde hunte a sow or twayne[15] out of this sorte.

IUP. What so ever his mynde be, let hym appere. 250
M.R. Now, good Mayster Horner, I pray you come nere.
GENT. I am no horner, knave, I wyll thou know yt.
M.R. I thought ye had, for when ye dyd blow yt,
Harde I never horeson make horne so goo.
As lefe ye kyste myne ars as blow my hole soo!
Come on your way before the god Iupyter,
And there for your selfe ye shall be sewter.
GENT. Moste myghty prynce, and god of every nacyon,
Pleasyth your hyghnes to vouchsave the herynge
Of me, whyche, accordynge to your proclamacyon, 260
Doth make apparaunce in way of besechynge,
Not sole for my selfe, but generally
For all come of noble and auncyent stock,
Whych sorte above all doth most thankfully
Dayly take payne for welth of the comen flocke,
Wyth dylygent study alway devysynge
To kepe them in order and unyte,
In peace to labour the encrees of theyr lyvynge,
Wherby eche man may prosper in plente.
Wherfore, good god, this is our hole desyrynge, 270
That for ease of our paynes, at tymes vacaunt,
In our recreacyon, whyche chyefely is huntynge,
It may please you to sende us wether pleasaunt,
Drye and not mysty, the wynde calme and styll,
That after our houndes yournynge so meryly,
Chasynge the dere over dale and hyll,
In herynge we may folow and to comfort the cry.
IUP. Ryght well we do perceyve your hole request,
Whyche shall not fayle to reste in memory,

255 *As lefe* rather   *kyste* kissed   275 *yournynge* journeying
277   *cry* pack of hounds

Wherfore we wyll ye set your selfe at rest,   280
Tyll we have herde eche man indyfferently,
And we shall take suche order, unyversally,
As best may stande to our honour infynyte,
For welth in commune, and ech mannys synguler profyte.

GENT. In heven and yerth honoured be the name
  Of Iupyter, whome of his godly goodnes
  Hath set this mater in so goodly frame,
  That every wyght shall have his desyre, doutles.
  And fyrst for us nobles and gentylmen,
  I doute not in his wysedome, to provyde   290
  Such wether as in our huntynge, now and then,
  We may both teyse and receyve[16] on every syde.
  Whyche thynge ones had, for our seyd recreacyon,
  Shall greatly prevayle you in preferrynge our helth:
  For what thynge more nedefull then our preservacyon,
  Beynge the weale and heddes of all comen welth?

M.R. Now I beseche your mashyp, whose hed be you?
GENT. Whose hed am I? Thy hed! What seyst thou now?
M.R. Nay, I thynke yt very trew, so God me helpe!
  For I have ever ben, of a lyttell whelpe,   300
  So full of fansyes, and in so many fyttes,
  So many smale reasons, and in so many wyttes,
  That, even as I stande, I pray God I be dede,
  If ever I thought them all mete for one hede.
  But syns I have one hed more then I knew,
  Blame not my reioycynge, I love all thynges new.
  And suer yt is a treasour of heddes to have store.
  One feate can I now that I never coude before.

GENT. What is that?
M.R.   By God, syns ye came hyther,
  I can set my hedde and my tayle togyther.   310
  This hed shall save mony, by Saynt Mary,
  From hens forth I wyll no potycary.

284 *synguler* particular   288 *wyght* man   294 *prevayle* benefit
296 *weale* origin, spring   312 *potycary* apothecary

For at all tymys, when suche thynges shall myster
My new hed shall geve myne olde tayle a glyster.
And after all this, then shall my hedde wayte
Uppon my tayle, and there stande at receyte.
Syr, for the reste I wyll not now move you,
But, yf we lyve, ye shall smell how I love yow.
And syr, towchyng your sewt here, depart when it please
 you,
For be ye suer, as I can, I wyll ease you.   320
GENT. Then gyve me thy hande. That promyse I take.
And yf for my sake any sewt thou do make,
I promyse thy payne to be requyted
More largely then now shall be recyted.
 [Exeat Gentleman]
M.R. Alas my necke! Goddes pyty, where is my hed?
By Saynt Yve[17], I feare me I shall be ded.
And yf I were, me thynke yt were no wonder,
Syns my hed and my body is so farre asonder.
 Entreth the Marchaunt
Mayster person, now welcome, by my lyfe!
I pray you, how doth my mastres, your wyfe?[18]   330
MARCHAUNTE Syr, for the presthod and wyfe that ye
 alledge,
I se ye speke more of dotage then knowledge.
But let pas, syr. I wolde to you be sewter
To brynge me, yf ye can, before Iupiter.
[M.R.] Yes, mary can I, and wyll do yt in dede.
Tary, and I shal make wey for your spede.
In fayth, good lord, yf it please your gracyous godshyp,
I muste have a worde or twayne wyth your lordshyp.
Syr, yonder is another man in place,
Who maketh great sewt to speke wyth your grace.   340
Your pleasure ones knowen, he commeth by and by.
IUP. Bryng hym before our presens, sone, hardely.
M.R. Why, where be you? Shall I not fynde ye?
Come away, I pray God the devyll blynde ye.

---

313 *myster* be needed   314 *glyster* enema   329 *person* parson

MARCH. Most myghty prynce, and lorde of lordes all,
Ryght humbly besecheth your maieste
Your marchaunt men thorow the worlde all,
That yt may please you, of your benygnyte,
In the dayly daunger of our goodes and lyfe,
Fyrste to consyder the desert of our request,   350
What welth we bryng the rest, to our great care and
    stryfe,
And then to rewarde us as ye shall thynke best.
What were the surplysage of eche commodyte,
Whyche groweth and encreaseth in every lande,
Excepte exchaunge by suche men as we be?
By wey of entercours, that lyeth on our hande,
We fraught from home thynges wherof there is plente;
And home we brynge such thynges as there be scant.
Who sholde afore us marchauntes accompted be?
For were not we, the worlde shuld wyshe and want   360
In many thynges, whych now shall lack rehersall.
And, brevely to conclude, we beseche your hyghnes
That of the benefyte proclaymed in generall
We may be parte takers, for comen encres,
Stablyshynge wether thus, pleasynge your grace:
Stormy nor mysty, the wynde mesurable,
That savely we may passe from place to place,
Berynge our seylys for spede moste vayleable;
And also the wynde to chaunge and to turne
Eest, west, north, and south, as beste may be set,   370
In any one place not to longe to soiourne,
For the length of our vyage may lese our market.

IUP. Ryght well have ye sayde, and we accept yt so;
And so shall we rewarde you ere we go hens.
But ye muste take pacyens tyll we have harde mo,
That we may indyfferently gyve sentens.

357 *fraught* carry, transport   358 *scant* want   359 *accompted*
considered   361 *rehersall* description   362 *brevely* briefly   368
seylys sails *vayleable* beneficial   372 *vyage* voyage *lese* lose
375 *harde* heard   376 *sentens* decision

There may passe by us no spot of neglygence,
But iustely to iudge eche thynge, so upryghte
That ech mans parte maye shyne in the selfe ryghte[19].

M.R. Now, syr, by your fayth, yf ye shulde be sworne,   380
Harde ye ever god speke so, syns ye were borne?
So wysely, so gentylly hys wordes be showd!

MARCH. I thanke hys grace, my sewte is well bestowd.

M.R. Syr, what vyage entende ye nexte to go?

MARCH. I truste or myd lente to be to Syo[20].

M.R. Ha, ha, is it your mynde to sayle at Syo?
Nay then, when ye wyll, byr lady, ye maye go,
And let me alone wyth thys. Be of good chere.
Ye maye truste me at Syo as well as here.
For though ye were fro me a thousande myle space,   390
I wolde do as myche as ye were here in place.
For syns that from hens it is so farre thyther,
I care not, though ye never come agayne hyther.

MARCH. Syr, yf ye remember me, when tyme shall come,
Though I requyte not all, I shall deserve some.

        Exeat Marchaunt

M.R. Now farre ye well, and God thanke you, by Saynt Anne.
I pray you, marke the fasshyon of thys honeste manne:
He putteth me in more truste at thys metynge here
Then he shall fynde cause why, thys twenty yere.

        Here entreth the Ranger[21]

RANGER God be here, now Cryst kepe thys company!   400

M.R. In fayth, ye be welcome, evyn very skantely:
Syr, for your comynge, what is the mater?

RANGER I wolde fayne speke wyth the god Iupyter.

M.R. That wyll not be; but ye may do thys –
Tell me your mynde, I am an offycer of hys.

RANGER Be ye so? Mary, I cry you marcy.
Your maystershyp may say I am homely,
But syns your mynde is to have reportyd
The cause wherfore I am now resortyd,
Pleasyth it your maystershyp it is so: 410
I come for my selfe and suche other mo
Rangers and kepers of certayne places,

As forestes, parkes, purlews, and chasys[22],
Where we be chargyd wyth all maner game.
Smale is our profyte and great is our blame.
Alas! For our wages, what be we the nere?[23]
What is forty shyllynges, or fyve marke[24] a yere?
Many tymes and oft, where we be flyttynge,
We spende forty pens a pece at a syttynge.
Now for our vauntage – whyche chefely is wyndefale –   420
That is ryght nought there blowyth no wynde at all;
Whyche is the thynge wherin we fynde most grefe,
And cause of my commynge to sew for relefe,
That the god, of pyty, all thys thynge knowynge,
Maye sende us good rage of blustryng and blowynge,
And yf I can not get god to do some good,
I wolde hyer the devyll to runne thorow the wood,
The rootes to turne up, the toppys to brynge under.
A myschyefe upon them and a wylde thunder!
M.R. Very well sayd. I set by your charyte   430
As mych, in a maner, as by your honeste.
I shall set you somwhat in ease anone.
Ye shall putte on your cappe, when I am gone,
For I se ye care not who wyn or lese,
So ye maye fynde meanys to wyn your fees.
RANGER Syr, as in that, ye speke as it please ye.
But let me speke wyth the god, yf it maye be.
I pray you, lette me passe ye.
M.R. Why, nay, syr, by the masse ye –
RANGER Then wyll I leve you evyn as I founde ye.   440
M.R. Go when ye wyll, no man here hath bounde ye.

    Here entreth the Water Myller, and the Ranger
    goth out

WATER MYLLER What the devyll shold skyl[25], though all
    the world were dum,
Syns in all our spekynge we never be harde?
We crye out for rayne, the devyll sped drop wyll cum.
We water myllers be nothynge in regarde,

    418 *flyttynge* on the road   440 *leve* leave

No water have we to grynde at any stynt,
The wynde is so stronge the rayne can not fall,
Whyche kepeth our myldams as drye as a flynt.
We are undone, we grynde nothynge at all,
The greter is the pyte, as thynketh me.   450
For what avayleth to eche man hys corne,
Tyll it be grounde by such men as we be?
There is the losse, yf we be forborne.
For touchynge ourselfes, we are but drudgys,
And very beggers, save onely our tole,
Whyche is ryght smale, and yet many grudges
For gryste of a bushell to gyve a quarte bole.[26]
Yet, were not reparacyons, we myght do wele.
Our mylstons, our whele with her kogges, and our
        trindill,
Our floodgate, our mylpooll, our water whele,   460
Our hopper, our extre, our yren spyndyll,
In thys and mych more so great is our charge,
That we wolde not recke though no water ware,
Save onely it toucheth eche man so large,
And ech for our neyghbour Cryste byddeth us care.
Wherfore my conscyence hath prycked me hyther,
In thys to sewe, accordynge to the cry,
For plente of rayne, to the god Iupiter
To whose presence I wyll go evyn boldely.

M.R. Syr, I dowt nothynge your audacyte,   470
But I feare me ye lacke capacyte,
For, yf ye were wyse, ye myghte well espye,
How rudely ye erre from rewls of curtesye.
What, ye come in revelynge and reheytynge
Evyn as a knave myght go to a beare beytynge!

W.M. All you bere recorde what favour I have!
Herke how famylyerly he calleth me knave!

---

446 *stynt* allotted portion   448 *myldams* mill-dams   455 *tole* toll
458 *reparacyons* repairs   459 *trindill* trindle, lantern wheel
461 *extre* axle-tree   *yren* iron   *spyndyll* spindle   474 *revelynge*
grumbling   *reheytynge* scolding   475 *beytynge* baiting

Dowtles the gentylman is universall!
But marke thys lesson, syr: you shulde never call
Your felow knave, nor your brother horeson;   480
For nought can ye get by it, when ye have done.

M.R. Thou arte nother brother nor felowe to me,
For I am goddes servaunt, mayst thou not se?
Wolde ye presume to speke wyth the great god?
Nay, dyscrecyon and you be to farre od!
Byr lady, these knavys muste be tyed shorter.
Syr, who let you in? Spake ye wyth the porter?

W.M. Nay, by my trouth, nor wyth no nother man
Yet I saw you well, when I fyrst began.
How be it, so helpe me God and holydam,   490
I toke you but for a knave, as I am.
But mary, now, syns I knowe what ye be,
I muste and wyll obey your authoryte.
And yf I maye not speke wyth Iupiter
I beseche you be my solycyter.

M.R. As in that, I wylbe your well wyller.
I perceyve you be a water myller,
And your hole desyre, as I take the mater,
Is plente of rayne for encres of water.
The let wherof, ye affyrme determynately,   500
Is onely the wynde, your mortall enemy.

W.M. Trouth it is, for it blowyth so alofte,
We never have rayne, or at the most, not ofte.
Wherfore, I praye you, put the god in mynde
Clerely for ever to banysh the wynde.

> *Entreth the Wynd Myller*

WYND MYLLER How! Is all the wether gone or I come?
For the passyon of God, helpe me to some!
I am a wynd myller, as many mo be.
No wretch in wretchydnes so wrechyd as we!
The hole sorte of my crafte be all mard at onys,   510
The wynde is so weyke, it sturryth not our stonys,

---

478 *universall* a know-all   495 *solycyter* advocate   500 *let* hindrance   510 *sorte* company   511 *weyke* weak

Nor skantely can shatter the shyttyn sayle
That hangeth shatterynge at a womans tayle.
The rayne never resteth, so longe be the showres,
From tyme of begynnyng, tyll foure and twenty howres;
And, ende whan it shall, at nyght or at none,
Another begynneth as soone as that is done.
Such revell of rayne, ye knowe well inough,
Destroyeth the wynde, be it never so rough,
Wherby, syns our myllys be come to styll standynge, 520
Now maye we wynd myllers go evyn to hangynge.
A myller! Wyth a moryn and a myschyefe,
Who wolde be a myller? As good be a thefe!
Yet in tyme past, when gryndynge was plente,
Who were so lyke Goddys felows as we?
As faste as God made corne, we myllers made meale.
Whyche myght be best forborne for comyn weale?
But let that gere passe, for I feare our pryde
Is cause of the care whyche God doth us provyde.
Wherfore I submyt me, entendynge to se 530
What comforte maye come by humylyte.
And now, at thys tyme, they sayd in the crye,
The god is come downe to shape remedye.

M. R. No doute, he is here, even in yonder trone.
But in your mater, he trusteth me alone.
Wherin I do perceyve, by your complaynte,
Oppressyon of rayne doth make the wynde so faynte,
That ye wynde myllers be clene caste away.

WYND MYLLER If Iupyter helpe not, yt is as ye say.
But, in few wordes, to tell you my mynde rounde, 540
Uppon this condycyon I wolde be bounde,
Day by day to say Our Ladyes sauter,
That in this world were no drope of water,
Nor never rayne, but wynde contynuall,

---

512 *skantely* hardly *shatter* wave 516 *none* noon 518 *revell* riotous outburst 522 *moryn* plague 527 *forborne* done without 533 *shape* plan 534 *trone* throne 540 *rounde* whole 542 *sauter* psalter

Then shold we wynde myllers be lordes over all.

M.R. Come on and assay how you twayne can agre —
A brother of yours, a myller, as ye be.

WATER MYLLER By meane of our craft we may be brothers,
But whyles we lyve shall we never be lovers.
We be of one crafte, but not of one kynde: 550
I lyve by water and he by the wynde.

Here Mery Reporte goth out

And syr, as ye desyre wynde contynuall,
So wolde I have rayne ever more to fall,
Whyche two in experyence, ryght well ye se,
Ryght selde, or never, together can be.
For as long as the wynde rewleth, yt is playne,
Twenty to one ye get no drop of rayne.
And when the element is to farre opprest,
Downe commeth the rayne, and setteth the wynde at rest.
By this ye se we cannot both obtayne,   560
For ye must lacke wynde, or I must lacke rayne.
Wherfore I thynke good, before this audyens,
Eche for our selfe to say, or we go hens;
And whom is thought weykest, when we have fynysht,
Leve of his sewt and content to be banysht.

WYND MYLLER In fayth, agreed, but then, by your lycens,
Our mylles for a tyme shall hange in suspens.
Syns water and wynde is chyefely our sewt,
Whyche best may be spared we woll fyrst dyspute.
Wherfore to the see my reason shall resorte,   570
Where shyppes by meane of wynd try from port to port,
From lande to lande, in dystaunce many a myle,
Great is the passage and smale is the whyle.
So great is the profyte, as to me doth seme,
That no mans wysdome the welth can exteme.
And syns the wynde is conveyer of all
Who but the wynde shulde have thanke above all?

WATER MYLLER Amytte in thys place a tree here to growe,
And therat the wynde in great rage to blowe.

555 *selde* seldom   575 *exteme* estimate   578 *Amytte* allow

When it hath all blowen, thys is a clere case, 580
The tre removyth no here-bred from hys place.
No more wolde the shyppys, blow the best it cowde,
All though it wolde blow downe both mast and shrowde,
Except the shyppe flete uppon the water
The wynde can ryght nought do – a playne mater.
Yet maye ye on water, wythout any wynde,
Row forth your vessell where men wyll have her synde.
Nothynge more reioyceth the maryner,
Then meane coolys of wynde and plente of water.
For commenly the cause of every wracke 590
Is excesse of wynde, where water doth lacke.
In rage of these stormys the perell is suche
That better were no wynde then so farre to muche.

WYND MYLLER Well, yf my reason in thys may not stande,
I wyll forsake the see and lepe to the lande.
In every chyrche where Goddys servyce is
The organs beare brunt of halfe the quere, i-wys.
Whyche causyth the sounde, or²⁷ water or wynde?
More over for wynde thys thynge I fynde –
For the most parte all maner mynstrelsy, 600
By wynde they delyver theyr sound chefly.
Fyll me a bagpype of your water full,
As swetly shall it sounde as it were stuffyd with wull.

WATER MYLLER On my fayth, I thynke the moone be at the
full,
For frantyke fansyes be then most plentefull,
Whych are at the pryde of theyr sprynge in your hed –
So farre from our mater he is now fled –
As for the wynde in any instrument,
It is no percell of our argument.
We spake of wynde that comyth naturally 610
And that is wynde forcyd artyfycyally,
Whyche is not to purpose: but yf it were

---

581 *here-bred* hairbreadth   584 *flete* float   587 *synde* assigned
589 *coolys* breezes   597 *quere* choir   603 *wull* wool   609 *percell*
part

And water, in dede, ryght nought coulde do there,
Yet I thynke organs no suche commodyte,
Wherby the water shulde banyshed be:
And for your bagpypes, I take them as nyfuls;
Your mater is all in fansyes and tryfuls.

WYND MYLLER By God, but ye shall not tryfull me of so!
Yf these thynges serve not, I wyll reherse mo.
And now to mynde there is one olde proverbe come,   620
'One bushell of March dust is worth a kynges
          raunsome'[28];
What is a hundreth thousande bushels worth than?

WATER MYLLER Not one myte, for the thynge selfe, to
          no man.

WYND MYLLER Why shall wynde every where thus be
          obiecte?
Nay, in the hye wayes he shall take effecte,
Where as the rayne doth never good, but hurt,
For wynde maketh but dust, and water maketh durt.
Powder, or syrop, syrs, whyche lycke ye beste?
Who lycketh not the tone maye lycke up the reste.
But sure who so ever hath assayed such syppes,   630
Had lever have dusty eyes then durty lyppes.
And it is sayd syns afore we were borne,
That drought doth never make derth of corne.
And well it is knowen, to the most foole here,
How rayne hath pryced[29] corne within this vii yere.

WATER MYLLER Syr, I pray the, spare me a lytyll season,
And I shall brevely conclude the wyth reason[30].
Put case on somers day wythout wynde to be,
And ragyous wynde in wynter dayes two or thre,
Mych more shall dry that one calme daye in somer   640
Then shall those thre wyndy dayes in wynter.
Whom shall we thanke for thys, when all is done?
The thanke to wynde? Nay, thanke chyefely the sone.
And so for drought, yf corne therby encres,

616 *nyfuls* trivialities   624 *obiecte* complained about   629 *the tone*
the one   631 *lever* rather

The sone doth comforte and rype all dowtles;
And oft the wynde so lyeth the corne, God wot,
That never after can it rype, but rot.
Yf drought toke place, as ye say, yet maye ye se
Lytell helpeth the wynde in thys commodyte.
But now, syr, I deny your pryncypyll. 650
Yf drought ever were, it were impossybyll
To have one grayne, for, or it can grow,
Ye must plow your lande, harrow and sow,
Whyche wyll not be, except ye maye have rayne
To temper the grounde, and after agayne
For spryngynge and plumpyng all maner corne
Yet muste ye have water, or all is forlorne.
Yf ye take water for no commodyte
Yet must ye take it for thynge of necessyte,
For washynge, for skowrynge, all fylth clensynge; 660
Where water lacketh, what bestely beynge!
In brewyng, in bakynge, in dressynge of meate,
Yf ye lacke water, what coulde ye drynke or eate?
Wythout water coulde lyve neyther man nor best,
For water preservyth both moste and lest.
For water coulde I say a thousande thynges mo,
Savynge as now the tyme wyll not serve so.
And as for that wynde that you do sew fore,
Is good for your wyndemyll, and for no more.
Syr, syth all thys in experyence is tryde, 670
I say thys mater standeth clere on my syde.
WYND MYLLER Well, syns thys wyll not serve, I wyll
   alledge the reste.
Syr, for our myllys, I saye myne is the beste.
My wyndmyll shall grynd more corne in one our
Then thy watermyll shall in thre or foure,
Ye, more then thyne shulde in a hole yere,
Yf thou myghtest have as thou hast wyshyd here.
For thou desyrest to have excesse of rayne,

646 *lyeth* flattens 649 *commodyte* respect 658 *commodyte* advantage 660 *skowrynge* scouring 674 *our* hour

162

Whych thyng to the were the worst thou coudyst
    obtayne.
For, yf thou dydyst, it were a playne induccyon[31]   680
To make thyne owne desyer thyne owne destruccyon;
For in excesse of rayne at any flood
Your myllys must stande styll, they can do no good.
And whan the wynde doth blow the uttermost
Our wyndmylles walke a-mayne[32] in every cost.
For, as we se the wynde in hys estate,
We moder our saylys after the same rate.
Syns our myllys grynde so farre faster then yours,
And also they may grynde all tymes and howrs,
I say we nede no watermylles at all,   690
For wyndmylles be suffycyent to serve all.
WATER MYLLER Thou spekest of all and consyderest not
    halfe.
In boste of thy gryste thou arte wyse as a calfe.
For, though above us your mylles grynde farre faster,
What helpe to those from whome ye be myche farther?
And, of two sortes, yf the tone shold be conserved,
I thynke yt mete the moste nomber be served.
In vales and weldes where moste commodyte is,
There is most people, ye must graunte me this.
On hylles and downes, whyche partes are moste barayne,   700
There muste be few, yt can no more sustayne.
I darre well say, yf yt were tryed even now,
That there is ten of us to one of you.
And where shuld chyefely all necessaryes be,
But there as people are moste in plente?
More reason that you come vii myle to myll
Then all we of the vale sholde clyme the hyll.
If rayne come reasonable, as I requyre yt,
We sholde of your wyndemylles have nede no whyt.
    Entreth Mery Reporte
M.R. Stop, folysh knaves, for your reasonynge is suche   710

685 *cost* place   687 *moder* adjust   693 *boste* boast   698 *weldes*
wealds

That ye have reasoned even ynough and to much.
I hard all the wordes that ye both have hadde.
So helpe me God, the knaves be more then madde!
Nother of them both that hath wyt nor grace,
To perceyve that both myllys may serve in place.
Betwene water and wynde there is no suche let,
But eche myll may have tyme to use his fet.
Whyche thynge I can tell by experyens,
For I have of myne owne, not farre from hens,
In a corner together, a couple of myllys,   720
Standynge in a marres betwene two hyllys,
Not of inherytaunce, but by my wyfe –
She is feofed in the tayle for terme of her lyfe –
The one for wynde, the other for water.
And of them both, I thanke God, there standeth nother;
For, in a good hour be yt spoken,
The water gate is no soner open,
But clap, sayth the wyndmyll, even strayght behynde!
There is good spedde the devyll and all they grynde!
But whether that the hopper be dusty,   730
Or that the mylstonys be sumwhat rusty,
By the mas, the meale is myschevous musty.
And yf ye thynke my tayle be not trusty,
I make ye trew promyse: come when ye lyst,
We shall fynde meane ye shall taste of the gryst.

WATER MYLLER The corne at receyt happely is not good.

M.R. There can be no sweeter, by the sweet rood.
     Another thynge yet, whyche shall not be cloked,
     My water myll many tymes is choked.

WATER MYLLER So wyll she be, though ye shuld burste
                                               your bones,   740
Except ye be perfyt in settynge your stones.
Fere not the lydger, beware your ronner;
Yet this for the lydger or ye have wonne her,

---

716 *let* obstacle   717 *fet* action, function   721 *marres* marsh
723 *feofed* legally possessed   *tayle* entail   742 *Fere* fear   *lydger*
ledger, lower millstone   *ronner* upper millstone

Perchaunce your lydger doth lacke good peckyng[33].
M.R. So sayth my wyfe, and that maketh all our checkyng.
She wolde have the myll peckt, peckt, peckt, every day!
But, by God, myllers muste pecke when they may.
So oft have we peckt that our stones wax ryght thyn,
And all our other gere not worth a pyn.
For wyth peckynge and peckyng I have so wrought   750
That I have peckt a good peckynge-yron to nought.
How be yt, yf I stycke no better tyll her,
My wyfe sayth she wyll have a new myller.
But let yt passe, and now to our mater;
I say my myllys lack nother wynde nor water;
No more do yours, as farre as nede doth requyre.
But syns ye can not agree, I wyll desyre
Iupyter to set you both in suche rest
As to your welth and his honour may stande best.
WATER MYLLER I pray you hertely remember me.   760
WYND MYLLER Let not me be forgoten, I beseche ye.
        Both Myllers go forth
M.R. If I remember you not both a-lyke
I wolde ye were over the eares in the dyke.
Now be we ryd of two knaves at one chaunce:
By Saynt Thomas, yt is a knavyshe ryddaunce.
        The Gentylwoman entreth
GENTYLWOMAN Now, good god, what foly is this?
What sholde I do where so mych people is?
I know not how to passe in to the god now.
M.R. No, but ye know how he may passe into you.
GENTYLWOMAN I pray you let me in at the backe syde.   770
M.R. Ye, shall I so, and your foresyde so wyde?
Nay, not yet; but syns ye love to be alone,
We twayne wyll into a corner anone.
But fyrste, I pray you, come your way hyther,
And let us twayne chat a whyle togyther.
GENTYLWOMAN Syr, as to you, I have lyttell mater.
My commynge is to speke wyth Iupiter.

745 *checkyng* quarrelling

165

M.R. Stande ye styll a whyle, and I wyll go prove
Whether that the god wyll be brought in love.
My lorde, how now, loke uppe lustely!   780
Here is a derlynge come, by Saynt Antony.
And yf yt be your pleasure to mary,
Speke quyckly; for she may not tary.
In fayth, I thynke ye may wynne her anone,
For she wolde speke wyth your lordshyp alone.

IUP. Sonne, that is not the thynge at this tyme ment.
If her sewt concerne no cause of our hyther resorte,
Sende her out of place. But yf she be bent
To that purpose, heare her and make us reporte.

M.R. I count women lost, yf we love them not well,   790
For ye se god loveth them never a dele.
Maystres, ye can not speke wyth the god.

GENTYLWOMAN No, why?

M.R. By my fayth, for his lordshyp is ryght besy
Wyth a pece of worke that nedes must be doone:
Even now is he makynge of a new moone.
He sayth your old moones be so farre tasted[34]
That all the goodness of them is wasted,
Whyche of the great wete hath ben moste mater
For olde moones be leake, they can holde no water.   800
But for this new mone, I durst lay my gowne,
Except a few droppes at her goyng downe,
Ye get no rayne tyll her arysynge,
Wythout yt nede, and then no mans devysynge
Coulde wyshe the fashyon of rayne to be so good;
Not gushynge out lyke gutters of Noyes flood[35],
But smale droppes sprynklyng softly on the grounde.
Though they fell on a sponge, they wold gyve no sounde.
This new moone shal make a thing spryng more in this
    while
Then a old moone shal while a man may go a mile.   810
By that tyme the god hath all made an ende,
Ye shall se how the wether wyll amende.

799 *wete* flood

By Saynt Anne, he goth to worke even boldely.
I thynke hym wyse ynough, for he loketh oldely.
Wherfore, maystres, be ye now of good chere,
For though in his presens ye can not appere
Tell me your mater and let me alone.
May happe I wyll thynke on you when you be gone.

GENTYLWOMAN Forsoth, the cause of my commynge is this:
    I am a woman ryght fayre, as ye se;   820
    In no creature more beauty then in me is.
    And syns I am fayre, fayre wolde I kepe me,
    But the sonne in somer so sore doth burne me,
    In wynter the wynde on every syde me,
    No parte of the yere wote I where to turne me,
    But even in my house am I fayne to hyde me.
    And so do all other that beuty have;
    In whose name at this tyme this sewt I make,
    Besechynge Iupyter to graunt that I crave:
    Whyche is this, that yt may please hym, for our sake,   830
    To sende us wether close and temperate,
    No sonne-shyne, no frost, nor no wynde to blow;
    Then wolde we get the stretes as trym as a parate.
    Ye shold se how we wolde set our-selfe to show.

M.R. Iet where ye wyll, I swere by Saynte Quintyne,
    Ye passe them all, both in your owne conceyt and myne.

GENTYLWOMAN If we had wether to walke at our
          pleasure,
    Our lyves wolde be mery out of measure:
    One parte of the day for our apparellynge,
    Another parte for eatynge and drynkynge,   840
    And all the reste in stretes to be walkynge,
    Or in the house to passe tyme wyth talkynge.

M.R. When serve ye God?

GENTYLWOMAN   Who bosteth in vertue are but daws.

M.R. Ye do the better, namely syns there is no cause.
    How spende ye the nyght?

833 *get* swagger, parade *parate* parrot 836 *conceyt* imagination
843 *daws* jackdaws (fools)

GENTYLWOMAN   In daunsynge and syngynge
  Tyll mydnyght, and then fall to slepynge.
M.R. Why, swete herte, by your false fayth can ye syng?
GENTYLWOMAN Nay, nay, but I love yt above all thynge.
M.R. Now, by my trouth, for the love that I owe you,
  You shall here what pleasure I can shew you.   850
  One songe have I for you, suche as yt is,
  And yf yt were better, ye shold have yt, by gys.
GENTYLWOMAN Mary, syr, I thanke you even hartely.
M.R. Come on, syrs, but now let us synge lustly.
    Here they synge
GENTYLWOMAN Syr, this is well done, I hertely thanke you.
  Ye have done me pleasure, I make God a vowe.
  Ones in a nyght I longe for suche a fyt,
  For longe tyme have I ben brought up in yt.
M.R. Oft tyme yt is sene both in court and towne,
  Longe be women a bryngyng up, and sone brought down. 860
  So fete yt is, so nete yt is, so nyse yt is,
  So trycke yt is, so quycke yt is, so wyse yt is,
  I fere my selfe, excepte I may entreat her,
  I am so farre in love, I shall forget her.
  Now, good maystres, I pray you let me kys ye.
GENTYLWOMAN Kys me, quoth a? Why nay, syr, I wys ye.
M.R. What! yes, hardely, kys me ons and no more.
  I never desyred to kys you before.
    Here the Launder[36] *cometh in*
LAUNDER Why, have ye alway kyst her behynde?
  In fayth, good inough, yf yt be your mynde.   870
  And yf your appetyte serve you so to do,
  Byr lady, I wolde ye had kyst myne ars to.
M.R. To whom dost thou speke, foule hore, canst thou tell?
LAUNDER Nay, by my trouth, I, syr? Not very well.
  But by coniecture this ges I have,
  That I do speke to an olde baudy knave.
  I saw you dally wyth your symper de cokket[37];

---

852 *gys* Jesus   857 *fyt* strain of music   861 *fete* graceful
862 *trycke* decked out   863 *entreat* court

THE PLAY OF THE WETHER

I rede you beware she pyck not your pokket.
Such ydyll huswyfes do now and than
Thynke all well wonne that they pyck from a man.   880
Yet such of some men shall have more favour
Then we that for them dayly toyle and labour.
But I trust the god wyll be so indyfferent
That she shall fayle some parte of her entent.

M.R. No dout he wyll deale so gracyously
That all folke shall be served indyfferently.
How be yt, I tell the trewth, my offyce is suche
That I muste reporte eche sewt, lyttell or muche.
Wherfore, wyth the god syns thou canst not speke,
Trust me wyth thy sewt, I wyll not fayle yt to breke.   890

LAUNDER Then leane not to myche to yonder gyglet,
For her desyre contrary to myne is set.
I herde by her tale she wolde banyshe the sonne,
And then were we pore launders all undonne.
Excepte the sonne shyne that our clothes may dry,
We can do ryght nought in our laundry.
Another maner losse, yf we sholde mys,
Then of such nycebyceters[38] as she is.

GENTYLWOMAN I thynke yt better that thou envy me
Then I sholde stande at rewarde of thy pytte.   900
It is the guyse of such grose queynes as thou art
Wyth such as I am evermore to thwart.
Bycause that no beauty ye can obtayne,
Therfore ye have us that be fayre in dysdayne.

LAUNDER When I was as yonge as thou art now,
I was wythin lyttel as fayre as thou,
And so myght have kept me, yf I hadde wolde,
And as derely my youth I myght have solde
As the tryckest and fayrest of you all.
But I feared parels that after myght fall,   910
Wherfore some besynes I dyd me provyde,
Lest vyce myght enter on every syde,

---

878 *rede* advise   890 *breke* deliver   891 *gyglet* wanton   901 *queynes*
harlots   902 *thwart* oppose   910 *parels* perils

Whyche hath fre entre where ydylnesse doth reyne.
It is not thy beauty that I dysdeyne,
But thyne ydyll lyfe that thou hast rehersed,
Whych any good womans hert wolde have perced.
For I perceyve in daunsynge and syngynge,
In eatyng and drynkynge and thyne apparellynge
Is all the ioye wherin thy herte is set.
But nought of all this doth thyne owne labour get.   920
For haddest thou nothyng but of thyne owne travayle,
Thou myghtest go as naked as my nayle.
Me thynke thou shuldest abhorre suche ydylnes
And passe thy tyme in some honest besynes.
Better to lese some parte of thy beaute
Then so oft to ieoberd all thyne honeste.
But I thynke rather then thou woldest so do,
Thou haddest lever have us lyve ydylly to.
And so, no doute, we shulde, yf thou myghtest have
The clere sone banysht, as thou dost crave.   930
Then were we launders marde, and unto the
Thyne owne request were smale commodyte.
For of these twayne I thynke yt farre better
Thy face were sone-burned, and thy clothis the swetter,
Then that the sonne from shynynge sholde be smytten,
To kepe thy face fayre and thy smocke beshytten.
Syr, how lycke ye my reason in her case?

M.R. Such a raylynge hore, by the holy mas,
I never herde, in all my lyfe, tyll now.
In dede I love ryght well the ton of you,   940
But, or I wolde kepe you both, by Goddes mother,
The devyll shall have the tone to fet the tother.

LAUNDER Promise me to speke that the sone may shyne
            bryght,
And I wyll be gone quyckly for all nyght.

M.R. Get you both hens, I pray you hartely.
Your sewtes I perceyve and wyll reporte them trewly

---

913 *entre* entry   916 *perced* pierced   926 *ieoberd* risk   936 *be-*
shytten dirty   940 *the ton,* 942 *the tone* the one   942 *fet* fetch

Unto Iupyter, at the next leysure,
And in the same desyre to know his pleasure;
Whyche knowledge hadde, even as he doth show yt,
Feare ye not, tyme inough ye shall know yt.   950
GENTYLWOMAN Syr, yf ye medyll, remember me fyrste.
LAUNDER Then in this medlynge my parte shalbe the wurst.

Here the Gentylwoman goth forth

M.R. Now, I beseche our lorde, the devyll the burst.
Who medlyth wyth many I hold hym accurst.
Thou hore, can I medyl wyth you both at ones?
LAUNDER By the mas, knave, I wold I had both thy stones
In my purs, yf thou medyl not indyfferently,
That both our maters in yssew may be lyckly.
M.R. Many wordes, lyttell mater, and to no purpose;
Suche is the effect that thou dost dysclose;   960
The more ye byb, the more ye babyll,
The more ye babyll, the more ye fabyll,
The more ye fabyll, the more unstabyll,
The more unstabyll, the more unabyll
In any maner thynge to do any good.
No hurt though ye were hanged, by the holy rood!
LAUNDER The les your sylence, the lesse your credence,
The les your credens, the les your honeste,
The les your honeste, the les your assystens,
The les your assystens, the les abylyte   970
In you to do ought. Wherfore, so God me save,
No hurte in hangynge suche a raylynge knave.
M.R. What monster is this? I never harde none suche:
For loke how myche more I have made her to myche³⁰,
And so farre, at lest, she hath made me to lyttell.
Wher be ye launder? I thynke in some spyttell.
Ye shall washe me no gere, for feare of fretynge.
I love no launders that shrynke my gere in wettynge.
I pray the go hens, and let me be in rest.
I wyll do thyne erand as I thynke best.   980

956 *stones* testicles 961 *byb* chatter 976 *spyttell* lazar-house
977 *fretynge* fraying

LAUNDER Now wolde I take my leve, yf I wyste how.
  The lenger I lyve, the more knave you.
    [*Exeat Launder*]
M.R. The lenger thou lyvest, the pyte the gretter;
  The soner thou be ryd, the tydynges the better!
  Is not this a swete offyce that I have,
  When every drab shall prove me a knave?
  Every man knoweth not what goddes servyce is,
  Nor I my selfe knew yt not before this.
  I thynke goddes servauntes may lyve holyly,
  But the devyls servauntes lyve more meryly.   990
  I know not what God geveth in standynges fees,
  But the devyls servauntes have casweltees
  A hundred tymes mo then Goddes servauntes have.
  For though ye be never so starke a knave,
  If ye lacke money the devyll wyll do no wurse
  But brynge you strayght to another mans purse.
  Then wyll the devyll promote you here in this world,
  As unto suche ryche yt doth moste accord.
  Fyrste *Pater noster qui es in celis*,
  And then ye shall sens the shryfe wyth your helys[40].   1000
  The greatest frende ye have in felde or towne
  Standynge a typ-to shall not reche your crowne.
    The Boy comyth in, the lest that can play[41]
BOY This same is even he, by al lycklyhod:
  Syr, I pray you, be not you master god?
M.R. No, in good fayth, sonne; but I may say to the
  I am suche a man that god may not mysse me.
  Wherfore wyth the god yf thou woldest have ought done
  Tell me thy mynde, and I shall shew yt, sone.
BOY Forsothe, syr, my mynde is thys, at few wordes;
  All my pleasure is in catchynge of byrdes   1010
  And makynge of snow ballys, and throwyng the same.
  For the whyche purpose to have set in frame,
  Wyth my godfather god I wolde fayne have spoken,

992 *casweltees* casual sums of money   994 *starke* complete
1000 *helys* heels   1012 *frame* order

Desyrynge hym to have sent me by some token
Where I myghte have had great frost for my pytfallys,
And plente of snow to make my snow ballys.
This onys had, boyes lyvis be such as no man leddys.
O, to se my snow ballys lyght on my felowes heddys,
And to here the byrdes how they flycker theyr wynges
In the pytfale, I say yt passeth all thynges.   1020
Syr, yf ye be goddes servaunt, or his kynsman,
I pray you helpe me in this, yf ye can.
M.R. Alas, pore boy, who sent the hether?
BOY A hundred boys that stode together
Where they herde one say in a cry
That my godfather, god almyghty,
Was come from heven, by his owne accorde,
This nyght to suppe here wyth my lorde[42],
And farther he sayde, come whoso wull,
They shall sure have theyr bellyes full.   1030
Of all wethers who lyste to crave,
Eche sorte suche wether as they lyste to have.
And when my felowes thought this wolde be had,
And saw me so prety a pratelynge lad,
Uppon agrement wyth a great noys,
'Sende lyttell Dycke,' cryed all the boys.
By whose assent I am purveyd
To sew for the wether afore seyd.
Wherin I pray you to be good as thus
To helpe that god may gyve yt us.   1040
M.R. Gyve boys wether, quoth a! Nonny, nonny!
BOY If god of his wether wyll gyve nonny,
I pray you, wyll he sell ony?
Or lend us a bushell of snow or twayne,
And poynt us a day to pay hym agayne?
M.R. I can not tell, for by thys lyght,
I chept nor borowed none of hym this nyght.

1015 *pytfallys* trap in form of a pit   1017 *onys* once   *leddys* leads
1037 *purveyd* sent   1045 *poynt* appoint   1047 *chept* bought and
sold

But by suche shyfte as I wyll make
Thou shalte se soone what waye he wyll take.
BOY Syr, I thanke you: then I may departe.   1050
    The Boye goth forth
M.R. Ye. Farewell, good sonne, wyth all my harte.
Now such an other sorte as here hath bene
In all the dayes of my lyfe I have not sene.
No sewters now but women, knavys, and boys,
And all theyr sewtys are in fansyes and toys.
Yf that there come no wyser after thys cry
I wyll to the god and make an ende quyckely.
    Oyes[43], yf that any knave here
    Be wyllynge to appere,
    For wether fowle or clere,   1060
    Come in before thys flocke,
    And be he hole or syckly,
    Come shew hys mynde quyckly,
    And yf hys tale be not lyckly
    Ye shall lycke my tayle in the nocke.
All thys tyme I perceyve is spent in wast,
To wayte for mo sewters; I se none make hast.
Wherfore I wyll shew the god all thys procys
And be delyvered of my symple offys.
Now, lorde, accordynge to your commaundement,   1070
Attendynge sewters I have ben dylygent,
And at begynnyng as your wyll was I sholde,
I come now at ende to shewe what eche man wolde.
The fyrst sewter before yourselfe dyd appere,
A gentylman desyrynge wether clere,
Clowdy, nor mysty, nor no wynde to blow
For hurt in hys huntynge; and then, as ye know,
The marchaunt sewde for all of that kynde,
For wether clere and mesurable wynde
As they maye best bere theyr saylys to make spede.   1080
And streyght after thys there came to me, in dede,

1052 *sorte* collection, crowd   1065 *nocke* crevice   1068 *procys*
proceeding

Another man who namyd hymselfe a ranger,
And sayd all of hys crafte be farre brought in daunger,
For lacke of lyvynge, whyche chefely ys wynde fall.
But he playnely sayth there bloweth no wynde at al,
Wherfore he desyreth, for encrease of theyr fleesys,
Extreme rage of wynde, trees to tere in peces.
Then came a water myller and he cryed out
For water and sayde the wynde was so stout
The rayne could not fale, wherfore he made request   1090
For plenty of rayne, to set the wynde at rest.
And then, syr, there came a wynde myller in,
Who sayde for the rayne he could no wynde wyn;
The water he wysht to be banysht all,
Besechynge your grace of wynde contynuall.
Then came there another that wolde banysh all this,
A goodly dame, an ydyll thynge, iwys.
Wynde, rayne, nor froste, nor sonshyne wold she have,
But fayre close wether, her beautye to save.
Then came there another that lyveth by laundry,   1100
Who muste have wether hote and clere here clothys to dry.
Then came there a boy for froste and snow contynuall,
Snow to make snowballys and frost for his pytfale,
For whyche, god wote, he seweth full gredely.
Your fyrst man wold have wether clere and not wyndy;
The seconde the same, save cooles to blow meanly;
The thyrd desyred stormes and wynde most extremely;
The fourth all in water, and wolde have no wynde;
The fyft no water but all wynde to grynde;
The syxst wold have none of all these, nor no bright son;   1110
The seventh extremely the hote son wold have wonne;
The eyght and the last for frost and snow he prayd.
Byr Lady, we shall take shame, I am afrayd.
Who marketh in what maner this sort is led
May thynke yt impossyble all to be sped.
This nomber is smale, there lacketh twayne of ten,

1086 *fleesys* incomes   1106 *meanly* moderately   1115 *sped* successful

And yet, by the masse, amonge ten thousand men
No one thynge could stand more wyde from the tother.
Not one of theyr sewtes agreeth wyth an other.
I promyse you, here is a shrewed pece of warke;   1120
This gere wyll trye wether ye be a clarke.
If ye trust to me, yt is a great foly,
For yt passeth my braynes, by Goddes body.

IUP.

    Son, thou haste ben dylygent and done so well
That thy labour is ryght myche thanke worthy.
But be thou suer we nede no whyt thy counsell,
For in our selfe we have foresene remedy,
Whyche thou shalt se. But fyrste, depart hens quyckly
To the gentylman and all other sewters here,
And commaunde them all before us to appere.   1130

M.R. That shall be no lenger in doynge
Then I am in commynge and goynge.
    Mery Report goth out

IUP.

    Suche debate as from above ye have harde,
Suche debate beneth amonge your selfes ye se;
As longe as heddes from temperaunce[44] be deferd,
So longe the bodyes in dystemperaunce be,
This perceyve ye all, but none can helpe save we.
But we as there have made peace concordantly,
So woll we here now gyve you remedy.

    Mery Reporte and all the Sewters entreth

M.R. If I hadde caught them   1140
Or ever I raught them,
I wolde have taught them
    To be nere me.
Full dere have I bought them,
Lorde, so I sought them,
Yet have I brought them,
    Suche as they be.

      1121 *clarke* learned man   1141 *raught* reached

GENTYLMAN Pleaseth your maieste, lorde, so yt is,
We, as your subiectes and humble sewters all,
Accordynge as we here your pleasure is,   1150
Are presyd to your presens, beynge pryncypall,
Hed, and governour of all in every place;
Who ioyeth not in your syght, no ioy can have.
Wherfore we all commyt us to your grace
As lorde of lordes us to peryshe or save.

IUP.
    As longe as dyscrecyon so well doth you gyde
Obedyently to use your dewte,
Dout ye not we shall your savete provyde,
Your grevys we have harde, wherfore we sent for ye
To receyve answere, eche man in his degre.   1160
And fyrst to content most reason yt is,
The fyrste man that sewde, wherfore marke ye this:

    Oft shall ye have the wether clere and styll
To hunt in for recompens of your payne.
Also you merchauntes shall have myche your wyll.
For oft tymes when no wynde on lande doth remayne,
Yet on the see plesaunt cooles you shall obtayne.
And syns your huntynge maye reste in the nyght,
Oft shall the wynde then ryse, and before day-lyght

    It shall ratyll downe the wood, in suche case   1170
That all ye rangers the better lyve may.
And ye water myllers shall obteyne this grace
Many tymes the rayne to fall in the valey,
When at the self tymes on hyllys we shall purvey
Fayre wether for your wyndmilles, with such coolys of
            wynde
As in one instant both kyndes of mylles may grynde.

    And for ye fayre women, that close wether wold have,
We shall provyde that ye may suffycyently
Have tyme to walke in, and your beauty save

1151 *presyd* thronged   1155 *peryshe* destroy   1159 *grevys* complaints

177

And yet shall ye have, that lyveth by laundry,   1180
The hote sonne oft ynough your clothes to dry.
Also ye, praty chylde, shall have both frost and snow,
Now marke this conclusyon, we charge you arow.

 Myche better have we now devysed for ye all
Then ye all can perceyve, or coude desyre.
Eche of you sewd to have contynuall
Suche wether as his crafte onely doth requyre.
All wethers in all places yf men all tymes myght hyer,
Who could lyve by other? What is this neglygens
Us to atempt in suche inconvenyens?   1190

 Now, on the tother syde, yf we had graunted
The full of some one sewt and no mo,
And from all the rest the wether had forbyd,
Yet who so hadde obtayned had wonne his owne wo.
There is no one craft can preserve man so,
But by other craftes, of necessyte,
He muste have myche parte of his commodyte.

 All to serve at ones and one destroy another,
Or ellys to serve one and destroy all the rest,
Nother wyll we do the tone nor the tother   1200
But serve as many, or as few, as we thynke best.
And where, or what tyme, to serve moste or lest,
The dyreccyon of that doutles shall stande
Perpetually in the power of our hande.

 Wherfore we wyll the hole worlde to attende
Eche sorte on suche wether as for them doth fall,
Now one, now other, as lyketh us to sende.
Who that hath yt, ply yt, and suer we shall
So gyde the wether in course to you all,
That eche wyth other ye shall hole remayne   1210
In pleasure and plentyfull welth, certayne.

GENTYLMAN Blessyd was the tyme wherin we were borne!
 Fyrst for the blysfull chaunce of your godly presens;

   1208 *ply* make the best use of 1210 *hole* whole

178

Next for our sewt – was there never man beforne
That ever harde so excellent a sentens
As your grace hath gevyn to us all arow,
Wherin your hyghnes hath so bountyfully
Dystrybuted my parte that your grace shall know,
Your selfe sooll possessed of hertes of all chyvalry?

MARCHAUNT Lyke wyse we marchauntes shall yeld us holy,   1220
Onely to laude the name of Iupyter
As god of all goddes, you to serve soolly
For of every thynge, I se, you are norysher.

RANGER No dout yt is so, for so we now fynde;
Wherin your grace us rangers so doth bynde,
That we shall gyve you our hertes with one accorde,
For knowledge to know you as our onely lorde.

WATER MYLLER Well, I can no more, but, for our water,
We shall geve your lordshyp Our Ladyes sauter.

WYND MYLLER Myche have ye bounde us, for, as I be saved,   1230
We have all obteyned better then we craved.

GENTYLWOMAN That is trew, wherfore your grace shall trewly
The hertes of such as I am have surely.

LAUNDER And such as I am, who be as good as you,
His hyghnes shall be suer on, I make a vow.

BOY Godfather god, I wyll do somwhat for you agayne:
By Cryste, ye may happe to have a byrd or twayne,
And I promyse you, yf any snow come,
When I make my snow ballys ye shall have some.

M.R. God thanke your lordship. Lo, how this is brought to pas!   1240
Syrs, now shall ye have the wether even as yt was.

IUP.
We nede no whyte our selfe any farther to bost,
For our dedes declare us apparauntly.

1219 *sooll* fully   1220 *holy* wholly   1222 *soolly* fully   1243 *apparauntly* for all to see

Not onely here on yerth in every cost,
But also above in the hevynly company,
Our prudens hath made peace unyversally,
Whyche thynge, we sey, recordeth us as pryncypall
God and governour of heven, yerth, and all.

   Now unto that heven we woll make retourne,
Where we be gloryfyed most tryumphantly;   1250
Also we woll all ye that on yerth soiourne,
Syns cause gyveth cause, to know us your lord onely,
And now here to synge moste ioyfully,
Reioycynge in us, and in meane tyme we shall
Ascende into our trone celestyall.

    [Exeunt]

WIT AND SCIENCE

The manuscript of this play is part of what appears to be a common-place book containing other dramatic fragments, some music and some poems (B.M. Additional MS. 15233), written out some time before 1550. John Redford's authorship of *Wit and Science* is attested by the colophon. He was Master of the Choristers at St Paul's from 1531 until 1534, and died in 1547. It is likely that the play was written at some point in this period, and intended for performance at court by the boys. For a time he was an associate of John Heywood.

Three leaves at the beginning of the manuscript are lost, but it is possible, from the two later versions of the play and from the development of the plot in Redford's version, to suggest the following reconstruction of events: Wit, son of Nature, seeks the hand of Science, daughter of Reason and Experience. Reason agrees to the match provided that Wit overcomes the monster Tediousness and journeys to Mount Parnassus. Wit is helped by Confidence, a servant provided by Nature, and by Instruction, Study, and Diligence, appointed by Reason. As the text begins, Reason is presenting Wit with a mirror.

Titles of the songs are given in the stage directions, but the texts were written out by a different scribe later in the manuscript. They have been inserted at the appropriate place in this edition.

The present text derives from the manuscript, and the following modern editions:

J. M. Manly, *Specimens of the Pre-Shakespearean Drama*, 1897
J. S. Farmer, '*Lost*' *Tudor Plays*, 1907
J. Q. Adams, *Chief Pre-Shakespearean Dramas*, Boston, 1924
A. Brown, *Malone Society Reprint*, 1951

The play was successful enough to inspire two later versions:

The Marriage of Wit and Science (anon.), printed by Thomas Marshe, *c.* 1569–70
Francis Merbury, *A Marriage between Wit and Wisdom*, B.M. Additional MS. 26782, 1570 or 1579

The interlude performed in *Sir Thomas More* is allegedly *The Marriage of Witt and Wisedom*, but the lines quoted come from elsewhere (see below, p. 416, note 3, and p. 417, note 14).

Wit and Science

REASON Then in remembrance of Reson hold yee
  A glas of Reson, wherein beholde yee
  Youre-sealfe to youre-selfe. Namely when ye
  Cum neere my dowghter, Science, then see
  That all thynges be cleane and trycke abowte ye,
  Least of sum sloogyshnes she myght dowte ye[1].
  Thys glas of Reason shall show ye all:
  Whyle ye have that, ye have me, and shall.
  Get ye foorth, now. Instruccion, fare well.
INSTRUCCION Syr, God keepe ye.
RESON   And ye all from parell.   10
     Heere all go out save Resone
  If anye man now marvell that I
  Woolde bestowe my dowghter thus baselye,
  Of truth I, Reson, am of thys mynde:
  Where partyes together be enclynde
  By gyftes of graces to love ech other,
  There let them ioyne the tone wyth the toother.
  Thys Wyt such gyftes of graces hath in hym
  That makth my dowghter to wysh to wyn hym.
  Yoong, paynefull, tractable, and capax —
  Thes be Wytes gyftes whych Science doth axe.   20
  And as for her, as soone as Wyt sees her,
  For all the world he woold not then leese her.
  Wherfore syns they both be so meete matches

2 *glas* mirror 5 *trycke* smart 10 *parell* peril 12 *baselye* below her proper rank 16 *the tone* the one *the toother* the other 19 *paynefull* careful *capax* capable 20 *axe* ask 22 *leese* lose

To love ech other, strawe for the patches
Of wo[r]ldly mucke![2] Syence hath inowghe
For them both to lyve. Yf Wyt be throwhe
Stryken in love, as he synes hath showde,
I dowte not my dowghter welbestowde.
Thende of hys iornay wyll aprove all.
Yf Wyt hold owte, no more proofe can fall.   30
And that the better hold out he[3] may,
To refresh my soone, Wyt, now by the way
Sum solas for hym I wyll provyde.
An honest woman dwellth here besyde,
Whose name is cald Honest Recreacion.
As men report, for Wytes consolacion
She hath no peere: yf Wyt were halfe deade
She cowld revyve hym – thus is yt sed.
Wherfore yf monye or love can hyre her,
To hye after Wyt I wyll desyre her.   40

    [Exit]
    Confydence cumth in with a pycture of Wyt
[CONFIDENCE] Ah, syr, what tyme of day yst, who can tell?
The day ys not far past, I wot well,
For I have gone fast, and yet I see
I am far from where as I wold be.
Well, I have day inowgh yet, I spye.
Wherfore, or I pas hens, now must I
See thys same token heere, a playne case,
What Wyt hath sent to my ladyes grace.
Now wyll ye see a goodly pycture
Of Wyt hym-sealfe, hys owne image sure –   50
Face, bodye, armes, legges, both lym and ioynt –
As lyke hym as can be in every poynt;
Yt lakth but lyfe. Well I can hym thanke
Thys token in-deede shall make sum cranke[4].
For, what wyth thys pycture so well faverde,
And what wyth those sweete woordes so well saverd

26 *throwhe* through   27 *synes* signs   32 *soone* son   40 *hye* go
46 *or* before   55 *well faverde* handsome

Dystyllyng from the mowth of Confydence,
Shall not thys apese[5] the hart of Science?
Yes, I thanke God, I am of that nature
Able to compas thys matter sure,   60
As ye shall see now, who lyst to marke yt,
How neately and feately I shall warke yt.
    [Exit]
    Wyt cumth in without Instruccion, wyth Study &c.
[WIT] Now, syrs, cum on. Whyche is the way now?
Thys way or that way? Studye, how say you?
Speake, Dylygence, whyle he hath bethowghte hym.
DYLYGENCE That way, belyke: most usage hath wrowht
    hym[6].
STUDYE Ye, hold your pease! Best we here now stay
For Instruccion. I lyke not that waye.
WYT Instruccion, Studye! I weene we have lost hym.
    Instruccion cumth in
[INSTRUCTION] In deade, ful lgently abowte ye have tost
    hym.   70
What mene you, Wyt, styll to delyghte
Runnynge before thus, styll owt of syghte.
And therby out of your way now quyghte?
What doo ye here, excepte ye woold fyghte?
Cum back a-gayne, Wyt, for I must choose ye
An esyer way then thys, or ells loose ye.
WYT What ayleth thys way? Parell here is none.
INSTRUCCION But as much as your lyfe standth upon[7].
Your enmye, man, lyeth heere before ye,
Tedyousnes, to brayne or to gore ye!   80
WYT Tedyousnes? Doth that tyrant rest
In my way now? Lord, how am I blest
That occacion so nere me sturres
For my dere hartes sake to wynne my spurres.
Ser, woold ye fere me wyth that fowle theeafe,
Wyth whome to mete my desyre is cheafe?

62 *feately* cleverly *warke* work 69 *weene* think 83 *occacion*
opportunity *sturres* arises

INSTRUCCION And what woold ye doo, you havyng
   nowghte
 For your defence? For thowgh ye have cawghte
 Garmentes of Science upon your backe,
 Yet wepons of Science ye do lak.   90
WYT What wepons of Science shuld I have?
INSTRUCCION Such as all lovers of ther looves crave,
 A token from Ladye Science, wherbye
 Hope of her favor may spryng, and therbye
 Comforte, whych is the weapon, dowteles,
 That must serve youe agaynst Tedyousnes.
WYT Yf Hope or Comfort may be my weapen
 Then never with Tedyousnes mee threten;
 For, as for hope of my deere hartes faver,
 And therby comfort, inowghe I gather.   100
INSTRUCCION Wyt, here me. Tyll I see Confydence
 Have browght sum token from Ladye Science,
 That I may feele that she favorth you,
 Ye pas not thys way, I tell you trew.
WYT Whych way than?
INSTRUCCION   A playner way I told ye,
 Out of danger from youre foe to hold ye.
WYT Instruccion, here me. Or my swete hart
 Shall here that Wyt from that wreche shall start
 One foote, thys bodye and all shall cracke!
 Foorth I wyll, sure, what ever I lacke.   110
DYLYGENCE Yf ye lacke weapon, syr, here is one.
WYT Well sayde, Dylygence, thowe art alone!
 How say ye, syr, is not here weapon?
INSTRUCCION Wyth that weapon your enmy never threton,
 For wythowt the returne of Confydence
 Ye may be slayne, sure, for all Dylygence.
DYLYGENCE God, syr! and Dylygence, I tell you playne
 Wyll play the man, or my master be slayne.
INSTRUCCION Ye, but what sayth Studye? No wurde to
   thys?

88 *cawghte* obtained

WYT No, syr. Ye knowe Studyes ofyce is   120
   Meete for the chamber, not for the feeld.
   But tell me, Studye, wylt thow now yeld?
STUDYE My hed akth sore: I wold wee returnd.
WYT Thy hed ake now? I wold it were burnd.
   Cum on – walkyng may hap to ese the.
INSTRUCCION And wyll ye be gone then, wythout mee?
WYT Ye, by my fayth, except ye hy ye after,
   Reson shall know yee are but an hafter.
     Exceat Wyt, Study and Dylygence
INSTRUCCION Well, go your way. Whan your father Reson
   Heerth how ye obay me at thys season   130
   I thynke he wyll thynke hys dowghter now
   May mary an other man for you.
   When wytes stand so in ther owne conceite,
   Best let them go tyll pryde at hys heyghte
   Turne and cast them downe hedlong agayne,
   As ye shall see provyd by thys Wyt playne.
   Yf Reson hap not to cum the rather
   Hys owne dystruccion he wyll sure gather.
   Wherfore to Reson wyll I now get me,
   Levyng that charge where abowt he set mee.   140
     Exceat Instruccion
     Tedyousnes cumth in with a vyser over hys hed
TEDYOUSNES Oh the body of me,
   What kaytyves be those
   That wyll not once flee
   From Tediousnes nose,
   But thus dysese me
   Out of my nest,
   When I shoold ese mee
   Thys body to rest!
   That Wyt, that vylayne,
   That wrech, a shame take hym,   150
   Yt is he playne

128 *hafter* dodger   137 *rather* more quickly   140 *vyser* visor
145 *dysese* disturb

That thus bold doth make hym,
Wythowt my lycence
To stalke by my doore
To that drab, Syence,
To wed that whore.
But I defye her[8],
And for that drabes sake,
Or Wyt cum ny her
The knaves hed shall ake.   160
Thes bones, this mall
Shall bete hym to dust
Or that drab shall
Once quench that knaves lust.
But, hah! Mee thynkes
I am not halfe lustye;
Thes io[y]ntes, thes lynkes,
Be ruffe, and halfe rustye.
I must go shake them,
Supple to make them.   170
Stand back, ye wrechys!
Beware the fechys
Of Tediousnes
Thes kaytyves to bles!
Make roome, I say!
Rownd evry way!
Thys way! That way!
What care I what way?
Before me, behynd me,
Rownd abowt wynd me!   180
Now I begyn
To swete in my skin.
Now am I nemble
To make them tremble.
Pash hed! Pash brayne!
The knaves are slayne,

161 *mall* club   167 *lynkes* links (of chain armour)   168 *ruffe* rough
172 *fechys* devices   182 *swete* sweat   185 *Pash* crush

189

All that I hyt.
Where art thow, Wyt?
Thow art but deade!
Of goth thy hed   190
A[t] the fyrst blo!
Ho, ho, ho, ho!
  Wyt spekyth at the dore
[WIT] Studye!
STUDYE   Here, syr!⁹
WYT   How? Doth thy hed ake?
STUDYE Ye, God wot, syr. Much payne I do take.
WYT Dylygens!
DYLYGENCE   Here, syr, here!
WYT   How dost thow?
  Doth thy stomak¹⁰ serve the to fyght now?
DYLYGENCE Ye, syr, wyth yonder wrech – a vengans on
        hym,
  That thretneth you thus. Set evyn upon hym!
STUDYE Upon hym, Dylygence? Better nay.
DYLYGENCE Better nay, Studye? Why shoold we fray?   200
STUDYE For I am wery: my hed akth sore.
DYLYGENCE Why, folysh Studye, thow shalt doo no more
  But ayde my master wyth thy presens.
WYT No more shalt thow nether, Dylygence.
  Ayde me wyth your presence, both you twayne,
  And, for my love, my selfe shall take payne.
STUDYE Syr, we be redye to ayde you so.
WYT I axe no more, Studye. Cum, then; goe!
  Tedyiousnes rysyth up
[TEDIOUSNESS] Why art thow cum?
WYT   Ye, wrech, to thy payne.
TEDIOUSNES Then have at the!
WYT   Have at the agayne!   210
  Here Wyt fallyth downe and dyeth
TEDIOUSNES Lye thow there. Now have at ye, kaytyves!
  [Study and Diligence run away]

200 *fray* fear

Do ye fle, i[n] fayth? A, horeson theves![11]
By Mahowndes bones, had the wreches taryd,
Ther neckes wythowt hedes they showld have caryd!
Ye, by Mahowndes nose, myght I have patted them,
In twenty gobbetes I showld have squatted them,
To teche the knaves to cum neere the snowte
Of Tediousnes. Walke furder abowte
I trow now they wyll. And as for thee,
Thow wylt no more now troble mee.   220
Yet lest the knave be not safe inowghe,
The horeson shall bere me an-other kuffe.
Now ly styll, kaytyv, and take thy rest
Whyle I take myne in myne owne nest.

> *Exceat Tedyousnes*
> *Here cumth in Honest Recreacion, Cumfort, Quycknes,*
> *and Strenght, and go and knele abowt Wyt [and sing*
> *the First Song[12]]*

When travelles grete in matters thycke
Have duld your wyttes and made them sycke
What medson than your wyttes to quycke?
Yf ye wyll know, the best phisycke
Is to geve place to Honest Recreacion.
Gyve place, we say, now for thy consolacion.   230

Where is that Wyt that we seeke than?
Alas he lyeth here pale and wan!
Helpe hym at once now, yf we can.
O Wyt, how doest thow? Looke up, man!
O Wyt, geve place to Honest Recreacion.
Gyve place, we say, now for thy consolacion.

After place gyvyn, let eare obay.
Gyve an eare, O Wyt, now we the pray;
Gyve eare to that we syng and say;

---

215 *patted* struck 216 *gobbetes* pieces *squatted* squashed 222 *kuffe*
blow 225 *travelles* labours *grete* great 227 *medson* medicine
than then *quycke* bring to life

Gyve an eare and healp wyll cum strayghteway;   240
Gyve an eare to Honest Recreacion.
Gyve an eare, now, for thy consolacion.

After eare gyvyn, now gyve an eye.
Behold thy freendes abowte the lye –
Recreacion I, and Comfort I,
Quicknes am I, and Strength herebye.
Gyve an eye to Honest Recreacion.
Gyve an eye, now, for thy consolacion.

After an eye gyvyn, an hand gyve ye.
Gyve an hand, O Wyt, feele that ye see –   250
Recreacion feele, feele Comfort fre,
Feele Quicknes here, feale Strength to the.
Gyve an hand to Honest Recreacion.
Gyve an hand, now, for thy consolacion.

Upon his feete woold God he were!
To rayse hym now we neede not fere.
Stay you hys handes whyle we here[13] bere.
Now all at once upryght him rere.
O Wyt, gyve place to Honest Recreacion.
Gyve place, we say, now for thy consolacion.   260

> *And at the last verce reysyth hym up upon hys feete[14],*
> *and so make an end. And than Honest Recreacion sayth*
> *as folowyth*

HONEST RECREACION Now, Wyt, how do ye? Wyll ye
be lustye?
WYT The lustier for you, needes be must I.
HONEST RECREACION Be ye all hole yet after your fall?
WYT As ever I was, thankes to you all.
> *Reson cummth in and sayth as folowyth*
[REASON] Ye myght thanke Reson that sent them to ye.
But syns the[y] have done that the[y] shoold, do ye
Send them home, soonne, and get ye forwarde.
WYT Oh father Reson, I have had an hard

260 *reysyth* lift   267 *soonne* son

Chance synce ye saw me.

RESON   I wot well that.
The more to blame ye when ye wold not   270
Obay Instruccion, as Reson wyld ye.
What marvell thowgh Tedyousnes had kyld ye?
But let pas now, synce ye ar well agayne.
Set forward agayne, Syence to attayne!

WYT Good father Reson, be not to hastye.
In honest cumpany no tyme wast I.
I shall to yowre dowghter all at leyser.

RESON Ye, Wyt, is that the grete love ye rayse her?
I say yf ye love my dowghter Science,
Get ye foorth at once, and get ye hence.   280

     Here Comfort, Quiknes and Strength go out

WYT Nay, by Saynt George, they go not all yet!

RESON No? Wyll ye dysobey Reson, Wyt?

WYT Father Reson, I pray ye content ye,
For we parte not yet.

RESON   Well, Wyt, I went ye
Had bene no such man as now I see.
Fare-well.

     Exceat

HONEST RECREACION He ys angry.

WYT   Ye, let hym be.
I doo not passe!
Cum now, a basse.

HONEST RECREACION Nay, syr, as for bassys,
From hence none passys   290
But as in gage
Of mary-age.

WYT Mary, evyn so:
A bargayne, lo!

HONEST RECREACION What, wythout lysence
Of Ladye Science?

WYT Shall I tell you trothe?

---

271 *wyld* willed, ordered   277 *leyser* leisure   278 *rayse* bring
into being (for)   284 *went* thought   287 *passe* care   288 *basse* kiss

I never lovde her.

HONEST RECREACION The common voyce goth
That mariage ye movd her.   300

WYT Promyse hath she none;
Yf we shalbe wone,
Wythout mo wurdes grawnt.

HONEST RECREACION What! Upon this soodayne?
Then myghte ye playne
Byd me avawnt.
Nay, let me see
In honeste
What ye can doo
To wyn Recreacion.   310
Upon that probacion
I grawnt therto.

WYT Small be my dooinges,
But apt to all thynges
I am, I trust.

HONEST RECREACION Can ye dawnce than?

WYT Evyn as I can,
Prove me ye must.

HONEST RECREACYON Then for a whyle
Ye must excyle   320
This garment cumbryng.

WYT In-deede, as ye say,
This cumbrus aray
Woold make Wyt slumbryng.

HONEST RECREACION Yt is gay geere
Of Science cleere;
Yt seemth her aray.

WYT Whose ever it were
Yt lythe now there.
        [*Throws off his gown*]

HONEST RECREACION Go to, my men, play!   330

300 *movd* urged   302 *wone* one   303 *grawnt* grant   311 *probacion*
proof, test   320 *excyle* take off

Here they dawnce, and in the mene-whyle Idellnes
cumth in and sytth downe; and when the galyard[15] is
doone, Wyt sayth as folowyth, and so falyth downe in
Idellnes lap

WYT Sweete hart, gramercys.

HONEST RECREACION Why, whether now? Have ye doone
    synce?

WYT Ye, in fayth, with wery bones ye have possest me;
  Among thes damselles now wyll I rest me.

HONEST RECREACION What, there?

WYT   Ye, here: I wylbe so bold.

IDLENES Ye, and wellcum, by hym that God sold.

HONEST RECREACION Yt ys an harlot, may ye not see?

IDLENES As honest a woman as ye be.

HONEST RECREACION Her name is Idlenes. Wyt, what
    mene you?

IDLENES Nay, what meane you to scolde thus, you
    quene, you?   340

WYT Ther, go to! Lo, now for the best game.
  Whille I take my ese, youre toonges now frame.

HONEST RECREACION Ye, Wyt, by youre fayth, is that
    youre facion?
  Wyll ye leave me, Honest Recreacion,
  For that common strumpet, Idellnes,
  The verye roote of all vyciousnes?

WYT She sayth she is as honest as ye.
  Declare your-selves[16] both now as ye be.

HONEST RECREACION What woolde ye more for my
    declaracion
  Then evyn my name, Honest Recreacion?   350
  And what wold ye more her to expres
  Then evyn her name, to, Idlenes,
  Dystruccion of all that wyth her tarye?
  Wherfore cum away, Wyt: she wyll mar ye.

IDELNES Wyll I mar hym, drabb, thow calat, thow,
  When thow hast mard hym all redye now?

---

340 *quene* strumpet   350 *Then* than   355 *calat* strumpet

Cawlyst thow thy sealfe Honest Recreacion,
Ordryng a poore man after thys facion,
To lame hym thus, and make his lymmes fayle
Evyn wyth the swyngyng there of thy tayle?   360
The dyvyll set fyre one the! For now must I,
Idlenes, hele hym agayne, I spye.
I must now lull hym, rock hym, and frame hym
To hys lust agayne[17], where thow dydst lame hym.
Am I the roote, sayst thow, of vyciousnes?
Nay, thow art roote of all vyce dowteles.
Thow art occacion, lo, of more evyll
Then I, poore gerle, nay more then the dyvyll!
The dyvyll and hys dam can not devyse
More devlyshnes then by the doth ryse   370
Under the name of Honest Recreacion:
She, lo, bryngth in her abhominacion!
Mark her dawnsyng, her maskyng and mummyng[18].
Where more concupyscence then ther cummyng?
Her cardyng, her dycyng, dayly and nyghtlye –
Where fynd ye more falcehod then there? Not lyghtly.
Wyth lyeng and sweryng by no poppetes,
But teryng God in a thowsand gobbetes.
As for her syngyng, pypyng, and fydlyng,
What unthryftynes therin is twydlyng!   380
Serche the tavernes and ye shall here cleere
Such bawdry as bestes wold spue to heere.
And yet thys is kald Honest Recreacion,
And I, poore Idlenes, abhomynacion.
But whych is wurst of us twayne, now iud[ge] Wy[t].
WYT Byrladye, not thow, wench, I iudge yet.
HONEST RECREACION No? Ys youre iudgment such then
        that ye
Can neyther pe[r]seve that best how she
Goth abowte to dyceve you, nor yet
Remembre how I savyd youre lyfe, Wyt?   390

360 *tayle* bottom   362 *hele* heal   377 *poppetes* idols   380 *twydlyng*
concerned with trifles   382 *bestes* beasts

Thynke you her meete wyth mee to compare
By whome so manye wytes curyd are?
When wyll she doo such an act as I dyd,
Savynge your lyfe when I you revyved?
And as I savyd you, so save I all
That in lyke ieoperdy chance to fall.
When Tediousnes to grownd hath smytten them
Honest Recreacion up doth quyken them
Wyth such honest pastymes, sportes or games,
As unto myne honest nature frames,   400
And not, as she sayth, wyth pastymes suche
As be abusyd, lytell or muche.
For where honest pastymes be abusyd
Honest Recreacion is refused;
Honest Recreacion is present never
But where honest pastymes be well usyd ever.
But in-deede Idlenes, she is cawse
Of all such abuses; she, lo, drawes
Her sort to abuse myne honest games,
And therby full falsly my name defames.   410
Under the name of Honest Recreacion
She bryngth in all her abhomynacion,
Dystroyng all wytes that her imbrace,
As youre-selfe shall see wyth-in short space.
She wyll bryng you to shamefull end, Wyt,
Except the sooner from her ye flyt.
Wherefore cum away, Wyt, out of her pawse.
Hence, drabb, let hym go out of thy clawse.
IDLENES Wyll ye get ye hence? Or by the mace,
Thes clawes shall clawe you by youre drabbes face.   420
HONEST RECREACION Yt shall not neade: syns Wyt
        lyethe as wone
That neyther heerth nor seeth, I am gone.
        Exceat
IDLENES Ye, so, fare-well! And well fare thow, toonge!

391 *meete* good enough   400 *frames* suits   419 *mace* mass
421 *wone* one

Of a short pele, this pele was well roong,
To ryng her hence, and hym fast a-sleepe
As full of sloth as the knave can kreepe.
How, Wyt! Awake! How doth my babye?
Neque vox neque sensus[19], byr Ladye.
A meete man for Idlenes, no dowte.
Hark, my pygg! How the knave dooth rowte!   430
Well, whyle he sleepth in Idlenes lappe,
Idlenes marke on hym shall I clappe.
Sum say that Idlenes can not warke,
But those that so say, now let them marke.
I trowe they shall see that Idlenes
Can set her-sealfe abowt sum busynes,
Or, at the lest, ye shall see her tryde,
Nother idle, nor yet well ocupyde.
Lo, syr, yet ye lak an-other toye[20].
Wher is my whystell to call my boye?   440

> *Here she whystleth, and Ingnorance cumth in*

[IGNORANCE] I cum! I cum!

IDLENES   Coomme on, ye foole.
All thys day or ye can cum to scoole.

INGNORANCE Um, mother wyll not let me cum.

IDLENES I woold thy mother had kyst thy bum!
She wyll never let the thryve, I trow.
Cum on, goose. Now, lo, men shall know
That Idlenes can do sumwhat, ye,
And play the scoolemystres, to, yf neade bee.
Mark what doctryne by Idlenes cummes.
Say thy lesson, foole.

INGNORANCE   Upon my thummes?   450

IDELLNES Ye, upon thy thummes. Ys not there thy name?

INGNORANCE Yeas.

IDELLNES   Go to, than; spell me that same.
Wher was thou borne?

INGNORANCE Chwas i-bore in Ingland, mother sed.

---

424 *pele* peal (of bells)   430 *rowte* snore   437 *tryde* tested
454 *Chwas* I was

IDLENES In Ingland?

INGNORANCE Yea.

IDLENES And whates half 'Inglande'?
  Heeres 'Ing', and heeres 'land'. Whates tys?

INGNORANCE Whates tys?

IDELLNES Whates tys, horeson? Whates tys?   460
  Heeres 'Ing', and heers 'land'. Whates tys?

INGNORANCE Tys my thum.

IDELLNES Thy thum! 'Yng', horeson, 'ing', 'ing'!

INGNORANCE Yng, yng, yng, yng.

IDELLNES Foorth! Shal I bete thy narse now?

INGNORANCE Ummm.

IDELLNES Shall I not bete thy narse now?

INGNORANCE Ummm.

IDELLNES Say 'no', foole, say 'no'.

INGNORANCE Noo, noo, noo, noo, noo!   470

IDLENES Go to, put together ... 'yng'.

INGNORANCE 'Yng'.

IDELLNES 'No'.

INGNORANCE 'Noo'.

IDELLNES Forth now! What sayth the dog?

INGNORANCE Dog barke.

IDLENES Dog barke? Dog ran, horeson, dog ran, dog ran.

INGNORANCE Dog ran, horson, dog ran, dog ran.

IDELLNES Put together ... 'ing'.

INGNORANCE 'Yng'.   480

IDELLNES 'No'.

INGNORANCE 'Noo'.

IDELLNES 'Ran'.

INGNORANCE 'Ran'.

IDLENES Foorth now! What seyth the goose?

INGNORANCE Lag! Lag!

IDLENES 'Hys', horson, 'hys'.

INGNORANCE Hys, hys-s-s-s-s.

IDLENES Go to, put together ... 'ing'.

INGNORANCE 'Ing'.   490

IDLENES 'No'.

INGNORANCE 'Noo'.

IDLENES 'Ran'.
INGNORANCE 'Ran'.
IDLENES 'Hys'.
INGNORANCE 'Hys-s-s-s-s-s'.
IDLENES No[w], who is a good boy?
INGNORANCE I, I, I, I, I, I.
IDLENES Go to, put together ... 'ing'.
INGNORANCE 'Ing'.   500
IDLENES 'No'.
INGNORANCE 'Noo'.
IDELLNES 'Ran'.
INGNORANCE 'Ran'.
IDELLNES 'His'.
INGNORANCE 'Hys-s-s-s-s-s'.
IDELLNES 'I'.
INGNORANCE 'I'.
IDELLNES 'Ing-no-ran-his-I'.
INGNORANCE 'Ing-no-ran-hys-s-s-s ...'   510
IDLENES 'I'.
INGNORANCE 'I'.
IDELLNES 'Ing'.
INGNORANCE 'Ing ...'
IDELLNES Foorth!
INGNORANCE 'Hys-s-s-s'.
IDELNES Ye! 'No', horeson, 'no'.
INGNORANCE 'Noo, noo, noo, noo'.
IDLENES 'Ing-no'.
INGNORANCE 'Ing-noo'.   520
IDELLNES Forth now!
INGNORANCE 'Hys-s-s-s-s-s'.
IDELLNES Yet agayne! 'Ran', horson, 'ran, ran'.
INGNORANCE 'Ran, horson, ran, ran'.
IDELLNES 'Ran', say.
INGNORANCE 'Ran-say'.
IDLENES 'Ran', horson.
INGNORANCE 'Ran-horeson'.
IDELLNES 'Ran'.
INGNORANCE 'Ran'.   530

IDELLNES 'Ing-no-ran'.

INGNORANCE 'Ing-no-ran'.

IDELLNES Foorth now. What sayd the goose?

INGNORANCE Dog barke.

IDLENES Dog barke? 'Hys', horson, 'hys-s-s-s-s-s'.

INGNORANCE 'Hys-s-s-s-s-s'.

IDLENES 'I'.

INGNORANCE 'I'.

IDELLNES 'Ing-no-ran-hys-I'.

INGNORANCE 'Ing-no-ran-hys-s-s-s'.   540

IDELLNES 'I'.

INGNORANCE 'I'.

IDELLNES How sayst now, foole? Is not there thy name?

INGNORANCE Yea.

IDELLNES Well than, cun me that same.
   What hast thow lernd?

INGNORANCE Ich can not tell.

IDELLNES 'Ich can not tell'? Thow sayst evyn very well,
   For yf thow cowldst tell then had I not well
   Towght the thy lesson whych must be tawghte,   550
   To tell all when thow canst tell ryghte noght[21].

INGNORANCE Ich can my lesson.

IDELLNES   Ye, and therfore
   Shalt have a new cote, by God I swore.

INGNORANCE A new cote?

IDELLNES   Ye, a new cote by-and-by.
   Of wyth thys old cote; 'a new cote', crye.

INGNORANCE A new cote! A new cote! A new cote!

IDELLNES   Pease, horson foole!
   Wylt thow wake hym now? Unbuttun thy cote, foole.
   Canst thow do nothyng?

INGNORANCE   I note how choold be.

IDELLNES 'I note how choold be'! A foole betyde the.
   So wysly hyt speketh. Cum on now. Whan!   560
   Put bak[22] thyne arme, foole.

INGNORANCE   Put backe.

---

545 *cun* repeat by heart   558 *note* know not   *choold* I should

IDELLNES So, lo! Now let me see how thys geere
  Wyll trym this ientle-man that lyeth heere.
  Ah, God save hyt, so sweetly hyt doth sleepe.
  Whyle on your back thys gay cote can creepe
  As feete as can be for this one arme.

INGNORANCE Oh, cham a-cold.

IDELLNES   Hold, foole, keepe the warme.
  And cum hyther; hold this hed here. Softe now, for
        wakyng.
  Ye shall see wone here browgght in such takynge
  That he shall soone scantlye knowe hym sealfe.   570
  Heere is a cote as fyt for this elfe
  As it had bene made evyn for this bodye.
     [*Dresses Wit in Ignorance's coat*]
  So, yt begynth to looke lyke a noddye.

INGNORANCE Ummmm.

IDELLNES What aylest now, foole?

INGNORANCE   Now cote is gone.

IDLENES And why is it gone?

INGNORANCE   Twoollnot byde on.

IDELLNES 'Twoolnot byde on'? Twoold if it cowlde.
  But marvell it were that byde it shoold –
  Sciens garment on Ingnorance bak!
    [*To Wit*]
  But now letes se, syr, what do ye lak?   580
  No-thyng but evin to bukell heere this throte,
  So well this Wyt becumthe a fooles cote.

INGNORANCE He is I now.

IDELLNES   Ye, how lykste him now?
  Is he not a foole as well as thow?

INGNORANCE Yeas.

IDELLNES   Well than, won foole keepe another.
  Geve me this and take thow that brother.

INGNORANCE Umm.

IDLENES   Pyke[23] the home, go!

INGNORANCE Chyll go tell my moother.

---

    566 *feete* fine   570 *scantlye* scarcely

IDELLNES   Yea, doo.

    [*Exit Ignorance*]
But yet to take my leve of my deere, lo,
Wyth a skyp or twayne, heere, lo, and heer, lo.   590
And heere agayne, and now this heele,
To bles this weake brayne. Now are ye weele,
By vertu of Idellnes blessyng toole,
Cuniurd from Wyt unto a starke foole.
    [*Exit Idleness*]
    Confydence cumth in with a swoord by his syde, and
    sayth as folowyth

[CONFIDENCE] I seake and seake, as won on no grownde
Can rest, but lyke a masterles hownde
Wandryng all abowt, seakyng his master.
Alas, ientle Wyt, I feare the fasster
That my tru servyce clevth unto thee,
The slakker thy mynd cleevth unto mee.   600
I have doone thye message in such sorte
That I not onlye for thy comfort
To vanquishe thyne enmy have browght heere
A swoord of comfort from thy love deere,
But also furder, I have so enclynd her
That upon my wurdes she hath assynd her
In her owne parson half-way to meete thee,
And hytherward she came for to greete thee.
And sure, except she be turned agayne
Hyther wyll she cum or be long playne[24],   610
To seake to meate the, heere in this cost.
But now, alas, thy-selfe thow hast lost,
Or at the least, thow wylt not be fownd.
Alas, ientle Wyt, how doost thow woonde
Thy trusty and tru servant, Confidence,
To lease my credence to Ladye Science.
Thow lesyst me, to, for yf I can not
Fynd the shortly, lenger lyve I ma not,

594 *Cuniurd* charmed by a spell   600 *slakker* slacker   607 *parson*
person   611 *cost* place   616 *lease* destroy   617 *lesyst* losest

But shortly get me evyn in to a corner
And dye for sorowe throwhe such a scorner.   620
    Exceat
    Here [*Fame, Favour, Riches, and Worship*] *cum in*
    with vyoles[25] [*followed by Experience and Science*]

FAME Cum, syrs, let us not disdayne to do
That the World hath apoynted us too.

FAVOR Syns to serve Science the World hath sent us,
As the World wylth us, let us content us.

RYCHES Content us we may, synce we be assynde
To the fayrest lady that lyvth, in my mynde.

WOORSHYP Then let us not stay here muet and mum,
But tast we thes instrumentes tyll she cum.
    Here the[*y*] *syng 'Excedynge Mesure'*

Exceedyng mesure, wyth paynes continewall,
Langueshyng in absens, alas, what shall I doe,   630
Infortunate wretch, devoyde of ioyes all,
Syghes upon syghes, redooblyng my woe,
And teres downe fallyng fro myne eyes toe?
    Bewty wyth truth so doth me constrayne
    Ever to sue where I may not attayne.

Truth byndyth me ever to be true,
How so that fortune faverth my chance.
Duryng my lyfe none other but you
Of my tru hart shall have the governance.
O good swete hart, have you remembrance   640
    Now of your owne whych for no smart
    Exyle shall yow fro my tru hart.

EXPERYENCE Dowghter, what meanyth that ye dyd not
       syng?
SCIENCE Oh mother, for heere remaynth a thynge.
Freendes, we thanke you for thes your plesures,
Takyn on us as chance to us measures.

624 *wylth* wishes   628 *tast* enjoy, use   633 *toe* two   637 *How so that* irrespective of how

WOORSHYPPE Ladye, thes our plesures, and parsons too,
  Ar sente to you, you servyce to doo.
FAME Ladye Science, to set foorth your name,
  The World, to wayte on you, hath sent me, Fame.   650
FAVOR Ladye Science, for your vertues most plentye
  The World, to cherysh you, Favor hath sent ye.
RYCHES Lady Science, for youre benefytes knowne
  The World, to mayntayne you, Ryches hath thrown.
WOORSHYP And as the World hath sent you thes three,
  So he sendth mee, Woorshypp, to avawnce you[r] degre.
SCIENCE I thank the World; but cheefly God be praysed
  That in the World such love to Science hath raysed.
  But yet, to tell you playne, ye iiij ar suche
  As Science lookth for lytell nor muche.   660
  For beyng as I am a lone wooman,
  Neede of your servyce I nether have nor can.
  But, thankyng the World, and you for your payn,
  I send ye to the World evyn now agayne.
WOORSHYPPE Why, ladye, set ye no more store by mee,
  Woorshypp? Ye set nowght by your selfe, I se.
FAME She setth nowght by Fame, wherby I spye her;
  She carethe not what the World sayth by her.
FAVOR She setthe nowght by Favor, wherby I trye her;
  She caryth not what the World sayth or dooth by her.   670
RYCHES She setth nowght by Ryches, whych dooth showe
  She careth not for the World. Cum, let us goe.
    [*Exeunt Worship, Fame, Favour, and Riches*]
SCIENCE In-deede smalle cawse gevyn to care for the
        Worldes faveryng.
  Seeyng the wyttes of Worlde be so waveryng.
EXPERYENCE What is the matter, dowghter, that ye
  Be so sad? Open your mynd to mee.
SCIENCE My marvell is no les, my good moother,
  Then my greefe is greate, to see, of all other,
  The prowde scorne of Wyt, soone to Dame Nature,
  Who sent me a pycture of hys stature   680

656 *avawnce* advance   679 *soone* son

205

Wyth all the shape of hym-selfe there openyng,
Hys amorous love, therby betokenyng,
Borne toward me in abundant facion;
And also furder to make ryght relacion
Of this hys love, he put in commyshion
Such a messenger as no suspicion
Cowlde growe in mee of hym – Confydence.

EXPERIENCE Um.

S[C]YENCE   Who, I ensure ye, wyth such vehemence
And faythfull behavoure in hys movynge
Set foorth the pyth of hys masters lovynge   690
That no lyvyng creature cowld coniecte
But that pure love dyd that Wyt dyrect.

EXPERIENCE So?

SCIENCE   Now, this beinge synce the space
Of three tymes sendyng from place to place
Betwene Wyt and his man, I here no more
Nether of Wyt, nor his love so sore.
How thynk you by thys, my nowne deere mother?

EXPERIENCE Dowghter, in this I can thynke none oother
But that it is true, thys proverbe old:
'Hastye love is soone hot and soone cold.'   700
Take hede, dowghter, how you put youre trust
To lyght lovers to hot at the furst.
For had this love of Wyt bene growndyd
And on a sure fowndashyon fowndyd
Lytell voyde tyme wold have bene betwene ye
But that this Wyt wolde have sent or seene ye.

SCIENCE I thynke so.

EXPERIENCE   Ye, thynke ye so or no,
Youre mother, Experience, proofe shall showe
That Wyt hath set hys love – I dare say
And make ye warrantyse – another way.   710

> *Wyt cumth before [with his face blackened, and
> wearing Ignorance's clothes]*

681 *openyng* revealing   690 *pyth* strength   691 *coniecte* conceive
705 *voyde* vacant   710 *warrantyse* guarantee

[WIT] But your warrantyse warrant no trothe.
    Fayre ladye, I praye you be not wrothe
    Tyll you here more; for, deere Ladye Science,
    Had your lover Wyt – ye, or Confydence
    Hys man – bene in helth all this tyme spent,
    Long or this tyme had cumme or sent.
    But the trothe is they have bene both sykke,
    Wyt and hys man, ye, and wyth paynes thycke
    Bothe stayde by the way, so that your lover
    Could neyther cum nor send by none other.   720
    Wherefore blame not hym, but chance of syknes.
SCIENCE Who is this?
EXPERIENCE   Ingnorance, or his lykenes.
SCIENCE What, the common foole?
EXPERYENCE   Yt is much lyke him.
SCIENCE By my soothe, his toong servth him now trym.
    What sayst thow, Ingnorance? Speak agayn.
WYT Nay, ladye, I am not Ingnorance, playne,
    But I am your owne deere lover, Wytt,
    That hath long lovd you, and lovth you yet.
    Wherefore, I pray the now, my nowne swetyng,
    Let me have a kys at this our meetyng.   730
SCIENCE Ye, so ye shall anone, but not yet.
    Ah, syr, this foole here hath got sum wyt.
    Fall you to kyssyng, syr, nowadayes?
    Your mother shall charme you. Go your wayes.
WYT What nedth all this, my love of long growne?
    Wyll ye be so strang to me your owne?
    Youre aquayntance to me was thowht esye,
    But now your woordes make my harte all quesye,
    Youre dartes at me so strangely be shott.
SCIENCE Heere ye what termes this foole here hath got?   740
WYT Well, I perseve my foolyshnes now;
    Indeede, ladyes, no dasterdes alowe.
    I wylbe bolde wyth my nowne darlyng.

---

711 *warrant* is worth   736 *strang* strange   737 *thowht* thought
740 *termes* clever language

Cum now, a bas, my nowne proper sparlyng!²⁶

SCIENCE What wylt thow, arrand foole?

WYT   Nay, by the mas,
  I wyll have a bas or I hence pas.

SCIENCE What wylt thow, arrande foole? Hence, foole,
      I say!

WYT What! Nothyng but 'foole', and 'foole' all this day?
  By the mas, madam, ye can no good.

SCIENCE Art a-sweryng, to? Now, by my hood,   750
  Youre foolyshe knaves breeche vj strypes shall bere.

WYT Ye, Godes bones! 'Foole' and 'knave' to? Be ye there?
  By the mas, call me foole once agayne
  And thow shalt sure call a blo or twayne.

EXPERIENCE Cum away, dowghter. The foole is mad.

WYT Nay, not yet nether hence ye shall gad.
  We wyll gre better or ye pas hence.
  I praye the now, good swete Ladye Science,
  All this strange maner now hyde and cover,
  And play the goodfelowe wyth thy lover.   760

SCIENCE What good felowshyppe wold ye of me,
  Whome ye knowe not, nether yet I knowe ye?

WYT Know ye not me?

SCIENCE   No; how shoold I know ye?

WYT Dooth not my pycture my parson shoow ye?

SCIENCE Your pycture?

WYT   Ye, my picture, ladye,
  That ye spake of. Who sent it but I?

SCIENCE Yf that be youre pycture, then shall we
  Soone se how you and your pycture agree.
  Lo, here, the pycture that I named is this.

WYT Ye, mary, myne owne lykenes this is.   770
  You havyng this, ladye, and so lothe
  To knowe me whych this so playne showthe!

SCIENCE Why, you are nothyng lyke, in myne eie.

WYT No? How say ye?

---

744 *bas* kiss   745 *arrand(e)* arrant, downright   756 *gad* flee
757 *gre* agree

EXPERIENCE As she sayth, so say I.

WYT By the mas, than are ye both starke blynde.
What dyference betwene this and this can ye fynd?

EXPERIENCE Marye, this is fayer, plesant, and goodlye,
And ye are fowle, dysplesant, and uglye.

WYT Mary, avawnt, thow fowle, ugly whoore!

SCIENCE So, lo! Now I perseve ye more and more.   780

WYT What, perseve you me, as ye wold make me,
A naturall foole?²⁷

SCIENCE Nay, ye mys-take me:
I take ye for no foole naturall,
But I take ye thus – shall I tell all?

WYT Ye, marye, tell me youre mynd, I pray ye,
Wher-to I shall trust. No more delay ye.

SCIENCE I take ye for no naturall foole
Browght up a-mong the innocentes scoole,
But for a nawghty vycious foole,
Browght up wyth Idellnes in her scoole.   790
Of all arrogant fooles thow art one.

WYT Ye! Goges bodye!

EXPERIENCE Cum, let us be gone.
    [Exeunt Science and Experience]

WYT My swerd! Is yt gone? A vengeance on them!
Be they gone, to, and ther hedes upon them?
But, prowde quenes, the dyvyll go wyth you both!
Not one poynt of curtesye in them gothe.
A man is well at ease by sute to payne him
For such a drab, that so doth dysdayne hym.
So mokte, so lowted, so made a sot,
Never was I erst synce I was begot!   800
Am I so fowle as those drabes wold make me?
Wher is my glas that Reson dyd take me?
Now shall this glas of Reson soone trye me
As fayre as those drabes that so doth belye me.
    [Looks at his reflection]
Hah! Goges sowle! What have we here? A dyvyll?

797 *sute* suit   799 *lowted* flouted   802 *take* give

This glas, I se well, hath bene kept evyll.
Goges sowle, a foole! A foole, by the mas!
What a very vengeance aylth this glas?
Other this glas is shamefully spotted,
Or els am I to shamefully blotted.   810
Nay, by Goges armes, I am so, no dowte.
How looke ther facis²⁸ heere rownd abowte?
All fayre and cleere they, evry-chone,
And I, by the mas, a foole alone,
Deckt, by Goges bones, lyke a very asse.
Ingnorance cote, hoode, eares – ye, by the masse,
Kokscome and all – I lak but a bable²⁹.
And as for this face, [it] is abhominable,
As black as the devyll. God, for his passion,
Where have I bene rayde affter this fassyon?   820
This same is Idlenes, a shame take her!
This same is her wurke, the devill in hell rake her!
The whoore hath shamd me for ever, I trow.
I trow? Nay, verely I knowe.
Now it is so: the stark foole I playe
Before all people. Now se it I maye.
Evrye man I se lawhe me to scorne.
Alas, alas, that ever I was borne!
Yt was not for nowght, now well I se,
That those too ladyes dysdayned me.   830
Alas, Ladye Science, of all oother,
How have I rayld on her and her moother.
Alas, that lady I have now lost
Whome all the world lovth and honoryth most.
Alas, from Reson had I not varyd
Ladye Science or this I had maryd.
And those fower gyftes which the World gave her
I had woon, to, had I kept her favor;
Wher now in stede of that lady bryght
Wyth all those gallantes seene in my syght –   840
Favor, Ryches, ye, Worship and Fame –

817 *Kokscome* coxcomb   820 *rayde* arrayed   827 *lawhe* laugh

I have woone Hatred, Beggry, and Open Shame.

Shame cumth in with a whyppe [followed by Reason]

WYT Out upon the, Shame! What doost thowe heere?

RESON Mary, I, Reason, bad hym heere appeere.

Upon hym, Shame, wyth stryppes inow smitten,
While I reherce his fawtes herein wrytten:
Fyrst, he hath broken his promyse formerly
Made to me, Reson, my dowghter to marye;
Nexte, he hath broken his promyse promisyd
To obay Instruccion, and him dyspised; 850
Thurdlye, my dowghter Science to reprove,
Upon Idlenes he hath set his love;
Forthlye, he hath folowed Idellnes scoole
Tyll she hath made him a verye starke foole;
Lastlye, offendyng both God and man,
Sweryng grete othes as any man can,
He hath abused himselfe to the grete shame
Of all his kynred and los of his good name.
Wherfore, spare him not, Shame! Bete him well there!
He hath deservyd more then he can beare. 860

Wyt knelith downe

[WIT] Oh father Reson, be good unto mee.
Alas, thes strypes of Shame will undo mee!

RESON Be still a while, Shame. Wyt, what sayst thow?

WYT Oh syr, forgeve me, I beseech you.

RESON Yf I forgeve the thy ponyshment,
Wylt thow than folow thy fyrst entent
And promyse made, my dowghter to marye?

WYT Oh syr, I am not woorthy to carye
The dust out where your dowghter shoold syt.

RESON I wot well that. But yf I admyt 870
The unwoorthy, agayne to her wooer,
Wylt thow then folow thy sewte unto her?

WYT Ye, syr, I promyse you while lyfe enduryth.

RESON Cum neere, masters, heere is wone ensuryth
In woordes to becum an honest man.

Here cumth Instrucion, Studye and Diligens in

Take him, Instruccion; do what ye can.

INSTRUCCION What, to the purpose he went before?

RESON Ye, to my dowghter prove him once more.
Take him and trym hym in new aparell,
And geve that to Shame there to his farewell.   880
  [Shame is paid and goes out]

INSTRUCCION Cum on your way, Wyt. Be of good cheere:
After stormy clowdes, cumth wether clere.
  Instrucion, Study, Wyt, and Dyligens go out

RESON Who lyst to marke now this chance heere doon
May se what Wyt is wythout Reson.
What was this Wyt better then an asse,
Being from Reson strayde as he was?
But let pas now, synce he is well poonyshyd,
And therby, I trust, meetely well monyshyd.
Ye, and I lyke him never the wurs, I,
Thowgh Shame hath handled hym shamefully.   890
For lyke as yf Wyt had prowdly bent hym
To resyst Shame to make Shame absent hym,
I wold have thowght than that Wyt had bene,
As the sayeng is, and daylye seene,
'Past shame once, and past all amendment':
So, contrarye, syns he dyd relent,
To Shame when Shame ponysht him evyn yll,
I have, I say, good hope in him styll,
And thynke, as I thowght, yf ioyne thei can,
My dowghter welbestowd on this man.   900
. . . but [30] all the dowte now is to thynke how
My dowghter takth this. For, I may tell you,
I thynk she knew this Wyt, evyn as weele
As she seemd heere to know him no deele.
For lak of knoledge in Science there is none;
Wherfore, she knew him: and therupon
His mysbehaver perchance evyn strykyng
Her hart agaynst him, she now myslykyng,
As women oft tymes wylbe hard hartyd,
Wylbe the stranger to be revertyd[31].   910

  888 *monyshyd* admonished 904 *no deele* not a bit

This must I helpe. Reson must now walke
On Wytes part wyth my Science to talke.
A neere way to her know I, wherebye
My soonnes cummyng prevent now must I.
Perchance I may bryng my dowghter hyther;
Yf so, I dowght not to ioyne them to-gether.
    Exceat Reson
    Confydence cumth in
[CONFIDENCE[32]] I thanke God, yet at last I have fownd
    hym.
I was afrayde sum myschance had drownd him,
My master, Wyt, wyth whome I have spoken,
Ye, and deliverd token for token,   920
And have an oother to Science agayne,
A hart of gold, syngnifyeng playne
That Science hath wun Wytes hart for ever.
Whereby I trust, by my good endever
To that good ladye, so sweete and so sortly,
A maryage betwene them ye shall see shortlye.
    Confydens exceat
    Instruccion cumth in wyth Wyt, Study, and Dylygence
[INSTRUCTION[32]] Lo, syr, now ye be entryd agayne
Toward that passage where dooth remayne
Tedyousnes, your mortall enmy.
Now may ye choose whether ye wyll trye   930
Your handes agayne on that tyrant stowte
Or els, walkyng a lytell abowte –
WYT Nay, for Godes pashion, syr, let me meete him!
Ye se I am able now for to greete him.
This sword of cumfort, sent fro my love,
Upon her enmy needes must I proove.
INSTRUCCION Then foorth there; and turne on your ryght
    hand,
Up that mownt before ye shall see stand.
But heere ye: yf your enmye chance to ryse,
Folowe my cowncell in anye wyse;   940

914 *soonnes* son's   925 *sortly* appropriate

Let Studye and Dyligence flee ther towche[33]
The stroke of Tediousnes, and then cowche
Them-selves as I told ye – ye wot how.

WYT Ye, syr, for that how, marke the proofe now.

INSTRUCCION To mark it in deede, heere wyll I abyde,
To see what chance of them wyll betyde,
For heere cumth the pyth, lo, of this iornaye.
That mowntayne before which they must assaye
Is cald in Laten *Mons Pernassus*[34],
Which mowntayne, as old auctors dyscus,   950
Who attaynth ones to sleepe on that mownt
Ladye Science his owne he may cownt.
But or he cum there, ye shall see fowght
A fyght with no les polycye wrowght
Then strength, I trow – if that may be praysed.

TEDIOUSNES Oh! ho! ho!

INSTRUCCION   Hark!

TEDIOUSNES   Out, ye kaytyves!

INSTRUCION   The feend is raysyd!

TEDIOUSNES Out, ye vilaynes! Be ye cum agayne?
Have at ye, wretches!

WYT   Fle, syrs, ye twayne!
[*Whilst Tediousness pursues Study and Diligence, Wit
attacks him*]

TEDIOUSNES Thei fle not far hens.

DYLIGENS Turne agayne, Studye!

STUDYE   Now, Dylygence!   960

INSTRUCCION Well sayde, holde fast now!

STUDYE   He fleeth.

DYLIGENCE   Then folowe!

INSTRUCCION Wyth his owne weapon now wurke him
sorow.
Wyt lyth at reseyte.

TEDIOUSNES   Oh! ho! ho!
Dyeth

INSTRUCION   Hark! He dyeth!

950 *auctors* authors   963 *reseyte* waiting for game (hunting)

Where Strength lackth, policye ssupplieth.

> *Heere Wyt cumth in, and bryngth in the hed upon his swoorde, and sayth as folowyth*

WYT I can ye thanke, syrs: this was well doone.

STUDYE Nay, yours is the deede.

DYLIGENCE   To you is the thank.

INSTRUCCION I can ye thank all: this was well doone.

WYT How say ye, man? Is this feelde well woonne?

> *Confydence cumth running in*

[CONFIDENCE] Ye, by my fayth, so sayth your deere hart.

WYT Why, where is she, that here now thow art?   970

CONFYDENS Upon yonder mowntayne, on hye,
She saw ye strike that hed from the bodye:
Wherby ye have woonne her, bodye and all!
In token whereof reseve heere ye shall
A gowne of knoledge, wherin you must
Reseve her here strayght.

WYT   But sayst thow iust?

[CONFIDENCE] So iust I say that except ye hye ye
Or ye be redye she wylbe by ye.

WYT Holde! Present unto her this hed heere,
And gyve me warning when she cumth nere.   980

> [*Exit Confidence*]

Instruccion, wyll ye helpe to devyse
To trim this geere now in the best wyse?

INSTRUCCION Geve me that gowne, and cum wyth me all.

DYLIGENCE Oh how this gere to the purpose dooth fall!

> *Confidens cumth running in*

[CONFIDENCE] How, master, master! Where be ye now?

WYT Here, Confydence; what tidynges bryngst thow?

CONFYDENS My ladye at hand heere dooth abyde ye.
Byd her wellcum. What, do ye hide ye?

> *Here Wyt, Instruccion, Studye, and Diligence syng
> 'Wellcum, my nowne', and Syence, Experience, Reson,
> and Confidence cum in at 'As . . .', and answer evre
> second verse*

The thyrd song

WYT AND HIS CUMPANYE

O ladye deere,
Be ye so neere   990
    To be knowne?
My hart yow cheere
Your voyce to here.
    Welcum, myne owne!

S[C]IENCE AND HIR CUMPANYE

As ye reioyse
To here my voyce
    Fro me thus blowne,
So in my choyce
I show my voyce
    To be your owne.   1000

WYT AND HIS CUMPANYE

Then drawe we neere
To see and heere
    My love long growne.
Where is my deere?
Here I apeere
    To see myne owne.

S[C]IENCE AND HIR CUMPANYE

To se and try
Your love truly
    Till deth be flowne,
Lo, here am I,   1010
That ye may spie
    I am your owne.

WYT AND HIS CUMPANYE

Then let us meete,
My love so sweete,
    Halfe-way heere throwne.

S[C]IENS AND HIR CUMPANYE

I wyll not fleete

1016 *fleete* fly

216

My love to greete.
   Welcum, myne owne.

WYT AND HIS CUMPANYE
      Welcum myne owne!

ALL SING
         Welcum, myne owne!   1020
   And when the song is doone, Reson sendyth
   Instruccion, Studye, and Dyligence and Confidens
   out; and then standyng in the myddell of the place,
   Wyt sayth as folowyth

WYT Wellcum, myne owne, wyth all my hole harte,
   Whych shalbe your owne till deth us depart.
   I trust, ladye, this knot evyn syns knyt.

SCIENCE I trust the same; for syns ye have smitt
   Downe my grete enmye, Tedyousnes,
   Ye have woon me for ever dowghtles –
   All thowgh ye have woon a clogg wyth all.

WYT A clogg, sweete hart? What?

SCIENCE   Such as doth fall
   To all men that ioyne them-selves in mariage,
   In kepyng ther wyves. A carefull cariage!   1030

WYT Carefull? Nay, ladye, that care shall imploye
   No clogg, but a key of my most ioye.
   To kepe you, swete hart, as shall be fyt
   Shalbe no care, but most ioy to Wyt.

SCIENCE Well, yet I say – mark well what I saye –
   My presence brynghth you a clogg, no naye,
   Not in the kepynge of me onelye,
   But in the use of Science cheeflye.
   For I, Science, am in this degree
   As all, or most part, of woomen bee –   1040
   Yf ye use me well in a good sorte,
   Then shall I be youre ioy and comfort;
   But yf ye use me not well, then dowt me,
   For, sure, ye were better then wyth-out me.

WYT Why, ladye, thinke you me such a wyt

1027 *clogg* hindrance   1030 *carefull* full of care   *cariage* load

217

As being avansyd by you, and yet
Wold mysuse ye? Nay, yf ye dowt that,
Heere is wone lovth thee more then sumwhat;
Yf Wyt my[s]use ye at any season,
Correct me then your owne father, Reson.   1050

RESON Lo, dowghter, can ye desyre any more?
What neede thes dowtes? Avoyde them therfore.

EXPERIENCE Byrlakyn, syr, but, under your favor,
This dowgt our dowghter doth well to gather,
For a good warnyng now at begynnynge
What Wyt in the end shall looke for in wynning;
Whych shalbe this, syr: yf Science here,
Whych is Godes gyft, wyll be usyd meere
Unto Godes honor, and profyt both
Of you and your neybowre, whych goth   1060
In her of kynd to do good to all,
This seene to, Experience, I, shall
Set you forth, Wyt, by her to imploye
Doble encrece to your doble ioye.
But yf you use her contrary wyse
To her good nature, and so devyse
To evyll effectes to wrest and to wry her,
Ye, and cast her of, and set nowght by her,
Be sure I, Experience, shall than
Declare you so before God and man   1070
That thys talent from you shalbe taken
And you ponysht for your gayne forsaken.

WYT 'Once warnd, half armd', folk say, namely whan
Experience shall warne a man, than
Tyme to take heede. Mother Experience,
Towchyng youre dowghter, my deere hart S[c]iens,
As I am sertayne that to abuse her
I brede myne owne sorow, and well to use her
I encrece my ioy; and so to make yt
Godes grace is redye, yf I wyll take yt.   1080

1053 *Byrlakyn* by Our Lady   1054 *dowgt* doubt   1058 *meere*
entirely   1067 *wrest* twist   *wry* distort

218

Then, but ye cownt me no wyt at all,
Let never thes dowtes into your hed fall;
But as your-selfe, Experience, cleryng
All dowtes at lenght, so, tyll tyme aperyng,
Trust ye wyth me in God. And, swete hart,
Whyle your father Reson takth Wyts parte³⁵
To reseve Godes grace as God shall send it,
Dowte ye not our ioy tyll lyves end end yt.

SCIENCE Well than, for the end of all dowtes past,
And to that end whiche ye spake of last,   1090
Among our weddyng matters heere rendryng,
Thend of our lyves wold be in remembryng;
Which remembrance, Wyt, shall sure defend ye³⁶
From the mysuse of Science, and send ye
The gayne my mother to mynd did call,
Ioy wyth-out end – that wysh I to all.

RESON Well sayd! And as ye, dowghter, wyshe it
That ioy to all folke in generall,
So wysh I, Reson, the same. But yet
Fyrst in this lyfe wysh I here to fall   1100
To our most noble Kyng and Quene in especiall,
To ther honorable Cowncell, and then to all the rest,
Such ioy as long may reioyse them all best.

ALL *say* Amen.

> *Heere cumth in fowre wyth violes, and syng*
> *'Remembreance'³⁷, and, at the last, quere³⁸ all make*
> *cur[t]sye, and so goe forth syngyng.*

Thus endyth the play of 'Wyt and Science' made by
Master Ihon Redford

FINIS

🐦 🐦 🐦

1081 *but* unless   1091 *rendryng* being accomplished

RESPUBLICA

The manuscript states that the play was written in 1553, though the copy is probably a little later. The heading of the play is given below, together with the original list of characters. The authorship is unknown, though a strong case has been made for Nicholas Udall, who achieved eminence at the court of Queen Mary for his part in dramatic productions, and who is known to have written *Ralph Roister Doister* at about the same time. The Prologue indicates that the play was intended for performance by children at Christmas, presumably at court. The manuscript was perhaps written as a record of this production, and does not seem to have been intended for publication.

The manuscript is now in America (Library of Carl H. Pforzheimer, MS. 40 A). There have been six modern editions:

J. P. Collier, *Illustrations of Old English Literature*, 1866

A. Brandl, *Quellen des weltlichen Dramas in England vor Shakespeare*, Strassburg, 1898.

L. A. Magnus, Early English Text Society, 1905, Extra Series 94

J. S. Farmer, *'Lost' Tudor Plays*, 1907

J. S. Farmer, facsimile, 1908

W. W. Greg, Early English Text Society, 1952, original series 226

This edition is based upon those of Brandl, Magnus, and Greg. In general it follows the spelling of the original, which is often inconsistent, in a period of considerable linguistic uncertainty. Punctuation and capital letters have been modernized to some extent.

Two extracts are included. The first (Acts I and II) contains the exposition of the vices, and shows the relationship established between them and Respublica. The second (Act V, scene iii to end) shows how the conventions of the morality play are employed to bring about a morally acceptable ending. There is a distinct political purpose to the play. The Prologue refers to a political allegory, and the date of the play makes it likely that the author intended to show that the corruption of the previous reign was now to be put right by the new regime of Queen Mary.

A Merye enterlude entitled Respublica made in the yeare of oure Lorde 1553, and the first yeare of the moost prosperous Reigne of our moste gracious Soverainge Quene Marye the first.

The Partes and Names of the Plaiers.

The Prologue. a Poete.
Avarice. allias policie[1], The vice[2] of the plaie.
Insolence. allias Authoritie, The chief galaunt.
Oppression. allias Reformation, an other gallaunt.
Adulation. allias Honestie, The third gallaunt.
People. representing the poore Commontie.
Respublica. wydowe.
Misericordia. ⎞
Veritas. ⎟
Iusticia. ⎬ fowre Ladies
Pax. ⎠
Nemesis. the goddess of redresse and correction. A goddesse.

Respublica

Actus Primi, scena prima[3]

AVARYCE Now goddiggod every chone, bothe greate and
　　　　smale,
　From highest to lowest goddiggod to yowe all!
　Goddiggod, what sholde I saie? even or morowe?
　If I marke howe the daie goeth, god geve me sorowe!
　But goddiggod echone twentie and twentie skore:
　Of that ye most longe for, what wolde ye have more?[4]
　Ye muste pardoune my wyttes, for I tell you plaine:
　I have a hive of humble bees swarmynge in my braine,

1 *goddiggod* God give you good day　*every chone* every one
5 *echone* each one　*skore* score

And he that hath the compace to fetch that I must
     fetche[5],
I maie saie in counsaile, had nede his wyttes to stretche.   10

But nowe, what my name is and what is my purpose,
Takinge youe all for frendes, I feare not to disclose:
My veray trewe unchristen[6] Name ys Avarice,
Which I may not have openlye knowen in no wise;
For though to moste men I am founde commodius,
Yet to those that use me my name is odius.
For who is so foolishe that the evell he hath wrought
For his owen behouff he wolde to light sholde be
        brought?[7]
Or who had not rather his ill doinges to hide
Thenne to have the same bruted on everye syde?   20
Therefore to worke my feate I will my name disguise
And call my name Polycie in stede of Covetise.
The name of Policie ys praised of eche one,
But to rake grumle sede[8] Avaryce ys alone;
The name of Policie is of none suspected;
Polycye is ner of any cryme detected:
So that under the name and cloke of Policie
Avaryce maie weorke factes and scape all ielousie.
And nowe ys the tyme come that – except I be a beaste –
Een to make up my mouth and to feather my neste[9],   30
A tyme that I have wayted for a greate longe space,
And nowe maie spede my purpose, if I have grace.

For heare ye, sirrha? our greate graund Ladie Mother,
Noble Dame Respublica, she and none other
Of all the offalles, the refuse, the ragges, the paringes,
The baggage, the trashe, the fragmentes, the sharinges,
The od endes, the crumes, the dribletes, the chippinges,

---

9 *compace* plan   15 *commodius* profitable   18 *behouff* advantage,
benefit   20 *Thenne* than   *bruted* shouted about   21 *feate* purpose
24 *rake* gather   26 *ner* never   28 *factes* crimes   *ielousie* suspicion
29 *except* unless   30 *Een* even   36 *sharinges* shearings   37 *crumes*
crumbs

The patches, the peces, the broklettes, the drippinges,
The fliettance, the scrapinges, the wilde wai[v]es and
    straies[10],
The skimmynges, the gubbins of booties and praies,   40
The glenynges, the casualties, the blynde excheates,
The forginge of forfayctes, the scape of extraietes[11],
Thexcesse, the waste, the spoile, the superfluites,
The windefalles, the shriddinges, the flycinges, the petie
    fees,
With a thowsaunde thinges mo which she maye right well
    lacke,
Woulde fyll all these same purses[12] that hange att my
    bakke;
Yea, and tenne tymes as manye moo bagges as these
Which sholde be but a flea bytinge for hir to lese,
That if I maie have the grace and happe to blynde her,
I doubte not, a shewete ladye I shall fynde hir.   50
To hir ytt wer nothing; yet manye a smale makith a greate
And all thinge wolde helpe me what ever I maye geate.
Full lytle knowe men the greate nede that I am yn.
Doo not I spende dailie of that that I doo wynne?
Then age cometh on and what ys a lytle golde
To kepe a man by drede that is feble and olde?[13]
No man therefore blame me thoughe I wolde have more.
The worlde waxeth harde, and store (thei saie) is no sore.
Nowe the chaunce of theves, in goode houre be ytt
    spoken –
Owte alas, I feare I lefte my cofer open.   60
I am surelye undoone! alas, where be my Cayes?
It[14] ys gone, that I have swette for all my lyve daies.
Wo worthe all whoreson theves, and suche covetous
    knaves

38 *broklettes* fragments   39 *fliettance* driftwood, flotsam   40 *gubbins* fragments *praies* preys   41 *casualties* legal payments *excheates* forfeits   44 *shriddinges* prunings *flycinges* fleecings (shares from extortion) *petie* petty   48 *lese* lose   50 *shewete* sweet   52 *geate* get   58 *sore* trouble   61 *Cayes* keys   62 *swette* sweated   63 *Wo worthe* a curse upon

That for theire wyndinge sheete wolde scrape men owt of
    theire graves.
Exeat

Actus Primi, scena secunda

Adulacion, Insolence, Oppressyon Intrant Cantantes[15]

ADULACION Oh noble Insolence, if I coulde singe as well
I wolde looke in heaven emonge angells to dwell.

INSOLENCE Sing? howe doo I sing, but as other manye doe?

ADUL. Yes, an angels voice ye have to herken unto.

INSO. Yea, but what availeth that to highe dignitie?

OPPRESSION By his[16] armes, not a whitte, as farre as I can
    see.

INSO. Or what helpeth that thinge, to sett a man a lofte?

OPPR. By his[16] woundes, not a strawe so have I tolde yowe
    ofte.

ADUL. No, but ye are one of suche goodlye personage,
Of suche wytte and beawtye and of sage parentage,   10
So excelente in all poyntes of everye arte –

INSO. In dede, god and nature in me have done theire
    parte.

ADUL. That yf ye wille putte yourselfe forwarde to the
    mooste,
Ye maie throughowte the whole land rewle all the roste.
Howe saie yowe, Oppression? ys ytt not even so?

OPPR. Thowe saiest soothe, Adulacion, so mowte I goe[17].
If he wer disposed to take the charge in hande,
I warraunte hym a chive to rewle all the whole lande.

ADUL. Lo, Maister Insolence, ye heare Oppression.

INSO. I thanke boothe hime and thee, goode Adulacion.   20
And long have I dreamed of suche an enterpryse;
But howe or where to begynne I cannot devise.

OPPR. Wherefore serve frendes, but your enterpryse to
    allowe?[18]

---

14 *roste* roost ('rule the roost' proverbial)   17 *charge* responsibility,
office   18 *hym a chive* he shall achieve

ADUL. And than must youe supporte them, as thei muste
    maintayne youe.

OPPR. And wherefore do frendes serve, but to sett youe yn?

ADUL. Ye shall have all my healpe whan ever ye beginne.

INSO. But we maie herein nothing attempte in no wyse
    Withowte the counsaile of our fownder Avaryce.

ADUL. He muste directe all this geare by his holye gooste.

OPPR. For he knowith whatt ys to be done in eche cooste;   30
    He knoweth where and howe that money is to be hadde;
    And yonder he cometh — me thinketh more then half
        madde.
    Intrat Avarice[19]

Actus Primi, scena tertia

Avarice, Insolence, Oppression, Adulacion

AVARICE It was a faire grace that I was not undooen clene;
    Yet my kye was safe lockt under nyne lockes, I wene.
    But een as against suche a thing my harte wyll throbbe:
    I fownde knaves abowte my howse readye me to robbe.
    Theare was suche a tooting, suche looking, and such
        priinge,
    Suche herkenynge, suche stalking, suche watching, suche
        spyinge:
    What wolde ye, my maisters? — We looke after a catte[20].
    Whatt make ye heare abowt? — We have smelled a rat.
    Nowe a wheale on suche noses, thought I by and by,
    That so quicklye canne sente where hidden golde dothe
        lye.   10
    But had I not comme when I did, with owte all failles
    I thinke theye had digged up my walles with theire nailes.

INSOLENCE Let us speake to hym and breake his chafing
    talke.

AVAR. Suche gredinesse of money emonge men dothe walke.

---

24 *than* then   29 *geare* affair (commonly, crimes) *gooste* spirit
30 *cooste* part   32 *then* than   2 *kye* key *wene* think   5 *tooting*
prying   9 *wheale* blow, or sore   10 *sente* scent

That have yt they will, eyther by hooke or by crooke[21].

OPPRESSION Lett us call to hym that he maye this waye looke.

AVAR. Whether by right or by wronge, in feith, some care not:

Therefore catche that catche maye hardely[22] and spare not.

ADULATION All haille oure fownder and chief, Maister Avaryce.

AVAR. The Devyll ys a knave, an I catche not a flyce.   20

ADUL. When ye see your tyme, looke this waie your frendes uppon.

AVAR. I doubte not to skamble and rake as well as one.

ADUL. Heare bee that wolde faine bee desiples of your arte.

AVAR. I wilnot bee behinde to gette a childes parte.

ADUL. Nowe if ye have done I pray youe looke this waye backe.

AVAR. Whoo buzzeth in myne eare so? what? ye sawecye Jacke.

ADUL. Are ye yet at leysure with your good frendes to talke?

AVAR. What clawest thowe myne elbowe, pratlinge merchaunt? walke.

Ye flaterabundus yowe, youe flyering clawbacke youe,

Youe the-crowe-is-white youe, youe the-swanne-is-blacke youe,   30

Youe John-Holde-my-stafe youe, youe what-is-the-clocke youe,

Youe *ait-aio* youe, yowe, *negat-nego*[23] yowe.

ADUL. I mervaile yowe speake to me in suche facion.

AVAR. Whi troublest thowe me then in my contemplacion?

ADUL. I came of right goode love, not mynding youe to lett.

AVAR. Thowe ner camst to anie man of good love yett.

ADUL. And these mennes myndes yt was I sholde soo dooe.

AVAR. As false wretches as thyne owen selfe, and falser tooe.

---

18 *hardely* boldly   20 *an* if   *flyce* fleece, share   22 *skamble* scramble   29 *flaterabundus* flatterer (mock Latin)   *flyering* mocking   *clawbacke* flatterer   35 *mynding* intending   *lett* hinder   36 *of* out of   37 *myndes* wishes

INSO. *and* OPPR. We have been loving to yowe and
    faithfull alwaye.

AVAR. For your owne profittes thenne and not myne, I dare
    saie, 40

And een verai youe three it was and others none

That wolde have robbed me, not yet haulf an howre gone.

INSO.

OPPR. }We never robbed any manne later or rather.

ADUL.

AVAR. Yes, manye a tyme and ofte your owne veraie father.

OPPR. And to yowe have we borne hartie favors alwaie.

AVAR. And I warraunte you hangd for your labours one
    daie.

OPPR. *and* ADUL. Even as oure God we have alwaie honored
    youe.

AVAR. And een as your God I have aie succoured youe.

OPPR. Wee call youe oure fowndur, by all holye halowes.

AVAR. Founder me no foundring, but beware the galowes. 50

INSO. I praie youe leave thes wordes and talke friendlie at
    laste.

AVAR. Content, at your request my fume is nowe well
    paste.

And in faith, what saithe our frende Adulacion?

ADUL. I wonder at your roughe communycacion,

That ye wolde to me use wordes of suche vehemence.

AVAR. Feyth, manne, I spake but even to prove your
    pacyence,

That yf thowe haddest grunted or stormed thereat –

ADUL. Naie, fewe times doe I use suche lewde manier as that.

AVAR. Come, shake handes and for ever we twoo bee at one.

ADUL. As for grutche in me there shall never remaine none. 60

AVAR. Nowe, Maister Insolence, to your ghostelye purpose.

INSO. We accordyd a matier to youe to disclosse.

AVAR. I understande all youre agreemente and accorde,

---

41 *verai* certainly   43 *rather* earlier   48 *aie* always   49 *halowes*
saints   52 *fume* anger   57 *That yf* to see if   60 *grutche* complaint
61 *ghostelye* spiritual (irony)   62 *accordyd* agreed

For I laie in your bosoms when ye spake the worde.
And I like well the advise of Oppression,
And eke of Flatterie, for your progression.

INSO. If there were matier whereon to worke, I care not.

AVAR. Ye shall have matier enoughe; bee doinge, spare not!

INSO. What? to come to honour and welthe for us all three?

AVAR. Ah! than ye could be well content to leave owt me.   70

INSO. No; for I knowe ye can for yourselfe well provyde.

AVAR. Yea, that I can, and for twentye hundreth besyde.

ADUL. Oh, wolde Christe, good fownder, ye wolde that
    thing open.

AVAR. Bones, knave; wilt thowe have ytt ere yt can be
    spoken?

OPPR. For the passion of god, tell ytt us with all spede.

AVAR. By the crosse, not a worde! here is haste made in dede.

INSO. Yes, good swete Avarice, despatch and tell att once.

AVAR. Naie, then cutte my throte, ye are felowes for the
    nonce.
Will ye have a matier before ytt can be tolde?
If ye will have me tell ytt ye shall your tonges holde.   80
Whiste, silence, not a worde! Mum, leatte your clatter
    sease!
Are ye with childe to heare and cannot holde your pease?
So, sir, nowe Respublica, the ladie of estate,
Ye knowe nowe latelye is left almoost desolate.
Hir welthe ys decayed, hir comforte cleane a goe,
And she att hir wittes endes what for to saie or doe.
Fayne wolde she have succoure and easemente of hir
    griefe
And highlye advaunce them that wolde promise reliefe.
Suche as wolde warraunte hir spirites to revive
Mowght mounte to highe eastate and be most sure to
    thrive.   90

INSO. So[24].

ADUL.   Well saide.

---

66 *eke* also   70 *than* then   74 *Bones* by God's bones   78 *for the nonce* in a hurry   85 *a goe* gone   90 *Mowght* might

OPPR.   Hah!

AVAR.   What is this hum, hah? hum?

INSO. Onn forth.

ADUL.   Goe too.

OPPR.   Tell on.

AVAR.   Bodye of me.

ADUL.   Mum.

AVAR. What saie ye?

INSO.   Hake.

ADUL.   Tuff.

OPPR.   Hem[25].

AVAR.   Who haken tuffa hum?
What saie ye?

OPPR.   Nothing.

INSO.   Not a worde.

AVAR.   Nor youe neither.

ADUL.   Mum.

AVAR. Dyd ye speake or not?

INSO.   No.

OPPR.   No.

ADUL.   No.

AVAR.   Nor yet doo not?

INSO. No.

OPPR.   No.

ADUL.   No.

OPPR.   No.

INSO.   No.

ADUL.   No.

AVAR.   That, that, that, that, that, that.
Sir, I entend Dame Respublica tassaille
And so to crepe in, to bee of hir counsaille.
I hope well to bring hir suche a paradise
That hir selfe shall sue me to have my service.   100
Than shall I have tyme and poure to bringe in youe three.

OPPR. Do this owte of hande, founder, and first speake for
        me.

Bring me in credyte, that my hande be in the pye.
An I gett not elbowe rowme emong them, let me lye.

AVAR. Naie, see an Oppression, this eager elfe;
Be not sens more covetous then covetous selfe!
Softe, be not so hastie, I praie youe, sir, softe a while;
Youe will over the hedge ere ye come att the stile.

OPPR. I wolde fayne be shouldering and rumbeling emonge
them.

AVAR. Naie, I will helpe iavels as shall wrong them.   110

ADUL. I praie youe, goode foundre, let not me be the laste.

AVAR. Thowe shalte be well placed where to thrive verai
faste.

ADUL. I thanke youe, Maister Avarice, with all my harte.

AVAR. And when thoue arte in place, see thowe plaie well
thie parte.
Whan ye clawe hir elbowe, remembre your best frende,
And lett my commendacions be ever att one ende.

ADUL. I warraunte youe.

INSO.   And what, shall I be left cleane owte?

AVAR. No syr, ye shall bee chiefe to bring all thinges abowte.
Ye shall emonges us have the chiefe preeminence,
And we to youe, as yt were, oughe obedience.   120
Ye shalbe our leader, our captaine, and our guyde.
Than muste ye looke a lofte with thandes under the side[26].
I shall tell Respublica, ye can beste governe;
Bee not ye than skeymishe to take in hand the stern:
Than shall we assiste youe as frendes of perfitte truste,
To doe and to undoe and commaunde what ye luste.
And when youe have all att your owne will and pleasure,
Parte of your lyvinges to your frendes ye maie measure
And punishe the prowdeste of theim that will resiste.

OPPR. He that ones wincheth shall fele the waite of my
fiste.   130

---

106 *sens* already   110 *iavels* rascals   120 *oughe* owe   124 *skey-mishe* squeamish *stern* rudder, helm   126 *luste* wish   130 *wincheth* hesitates

ADUL. Yea, we muste all holde and cleve togither like
      burres.

AVAR. Yea, see ye three, hang and drawe togither like
      furres.

OPPR. And so shall we be sure to gett store of money,
  Sweter then sugar!

AVAR.   Sweter then enie honey.

INSO. Verai well spoken! This geare will right well accorde.

ADUL. Did not I saye ye were worthie to be a lorde?

AVAR. I will make Insolence a lorde of highe eastate.

INSO. And I will take uppon me well bothe earely and late.

OPPR. But, Insolence, when you come to the encrochinge
      of landes,

  Ye maie not take all alone into youre handes;   140

  I will looke to have parte of goodes, landes and plate.

INSO. Ye shall have enoughe, eche bodye after his rate.

ADUL. I must have parte too; ye muste not have all alone.

INSO. Thowe shalte bee laden tyll thye shoulders shall
      cracke and grone.

ADUL. I praie youe, lett me have a goode lordship or twoo.

INSO. Respublica shall feede the tyll thowe wilte saie hoo.

ADUL. And I muste have good mannour places, twoo or
      three.

INSO. But the chiefe and beste lordship muste remaine to me.

OPPR. Masse, and I will loke to be served of the beste.

  Orels some folke some where shall sytt but in smale reste.   150

INSO. I muste have castels and townes in everye shiere.

ADUL. And I a chaunge of howses, one heare and another
      there.

INSO. And I muste have pastures and townships and woodes.

OPPR. And I muste needes have store of golde and other
      goodes.

INSO. And I must have chaunge of farmes and pastures for
      shepe,

  With dailie revenues my lustye porte for to kepe.

---

132 *furres* thieves   141 *looke* expect   146 *hoo* stop, enough   150 *Orels*
or else   156 *lustye* pleasant   *porte* style of living

AVAR. I wolde have a bone here rather then a grote,
 To make thes snarling curres gnawe owte others throte.
 Here, be eager, whelpes, loe: to yt, Boye, box him, Ball![27]
 Poore I maie picke strawes these hungri dogges will
  snatche all.   160
OPPR. Eche man snatche for hym selfe; by gosse, I wilbe
  spedde.
AVAR. Lacke who lacke shall, Oppression wilbe corne
  fedde.[28]
 Is not Dame Respublica sure of goode handlinge
 Whan theis whelpes, ere thei have ytt, fall thus to
  skambling?
 And me, their chiefe founder, thei have een syns forgotte.
INSO. Thowe shalte have golde and silver enoughe to thy
  lotte.
 Respublica hath enough to fill all owre lappes.
ADUL. Than, I praie youe, sir, leate our fownder have some
  scrappes!
AVAR. Scrappes, ye doultishe lowte! fede youe your founder
  with scrappes?
 Yf youe were well served youre head wolde have some
  rappes.   170
ADUL. I spake of goode will.
INSO.   Naie, fight not, good Avarice.
OPPR. What enie of us getteth thoue haste the chiefe price.
AVAR. Than what ever ye doe, ye will remember me?

INSO. ⎫
OPPR. ⎬ Yea.
ADUL. ⎭

AVAR.   Well so doe than, and I forgeve youe all three.
INSO. But when doe wee enter everye man his charge?
AVAR. As soone as I can spye Respublica att large
 I will bourde hir, and, I trowe, so wynne hir favoure
 That she shall hire me and paie well for my laboure.

157 *grote* groat   161 *gosse* god   164 *skambling* quarrelling
177 *bourde* board, accost

Than wyll I comende the vertues of youe three
That she shall praie and wishe under our rewle to bee.   180
Therefore from this houre bee ye all in readinesse.
OPPR. Doubte not of us; thowe seeste all oure gredinesse.
INSO. If ytt bee at midnight, I come att the firste call.
  They go foorthwarde one after other
ADUL. Doe but whistle for me, and I come forth with all.
AVAR. That is well spoken. I love suche a towarde twygg.
  He whistleth
ADUL. I come, fownder.
AVAR.   That is myne owne good spaignell Rigg[29].
  And come on backe againe all three, come bakke agayne!
INSO. Oure founder calleth us backe.
OPPR.   Retourne then amaigne.

Actus Primi, scena quarta[30]

Avaryce, Adulacion, Insolence, Oppresion

AVAR. Come on, syrs, all three. And first to youe, best be
  truste:
What is your brainpan stufte with all? wull or sawe
  duste?
ADUL. Why so?
AVAR.   What is your name?
ADUL.   Flatterie.
AVAR.   Een so just!
ADUL. Yea, orels Adulacion, if youe so luste.
Either name is well knowne to mannye a bodye.
AVAR. An honest mome; ah, ye dolt, ye lowte, ye nodye.
Shall Respublica here yore commendacion
By the name of Flatterie or Adulacion?
Or when ye commende me to hir, will ye saie this:
Forsouthe, his name is Avarice or Covetise?   10
And youe that sholde have wytte, yst your discretion

---

185 *towarde* 'hopeful', promising   *twygg* youngster   186 *spaignell*
spaniel   188 *amaigne* immediately   2 *wull* wool   6 *mome* fool
11 *yst* is it

Bluntlye to goe forth and be called Oppression?
And youe, Insolence, doe ye thinke yt wolde well frame
If ye were presented to hir under that name?

INSO. I thought nothing thereupon, by my holydome.

OPPR. My mynde was an other waie, by my christendome.

ADUL. That thing was lest parte of my thought, by
   Saincte Denie.

AVAR. No, marie: your myndes were all on your haulfe penie.
But, my maisters, I must on myne honestie passe
And not ronne on heade, like a brute beaste or an asse, 20
For is not Oppression eche where sore hated?
And is not Flaterie openly rahated?
And am not I, Avarice, styll cryed owte uppon?

ADUL. Yes; I coulde have tolde youe that, a greate while
   agone.
But I woulde not displease youe.

AVAR.   And youe, Insolence,
I have harde you ill spoken of a greate waie hens.

ADUL. In my consciens the Devill hym selfe dothe love youe.

AVAR. But, chaungeynge your yll name, fewer shall
   reprove youe,
As I myne owen self, where my name is knowen,
Am right sore assailed to be overthrowen; '30
But dooing as I wyll nowe, countrefaicte my name,
I spede all my purposes and yet escape blame.

INSO. Lett us then have newe names, eche manne withoute
   delaye.

AVAR. Els will some of youe make good hanging stuff one
   daie.

OPPR. Thowe must newe christen us.

INSO.   First: what shall my name bee?

AVAR. Faithe, sir, your name shalbe Mounsyre Authoritie.

OPPR. And for me what ys your determinacyon?

AVAR. Marye, sir, ye shalbe called Reformacyon.

---

15 *holydome* holy relic 17 *lest* the least 19 *passe* pause 20 *ronne*
run 21 *eche where* everywhere 22 *rahated* reproved 24 *agone*
ago 31 *countrefaicte* disguise

ADUL. Nowe I praie yowe, devise for me an honest name.

AVAR. Thowe arte suche a beast, I cannot for veray shame.   40

ADUL. If ye thinke good, lett me be called Policie.

AVAR. Policie – a rope ye shall. Naye, Hipocrisie.

ADUL. Fy, that were as slaunderous a name as Flatterye.

AVAR. And I kepe for myselfe the name of Policie.

But if I devise for thee, wilte thou not shame me?

ADUL. Naie, I will make the prowde of me, orels blame me.

AVAR. Well than, for this tyme thy name shalbe Honestie.

ADUL. I thanke youe, Avaryce – Honestie, Honestie.

AVAR. Avaryce, ye whooresone? Policye, I tell thee.

ADUL. I thanke youe, Policye, Honestie, Honestie.   50

Howe saie youe, Insolence? I am nowe Honestie.

AVAR. We shall att length have a knave of youe, Honestie.

Saide I not he shoulde be called Mounsier Authoritye?

ADUL. Oh, frende Oppression, Honestie, Honestie.

AVAR. Oppression? hah! is the devyll in thye brayne?

Take hede, or, in faithe, ye are Flatterye againe.

Policie. Reformacion. Authorytie.

ADUL. Hipocrisye, Diffamacion, Authorytie.

AVAR. Hipocrisye, hah? Hipocrisie, ye dull asse?

ADUL. Thowe namedste Hipocrisie even nowe, by the

Masse.   60

AVAR. Polycye, I saide. Policye, knave, Polycye!

Nowe saye as I sayd.

ADUL.   Policie, knave, Policie.

AVAR. And what callest thowe hym here?

ADUL.   Dyffamacion.

AVAR. I tolde the, he shoulde be called Reformacion.

ADUL. Veraye well.

AVAR.   What ys he nowe?

ADUL.   Deformacion.

AVAR. Was ever the like asse borne in all nacions?

ADUL. A pestell on hym, he comes of the Acyons.

AVAR. Come on, ye shall learne to solfe: Reformacion!

Sing on nowe: Re.

67 *pestell* plague   *Acyons* (?) Asians   68 *solfe* to sing solfa

238

ADUL.   Re.

AVAR.   Refor.

ADUL.   Reformacion.

AVAR. Policie, Reformacion, Authorytie.   70

ADUL. Polycie, Reformacion, and Honestie.

AVAR. In faithe, ye asse, yf your tong make enie moo trips,
    Ye shall bothe be flatterie and have on the lips[31].
    And now, Mounsyre Authoritie, against I youe call[32]
    Ye muste have other garmentes, and soo muste ye all.
    Ye muste, for the season, counterfaite gravitee.

INSO. *and* OPPR. Yes, what else?

ADUL.   And I must counterfaite honestie.

AVAR. And I must tourne my gowne in and owte, I wene;
    For theise gaping purses maie in no wyse be seen.
    I will tourne ytt een here; come helpe me, Honestye.   80

ADUL. Here at hande.

AVAR.   Why, how now? plaie the knave, Honestie?
    Helpe, what dooest thowe nowe?

ADUL.   I counterfaicte honestie.

AVAR. Why, than, come thowe, helpe me, my frende
        Oppression!
    What helpe calle youe that?

OPPR.   Fytt for your discrecion.

AVAR. Oh, I shoulde have sayde: helpe, sir Reformacyon.

OPPR. Yea, marye, sir, that is my nomynacion.

AVAR. And whan yowe are in your robe, keape yt afore
        close.

OPPR. I praie youe, Maister Policie, for what purpose?

AVAR. All folke wyll take youe, if theye piepe under your
        gowne,
    For the veriest catif in countrey or towne.   90
    Now goe, and when I call, see that ye readie be.

INSO. I will.

OPPR.   And I wyll.

ADUL.   And so will I, Honestie.

    Exeant

89 *piepe* peep   90 *catif* villain

239

AVAR. Well, nowe will I departe hens also for a space
And to bourde Respublica waite a tyme of grace.
Wherever I fynde hir a tyme convenient,
I shall saie and dooe that maie bee expedient!
 Exeat Avarice

Actus Secundi, scena prima

RESPUBLICA[33] Lorde, what yearethlye thinge is permanent
  or stable,
Or what is all this worlde but a lumpe mutable?
Who woulde have thought that I from so florent estate
Coulde have been browght so base as I am made of
  late?
But as the waving seas doe flowe and ebbe by course,
So all thinges els doe chaunge to better and to wurse.
Greate cyties and their fame in tyme dooe fade and
  passe.
Nowe is a champion fielde where noble Troie was.
Where is the greate empire of the Medes and Persans?
Where bee tholde conquestes of the puissaunt Grecians? 10
Where Babilon? where Athennes? where Corinth so wyde?
Are thei not consumed, with all their pompe and pryde?
What is the cause heareof, mannes wytte cannot discusse;
But of long contyunuance the thing is founde thus.
Yet by all experience thus much is well seen
That in common weales, while goode governors have been,
All thing hath prospered, and where such men dooe lacke,
Common weales decaye and all thinges doe goe backe.
What mervaile then yf I wanting a perfecte staigh
From mooste flourishing welth bee falen in decaye, 20
But lyke as by default quicke ruine dothe befalle,
So maie good governemente att ons recover all.
 Intrat Avarice cogitabundus et ludibundus[34]

---

1 *yearethlye* earthly   2 *mutable* changing   3 *florent* flourishing
13 *discusse* conceive   19 *staigh* support

Actus Secundi, scena secunda

Avaricia, Respublica

AVAR. Alas, my swete bages, howe lanke and emptye ye bee;
But, in faithe and trawth, sirs, the fawlte ys not in mee.

RESP. Well, my helpe and comforte, oh lorde, muste come
from thee.

AVAR. And my swete purses heare I praie youe all see, see,
How the litle fooles gaspe and gape for grumble sede.

RESP. Iff ytt be thie will, lorde, send some redresse with
spede.

AVAR. But, in faithe, goode swete fooles, yt shall cost me a
fall.
But I will shortelye fyll youe, and stoppe your mouthes
all.

RESP. Oh, that ytt were my happe, on frendelye frendes
to light!

AVAR. Hahe? who is that same that speaketh yonder in
sight?   10
Who ist? Respublica? yea, by the Marye Masse[35].

RESP. Than might I bee againe as well as ere I was.

AVAR. Hide up these pipes; nowe I praie God she bee
blynde.
I am haulf afraide leste she have an yei behynde.
We must nowe chaunge our coppie: oh lorde, whowe I
fraie[36],
Lest she sawe my toyes and harde whatt I dyd saie!

RESP. Is there no good manne that on me wyll have
mercye?

AVAR. Remembre nowe, my name ys Maister Polycie.
All thing, I tell yowe, muste nowe goe by polycie.

RESP. Herke, me thinke I heare the name of Polycie.   20

AVAR. Hooe calleth Conscience? heare am I, Polycie.

RESP. I praie youe come to me, if youe bee Polycie.

AVAR. Yea forsouth, yea forsouthe, my name ys Polycie.

5 *grumble sede* money   9 *happe* fortune   13 *pipes* purses   14 *yei*
eye   15 *coppie* behaviour   16 *harde* heard

RESP. I am sore decaied throughe defalte of Polycie.

AVAR. Yea, moost noble Respublica, I knowe that well,
And doe more lament yt, then enie tong can tell.
For an if goode Polycie had had youe in hande,
Ye had nowe been the wealthiest in anye lande.
But good Polycie hath long been putte to exile.

RESP. Yea, God wotte, ye have been bard from me a greate
while.   30

AVAR. Yea, I have been putte backe, as one cleane of shaken[37],
And what can a man doe tyll he be forthe taken?

RESP. Well, I fele the lacke of your helping hande, by the
roode.

AVAR. Alacke, noble ladye, I woulde I coulde doe youe
goode.

RESP. Yes, Polycie, ye might amende all, if youe luste.

AVAR. Yea, feithe, I durste put miself to youe of truste.
But there bee enough that for youe coulde shifte make.

RESP. Yet none like to yowe, if yowe woulde yt undertake.
And I will putt miselfe whollye into your handes:
Metall, graine, cataill, treasure, goodes and landes.   40

AVAR. Well, I will take some paine; but this to youe be
knowen:
I will doe ytt, not for your sake, and but myne owne[38].

RESP. Howe saie ye that, Polycie?

AVAR.   This to yowe bee knowen:
I will doe all for your sake, and not for myne owen.

RESP. I thanke youe, Polycie.

AVAR.   Naie, I thanke youe, ladye,
And I trust ere long to ease all oure maladie.
Will ye putte yourselfe nowe wholye into my handes?

RESP. Ordre me as youe wyll.

AVAR.   Treasure, goodes and landes?

RESP. Yea, everye whitte.

AVAR.   Well, I thanke youe ons againe,

---

30 *bard* excluded   31 *of* off   40 *Metall* gold   *cataill* cattle   49 *ons*
once

But nowe, that youe maie thinke my dealing trewe and
    plaine,   50
And because one cannot doe so well as mannye,
Ye muste associate me with mo compaignie,
And first, by my will, ye shall sette up Honestie.
RESP. Marye, withall my veraie harte: but where is he?
AVAR. Veray hard to fynde: but I thinke I coulde fetche hym.
RESP. Call hym straight waies hither; see that nothing lett
    hym.
AVAR. It were best if I shall goe fett men for the nones,
To make but one viage and bring them all att ones.
RESP. Whome more then hym?
AVAR.   Ye muste stablishe Authoritie.
RESP. That muste needes bee doen.
AVAR.   And eke Reformacion.   60
Wee fowre will rewle thinges of another facion.
RESP. Polycie, I praie youe goe fette all these straight waye.
AVAR. Yes, for this your present case maie byde no delaye.
I will goe and come wyth all festinacion.
    Exeat
RESP. I like well this trade of administracion:
Polycie for to devise for my comoditie;
No personne to be advaunced but Honestye;
Then Reformacion good holsome lawes to make,
And Auctorytie see the same effecte maie take;
What comon weale shall then bee so happie as I?   70
For this (I perceive) is the drift of Polycie.
    Intrat Avarice, adducens[39] *Insolence, Oppression et
    Adulacion*
And beholde, where he is retourned againe seens;
Hee shewith himselfe a man of muche diligence.

---

52 *mo* more   56 *lett* hinder   57 *fett* fetch   *for the nones* at once
58 *viage* journey   63 *byde* brook (verb)   64 *festinacion* speed
66 *comoditie* advantage   72 *seens* already

Actus Secundi, scena tertia

Adulacion, Avaryce, Respublica, Insolence, Oppression

ADUL. I will doe hir double servis to another.

AVAR. Ye, double knave youe, will ye never be other?

ADUL. She schall have triple service of me, Honestie.

AVAR. Ye quadrible knave, will ye ner use modestie?
Thowe dronken whoresone, doest thoue not see nor
perceive
Where Respublica standes readie us to receyve?

RESP. What talke have theye yonder emong themselves
togither?

ADUL. I have spied hir nowe. Shal I first to hir thither?

AVAR. Softe, lett me present yowe.

RESP.   I weene thei bee in feare.
Polycie, approche, and bring my goode frendes nere.   10

AVAR. Come on, my deare frendes, and execute with good
wyll
Suche offyce as eche of youe shall be putt untyll.
Dame Respublica yt ys, that for youe hath sent.
Come on, frendes, I will youe unto her greace present.

INSO. *and* OPPR. To serve her we are preast with harte and
whole entent.

AVAR. Madame, I have brought youe these men for whom
I went.

RESP. Polycie, I thanke youe, ye have made spiede spede.
Therefore ye be double welcome, and welcome frendes
in dede.

AVAR. Madame, your grace to serve we all are fullye bente.

ADUL. And Madame, ye shall fynde me double diligente.   20

RESP. That is spoken of a goode harte; but who bee ye?

ADUL. Forsouthe, madame, my name ys Maister Honestie.

RESP. Honestie? well saide.

AVAR.   Madame, this is Honestie.

ADUL. Yea forsouth, an please your grace, I am Honestie.

---

4 *ner* never   12 *untyll* to   14 *greace* grace   15 *preast* ready   *entent*
intention   17 *spiede* speedy   19 *bente* devoted

AVAR. Madame, he is for youe: on my woorde regarde hym.
RESP. Yes, and with large preferment I will rewarde hym.
ADUL. I thanke your Grace, and I will for youe take suche
     paine
  That ere I deserve one ye shall geve me twayne.
AVAR. Honestie, your tong tripth.
RESP.   Howe saide ye, take suche paine —
ADUL. That ere ye geve me one I will deserve twaine —   30
  By your lycence, Madame, to take awaie this mote.
AVAR. Naie, Honestie will not see a wemme on your cote.
  Nowe unto youe I commende Reformacion.
RESP. Of hym is no small nede nowe in this nacion.
OPPR. Well, nowe that ye bydde me abuses to redresse
  I doubte not all enormitis so to represse,
  As shall redowne to your wealth and honour att length.
RESP. There to shall Authoritee ayde youe with his
     strength.
AVAR. Yea, for Authoritee to governe ys mooste fytte.
INSO. Yf ye, Dame Respublica, doe me so admytte,   40
  I doubte not to hamper the prowdeste of them all.
RESP. And emong youe destroye Avarice.
ADUL.   Hem!
INSO. *and* OPPR.   We shall.
RESP. Vanquishe Oppression and Adulacion,
  For those three have nighe wrought my desolacion.
AVAR. Hem, sirs, hem; there, kepe your gownes close
     afore, I saie;
  Have ye forgotten nowe that I tolde youe one daye?
  There is another too that wolde bee chaced hens.
RESP. Who is that?
AVAR.   Lucifers sonne, called Insolence.
RESP. Ye saie truth and manye naughtie ones moo then he.
INSO. *and* OPPR. If ye dare truste us —
INSO.   All —
OPPR.   All shall reformed bee.   50

  29 *tripth* trips over   31 *mote* speck   32 *wemme* blemish   37 *re-downe* add

RESP. I thanke youe and I truste youe for my maintenaunce
  To bee administer for your goode governaunce.
INSO. Than withowte feare or care ye maie yourselfe
      repose.
OPPR. And lett us alone withall suche mattiers as those.
RESP. Than I leave yowe heare, on our affaires to consoulte.
    Exeat Respublica
INSO. Whan youe please, in godes name.
OPPR.   We muste bothe sifte and boulte[40].
ADUL. She is gone.
AVAR.   Well then, sirs, lett us make no delaye
  But abowte our markett departe eche manne his waye.
ADUL. Naie, first lett us sing a song to lighten our hartes.
AVAR. Then are ye like for me to sing but of three partes.   60
  Canne Avarice hart bee sett on a merie pynne,
  And see no gaine, no profitte att all coming in?
INSO. We shall have enoughe to drive awaie all sorowe.
AVAR. Than sing wee on bowne viage, and Saincte
      George the borowe.
    *Cantent 'Bring ye to me' and 'I to ye etc.' & sic
    exeant*[41]

.   .   .

Actus Quinti, scena tertia

Misericordia, Veritas, Respublica
MISERICORDIA I dare saie Respublica thinketh the tyme
      long.
VERITAS Who can blame hir, having endured so muche
      wrong?
  But as meate and drinke and other bodylye foode
  Is never founde to bee so pleasaunte nor so goode
  As whan fretting hongre and thirste hathe pincht afore,
  And as health after sickenes is sweeter evermore,
  So after decaye and adversytee overcome,
  Welth and prospiritee shalbe double welcome.

52 *administer* administrator 61 *pynne* note, pitch 64 *the* thee
borowe ransome, save 5 *fretting* wearing

MISER. How nowe, Respublica? Have I not been long hens?

RESP. Come ye first or laste, ye blisse me with your
        presence.   10

MISER. As I was commaunded, I bringe yowe Veritee
  To helpe youe, youre people, and theire posteritee.

VER. Dere iewell Respublica, I dooe youe enbrace.

RESP. I thanke your goodnesse and submitte me to your
        grace.

MISER. Enbrace Veritee for ever, Respublica,
  And cleve fast to hir.

RESP.   Yes, Misericordia.

MISER. Nowe please yt yow to declare, sister Veritee,
  How she maie recover hir olde prospiritee,
  Hir honour, hir wealth, hir riches, hyr substaunce,
  Hir comons, hyr people, hir strength, and hyr puissance.   20

VER. All this wilbee recovered incontinent
  And to better state also by good governement.

RESP. No ladie of my name upon yearth, I esteme,
  Hath had better administers then myne have been,
  Policie, Reformacion, and Authoritie.

MISER. Thes three bee veray good.

RESP.   And the foure[th] Honestee.

VER. But what if these which have had youe and yours
        to kepe
  Have been ravnyng woulves in the clothing of sheep?

RESP. If I hard not youe, Verytee, suche sentence geve,
  By no mans perswasion I could ytt beeleve.   30

VER. Ah, good Respublica, thow haste been abused.
  Whom thowe chosest are vices to be refused:
  Whom thow calst Honestee ys Adulacion,
  And he that in pretence was Reformacyon
  Is indede Oppression and houge Violence;
  Whom thowe calst Authoritee is prowde Insolence.
  Than he that was Policie, the chiefe manne of price,

10 *blisse* bless   13 *enbrace* embrace   21 *incontinent* speedily
23 *yearth* earth   28 *ravnyng* ravening   29 *sentence* opinion   35 *houge*
huge   37 *price* esteem

Indede is moost stinking and filthie Avarice.
He firste enveigled thee, and his purpose to frame
Cloked eche of these vices with a vertuous name.   40
RESP. *Benedicite*[42], is this a possible case?
VER. Ye shall see yt proved trewe before your owne face.
Thei shalbe convinced before youe one by one.
RESP. O Lorde, what mervail if my thrifte wer well nighe
    gon?
But what redresse shall I have hereof? and whan?
MISER. Suche as maie bee mooste fitte, and as soone as we
    can.
Iustice and Peace are appointed to descende,
Thone to kepe youe quiete, the other youe to defende.
As soone as wee fowre sisters togither shalbe mette,
An ordre for your establishment shall bee sett   50
By the eternall providence; yt is decreed soo.
RESP. O mooste mercifull lorde, all prayse bee thee unto.
MISER. I will leave youe here with my syster Veritee
And learne of their coming wyth all celerytee.
VER. Ye nede not, for I knowe thei bee nowe veray nere,
And beholde they begynne alreadie to appeare.

Actus Quinti, scena quarta

Pax, Iustitia, Veritas, Misericordia, Respublica

PAX Nowe ons againe in God leat us twoo systers kisse
In token of oure ioynynge to make a perfytte blysse[43].
IUSTITIA And now leate us never bee soondred any more
Tyll we maie Respublica perfectelye restore.
VER. Leate us meet theym, sister Misericordia.
MISER. And unto theire sight present Respublica.
IUS. *and* PAX All haile, mooste deare systers, Mercye and
    Verytee,
And all haile, Respublica, with all sincerytee.
RESP. O ye ladies celestiall, howe muche am I bounde

39 *enveigled* deceived   43 *convinced* convicted   44 *thrifte* fortune
48 *Thone* the one   3 *soondred* parted

With thankes to fall flatte before youe on the grownde   10
That ye thus vouchesalve a forlorne creature
By youre heave[n]lye protection to recure.

ıus. I, Iustice from heaven, am come youe to visytte.

pax And I, Peace, for ever with yowe to enhabite.

miser. And all wee fowre systers, to thutmooste of oure
         poure,
Shall restore, establishe, and defend youre honnour.

ıus. We shall firste restore your moste happie eastate,
And suppresse all them that had made youe desolate.

ver. Verytee shall all trueth open as ytt ys.

ıus. I, Iustice, shall redresse what er is founde amisse.   20

miser. I, Mercye, where the membre maie recured bee,
Shall temper the rigoure, and slake extremitee.

pax I, Peace, whan thuncurable is clene cutte awaie,
And thyll made goode, shall flourishe for ever and aie.

resp. And I, which cannot otherwise your goodnes deserve,
Shall your holsome directions dewlie observe.
And what yf Insolence shall come, or Avarice?

ver. Detest them, abhore them, and refuse their service.
I doubte not but thei wilbe styll haunting hither
Tyll we fowre shall theim fowre take here altogither.   30

miser. Nowe, sisters, goe wee, and Respublica with us,
To bee newe appareled[44] otherwyse then thus.

ıus. Come on, Respublica, with us to wealth from wooe:
Godde hathe geven us in charge that yt muste bee soo.

ver. The blysfull renovacion ye shall reigne in
Muste from hensfoorthe nowe immediatelye begynne.

     Cantent 'The mercye of God et cetera' et exeant

Actus Quinti, scena quinta

Avarice, Adulacion

avar. Suche gredie covetous folke as nowe of daies been
I trowe before these present daies wer never seen.

11 *vouchesalve* vouchsafe   12 *recure* restore   15 *thutmooste* the
utmost   20 *er* ever   22 *slake* mitigate   23 *thuncurable* the uncurable   35 *renovacion* restoration

An honest man can goe in no place of the strete
But he shall, I thinke, with an hundred beggers mete.
'Geve for goddes sake, geve for Saincte Charitee,
Geve for Our Ladies sake, geve for the Trenitee,
Geve in the waye of your good spede, geve, geve, geve,
    geve.'[45]
Finde we oure money in the strete, doo theye beeleve?
If I had not a speciall grace to saie naye
I wer but undooen emongst them in one daie.   10
But who cometh yond? Honestee? He cometh in haste.

ADUL. I seke Policie.

AVAR.   Here, boye.

ADUL.   All is in waste.

AVAR. Howe so?

ADUL.   We strive againste the streame all that we doo.

AVAR. Wherein?

ADUL.   That Veritee come not this place untoo.
For wotte ye what?

AVAR.   I shall whan ye have spake the woorde.

ADUL. Iustice and Peace too with full consent and accorde
Are come downe from heaven and have kyste together.

AVAR. God geve grace that theye twayne also come not
    hither.

ADUL. As Mercye and Trueth *sibi obviaverunt*,
So *Iustitia et Pax osculatae sunt*[46].   20

AVAR. Is yt trewe? Are they come?

ADUL.   And have kist together.

AVAR. Than carrye yn apace for feare of fowle weather.
Have they kyssed together?

ADUL.   Yea.

AVAR.   What nedeth that?
Men shoulde kysse woomen. And what poincte bee theye
    att?

ADUL. All the foure sisters, I doo you tunderstaunde,
Have alreadie taken Respublica in hand.
Theye fowre progresse with hir in everye border,

    15 *wotte* know   22 *carrye yn* take care   *apace* quickly

And marre all that ever we have sette in order.

AVAR. And what doeth Insolence, or what saieth he to that?

ADUL. He stampeth, he stareth, and snuffeth sore theareat.   30

AVAR. I advise hym to storme, and to shewe himselfe
       stowte;

Thei bee weemen and perchaunce maye bee faced owte,

And Peace is an honest ladie and a quiete.

ADUL. Veritee and Iustice are not for oure dyete.

AVAR. Then Mercye ys a goode one. I like hir well.

ADUL. Yet oft turnth she hyr face awaie, and will not mell.

AVAR. Well, fall backe, fall edge, I am ons att a poincte

If Respublica come tadventure a ioyncte[47].

ADUL. She is freshe and gaye, and flourissheth who but she?

AVAR. Who brought yt to suche passe, will I tell hir, but
       wee?   40

Orels, making these newe ladies of hir werie,

Wee shoulde thrihumphe and reigne.

ADUL.   Oh never so merye.

AVAR. Well, go to our compaignie; I will remaine here.

I maie perhaps see Dame Respublica appere.

I wilbe in hande with hir and make a goode face.

ADUL. And what shall I doe?

AVAR.   Geve warning in the meane space

That Insolence shrinke not, but plaie the stowte man.

ADUL. That I knowe he will doo, for ons I knowe he can.

AVAR. And that youe all three be prest to come hether,

Whan nede shall require we laye our heades together.   50

Whye arte thowe heare yet?

ADUL.   I am gon withall my might.

     Exeat

     Intrat Respublica

AVAR. And loe where Respublica appereth in sight.

She is nowe att hyr nymphes bearing upp hir traine.

I will stande asyde, and lysten a woorde or twaine.

30 *snuffeth* snorts *sore* vigorously 31 *stowte* brave 36 *mell*
interfere 41 *Orels* or else *werie* weary 49 *prest* ready

Actus Quinti, scena sexta

Respublica, Avarice

RESP. O Lorde, thy mercies shall I sing evermore
Whiche dooeste soo tenderlie thie handemaide restore.
But what creature woulde suspicion have had
That my late administers had been men so bad?
Or who woulde have thowght theim counterfaictes to
    have been
That had harde their woordes and their countenaunce
    seen?
And chieflye Avarice which dyd the matier breake?

AVAR. That woorde towcheth mee: now is tyme for me to
    speake.

RESP. I thought hym Policie, as iuste and true as stele.

AVAR. I am gladde that by me ye doo suche goodnesse fele.   10

RESP. And that my wealth dyd growe, as it hath growne of
    late.

AVAR. I ever tolde ye youe shoulde growe to this eastate.

RESP. Thowe tell me?

AVAR.   Yea, I tolde youe soo in veraie dede:
And highlie I reioyce yt doeth so well succede.
And '*Salve festa dies*'[48] upon youe, Madame!
I am glad ye have gotte a newe robe, so I am.
What saincte in the callender doe we serve todaye
That ye bee so gorgeouslye decked and so gaye?

RESP. In reioycing that I shalbe cleane ryd of thee.

AVAR. Naie, by this crosse ye shall never be rydde, for me[49].   20

RESP. And of thy compares.

AVAR.   Well, leate them doo as thei luste.
I will ryde uppon Iyll, myne owne mare: that is iuste.
Other waies I shall doe yowe service of the beste.

RESP. Thowe wicked wretche, dareste thowe with me to
    ieste?

AVAR. What? I now see *honores mutant mores*,

4 *administers* ministers   6 *harde* heard   7 *breake* initiate   21 *compares* companions

But, as semeth here, *raro in meliores*[50].

RESP. Thee and all thy service I doe from me exile.

AVAR. Is that the highe rewarde ye promist me ere while?
Is not this a wise woman and mynded to thrive
That woulde me, Policie, owte of the countrie drive? 30

RESP. Thee and thy complices from me I shall owte caste.

AVAR. Than I praie youe paie us for our paines that are
  paste.

RESP. Ye shalbe paide.

AVAR.   Ons I have doone the best I canne;
Authorytee also, he hath plaied the man;
Reformacion hath doen his parte, I canne tell;
If ye mystruste Honestie, feith, ye doo not well.
And as for Avarice, he is conveighed quite:
I bed hym gette hens or I woulde hym endyte.
I, Policie, have made hym to plucke in his hornes[51];
I sware I woulde els laie hym on prickels and thornes, 40
Where he shoulde take no rest neither daie nor night,
So he had as liefe bee hanged as come in sight.

RESP. I maie saie with Iob[52] howe vainelye doe ye cheare me,
Whan all the wordes ye geve from truth doeth disagree,
And with the wise man[53] I maie moost iustlye saye this:
Iusticia tamen non luxit in nobis;
Orels with the prophet[54], in mooste sorowfull moode,
The fruicte of our iustice is tourned into wormwoode.
Well, the best of youe is a detestable vice,
And thow for thie parte arte mooste stinking Avarice. 50

AVAR. Iesu, when were youe wonte so foule moothed to bee,
To geve suche nicknames? Ah, in feith, Dame Veritee
Hath had youe in scooling of late. Well, in Gods name,
I am sorie for yowe, een sorie, that [I am].
I wisse, I have wrowte to sett youe in goode state,
And watched for that purpose bothe earlie and late.
And I wis, if yowe woulde abyde my framynge

31 *complices* associates 37 *conveighed* removed 38 *bed* bade
endyte indict 42 *as liefe* rather 55 *wrowte* worked 57 *framynge*
planning

And not thus to have fall to checking and blamynge,
I woulde ere long of yowe have made suche carpenter
    weorke[55]
That ye shoulde have saide Policie had been a clerke.   60
Naie, youe shoulde have seen how I woulde have youe
    compacte.

RESP. Yea, no doubte, ye woulde have doone somme great
    and fyne acte.

AVAR. I woulde have browght haulfe Kent into
    Northumberlande,
And Somersett shiere should have raught to
    Cumberlande;
Than woulde I have stretched the countie of Warwicke
Uppon tainter hookes[56] and made ytt reache to Barwicke.
A pece of the Bisshoprique[57] shoulde have come
    southwarde —
Tut, tut, I tell yowe, I had wonderous feates towarde.

RESP. God hath placed me alreaddie in the best wise.

AVAR. Yea, but yet not haulfe so well as I coulde devise.   70
But no force. Well than, I see ye will none of mee.

RESP. No.

AVAR.   Than ye can be content I departe from yee.

RESP. Yea.

AVAR.   Well, yet and ye praie me, I will tarrye still.

RESP. No.

AVAR.   Well, speake me faire, and woo me yet, and I will.

RESP. No. Hens! Avaunt!

AVAR.   Have I had of youe suche a clogg,
And nowe youe byd me avaunte and make me a dogg?

RESP. Hens at ons.

AVAR.   Naie, tut, an ye will ha us, ha us.

RESP. Owte of my presence.

AVAR.   Well then, ye wilnot ha us.

RESP. No, avoide, I charge thee.

AVAR.   Than nedes departe I muste.

---

60 *clerke* learned man   61 *compacte* made successful   64 *raught*
reached   68 *towarde* impending   75 *clogg* obstacle

Adieu, in feith, I woulde have servyd youe of truste.   80
But sens Respublica hathe putt me to exile,
Where maye I goo kepe miselfe secrete for a while?
Is there never a goode chaplaine in all this towne,
That will for a while hide me under his gowne?
Never a goode farmer? never a goode merchaunte manne?
Well, I will goo pieke owt some corner yf I canne.
But first will I monishe my fellowes of this geare;
An we scape this plounge, I care not for the next yeare.
     Exeat
RESP. Nowe will I to Iustice and thother ladies three,
And praie that these vices maie all suppressed bee.   90
     Intrat People
But loe, heare cometh People. I will nowe torne againe
And firste knowe of his goode state by a woorde or
          twaine.

Actus Quinti, scena septima

Respublica, People

RESP. What standith he prying? Dareth he not entre?
PEOPLE Choulde vaine zee my ladie: but Isdare not venter[58].
RESP. Shrinke not backe from me, but drawe to me, my deare
          frend.
PEOPLE Chil virst knowe an ye bee alone, zo God me
          mende.
RESP. Come, here bee non but thie frends, me beleve.
PEOPLE Well, than, chil bee zo bolde to peake in by your
          leve.
RESP. How happeneth that thowe hast so long been me
          froo?
PEOPLE Marie, chill tell yowe: as soone as ye were agoe,
     Hither cam a zorte of courtnalls, harde men and zore;

---

81 *sens* since   86 *pieke* pick   87 *monishe* warn   88 *plounge* fall
2 *Choulde* I would   *venter* venture   4 *Chil* I will   *ʒo* so   *mende*
renew   6 *peake* peep   9 *ʒorte* group   *courtnalls* courtiers

Thei shaked me up, chwas ner zo rattled avore,   10
Theye vell all uppon me, catche awoorde that might
    catche,
Well was hym that at me, People, might geat a snatche.
Choulde have been at home rather then a newe grote.
Iche maie zedge to yowe, Isfearde pulling owte my
    throte.
They bade me pieke me home[59], and come att yowe no
    more.
An iche did, thei zware Isshoulde bee corrupt therefore.
Zo thieke prowte howrecop, what call ye hym?

RESP.   Insolence.
PEOPLE Yea, even thickesame, he vaire popt me to silence.
RESP. And howe ys it with youe now? better then it was?
PEOPLE All beginneth now to come gailie well to passe.   20
Wee heare of your goode vortune that goeth abowte,
Howe ye beeth permounted, which makithe all us proute.
And iche am hable sens to bie me a newe cote,
And Isthanke God chave in my purse a zilver grote.
I wis iche cowlde not zo zai these zixe yeares afore.
Who ever cawsed yt, ill thanke have they therefore.
RESP. Thei wilbe heare soone; byde youe theim here for a
    traine.
PEOPLE Masse, but I nynnat. Woulde ye have om sqwatte
    owt ons braine?
RESP. They shall not doe thee harme the value of a poincte.
PEOPLE Then an youe zaie the woorde, ichill ieoparde a
    ioincte.   30
RESP. If thei but offer thee wrong, they shall smarte
    therefore.
PEOPLE Naie, will ye bee zo goode to tye om up avore?
  And what shalche zai to om?

---

10 *chwas* I was *avore* before 12 *geat* get *snatche* grab 14 *zedge*
say 16 *corrupt* destroyed 17 *thieke* that *prowte* proud *howrecop* time-server 18 *popt* put 22 *permounted* advanced 24 *chave*
I have 28 *nynnat* will not *om* them *sqwatte* squash 30 *ieoparde*
risk *ioincte* limb

RESP.   Nothing but bee a bayte,
    Tyll 'take theim all here soodainelie I maie awayte.
        Exeat
PEOPLE Well, ytt shalbe doo. Choulde laugh and bothe my
            handes clappe,
    To zee Ricepuddingcakes[60] envies take in a trappe.
    And azee praie, if zome of om comnot yonder.
    Choulde my ladie had byd ner zo lytle longer[61].

Actus Quinti, scena octava

Insolence, Adulacion, Oppression, People, Avarice

INSO. Where is Avarice, howe? He doeth not nowe appere.
ADUL. He bydde me monishe youe that we might all mete
            here.
OPPR. But see where People staundeth.
ADUL.   What dothe he here now?
OPPR. Abought litle goodnes, I dare my woorde avowe.
INSO. Let us speake unto hym. People, wherefore and why,
    Like a loytring losell, standeste thowe heare idelye?
OPPR. Thowe comest to Respublica to make some mone.
ADUL. Orels some complainte.
PEOPLE   Youe all see cham here alone.
INSO. Ye muste have silver money, muste ye, ientilman?
    Youe cannot be content with suche coigne as wee can.   10
OPPR. We muste burne woode and cole: muste ye all of
            pleasaunce?
    Burne turves, or some of thy bedstrawe, with a vengeaunce.
ADUL. Ye muste eate freshe meate bowght from the
            shambles, muste ye?
    Eate garlike and onnyons and rootes or grasse, an luste ye.
INSO. In feith, I will whippe youe for this, ye peasaunte
            lowte.
ADUL. And twygge youe.

33 *bayte* bait   36 *envies* enemies   37 *azee* easy   4 *Abought* about
6 *loytring* loitering   *losell* vagabond   13 *shambles* meat market
16 *twygge* pull about

INSO.   Ere another yeare come abowte.

ADUL. But see where Avarice cometh rennyng veraie faste.

    Intrat Avarice

AVAR. I have trodde and scudde tyll my winde is almoste
       paste,

  Yet my mates are not where.

INSO. *et* ADUL.   We bee heare come of late.

AVAR. Be there not, trowe ye, honester men in Newgate?   20

INSO. No woordes of reproche, brother myne, I reade youe.

AVAR. None but goddigod eve, and goddigod spede youe.

  Fare ye well againe an ye bee faling owte nowe.

INSO. *et* ADUL. We mynde yt not.

AVAR.   Twere more neade to looke abowte youe.

INSO. Howe goethe all, tell us?

AVAR.   My Ladye is waxte froward.

  Our names bee all knowen, so there is araie towarde.

INSO. *et* OPPR. God spede us well.

AVAR.   Ons I am thruste owte of service.

ADUL. Alas, what maie I doe?

INSO. *et* OPPR.   Tell us thie best advise.

AVAR. Naie, I cannot have youe whan I woulde, none of
       yowe all;

  Therefore shifte for yourselves, eche one for me youe shall.   30

ADUL. Naie, for the pashe of God, tell us what beste to doo;

  Ye knowe I was ner slake to resorte youe untoo.

AVAR. Theis ladies that are come for comon weales reliefe

  Prepare to weorke us woo, and doo us all mischiefe.

INSO. Naie, by his precious populorum[62] I shwere

  Not the prowdest of them all can hurt me a heare.

OPPR. If theye offre of us to make theire gawdes or toyes,

  Theie shall [find], I trowe, we are no babes nor boyes.

AVAR. To prevaile againste them with force I doo despaire.

INSO. Bee that as bee maie.

ADUL.   I will fall to speaking faire.   40

---

18 *scudde* hurried   21 *reade* advise   22 *goddigod eve* God give you
good evening   25 *froward* perverse   26 *araie* trouble   31 *pashe*
passion   32 *slake* slack

Butte of all this trouble we maie thanke People, this
    wretche.

OPPR. Feith, vilaine, if wee scape, thow shalte an halter
    stretche.

ADUL. But what remedie therwhile?

AVAR.   Feith, all wilbe nawght.

ADUL. Tell us what to doo.

AVAR.   I will. Thei come. Wee are caught.

ADUL. Whether shall I renne?

AVAR.   Nowe sing a song, Honestie.

ADUL. I am past singing now.

AVAR.   Yes, one song, Honestie.
        Haye, haie, haie, haie,
        I wilbe merie while I maie.

Actus Quinti, scena nona

Veritee, Iustice, Avarice, Respublica, Adulacion,
Mercy, Peace, Insolence, Oppression, People

VER. Heare theye bee all fower. This is an happie chaunce.

AVAR. Take eche manne a ladie, sirs, and leate us goo daunce.

RESP. I leafte People heare for a traine to holde them talke.

AVAR. Alas that I coulde tell which waie beste hens to walke.
  What bee thes faire ladies? and whether will theye, trowe?

IUS. Wee arest youe, sirs, all fowre as ye stande in a rowe.
  Not so hardie in your hartes oure areste to gaine saie.

AVAR. Naie, we are content if ye let us gooe oure waie.

IUS. Noo, not a foote; we muste firste your reckeninge take.

AVAR. I nere bought nor solde with yowe, reckeninge to
    make,   10
  Nor I knowe not who yowe bee.

IUS.   Iustice is my name.

AVAR. Where is your dwelling?

IUS.   In heaven, and thens I came.

AVAR. Dwell ye in heaven, and so madde to come hither?
  All our hucking here is howe we maie geate thither.

---

3 *traine* time   14 *hucking* haggling

IUS. I bring heaven with me and make it where I am.

AVAR. Than, I praie youe, lett me bee your prentise, Madame.

   I wilbe at your becke.

IUS.   Ye shall ere ye departe.

AVAR. I woulde learne howe to make heaven withall my harte.

   Well, as for Ladie Misericordia,

   I remember I sawe youe with Respublica.   20

ADUL. Youe, if youe soo please, maie doo muche goode in this lande.

   Mannie att this howre dooe nede your goode helping hande.

AVAR. And ye cam downe from heaven too, I iudge.

MISER.   Yea sure.

AVAR. Why what folke are ye that cannot heaven endure?

   And what maie I call youe, ladie?

PAX   My name is Peace.

AVAR. Ye have long dwelte with us, wee have been long in peace.

PAX Cale ye it peace, sirrha, whan brother and brother

   Cannot bee content to live one by an other,

   Whan one for his howse, for his lande, yea for his grote,

   Is readie to strive, and plucke owte anothers throt?   30

   I will in all suche thinges make perfecte union.

AVAR. Than goode night the laweiers gaine, by Saincte Tronnion[63].

   Westminster Hale[64] might goo plaie if that cam to passe.

   Feithe, we must serve youe with a Supersideas[65].

VER. Well, leave vaine pratling, and nowe come aunswere to mee.

AVAR. I muste heare first what ye saie, and who ye bee.

VER. I am Dame Veritee.

AVAR.   What? the dawghter of Tyme?

VER. Yea.

AVAR.   I knowe my maister your father well afyne.

16 *prentise* apprentice   17 *becke* call

Welcome, faire ladie, swete ladie, litle ladye,
Plaine ladie, smoothe ladie, sometyme spittle[66] ladye,   40
Ladie longtong, ladye tell all, ladie make-bate,
And I beseche youe from whens are ye come of late?

VER. I am sproong owte of the earth.

AVAR.   What, ye doo butt ieste.

VER. The booke saieth *Veritas de terra orta est*[67].

AVAR. Happie is he which hathe that garden platte, I trowe,
Owte of which suche faire blossomes doe spring and
    growe.
Yet this one thing I saye –

VER.   What?

AVAR.   Ye are frende to fewe,
Preste to open all thinges and mennes manniers to shewe.

VER. If ye bee true and iuste that is your benefite.

AVAR. True or untrue, iuste or uniust, it is your spite,   50
And gladde ye are to take other folkes a tryppe
. . . . and than your owne selfe on the whippe[68].
Well ye might bee honeste of your tonge if yowe woulde.

VER. If your actes were honest, ye did but as ye shoulde.

AVAR. Who chargeth me with the cryme of anie vice?

VER. Thowe calst thieselfe Policie, and arte Avarice.

AVAR. Naie, I defie youre mallis; I am Policie.
Aske of my felowes here, am I not Policie?

VER. Ladies, will ye all see hym openlie tried?

IUS. If he bee an yll one, leate hym bee descryed.   60

VER. What haste thow in thie bosome?

AVAR.   Nothing I, truelie.

VER. Nothing trulie gotte, saie. Shewe ytt foorth openlie.

AVAR. What shoulde I shew foorth?

VER.   That bag in thie bosome hid.

AVAR. It lieth well, I thanke youe, as muche as thoughe
    I dyd.

VER. Naie, come on, owte with ytt.

---

40 *spittle* hospital (i.e. leper-house)   41 *make-bate* make-trouble
48 *Preste* quick   *manniers* manners, behaviour   51 *tryppe* error
57 *mallis* malice   60 *descryed* revealed

AVAR.   Loe, here tis for your fansie.

VER. Geve it me.

AVAR.   Yea, naie, I defie that polycye.

VER. Open yt.

AVAR.   Yea, that eche bodie might bee catching;
  Somes teeth I thinke water een sens to bee snatching.

VER. We muste nedes see what yt is.

AVAR.   Tis abag of rie.

VER. Rye, what rye?

AVAR.   A bag of rie.

VER.   Suche as men doe eate?   70

AVAR. A bag of rye flowre a greate deale better then
        wheate.

VER. Lett us see what rye ytt is; poore it owte in haste.

AVAR. Yea, shall? I trowe not. In dede soo might wee
        make waste.

VER. There is no remedie; powre ytt owte in my lappe.
  Naie, if there bee no choyse I will use myne owne cappe.

VER. So, a bag of rye, quod thoue?

AVAR.   Yea, so god me spede.

VER. Thou saiest even trueth; tis a bagg of rye[69] in dede:
  Usiree[70], periuree, pitcheree, patcherie,
  Pilferie, briberee, snatcherie, catcherie,
  Flatterie, robberie, clowterie, botcherie,   80
  Troumperye, harlotrie, myserie, tretcherie.

AVAR. There is too, an please youe, a litle sorcerie,
  Witcherie, bauderee, and suche other grosseree.

VER. And howe gotste thowe all this in thye possession?

AVAR. Pardon me, and I will make my confession.
  The worlde is harde and the bag is but veraie smale.
  I gotte it where I colde to goe on begging withall,
  A plaine true deling manne that loveth not to steale,

---

65 *fansie* whim   68 *Somes* some people's   78 *pitcheree* begging
with a pitcher *patcherie* clownish behaviour   80 *clowterie* shoddy
work *botcherie* clumsy work   81 *Troumperye* fraud *harlotrie*
prostitution *myserie* miserliness   83 *bauderee* procuring *grosseree* wickedness

And I durst not bee bolde to crave of comon weale.

VER. Now doe of thie gowne, and tourne the inside
        outwarde.   90

AVAR. Leate me alone and an angell[71] for a rewarde.

VER. Come of, atons: whan? come of. No more gawdies
        nor iapes.

AVAR. Muste I nedes whipp over the chaine like a iacke-a-
        napes.

RESP. Owte, in the vertue of God, what doo yee here see?

AVAR. All this had been loste, Respublica, but for me.

RESP. O lorde, where hast thow dragged up all these purses?

VER. Where he hathe had for theim manie thowsaunde
        curses.

RESP. Where hast thow gotten them? Tell trueth and do
        not lye.

AVAR. Where no honest manne coulde have gotten theym
        but I.

In blinde corners where some woulde have hourdd
        theim   100

Had I not take theym with the manier[72] and bouredened
        theym.

RESP. And whither was yt thine entent to conveigh theim
        now?

AVAR. I hidde them that I might bring theim safelie to
        youe.

I durst not beare theim openlie, to God I vowe;

I wis ye have harde me blame piekepurses or nowe.

And this is all yours.

VER.   It is hers in veraie dede.

AVAR. With sufferaunce I coulde gette mo to helpe hir
        nede.

VER. Howe saie ye, Respublica, nowe to Policie?

RESP. I ner suspecte hym nor hadde hym in zelosie.

VER. Een suche like counterfaictes shall all the rest appere.   110

---

89 *crave* beg 90 *doe of* take off 92 *atons* at once *gawdies*
pretences *iapes* tricks 93 *iacke-a-napes* monkey 100 *hourded*
hoarded 101 *bourdened* taken as a burden 109 *ʒelosie* mistrust

Sirs, doe of your utmoste robes eche one even heare.
Now what these are yee see plaine demonstration.

RESP. Insolence. Oppression. Adulacion.

O lorde, howe have I bee used these five yeres past?

PEOPLE Naie, Isner thought better of om, iche, by goddes
vast.

Vey Madame, my ladie, suche strussioners as these
Have ofte made youe beeleve the moone was a grene
chese.

VER. Nowe ye see what thei are, the punishment of this
Muste be referred to the goddesse Nemesis[73].

She is the mooste highe goddesse of correcçion,   120
Cleare of conscience and voide of affeccion.

She hath powre from above, and is newlie sent downe
To redresse all owtrages in cite and in towne.

She hath powre from Godde all practise to repeale
Which might bring annoyaunce to Ladie Comonweale.

To hir office belongeth the prowde toverthrowe
And suche to restore as iniurie hath browght lowe.

Tys hir powre to forbidde and punishe in all eastates
All presumptuous immoderate attemptates.

Hir cognisaunce therefore is a whele and wings to flye,   130
In token hir rewle extendeth ferre and nie.

A rudder eke she bearethe in hyr other hande,
As directrie of all thinges in everye lande.

Than pranketh she hir elbowes owte under hir side,
To keape backe the headie and to temper theire pride.

To hir therefore, dere sisters, we muste nowe resorte,
That she maie geve sentence uppon this nawghtie sorte.

She knowith what is fyttest for theire correction:
Nemesis muste therefore herin geve direction.

---

111 *utmoste* outermost 115 *Isner* I never *vast* face 116 *strus-sioners* destroyers (or 'deceivers' Magnus) 121 *affeccion* partiality
124 *practise* contriving *repeale* put right 129 *attemptates* attempts
130 *cognisaunce* sign 131 *ferre* far *nie* near 133 *directrie*
director 134 *pranketh* forces out 137 *nawghtie* wicked *sorte*
gang

ıus. Than, People, while we Ladie Nemesis doo fett,   140
All these offendours in thie custodie wee sett,
Theim to aprehende and kepe tyll wee come againe.

PEOPLE An ye geve me toritee chill kepe om that is plaine.

INSO. *et* OPPR. Shall People kepe us, of whom we have
been lordes?

PEOPLE Stande still, or by Iisse [chil] bynde youe vaste
with chordes.

Naie, sirs, iche ha youe nowe in my custoditee.

AVAR. Masse, I wilbe gone for myne owne comoditie.

PEOPLE Zoft, whether wilte thow? Nilt thowe not bee
roylled?

Stande styll, skitbraind theaff, or thy bones shall be
coilled.

Yond bee thei comyng nowe, che warte, that will tame ye. 150
A zee, arte thowe gon too? Come backe, and evill a thee.

Actus Quinti, scena decima

*Nemesis, Respublica, Misericordia, Veritas, Iusticia,
Pax, People, Insolence, Oppression, Adulacion,
Avarice*

NEMESIS Come foorth, Respublica, our derling mooste
dere.

RESP. At youre woorde, mooste gracious ladie, I am here.

NEMESIS Are these your trustie men that had youe in
govermente?

PEOPLE The skitbraines nold not bee roilled ner sens ye
wente.

NEMESIS People, whie art thow bashefull and standest soo
farre?

Bee of goode chere nowe, and I warraunte thee come ner.

---

143 *toritee* authority   145 *Iisse* Jesus   *vaste* fast   147 *comoditie*
advantage   148 *Nilt* wilt not   *roylled* ruled   149 *skitbraind*
harebrained   *coilled* beaten   150 *che warte* I assure [you]   151 *thee*
thrive   4 *nold* would not   *ner* (redundant) never   6 *ner* near

PEOPLE I nil come no nere: cha not bee haled up with
    states,
  But Iscannot bee fichaunte[74] enoughe emongst my
    mates.
NEMESIS Come nere whan I bydde thee.
PEOPLE   Marye, but I ninnat.
  I nam not worthye to perke with yowe, no I nam not.   10
NEMESIS Well, Respublica, are these youre late governoures,
  Whom ye tooke for faithfull and trustie counsailours?
RESP. Yea, forsouth, Madame.
AVAR.   These three bee, but I am none,
  For I was discharged nigh haulfe an howre agone.
NEMESIS Come firste stande foorth here, thow Adulacion.
ADUL. Speake a goode woorde for me, Ladie Compassion.
PEOPLE Naie, she shall not nede; I chill speake for the
    miselfe.
  Madame, take goode hede, for this is a naughtie elfe.
ADUL. Naie, Madame, the cause of all this was Avarice.
  He forged us newe names and dyd us all entice.   20
OPPR. Wee neither dyd nor coulde weorke but by his
    advise.
ADUL. Because I gotte no more he chidde me ones or twise.
INSO. Madame, onlye Avarice made us all to fall.
AVAR. Yea? Falle to peaching? naie, then will I tell all.
  Madame, ere I had taught these merchauntes enie while,
  Thei were conynger then I, all men to beeguile.
  And Veritee sawe myne were small purses and baggs
  Tottering looce abought me like windshaken rags.
  But he that shoulde have bagged that Insolence dyd winne
  Muste have made a poke to putt five or six shiers in;   30
  He muste have wyde sackes for castells, townes, and
    woodes.
  The canvesse to make them of were woorth ten tymes
    my goodes.

7 *cha* I have   *haled* brought   *states* people of rank   9 *ninnat* will
not   10 *perke* show off   18 *elfe* mischief-maker   24 *peaching*
informing   26 *conynger* more cunning   28 *Tottering* hanging
looce loose   30 *poke* bag   *shiers* shires   32 *canvesse* canvas

Than Oppression here, to feather well his neaste,
Cared not of theire liuelood whom he dispossste.
Bisshops, deanes, prouestes, yea poore folke from the
      spittle,
Landes with churche and chapple, all was for him to litle.
Poore I did not soo; I scraped but lytle crummes
And here and there, with odde endes, patchid up my
      summes.
Flatterye gotte his thrifte by counterfaicte honestie,
Yet by these tenne bones[75], I bydde hym use modestie.   40
Therefore spare not hym, he will ner come to goode
      passe:
But I maie welbe mended by the Marye Masse.
MISER. Ladie Nemesis, now have yee occasion
And matier to shewe youre commiseracion.
It is muche more glorie, and standith with more skyll,
Loste shepe to recover then the scabye to spill.
IUS. But howe shall this redresse bee well prosecuted,
If Iustice with Mercye shalbee executed?
Streight Iustice muste suche greate enormiteis redresse;
Severitee muste putt men in feare to transgresse.   50
Iustice muste geve eche manne that he dothe deserve.
MISER. If offendours were not, wherefore might Mercye
      serve?
AVAR. Stike harde to it, goode shwete Ladie Compassion;
We are els undoone, by cockes bytter passion.
MISER. Veritee, how saie youe? have I not spoken well?
VER. Mercie in one place with Iustice sometyme maie dwell,
And right well agree togither. Howe saie youe, Peace?
PAX Where althing is well emended I doo encreace.
NEMESIS Ladies, we have harde all your descrete advises,
And eche one shall have some parte of youre devises;   60
Neither all nor none shall taste of severitee.
But as theye are nowe knowen throughe Ladie Veritee,

---

38 *summes* amounts   39 *thrifte* fortune   44 *commiseracion*
sympathy   46 *scabye* scoundrel *spill* destroy   54 *cockes* God's
58 *emended* amended   59 *advises* counsels

So shall theye receyve oure mercie or our ire,
As the wealthe of Respublica shall best require.
Now, Adulacion, what saieth youe in this case?

ADUL. Nought in myne excuse, but submitte me to your
grace.
Onelie this: I promise, if I maie Mercye fynde,
Utterlie for ever to chaunge my wicked mynde.
I nere sought afore myne owne private gayne so muche,
But I will ferther Commonweales tenne tymes so muche.   70

NEMESIS Well thowe maiest become a worthie subiecte,
yt ys plaine.

ADUL. Els ye knowe at all tymes howe to reache me againe.

NEMESIS Thowe mightest swerve of frailtee, thow mightst
doo too please,
Thow mightst doo for feare, thow mightst doo too lyve
in ease.
Well uppon thie promyse for ones wee pardon thee;
Goo, and see that from hensfoorthe thow bee perfeicte
Honestee.

ADUL. So long as shall please God to geve me life and heale
I shall mooste duelie serve God and the Commonweale.

AVAR. Nowe to thee, Avarice, have att thye petticote[76].

NEMESIS Now, the plague of Comonweales, as all men
doo note,   80
Come foorth, Avarice: to spare thee wilbe no boote;
Thow muste bee plucked upp een bye the veraie roote,
Because thowe scrapedst up what ever thow mightst geate.

AVAR. In dede, I thanke God, there is no man in my debte.

NEMESIS And because thowe caughtst yt, by wrong
contribucion,
Thow shalte firste and formooste make restitucion.

AVAR. Leat me than with pardon goe hens abowte yt
lightlye.

NEMESIS No, ye shall have helpe to see it doon
uprightlie.
People, take this felowe –

---

79 *petticote* under-garment   81 *boote* advantage

AVAR.   Godde save me from this plounge.
NEMESIS That he maie bee pressed, as men doo presse a
                    spounge,   90
  That he maie droppe ought teverye man hys lotte,
  To the utmooste ferthing that he hath falslie gotte.
PEOPLE An ye bydde mee, chill squease hym as drie as a
                    kyxe.
AVAR. Naye, the pashe of godde, I shall then die of the flixe.
NEMESIS Naie, thowe shalte deliver hym to the hedd
                    officer,
  Which hathe authoritee, iustice to mynister.
PEOPLE Chil lyver hym to the counstable and come againe.
NEMESIS Now, Iustice, for these twoo that doe here remaine,
  Because the faulte of Insolence is hainous and greate,
  Lucifers owne faulte taspire to the highest seate,   100
  And because Oppression hath wronged men so sore
  That he spoiled innocentes of all thei had and more,
  People shall deliver them unto safe costodie
  Where thei maie no farther anoye anie bodie.
  Whan the tyme maie serve texamine and trie their cause,
  Call them bothe before youe, and iudge them by the lawse.
PEOPLE And shalche carrie awaie these same twoo men also?
NEMESIS Yea, goe deliver them to an officer, goe.
  Now, dearling Respublica, ye are in tholde goode eastate
  And they taken awaie that spoiled youe of late.   110
  Nowe cleve to these ladies from heaven to youe directe:
  They from all corruption will youe safe protecte.
  Well, I muste goe hens to an other countreye nowe,
  That hathe of redresse the like case that was in youe.
  I leave youe for thys tyme, immortall thankes to geve
  To Godde and your Soveraigne which doo youe thus
                    relieve.
RESP. Thankes be to thee, O Lorde, which haste this worlde
                    wrowght,

89 *plounge* plunge, fall 90 *spounge* sponge 93 *kyxe* dry stalk
94 *flixe* 'the runs', dysentery 97 *lyver* deliver 99 *hainous*
criminal

And hast me too this state from utter ruine brought.

PAX Now leat us all togither, bothe with harte and voice,
In God and in Quene Marie mooste ioyfullie reioyce.   120

VER. Praying that hir reigne mooste graciouslye begonne
Maie long yeares endure as hithertoo yt hath doone.

MISER. Praie wee forre hir Counsaile to have long life and
       healthe.

IUS. Theire Soveraigne to serve.

PAX   And to mainteine Comonwealthe.

OMNES *Amen.*

    Cantent et exeant

▶ ▶ ▶

A new Tragicall Comedie of *Apius and Virginia*,

Wherein is liuely expressed a rare
example of the vertue of Chastitie,
by Virginias constancy, in wishing
rather to be slaine at her owne Fathers handes, then to be deflowred of the wicked Iudge
Apius.

By R. B.

The Players names.

Virginius.	Conscience.
Mater.	Iustice.
Virginia:	Claudius.
Haphazard.	Rumour.
Mansipulus.	Comforte.
Mansipula.	Rewarde.
Subseruus.	Doctrina.
Apius.	Memorie.

Imprinted at London, by Wil-
liam How, for Richard Ihones.
1575.

Facsimile of the title-page of the 1575 edition of Apius and Virginia

The play was entered in the Stationers' Register in 1567, but the only known edition was printed by William How for Richard Jones in 1575. Three copies of this survive, the one in the British Museum (C.34.b.2) being the basis for the present edition. The title-page reads:

A new Tragicall Comedie of Apius and Virginia, Wherein is lively expressed a rare example of the vertue of Chastitie, by Virginias constancy, in wishing rather to be slaine at her owne Fathers handes, then to be deflowred of the wicked Iudge Apius.
By R.B.
The Players names.

Virginius.	Conscience.
Mater.	Iustice.
Virginia.	Claudius.
Haphazard.	Rumour.
Mansipulus.	Comforte.
Mansipula.	Rewarde.
Subservus.	Doctrina.
Apius.	Memorie.

It has been suggested that the author was Richard Bower, who was Master of the Chapel Royal in the years 1561–6, but there is not a great deal of evidence to support this. The list of players is not divided for doubling, and this may suggest that the first actors were indeed boys.

The most useful modern editions are:

R. Dodsley, *A Select Collection of Old Plays*, ed. W. C. Hazlitt, Vol. 4, 1874

J. S. Farmer, (1) *Five Anonymous Plays*, Fourth Series, 1905; (2) *Tudor Facsimile Text*, 1908

W. W. Greg and R. B. McKerrow, *Malone Society Reprint*, 1911 (this edition takes account of corrections from the two copies in U.S.A.)

The chief source of the play is Chaucer's *Phisicien's Tale*, which it follows closely, though there are a number of modifications and expansions which are intended to clarify the author's particular moral and tragic objectives. The author shows considerable skill in converting the narrative poem into dramatic terms.

It will be observed that the text is well provided with stage directions. The modifications which I have made, together with modern scene headings, are printed in brackets.

Apius and Virginia

THE PROLOGUE[1]

Qui cupis aethereas et summas scandere sedes
    Vim simul ac fraudem discute, care, tibi:
Fraus nulla iuvat, non fortia facta iuvabunt;
    Sola Dei tua te trahet tersa fides.
Qui placet in terris intactae Palladis instar
    Vivere Virginiam nitore, virgo, sequi.
Quem tulit et lustus discas gaudia magna
    Vitae dum Parcae scindere fila parent.
Huc ades, O virgo, pariter moritura sepulchro.
    Sic ait et facies pallida morte mutat.   10

Who doth desire the trump of fame to sound unto the
    skies,
Or els who seekes the holy place where mighty Ioue he
    lies,
He must not by deceitfull mind, nor yet by puissant
    strength,
But by the faith and sacred lyfe he must it win at length,
And what she be that virgins lyfe on earth wold gladly
    leade
The fluds that Virginia did fall I wish her reade,
Her doller and hir dolefull losse, and yet her ioyes at
    death.

16 *reade* consider   17 *doller* dolour, grief

'Come, virgins pure, to grave with mee,' quoth she with
    latest breath.
You lordings all, that present be this tragidie to heare,
Note well what zeale and love heerein doth well appeare.   20
And ladies you, that linked are in wedlocke bandes for
    ever,
Do imitate the life you see, whose fame will perish never.
But virgins you, oh ladies faire, for honour of your
    name,
Doo lead the life apparent heere to win immortall fame.
Let not the blinded God of Love, as poets tearme him so,
Nor Venus with her venery, nor lechors, cause of wo,
Your virgins name to spot or file: deare dames, observe
    the like
That faire Verginia did observe, who rather wish the
    knife
Of fathers hand hir life to ende then spot her chastety.
As she did waile, waile you her want, you maids of
    courtesie[2].   30
If any by example heere would shun that great anoy,
Our authour would reioyce in hart, and we would leap
    for ioy.
Would Gods that our indever may as well to please your
    eares
As is our auctors meaning heere; then were we voyde of
    feares:
But paciently wee wish you beare with this our first
    attempt,
Which surely will to do our best, then yeeld us no
    contempt.
And as you please in pacient wise our first for to
    receive,
Ere long a better shall you win, if God do graunt us leave.

FINIS

26 *venery* lust   27 *file* defile   29 *then* than   31 *anoy* harm
34 *auctors* author's

[Scene i. Outside the house of Virginius]

VIRGINIUS

Before the time that Fortunes lot dyd shew ech fate his
  dome,
Or byrde, or beast, or fish, or foule, on earth had taken
  rome,   40
The Gods they did decree to frame, the thing is ended
  now,
The heavens, and the planets eke, and moyst from ayre to
  bow[3].
Then framed they the man of mould and clay, and gave
  him time to raign,
As seemed best their sacred minds to runne and turne
  againe.
They framed also after this, out of his tender side,
A peece of much formositie with him for to abide,
From infansie to lusty youth, and so to raigne awhile,
And well to live, tyl Etas[4] he unwares do hym begyle.
And sith to see these giftes of them, on grounded cau[s]e
  to vew
Not daintyly to deck them up, which after they may rew: 50
Wherfore I thank the Gods above, that yeeld to mee
  such fate,
To lincke to mee so iust a spouse, and eke so loving mate.
By her I have a virgin pure, an ympe of heavenly race,
Both sober, meeke, and modest too, and vertuous in lyke
  case.
To Temple will I wend therfore, to yeeld the Gods their
  praise
For that they have thus luckely anexed with my daies.
But stay, behold the peerelesse sparks wherof my tongue
  dyd talke
Approch in presence of my sight; to church I deeme they
  walk.

39 *dome* judgement   46 *formositie* beauty   52 *eke* also   53 *ympe*
child   56 *anexed* linked

But stay I wyll, and shroud me secretly a while
To see what witte, or counsell grave, proceedeth from
      their stile.   60

   Heere entreth Mater and Virginia

[MATER]

The perte and pricking prime of youth ought
      chastisment to have,
But thou, deare daughter, needest not; thy self doth
      shew thee grave.
To see how Phoebus with his beames hath youth so
      much infected,
It doth me woe to see them crave; the thing should be
      detected[5].
I draw to grave, and naught can leave of thee to be
      desired
As much as duty to thy deare, as reason hath required,
Thy sufferent lord and frindly feare, Virginius, father
      thine,
To nourse as doth become a childe, when boanes are
      buried mine.

VIRGINIA[6]

Refel your minde of mourning plaints, deare mother; rest
      your minde.
For though that duty dainty were, Dame Nature will
      me binde   70
So much to do, and further force of Gods that rule the
      skies,
The globe and eke the element, they would me els
      dispies.

MATER

Then if the Gods have graunted thee such grace to love
      thy syer,
When time shall choose thee out a make, be constant, I
      requier.

60 *stile* mode of conversation   61 *pricking* vigorous   67 *sufferent* patient, tolerant   69 *Refel ... of* dispel from   70 *dainty* over-nice   72 *element* atmosphere   74 *make* mate

Love, live, and lyke him well before you graunt him
     grace or faith,
So shall your love continue long: experience thus he saith.

VIRGINIA

I graunt, deare Dame, I doo agree,
When time shall so provide:
But tender youth and infansie
Doth rather with me bide.   80
What should I lose Dianas gifte,
And eke the spring to shun
By which Acteon[7] fateally
His finall race did run,
Should I as abiect be esteemed
Throughout Pernassus[8] hill,
Or should my virgins name be filde
It were to great a skyll.
But yet it is unspotted, loe,
Right well I doo conceave.   90
When wedlocke doth require the same
With parents love and leave,
Yet obstinate I wyll not be,
But willing will me yeeld
When you commaund and not before:
Then duety shall me sheeld.

VIRGINIUS

Ah, Gods that rule and raine in heavens, in seas, in
     flods, and lands,
Two couple such I surely deeme you never made with
     hands.
A, Gods, why doo ye not compel eche Dame the lyke to
     showe?
And every Impe of her againe, her duty thus to know?   100
I cannot stay my tounge from talke; I needes must call
     my deare.
Oh spouse wel met, and daughter to, what newes? how
     do you cheare?

87 *filde* defiled   88 *skyll* matter

MATER

O deare Virginius, ioy to me, oh pearelesse spouse and
  mate,
In health I praise the Gods I am, and ioifull for thy
  state.

VIRGINIUS

Virginia, my daughter deare,
How standeth all with thee?

VIRGINIA

Like happie state as mother tolde,
Like ioyfull sight to mee.

VIRGINIUS

By the Gods, wife, I ioy me, that have such a treasure⁹,
Such gemme and such iuell, surmounting all measure,   110
Such a happy spouse, such a fortunate dame,
That no blot or staine can impayre her fame
Against such an Impe and graffe of my tree
As cleare doth surmount all others that bee.

MATER

Nay rather, deare spouse, how much is my case
To be now advaunced by such happy grace
Doth dayly distill my husband so loving,
Graunting and geving to all thing behoving,
Ioying in me and in the fruicte of my wombe.
Who would not requit it, the Gods yeelde their dome.   120
And if it be I, the Gods doo destroy mee
Rather then sinne so sore should annoy me.

VIRGINIUS

Oh wife, refell thy wishing for woe,
My selfe thy faute right well do know.
And rather I wish my selfe to be slaine,
Then thou or thy daughter ought wo should sustaine.

VIRGINIA

Oh father, my comfort, oh mother, my ioy,
O deare, and O sufferaigne, do cease to employ

---

109 *ioy* rejoice   110 *iuell* jewel   113 *graffe* branch   128 *sufferaigne*
sovereign

Such dolorus talking where dangers are none.
Where ioyes are attendant what needeth this mone?   130
You matron, you spouse, you nurse, and you wife,
You comfort, you only the some of his lyfe:
You housband, you harte, you ioye, and you pleasure,
You king and you keyser, to her only treasure:
You father, you mother, my lyfe doth sustaine,
I babe and I blisse your health am againe[10].
Forbeare then your dolor, let mirth be frequented.
Let sorow departe, and be not attempted.

VIRGINIUS

Oh wife, oh spouse, I am contente.

MATER

Oh husband.

VIRGINIA

             Oh father we doo consent.   140
   Sing heere

ALL *singe this*

The trustiest treasure in earth as wee see
Is man, wife, and children in one to agree.
Then friendly and kindly, let measure be mixed
With reason, in season, where friendship is fixed.

VIRGINIUS

When nature nursed first of all yong Alexander
    learned,
Of whom the poets mencion make in iudgement so
    deserned,
Oh, what did want that love procured his vital end well
    neare?
This is the hope where parents love their children do not
    feare.

ALL *sing this*

The trustiest treasure in earth as wee see
Is man, wife, and children &c.   150

134 *keyser* caesar (emperor)   143 *kindly* according to natural
affection   146 *deserned* discerning

MATER

When time King Nisus[11] would not let his daughter to
    be taught,
Of any one correcting hand to nurture[12] to be brought,
She, void of duty, cut his lockes and golden tresses cleare,
Whereby his realme was overrun, and she was payd her
    hier.

ALL *sing this*

The trustiest treasure in earth as we see
Is man, wife, and children &c.

VIRGINIA

When Dedalus[13] from Creete did flie
With Icarus his ioy,
He, naught regarding fathers words,
Did seeke his owne anoy.   160
He mounted up into the skies,
Wherat the Gods did frowne,
And Phoebus sore his winges did frie,
And hedlonge flings him downe.

ALL *sing this*

The trustiest treasure in earth as we see
Is man, wife, and children &c.

VIRGINIUS

Then sith that persualitie[14] doth partly discorde move,
And hatred often times doth creepe where overmuch wee
    love,
And if we love no whit at all the faming trump will
    sound,
Come wife, come spouse, come daughter deare, let measure
    beate the ground.   170

ALL *sing this*

The trustiest treasure in earth as we see
Is man, wife, and children in one to agree.
Then friendly and kindly, let measure be mixed
With reason, in season, where frindship is fixed.

    [*Exeunt*]

[Scene ii. The same]

Here entreth Haphazard the Vice

[HAPHAZARD]

Very well, sir, very well, sir, it shalbe doone,
As fast as ever I can prepare.
Who dippes with the Divel, he had neede have a long
    spoone[15],
Or els full smale will be his fare.
Yet a proper gentleman I am of truthe.
Yea, that may yee see by my long side gowne[16].   180
Yea, but what am I; a scholer, or a scholemaister, or els
    some youth,
A lawier, a studient, or els a countrie cloune,
A brumman[17], a baskit maker, or a baker of pies,
A flesh or a fishmonger, or a sower of lies,
A louse or a louser, a leeke or a larke,
A dreamer, a drommell, a fire or a sparke,
A caitife, a cutthrote, a creper in corners,
A herbraine, a hangman, or a grafter of horners[18];
By the Gods, I know not how best to devise,
My name or my property, well to disguise;   190
A marchaunte, a may poole, a man or a mackrell,
A crab or a crevise, a crane or a cockerell.
Most of all these my nature doth inioy,
Somtime I advaunce them, somtime I destroy:
A mayde or a mussell bote, a wife or a wilde ducke,
As bolde as blinde bayerd[19], as wise as a wood cocke,
As fine as phippence[20], as proude as a pecocke,
As stout as a stockefish, as meeke as a mecocke,
As bigge as a begger, as fat as a foole,
As true as a tinker, as riche as an owle.   200
With hey tricke, how trowle[21], trey trip, and trey trace,
Trowle hazard in a vengeance, I beshrew his knaves face;

---

186 *drommell* sleepy-head   188 *herbraine* harebrain   192 *crevise*
crayfish   198 *stockefishe* dried cod *mecocke* coward

For tro and trowle hazard, keepe such a range,
That poore Haphazard was never so strange.
But yet, Haphazard, be of good cheere,
Goe play and repast thee, man; be mery to yeere.
Though vittaile be dainty and hard for to get
Yet perhaps a number will die of the swet[22];
Though it be in hazard, yet happely I may,
Though mony be lacking, yet one day go gay.   210
    Enter Mansipulus and Mansipula

MANSIPULUS

When[23], Maud, with a pestelence, what makst thou no
    hast?
Of Baybery insence[24] belike thou wouldest tast.
By the Gods, I have stayed a full great while;
My lorde he is neare hand by this at the Church stile,
And al for Maud mumble turde, that mampodding
    madge[25].
By the Gods, if she hie not, ile geve her my badge.

MANSIPULA

What, drake-nosed[26] drivell, begin you to floute?
Ile fry you in a fagot sticke, by cocke, goodman loute.
You boaster, you bragger, you brawling knave,
Ile pay thee thy fortypence, thou brawling slave.   220
My ladies great busines belike is at ende
When you, goodman dawcocke, lust for to wend.
You codshed, you crackerope[27], you chattering pye,
Have with ye, have at ye, your manhode to try.

HAPHAZARD

What holde your hands, masters, what? Fie, for shame,
    fie.
What culling? what lulling? what stur have wee here?
What tugging? what lugging? what pugging by the eare?
What, part and be friends and ende all this strife.

---

203 *tro* trust   216 *badge* blow   217 *drivell* imbecile   222 *dawcocke*
simpleton   226 *culling* hugging   *lulling* soothing   227 *pugging*
pulling

MANSIPULUS

Nay, rather I wishe hir the end of my knife.

MANSIPULA

Drawe it; geve mee it. I will it receave   230
So that for to place it I might have good leave.
By the Gods, but for losing my land, lyfe and living,
It should be so placed he should have ill thrivinge.

MANSIPULUS

By the Gods, how ungraciously the vicksen she chatteth.

MANSIPULA

And he even as knavishly my answer he patteth.

HAPHAZARD

Here is naught els but railing of words out of reason,
Now tugging, now tattling, now musling in season.
For shame, be contented and leave of this brawling.

MANSIPULUS

Content, for I shall repent it for this my tonge wralling.

MANSIPULA

Thow knave, but for thee, ere this time of day,   240
My ladies faire pue had been strawed full gay
With primroses, couslips, and violets sweete,
With mints and with marigolds, and margerum meete,
Which now lyeth uncleanly and all long of thee,
That a shame recompence thee, for hindring mee.

MANSIPULUS

Ah, pretie pranck parnel, the coushen and booke
Whereon he shoulde reade and kneele are present here,
        looke.
My lorde, when he seeth mee, he will cast such an eye
As pinch wyll my hart neare ready to die,
And thus wise, and thus wise, his hand wyll be walking;   250
With 'Thou precious knave, away, get thee packing!'
        Here let hym fight

HAPHAZARD

Nay then, by the masse, its time to be knacking.

239 *wralling* railing   241 *pue* pew   *strawed* strewn   243 *margerum*
marjoram (Origanum vulgare)   246 *pranck* adorned   *parnel* wanton

No words at all but to me he is poynting.
Nay, have at you againe, you shall have your
    annoynting.

MANSIPULA

Body of me, hold yf ye can!
What, will you kill such a proper man?

HAPHAZARD

Nay, sure I have done when women do speake.
Why would the knave my pacience so breake?

MANSIPULUS

Well, I must begon, there is no remedy,
For feare my tayle makes buttons[28], by mine honesty.   260

HAPHAZARD

For reverence on your face, your nose and your chin,
By the Gods, have ye hard such an unmannerly villin?

MANSIPULA

I never heard one so rancke of rudnesse.

MANSIPULUS

In faith it is but for lacke of lewdnesse;
But here I burne day light, while thus I am talking.
Away, come Mansipula, let us be walking.

MANSIPULA

Contented Mansipulus, have with thee with speede.

HAPHAZARD

Nay, stay yet, my freendes, I am not agreede.

MANSIPULA

Wee dare not tary, by God wee sweare.

HAPHAZARD

Nay, tary, take comfort with you for to beare.   270
It is but in hazard and yf you be mist,
And so it may happen you feele not his fist.
Perhaps he is stayde by talke with some friend.
It is but in hazarde: then sing you or you wend.
Let hope be your helper, your care to defend.

252 *knacking* beating   263 *rancke* abundant   264 *lewdnesse* knowledge

MANSIPULUS

    By hap or by hazard, we singe or we crie.

    Then singe let us say so, let sorow go by.

MANSIPULA

    We can but be beaten, that is the worst.

       Enter Subservus

SUBSERVUS

    What, how, Mansipulus, thou knave, art thou curst?

    My lorde standeth talking and I gape for thee.   280

    Come away with a wannion, runne, hast and hie.

MANSIPULUS

    Nay, herken, Subservus, stay, I pray thee.

    Let us have a song and then have with thee.

SUBSERVUS

    Content if thou hie thee.

Sing heere ALL

    Hope so, and hap so, in hazard of thretninge,

    The worst that can hap, lo, in end is but beating.

MANSIPULUS

    What if my lordinge doo chaunce for to misse me,

       The worst that can happen is cudgell will kisse mee.

    In such kinde of sweetnes, I sweare by Gods mother,

    It will please me better, it were on some other,   290

       With thwicke thwack, with thump thump,

         With bobbing and bum,

       Our syde saddle shoulders shal sheilde that doth come.

         Hope so, and hap so, in hazarde &c.

MANSIPULA

    If case that my lady do threaten my case,

    No cause to contrary, but beare hir a space,

    Untill she draw home, lo, where so she will use me,

    As docters doth doubt it, how should I excuse me,

       With thwicke thwack, with thump thump,

         With bobbing and bum,   300

       Our side saddle shoulders shal sheilde that doth come.

         Hope so, and hap so, in hazard &c.

281 *wannion* vengeance

SUBSERVUS
  What if your company cause me have woo,
  I minde not companyons so soone to forgo.
  Let hope holde the helmet till brunt it be past,
  For bloes are but buffits, and words but a blast,
    With thwick thwack, with thump thump,
      With bobbing and bum,
    Our side saddle shoulders shal sheild that doth come.
      Hope so, and hap so, in hazard &c.   310

HAPHAZARD
  Then let us be mery, it is but by hap;
  A hazardly chaunce may harbor a clap.
  Bestur ye, be mery, be glad and be ioying,
  For bloes are but buffits, and smale time annoying,
    With thwick thwack, with thump thump,
      With bobbing and bum,
    Our side saddle shoulders shal sheild that doth
      come.
      Hope so, and hap so, in hazard &c.
      The end of the song

ALL *speaketh this*
  Haphazard, farewell; the Gods do thanke thee.
    Exiunt

HAPHAZARD
  Farewell, my friends, farwell, goe prancke yee.   320
  By the Gods, Haphazard, these men have tried thee.
  Who sayd thou wast no man, sure he belied thee.
  By Ioue, master marchaunt by sea or by land
  Would get but smale argent if I did not stand
  His very good master: I may say to you
  When he hazards in hope what hap will insue.
  In court I am no man. By cocke, sir, ye lie:
  A plowman perhaps, or ere that he die,
  May hap be a gentleman, a courtier or captaine,
  And hap may so hazard he may goe a begging.   330
  Perhap that a gentleman heyre to great land,

320 prancke dance   324 argent money

Which selleth his living for mony in hand,
In hazard it is the bying of more,
Perhaps he may ride when spent is the store.
Hap may so hazard, the moone may so chaunge,
That men may be masters, and wives will not raunge.
But in hazard it is in many a grange
Lest wives were the codpiece, and maydens coy straunge[29].
As pecockes sit perking by chaunce in the plomtree,
So maides would be masters, by the guise of this countrey. 340
Haphazard eche state full well that he markes
If hap the skie fall, we hap may have larkes.
Well, fare ye well now, for better or worse,
Put hands to your pockets, have minde to your purse.

 Exit

[Scene iii. The house of Apius]

 Enter Judge Apius

[APIUS]
 The forowed face of Fortunes force my pinching paine
   doth move:
 I, setled ruler of my realme, inforced am to love.
 Judge Apius I, the princelest judge that raigneth under
   sonne,
 And have bene so esteemed long, but now my force is
   done:
 I rule no more, but ruled am; I do not judge but am
   judged.
 By beauty of Virginia my wisdome all is trudged.   350
 Oh perelesse dame, Oh passing peece, Oh face of such a
   feature
 That never erst with bewty such matched was by nature!
 Oh fond Apelles[30], pratling foole, why boastest thou so
   much

---

336 *raunge* go free 345 *forowed* furrowed 347 *princelest* most
princely 350 *trudged* (?) conquered

The famost peece thou madst in Greece whose liments
      were such?
Or why didst thou, deceved man, for beuty of thy worke,
In such a sort, with fond desire where no kinde lyfe
      dyd lurke,
With raging fits thou, foole, ran mad, oh fond
      Pigmalion?[31]
Yet sure if that thou sawest my deare, the like thou
      couldst make none.
Then what may I, oh Gods above, bend downe to heare
      my crie,
As once ye[32] did to Salmasis[33] in pond hard Lyzia by.   360
Oh that Virginia were in case as somtime Salmasis,
And in Hermafroditus steede my selfe might seeke my
      blisse!
Ah Gods, would I unfolde her armes complecting of my
      necke?
Or would I hurt her nimble hand, or yeelde her such a
      checke?
Would I gainsay hir tender skinne to baath where I do
      washe?
Or els refuse hir soft sweete lippes to touch my naked
      fleshe?
Nay, oh the Gods do know my minde, I rather would
      requier
To sue, to serve, to crouch, to kneele, to crave for my
      desier.
But out ye Gods, ye bende your browes and frowne to
      see me fare.
Ye do not force my fickle fate; ye do not way my care.   370
Unrighteous and unequall Gods, uniust and eke unsure,
Woe worth the time ye made me live to see this haplesse
      houre.
Dyd Iphis[34] hang himselfe for love of lady not so faire?

---

354 *liments* lineaments   356 *kinde* natural   362 *steede* stead, place
363 *complecting* enfolding

Or els did Iove[35] the cloudie mistes bend downe from
    lightsome ayre?
Or as the poets mencion make of Inachs daughter[36]
    meeke
For love dyd he to make a cowe whom Inach long dyd
    seeke?
Is love so great to cause the quicke to enter into Hell,
As stout Orpheus[37] did attempt, as histories do tell?
Then what is it that love cannot? Why, love dyd pearce
    the skies.
Why, Phebus and famous Mercury with love had blinded
    eies.   380
But I, a judge of grounded yeeres, shall reape to me such
    name
As shall resounde dishonour great with trump of
    carelesse fame.
Oh that my yeeres were youthfull yet, or that I were
    unwedded!
    Here entreth Haphazard

HAPHAZARD
Why, cease, sir knight; for why, perhaps, of you she
    shalbe bedded.
For folow my counsell, so may you me please,
That of carefull resurging your hart shall have ease.

APIUS
Oh, thundring Gods, that threaten yre
    And plague for eche offence,
Yourselves, I deeme, would counsell crave
    In this so fit pretence.   390
And eke your nimble stretched armes
    With great rewards would flie
To purchase faire Virginia,
    So deare a wight to me,
And, friend, I sweare by Iupiter,
    And eke by Iunos seate,

---

381 *grounded* established   386 *carefull* full of care   *resurging*
beating   394 *wight* person

And eke by all the misteries
   Where on thou canst intreate,
Thou shalt possesse and have,
   I will thee graunt and geve,   400
The greatest part of all my realme
   For aye thee to releeve.

HAPHAZARD

Well then, this is my counsell, thus standeth the case,
Perhaps such a fetche as may please your grace:
There is no more wayes, but hap or hap not,
Either hap, or els haplesse, to knit up the knot.
And if you will hazard to venter what falles,
Perhaps that Haphazard will end al your thralles.

APIUS

I meane so, I will so, if thou do perswade me,
To hap or to hazard what thing shall envade me.   410
I King, and I Keyser, I rule and overwhealme;
I do what it please me within this my realme,
Wherfore in thy iudgement see that thou do enter.
Hap life or hap death I surely will venter.

HAPHAZARD

Then this, and in this sorte, standeth the matter;
What neede many wordes, unlesse I should flatter.
Full many there be will hazarde their life
Happely to ease your grace of all your strife.
Of this kind of conspirasie now let us common:
Some man Virginius before you must summon,   420
And say[38] that Virginia is none of his daughter,
But that Virginius by night away caught her.
Then charge you the father his daughter to bringe.
Then do you detayne hir till proved be the thing;
Which well you may win hir, she present in house,
It is but Haphazard, a man or a mouse.

APIUS

I finde it, I minde it, I sweare that I will,

404 *fetche* device   407 *venter* risk   408 *thralles* troubles   419 *common* commune, discuss

Though shame, or defame, do happen no skill.
> *Here let him make as thogh he went out and let*
> *Conscience and Iustice come out of him, and let*
> *Conscience hold in his hande a lamp burning, and let*
> *Iustice have a sworde and hold it before Apius brest*

But out, I am wounded; how am I devided?
Two states of my life from me are now glided: 430
For Conscience he pricketh me contempned,
And Iustice saith Iudgement wold have me condemned;
Conscience saith crueltye sure will detest me,
And Iustice saith death in thende will molest me;
And both in one sodden me thinkes they do crie,
That fier eternall my soule shall destroy.

HAPHAZARD

Why, these are but thoughts, man! Why, fie, for
    shame, fie!
For Conscience was carelesse, and sayling by seas
Was drowned in a basket and had a disease.
Sore mooved for pitye when he would graunt none   440
For beyng hard harted was turned to a stone,
And sayling by Sandwitche he sunke for his sin.
Then care not for Conscience the worth of a pin.
And Iudgement iudge Iustice to have a reward
For iudging still iustly, but all is now marde,
For giftes they are geven wher iudgement is none.
Thus Iudgement and Iustice a wronge way hath gone.
Then care not for Conscience the worth of a fable:
Iustice is no man, nor nought to do able.

APIUS

And saiest thou so, my sured freende, then hap as hap
    shall hit.   450
Let Conscience grope, and Iudgement crave, I wil not shrink
    one whit.
I will persever in my thought, I will deflower hir youth,
I will not sure reverted be; my hart shall have no ruth.

428 *skill* matter   445 *marde* spoiled   453 *reverted* turned aside
ruth pity

Come on, proceede, and wayte on me; I will hap woe or
      wealth.
Hap blunt, hap sharp, hap life, hap death, though
      Haphazard be of health.

HAPHAZARD

At hand (quoth Picke Purse), here redy am I.
See well to the Cut Purse; be ruled by me.
   Exit. Go out here

CONSCIENCE

O cleare unspotted giftes of Ioue,
How haps thou art refused?
Oh Conscience cleare, what cruell minde   460
Thy truth hath thus misused?
I spotted am by wilfull will,
By lawles love and luste,
By dreadfull daunger of the life,
By faith that is uniust.

IUSTICE

Ah gift of Ioue, ah Fortunes face,
Ah state of steddy life,
I Iustice am and prince of peeres,
The end of lawes and strife,
A guider of the common weale,   470
A gwerdon to the poore,
And yet hath filthy lust supprest
My vertues in one houre.
Well, well, this is the most to trust:
In ende we shall espire
To see the end of these our foes
With sword and eke with fire.

CONSCIENCE

Oh help, ye Gods, we members require.
   Exeunt

[Scene iv. The same]

Enter Haphazard
[HAPHAZARD]
When gayne is no gransier,
And gaudes naught set by,   480
Nor puddings nor pie meate
Poore knaves will come nie,
Then hap and Haphazard
Shall have a new cote:
And so it may happen
To cut covetousnesse throte.
Yea, then shall Iudge Apius
Virginia obtayne,
And geese shall cracke mussels
Perhaps in the rayne;   490
Lerkes shalbe leverets
And skip to and fro,
And chourles shalbe codsheads
Perhaps and also.
But peace for mans body,
Haphazard, be mum.
Fie, pratlyng noddy,
Iudge Apius is come.
Here entreth Iudge Apius and Claudius
[APIUS]
The Furies[39] fell of Lymbo[40] Lake
My princely daies doo shorte.   500
All drownde in deadly woes I live
That once dyd ioy in sport.
I live and languish in my lyfe
as doth the wounded deare.
I thirst, I crave, I call and crie,
And yet am naught the neare.

---

479 *gransier* grandfather   480 *gaudes* tricks   493 *chourles* common
men (perhaps 'boors')   504 *deare* deer

And yet I have that me so match
  within the realme of mine[41].
But Tantalus[42] amids my care
  I hunger, sterve and pine;   510
As Sifsifus[43] I roule the stone
  in vaine to top of hill,
That evermore uncertainly
  revolving slideth still.
Oh as if to her it were to me
  what labours would I flie?
What raging seas would I not plow
  to her commoditie?
But out, alas, I doubt it sore
  lest drousy Morpheus[44]   520
His slumbry kingdomes graunted hath
  with dewes and bewtious[45].
Oh Gods above, that rule the skies,
  ye Babes, that bragge in blisse,
Ye Goddesses, ye Graces, you,
  what burning brunt is this?
Bend downe your ire, destroy me quicke,
  or els to graunt me grace
No more but that my burning breste
  Virginia may imbrace.   530
If case[46] your eares be dead and deafe,
  the Feende and sprites beloe,
You carelesse carls of Limbo Lake,
  your forced mightes doo shoe.
Thou caitife Kinge of darksome den,
  thou Pluto, plaged knave,
Send forth thy sacred vengeaunce straight;
  consume them to the grave
That will not aide my case.

CLAUDIUS

Content, and if it like your grace,   540

---

510 *sterve* starve   514 *still* continuously   518 *commoditie* advantage   526 *brunt* blow

I will attempt the deede.
I sommon will Virginius
  before your seat with speede.

HAPHAZARD

Do so, my lorde; be you not afrayde,
And so you may happen to Hazard the mayde.
It is but in Hazard, and may come by hap,
Win her, or lose her, trie you the trap.

APIUS

By the Gods, I consent to thee, Claudius, now.
Prepare the in haste Virginius unto.
Charge him, commaund him, upon his alegeance,   550
With all kinde of speede to yeelde his obeysance
Before my seate, in my consistary[47],
Subpene[48] of lande, life and treasurie.
    Here let Claudius go out with Haphazard

CLAUDIUS

No let, no stay, nor ought perturbraunce
Shall cause me to omit the furtheraunce
Of this my waighty charge.
    Exit[49]

APIUS

Well, now I range at large, my will for to expresse,
For looke how Torquin[50] Lucres faire by force did
          once oppresse,
Even so will I Virginia use.

Here let CONSCIENCE *speake within*

Iudge Apius prince, oh stay, refuse,   560
Be ruled by thy friende.
What bloudy death with open shame
Did Torquin gaine in ende?

APIUS

Whence doth this pinching sounde desende?

CONSCIENCE

From contrit Conscience, pricked on
By member of thy lyfe[51],

558 *looke how* just as

Enforced for to cry and call,
And all to ende our strife.

APIUS

What art thou, then? Declare, be breefe.

CONSCIENCE

Not flesh nor filthy lust I am,   570
But secret Conscience I,
Compeld to crie with trimbling soule
At point nere hand to die.

APIUS

Why, no disease doth me aproche, no griefe doth make
    me grudge,
But want of faire Virginia, whose beauty is my iudge.
By hir I live, by hir I die, for hir I ioy or woe,
For hir my soule doth sinke or swimme, for hir I swere
    I goe.

CONSCIENCE

Ah Gods, what wittes doth raine, and yet to you
    unknowen?
I die the death, and soule doth sinke, this filthy flesh
    hath sowen.

APIUS

I force it not, I wyll attempt; I stay for Claudius
    heare.   580
Yet wyll I goe to meete with him, to know what newes
    and cheare.

    Exeunt

[*Scene v. Outside the house of Virginius*]

    Here entreth Haphazard

[HAPHAZARD]

Hast for a hangman, in hazard of hempe;
Runne for a ridducke, there is no such impe.
Claudius is knocking with hammer and stone
At Virginius gate, as hard as he can lay one.

            580 *force* consider   583 *ridducke* gold coin

By the Gods, my maisters, Haphazard is hardy,
For he will run rashly, be they never so many.
Yea, he will singe sowsnout[52] and sknap with the best.
But peace; who comes yonder, what ioly good gest?

Here enter in with a songe [MANSIPULUS, MANSIPULA
and SUBSERVUS]

When men will seeme misdoubtfully,   590
Without an why, to call and cry,
And fearing with temerety, its ieopardy, of libertie,
Wee wish him take, to chere his hart, Haphazard,
Boulde blinde bayarde.
A fygge for his uncourtesie
That seekes to shun good company.

MANSIPULUS

What if case that cruelty should bussell me, and
iussell mee,
And holywand should tickle me, for keeping of good
companye,
Ile folow by my honestie hap Haphazard, bould blinde
bayard,
A figge for his uncourtesie that seekes to shun good
companie.   600

ALL *singe this*

When men wyll seeme misdoubtfully,
Without an why, to call and crie, &c.

MANSIPULA

Never was that misteris so furious, nor curious,
Nor yet hir bloes so boisterous, nor roisterous, nor
dolorous,
But sure I would venterous hap Haphazard, boulde
blinde bayard,
A figge for his uncourtesie that seekes to shun good
companie.

ALL *singe this*

When men wyll seeme misdoubtfully,
Without an why, to call and crie, &c.

588 *sknap* (?) quarrel

HAPHAZARD

Then wend ye on and folow me, Mansipulus, Mansipula.
Let cropyng cares[53] be cast away, come folow me, come
    folow me.   610
Subservus is a ioyly loute, brace Haphazard, bould
    blinde bayarde,
A figge for his uncourtesie that seekes to shun good
    company.

ALL *sing this*

When men will seeme misdoubtfully,
Without an why, to call and cry, &c.
    The end of the song

Heere HAPHAZARD *speaketh*

I, by the Gods, my maysters, I tould you plaine,
Who companyes with me will desire me agayne.
But how dyd ye speede, I pray ye shew me?
Was all well agreed, did no body blow ye?

MANSIPULUS

Masse, syr, hap dyd so happen that my lorde and
    maister
Staied in beholding and viewing the pasture.   620
Which when I perceived, what excuse did I make?
I came in the crosse way on the nerside the forlake,
Hard by Hodges halfe aker, at gaffer Millers stile,
The next way round about, by the space of a mile,
And at Symkins side ridge my lord stoode talking
And angerly to me quoth he 'Wher hast thou ben
    walking?'
Without any staggeryng, I had ready my lye.
'Out at Bridgemedow, and at Benols lease,' quoth I;
'Your fatlings are feding well, sir, the Gods be praised;
A goodly loume of beef on them is all redy raised.'   630
Then out steps one Frauncis Fabulator that was never
    my friende.
'How, past you Carters hay cocke at long medow ende?
There might one,' quoth he, 'within this few dayes

---

611 *brace* bold, shameless   628 *lease* pasture   630 *loume* loin

With a cast net had geven iiii knaves great assayes
Under the hedge with a payre of new cardes[54] both rip
    and sledge.'
'Is it true?' quoth my lorde, 'will this geare never be
    lefte?'
'This causes swearing and staring, proling and thefte.'
'Well,' quoth my lorde, 'take hede least I finde it.'
And so past his way, and did no more minde it.

HAPHAZARD

By the Gods, that was sport, ye, and sport alone.   640

MANSIPULA

Yea, but I was in worse case, by Saint Jhon.
My lady in church was set full devout,
And hearing my comming, she tourned aboute.
But as soone as I heard hir snappishly sounde
In this sorte I crouched me downe to the grounde,
And mannerly Maude, as though I were sad,
As soone as the pue then strawed I had
She gave me a wincke and frowardly frowne,
Wherby I do iudge she woulde cougell my gowne.
Then I dyd devise a prety fine pranke,   650
A meane whereby to picke me a thanke,
Of Margery Mildon, the maide of the milke house
And Stainer the stutter, the guid of the store house.
Then was my ladies anger well gone
And wilbe so still, and the truthe be not knowne[55].

HAPHAZARD

Ber lady barefoote, this bakes trimly.

SUBSERVUS

Nay, but I escaped more finely,
For I under this hedge one while dyd stay,
Then in this bushe, then in that way.
Then slipt I behind them among all the rest,   660
And seemed to common to of things with the best[56].
But so it did happen that all things were well,

---

635 *sledge* strike   637 *proling* prowling   649 *cougell* cudgel
653 *stutter* stutterer   *guid* guide

But hazard it is least time will truth tell.

HAPHAZARD

  Tut, tut, that was but by hap, and if it be so,

  Well, sith it was in hazard then let it goo.

SUBSERVUS

  Content, by my honestie; then farewell all wo.

MANSIPULUS

  Come out, dogge; ye speake happely of truth, if it be so.

ALL *speake*

  Now, master Haphazard, fare you well for a season.

HAPHAZARD

  Let my councell at no time with you be geason.

ALL *speaketh*

  No, by the Gods, be sure not so.   670

HAPHAZARD

  Well, sith here is no company, have with ye to Ierico[57].

    Exit

[Scene vi. The Court of Apius]

  Enter Virginius

[VIRGINIUS]

  What so the Gods they have decreed to worke and do
        by me,

  I mervaile why Iudge Apius he such gretings lets me see.

  I served have his seate and state, I have maintaind his
        weale,

  I have supprest the rebels stoute, I beare to him such
        zeale,

  And now he sends to me such charge, upon my life and
        lands,

  Without demur or further pause, or ere ought things
        be scand,

  That I in hast, with posting speede, to Court I do
        repaire

  To aunswer that aleaged is before his iudgement chaire.

665 *sith* since   669 *geason* scarce

Some histories they do expresse when such mishaps do
    fall 680
They should have tokens many a one: I have not one
    but all.
My juels somtime precious do vade and beare no hewe,
My sences they do shun there course, my lights do
    burne as blewe,
My willing wights are waxed slow, that once were swifte
    in speede,
My hart it throbs in wonderous sort, my nose doth
    often bleede,
My dreadfull dreames do draw my woe and hatefull
    hazard hale:
These tokens be of evell hap, this is the old wives tale.
But yet, O thou Virginius, whose hoary heares are olde,
Didst treason never yet commit, of this thou maist be
    bould.
In Mars his games, in marshall feates, thou wast his only
    aide, 690
The huge Carrebd[58] his hazards thou for him was ofte
    assaide.
Was Sillas[59] force by thee oft shunde, or yet Adrice[60]
    lande?
Laceface[61] childe, that Minnotaur, did cause thee ever
    stande
To pleasure him, to serve thy leach, to keepe all things
    upright.
Thou God above, then what is it that yeeldeth me this
    spight?
Sith nothing neede misdoubted be where grounded
    cause is none,
I enter will Iudge Apius gate, reiecting care and mone.
But stay, Virginius, loe, thy Prince doth enter into
    place.

682 *vade* fade, tarnish   684 *wights* wits   686 *hale* drag, bring
694 *leach* (?) liege

Oh sufferant lord, and rightful iudge, the Gods do save
    thy grace.
    Here entreth Iudge Apius and Claudius

APIUS

With tender hart, Virginius, thou welcome art to me.   700
I sory am to utter out the things I here of thee,
For Claudius, a subiecte here, a man of mickle fame,
Appealeth thee before my Courte in deede of open
    shame,
And though in deede I love thee so, as thy deserts desier,
Yet not so but I must iudgement geve, as Iustice doth
    require.

VIRGINIUS

My lord, and reason good it is, your servaunt doth
    request
No parciall hand to aide his cause, no parciall minde or
    brest.
If ought I have offended you, your Courte, or eke
    your Crowne,
From lofty top of turret hie persupetat me downe.
If treason none by me be done, or any fault committed,   710
Let my accusers beare the blame, and let me be remitted.

APIUS

Good reason to, Virginius. Come, Claudius, shew thy
    minde;
Let Iustice here, if Iudgement may, Virginius gilty
    finde.

CLAUDIUS

Thou sufferant Lord, and rightfull Iudge, this standeth
    now the case:
In tender youth, not long agone, nere sixtene yeares of
    space,
Virginius a thrall of mine, a childe and infant yonge,
From me did take by subtell meane, and keepes by arme
    full strong.

702 *mickle* great   709 *persupetat* precipitate   716 *thrall* slave

And here before your grace I crave that iustice be
    extended
That I may have my thrall agayne and faultes may be
    amended.

VIRGINIUS

Ah Gods, that guide the globe above, what forged tales
    I here!   720
Oh Iudge Apius, bend your eares while this my crime
    I cleare.
She is my child, and of my wife her tender corpes did
    springe.
Let all the countrey where I dwell beare witnesse of
    the thing.

Apius and Claudius go forth, but APIUS *speaketh this*

Nay, by the Gods, not so, my friend; I do not so
    decree.
I charge thee here, in paine of death, thou bring the
    maide to mee.
In chamber close, in prison sound, the secret shall abide
And no kinde of wight shall talke with her untill the
    truth be tride.
This doo I charge, this I commaund, in paine of death
    let see,
Without any let, that she be brought as prisoner unto me.
    Exit
    Here let Virginius go about the scaffold[62]

[VIRGINIUS]

Ah fickle faule, unhappy dome, oh most uncertaine rate   730
That ever chaunce so churlishly, that never staide in
    state.
What Iudge is this? what cruell wretch? what faith doth
    Claudius finde?
The Gods do recompence with shame his false and
    faithles minde.
Well, home I must, no remedy, where shall my soking
    teares

    722 *corpes* body   730 *faule* fall   *rate* portion, lot

Augment my woes, decrease my ioyes, while death do rid
    my feares.
    [*Exit*]
    Here entreth Rumour
[RUMOUR]
Come, Ventus, come, blow forth thy blast.
    Prince Eol[63], listen well.
The filthiest fackte that ever was
    I, Rumor, now shall tell.
You Gods, bend downe to here my crie;   740
    revengemente duly showe,
Thy Rumor craves. Did Claudius lay[64]
    and bring Iudge Apius loe?
That wicked man, that fleshly iudge,
    hath hiered Claudius
To claime a childe, the only heyre
    of olde Virginius,
A virgin pure, a queene in life,
    whose state may be deplored;
For why, the queene of chaste life   750
    is like to be defloured
By false Iudge Apius, cruell wretche,
    who straightly hath commaunded
That she to keping his be brought:
    Prince Pluto[65] this demaunded.
To skies I flie to blase abrode
    the trompe of depe defame.
Revenge, you Gods, this Rumor craves,
    this bloud and bloddy shame.
Have through the ayre, geve place you ayres.   760
    This is my dutye done.
The Gods confound such lecherers,
    loe, Rumor, this I run.
        [*Exit*]

738 *fackte* crime

[Scene vii. The house of Virginius]

[Enter Virginius]

VIRGINIUS

O man, O mould, Oh mucke, O clay, O Hell, O
    hellish hounde,
O faulse Iudge Apius, wrablinge wretch, is this thy
    treason found?
Woe worth the man that gave the seede wherby thou
    first didst spring,
Woe worth the wombe that bare the babe to meane this
    bluddy thing,
Woe worth the paps that gave thee sucke, woe worth
    the fosters eke,
Woe worth all such as ever did thy health or liking
    seeke.
Oh that the graved yeares of mine were covered in the
    clay.   770
   Here entreth Virginia

VIRGINIA

Let pacience, deare father mine, your rigor something
    stay.
Why do you waile in such a sorte? why do you weepe
    and mone?

VIRGINIUS

Oh doughter deare and only heyre, my life is neare
    forgone,
And all for love of thee.

VIRGINIA

A Gods, how may this be?
Deare father, do withdraw your dread, and let me know
    the cause.
Myselfe wyll ayde with lyfe or death without demur or
    pause:
Then tender your childe that craveth this bound.

765 *wrablinge* gabbling 768 *fosters* foster nurses 770 *graved*
buried 778 *bound* boon

VIRGINIUS

    Oh hearken, deare daughter, attend thou my sounde.
    Iudge Apius, prickt forth with filthy desire,   780
    Thy person as lemmon doth greatly require,
    And no kinde of intreatie, no feare nor no shame,
    Will he heare aledge defending the same.
    And straight without staying, in paine of my death,
    I must bring thee thither; wherfore stop my breath,
    O Sisters; I search, I seeke and I crave
    No more at your handes but death for to have,
    Rather then see my daughter deflourde,
    Or els in ill sorte so vildely devourde.

VIRGINIA

    Oh father, oh friendship, oh fatherly favour,   790
    Whose dulset words so sweetly do savour,
    On knees I beseeche thee to graunt my request,
    In all things according as lyketh thee best.
    Thou knowest, O my father, if I be once spotted,
    My name and my kindred then forth wilbe blotted;
    And if thou my father should die for my cause
    The world would accompt me as gilty in cause.
    Then rather, deare father, if it be thy pleasure,
    Graunt me the death; then keepe I my treasure,
    My lampe, my light, my life undefiled: 800
    And so may Iudge Apius of flesh be begiled.
    This upon my knees with humble beheste,
    Graunt me, O father, my instant requeste.

VIRGINIUS

    Then ryse up, my daughter, my aunswere doo note,
    From mouth of thy father whose eyes do now flote.
    O daughter, oh deare, oh darling, oh dame,
    Dispatch me[66], I pray thee; regarde not my name.
    But yet, as thou saiest, sith remedy none
    But lemmon thou must be if I were gone,
    And better it is to dye with good fame   810
    Then longer to live to reape us but shame:

781 *lemmon* lover   786 *Sisters* the Fates   789 *vildely* vilely

But if thou do dye, no doubt is at all
But presently after myselfe folow shall.
Then end without shame so let us persever,
With trompe of good fame so dye shall we never.
    Virginia here kneeleth

VIRGINIA

Then, tender armes, complect the neck; doo dry thy
      fathers teares,
You nimble handes, for wo whereof my loving hart it
      weares.
Oh father mine, refraine no whit, your sharped knife to
      take
From giltles sheath my shame to ende and body dead to
      make.
Let not the shameles blouddy iudge defile my virgins
      life.   820
Doe take my head and send it him upon your bloudy
      knife.
Bid him imbrue his bloudy handes in giltles bloud of mee.
I virgin dye, he leacher lives; he was my ende, you see.
No more delayes; lo, kisse me first, then stretch your
      strongest arme,
Do ryd my woe, increase my ioy, do ease your childe of
      harme.

VIRGINIUS

O weary wittes of wo or wealth, oh feble aged man,
How can thy arme geve such a blow; thy death I
      wishe thee than:
But sith that shame with endles trompe wil sounde if
      case thou ioy,
By meanes of false Iudge Apius he, my selfe will thee
      destroy.
Forgeve me, babe, this bloudy deede, and meekely take
      thy ende.   830
    Here let him profer a blowe

[VIRGINIA]

The Gods forgeve thee, father deare; farewell, thy blow
      do bend.

Yet stay a whyle, O father deare, for fleash to death is
    fraile.
Let first my wimple[67] bind my eyes, and then thy blow
    assaile.
Now father, worke thy will on me, that life I may inioy.
    Here tye a handcarcher aboute hir eyes, and then
    strike of hir heade

VIRGINIUS

Now stretch thy hand, Virginius, that loth would flesh
    distroy.
O cruell handes, or blouddy knife, O man, what hast
    thou done?
Thy daughter deare, and onely heyre, hir vitall ende
    hath wone.
Come, fatall blade, make lyke dispatche, come Atropos[68],
    come ende,
Strike home thou careles arme with speede; of death be
    not afrayde.
    Here entreth Comfort

COMFORT

Oh noble knight Virginius, do stay; be not dismayde.   840
I curing Comfort present am, your doller to ayde.

VIRGINIUS

Sith ioy is gone, sith life is deade,
What comfort can there be?
No more there is but deepe dispaire
And deadly death to me.

COMFORT

No more, Sir knight, but take the head, and wende a
    while with me.
It shalbe sent to court for that Iudge Apius may it se:
In recompence of lechors lust this present let him have,
And stay your corps for certaine space in coping[69] from
    the grave.
So shall you see the end of him and all his whole consent. 850
This wilbe comfort to your harte, Virginius; be content.

VIRGINIUS

Of truth even so, for Comfort els, I know right well, is
    none.
Wherefore I do consent with you; come on, let us be
    gone.
But messenger my selfe wyll bee, myself will geve the
    gifte.
Come on, good Comfort, wend we then; there is no other
    shifte.

   Exeunt

[Scene viii. The Court of Apius]

Here entreth Iudge Apius

[APIUS]

Well hap as can hap, or no;
In hazard it is, but let that goe.
I wyll what so happen persue on still;
Why, none there is living can let me my wyll.
I will have Virginia, I will hir defloure,   860
Els rigorous sword hir hart shall devoure.

   Heere entreth Haphazard

HAPHAZARD

I came from Caleco[70] even the same houre,
And hap was hyred to Hackney in hempstrid[71].
In hazard he was of riding on beamestrid,
Then crow crop on tree top hoist up the sayle,
Then groned their neckes, by the weight of their tayle:
Then dyd Carnifex[72] put these three together,
Payd them their pasporte for clustring thither.

APIUS

Why, how now, Haphazard, of what doest thou speake?
Me thinks in mad sort; thy talke thou doest breake.   870
Those three words chopt all in one
Is Carnifex, that signifieth a hangman.
Peace, no such words before me do utter.

864 *beamestrid* astride a beam

HAPHAZARD

Nay, I lye as still as a cat in a gutter.
Go to, Iudge Apius, go forward, good Prince;
Perhaps ye may have that the which wyll not blince.

APIUS

What is the man that liveth now so neare to doore of
    death
As I for lust of lady faire, whose lacke will stop my breth.
But long I shall not want her sight; I stay her comming
    heere.
Oh lucky light, lo, present heere hir father doth appeare.   880
Oh how I ioy; yet bragge thou not, Dame Beuty bides
    behinde.
Virginius, where is the maide? How haps thou breakes
    my minde?
    Here entreth Virginius

VIRGINIUS

Ah wicked Iudge, the virgin chaste
Hath sent her beutious face
In recompence of lechour gaine
To thee so voide of grace.
She bids thee imbrue thy bloudy handes
And filthy lecherous minde
With Venus damsels voyde of shame
Where such thou haps to finde;   890
But thou as with Dianas ympes
Shalt never be aquainted;
They rather wishe the naked knife
Then virgins life attainted.
In ende iust profe whereof,
Beholde Virginias heade.
She sought hir fame, thou soughts hir shame,
This arme hath smit her dead.

APIUS

Oh curst and cruell cankerd churle, oh carll unnaturall,

Which hast the seede of thine owne lym thrust forth to
    funerall.   900
Ye Gods, bend downe your yre; do plague him for his
    deede.
You sprites below, you hellish houndes, do geve him
    gaule for meed.
Myselfe will se his latter end. I iudge him to the death;
Like death that faire Virginia toke, the lyke shall stop his
    breath.
Then flasky feends of Lymbo Lake his ghost do so tormoyle
That he have neede of Carons[73] helpe, for all his filthy
    toyle.
Come, Iustice, then, come on, Rewarde, come ayde me in
    my neede.
Thou, wicked knight, shal slaughterd be with self same
    knife with speed.

VIRGINIUS

Sith she, a virgine pure and chast, in heaven leades hir
    life,
Content I am to dye with her, and dye upon her knife.   910

APIUS

Come, Iustice, then, come on, Reward, when Iudgement
    now doth cal.

Heere entreth IUSTICE *and* REWARD, *and they both speake
    this*

We both are ready here at hande to worke thy fatall fall.

IUSTICE

O gorgan[74] Iudge, what lawles life hast thou most
    wicked led?
Thy soking sinne hath sonke thy soule; thy vertues all
    are fled.
Thou chast and undefiled life didest seeke for to have
    spotted,
And thy Reward is ready here, by Iustice now alotted.

902 *meed* reward   905 *flasky* (?) inconstant   *tormoyle* torment

REWARDE

    Thy iust Reward is deadly death, wherfore come wend
        away;

    To death I straight will do thy corps, then lust shall have
        his pray.

    Virginius, thou wofull knight, come neare and take thy
        foe;

    In prison thou make him fast, no more let him do so.   920

    Let Claudius for tirrany be hanged on a tree.

VIRGINIUS

    Ah right Reward, the Gods be blist
    This day I chaunce to see.

HAPHAZARD

    Why, how now, my lord Apius, what cheare?
    Why, where is my Reward for this geare?
    Why dyd I ride, run and revell,
    And for all my iaunting now am made a iavell.
    Why run, sir knave, and call me Claudius,
    Then run with a vengeaunce, watch Virginius,
    Then ride, sirra, is Virginia at church,   930
    Then gallope to see where her father doth lurche,
    Then up, sirra, now what counsell,
    Of Dame Bewty what newes canst thou tell?
    Thus in hurly burly from piller to poste
    Poore Haphazard daily was toste,
    And now with Virginius he goes sadly walking,
    And nothing at all will listen my talking.
    But shall I be so used at his hands?
    As leve I were neare in Limbo bands;
    That dronel, that drowsy drakenosed drivill,   940
    He never learned his manners in Sivill[75].

    A Iudge may cause a gentleman, a gentleman nay a iack
        hearinge,

    As honest as he that caries his hose on his neck for feare
        of wering[76],

    A caitife, a cutthrote, a churle worthy blame,

       927 *iavell* rascal   931 *lurche* stay   940 *dronel* sluggard

I wyll serve him no longer; the Devill geve him shame.
Yet, by the mouse foote, I am not content;
I will have a reward sure els will I repent.
To Master Reward I straight waies will go;
The worst that can hap is but a noo.
But sure I know his honesty is such   950
That he will recompence me with little or much;
And well this proverb commeth in my head,
Birlady, halfe a loafe is better then nere a whit of bread.
Therfore hap, and be happely, hap that hap may,
I wyll put it in hazard; I geve it assay.
Alhayle, Maister Reward and rightuous Iustice.
I beseech you, let me be recompenced to, according to
          my service,
For why all this long time I have lived in hope.

REWARDE

Then, for thy reward, then here is rope.

HAPHAZARD

Nay, softe, my maisters, by Saincte Thomas of trunions,   960
I am not disposed to by of your onions.
A rope, quoth you; away with that showing.
It would greve a man having two plowes goyng.
Nay, stay, I pray you, and let the cat winke,
It is naught in dry sommer for letting my drinke[77].

IUSTICE

Let or no let, there is no remedy; hanging shalbe thy
          reward, verely.

HAPHAZARD

Is there nothing but hanging to my lot doth fall?
Then take you my rewarde; much good doo it you withall.
I am not so hasty, although I be clayming,
But that I can aford you the most of my gayning.   970
I wyll set, let, graunt, yelde, permit and promise
All the revenewes to you of my service.
I am friendly, I am kindly, I proffer you faire;
You shall be my ful executor and heyre.

960 *trunions* i.e. the Trinity

REWARD

Nay, make you ready first to dye by the roode,
Then we will dispose it as we think it good.
Then those that with you to this dyd consent,
[Th]e lyke reward shall cause them repent.

IUSTICE

Nay, stay a while; Virginius is comming.

Prece to go foorth

Nay, soft, Haphazard, you are not so cunning,   980
Thus to escape without punishment.

REWARDE

No, certis, it is not so expedient.

Here entreth Virginius

VIRGINIUS

Oh noble Iustice, duty done, behold I come againe
To shew you that Apius he himselfe hath lewdly slaine.
As soone as he in prison was enclosed out of sight,
He, desperate for bluddy deede, did slea himselfe out right,
And Claudius doth mercy crave who did the deede for feare:
Voutchsafe, Oh Iudge, to save his life, though countrie he
        forbeare.

IUSTICE

We graunt him grace at thy request, but bannish him the
        lande;
And see that death be done out right on him that here
        doth stand.   990

HAPHAZARD

Nay, M[aister] Virginius, take him by the hande;
I crave not for service the thing worth ought.
Hanging, quoth you; it is the last end of my thought.
Fye, for shame, fye; stay by my fathers soule.
Why, this is like to Tom Turners doule[78],
Hang one man, and save all the rest.
Take part one with another; plaine dealing is best.

REWARDE

This is our dealing, thus deale we with thee:

979 *Prece* press (i.e. attempt)   984 *lewdly* wickedly

Take him hence, Virginius, goe trusse him to a tree.

HAPHAZARD

Ye shall in a ropes name whether away with me.   1000

VIRGINIUS

Come, wend thou in haste, thy death for to take.

To the hangman I will leade thee, a quicke dispatch to
make.

HAPHAZARD

Must I needes hange? By the Gods, it doth spight me

To thinke how crabbedly this silke lase will bite me.

Then come, cosin Cutpurse, come runne haste and folow
me;

Haphazard must hange; come folow the lyverie.

Exit

IUSTICE

Well, wende we now; the finall ende of fleshly lust wee
see.

REWARDE

Content, Rewarde is ready bent with Iustice to agree.

Here entreth Fame[79]

[FAME]

Oh stay, you noble Iustice, stay. Reward, do make no
haste.

We ladies three have brought the corse in earth that must
be plaste.   1010

Doctrina and Memorie and Virginius bring a tome

[DOCTRINA]

We have brought backe Virginius, the funerall to see.

I graunt him that the learned pen shall have the ayde of
mee

To wright in learned verse the honor of hir name.

FAME

And eke it shall resownd by trompe of me, Dame Fame.

Here let MEMORIE *wright on the tome*

I, Memorie, will minde hir life, hir death shall ever raine,

1010 *corse* corpse   *plaste* placed   *tome* tomb (tombstone)

316

Within the mouth and minde of man from age to age
    againe.

IUSTICE

And Iustice sure will ayde all those that immitate hir
    lyfe.

REWARDE[80]

. . . [Re]warde will punnish those that move such dames
    to stryf.

FAME

Then sing we round about the Tome in honour of hir
    name.

REWARDE

Content we are with willing minde to sing with sound
    of Fame.   1020

THE EPILOGUE

As earthly life is graunted none for evermore to raigne,
But denting death wil cause them al to grant this world
    as vain,
Right worshipfull, sith sure it is that mortall life must
    vade,
Do practise then to winne his love that all in all hath made,
And by this Poets faining here, example do you take
Of Virginias life, of chastetie, of duty to thy make,
Of love to wife, of love to spouse, of love to husband
    deare,
Of bringing up of tender youth[81], all these are noted
    heare.
I doubt it not, right worshipful, but well you do conceive
The matter that is ended now, and thus I take my leave,   1030
Beseeching God, as dutie is, our gracious Queene to save,
The Nobles, and the Commons eke, with prosperous life,
    I crave.
    [*Exeunt*]

¶An Enterlude Intituled,

ke wil to like quod the Deuel to the Colier, vn-
godly and ful of pleſant mirth. Wherin is declared not onely what puniſhment followeth thoſe that wil rather followe licentious liuing, then to eſteem & followe good
counſel: and what great benefits and commodi
ties they receiue that apply them vnto
vertuous liuing and good exerciſes.
Made by Vlpian Fulwel.

¶Fiue may eaſely play this enterlude.

¶The names of the players.

¶The Prologue			¶Chance,	
Tom Tolpot			Uertuous life	
Hankin hangman	for one.		Gods promiſes	for one.
Tom Colier.			Cutbert cutpurs	
¶Lucifer			Philip Fleming	
Ralfe Roiſter.	for one.		Pierce Pickpurs	for another.
Gods ſame			Honour	
Seueritis.				

Nichol newfangle the vice.

¶Imprinted at London at
the long ſhop adioyning vnto S. Mildreds Churche
in the Pultrie by John Allde.
Anno Domini 1568.

Facsimile of the title-page of the 1568 edition of Like Will to Like

The present edition of this play is based upon that printed by Edward Allde in 1587. A copy is in the British Museum (C.34.c.36). The title-page reads:

A pleasant Enterlude intituled Like will to Like quoth the Devill to the Collier. Wherin is declared what punishments followe those that will rather live licentiously then esteeme and followe good Councell. And what benefits they receive that apply themselves to vertuous living and good exercises. Made by Ulpian Fulwel.

Five may easily play this Enterlude.

The Prologue		Haunce	
Tom Tospot		Vertuous Life	
Hankin Hangman	For one.	Gods Promise	For one.
Tom Collier		Cutbert Cutpurs	

Lucifer		Philip Fleming	
Rafe Roister		Pierce Pickpurs	
Good Fame	For one.	Honour	For one.
Severitie			

Nichol Newfangle the Vice.

A copy of an earlier edition (1568) by John Allde is in the Bodleian Library (Malone 231 (3)). The two versions are substantially the same. As most of the variants are unimportant, I have followed the 1587 edition closely, and I have listed below (pp. 415–16) readings from 1568 which might be of interest.

There are three modern editions:

R. Dodsley, *A Select Collection of Old Plays*, ed. W. C. Hazlitt, Vol. 3, 1874

J. S. Farmer, (1) *Dramatic Writings of Ulpian Fulwell*, 1906; (2) *Tudor Facsimile Text*, 1909

Little is known of Ulpian Fulwell. Son of a farmer, he was rector of Naunton in Gloucestershire from 1570 until his death in 1586 (the year before Edward Allde's edition of his play). During this time he married, had a family, and studied at Oxford in 1578.

Like Will to Like

Cicero in his book *De Amicitia*[1] these woords dooth
    expresse,
Saying nothing is more desirous then like is unto like;
Whose woords are most true and of a certainty doubtles:
For the vertuous doo not the vertuous company mislike.
But the vicious dooth the vertuous company eschue:
And like wil unto like, this is most true.

It is not my meaning your eares for to wery
With harkening what is the effect of our matter:
But our pretence is to moove you to be mery,
Merily to speak, meaning no man to flatter;   10
The name of this matter, as I said while ere,
Is '*Like wil to like,*' quod the Devil to the Collier[2].

Sith pithie proverbs in our English tung doo abound,
Our author thought good such a one for to chuse,
As may shew good example, and mirth may eke be found;
But no lascivious toyes he purposeth to use.
Heerin, as it were in a glasse, see you may
The advauncement of vertue, and of vice the decay.

To what ruin ruffins[3] and roisters are brought
You may heer see of them the finall end.   20
Begging is the best though that end be naught;
But hanging is woorse if they doo not amend.
The vertuous life is brought to honor and dignitie,
And at the last to everlasting eternitie.

And because divers men of divers mindes be,
Some doo matters of mirth and pastime require:
Other some are delighted with matters of gravitie.

2 *then* than   8 *effect* significance   9 *pretence* intention   12 *quod*
said   16 *toyes* trifles   19 *roisters* swaggerers, revellers

To please all men is our authors cheef desire,
Wherfore mirth with mesure to sadnes is annexed,
Desiring that none heer at our matter wil be parplexed.　　30

Thus, as I said, I wil be short and breef,
Because that from this dump you shall releeved be;
And the Devil with the Colier, the theef that seeks the
　　　　theef,
Shall soon make you merry, as shortly you shall see;
And sith mirth for sadnes is a sauce most sweet,
Take mirth then with measure that best sauceth it.
　　　Finis

Heer entreth Nichol Newfangle, the Vice, laughing, and
hath a knave of clubs in his hand, which as soon as he
speaketh he offreth unto one of the men or boyes standing
by

[NEWFANGLE] Ha, ha, ha, ha, now like unto like: it wil be
　　　none other.
Stoup[4], gentle knave, and take up your brother.
Why, is it so? and is it even so indeed?
Why, then, may I say God send us good speed!　　40
And is every one heer so greatly unkinde,
And I am no sooner out of sight, but quite out of minde?
Mary, this wil make a man even weep for woe,
That on such a sodain no man wil him knowe,
Though men be so dangerous now at this day:
Yet are women kinde woorms, I dare wel say.
How say you, woman, you, that stand in the angle[5],
Were you never acquainted with Nichol Newfangle?
Then I see Nichol Newfangle is quite forgot;
Yet you wil know me anon, I dare ieopard a grote.　　50
Nichol Newfangle is my name; doo you me not knowe?
My whole education to you I wil showe.
For first, before I was born, I remember very well
That my gransier and I made a iourney into hell,

45 *dangerous* difficult to please　46 *woorms* creatures (term of
affection)　50 *ieopard* risk, bet

Where I was bound prentice before my nativitie
To Lucifer himself, such was mine agilitie.
All kinde of sciences he taught unto me,
That to the maintenance of pride might best agree.
I learned to make gowns with long sleeves and winges;
I learned to make ruffs like calves chitterlings,   60
Caps, hats, cotes, and all kinde of apparails,
And especially breeches as big as good barrels.
Shoos, boots, buskins, with many prity toyes;
All kinde of garments for men, women, and boyes.
Know ye me not now? I thought that at the last
All acquaintance from Nichol Newfangle is not past.
Nichol Newfangle was, and is, and ever shalbe;
And there are but few that are not acquainted with me,
For so soon as my prentishood was once come out
I went by and by the whole world about.   70

Heer the Devil entreth but speaketh not yet
Sancte benedicite, who have we heere?
Tom Tumbler, or els some dauncing beare?
Body of me, it were best goe no neere:
For ought that I see, it is my godfather Lucifer,
Whose prentice I have been this many a day,
But no more words but mum, you shall heare what he wil
    say.
    This name Lucifer must be written on his back and on
    his brest

LUCIFER Howe, mine own boy, I am glad that thou art
    heere!
NEWFANGLE He speaketh to you, sir, I pray you come neer.
    Pointing to one standing by
LUC. Nay, thou art even he of whom I am wel appaid.
NEW. Then speak aloof of[6]; to come nie I am afraid.   80
LUC. Why lo, my boy, as though thou didst never see me?

---

60 *chitterlings* intestines (i.e. frilly)   61 *apparails* decorated or
ornamental clothing   73 *neere* nearer   79 *appaid* rewarded   80 *nie*
near

NEW. Yes, godfather, but I am afraid it is now as often
      times it is with thee.
  For if my dame and thou hast been tumbling by the eares,
  As oftentimes you doo, like a couple of great beares,
  Thou carest not whom thou killest in thy raging minde.
  Doost thou not remember since thou brusedst me behinde?
  This hole in thy fury didst thou disclose,
  That now may a tent be put in, as big as thy nose.
  This was when my dame called thee bottle-nosed[7] knave,
  But I am like to cary the mark to my grave.   90
LUC. Oh my good boy, be not afraid,
  For no such thing hath happened as thou hast saide.
  But come to me, my boye, and blesse thee I wil,
  And see that my precepts thou doo fulfill.
NEW. Wel, godfather, if you will say ought to me in this
      case.
  Speak, for in faith I meane not to kneell to that ill face.
  If our Lady of Walsingham[8] had no fairer face and
      visage,
  By the masse, they were fooles that would goe to her on
      pilgremage.
LUC. Wel, boy, it shall not greatly skil
  Whether thou stand, or whether thou kneele.   100
  Thou knowest what sciences I have thee taught,
  Which are able to bring the world to nought.
  For thou knowest that through pride from heaven I was
      cast,
  Even unto hell, wherfore see thou make haste
  Such pride through new fashions in mens harts for to
      sowe
  That those that use it may have the like overthrowe.
  From vertue procure men to set their minds aside,
  And wholy imploy it to all sinne and pride.
  Let thy newfangled fashions bear such a sway
  That a rascall be as proud as he that best may.   110
NEW. Tush, tush, that is alredy brought to passe,

88 *tent* probe 99 *skil* matter

For a very skip-iack is prouder, I swere by the mas,
And seeketh to goe more gayer and brave,
Then dooth a lord, though himselfe be a knave.

LUC. I can thee thank, that so wel thou hast plaid thy part;
Such as doo so shall soon feel the smart.
Sith that thou hast thus doon, there remaineth behinde
That thou in another thing shew thy right kinde.

NEW. Then, good godfather, let me heare thy minde.

LUC. Thou knowest that I am bothe proud and arrogant,   120
And with the proud I wil ever be conversant;
I cannot abide to see men that are vicious
Accompany themselves with such as be vertuous,
Wherfore my minde is, sith thou thy part canst play,
That thou adioyne like to like alway.

NEW. I never loved that wel, I swere by this day.

LUC. What, my boy?

NEW. Your minde is, sith I fast three meales every Good
        Friday,
That I eat nothing but onions and leekes alway.

LUC. Nay, my minde is, sith thou thy part canst play,   130
That thou adioyne like to like alway.

NEW. Tush, tush, godfather Devil, for that have thou no
        care:
Thou knowest that like wil to like, quod the Devil to the
        Colier.
And thou shalt see that such a match I shall make anon
That thou shalt say I am thy good, good, sweet, sweet
        godson.

LUC. I wil give thee thanks when thou hast so doon.
        Heer entreth the Colier

NEW. Wel, godfather, no more words, but mum,
For yonder comes the Collier, as seemeth me.
By the mas, he wil make a good mate⁹ for thee.
What, olde acquaintance, small remembraunce?   140
Welcome to town with a very vengeance!
Now welcome, Tom Colier, give me thy hand:

        112 *skip-iack* fop   118 *kinde* breeding

As very a knave as any in England.

COLL. By masse, God amarcy, my vreend Nichol!

NEW. By God, and welcome, ientle Tom Lickhole!

COLL. Cham glad to zee thee mery, my vreend Nickol.
And how doost thou now a dayes, good Nickole?

NEW. And nothing els but even plain Nichol?

COLL. I pray thee tell me how doost, good vreend
   Lickhole.

NEW. It is turned from Nichol to Lick hole with Tom
   Colier.   150
I say no more, Tom, but hold thy nose there.

COLL. Nay, hold thy tung, Nichol, til my nose dooth come:
So thou shalt take part, and I shall take zome.

NEW. Wel, Tom Colier, let these thinges passe away;
Tel me what market thou hast made of thy coles today.

COLL. To every bushel cha zolde three peck[10];
Loe, here be the empty zacks on my neck.
Cha begilde the whorsons that of me ha bought:
But to begile me was their whole thought.

NEW. But hast thou no conscience to begile thy poore
   neighbour?   160

COLL. No, mary, zo I may gain vor my labour.
It is a common trade now a daies, this is plain,
To cut one anothers throte vor lucar and gaine.
A small vaut as the world is now brought to passe.

NEW. Thou art a good fellow. I swere by the masse;
As fit a companion for the Devil as may be.
Lo, good father Devil, this felow wil I match with thee.

LUC. And good Tom Collier, thou art welcom to me.
  He taketh him by the hand

COLL. God a mercy, good Devil, cham glad of thy
   company.

LUC. Like wil to like, I see very wel.   170

NEW. Godfather, wilt thou daunce a little, before thou goe
   home to hell?

LUC. I am content, so that Tom Colier doo agree.

145 *ientle* gentle 146 *Cham* I am 156 *cha* I have 164 *vaut* fault

COLL. I wil never refuse, Devil, to daunce with thee.
NEW. Then, godfather, name what the daunce shall be.
LUC. Tom Colier of Croydon hath solde his cole.
NEW. Why then, have at it, by my fathers soule!

> *Nichol Newfangle must have a gittern[11] or some other*
> *Instrument, if he may, but if they have none they must*
> *daunce about the place all three, and sing this song*
> *that followeth, which must be doon though they have an*
> *instrument*

The Song

Tom Colier of Croydon hath solde his coles,
  and made his market today:
And now he daunceth with the Devil,
  for like wil to like alway.   180
Wherfore let us reioyce and sing,
  let us be mery and glad:
Sith that the Colier and the Devill
  this match and daunce hath made.
Now of this daunce we make an end,
  with mirth and eke with ioy:
The Colier and the Devill wil be
  much like to like alway.
  Finis

NEW. Aha, mary, this is trim singing!
I had not thought the Devil to be so cunning.   190
And, by the mas, Tom Colier is as good as he:
I see that like with like wil ever agree.
COLL. Var-wel, maister Devil, vor ich must be gone.
  Exit Tom Collier
LUC. Why then, farwel, my gentle freend Tom.
NEW. Farwel, Tom Colier, a knave be thy comfort!
How saist thou, godfather, is not this trim sport?
LUC. Thou art mine own boy; my blessing thou shalt
  have.
NEW. By my troth, godfather, that blessing I doo not
  crave.

193 *Var-wel* farewell

But if you goe your way, I wil doo my diligence,
As wel in your absence as in your presence.   200

LUC. But thou shalt salute me, or I goe doutles,
That in thy dooings thou maist have the better successe.
Wherfore kneel down and say after me.

NEW. When the Devil wil have it so, it must needs so be.
He kneleth downe
What shal I say, bottel nosed godfather, canst thou tel?

LUC. All haile, Oh noble prince of hel.

NEW. All my dames cow tailes fel down into the wel.

LUC. I wil exalt thee above the clowdes.

NEW. I wil sault thee, and hang thee in the shrowdes.

LUC. Thou art the inhauncer of my renowne.   210

NEW. Thou art Haunce, the hangman of Callis town[12].

LUC. To thee be honour alone.

NEW. To thee shall come our hobling Jone.

LUC. Amen.

NEW. Amen.

LUC. Now farwel, my boy, farwel hartely.

NEW. Is there never a knave heer wil keep the Devil
company?
Farwel, godfather, for thou must goe alone:
I pray thee come hether again anon.
Exit Lucifer
Mary, heere was a benediction of the Devils good grace: 220
Body of me, I was so afrayd, I was like to bestench the
place!
My buttocks made buttons[13] of the new fashion
While the whorson Devil was making his salutation.
But, by the masse, I am as glad as ever was Madge Mare
That the whorson Devil is ioyned with the knave
Coliar.
As fit a match as ever could be pickt out:
What saist thou, Jone, with the long snout?
Tom Tospot commeth in with a fether in his hat
But who comes yonder, puffing as whot as a black
pudding?
I holde xx.li it is a ruffin, if a goose goe a gooding[14].

TOSSPOT Gogs hart and his guts, is not this too bad?   230
  Bloud, wounds and nailes, it wil make a man mad!
NEW. I warant you heere is a lusty one, very brave.
  I think anon he wil swere himself a knave.
TOSSPOT Many a mile have I ridden, and many a mile
       have I gone,
  Yet can I not finde for me a fit companion.
  Many there be which my company would frequent,
  If to doo as they doo I would be content.
  They would have me leave off my pride and swearing,
  My new fangled fashions, and leave of this wearing.
  But rather then I such companions wil have,   240
  I wil see a thousand of them laid in their grave.
  Similis similem sibi quaerit[15], such a one doo I seek,
  As unto my self in every condition is like.
NEW. Sir, you are welcome; ye seem to be an honest man,
  And I wil help you in this matter as much as I can:
  If you tary heer a while, I tel you in good sooth,
  I wil finde one as fit for you as a pudding for a friers
      mouth.[16]
TOSSPOT I thank you, my freend, for your gentle offer to
      me.
  I pray you, tell me what your name may be.
NEW. Me think by your apparell you have had me in
      regard: 250
  I pray you, of Nichol Newfangle have you never heard?
TOSSPOT Nichole Newfangle? Why, we are of olde
      acquaintance.
NEW. By my troth, your name is quite out of my
      remembrance!
TOSSPOT At your first comming into England, wel I wot,
  You were very wel acquainted with Tom Tospot.
NEW. Tom Tospot? *Sancti amen*, how you were out of my
      minde!
TOSSPOT You know when you brought into England this
      new fangled kinde,
  That Tospots and Ruffins with you were first
      acquainted.

NEW. It is even so, Tom Tospot, as thou hast saide.

TOSSPOT It is an olde saying, that mountains and hills
    never meet,   260
 But I see that men shall meet though they doo not seek,
 And I promise you more ioy in my hart I have found
 Then if I had gained an hundred pound.

NEW. But I am as glad as one had given me a grote,
 That I have met with thee, Tom Tospot.
 And seeing a mate thou wouldst so faine have,
 I wil ioyne thee with one that shalbe as very a knave
 As thou art thyselfe, you may beleeve me;
 Thou shalt see anon what I wil doo for thee.
 For you seek as very a knave as you yourselfe are: 270
 For like wil to like, quod the Devil to the Coliar.

TOSSPOT Indeed, Nichole Newfangle, ye say the veritie,
 For like wil to like; it wil none otherwise be.

  Heer entreth Rafe Roister

NEW. Beholde, Tom Tospot, even in pudding time[17],
 Yonder commeth Rafe Roister, an olde freend of mine.
 By the mas, for thee he is so fit a mate
 As Tom and Tib for Kit and Kate.
 Now welcome, my freend Rafe Roister, by the masse.

ROISTER And I am glad to see you heere in this place.

NEW. Bid him welcome; hark, he can play a knaves part. 280

TOSSPOT My freend, you are welcome with all my hart.

ROISTER God a mercy, good fellowe, tel me what thou art.

NEW. As very a knave as thou, though the best be to bad.

TOSSPOT I am one which of thy company would be very
  glad.

ROISTER And I wil not your company refuse of a
  certaintie,
 So that to my conditions your maners doo agree.

TOSSPOT It should appeere, by your sayings, that we are of
  one mind,
 For I knowe that roisters and tospots come of one kinde.
 And as our names be much of one accord, and much like,

     286 *conditions* character

So I think our condicions be not far unlike. 290

ROISTER If your name to me you will declare and showe,
   You may in this matter my minde the sooner knowe.

TOSSPOT Few woords are best among freends, this is true;
   Wherfore I shall breefly shew my name unto you.
   Tom Tospot it is, it need not be painted,
   Wherfore with Rafe Roister I must needs be acquainted.

NEW. In faith, Rafe Roister, if thou wilt be ruled by me,
   We wil daunce hand in hand, like knaves all three.
   It is as unpossible for thee his company to deny
   As it is for a cammel to creep through a needles eye. 300
   Therfore bid him welcome, like a knave as thou art.

ROISTER By my troth, Tom Tospot, you are welcome with
      all my hart.

TOSSPOT I thank you that mine acquaintance you wil take
      in good part,
   And, by my troth, I wil be your sworn brother.

NEW. Tush, like wil to like, it wil be none other.
   For the vertuous wil alwaies the vertuous company seek
      out:
   A gentleman never seeketh the company of a lout;
   And roisters and ruffians do sober company eschue:
   For like wil ever to like, this is moste true.

ROISTER Now, freend Tom Tospot, seeing that we are
      bretheren sworne, 310
   And neither of our companies from other may be
      forborne,
   The whole trade of my life to thee I wil declare.

TOSSPOT And to tell you my properties also I shall not
      spare.

NEW. Then, my maisters, if you will awhile abide it,
   Ye shall see two such knaves so lively described
   That, if hel should be raked even by and by indeed,
   Such another couple cannot be found, I swere by my
      creed.
   Go to, sirs, say on your whole mindes,

295 *painted* elaborated   311 *forborne* withheld   316 *raked* dragged

And I shall paint you out in your right kindes.
First, Tom Tospot, plead thou thy cause and thy name,   320
And I wil sit in this chaire and give sentence on the
    same.
I will play the Iudge, and in this matter give iudgement.
How say you, my maisters, are you so content?

ROISTER By my troth, for my part, therto I doo agree.

TOSSPOT I were to blame if any fault should be in me.

NEW. Then that I be in office, neither of you doo grudge?

BOTH No, indeed.

NEW. Where learned you to stand capt before a Iudge?
You sowterly knaves, shew you all your manners at once?

ROISTER Why, Nichole, all we are content.   330

NEW. And am I plaine Nichole? and yet it is my arbitrement
To iudge which of you two is the veriest knave?
I am Maister Nichole Newfangle, both gay and brave.
For seeing you make me your Iudge, I trowe,
I shall teach you both your leripup to knowe[18].
    He fighteth

TOSSPOT Stay yourself, I pray you hartely.

ROISTER I pray you, be content, and we wil be more
    manerly.

NEW. Nay, I cannot put up such an iniury;
For, seing I am in office, I wil be known therfore:
Fend your heds, sirs, for I wil fight once more.   340
    He fighteth againe

ROISTER I pray you be content, good gentle maister
    Nichole.

TOSSPOT I never saw the like, by gogs soule.

NEW. Wel, my maisters, because you doo intend
To learn good manners, and your conditions to amend,
I wil have but one fit more, and so make an end.
    He fighteth againe

ROISTER I pray you, sir, let us no more contend.

NEW. Mary, this hath brethed me very wel:

---

328 *capt* wearing a hat   329 *sowterly* vulgar   337 *manerly* well
behaved   340 *Fend* defend   345 *fit* bout, round

Now let me heare how you your tales can tel.
And I, maister Iudge, wil so bring to passe,
That I wil iudge who shalbe Knave of Clubs at
    Christmas.   350

TOSSPOT Gogs wounds, I am like Phalaris[19], that made a bul
    of brasse –

NEW. Thou art like a false knave now, and ever more was.

TOSSPOT Nay, I am like Phalaris that made a bul of
    brasse,
As a cruell torment for such as did offend,
And he himself first therin put was:
Even so are we brought to this end
In ordaining him a iudge, who wil be honored as a God,
So for our own tailes we have made a rod.

ROISTER And I am served as Haman[20], that preparde –

NEW. How was he served, I pray thee, doo me tel?   360

ROISTER Whom I speak of thou knowest not wel.

NEW. Thou art served as Hary hangman, captain of the
    black garde.

ROISTER Nay, I am served as Haman, that preparde
A high paire of gallous for Mardocneus the Jew,
And was the first that theron was hanged:
So I feele the smart of mine owne rod, this is true.
But heerafter I wil learn to be wise,
And ere I leap once, I wil look twice.

NEW. Wel, Tom Tosspot, first let me heare thee.
How canst thou prove thyself a verier knave then he?   370

TOSSPOT You know that Tom Tospot men doo me call?

NEW. A knave thou hast alwaies been, and ever shall.

TOSSPOT My conditions, I am sure, ye know as wel as I.

NEW. A knave thou wast born, and so shalt thou dye.

TOSSPOT But that you are a iudge, I would say unto you,
Knaves are Christen men, els you are a Jew.

NEW. He calleth me knave by craft, doo you not see?
Sirra, I wil remember it when you think not on me.
Wel, say what thou canst for thine own behoof:

379 *behoof* advantage

334

If thou prove thyself the verier knave by good proof,   380
Thou must be the elder brother and have the patrimony.
And when he hath said, then doo thou reply.
Even Thomas a Watrings[21] or Tiburn hil
To the falsest theef of you both, by my fathers wil.

ROISTER I pray you, sir, what is that patrimony?

NEW. I pray you, leave your curtesie, and I will tel you by
     and by.
If he be the more knave, the patrimony he must have;
But thou shalt have it, if thou prove thyself the verier
     knave.
A peece of ground it is, that on beggers maner doth
     holde,
And whoso deserves it, shal have it, ye may be bolde,   390
Called Saint Thomas a Watrings, or els Tiburn Hil,
Given and so bequethed to the falsest knave by wil.

TOSSPOT Then I trow I am he that this patrimony shal
     possesse,
For I am Tom Tospot to use this trade doutles:
From morning til night I sit tossing the black bole,
Then come I home, and pray for my fathers soule,
Saying my praiers with wounds, bloud, guts and hart,
Swearing and staring; thus play I my parte.
If any poore man have in a whole week earn'd a grote,
He shal spend it in one houre in tossing the pot.   400
I use to call servants and poore men to my company,
And make them spend all they have unthriftily;
So that my company they think to be so good,
That in short space their haire growes through their
     hood.

NEW. But wil no gossips keep thee company now and
     than?

TOSSPOT Tush, I am acquainted with many a woman,
That with me wil sit in every house and place:
But then their husbands had need to fend their face.
For when they come home, they wil not be afeard

389 *maner* manor   395 *bole* bowl

To shake the goodman, and sometime shave his beard.　　410
And as for Flemish servants, I have such a train,
That wil quasse and carous, and therin spend their gain.
From week to week I have [all] this company;
Wherfore I am woorthy to have the patrimony.

NEW. Thus thou maist be called a knave in graine,
And where knaves be scant, thou maist goe for twaine.
But now, Rafe Roister, let me heare what thou canst say.

ROISTER You know that Rafe Roister I am called alway,
And my conditions in knavery so far doo surmount
That to have this patrimony I make mine account.　　420
For I intice yong gentlemen all vertue to eschewe,
And to give them to riotousnes, this is true.
Serving men by me are also seduced,
That all in bravery their mindes are confused.
Then, if they have not themselves to maintaine,
To pick and to steale they must be fain.
And I may say to you, I have such a traine
That some time I pitch a feeld on Salisbury Plain[22].
And much more, if need were, I could say verily;
Wherfore I am woorthy to have the patrimony.　　430

NEW. He that should iudge this matter had need have
　　　more wit then I;
But seeing that you have referred it unto my arbitrement,
In faith I wil give such equall iudgement
That both of you shall be wel pleased and content.

ROISTER Nay, I have not doon, for I can say much more.

NEW. Wel, I will not have you contend any more;
But this farme which to beggers manner dooth appertaine
I wil equally devide betweene you twaine.
Are you not content that so it shall be?

BOTH As it pleaseth you, so shall we agree.　　440

NEW. Then see that anon you come bothe unto me.

ROISTER Sir, for my parte, I thank you hartely.
I promised of late to come unto a company,

---

412 *quasse* drink deeply　415 *in graine* thorough (from dyeing)
416 *scant* scarce　426 *pick* filch

Which at Hob Filchers for me doo remain:
God be with you, and anon I wil come again.

TOSSPOT Farwel, brother Rafe, I wil come to you anon.

NEW. Cum again, for you shal not so sodainly be gon.
See you not who cums yonder? An old frend of yours;
One that is redy to quasse at all houres.

Heer entreth Haunce with a pot, and singeth as
foloweth. He singeth the first two lines, and
speaketh the rest as stammering as may be

HAUNCE

Quas in hart and quas again, and quas about the house a,   450
And tosse the black bole to and fro, and I brinks them
    all carous a.

Be go-go-gogs nowns²³, cha-cha drunk zo-zo much
    today
That, be-be-be masse, I cham a moste drunk, ich da-da-
    dare zay,
Chud spe-spe-spend a goo-goo-good grote
Tha-that ich cud vi-vinde my ca-ca-chaptain To-to-tom
    Tospot.

NEW. Sit down, good Haunce, lest thou lye on the ground.
    He seteth him in the chaire
He knoweth not Tom Tospot, I dare ieopard twenty
    pound.

TOSSPOT He will know me by and by, I holde you a
    crown.
How doost thou, servaunt Haunce? How commeth this to
    passe?

HAUNCE Ma-ma-master To-to-tom, cha-cha-cham glad,
    by mas —   460
Ca-ca-carouse to-to thee, goo-goo-good Tom.
    He drinketh

TOSSPOT Holde up, Haunce, I will pledg thee anon.

ROISTER Wel, there is no remedy but I must be gone.

HAUNCE Ta-ta-tary, good velow, a wo-wo-word or twaine:

452 *cha-cha* I-I-have   455 *vinde* find

337

If tho-tho-thou thi self do-do-doo not come againe,
Bi-bi-bid Philip Fleming cu-cu-cum hether to me,
Vo-vo-vor he must lead me home, now ich doo zee.

ROISTER Then farwel, Haunce, I wil remember thy
errant:
He wilbe heer by and by, I dare be his warrant.
Exit Rafe Roister

NEW. Farwel, Rafe Roister, with all my hart: 470
Come anon, and I wil deliver thee thy part.

TOSSPOT Now, Haunce, right now thou drankst to me;
Drink again, and I wil pledge thee.

HAUNCE *Omni-po-po-potenti,* all the po-po-pot is emptie.

NEW. Why, Haunce, thou hast Latin in thy belly, me think:
I thought there was no room for Latin, there is so much
drink.

HAUNCE Ich le-le-lernd zome La-la-laten when ich was a
la-la-lad:
Ich ca-ca-can zay *tu es nebulo*[24], ich learnd of my dad.
And ich did once he-he-help the pre-pre-preest to zay
masse:
By gis[25], ma-man, ich ha been cunning when twas.   480

TOSSPOT I knew Haunce when he was as he saith,
For he was once a scholler in good faith.
But through my company he was withdrawn from
thence,
Through his riote and excessive expence,
Unto this trade which now you doo in him see:
So that now he is wholy addicted to followe me,
And one of my garde he is now become.
Wel, Haunce, wel, thou wast once a white sonne![26]

NEW. Now, so God help me, thou art a pritty felowe,
Haunce,
A clene-legged gentleman, and as proper a praunce   490
As any I know between this and Fraunce.

HAUNCE Yes, by-by God, ich cud once daunce.

NEW. I speak of no dauncing, little belied Haunce,
But, seing thou saist thou canst so wel daunce,
Let me see where thou canst daunce lively.

HAUNCE Tha-tha-that ca-ca-can ich doo ful trimly.
>   *He daunceth as evill favoured as may be devised, and*
>   *in the dauncing he falleth down, and when he riseth*
>   *he must grone*

NEW. Rise again, Haunce, thou hadst almost got a fall:
But thou dauncest trimly, leggs and all.
Body of me, Haunce, how dooth thy belly, canst thou
tel?
By the masse, he hath beraid his breeches, me think by
the smell.   500

TOSSPOT I wil help thee up, Haunce; give me thy hand.
>   *He riseth*

HAUNCE By-by mas, ch-ch-chwas almost down, I think
verily.

NEW. Wast thou almost down, Haunce? So think I.
But thou art sick, me think by thy groning:
He grones like a beare when he is a-moning.
Hark how his head akes, and his pulses doo beat:
I think he wil be hanged, his belly is so great.

HAUNCE Go-go-god a mercy, Tom, with all my hart.

NEW. If thou canst not leap, Haunce, let me see thee drink
a quart,
And get thee out abroad into the aire.   510

TOSSPOT Tush, he had more need to keep his chaire.
Sit down, Haunce, and thou shalt see anon
Philip Fleming wil come and fetch thee home.
>   *Haunce sitteth in the chaire, and snorteth as though*
>   *he were fast asleep*

NEW. I pray thee, Tom Tospot, is this one of thy men?

TOSSPOT He is a companion of mine now and then.

NEW. By the faith of my body, such carpenter, such chips;
And as the wise man saith, such letice, such lips[27].
For like maister, like men; like tutor, like scholer;
And like wil to like, quoth the Devil to the Colier.

TOSSPOT There is no remedy, for it must needs so be;   520
Like wil to like, you may beleeve me.

496 *evill favoured* grotesquely   500 *beraid* befouled

339

Philip Fleming entreth with a pot in his hand

NEW. Loe, where Phillip Fleming commeth even in pudding
    time!

TOSSPOT He bringeth in his hand either good ale or els
    good wine.

PHILLIP FLEMING *singeth these foure lines following*
    Troll the bole and drink to me, and troll the bole
      again-a,
    And put a browne tost[28] in the pot, for Phillip
      Flemmings brain-a,
    And I shall tosse it to and fro, even round about the
      house-a:
    Good hostice, now let it be so, I brinks them all
      carous-a.

FLEMING Mary, heer is a pot of nappy good ale,
    As pure as christall, pure and stale.
    Now a crab in the fire were woorth a good grote,   530
    That I might quasse with my captain Tom Tospot.
    What, I can no sooner wish, but by and by have!
    God save mine eyesight, me think I see a knave.
    What captain, how goeth the world with you?

TOSSPOT Why, now I see the olde proverb to be true,
    Like wil to like, both with Christian, Turk, and Jew.
    Mary, Phillip, even as I was wont to doo.

FLEMING Rafe Roister tolde me I should finde Haunce
    heere.
    Where is he, that he dooth not appeere?

NEW. I holde twenty pound the knave is blinde.   540
    Turn about, Phillip Fleming, and look behinde.
    Hast thou drunk so much that thine eyes be out?
    Lo, how he snorteth like a lazy lout.
    Goe to him, for he sleepeth sound.
    Two such paunches in all England can scant be found.

FLEMING Why, Haunce, art thou in thy praiers so
      devoutly?

---

524 *Troll* pass   527 *hostice* hostess   528 *nappy* foaming   529 *stale*
still and strong   530 *crab* apple

Awake, man, and we two wil quasse togither stoutly.

HAUNCE *Domine dominus noster,*

Me think I cha spide three knaves in a cluster.

NEW. Stay a while, for he saith his *Pater Noster.* 550

HAUNCE *Sanctum Benedicitum,* what have I dremed?

By gogs nowns, chad thought ich had been in my bed.

Cha dremed such a dreme that thou wilt mervaile to
heere.

Me thought ich was drowned in a barell of beere,

And by and by the barrel was turned to a ship,

Which me thought the winde made lively to skip.

And ich did sail therin from Flaunders to Fraunce[29]:

At last ich was brought hether among a sort of knaves
by chaunce.

NEW. Lo, Haunce, heer is Phillip Fleming come now;

We wil goe drink togither now, how saist thou? 560

HAUNCE I pray thee, god Vilip, lead me away.

FLEMING Give me thy hand, and I wil thee stay.

HAUNCE How say you, maister Nichol, wil you keep us
company?

NEW. Goe before, maister lickhole, and I wil come by
and by.

Mates matched togither, departe you three;

I wil come after, you may beleeve me.

*They three are gone togither, and Nichole Newfangle
remaineth behinde, but he must not speak til they be
within*

Ha, ha, ha, ha, ha, ha, ha, ha.

Now three knaves are gone, and I am left alone,

My selfe heere to solace;

Wel doon, gentle Ione, why begin you to mone? 570

Though they be gone, I am in place.

And now I wil daunce, now wil I praunce,

For why I have none other woork:

Snip, snap, butter is no bone meat;

Knaves flesh is no porke.

558 *sort* company, collection

Hey tisty tosty, an ole is a bird:
    Iack-a-napes[30] hath an olde face.
You may beleeve me at one bare woord;
    How like you this mery cace?
A peece of ground they think they have found,   580
    I wil tel you what it is:
For I them tolde that of beggars maner it did holde,
    A staffe and a wallet, I wis.
Which in short space, even in this place,
    Of me they shall receive:
For when that their drift hath spent all their thrift,
    Their mindes I shall deceive.
I trowe you shall see more knaves come to me,
    Which whensoever they doo,
They shall have their meed, as they deserve indeed,   590
    As you shal shortly see these two.
When they doo pretend to have a good end
    Mark wel, then, what shall insue:
A bag and a bottle, or els a rope knottle,
    This shall they prove to true.
But mark wel this game; I see this geer frame.
    Lo, who cometh now in such hast?
It is Cuthbert Cutpurse and Pierce Pickpurse,
    Give room now a little cast.
       Heere entreth Cuthbert Cutpurse and Pierce Pickpurse.
       Cuthbert Cutpurse must have in his hand a purse of
       money or counters in it, and a knife in one hand and a
       whetstone in the other, and Pierce must have money
       or counters in his hand and gingle it as he commeth in
CUTPURSE By Gogs wounds, it dooth me good to the
       hart   600
To see how clenly I plaid this parte.
While they stood thrusting togither in the throng,
I began to goe them among;
And with this knife, which heere you doo see,

576 *ole* owl   579 *cace* arrangement   583 *wallet* pack, scrip   599
cast space   *gingle* jingle

I cut away his purse clenly.

NEW. See to your purses, my maisters; be ruled by me,
  For knaves are abroad; therfore beware.
  You are warned; and ye take not heed, I doo not care.

PICKPURSE And also so soon as I had espied
  A woman in the throng, whose purse was fat,   610
  I took it by the strings, and clenly it untide:
  She knew no more of it then Gib our cat.
  Yet at the last she hied apace,
  And said the money in my hand she saw.
  'Thou whore,' said I, 'I wil have an action of the case,
  And seing thou saist so, I will trye the lawe.'

CUTPURSE How saist thou Pierce Pickpurse, art thou not
        agreed
  These two booties equally to devide?

PICKPURSE Then let us count the totall summe,
  And devide it equally when we have doone.   620

NEW. My maisters, heere is a good fellowe that would faine
        have some.

CUTPURSE What, Nicole Newfangle, be you heere?
  So God help me, I am glad with all my hart.

PICKPURSE Then ere we depart, we wil have some cheere,
  And of this booty you shall have your parte.

NEW. I thank you both hartely,
  And I will doo somewhat for you by and by.
  Are not you two sworn brothers in every bootye?

BOTH Yes, that we are truely.

NEW. Then will I tell you newes, which you doo not
        knowe,   630
  Such newes as wil make you glad, I trowe.
  But first tel me this, Pierce Pickpurse,
  Whether is the elder, thou or Cuthbert Cutpurse.

PICKPURSE In faith, I think we are both of one age, wel
        nye.

CUTPURSE I suppose there is no great difference, truely,
  But wherfore ask you? I pray thee, tell me why.

  608 *and* if   633 *Whether* which of the two

NEW. I wil tell you the cause without delay:
    For a peece of land is fallen, as I heare say,
    A proper plot it is, this is most true,
    Which by succession must come to one of you.   640
    For thou, Cuthbert Cutpurse, wast Cuthbert Cutthrotes
        sonne,
    And thou, Pierce Pickpurse, by that time thou hast doon,
    Canst derive thy pedigree from an ancient house:
    Thy father was Tom Theef, thy mother Tib Louse.
    This peece of land, wherto you inheritours are,
    Is called the land of the two-legged mare[31]:
    In this peece of ground there is a mare in deed,
    Which is the quickest mare in England for speede.
    Therfore, if you will come anon unto me,
    I will put you in possession, and that you shall see.   650
CUTPURSE I cannot beleeve that such luck is happened unto
    us.
NEW. It is true, that I to you doo discusse.
PICKPURSE If you wil help us to this peece of ground,
    Bothe of us to you shal think ourselves bound.
NEW. Yes, in faith, you shall have it, you may beleeve me;
    I will be as good as my woord, as shortly you shall see.
CUTPURSE Then, brother Pierce, we may think ourselves
       happy
    That ever we were with him acquainted.
PICKPURSE Even so, we may of certaintie,
    That such good luck unto us hath happened.   660
    But, brother Cuthbert, is it not best
    To goe in for a while, and distribute this booty?
    Where we three wil make some feast,
    And quasse togither, and be mery.
CUTPURSE What say you, Nichol?
NEW.   I doo agree[32].
     Heere entreth Vertuous Living.
NEW. But soft a while; be ruled by me.
    Look yonder a little. Doo you not see

652 *discusse* describe

Who commeth yonder? A while we wil abide;
Let him say his pleasure, and we wil stand aside.

V.L. Oh gratious God, how wonderfull are thy woorks.   670
How highly art thou of all men to be praised.
Of Christians, Sarasins, Iewes and also Turks
Thy glory ought to be erected and raised.
What ioyes hast thou prepared for the vertuous life,
And such as have thy name in love and awe.
Thou hast promised salvation to man, childe, and wife
That thy precepts observe and keep wel thy law.
And to the vertuous life what dooth insue?
Vertutis premium honor, Tully[33] dooth saye:
Honour is the guerdon for vertue due,   680
And eternall salvation at the latter day.
How cleere in conscience is the vertuous life!
The vicious hath consciences so heavy as lead;
Their conscience and their dooings is alway at strife,
And although they live, yet in sin they are dead.

NEW. God give you good morow, sir; how doo you today?

V.L. God blesse you also, both now and alway.
I pray you, with me have you any acquaintance?

NEW. Yea, mary, I am an olde freend of yours, perchaunce.

V.L. If it be so, I mervaile very much   690
That the dulnes of my wit should be such
That you should be altogither out of my memory.
Tell me your name, I pray you hartely.

NEW. By the faith of my body, you wil appose me by and
            by;
But indeed I was but little when I was first borne,
And my mother to tell me my name thought it scorne.

V.L. I wil never acquaint me with such in any place
As are ashamed of their names, by Gods grace.

NEW. I remember my name, now it is come to minde:
I have mused much before I could it finde.   700
Nichole Newfangle it is; I am your olde freend.

V.L. My freend! Mary, I doo thee defye,

680 *guerdon* reward   694 *appose* cross-examine

And all such company I doo deny.
For thou art a companion for roisters and ruffins,
And not fit for any vertuous companions.
NEW. And, in faith, art thou at plaine defiaunce?
Then I see that I must goe to mine olde acquaintaunce.
Wel, Cuthbert Cutpurse and Pierce Pickpurse, we must
    goe togither,
For like wil to like, quoth the Devil to the Colier.
V.L. Indeed, thou saist true; it must needs be so, 710
For like wil ever to like goe.
And my conditions and thine so farre doo disagree
That no familiarity between us may be.
For thou nourishest vice both day and night:
My name is Vertuous Life, and in vertue is my delight.
So vice and vertue cannot togither be united:
But the one the other hath alwaies spighted.
For as water quencheth fier, and the flame dooth suppres,
So vertue hateth vice, and seeketh a redres.
PICKPURSE Tush, if he be so dangerous, let us not him
    esteem, 720
And he is not for our company, I see very wel.
For if he be so holy as he dooth seem,
We and he differ as much as Heaven and Hell.
NEW. You knowe that like wil to like alway,
And you see how holily he is now bent;
To seek his company why doo we assay?
PICKPURSE I promise you, doo what you wil, I wil not
    consent:
For I passe not for him, be he better or be he wursse.
NEW. Freend, if you be wise, beware of your purse.
For this fellow may doo you good when all comes to
    all, 730
If you chaunce to loose your purse in Cutpurse Hall.
But, in faith, fare ye wel, sith of our company you be
    wery;
We wil goe to a place where we wil make mery.

728 *passe* care

For I see your company and ours doo far differ,
For like wil to like, quoth the Devil to the Colier.

CUTPURSE Well, let us be gone, and bid him adue,
For I see this proverb proveth very true.

PICKPURSE Then let us goe to Hob Filchers house
Where we wil be mery, and quasse carous,
And there shall we finde Tom Tospot, with othermoe,　　　740
Meet mates for us, therfore let us goe.

NEW. Then, seeing we are all of one minde,
Let us three go, and leave a knave heer behinde.

　　　Exeunt they three
　　　They sing this song as they goe out from the place

Good hostes, lay a crab in the fire, and broil a messe of
　　　sous-a,
　　That we may tosse the bole to and fro, and brinks
　　　them all carous-a.

And I wil pledge Tom Tospot, til I be as drunk as a
　　　mouse-a;
　　Who so wil drink to me all day, I wil pledge them all
　　　carous-a.

Then we wil not spare for any cost, so long as we be in
　　　a house-a,
　　Then hostes, fil the pot again, for I pledge them all
　　　carous-a.

　　　Finis

V.L. Oh wicked imps, that have such delight　　　750
In evil conversation, wicked and abhominable;
And from vertues lore withdraw yourselves quite,
And lean to vice most vile and detestable!
How prone and redy we are vice to insue!
How defe we be good counsaile to heare!
How strange we make it our harts to renue!
How little we have Gods threats in feare!

　　　When this is spoken he must pause and then say as
　　　followeth

739 *carous* in a toast　740 *othermoe* others of the same kind　744
sous pickles　750 *imps* fools　754 *insue* follow

347

Saint Augustine saith in his fifth book *De Civitate Dei*[34],
Coniuncta sunt aedes Vertutis et Honoris, saith he:
The house of Vertue and Honour ioyned togither be.   760
And so the way to Honours house is disposed
That through Vertues house he must needs passe,
Or else from honour he shall soone be deposed,
And brought to that point that he before was.
    But if through vertue, honour be attained,
    The path to salvation may soon be gained.
Some there be that doo fortune prefer,
Some esteem plesure more then vertuous life;
But in mine opinion all such doo erre,
For vertue and fortune be not at strife.   770
    Where vertue is, fortune must needs growe:
    But fortune without vertue hath soone the overthrowe.
Thrice happy are they that doo vertue imbrace,
For a crowne of glory shall be their rewarde:
Sathan at no time may him any thing deface,
For God over him wil have such regarde
    That his foes he shall soon tread under his foot,
    And by Gods permission pluck them up by the root.
It booteth not vice against vertue to stur,
For why vice is feeble and of no force: 780
But *Virtus eterna preclaraque habetur*.
Wherfore I would all men would have a remorse,
    And eschue evil company vile and pernicious:
And as the end of vertue is honour and felicitie,
So mark wel the end of wickednes and vice:
Shame in this world and pain eternally;
Wherfore you that are heere learn to be wise,
And the end of the one with the other waye,
By that time you have heard the end of this play.
But why doo I thus much say in the praise of vertue   790
Sith the thing praiseworthy need no praise at all?
It praiseth it self sufficiently, this is true,
Which chaseth away sinne as bitter as gall.
And where vertue is, need not to be praised,
For the renowne therof shall soon be raised.

Intrat Good Fame

G.F. Oh Vertuous Life, God rest you mery;
  To you I am come to attend.

V.L. Good Fame, you are welcome hartely.
  I pray you, who did you hether send?

G.F. Even Gods Promise hath sent me unto you,   800
  Willing me not from you to depart,
  But alwaies to give attendance due,
  And in no wise from you to start.
  For God of his promise hath moste liberally
  Sent me, Good Fame, to you, Vertuous Life.
  Wherby it may be seene manifestly
  Gods great zeale to vertue both in man and wife.
  For why they may be sure that I, Good Fame,
  From the Vertuous Life will not stray.
  Wherby honour and renown may grow to their name,   810
  And eternall salvation at the latter day.

V.L. God is gratious and full of great mercy
  To such as in vertue set their whole delight,
  Powring his benefites upon them aboundantly.
  Oh man, what meanest thou with saviour to fight?
  Come unto him, for he is full of mercy,
  The fountain of vertue and of godlines the spring:
  Come unto me and thou shalt live everlastingly,
  He dooth not require thee any price to bring.
  Venite ad me omnes qui laboratis et onerati estis et ego
      reficiam vos[35].   820
  Come unto me ye that travaile, saith he,
  And such as with sinne are hevily laden,
  And of myselfe refreshed you shall be.
  Repent, repent; your deeds shall be down troden.
  Wel, Good Fame, sith God of his goodnes
  Hath hether sent you on me to attend,
  Let us give thanks to him with humblenes,
  And perswade with all men their lives to amend.

G.F. Vertuous Life, therto I doo agree,

814 *Powring* pouring

349

For it becommeth all men to doo so.   830
But beholde, yonder commeth Gods Promise, as seemeth
    to me,
And Honour with him commeth also.

Enter Gods Promises and Honour with him

v.l. Such godly company liketh me very wel,
For vicious men from our company we woulde expel.
g.prom. God rest you mery both, and God be your guide.
honour We are now come to the place where we must
    abide,
For from you, Vertuous Life, I, Honour, may not slide.
g.prom. I am Gods Promise, which is a thing etern,
And nothing more surer then his promises may be,
A sure foundation to such as wil learn   840
Gods precepts to observe: then must they needs see
Honour in this world, and at last a crown of glorye;
Ever in ioy and mirth, and never to be sory.
Wherfore, Oh Vertuous Life, to thee we doo repaire,
As messengers from God, his promise to fulfil;
And therfore sit you downe in this chaire,
For to indue you with honour it is Gods promise and wil.

Vertuous Living sitteth downe in the chaire

honour Now take this swoord in hand as a token of
    victorye;
This crowne from my head to you I shall give.
I crowne you with it as one moste woorthy;   850
And see that all vice ye doo punish and greeve.
For in this world I, Honour, with you shall remain,
And Good Fame from you cannot refrain:
And after this life, a greater crown you shall attain.
g.prom. What hart can think, or what tung can expresse
The great goodnes of God, which is almightye?
Who seeth this, and seeketh not vice to suppresse,
Honour, Good Fame, yea, and life everlastingly?
    Thy name be praised, oh Lord, therfore,
    And to thee only be glory and honour!   860
g.f. Sith Gods Promise hath brought Honour into this
    place,

I will for a while leave you three alone:
For I must depart now for a litle space,
But I shal come to you again anon.
    Exit Good Fame

G. PROM. Gods Promise is infallible; his woord is most
      true;
And to ground theron a man may be bolde:
As Scripture dooth testifye and declare unto you,
On which foundation your building you may beholde.
  For vertuous rulers the fruit of felicitie doo reap,
    And the reward of Fame and Honour to themselves
    they heap.   870

HONOUR Seing we have now indued him with the crown
    and swoord,
Which is due unto him by Gods promise and woord,
Let us three sing unto God with one accord.

G. PROM. To sing praises unto God it liketh wel me.

V. L. And I also with you therto doo agree.
A plesant noise to Gods eares it must needs bring
That Gods Promise, Honour, and Vertuous Life doo sing.
    They sing this song folowing
    This must be sung after every verse
    Life is but short; hope not therin;
    Vertue immortall seek for to win.

Who so to vertue dooth apply,   880
    Good Fame and Honour must obtaine,
And also live eternally;
    For Vertuous Life this is the gaine.
          Life is but short, &c.

Gods Promise sure will never faile;
    His holy woord is a perfect ground:
The forte of vertue, oh man, assaile,
    Where tresure alway dooth abound.
          Life is but short, &c.

To thee alone be laud and praise,   890
    Oh Lord, thou art so mercifull:

Who never failed at all assaies,
   To aid and help the pitifull.
         Life is but short; hope not therin.

Finis
Exeunt omnes
Heere entreth Nichole Newfangle and bringeth in
with him a bagge, a staffe, a bottle, and two halters,
going about the place shewing it to the audience, and
singing this

[NEW.] Trim marchandise, trim, trim, trim marchandise,
    trim, trim[36].

   He may sing this as oft as he thinketh good

Mary, heer is merchandise, who list for to buy any:
Come see for your love, and buy for your money.
This is the land which I must distribute anon
According to my promise, or I begon.
For why Tom Tospot, since he went hence,   900
Hath increased a noble[37] iust unto ninepence;
And Rafe Roister, it may none otherwise be chosen,
Hath brought a pack of wul to a faire paire of hosen:
This is good thrift, learn it who shall.
And now a couple of felowes are come from Cutpurse
    Hall,
And there have they brought many a purse to wrack.
Loe, heer is geer that wil make their necks to crack,
For I promised Tom Tospot and Rafe Roister a peece
    of land;
Loe, heere it is redy in my right hand:
A wallet[38] and bottle, but it is not to be solde.   910
I tolde them before that of beggers maner it did holde;
And for Cuthbert Cutpurse and Pierce Pickpurse heere
    is good fare:
This is the land of the two legged mare,
Which I to them promised, and devide it with discretion.
Shortly you shall see I wil put them in possession.
How like you this marchandise, my maisters? Is not this
    trim?

      899 *or* before   903 *wul* wool

A wallet, a bottle, a staffe, and a string.
How saist thou, Wat Waghalter? Is not this a trim
    thing?[39]
In faith, Rafe Roister is in good case, as I suppose,
For he hath lost all that he hath, save his doublet and
    his hose;   920
And Tom Tospot is even at the same poynte,
For he would loose a lim or ieopard a ioynt.
But beholde, yonder they come bothe, now all is gone
    and spent,
I knowe their errand, and what is their intent.

> *Heere entreth Rafe Roister and Tom Tospot in their*
> *dublet and their hose, and no cap nor hat on their head,*
> *saving a night cap because the strings of the beards*
> *may not be seene, and Rafe Roister must cursse and ban*
> *as he commeth in*

ROISTER Wel, be as be may, is no banning:
But I feare that when this geere shall come to scanning,
The land to the which we did wholy trust
Shall be gone from us, and we cast in the dust.
TOSSPOT Gogs blood, if Nichol Newfangle serve us so,
We may say that we have had a shrewd blowe;   930
For all that I had is now lost at dice,
My swoord, my buckler, and all at sink and sice[40];
My cote, my cloke and my hat also;
And now in my dublet and my hose I am faine to goe.
Therfore, if Nichol Newfangle help not now at a pinch,
I am undoon, for land I have not an inch.
ROISTER By Gogs wounds, even so it is with me;
I am in my doublet and my hose, as ye see:
For all that I had dooth lye at pledge for ale.
By the masse, I am as bare as my naile,   940
Not a crosse[41] of money to blesse me have I;
But I trow we shall meet with Nichol Newfangle by and
    by.
NEW. Turn hether, turn hether, I say, sir knave;

924 *ban* curse   926 *scanning* judgement   930 *shrewd* severe

For I am even he, that you so fain would have.

ROISTER What, Maister Nichole, are you heer all this
while?

NEW. I think I am heere, or els I doo thee begile.

TOSSPOT So God help me, I am glad that you be in sight,
For in faith your presence hath made my hart light.

NEW. I wil make it lighter anon, I trowe.
My maisters, I have a peece of land for you, doo you
not knowe?   950

ROISTER Mary, that is the cause of our hether resort,
For now we are void of all ioy and comfort.

TOSSPOT You see in what care we now stand in,
And you heard us also even now, I ween.
Wherfore, good Maister Nichol, let us have this land
now,
And we shall think ourselves much bound unto you.

NEW. You know that I this land must devide,
Which I shall doo; but a while abide.
All thy goods for ale at pledge be,
And thou saist a paire of dice hath made thee free: 960
First, Rafe Roister, come thou unto me
Because thou hast lost every whit at dice,
Take thou this bag to cary bread and cheese,
*He giveth the bag to Rafe Roister, and the bottle to
Tom Tosspot*
And take thou this bottle, and mark what I shall say:
If he chaunce to eat the bread and cheese by the way,
Doo thou in this matter follow my councel,
Drink up the drink, and knock him about the head with
the bottle.
And because that Rafe is the elder knave,
This staffe also of me thou shalt have.

ROISTER But where is the land that to us you promised?   970

NEW. In faith, good fellowes, my promise is performed.

TOSSPOT By Gogs blood, I thought that it would be so.

NEW. This must you have, whether you wil or no,

962 *whit* small piece (of money)

Or els fall to woork with shovel and with spade;
For begging now must be your cheefest trade.

ROISTER Gods hart, can I away with this life
 To beg my bread from doore to doore?
 I wil rather cut my throte with a knife
 Then I will live thus beggerly and poore.
 By Gogs blood, rather then I wil it assay   980
 I wil rob and steale, and keep the hye way.

TOSSPOT Wel, Rafe Roister, seeing we be in this miserie,
 And labour we cannot, and to beg it is a shame,
 Yet better it is to beg most shamfully
 Then to be hanged, and to theevery ourselves to frame.

NEW. Now, my maisters, learn to beware;
 But like wil to like, quod the Devil to the Coliar.

ROISTER Oh Lord, why did not I consider this before,
 What should of roisting be the finall end?
 Now the horse is stolen, I shut the stable doore[42]. 990
 Alas, that I had time my life to amend!
 Time I have, I must needs confesse,
 But yet in misery that time must be spent,
 Seeing that my life I would not redresse,
 But wholy in riot I have it all spent:
 Wherfore I am now brought to this exigent.
 But the time past cannot be called again, this is no nay;
 Wherfore all you heere take example by me,
 Time tarieth no man, but passeth stil away.
 Take time while time is, for time dooth flee.   1000
 Use wel your youthful yeeres, and to vertues lore agree.
 For if I to vertue had any respect,
 This misfortune to me could not have chaunced;
 But because unto vice I was subiect,
 To no good fame I now be advaunced.
 My credit also is now quite staunched;
 Wherfore I would all men my wofull case might see,
 That I to them a mirrour might be.

TOSSPOT Oh all ye parents, to you I doo say,

996 *exigent* strait 1006 *staunched* dried up

Have respect to your children and for their education,　　　1010
Least you answere therfore at the latter day,
And your meed shall be eternall damnation.
If my parents had brought me up in vertue and
　　　learning,
I should not have had this shamefull end;
But all licenciously was my up bringing.
Wherfore learn by me your faults to amend.
But neither in vertue, learning, nor yet honest trade
Was I bred up my living for to get:
Therfore in misery my life away must fade.
For vicious persons beholde not the net;　　　1020
I am in the snare, I am caught with the gin,
And now it is too late, I cannot again begin.

NEW. This geere would have been looked too before,
But now, my maisters, you are upon the skore[43]
Be packing, I say, and get you hence:
Learn to say 'I pray, good maister, give me nine pence.'

ROISTER Thou, villain, art only the causer of this woe;
Therfore thou shalt have some thing of me ere I goe.

TOSSPOT Thou hast given me a bottle heere;
But thou shalt drink first of it, be it ale or beere.　　　1030

　　　Rafe Roister beateth him with the staffe, and Tom
　　　Tosspot with the bottell

ROISTER Take this of me, before I goe hence.

TOSSPOT Take this of me, in parte of recompence.

NEW. Now am I driven to play the maister of fence[44]
Come no neer me, you knaves, for your life,
Least I stick you both with this wood knife[45].
Back I say, back, thou sturdy beggar!
Body of me, they have tane away my daggar.

　　　They have him doun and beat him. He crieth for help

ROISTER Now, in faith, you whorson, take heed, I you
　　　advise,
How you doo any more yong men intice.

TOSSPOT Now, farwell, thou hast thy iust meed.　　　1040

1021 *gin* trap

ROISTER Now we goe a-begging, God send us good speed.
Rafe Roister and Tom Tosspot goeth out, and
Severitie the Iudge entreth. Nichol Newfangle lieth
on the ground groning

SEVERITY That upright iudgement without parcialitie
Be ministered duely to ill-dooers and offenders!
I am one whose name is Severitie,
Appointed a Iudge to suppresse evil-dooers,
Not for hatred, nor yet for malice,
But to advaunce vertue and suppresse vice.
Wherfore Isidorus[46] these woords dooth say,
Non est Iudex si in eo non est Iusticia:
He is not a Iudge that Iustice dooth want,   1050
But he that trueth and equitie dooth plant.
Tully also these woords dooth expresse,
Which woords are very true doubtlesse.
Semper iniquus est [Iudex] qui aut invidet aut favet:
They are unrightfull Iudges all,
That are either envious or els partiall.

NEW. Help me up, good sir, for I have got a fall.

SEVERITY What cause have you, my freend, thus heavily
to grone?

NEW. Oh sir, I have good cause to make great mone:
Heere were two fellowes, but right now,   1060
That I think have killed me, I make God a vow.
I pray you tel me, am I alive or am I dead?

SEVERITY Fellowe, it is more need for thee to be in thy
bed
Then to lye heere in such sort as thou doost.

NEW. In faith, I should have laid some of the knaves in
the dust
If I had had your swoord right now in presence;
I would have had a leg or an arme, ere they had gon
hence.

SEVERITY Who is it that hath doon thee this iniury?

NEW. A couple of beggers have doon me this vilany.

SEVERITY I see if severitie should not be executed,   1070
One man should not live by another.

357

If such iniuries should not be confuted,
The childe would not regard father nor mother.
Give me thy hand, and I wil help thee.
NEW. Hold fast your swoord then, I pray you hartely.
>*He riseth*
SEVERITY Now, freend, it appeereth unto me
That you have been a travailer of the cuntrie,
And such as doo travaile doo heare of things doon,
As wel in the cuntrie, as in the citie of London.
How say you, my freend; can you tel any newes? 1080
NEW. That can I, for I came lately from the stewes.
There are knaves abroad, you may beleeve me,
As in this place shortly you shall see.
No more woords but mum, and stand awhile aside:
Yonder commeth two knaves; therfore abide.
>*Enter Cuthbert Cutpurse and Pierce Pickpurse*
CUTPURSE By Gogs wounds, if he help not now, we are
>undoon:
By the mas, for my part I wot not where to run.
We be so pursued on every side
That, by Gogs hart, I wot not where to abide.
Every constable is charged to make privy search, 1090
So that if we may be got, we shalbe thrown over the
>perch.
PICKPURSE If Nichol Newfangle help not now in our
>need,
We are like in our busines ful evil to speed.
Therfore let us make no more delay,
But seek him out of hand, and be gone away.
NEW. Soft, my maisters, a while I you pray:
For I am heer for whom you doo seek;
For you know that like wil never from like.
I promised you of late a peece of land,
Which by and by shall fall into your hand. 1100
CUTPURSE What, maister Nichol, how doo you today?

1077 *travailer* traveller   1090 *privy* thorough (secret)   1091 *perch*
gallows

358

PICKPURSE For the passion of God, maister Nichol, help
   to rid us away;
 And help us to the land wherof you did say
 That we might make money of it by and by:
 For out of the realm we purpose to flee.
NEW. Mary, I wil help you, I swere by all hallowes:
 I wil not part from you till you come to the gallowes.
 Lo, noble Severitie, these be they, without doubt,
 On whom this rumor of theevery is gon about.
 Therfore, my maisters, heer is the snare,   1110
 That shall lead you to the land called the two-legged
   mare.
  He putteth about each of their necks an halter
SEVERITY My freend, holde them fast in that plight.
NEW. Then come, and help me with your sword, for I feare
   they wil fight.
SEVERITY Strive not, my maisters, for it shall not availe.
 But a while give eare unto my counsaile:
 Your owne woords have condemned you for to dye,
 Therfore to God make you yourselves redy.
 And by and by I wil send one which, for your abusion,
 Shall lead you to the place of execution.
NEW. Help to tye their hands before ye be gon.   1120
  He helpeth to tye them.
SEVERITY Now they are bound. I wil send one to you anon.
  Exit
NEW. Ah, my maisters, how like you this play?
 You shall take possession of your land today!
 I wil help to bridle the two-legged mare,
 And both you for to ride need not to spare.
 Now so God help me, I swere by this bread,
 I mervaile who shall play the knave when you twain be
   dead.
CUTPURSE Oh cursed caitive, borne in an ill hower,
 Woe unto me that ever I did thee knowe.
 For of all iniquitie thou art the bowre;   1130

1106 *hallowes* saints 1118 *abusion* law breaking 1128 *hower* hour

The seed of Sathan thou doost alwaies sowe.
Thou only hast given me the overthrowe.
Woe woorth the house wherin I was borne!
Woe woorth the time that ever I knew thee!
For now in misery I am forlorne.
Oh all youth, take example by me:
Flee from evill company as from the Serpent ye would
    flee,
For I to you all a mirrour may be.
I have been daintily and delicately bred,
But nothing at all in vertues lore: 1140
And now I am but a man dead;
Hanged I must be, which greeveth me full sore.
Note well the end of me therfore:
And you that fathers and mothers be,
Bring not up your children in to much libertie.

PICKPURSE Sith that by the law we are now condemned,
Let us call to God for his mercie and grace,
And exhort that all vice may be amended,
While we in this world have time and space.
And though our lives have licenciously been spent,   1150
Yet at the last to God let us call:
For he heareth such as are ready to repent,
And desireth not that sinners should fall.
Now are we ready to suffer, come when it shall.
    Heer entreth Hankin Hangman

NEW. Come, Hankin Hangman, let us two cast lots,
And between us devide a couple of coates.
Take thou the one, and the other shalbe mine.
Come, Hankin Hangman, thou camst in good time.
    They take off their cotes and devide them

HANGMAN Thou shouldst have one, Nichol, I swere by
    the masse,
For thou bringest woork for me dayly to passe,   1160
And through thy means I get more cotes in a yeere
Then all my living is woorth beside, I swere.

    1135 *forlorne* destroyed   1139 *daintily* carefully

Therfore, Nichol Newfangle, we wil depart never;
For like wil to like, quoth the Devil to the Collier.
NEW. Now farwel, Hankin Hangman, farwel to thee.
HANGMAN Farwel, Nichol Newfangle. Come you two with
        me.

> *Hankin goeth out and leadeth the one in his right*
> *hand, and the other in his left, having halters about*
> *their necks*

NEW.
Ha, ha, ha, there is a brace of hounds wel woorth a
        dozen crowns,
  Beholde the huntsman leadeth away!
I think in twenty towns, on hills, and eke on downs,
  They taken have their pray.   1170
So well liked was their hunting on hill and eke on
        mountain,
  That now they be up in a leace:
To keep within a string it is now a gay thing.
  Doo all you holde your peace?
Why then, good gentle boy, how likest thou this play?
  No more, but say thy minde.
I swere by this day, if thou wilt this assay,
  I wil to thee be kinde.
This is wel brought to passe of me, I swere by the
        masse,
  Some to hand, and other some to beg.   1180
I would I had Balams[47] asse to cary me where I was.
  How say you, little Meg?
Rafe Roister and Tom Tospot are not now woorth a
        grote,
  So wel with them it is.
I would I had a pot, for now I am so whot,
  By the masse, I must go pisse.
Philip Fleming and Haunce hath daunst a prity daunce,
  That all is now spent out;

1172 *leace* leash (for 'halter')

And now a great mischaunce came on while they did
    praunce:
  They lye sick of the gout;   1190
And in a spittle house[48] with little Laurence louse
  They be faine to dwell.
If they eate a morsel of souce, or els a rosted mouse,
  They think they doo fare well.
But as for Pierce Pickpurse and Cuthbert Cutpurse,
  You saw them both right now:
With them it is much wurse, for they doo ban and
    curse,
  For the halter shall them bow.
Now if I had my nag to see the world wag,
  I would straight ride about: 1200
Ginks doo fil the bag, I would not passe a rag
  To hit you on the snout.
    Heer entreth the Devil
LUC. Ho, ho, ho, mine own boy, make no more delay,
But leap upon my back straight way.
NEW. Then who shall holde my stirrop, while I goe to
    horse?
LUC. Tush, for that doo thou not force,
Leap up, I say, leap up, quickly.
NEW. Who, Ball, who, and I will come by and by.
Now for a paire of spurs I would give a good grote,
To try whether the iade dooth amble or trot!   1210
Farwel, my maisters, til I come again,
For now I must make a iourney into Spaine[49].
    He rideth away on the Devils back
    Heer entreth Vertuous Life and Honour
V.L. Oh woorthy diadem, oh iewel most precious,
Oh vertue, which dooth all worldly things excel:
How worthy a treasure thou art to the vertuous!
Thy praise no pen can write, ne tung tel.
For I, who am called Vertuous Life,

1193 *souce* pickles 1201 *Ginks* clinks (of money) 1208 *Who*
whoa! 1216 *ne* nor

Have in this world both honour and dignitie;
Immortall fame of man, childe, and wife
Dayly waiteth and attendeth on me.   1220
The commoditie of vertue in me you may behold;
The enormities of vice you have also seene:
Therfore to make an end we may be bolde,
And pray for our noble and vertuous Queene.

HONOUR To doo so, Vertuous Life, it is our bounden dutye,
   And because we must doo so before we doo end,
   To aid us therin Good Fame commeth verily,
   Which dayly and hourely on you dooth attend.
     Heer entreth Good Fame

G.F. Vertuous Life, doo what you list:
   To pray or to sing I wil you assist.   1230

V.L. O Lord of hostes, oh King almightye,
   Poure down thy grace upon our noble Queene!
   Vanquish her foes, Lord, that dayly and nightly
   Through her thy lawes may be sincerely seen.

HONOUR The honourable Counsaile also, O Lord,
      preserve,
   The Lords both of the Clergie and of the Temporalitie:
   Graunt that with meeknes they may thee serve,
   Submitting to thee with all humilitie.

G.F. Oh Lord, preserve the Commons of this realme also;
   Poure upon them thy heavenly grace,   1240
   To advaunce vertue and vice to overthrowe,
   That at the last in heaven with thee they may have a
     place.

AMEN

A Song[50]

Where like to like is matched so
   That vertue must of force decay:
There God with vengeance, plagues and woe
   By iudgement iust must needs repay.
     For like to like, the worldlings cry,
     Although both like doo grace defye.

And where as Sathan planted hath 1250
   In vicious mindes a sinful trade,
There like to like dooth walke this path,
   By which to him like they are made.
     So like with like reward obtain,
     To have their meed in endles paine.

Likewise in faith, where matched be
   And where as God hath planted grace,
There doo his children stil agree,
   And like to like doo run their race.
     Like Christe, like harts of Christian men: 1260
     As like to like wel coupled then.

Therfore like grace, like faith and love,
   Like vertue, springs of eche degree
Where like assistance from above
   Dooth make them like so right agree:
     A holy God, a Christ most iust,
     And so like soules in him to trust.

Then like as Christe above dooth raigne,
   In heaven high our Saviour best,
So like with him shal be our gain 1270
   In peace, and ioy, and endles rest,
     If we our selves like him doo frame,
     In feare of his most holy name.

To him be praise that grace dooth give,
   Wherby he fashineth us anew:
And make us holily to live,
   Like to himself in faith most true.
     Which our redemption sure hath wrought,
     Like him to be most deerly bought.

SIR THOMAS MORE

This play has survived in manuscript form and is in the British Museum (MS. Harley 7368). Studies of the handwriting have shown that five dramatists contributed to the play in its present form. It was originally the work of Anthony Munday (1560–1633) (Hand S), c.1590–93. His first version was rejected, on account of certain allegedly seditious passages, by the Master of the Revels, Edmund Tilney, whose handwriting appears on the manuscript. Revisions and additions were attempted by four other playwrights, probably in the years 1594–5. These have been identified as

Hand A: Henry Chettle (c. 1560–1607)
Hand B: Thomas Heywood (c.1572–1632)
Hand D: William Shakespeare (1564–1616)
Hand E: Thomas Dekker (c.1574–1641)

Hand C is that of a book-keeper who started to put the play in readiness for performance. But it was again rejected by Tilney, and there is no indication that a performance took place.

There are two modern editions:

C. F. Tucker Brooke, *The Shakespeare Apocrypha*, Oxford, 1908
W. W. Greg, *Malone Society Reprint*, 1911
See also Harold Jenkins, 'A Supplement to Sir Walter Greg's Edition of *Sir Thomas More*', *Malone Society Collections*, VI, 1962

The text of the present extract is based upon Greg's text, where it is designated Scene ix. Brooke, adopting a five-act structure, calls it Act IV, Scene i.

The plot of the play recounts More's rise and fall, with particular emphasis upon his justice and wit, and his attractive personality. This scene illustrates his hospitality, his good relations with the Lord Mayor, his witty inventiveness in the performance of the interlude, and his concern for justice even in small matters.

Sir Thomas More

*Enter Sir Thomas More, Mr Roper, and serving
men setting stooles*

MOORE Come, my good fellowes, stirre, be dilligent[1].
  Sloth is an ydle fellowe, leave him now;
  The time requires your expeditious service.
  Place me heere stooles to set the Ladyes on.
  Sonne Roper, you have given order for the banquet?
ROPER I have, my lord, and every thing is readie.
    Enter his Lady
MOORE Oh, welcome, wife! Give you direction
  How women should be plac'de; you knowe it best.
  Ffor my Lord Maior, his bretheren, and the rest,
  Let me alone; men best can order men.   10
LADY I warrant ye, my lord, all shalbe well.
  Ther's one without that stayes to speake with ye,
  And bad me tell ye that he is a player.
MOORE A player, wife? One of ye bid him come in.
    Exit one
  Nay, stirre there, fellowes; fye, ye are to slowe!
  See that your lights be in a readines;
  The banquet shalbe heere. Gods me, Madame,
  Leave my Lady Maioresse? Bothe of us from the boord?
  And my sonne Roper too? What may our guests thinke?
LADY My Lord, they are risen, and sitting by the fire.   20
MOORE Why, yet goe you and keepe them companie;
  It is not meete we should be absent bothe.
    Exit Lady
    Enter Player
  Welcome, good freend, what is your will with me?
PLAYER My Lord, my fellowes and my selfe
  Are come to tender ye our willing service,
  So please you to commaund us.
MOORE What, for a play, you meane?
  Whom doo you serve?

PLAYER My Lord Cardinalles² grace.

MOORE My Lord Cardinalls players? now trust me,
          welcome.   30
   You happen hether in a luckie time
   To pleasure me, and benefit your selves.
   The Maior of London, and some Aldermen,
   His Lady, and their wives, are my kinde guests
   This night at supper. Now, to have a play
   Before the banquet will be excellent.
   How thinke you, sonne Roper?

ROPER Twill doo well, my Lord,
   And be right pleasing pastime to your guests.

MOORE I prethee tell me, what playes have ye?   40

PLAYER Divers, my Lord: 'The Cradle of Securitie'³,
   'Hit Nayle o'th Head', 'Impacient Povertie',
   'The Play of Foure Pees', 'Dives and Lazarus',
   'Lustie Iuventus', and 'The Mariage of Witt and
          Wisedome'.

MOORE 'The Mariage of Witt and Wisedome'? That,
          my lads;
   Ile none but that; the theame is very good,
   And may maintaine a liberall argument.
   To marie Wit to Wisedome asks some cunning:
   Many have witt, that may come short of wisedome.
   Weele see how Mr Poet playes his part,   50
   And whether witt or wisedome grace his arte.
   Goe, make him drinke, and all his fellowes too,
   How manie are ye?

PLAYER Ffoure men and a boy⁴, sir.

MOORE But one boy? then I see
   Ther's but fewe women in the play.

PLAYER Three, my lord: Dame Science, Lady Vanitie,
   And Wisedome, she her selfe.

MOORE And one boy play them all? Bir Lady, hees loden⁵.

41 *Divers* several   47 *liberall* of educational value (for a gentleman)
argument theme   59 *Bir Lady* by Our Lady   *loden* loaded

369

Well, my good fellowe, get ye straite together,   60
And make ye readie with what haste ye may.
Provide their supper gainste the play be doone,
Else shall we stay our guests heere over long.
Make haste, I pray ye.
PLAYER We will, my lord.
    Exeunt Servant and Player
MOORE Where are the waytes? Goe, bid them play,
To spend the time awhile. How now, madame!
    Enter Lady
LADY My lord, th'are comming hether.
MOORE Th'are welcome. Wife, Ile tell ye one thing,
Our sporte is somewhat mended; we shall have   70
A play tonight: 'The Mariage of Witt and Wisedome',
And acted by my good Lord Cardinalles players.
How like ye that, wife?
LADY My lord, I like it well.
  See, they are comming.
    The waytes[6] *playes. Enters Lord Maior, so many*
    Aldermen as may, the Lady Maioresse in Scarlet, with
    other Ladyes and Sir Thomas Moores daughters,
    Servaunts carying lighted torches by them
MOORE Once agayne, welcome, welcome, my good
      Lord Maior,
And bretheren all, for once I was your brother[7],
And so am still in hart. It is not state
That can our loove from London seperate[8].
. . . . naught but pride.   80
But they that cast an eye still whence they came
Knowe how they rose, and how to use the same.
MAIOR My lord, you set a glosse on Londons fame
And make it happie ever by your name.
Needs must we say, when we remember Moore,
Twas he that drove rebellion from our doore,

With grave discretions, milde and gentle breath,
Sheelding a many subiects lives from death.
Oh, how our cittie is by you renownde,
And with your vertues our endevours crownde!   90

MOORE No more, my good Lord Maior: but thanks to all,
That on so short a summons you would come
To visite him that holdes your kindnesse deere.
Madame, you are not merie with my Lady Maioresse,
And these fayre Ladyes; pray ye, seate them all.
And heere, my Lord, let me appoint your place —
The rest to seate themselves. Nay, Ile wearie ye⁹;
You will not long in haste to visite me.

LADY Good madame, sit; in sooth, you shall sit heere.

MAIORESSE Good madame, pardon me; it may not be.   100

LADY In troth, Ile have it so; Ile sit heere by yee.
Good Ladyes, sit; more stooles here, hoe!

MAIORESSE It is your favour, madame, makes me thus
Presume aboove my merit.

LADY When we come to you,
Then shall you rule us, as we rule you heere.
Now must I tell ye, madame, we have a play,
To welcome ye withall: how good so ere,
That knowe not I; my lord will have it so.

MOORE Wife, hope the best; I am sure theyle doo their
        best;   110
They that would better comes not at their feaste.
My good Lord Cardinalles players, I thanke them for it,
Play us a play to lengthen out your welcome —
My good Lord Maior, and all my other freends¹⁰ —
They say it is 'The Mariage of Wit and Wisedome',
A theame of some importe, how ere it proove.
But if Arte faile, weele inche it out with loove.
What, are they readie?
        [*Enter Servant*]

SERVANT My lord, one of the players craves to speake
        with you.

---

117 *inch it out* supplement it

MOORE With me? Where is he?   120
    Enter Inclination the Vise[11], *readie*

INCL. Heere, my lord.

MOORE How now? What's the matter?

INCL. We would desire your honor but to stay a little; one of my fellowes is but run to Oagles[12] for a long beard for young Witt, and heele be heere presently.

MOORE A long beard for young Witt? Why, man, he may be without a beard till he come to mariage, for witt goes not all by the hayre[13]. When comes Witt in?

INCL. In the second scene, next to the Prologue, my   130
lord.

MOORE Why, play on till that sceane come, and by that time Witts beard will be growne, or else the fellowe returned with it. And what part plaist thou?

INCL. Inclination, the Vice, my lord.

MOORE Gramercies, now I may take the vice if I list. And wherfore hast thou that bridle in thy hand?

INCL. I must be bridled annon, my lord.

MOORE And thou beest not sadled too, it makes no matter, for then Witts inclination may gallop so fast   140
that he will outstrip wisedome, and fall to follie.

INCL. Indeed, so he does to Lady Vanitie: but we have no Follie in our play.

MOORE Then ther's no witt in't, Ile be sworne: ffollie waites on witt, as the shaddow[e] on the bodie; and where witt is ripest, there follie still is readiest. But beginne, I prethee; weele rather allowe a beardlesse Witt then witt all bearde to have no braine.

INCL. Nay, he has his apparell on too, my lord, and therfore he is the readier to enter.   150

MOORE Then, good Inclination, beginne at a venter.
    Exit Inclination
My Lord Maior, Witt lacks a beard, or else they would beginne;

134 *plaist* playest   149 *venter* risk

Ide lend him mine, but that is too thinne.
Silence, they come.

    The Trompet soundes. Enter the Prologue[14]

PRO. Now, for as much as in these latter dayes,
  Throughout the whole world in every land,
  Vice dooth encrease, and vertue decayes,
  Iniquitie having the upper hand;
  We therfore intend, good gentle audience,
  A prettie short Enterlude to play at this present,   160
  Desiring your leave and quiet silence,
  To shewe the same, as is meete and expedient.
  It is called 'The Mariage of Witt and Wisedome',
  A matter right pithie and pleasing to heare,
  Wherof in breefe we will shewe the whole summe;
  But I must begon, for Witt dooth appeare.

    Exit Prologue
    Enter Witt ruffling and Inclination the Vice

WITT In an arbour greene, asleepe where as I lay,
  The birdes sang sweetely in the midst of the day,
  I dreamed fast of mirthe and play –
  In youth is pleasure, in youthe is pleasure.   170
  Me thought I walked still to and fro,
  And from her companie I could not goe,
  But when I waked, it was not so –
  In youth is pleasure, in youth is pleasure.
  Therefore my hart is surely plight,
  Of her alone to have a sight,
  Which is my ioy and harts delight –
  In youth is pleasure, in youth is pleasure.

MOORE Marke ye, my Lord, this is Witt without a
  bearde. What will he be by that time he comes to the   180
  commoditie of a bearde?

INCL. Oh, sir, the ground is the better on which she
  dooth goe. Ffor she will make better cheere with a

---

166 *ruffling* bullying   169 *fast* fixedly   175 *plight* bound
181 *commoditie* distinction

373

little she can get then many a one can with a great
banquet of meat.

WITT And is her name Wisedome?

INCL. I, sir, a wife moste fitt
For you, my good maister, my daintie sweet Witt.

WITT To be in her companie my hart it is set:
Therfore I prethee to let us begon;   190
For unto Wisedome Witt hath inclination.

INCL. Oh, sir, she will come herselfe even annon.
Ffor I tolde her before where we would stand,
And then she sayd she would beck us with her hand.
Back with these boyes, and saucie great knaves!
          Florishing his dagger[15]
What, stand ye heere so bigge in your braves?
My dagger about your coxecombes shall walke,
If I may so much as heare ye chat or talke.

WITT But will she take paines to come for us hether?

INCL. I warrant ye; therfore you must be familiare with her   200
When she commeth in place.
You must her embrace,
Somewhat hansomely,
Least she thinke it daunger,
Because you are a straunger,
To come in your companie.

WITT I warrant thee, Inclination, I will be busie.
Oh, how Witt longs to be in Wisedomes companie!
          *Enter Lady Vanitie singing, and beckning with her
          hand*

VAN. Come hether, come hether, come hether, come:
Such cheere as I have, thou shalt have some.   210

MOORE This is Lady Vanitie, Ile holde my life.
Beware, good Witt, you take not her to wife.

INCL. What, unknowne honestie, a woord in your eare,
You shall not be gon as yet, I sweare.
          She offers to depart
Heere's none but your freends, you need not to fray;

196 *braves* fine clothes   215 *fray* fear

This young gentleman looves ye; therfore you must stay.

WITT I trust in me she will thinke no daunger,
    For I loove well the companie of fayre women:
    And though to you I am a straunger,
    Yet Witt may pleasure you now and then.   220

VAN. Who, you? Nay, you are such a holy man
    That to touche one you dare not be bolde.
    I thinke you would not kisse a young woman
    If one would give you twentie pound in golde.

WITT Yes, in good sadnesse, lady, that I would.
    I could finde in my hart to kisse you in your smock.

VAN. My back is broade enough to beare that mock.
    Ffor it hath bin tolde me many a time
    That you would be seene in no such companie as mine.

WITT Not Witt in the companie of Lady Wisedome?   230
    Oh Iove, for what doo I hether come?

INCL. Sir, she did this nothing else but to proove
    Whether a little thing would you moove
    To be angrie and frett.
    What, and if one sayd so,
    Let such trifling matters goe,
    And with a kinde kisse come out of her debt.

      Enter another player

    Is Luggins come yet with the beard?

PLAYER No, faith, he is not come. Alas, what shall we doo?

INCL. Fforsooth, we can goe no further till our fellowe   240
    Luggins come, for he plays Good Councell, and now
    he should enter to admonishe Witt that this is Lady
    Vanitie and not Lady Wisedome.

MOORE Nay, and it be no more but so, ye shall not tarie
    at a stand for that. Weele not have our play marde
    for lack of a little good councell. Till your fellowe
    come Ile give him the best councell that I can. Pardon
    me, my Lord Maior, I love to be merie[16].

        •   •   •

225 *sadnesse* seriousness   242 *admonishe* advise   245 *stand* delay
marde marred

MOORE Oh ... Witt, thou art nowe on the bowe hand[17], 250
And blindely in thine owne oppinion doost stand.
I tell thee, this naughtie lewde Inclination
Does lead thee amisse in a very straunge fashion.
This is not Wisedome, but Lady Vanitie.
Therfore list to Good Councell, and be ruled by me.

INCL. In troth, my lord, it is as right to Lugginses part
as can be. Speake, Witt.

MOORE Nay, we will not have our audience disappointed
if I can help it.

WITT Art thou Good Councell, and wilt tell me so?
Wouldst thou have Witt from Lady Wisedome to goe? 260
Thou art some deceiver, I tell thee verily,
In saying that this is Lady Vanitie.

MOORE Witt, iudge not things by the outwarde showe;
The eye oft mistakes, right well you doo knowe.
Good Councell assures thee, uppon his honestie,
That this is not Wisedome, but Lady Vanitie.
     Enter Luggins with the bearde

INCL. Oh, my lord, he is come; now we shall goe
forwarde.

MOORE Art thou come? Well, fellowe, I have holpe to
save thine honestie a little. Now, if thou canst give 270
Witt any better councell then I have done, spare not.
There, I leave him to thy mercie.
But by this time, I am sure our banquet's readie;
My Lord, and Ladyes, we will taste that first,
And then they shall begin the play againe,
Which, through the fellowes absence, and by me,
In sted of helping, hath bin hindered.
Prepare against we come. Lights there, I say!
Thus fooles oft times doo help to marre the play.
     [*Exeunt all, except the Players*[18]]

WITT Ffye, fellowe Luggins, you serve us hansomely, 280
doo ye not thinke ye?

LUG. Why, Oagle was not within, and his wife would

251 *naughtie* wicked 275 *againe* still

376

not let me have the beard; and by my troth I ran so
fast that I sweat againe.

INCL. Doo ye heare, fellowes? Would not my lord
make a rare player? Oh, he would upholde a companie
beyond all hope, better then Mason[19] among the
Kings Players. Did ye marke how extemprically he
fell to the matter, and spake Lugginses parte almoste
as it is the very booke set downe?   290

WITT Peace, doo ye knowe what ye say? My lord a
player? Let us not meddle with any such matters. Yet
I may be a little proude that my lord hath answerd
me in my parte. But come, let us goe, and be readie
to begin the play againe.

LUG. I, thats the best, for now we lack nothing.
        Enter a Serving Man[20]

MAN Wher be theis players?

ALL Heare, sir.

MAN My lord in poste is sent for to the courte,
And all the guests doo after supper parte;   300
And for he will not troble you againe,
By me, for your reward, a sends 8 angills,
With many thanks. But supp before you goe:
Yt is his will you should be farely entreatid.
Follow, I pray ye.

WITT This, Luggins, all is your neclegens:
Wanting Witts beard brought things into dislike.
For otherwies the playe had bin all seene
Wher now some curius cittisin disgraste itt,
And discommendinge ytt, all is dismiste.   310

INCL. Fore God, a sayes true. But heare ye, sirs: 8
angells, ha! My lord wold never gives 8 angells —
more, or elles for 12d: ether yt shold be 3.li, 5.li, or
tenn.li; thers 20s wantinge, suer[21].

---

288 *extemprically* without rehearsal 296 *I* aye (yes) 297 *theis*
these 299 *poste* speed 302 *a* he 304 *entreatid* entertained
309 *curius* over-critical *cittisin* citizen *disgraste* found fault
with 310 *discommendinge* disapproving of 314 *suer* sure

WITT Twenty to one, tis soe: I have a tricke – my lord
comes – stand aside.

Enter More with Attendaunts, with Purss and Mace

[MORE] In haist to Cownsell! Whats the busnes now,
That all so late his highnes sends for me?
What sekst thou, fellow?

WITT Nay, nothinge. Your lordship sent 8 angills by   320
your man, and I have lost too of them in the rishes.

[MORE] Wytt, looke to thatt. 8 angells? I did send them
tenn. [W]ho gavie yt them?

MAN I, my lord. I had no more aboute me,
But buy and buy they shall risseave the rest.

[MORE] Well, Witt, twas wieslye donne; thou plaist Witt
well endede,
Not to be thus disseavid of thy righte.
Am I a man by offis truely ordaind
Equally to devide true righte his owne,
And shall I have disseavers in my house?²²   330
Then what availes my bowntie, when such servants
Disseave the pore risseaver of what the master gives?
Goe one and pull his cote over his eares²³.
There are too manye such. Give them ther righte.
Witt, let thie fellowes thanke the; twas well dunn.
Thou now disserveste to match with Ladye Wisdome.

[Exit More with Attendants]

INCL. God a mersye, Wytt: sir, you had a maister, Sir
Thomas More, more; but now we shall have more.

LUG. God blesse him! I wold ther weare more of his
minde; a loves our qualletie. And yit hees a larnid   340
man, and knows what the world is.

CLOWN²⁴ Well, a kinde man, and more loving then
many other, but I thinke we ha mett with the first …

LUG. First served [he] his man that had our angills, and
he maye chaunce dine with Duke Homphrye²⁵

321 *rishes* rushes   325 *risseave* receive   326 *wieslye* wisely   *endede*
indeed   335 *thie* thy   340 *qualletie* fraternity (of actors)
larnid learned

tomorrow, beinge turnde away todaye. Come, lets
goe.

CLOWN And many such reward wold make us all ride,
and horsse us with the best nags in Smithfelde.

[*Exeunt*]

❧ ❧ ❧

Notes

The Pride of Life

p. 43

1. *Prologus*. Stage directions and speech headings in the manuscript were in Latin. In this edition the stage directions are translated in the Notes. The names of characters, which appeared in English in the text itself, are related as follows:

Rex, Rex Vivus: the King of Life.

Regina: Queen (Quen).

Primus Miles, Fortitudo: First Knight, Strength (Streynth).

Secundus Miles, Sanitas: Second Knight, Health (Hele).

Nuncius: Messenger (Messager, Mirth, Solas).

Episcopus: Bishop (Bicop, Bisschop).

2. *Pees*. The call for silence was a regular feature of early plays, and was probably necessary to settle the audience gathered informally around the acting area.

3. *horkynt*. This, according to Mills, is the spelling of scribe A; scribe B writes *herkenith* (line 6).

4. *weder*. weather. The play must have been written for the open air.

5. *proud*. Pride is an important theme in this play. It was commonly regarded as the first and greatest sin by medieval theologians, and as such finds an important place in moralities and interludes because of its homiletic significance. It also allowed considerable scope to the actor (cf. lines 113 ff.).

6. *stondith*. The characters probably appeared mute before the audience while Prologus described their significance. Cf. the Queen, line 41.

p. 44

7. *ne may he . . . misse*. 'and he cannot complain about or feel the want of any happiness'.

8. *bringe his bale . . . blisse*. 'make what torments him (*bale*) subject to his pleasure'.

9. *munith hir mac . . . ten*. 'has her mate constantly in mind, as far as she dares, for fear of vexing him'. She observes a proper respect for him.

p. 45

10. Having introduced the characters, Prologus now gives a sum-

mary of the plot. In some early plays (e.g. *The Castell of Perseverance*, and some mystery plays) the initial proclamation (the banns) was made some time before the performance, so as to warn the audience to be present. Here, however, the indications (especially lines 11–12 and 110) are that the performance followed closely upon the proclamation.

p. 46

11. *that al ... mit.* 'that whatever Death might do, he would not dare to come into the King's realm to try his strength upon the King'. The manuscript was apparently damaged here. This reading follows Holthausen. Waterhouse has:

[Deth did a me]ssenger than send
[Unto] the King of Lif.   (76)
[and] eny him wold do undirston
[that now] he may del and dit,
[he] wold cum into his ouin lond,
on him to kyt his mit.   (80)

12. The coming of Death had a twofold interest for medieval dramatists. It served a primary homiletic purpose by reminding the audience that all men were mortal. This is the theme of the Dance of Death, in which Death carries off people from all ranks of society. It also provided a powerful dramatic event: see *Ludus Coventriae*, XX, 'King Herod'.

13. *welle aghte al carye.* 'well may all be troubled by this!'

14. *beth togeder i-take.* 'encountered one another'.

p. 47

15. *i-kaghte* rhymes with *lafte* (line 108).

16. *place.* This is the usual word for 'stage' or 'acting area'.

17. The prayer is another conventional feature of the Prologue.

18. REX ... *dicendum.* 'The King of Life shall begin, saying this'. This first speech is a tyrant's boast, comparable to several in the mystery plays. Note the heavy alliteration, which is a common feature of such speeches (though it should also be noted that alliteration was a general poetic embellishment at this time).

p. 48

19. Lacuna. The missing portion appears to contain a dialogue between King and Queen. Brandl is probably correct in attributing lines 127–30 to the Queen.

p. 49

20. *curteyse* signified more than the modern 'courteous'. It summed up a number of knightly virtues, including loyalty, piety, courage, as well as noble and respectful attitudes towards women. Its origin lies in the conventions of Courtly Love.

21. *qwho is so gode.* 'who would be so good as to ...' (irony).

p. 50

22. *ffor bothe two thin eye.* 'for the sake of your two eyes'; probably only an asseveration (cf. line 242).

p. 51

23. *ne kepte I noghte.* 'I cared nothing for that'.

p. 52

24. *bot kinde . . . sorowe.* 'But from the time of our birth, Nature has taught you and me to weep and lament for fear of the power of death'.

25. *bothe loude and stille.* 'with persistence'.

26. *for his bothe eye.* cf. line 194.

p. 53

27. *bachelere.* man, warrior, squire (below the rank of knight).

p. 54

28. Mirth's role in the play is somewhat enigmatic. In this speech he flatters the King, drawing attention to the latter's foolish pride. At line 319 he accepts the Queen's instruction to summon the Bishop, ostensibly for the good of the King. But at line 417 he proclaims the King's challenge to Death, so bringing on the final conflict. To some extent he is a means of activating the plot, but his craftiness is sinister.

29. Berwick-upon-Tweed – chosen for its remoteness, in the far North.

p. 55

30. *Gailispire.* This has not been identified, so far as I have been able to check.

31. This earldom fell to the Crown in 1407, and the reference has been held by some editors as evidence for dating.

32. This, and the stage direction which follows, suggest that a booth with a front curtain was erected in the acting area. There is little evidence about the nature of such a booth, though the pageant

carts used for the mystery cycles and the 'scaffolds' of *The Castell of Perseverance* may give some clues. In the later development of the interlude, more formal stages were used, but it seems likely that temporary staging arrangements were often necessary.

33. *Et tunc . . . nuncio.* 'And then, with the booth closed, the Queen will say secretly to the Messenger'.

34. *of god . . . eye.* 'he has no care for God'. Cf. lines 188, 213.

p. 56

35. *Et cantat.* 'And he sings'. Messengers and Vices frequently sang in the interludes. The origin of this custom may be that many of the first professional actors were minstrels by training, but the dramatic effectiveness of song was much exploited in later interludes: see Nichol Newfangle in *Like Will to Like* (p. 352).

36. *bi-levyd:* probably 'believed', but the sense is obscure because of the lacuna which follows. The lost episode would contain Mirth's summons of the Bishop.

37. The Bishop's long speech is a sermon. It follows the contemporary custom of castigating the indulgences of the worldly, particularly in its allegorical references. Davis points out that the theme is exemplified in 'The Twelve abuses of the Age'. His emendation *geyl* (line 333) for *gocyl* (Mills) derives from this source. Dramatically the speech is interesting because it is addressed directly to the audience, so advancing the homiletic purpose of the play. At line 391 the Bishop turns his attention specifically to the King.

If the rhyme-scheme is to be consistent, line 337 should be exchanged with line 339.

38. *thes lau-is beth irerit.* 'These bad "laws" are the only ones raised.'

p. 57

39. *Slet* Davis; *Slot* MS.; *Sot* Waterhouse, for *Soth* = 'true'. The theme of the oppression of the poor has considerable importance in the literature of the time; cf. Wyclif and *Piers Plowman*.

p. 58

40. *maynpris . . . supersidias.* Legal devices such as these would not facilitate an escape from Hell.

41. *Tunc dicet regi.* 'Then he shall say to the King'.

p. 59

42. *lenust* MS., a doubtful reading; perhaps 'short-lived'.

NOTES

43. *Deth ... spar.* 'Death is not one to spare you for any reason'.

44. As lines 415–16 were written at the foot of the third column and again at the head of the fourth, there appears to be no lacuna here.

p. 60

45. *Thynk ... one othir ... son.* 'Think upon one other consolation (i.e. Christ) which you will soon feel the need of'.

46. *that mete is ffeyt and moide* MS.; *ther metis fleys and molde* Waterhouse; *thi mede is fylth on molde* Holthausen.

47. *Hic addet.* 'Here he shall add'.

p. 61

48. *Et eat platea.* 'And he will go from the place'. He probably did not disappear entirely, since he has the next speech. To walk about the acting area was often an indication of making a journey.

49. The proclamation here recalls the Prologue (line 1).

p. 62

50. The Prologue indicates that the rest of the plot contained the conflict between Life and Death, the death of the King, whose soul was carried off by the fiends, and the intercession by Our Lady on its behalf. From what is known of other moralities, one may doubt whether Christ and Our Lady actually appeared on the stage; the intercession could easily be enacted by Virtues as in *The Castell of Perseverance.*

TEXTUAL NOTE

The following list gives some of the readings by Mills not adopted here.

lines 33, 56, 135 *kyntis.*
47 *tun mit* (and munith).
58 *wyt* (Which), *bas* (bal).
68 *chont.*
73 *yam.*
81 *and* (he).
144 *feyfuli.*
174 *worth.*
206 *hen so ever.*
220 *qwherffore.*
248 *me* (may).
333 *gocyl* (Geyl).
342 *yis lan is bot irerit.*

384

343 *slot* (Slet), *blet* (beth).
353 *schanles*.
357 *far*.
360 *fot* (soth).
369 *him* (ham).
370 *daus*.
373 *derkyns*.
378 *yer* (they).
382 *pas*.
400 *thyar*.
413 *thit thou and he wer bot togidir*.
414 *irot*.
420 *thyng*.
422 *triwe*.
424 *wostoner*.
431 *thyng* (i.e. 'young', for 'kyng').
436 *tyng*.
444 *that mete is ffeyt and moide*.

Mankind

p. 67

1. *Mercy*. The play begins with the advice of Mercy, who warns Mankind against the temptations he will meet, especially Titivillus.

2. *And yf . . . lyke*. 'and if he wants compost, he may "bless" it with his excrement'.

3. *Marryde I was for colde*. 'I was perishing with cold.'

p. 68

4. *Nec . . . Dominus*. 'The Lord saveth not with sword and spear' (I Samuel 17.47).

5. *spadiibus . . . hedybus* (mock Latin). 'by spades . . . to heads'. The villains probably use scraps of Latin in mockery of priests, and of Mercy in particular.

6. *hyme that me bought*. i.e. the Redeemer.

7. *game* (cf. line 258). 'trick'; but also used for 'play' in the sense of drama.

8. *Clamant*. 'They shout.'

p. 69

9. *vene, vene*. 'come, come'.

10. *in nomine patris*. 'in the name of the Father'.

11. *one and one*. 'one after the other', referring to the threatened blows. *Ther wer on and on* Eccles.

12. The musical prelude and the shout from Titivillus (line 107) are preparations for his appearance. His appearance thus anticipated is made the excuse for a collection: *si dedero* (line 109), a Latin tag, refers to this. Note that some space is allowed in the text for the actors to collect the money (lines 110–27).

Titivillus was a devil whose function was to collect syllables lost during Mass. Later Mercy states that he 'syngnyfyth the Fend of helle'.

13. *Walsingham Wystyll*. Perhaps a pipe used at the shrine at Walsingham. The reference to Walsingham, which is in Norfolk, perhaps connects with the other place names below, lines 158–68.

p. 70

14. *He*. Titivillus.

15. *grotys*. groats, each worth fourpence.

16. *reyallys*. royals, coins worth ten shillings.

17. *Estis vos pecuniatus?* 'Have you been paid?'

18. *patus* (mock Latin). 'pate'.

19. *Ita vere, Magister*. 'Yes, indeed, Master.'

p. 71

20. *Ego . . . dominus*. 'I am the Lord of Lords.'

21. *Caveatis*. 'Have a care.'

22. *loquitur ad*. 'he speaks to'.

23. *Ego probo sic*. 'I will test him thus'.

24. *The deull . . . qwyll*. Perhaps 'thee' is omitted – 'May the Devil have you now.'

25. *Non nobis . . . .*'Not unto us, O Lord, not unto us (but unto thy name, give glory)' (Psalm 115).

26. *vii devyllys* Manly. *five vowellys* MS., perhaps a comic reference to the five wounds of Christ.

p. 72

27. *Saustone . . . Soffeham*. These villages are near Cambridge, and in Norfolk. Most of the men named have been traced (see Furnivall, p. 19, and Eccles, p. 222). The reference to these places suggests that the play was performed in the area, most probably in at least two locations. The names of local worthies would no doubt create lively interest.

28. *a noli me tangere*. 'one not to be touched'. This man was a Justice of the Peace (Eccles).

29. *in manus tuas*. 'into Thy hands' (said for the dying).

30. *qweke*. A choking sound. Lines 169 and 170 should perhaps be reversed.

31. *well ware and wethere* MS.

32. *neke-verse*. A verse of scripture which saved from hanging by benefit of clergy.

p. 73

33. *nett*. This suggests that a net, presumably for catching odd syllables at Mass, was part of his costume. Mercy has warned Mankind that Titivillus 'goth invysybull', and will 'cast a nett befor yowur eye'.

34. *In nomine . . . Sancti*. 'In the name of the Father, of the Son, and of the Holy Ghost'.

35. *Pater . . . celis*. 'Our Father, which art in heaven . . .'.

p. 74

36. The success gained by Titivillus is not only that he prevents Mankind from carrying out his due labour, but also that he interrupts his devotions. This relates to the function of Titivillus as a devil especially concerned with carelessness and misbehaviour in church. Mankind's saying his prayers out of church is also a sign of yielding to temptation. Note also the attention Titivillus pays to hiding Mankind's beads.

37. *power of Parysch*. powder of Paris, which might make brass appear to be silver in twilight.

38. *ad omnia quare*. 'whatever he may ask'.

p. 75

39. *kepe now yowur sylence*. Titivillus asks the audience to be quiet so as not to wake Mankind while he whispers lies about Mercy in his ear.

p. 76

40. *brethell*. (?) rascal. The sense would perhaps be clearer if we read *brethell, take* and assume that *brethell* is a verb: 'if your own wife plays you false, get yourself a mistress.'

Fulgens and Lucres

p. 81

1. *Intrat A dicens*. 'A enters, saying'.

2. *Non sunt loquele neque sermones*. 'There is no speech nor language where their voice is not heard' (Psalm 19.3).

3. *sprynge*. One line is missing here containing a verb, and a rhyme for *tell/damesell*.

4. *what calt*. 'whatever you call it'.

p. 82

5. *No man . . . for the maner sake*. 'No one will prevent you, unless it were necessary for the sake of fashion', i.e. no one will prevent you watching unless fashion demands it. B is speaking to A, who is doubtful whether he should watch the play.

6. *oon/Of them*. Though A and B pretend that they are not actors, they are really integral to the action, and at the same time make a great contribution to the rapport between actors and audience. The latter is a valuable indication of the professionalism demanded by this play. The joke about the actor's finery (lines 53–6) supports this.

7. *never a dell*. 'not at all'.

p. 83

8. *of counsell*. 'in the know'.

9. *No forse*. 'it does not matter'.

p. 84

10. *Perde* (a mild oath). 'by God'.

11. *dyner*. This refers to Part One of the play, which was enacted while the audience were seated for the first part of the meal.

12. *Loke whiche*. 'whichever'.

13. *impertinent*. The author does himself less than justice, for the comic subplot in Part One, which shows a contest between A and B for the favour of Lucres' maid, is a skilful anticipation of the plot in Part Two. Sixteenth-century critics argued at great length against the inclusion of comic material in serious plays: but playwrights generally ignored such strictures in practice, with great success in many instances.

p. 85

14. *almys*. alms. The phrase means 'It would be a kindness . . .'.

15. *had I . . . contynuaunce*. 'had I given an orderly account (without digression) . . .'.

p. 86

16. *One of you*. He invites one of the audience to admit the players.

17. *A man may . . . answere.* He means that no one can be bothered to open the door in spite of the vigorous knocking.

18. *I shrew my catt.* 'I curse my cat.'

19. *all be shrewyde!* (a mild oath). 'damn it all!'

20. *fayre prayde.* i.e. asked politely to return.

p. 87

21. *shrinke.* 'slink away'. Because of the long delay, he thinks some of the players may have disappeared.

22. *apoyntyth hym.* 'has decided to come'.

23. *mummynge.* The mummers wear masks (cf. *disgisyd*, line 120), and perform a dance. Mumming was traditional Christmas entertainment, and it may indicate that this play was written for Christmas.

p. 88

24. *in hand.* 'into conference'.

p. 89

25. *musc.* musk, secreted by the male musk-deer, and used as a perfume. The musk ball was probably a pomander, a case of gold or other precious material containing sweet-smelling substances.

p. 90

26. *chose he for me.* 'he may do the choosing as far as I am concerned.'

p. 93

27. *maysters:* for 'mistress'.

28. *Syrs . . . you.* He suggests that one of the audience may have picked up his paper.

29. *I shall . . . nere honde.* 'I shall come close to you' (to speak privately).

p. 94

30. *Et scalpens . . . dicat.* 'And scratching his head, he shall say after a moderate interval'.

31. *by that tyme I have spoken.* 'when I have spoken'.

32. *thappoyntement.* 'the appointment'. Similar elisions of 'the' occur in lines 458, 469, 484, 499.

p. 95

33. *bace daunce.* a slow and stately dance.

34. *I shall gyve . . . on.* 'I consent to watch it'.

35. *Spele . . . frelike.* 'Beat up drum, I bid you merrily'. The Flemish words here were probably meant as a compliment to some of the audience.

36. *Et deinde corisabunt.* 'And then they will dance.'

37. *Irissh Portyngales:* probably a fanciful description of Portuguese or Spanish dancing, thought to have influenced the Morris (Moorish) dance.

38. *Dicat Lucres.* 'Lucres will say.'

p. 96

39. *It may not be . . . precedent.* This circumspection about the judgement she will give is not surprising in view of the delicate political and social implications involved in placing the base-born above the aristocrat.

p. 97

40. *Cornelys.* the Cornelii, i.e. the patrician family named Cornelius.

41. *Thempire.* the dominions (not necessarily ruled by an emperor).

p. 98

42. *gestis of Arthur . . . Alexandyrs life.* The deeds of King Arthur and the story of Alexander the Great were source material for many medieval romances.

43. *Cipion.* Publius Cornelius Scipio Aemilianus Africanus (185–129 B.C.), who subdued Carthage to Roman rule.

44. *faders of the contrary.* Several of his ancestors had been honoured with the title *Pater patriae,* 'father of the nation'.

p. 99

45. *playest check mate.* 'cause ruin'.

p. 100

46. *an .L. £1.*

p. 101

47. *without it be . . . away.* 'except those maidens who do not mind throwing themselves away for little return'.

48. This speech is attributed to B in the original quarto.

p. 103

49. *he to wyteth me.* 'he alleges me to be'.

p. 106

50. *thopynyon of my sentence.* 'the choice I decide upon'.
51. *theffect of my desyre.* 'whether I shall accomplish my desire'.
52. *theffect of my sentence.* 'the import of my judgement'.
53. *I wot nere yet.* 'I do not yet know'.

p. 108

54. *Exit Lucres.* No exit is marked for Lucres in the original text, but she has clearly left the stage by line 831.
55. *for me.* 'as far as I am concerned'.
56. *made as an hare:* a proverbial expression (cf. mad March hares).
57. *in the mare name:* obscure, but 'mare' was used for an evil spirit (Incubus) later in the sixteenth century.

p. 110

58. *settyth a blank/By.* 'considers worth a blank' (a small French coin).
59. *konneth the thank.* 'gives you thanks'.
60. *I wot nere whan.* 'I do not know when'.

p. 111

61. *wit runnynge.* 'unrestrained invention'.

Youth

p. 116

1. *Qui . . . manet.* 'And he that dwelleth in love dwelleth in God' (I John 4.16).
2. *ye* Waley; *he* Copland. *Ye* may be the correct reading if, as seems likely, Charity is addressing the audience.
3. *A.B.C.* a spelling book or primer, which would contain simple elements of Christian doctrine, such as 'God is love' (I John 4.8).
4. *Maye singe no masse* Waley; *may not live* Copland (perhaps in deference to anti-Catholic feeling).

p. 117

5. *Abacke.* This call for room is a conventional feature of the interlude. It reflects the close proximity of the audience. The convention is also found in the mumming plays.
6. *bigge* Copland, Lambeth; *fayre* Waley.

p. 119

7. *Miserationes ... eius.* 'And his tender mercies are over all his works' (Psalm 145.9).

8. *mustarde with saltfysshe.* It was common practice to eat mustard as a sauce for fish, especially salt herring.

p. 120

9. This speech is given to Humility in the early editions, but he is not on the stage (see lines 184 and 293).

10. *Goddes faste.* 'by God's fast'.

p. 121

11. *thou wylte it rue* Copland; *I tell the true* Waley.

12. *Farewell ... :* addressed to the audience.

p. 122

13. Like other Vices, Riot is evil in a variety of ways. His name suggests two kinds of wickedness: wasteful living and dissipation (cf. Falstaff), and public violence and disorder.

14. *my lippes ... lyght:* proverbial, for foolish blindness.

15. *Newgate:* the famous medieval prison in the north-west of the City of London. It was rebuilt in 1770 and pulled down in 1902.

p. 123

16. *Tyborne.* Tyburn, near Marble Arch, used for public executions until 1783. It was customary for the condemned to speak, but Riot's speech would be outrageous.

17. *For to be ... colere.* i.e. to be hanged (for theft).

18. *cessions.* i.e. Judicial Sessions.

p. 124

19. *have adoo.* 'have done!'

20. *croked langage.* 'improper, impertinent language; abuse'.

p. 125

21. *do you servyce* Copland; *do good you servyce* Waley: perhaps 'do you good service'.

22. *fee:* probably a legal term, indicating that in return for allegiance and homage Pride would receive estates.

p. 127

23. *Intret ... Superbia.* 'Pride will enter with Lechery, and say'.

24. *nyset . . . pye.* Both words are terms of affection. The former is very rare, but it probably has licentious overtones; the latter is one of many words of affection which refer to birds, e.g. 'chicken', 'duck'.

p. 128

25. *farye* Waley; *farie* Copland: probably an error for 'fayre'.

26. *noble.* a coin worth 6s. 8d., or 10s.

27. *howe they fight.* McKerrow suggests that Youth is referring to coins in his purse rattling together; the spending on wine would separate them. But the idea of a brawl is more likely, particularly as Riot is leading Youth.

28. *so mote I the.* 'as I hope to thrive'.

p. 129

29. *Rector Chorye.* i.e. Rector chori, the choir master: often a butt in sixteenth-century literature. Dekker associates the phrase with thieves (*Works*, ed. Grosart, III, 82).

30. *Iohn-a-Pepo.* 'John who peeps' (a term of contempt).

31. *syr John:* a term of contempt for a priest.

p. 130

32. Lines 517–20 are more appropriate to Pride or Youth, commenting upon what Riot has achieved.

p. 131

33. *Beati . . . iusticiam.* 'Blessed are they which are persecuted for righteousness' sake' (Matthew 5.10).

p. 132

34. *speciall:* obscure. It usually means 'friend' or 'associate', but as Youth is boasting about his superiority we must suppose that he requires respect rather than familiar affection.

p. 133

35. *Trumpington.* a village south of Cambridge.

36. *Hogges Norton.* a village in Oxfordshire, proverbially inhabited by foolish rustics.

p. 135

37. *play at the dice. . . .* Both dicing and card playing were officially discouraged at the end of the fifteenth century, indicating that they were common amongst people of all classes.

Dicing

Queen's game depended upon the same number turning up at one throw.

Irish resembled modern backgammon.

Treygobet: 'trey' for 'three'; 'go bet' for 'go better' (*N.E.D.*): i.e. throw better than three.

Hazard. In this game the chances of a winning throw were complicated by a number of arbitrary rules.

Card Playing

Triump (spelt 'triunph' in Copland, perhaps from Italian 'triunfo'). This game, also known as 'Ruff', depended upon a trump suit, and was thus a forerunner of modern whist.

One and thirty. Every third card was dealt face upwards, the player with the highest winning the stake (the 'bone': the game was also known as 'bone-ace'). The chances of winning in this game were so remote that it was sometimes called 'the fool's game'.

Post (also known as 'post and pair'). Players received three cards, and bet upon them.

Pinion: known to be a card game, but the rules are now lost.

Aumsace ('ambsace'): both aces, the lowest possible score;

Dewsace: two ('deuce') and an ace. These two games seem to have been played with cards or dice. Both low scores were considered unlucky (see *Works of Chaucer*, ed. F. N. Robinson, 1957, p. 692, note to line 124).

Pinke: former name for a suit of cards, now diamonds. But the word may also mean 'thrust' or 'stab'.

Blanke: (?) target in archery. As the sport of archery was normally regarded as laudable, its inclusion here is surprising. One possible explanation may be gambling upon the scores.

For further information upon the games mentioned here see: H. Smith, *Festivals, Games and Amusements*, 1831; J. Strutt, *Sports and Pastimes of the People of England*, 1898; J. Brand and W. C. Hazlitt, *Popular Antiquities of Great Britain*, 1870.

38. *wyll con me thanke* (idiomatic). 'will give me thanks'.

p. 136

39. *tell me/Howe may thys be.* Dramatically this conversion is very sudden, and without motivation. It is hard to see why Youth should be persuaded by Charity at this point, having scorned him previously.

The Play of the Wether

p. 142

1. *our fathers fale.* This refers to the fall of his father, Saturn, whom he deposed in order to become the ruler of gods and men.

p. 143

2. *Saturne ... Phebus ... Eolus ... Phebe.* supernatural beings responsible, respectively, for frost, sun (Phoebus), wind, and rain (Phoebe).

3. *constellacyons.* i.e. appointed places in the universe.

4. *Hath ... entent.* 'has introduced arguments which served his purpose'.

5. *leyd in her reprovynge.* 'laid to her blame'.

p. 145

6. *Brother ... hyer:* addressed to one of the torch-bearers whom he passes as he enters through the audience.

7. *lyght ... araye.* His costume was probably reminiscent of a Fool's.

p. 146

8. *fryse.* 'frieze', a coarse woollen cloth with a nap.

p. 147

9. *We woll* Awdeley; *Well woll* Rastell.

10. *the reste.* ... Those not of high rank are to be intercepted by Mery Reporte.

11. *a fellyshyppe.* He requests them to make way for him out of fellowship.

p. 148

12. This journey is a conventional feature of the Fool's part, and is also found in the folk-play. The places named in the following lines are grouped together chiefly for reasons of alliteration, but it is notable that several of them are in Essex, where Heywood had family connections.

13. *Ynge Gyngiang Iayberd.* ... 'Inge Gynge Ioyberd Laundry' was a Manor in the parish of Butsbury, Essex, from which Heywood's brother William leased property (A. W. Reed, *Early Tudor Drama*, 1926, p. 31).

p. 149

14. *womens hornes.* This alludes to the horns of cuckoldry. Mery

Reporte works this joke to death in the next few lines. Jokes about cuckoldry are so common in sixteenth-century drama that they must have been held to be as hilarious as modern ones about mothers-in-law.

p. 150

15. *sow or twayne:* an impertinent reference to women in the audience.

p. 151

16. *Suche wether ... syde.* 'such weather that in our hunting, from time to time, we may pursue our quarry, and catch it'.

p. 152

17. *Yve.* Eve.

18. *your wyfe.* Parsons were not supposed to be married, though, as the Reformation developed, the Protestant clergy began to take wives.

p. 154

19. *shyne ... ryght.* 'be seen to be dealt with equitably'.

20. *Syo.* Chios, an island in the Aegean. Perhaps a topical allusion since international affairs made a voyage to Chios hazardous in late 1527, and impossible in 1528 (K. W. Cameron, *John Heywood's 'Play of the Wether'*, Raleigh, N. Carolina, 1941, p. 43).

21. *Ranger.* keeper of royal parks.

p. 155

22. *forestes.* woods set aside by law for hunting, with special laws and officers.

parkes. similar enclosures, without special laws and officers.

purlews (purlieus). land surrounding a forest, not included in it, but subject to its laws.

chasys. unenclosed hunting land.

23. *what be we the nere?* 'How near are we to receiving what we desire?'

24. *marke:* worth 13s. 4d.

25. *What ... shold skyl.* 'what the devil should it matter ... ?'

p. 156

26. *For gryste ... bole.* 'to pay a quart-sized bowl of corn in return for grinding one bushel.'

p. 160

27. *or* Adams; *of* Rastell.

p. 161

28. *March dust.* . . . 'It is proverbially said in England that a Peck of March Dust is worth a King's Ransom: so unfrequent is dry Weather during that Month in our Climate' (*N.E.D.*, *March*, sb². 2a, Boyle, 1685). Heywood appears to be the earliest recorded user of the proverb.

29. *pryced.* Heavy rain late in 1527 ruined crops and forced up the price of wheat.

30. *conclude the wyth reason.* 'confute you with a reason'.

p. 163

31. *a playne induccyon.* 'an obvious inference' (the water mill cannot turn if it is flooded).

32. *walke a-mayne.* 'work at full pressure'.

p. 165

33. *peckyng* refers to the pitted ('pecked') surface of the millstones, essential to grinding.

p. 166

34. *tasted:* metaphorical – the old moons have been sampled, and are now used up.

35. *Noyes flood.* Noah's flood.

p. 168

36. *Launder.* 'Laundress'.

37. *symper de cokket.* 'wanton'.

p. 169

38. *nycebyceters:* a term of contempt for affected women.

p. 171

39. *loke . . . to myche.* 'look how much I have exaggerated her importance'.

p. 172

40. *Fyrste . . . helys.* 'First say the Lord's Prayer, and then you shall cense the Sheriff with your heels' (as you are hanged).

41. *. . . the lest that can play.* This stage direction requires that the smallest possible actor take the part of the Boy.

p. 173

42. *my lorde:* a complimentary reference to the host, or perhaps to

the most important guest. This play, like *Fulgens and Lucres*, was entertainment for a feast.

p. 174

43. *Oyes.* 'hear ye', the traditional call for silence by an official making a proclamation.

p. 176

44. . . . *temperaunce.* This is the moral of the play, a plea for tolerance among different levels of society.

Wit and Science

p. 184

1. *Least . . . ye.* 'lest she suspect you of being lazy'.

p. 185

2. *strawe* (proverbial). 'worldly goods are worthless.'
3. *he* Manly; *ye* MS.
4. *cranke.* 'merry, sprightly' (Adams). The sense is probably that Wit will have cause to be confident because of the excellence of the picture.

p. 186

5. *apese* Adams; *apose* MS.
6. *most usage hath wrowht hym.* 'frequent use has made it the best way'.
7. *But . . . upon.* 'only as much as will endanger your life'.

p. 189

8. *her* Manly; *here* MS.

p. 190

9. *Here, syr. Here of* MS.
10. *stomak.* 'courage'. The stomach was thought to be the seat of the emotions.

p. 191

11. Tediousness rants like the tyrants in the mystery cycles, and his reference to Mahownde (line 213) probably derives from the same source.

12. The texts of this song, and of 'Exceedyng mesure' (lines 629 ff.) and 'Welcum myne owne' (lines 989 ff.) were written out later in the manuscript by a different scribe.

p. 192

13. *here* MS.; *hym* Manly.

14. The resurrection of Wit after his defeat by the monster Tediousness has an obvious parallel in the reviving of St George in the folk-play, where the hero is also slain by a monster, or by the Turkish Knight.

p. 195

15. *galyard.* galliard (a lively and popular dance).

16. *Declare your-selves.* Wit invites a dispute between Honest Recreation and Idleness in which they are to put their rival claims (cf. Mery Reporte and the two Millers, *Wether*, lines 546 ff.).

p. 196

17. *frame hym . . . agayne.* 'restore him'.

18. *. . . mummyng.* This attack by Idleness on Honest Recreation foreshadows the puritanical tone of much subsequent religious controversy.

p. 198

19. *Neque vox neque sensus.* 'neither voice nor feeling'.

20. At this point she blacks Wit's face (see line 819), and then calls Ignorance so as to exchange Wit's garments with the fool's.

p. 201

21. *noght.* If she has succeeded in teaching him his lesson, which is that he is ignorant, he cannot be expected to know anything at all.

22. *bak.* She is wrenching his arms out of the sleeves of his own coat in order to exchange it for Wit's.

p. 202

23. *Pyke:* perhaps from ME *picken*, adorn: 'go home in splendour'.

p. 203

24. *or be long playne.* 'without much ado'.

p. 204

25. *vyoles.* The viol is an obsolete musical instrument, having five, six, or seven strings, played with a bow.

p. 208

26. *sparlyng*. 'little fish' (a term of affection?).

p. 209

27. *naturall foole*. one born with deficient wits, causing merriment by ignorance and by the ingenuous folly of what he says and does. The 'arrogant foole' (line 791) is the fool who is intelligent enough to calculate his effects.

p. 210

28. *ther facis*. He looks at the reflections of the audience in his mirror.

29. *bable*. bauble (a stick with a bladder, carried by fools).

p. 212

30. *... but*. An erasure in MS.

31. *Wylbe ... revertyd*. 'will be the more reluctant to revive her affection'.

p. 213

32. No speaker's name in MS.

p. 214

33. *Let Studye. ...* Study and Diligence are to run away from the attack of Tediousness, while Wit lies in wait for him.

34. *Mons Pernassus*. Mount Parnassus, sacred to the worship of Apollo and the Muses.

p. 219

35. *Wyts parte*. *wyth parte* MS.

36. *ye* Manly; *you* MS.

37. *Remembreance*. There is no copy of this song anywhere in the manuscript, nor has it been traced elsewhere.

38. *quere*. 'choir', i.e. 'and after the last verse, the choir will bow and go out singing . . .'.

Respublica

p. 224

1. *policie*. This could mean wise statecraft, or ruthless, even blood-thirsty opportunism. Both senses were widely used, and this dramatist,

in common with many others, plays on them both. Respublica clearly interprets the word in the first sense at II.ii.18–24, and yet by then the audience has been reminded of the more sinister meaning, partly by the device of the disguise.

2. Avarice is an early example of 'the Vice'. This role, the leader of the group of evil characters and the principal schemer, became almost a virtuoso part as professionalism increased in the interludes of the next thirty years (see Nichol Newfangle, pp. 323 ff.).

3. The play is divided in the classical manner into Acts and Scenes. A new scene is marked when a character enters or leaves the stage, though this author is not entirely consistent (see I.iv).

4. *Of that . . . more?* This is the first of many proverbs in Avarice's part.

p. 225

5. *he . . . fetche.* 'he who has a plan to bring about what I am contriving . . .'.

6. *unchristen.* Avarice begins here to reveal his allegorical significance. This is characteristic of the Vice's first speech. Avarice is one of the Seven Deadly Sins.

7. *For who . . . brought?* 'for who is so foolish that he is willing to have made public all the evil he has committed for his own advantage?'

8. *grumle* (or *grumble*) *sede.* 'money'.

9. *make up . . . neste* (proverbial). 'make the most of my opportunities and take my profit'.

p. 226

10. *waives and straies.* 'unclaimed property'.

11. *scape of extraietes.* 'payment to avoid estreat' (fine). Several items in this list are examples of corrupt practice by lawyers. Greg has *extraictes.*

12. *purses.* The costume helps to clarify his allegorical function. The purses were real, and he has to conceal them later (I.iv.79–80).

13. *olde.* Avarice is traditionally the vice of the aged. It is Avaricia who finally corrupts the hero in *The Castell of Perseverance.*

14. *It.* i.e. 'that' (his treasure).

p. 227

15. *Intrant Cantantes.* 'enter singing'. Insolence represents conceit and self-importance. This scene shows Insolence, Oppression and Adulation in their true colours. Each exhibits his nominate vice.

16. '*his . . .*'. i.e. God's. These are oaths.

17. *so mowte I goe.* 'as I hope to thrive'.

18. *Wherefore . . . allowe?* 'what use are friends if not to advance your interests?'

p. 228

19. *Intrat Avarice.* 'Avarice enters', having made sure that his coffer is safe.

20. *We . . . catte.* Avarice repeats the excuses given by the loiterers.

p. 229

21. *have yt . . . crooke:* true of Avarice himself; the villain reveals his villainy. The comedy of the Vices largely depends upon this simple irony.

22. *catche that . . . hardely.* 'boldly grab what you can'.

23. *ait-aio . . . negat-nego.* These are ways of describing 'yes-men' and flatterers who are ready to say anything to please; *ait-aio* (Latin): 'he says yes, I say yes'; *negat-nego* (Latin): 'he says no, I say no'.

p. 231

24. This passage of clowning, depending upon rapid speech and skilful timing, suggests that the actors (boys in the first instance) had achieved a high degree of competence.

p. 232

25. *Hake. Tuffa. Hem.* These sounds are exclamatory, suggesting exhaling heavily, and clearing the throat.

p. 233

26. *thandes under the side:* obscure; perhaps a gesture suggesting boldness (Greg).

p. 235

27. *. . . box him, Ball!* He urges the 'dog' on (following *curres*, line 158).

28. *wilbe corne fedde.* i.e. will eat the best food.

p. 236

29. *Rigg.* dog's name.

30. This scene-change is unnecessary, as the characters do not leave the stage. Nevertheless the business of the following scene is a new phase in the development of the plot. The villains now assume the

aliases necessary for the deception of Respublica. The names chosen are politically significant.

p. 239

31. *have on the lips.* 'be struck on the mouth'. The connection with flattery is perhaps that the latter was considered to be smooth-tongued.

32. *against I youe call.* 'in preparation for when I call you'.

p. 240

33. This speech employs two themes important in Tudor thought and drama. The first is a development of the *Ubi sunt* theme, which laments the passing of the greatness of the past (either states or individuals), and contributes to the development of tragedy. The second is a political concept, stressing the need for good rulers who provide stability and civil order. Both themes were inherited by Elizabethan dramatists from their medieval predecessors.

34. *cogitabundus et ludibundus.* 'thinking and playing'. 'Playing' refers to Avarice's game with his purses which follows. He is so wrapped up in this by-play that he does not notice Respublica for ten lines.

p. 241

35. *Marye Masse.* Mass for the Virgin.

36. *whowe I fraie.* 'how afraid I am'.

p. 242

37. *I have ... shaken.* 'I have been cast aside as though completely rejected'.

38. Avarice's slip of the tongue is characteristic of the Vice, and serves as a reminder of his true nature (cf. II.iii.24–30). It is also comic, showing the foolish carelessness of the Vice, a development of the cosmic stupidity of the Devil.

p. 243

39. *adducens.* 'leading in'.

p. 246

40. *sifte and boulte.* 'examine matters and plan accordingly'.

41. *Cantent ... exeant.* 'They sing "Bring ye to me" and "I to ye etc.", and thus they go out'. The songs have not been traced. Magnus prints the quotation as a single title.

p. 248

42. *Benedicite.* 'Bless ye (the Lord)'.

43. *leat us ... blysse.* 'Mercy and truth are met together; Righteousness and peace have kissed each other. Truth shall spring out of the earth; And righteousness shall look down from heaven' (Psalm 85.10–11). This reconciliation of the daughters of God symbolized the establishment of the divine will, and was much used in devotional literature and the drama (see *The Macro Plays*, ed. Eccles, 1969, p. 200, note to line 312). Avarice is terrified when he hears of this (V.v.21 ff.).

p. 249

44. *appareled.* Respublica appears later (V.v.53) in her new garments, signifying the return of prosperity and the restoration of her true authority.

p. 250

45. *Geve. ...* Again Avarice mimics imaginary conversations.

46. *sibi ... sunt.* For translation see note 43.

p. 251

47. *fall backe ... a ioyncte.* 'whatever happens, I am already resolved what to do if Respublica comes to risk her limbs in a fight'.

p. 252

48. *'Salve festa dies'.* 'Hail festive day', a processional hymn, used for the dedication of churches. *York Processional* (*c.* 13th century); cf. Ovid, *Fasti*, 1.87.

49. *for me.* 'as far as I am concerned'.

p. 253

50. *honores mutant mores ... raro in meliores.* 'Honours change manners ...', and he adds bitterly 'rarely for the better'.

51. *plucke in his hornes* (like a snail).

52. *Iob.* Job was made to suffer by God to prove his faith. He successfully withstood the trial, but in a moment of despair he rejected the comforting of his friends (Job 21.34).

53. *wise man.* i.e. Solomon: 'but Justice does not shine on us' (Wisdom 1.15).

54. *prophet.* i.e. Amos: 'Ye who turn judgement to wormwood' (Amos 5.7). *Wormwood* was proverbial for its bitter taste, 'an emblem or type of what is bitter and grievous to the soul' (*O.E.D.*).

p. 254

55. *made ... carpenter weorke.* i.e. made a success for Respublica; but there is probably an ironic undertone referring to gallows or coffins.

56. *tainter hookes.* tenter hooks, used for stretching cloth: figuratively, 'the rack'.

57. *Bisshoprique.* i.e. Durham. Magnus suggests that this passage refers to the attempt of the Duke of Northumberland to dethrone Queen Mary by acquiring property in Kent and Cumberland, and by extending the power of Durham.

p. 255

58. People's dialect is based on south-western forms, possibly Hampshire or Wiltshire. It is comically ungrammatical. Among its chief features are elision of the first-person pronoun, '[i]ch[e]' for 'I'; substitution of 'v' for 'f', 'z' for 's', and 'a' for 'he'; and confusion of word-divisions. See Magnus, p. 73, where it is suggested that deliberate variations from London speech of the time are distinguishing features of this stage-dialect.

p. 256

59. *pieke me home.* (?) 'find my way home'.

p. 257

60. *Ricepuddingcakes:* a comic distortion of 'Respublica'.

61. *Choulde . . . longer.* 'I wish my lady had stayed nearby a little longer.' He sees the villains approaching.

p. 258

62. *by his . . . populorum:* a ludicrous, and probably meaningless oath.

p. 260

63. *Saincte Tronnion:* a corruption of 'the Holy Trinity'.

64. *Westminster Hale* (Hall). the Court of Justice, where the prosperity of lawyers would be much in evidence.

65. *Supersideas.* a writ staying legal proceedings; cf. *The Pride of Life,* line 380.

p. 261

66. *spittle* (from 'hospital') usually implies leprosy, as here.

67. *Veritas . . . est.* Psalm 85.11. For translation see note 43.

68. Damage to the first words in this line makes it virtually incomprehensible.

p. 262

69. *a bagg of rye.* Magnus suggests a pun on 'a bag awry', i.e. a bag of crooked deeds.

70. *Usiree.* Usury, taking money as interest on a loan, was a crime proscribed by Canon Law until the Reformation.

p. 263

71. *angell.* coin worth 10s.

72. *with the manier.* 'in the act'; cf. *The Winter's Tale*, IV. iv. 727–8 (Arden edition, note).

p. 264

73. *Nemesis:* originally the Greek goddess of retribution; used here allegorically as Correction. The Prologue draws a parallel with Queen Mary who is putting right the abuses of the previous (Protestant) reign: 'She is oure most wise and most worthie Nemesis' (Prologue, line 53).

p. 266

74. *fichaunte:* obscure. Greg suggests 'fitchant, nimble'.

p. 267

75. *by these tenne bones.* i.e. 'by these thumbs and fingers'.

p. 268

76. If this line is correctly attributed to Avarice, he must be afraid that, all having been revealed, he will now be beaten.

Apius and Virginia

p. 274

1. 'These Latin lines are full of false grammar, sense, and quantities, of which some are beyond conjecture' (Hazlitt). However, with a few corrections, the passage, which is roughly rendered in lines 11–18, may be translated: 'You who wish to ascend to the highest heavenly places, reject and abstain from both force and fraud: here no fraud helps, nor will your brave deeds support you; only your burnished faith in God will bring you there.

'You who wish to be the earthly image of pure Minerva, live, O virgin, following Virginia in brightness. And you who suffer grief shall learn great joys when the Fates prepare to cut the threads of life. "O virgin equally about to die, come here to the tomb." Thus she speaks, and her pale face is changed by death.'

The printed version (1575) reads: line 2 *chare*. 4 *trahat terse*.
5 *palludis*. 7 *Quos*. 8 *parce scinder*. 9 *paritere*. 11 *faciem*.

p. 275

2. *you maids of courtesie:* perhaps addressed to court ladies in the audience.

p. 276

3. *moyst from ayre to bow*. 'the dew to fall from the air'.
4. *Etas*. Aetas, Time (personified).

p. 277

5. *detected. detected* 1575. The lines are obscure: 'It pains me to see how Phoebus has so infected youth, and inspired lust: this is to be detested.'
6. *Virginia. Virginius* 1575.

p. 278

7. *Acteon*. Actaeon, a huntsman who came upon Diana and her nymphs bathing. He was turned into a stag and subsequently torn to pieces by his own hounds. As with most of the classical references in this play, the source for this is to be found in Ovid's *Metamorphoses*. Parts of this collection of myths were prescribed reading in schools.
8. *Pernassus*. Mount Parnassus, sacred to the Muses.

p. 279

9. *I ioy me.* .... This speech is probably meant as dangerous pride, provoking disaster.

p. 280

10. *I babe ... againe*. 'I, your babe, and I, your blessing, am health to you.' She means that there is no need for the gloomy thoughts of Virginius (lines 123–6); but the latter is meant for tragic foreboding.

p. 281

11. *Nisus*. His daughter Scylla cut off the lock of yellow hair upon which his fate depended, and so his city fell to her lover Minos.
12. *nurture. virtue* Hazlitt.
13. *Dedalus*. Daedalus, who flew from Crete with his son Icarus on wings fixed with wax. Icarus foolishly flew too near the sun (Phoebus) and the wax melted, with fatal results.
14. *persualitie*. 'partiality, strong affection'.

p. 282

15. *Who ... spoone:* proverbial. The Vice usually speaks many proverbs, and this one comes as a means of recognition on his first appearance.

16. *gowne.* He is probably wearing a long Fool's coat.

17. *brumman:* obscure. By 1637 the word 'Brummagen' (Birmingham) meant 'sham', 'counterfeit' (from counterfeit groats). But many of the items in this speech and others by the Vice are fanciful nonsense.

18. *horners.* cuckolds, wearing horns. The Vice would enjoy promoting cuckoldry.

19. *bayerd.* Bayard is the name of a magic horse given by Charlemagne to Rinaldo. Proverbially the name was given to blind recklessness, and so is appropriate to Haphazard.

20. *phippence.* 'fivepence'.

21. *trowle.* 'skip about'. At this point he breaks into a dance or caper to show how nimble he is.

But at lines 203–4 *trowle* could mean 'throw dice', associating his movement with dicing.

p. 283

22. *swet.* plague, which raged in London in 1563, according to Camden.

23. *When:* that is, 'when are you coming ... ?'

24. *Baybery insence.* berries from the bay tree. Perhaps she is seeking fame for talking so much.

25. *mampodding madge:* obscure; (?) 'woman who eats puddings'.

26. *drake-nosed.* with a turned-up nose (perhaps a broken nose from brawling).

27. *crackerope.* one who is hanged.

p. 285

28. *tayle makes buttons:* proverbial for incontinence due to vehement fear; see W. G. Smith, *The Oxford Dictionary of English Proverbs*, s.v. *breech.*

p. 288

29. *Lest wives ... straunge.* 'that wives wear the breeches and girls are unusually shy' (examples of strange behaviour which are all too frequent).

30. *Apelles.* the celebrated Greek painter, contemporary of Alexander; his most perfect picture was Venus Anadyomene.

p. 289

31. *Pigmalion*. Pygmalion, a sculptor, who fell in love with a marble statue he had made. Aphrodite turned it into a woman, whom he married.

32. *ye. he* 1575.

33. *Salmasis*. Salmacis, the nymph of a fountain in Caria, which adjoined Lycia, fell in love with Hermaphroditus, who rejected her. Embracing him, she begged the gods to make them one body, which they did.

34. *Iphis* loved Anaxarete, but was rebuffed so coldly that he hanged himself.

p. 290

35. *Iove* (Jove) visited his mistress, Io, concealed in a cloud.

36. *Inach's daughter*. Io, beloved by Jove, who turned her into a beautiful heifer to avoid the jealousy of Juno. She wandered over most of the earth pursued by Juno's gadfly.

37. *Orpheus*, with his miraculous musical powers, charmed his way into hell in an attempt to recover his dead wife Eurydice.

p. 291

38. *Some man . . . say*. 'a (false) plaintiff must summon Virginius to appear before you, and claim . . .'.

p. 294

39. *Furies*. the Gods' ministers of vengeance, who were seated round Pluto's throne in hell.

40. *Lymbo*. Limbo; here the pit of hell, Acheron, but it is a Christian conception, being the abode of the just and the innocent not fully received into the Church.

p. 295

41. *And yet . . . mine*. 'And yet, within this my kingdom, I find people that will challenge me'.

42. *Tantalus* was punished in hell with insatiable thirst.

43. *Sifsifus*. Sisyphus, who was punished in hell by being condemned to roll a stone to the summit of a hill whence it repeatedly fell down.

44. *Morpheus*. god of sleep and dreams.

45. *dewes and bewtious:* obscure; the sense seems to be that he will not obtain her unless in a dewy and beautiful sleep granted by Morpheus.

46. *If case*. 'if it be that'.

p. 296

47. *consistary.* 'consistory' (a tribunal).

48. *Subpene.* 'on pain of forfeit'.

49. *Exit.* The text marks the exit of Claudius twice, but the intention is probably that he says lines 555–7 while on his way out.

50. *Torquin.* Sextus Tarquinius, who gained access by a trick to the house of Lucretia, famous for her wifely virtues, and ravished her.

51. *By member of thy lyfe.* 'by one who is an essential part of thy life'.

p. 298

52. *sing sowsnout:* perhaps 'sing in a high-pitched tone'.

p. 299

53. *cropyng cares.* 'cares which cut down'.

p. 300

54. *cardes.* instruments with teeth, used in pairs to comb out wool.

55. *My lady . . . not knowne.* Much of this is elaborate nonsense, but Mansipula seems to have arrived late, and, while renewing rushes in the pew, to have aroused the wrath of her mistress; whereupon she diverted attention by telling some tale about the two other servants. What she alleged was not true, but it was taking a chance.

56. *And seemed . . . best.* 'and seemed to talk about general matters with everyone there'.

p. 301

57. *Ierico.* Jericho, chosen because of its remoteness (perhaps proverbial). The reference suggests the journeys often undertaken by the Vice.

p. 302

58. *Carrebd.* Charybdis, the famous whirlpool off the Italian coast.

59. *Silla.* Scylla, dangerous rocks close to Sicily, considered as the complementary danger to Charybdis.

60. *Adrice:* not identified.

61. *Laceface:* not identified. The Minotaur, half-man, half-bull, was the fruit of the unnatural love of Pasiphae, wife of Minos, for a white bull.

p. 304

62. *scaffold.* For the original performance some kind of stage must

have been erected. This seems to have been quite common in banqueting halls.

p. 305

63. *Eol.* Aeolus, king of storms and winds.
64. *craves. Did Claudius lay. craves bid Claudius stay* Hazlitt.
65. *Pluto.* king of the underworld.

p. 307

66. *Dispatch me.* .... At first Virginius asks her to kill him, but he realizes that this will not save her.

p. 309

67. *wimple.* a cloth covering the head, sides of the face, chin and neck.
68. *Atropos.* one of the three Fates; she cut the thread of life. cf. line 8.
69. *in coping:* obscure: (1) 'while you deal with him'; (2) 'in exchange' (*N.E.D. cope* v.3).

p. 310

70. *Caleco.* i.e. Calcutta (chosen because it is far distant).
71. *in hempstrid.* 'with a halter'.
72. *Carnifex.* a name for the hangman.

p. 312

73. *Caron.* Charon, the ferryman who took souls across the Styx.
74. *gorgan.* The Gorgons were mythical monsters. Anyone looking upon them was immediately turned to stone.

p. 313

75. *Sivill.* Seville (with a pun on 'civil').
76. *A Iudge ... wering.* Line 944 clearly refers to the meanness of Apius, but line 943, which seems intended to introduce it, seems corrupt.

p. 314

77. *It is ... drinke.* 'It is too bad of you to stop my drink in this dry weather by hanging me' (Hazlitt).

p. 315

78. *Tom Turners doule.* a bumpkin's lament.

p. 316

79. *Here entreth Fame.* In all probability the four actors came on

very close together, Fame preceding the other three, who carried the tomb, i.e. tombstone.

p. 317

80. The page is slightly damaged in the B.M. copy, on the left-hand corner.

81. *bringing up . . . youth.* The final speech reminds all of the need for careful nurture of the young, and of the ideal of domestic happiness.

Like Will to Like

p. 322

1. *De Amicitia.* one of Cicero's books of ethical philosophy, written c.44 B.C.

2. Many interludes at this time had a title proverb. The Vice is often the most frequent user of it, as he is in this play (see B. J. Whiting, *Proverbs in the Earlier English Drama*, Cambridge, Mass., 1938, pp. 127–30). 'Like will to like' goes back to Homer and Cicero, appears in Chaucer and Lydgate, and is to be found in sixteenth-century books which are background material for the interludes, such as S. Barclay, *The Ship of Fools*, 1509; see W. G. Smith, *The Oxford Dictionary of English Proverbs*, p. 368. The earliest appearance of the longer form used here is 'Lyke wyl to lyke as the devyl fyndeth out the colyer' (John Bale, *Apology*, c.1552). Colliers were notorious for their short measure, and so a by-word for cheating.

3. *ruffin.* The word 'ruffian' is probably analogous to *Ruffin,* the name of a fiend (1500).

p. 323

4. *Stoup.* 'stoop, bend down'. Newfangle's entry quickly establishes his knavish trickery. His name, which recalls Newguise in *Mankind,* suggests an extravagant style of costume signifying a preoccupation with fashionable novelties.

5. *angle:* a reference to part of the hall, a nook, perhaps the chimney corner.

p. 324

6. *aloof of.* 'from a distance'.

p. 325

7. *bottle-nosed.* with a nose swollen in the shape of a bottle.

8. *Lady of Walsingham*. The shrine of Our Lady at Walsingham, Norfolk, was much visited by pilgrims from its foundation in 1061 until the Dissolution.

p. 326

9. *mate*. The Collier is a good partner for the Devil because they both had black faces.

p. 327

10. *three peck*. There should be four pecks in a bushel.

p. 328

11. *gittern* (or 'cithern'). a type of guitar with wire strings.

p. 329

12. *Callis*. Calais, an English possession 1347–1558.
13. *buttons*. See note 28 on *Apius and Virginia* (line 261).
14. *if a . . . gooding*. This is alliterative near-nonsense, being merely an asseveration.

p. 330

15. *Similis similem sibi quaerit*. 'like seeks one like itself'.
16. *friers mouth:* proverbial, with reference to the alleged gluttony of friars.

p. 331

17. *pudding time*. time when puddings are to be had, i.e. time of good fortune.

p. 333

18. *teach . . . knowe*. 'teach you to know your places'.

p. 334

19. *Phalaris*. Perillus made a bull of brass for Phalaris, the tyrant of Agrigentum. Phalaris roasted Perillus and other victims in it; but he was finally subjected to the same fate himself.
20. *Haman*, like Phalaris, was hoist with his own petard. He prepared a gallows fifty cubits high for the Jew Mordecai (*Mardocneus* here), but after the intercession of Queen Esther he was condemned to be hanged there himself (Esther 3–7).

p. 335

21. *Thomas a Watrings*. Like Tyburn Hill, this was a place of execution for criminals; situated in Surrey, south-east of London.

p. 336

    22. *Salisbury Plain:* notorious as the haunt of footpads.

p. 337

    23. *Be . . . gogs nowns.* 'by God's wounds'.

p. 338

    24. *tu es nebulo.* 'you are a good-for-nothing'.
    25. *By gis.* 'by Jesus'.
    26. *white sonne* (term of endearment). 'favoured son'.

p. 339

    27. *such carpenter, such chips . . . such letice, such lips:* both proverbial, the former Heywood (1546), the latter classical.

p. 340

    28. *tost.* toast, bread browned in the fire and placed in wine or ale.

p. 341

    29. *Flaunders to Fraunce.* As these countries are contiguous, the voyage is probably a nonsense-journey.

p. 342

    30. *Iack-a-napes.* tame ape or monkey, but often used for an impertinent knave.

p. 344

    31. *two-legged mare.* the gallows.
    32. *I doo agree:* given to Cutpurse 1568, 1587.

p. 345

    33. *Tully.* Marcus Tullius Cicero (106–43 B.C.), known in England as 'Tully' for centuries.

p. 348

    34. *De Civitate Dei.* 'The City of God', written by St Augustine of Hippo (345–430).

p. 349

    35. *Venite . . . vos.* Matthew 11.38.

p. 352

    36. *Trim . . . trim.* This line has a stave of music in John Allde's edition.

NOTES

37. *noble:* worth 6s. 8d.
38. *wallet.* 'pack'; not mentioned in the stage direction.

p. 353
39. *How ... thing:* omitted 1587.
40. *sink and sice:* proverbial for setting all at risk, probably from an obsolete card game involving throws of five and six.
41. *crosse.* any coin; with a pun on 'cross oneself' (bless oneself).

p. 355
42. *horse. ... :* proverbial.

p. 356
43. *skore.* 'moment of reckoning', from 'score', the innkeeper's tally of debt.
44. *maister of fence.* 'master of sword-play'.
45. *wood knife:* the wooden dagger for which Vices were famous; cf. *dagger of lath.*

p. 357
46. *Isidorus.* Isidore of Seville (c.560–636), bishop and theologian.

p. 361
47. *Balam.* Balaam's ass saved him from being killed by the angel of the Lord. Instead of denouncing the Jews, as King Balaak wished, Balaam was inspired to prophesy the coming of Christ (Numbers 23–4). See also *The Chester Plays,* v. *Balaam and Balak.*

p. 362
48. *spittle house.* hospital for the poor, infested with lice.
49. *I must ... Spaine:* perhaps an anti-Catholic thrust; the journey to Spain and other Catholic countries is something the Vice shares with the Fool in the folk-play.

p. 363
50. *Song.* There is no division into parts, but each verse was probably sung by a different actor.

SELECTED VARIANTS IN JOHN ALLDE'S EDITION
OF 1568
line 44 wil *me* knowe.
80 of, *for* to come.

415

207 *cowes* tailes.

266 And seeing *that thou wouldst a mate* so fain have.

323 are you *not* so content.

332 the *veryer* knave.

336 your self *sir* I pray.

364 *Mardocheus*

365 first *himself* that.

394 For I Tom Tospot *doo* use.

423 Serving men *also* by me are *so* seduced.

511 to *sleep in this* chair.

520 *It* is no remedy.

529 As *cleer* as Christall.

532 by and by *I* have.

543 *snoreth*.

639 and 640 (reversed).

685 yet *to* sin.

818 Come unto *him*.

820 ego *refossilabo* vos.

824 your *sinnes* shalbe.

834 we *should* expel.

904 thrift *sirs* learn it.

932 sink and *cise*.

937 it is *now* with me.

1028 some *what* of me *or ere* I go.

1032 Take *that* of me.

Sir Thomas More

p. 368

1. The first part of this extract, up to line 296, is written in Hand S, identified as Anthony Munday. See also note 20 below.

p. 369

2. *My Lord Cardinall:* presumably Thomas Wolsey, Cardinal 1515–30.

3. '*The Cradle of Securitie*': lost; perhaps identical with another lost play *The Castle of Securitie*, c.1570.

'*Hit Nayle o'th Head*'. This is the only reference to this lost play.

'*Impacient Povertie*'. anon., ?1547. Printed 1560.

'*The Play of Foure Pees*'. John Heywood, c.1520–22. Printed 1541–7, 1549–69, and 1569.

'*Dives and Lazarus*': lost; *c.*1570.

'*Lustie Iuventus*'. R. Wever, *c.* 1547–63. Printed 1549–69 and 1548–86.

'*The Mariage of Witt and Wisedome*'. Perhaps an adaptation of John Redford's *Wit and Science*; cf. *Marriage of Wit and Science*, anon., 1569–70, and Francis Merbury, *A Marriage between Wit and Wisdom*, 1570. The lines of the interlude attempted by the actors come from none of these: see note 14 below.

4. *Ffoure men and a boy*. Though there were undoubtedly companies of this size, the doubling schemes of other plays suggest that companies of six or more were common.

5. *hees loden*. This should not be taken as proof that all the female parts in the earlier interludes were played by boys. Bevington has shown that they frequently doubled male parts, and that men also played female parts (*From 'Mankind' to Marlowe*, pp. 74–8).

p. 370

6. *waytes*. 'Waites play here' added in margin by Hand C.

7. *your brother*: probably a reference to his appointment as Sheriff, from which he had been elevated to the Chancellorship for his successful outwitting of the rebels (as shown earlier in the play).

8. *seperate*. One line is missing.

p. 371

9. *Ile wearie . . . ye*. He apologizes for his attention to etiquette, which he fears may make his guests uncomfortable.

10. *My good . . . freends*: deleted in MS.

p. 372

11. *the Vise*: usually played by the most important actor, who often acted as presenter as well. Here he is clearly the spokesman of the company.

12. *Oagle*: known as a theatrical furnisher between 1570 and 1600.

13. *witt . . . by the hayre*. i.e. it is not only the old who are wise or witty.

p. 373

14. The incomplete interlude which follows is an ingenious conflation of several plays. Part of the Prologue, lines 155–62, is taken from Thomas Ingelend's *The Disobedient Child*, *c.*1560. Witt's song, lines 167–74, comes from R. Wever's *Lusty Iuventus*, which also contains a character called Good Counsell. Inclination, the Vice,

appears in *The Triall of Treasure*, 1567, where he is bridled and led away by Just.

p. 374

15. *dagger*. Here the Vice's notorious wooden dagger is used as a means of menacing the audience in addition to its usual function of symbolizing his depravity.

p. 375

16. *merie*. This is the end of the leaf in the manuscript, and the first words of the next leaf (Fol. 17a) are obscured.

p. 376

17. *on the bowe hand*. 'wide of the mark'.
18. *Exeunt . . . Players*. *exeunt ma[nent] players* MS.

p. 377

19. *Mason* received a royal payment on 6 January 1515.
20. *Enter a Serving Man*. This stage direction is in Hand C, that of the book-keeper who worked over the play, assembling the additions and revisions, and preparing it for a performance. The rest of the extract is written by Hand B (Thomas Heywood), and the addition is marked for insertion at this point.
21. *My . . . suer*. The player means that More could be expected to give them £3, £5, or £10. If an angel was worth 10s., they have so far received £4, and the player is prepared to bet 12d. that this is £1 short.

p. 378

22. *Am I . . . house?* 'Am I, a man whose office is to secure the rights of every man, to have deceivers in my own household?'
23. *pull . . . eares*. ' "sack" him'.
24. *Clown*. This is possibly meant for the Vice.
25. *dine with Duke Homphrye:* proverbial for going without food (*N.E.D. dine* v).

Glossary

A

a he, she.

abashe be ashamed.

abhomynabull unnatural.

abought about.

abought paid for.

abroche open.

abusion law breaking.

accompted considered.

accordyd agreed.

accordynge suitable, as is appropriate.

acerteyned informed.

administer (n.) administrator, minister.

admonish advise.

advayle avail.

advise counsels.

afer, affere frighten.

affeccion, affeccyon emotion, partiality.

againe, agayne against, still.

agate on the road.

aghte was bound.

agone ago.

aie always.

al whatever.

alond along.

alyng wholly.

amaigne immediately.

amonge at this same time.

amonge commonly.

amytte allow.

an, and if.

anexed linked.

a-none at once.

anoy harm.

apace, apase quickly.

apayde, appaid rewarded, satisfied.

apparauntly for all to see.

appose cross-examine.

ar before.

araie trouble.

a-rere raise up.

argent money.

argument theme.

arow in succession.

arrand(e) arrant, downright.

artou art thou.

ascribede subjected.

aslawe slain.

assoyle solve.

assynge establish.

attemperynge moderating.

attemptates attempts.

aucto(u)rs authors, ancestors.

auncetours ancestors.

avantage booty.

avaunsyd advanced.

avawnce advance.

avent relieve.

avore before.

avoyde go away.

axe ask.

axyd asked.

aʒee easy.

B

bachelere warrior.

badge blow.

bal(e) injury, pain.

baldlich bravely.

ban curse.

ban(n)s proclamation.

bard excluded.

bargene bargain.

bas(se) kiss.

basely below proper rank.

bauderee procuring.

bayte bait.

be been.

beamestrid astride a beam.

419

becke call.
bed bade.
bedes beads.
behoof, *behouff*, *behove* advantage.
ben been.
bente devoted.
beschrew curse.
beshytten dirty.
bestes beasts.
besynes trouble.
bet better.
beth are.
bet-ith beats.
betyme soon.
betynge baiting.
be-ware be aware.
bi-lent settled.
bi-levyd believed.
bisey careful.
bit bade, told.
bi-went established
bled (n.) flower.
blench deceive.
blince cheat.
blisse bless.
blod blood.
blyne desist.
blyve quickly.
bode threaten.
bole bowl.
bolhead blockhead.
bon bone.
bonde bonds.
boote advantage.
borde board.
bore born.
borow (n.) protector.
borow(e) (v.) ransom, save, get.
bost(e) boast.
bot remedy.
bot, *but* but, unless.
botcherie clumsy work.
boun bound.
bound boon.
bourde board.
bourdened taken as a burden.

brallynge brawling.
braves in fine clothes.
breake initiate.
bred breadth.
bredynge reproach.
breke deliver.
breve(ly) brief(ly).
brit bright.
broklettes fragments.
brond(e), *brondis* sword(s).
browke break.
brunt blow.
bruted shouted.
bushed well grown.
but unless.
by-and-by nearby.
byb chatter.
by-comin descended.
byde (v.) brook.
byrlakin by Our Lady.

C

cace arrangement.
ca(i)tif villain.
cal(l)at strumpet.
can began.
cankerd corrupted.
canvesse canvas.
capax capable.
capt with a cap.
carefull full of care.
cariage load.
carye care.
cast (v.) spew.
cartely boorish.
casualties, *casweltees* casual sums
  of money, fees.
catail cattle.
cawghte obtained.
cayes keys.
cayser caesar, emperor.
cepman merchant.
chagler cackler.
cham came.
char care.

charge responsibility.
charp talk.
chave I have.
checkyng quarrelling.
cheke (n.) throttling.
chept bought and sold.
chil I will.
chise chose.
chitterlings intestines.
chive achieve.
chong(e) change.
choold I should.
chourles common men.
chout knew.
churg church.
chwas I was.
cildrin children.
cittisin citizen.
clarke, clerk(e) priest, learned man.
clogg(e) hindrance, obstacle.
clowterie shoddy work.
cognisaunce sign.
coilled beaten.
commaunde commend.
commiseracion sympathy.
commoditie, com(m)odyte distinction, respect, advantage.
commodius profitable.
common (v.) commune, discuss.
compace plan.
compacte made successful.
compare companion.
compasse compost.
complecting enfolding.
complices associates.
con learn, know.
conceyt imagination.
conditions inclinations, character.
condyscend agree.
coniecte conceive.
coniured charmed.
connynge skill, craft.
consent (n.) following.
contenance style.
contray country.
conveighed removed.

convenience suitability.
convinced convicted.
convycte (v.) conquer.
conynger more cunning.
coolys breezes.
cooste part.
coppie behaviour, pattern.
cornecles chronicles.
corpes body.
corroupt destroyed.
cors(e) body.
cost place.
cot cat.
cougell cudgell.
countrefaicte disguise.
courtnalls courtiers.
couthe knew.
cowardy cowardice.
crab apple.
crake chatter, boast.
crave beg.
creatours creatures.
credence credit.
crevise crayfish.
crum(m)es crumbs, amounts.
cry pack of hounds.
culling lugging.
cumlich handsome, beautiful.
cun repeat by heart.
cuniurd charmed.
curius over-critical.
curteyse courteous, knightly.

D

daintily carefully.
dainty fastidious, particular.
dam lady.
dangerous difficult to please.
dar dares.
dau, dauis day, days.
daunger power, risk.
dawcocke simpleton.
dawe jackdaw, dolt.
deare deer.
dede dead.
deit dead.

del act.
delful full of devils.
demisman judge.
depart separate.
derysyone scorn.
descryed revealed.
deserned discerning.
deull devil.
dever duty.
deye die.
directrie director.
discommending disapproving.
discusse conceive, describe.
disgraste found fault with.
dispice despise.
disport(is) entertainment(s).
dispyte pity.
dit do.
divers several.
do make, cause to.
doghtely bravely.
doghti brave.
doller dolour, grief.
dome judgement.
douce sweet.
dout, dowte fear.
dowgt doubt.
dradd afraid.
drawke weed.
dremit dreamed.
drivell imbecile.
drommell sleepy-head.
dronel sluggard.
druge drudge.
dryffe drive.
dur dare.
durnell darnel.
dyffyne decide.
dynge strike.
dysese (v.) disturb.
dyssever depart.

E

eche, eche a each, every.
echewhere everywhere.
echone each one.

edifye erect.
een even.
effect significance.
effectually with due care.
egally equally.
eke also.
element atmosphere.
elfe mischievous child, mischief-maker.
emended amended.
empire rule.
enbrace embrace.
endede indeed.
endyte indict.
enormytees irregularities.
entent intention.
entre entry.
entreat (v.) court.
entreatid entertained.
enveigled deceived.
envies enemies.
equyte impartiality.
er ever.
ere ear.
erme arm.
etyn eaten.
everyche every.
everychone every one.
evyne evening.
except unless.
excheates forfeits.
excyle take off.
exigent strait.
exteme estimate.
extemprically without rehearsal.
extre axle-tree.
eye fear.

F

facte(s), fackte crime(s).
faie faith.
fale many.
fallith occurs.
fande found.
fansie whim.
fantasie inclination.

fare (adv.) far.
fare (v.) proceed, go, travel.
fare (n.) fortune, luck.
fast fixedly.
faule fall.
fautys faults.
fayer fair.
fayle fall short.
fayn content.
fayne willingly.
feate purpose.
feately cleverly, skilfully.
fechys, fetches devices.
fee property.
feete fine, handsome.
fel terrible, cruel.
fend defend.
feofed legally possessed.
fer for.
fere fear.
ferre far, farther.
festinacion speed.
fet action.
fete graceful.
fethfulich faithfully.
fetred fettered.
fet(te) fetch.
ffare make out, go.
ffel skin.
ffinde reveal.
ffonde try.
fforlore, forlorne utterly lost,
   destroyed.
ficis fish (pl.).
file, filde defile, defiled.

flaterabundus flatterer.
fleece, fleecys illegal income(s).
fleete fly.
flete float.
flewte flute.
fleys flies.
fliettance flotsam.
flixe dysentery.
florent flourishing.
flour(e) flower.
flyce fleece, share.

flycinges extortions.
flyering mocking.
flyttynge on the road.
fond found.
fone foes.
foppe fool.
forbere lose.
forborne withheld.
force consider.
forceth care.
forseyde aforesaid.
formositee beauty.
forowed furrowed.
forthink regret.
foster foster nurse.
fote-mette measure.
frame (n.) device.
frame (v.) order.
frames (v.) suits, fits.
framynge planning.
fraught carry.
fray fear.
fre from.
fre (adj.) noble.
fremit stranger.
fretynge fraying.
fresshly gaily.
fretting wearing (out).
fretyth wears.
froward perverse.
fume anger.
furres thieves.
fyne conclusion.
fyrmament sky.
fyt, fit strain of music.

G

gad flee.
gainste in readiness for.
galandis gallants.
galouse gallows.
gam(e) play.
gapys stares.
gaudes tricks.
gawdies pretences.
geare: see gere.

geason scarce.

geat get.

geett get.

gere, geare matter, affair, plot.

gest fellow.

gestis deeds.

get swagger, parade.

geyl cunning.

ghostelye spiritual.

gingerlie daintily.

gingle jingle.

ginks clinks.

gird smite.

glade (v.) please.

glas mirror.

glyster enema.

gobbetes pieces.

gode good.

goddiggod God give you good day.

goddigod eve God give you good evening.

gooste spirit.

gosse god.

gostlich spiritually.

governance behaviour.

graffe branch.

gransier grandfather.

graved buried.

graven buried.

grawnt grant.

gre agree.

greace grace.

grete great.

grete (v.) weep.

greve disappoint.

grevys complaints.

grisful wretched.

grone groan.

grosseree wickedness.

grote groat.

grou grieve.

grounded established.

grue grew.

grumble sede money.

grutche complaint.

gubbins fragments.

guerdon, gwerdon reward, recompense.

guid guide.

gyglet wanton.

gys Jesus.

gyse custom.

H

hafter dodger.

hainous criminal.

hal all.

hal wholly.

hal (n.) hall.

hale drag.

hallowes saints.

ham them.

happe chance, fortune.

har, her their.

harde (n.) heart.

harde (v.) heard.

hardely truly.

hardely bravely, boldly.

harlotrie prostitution.

he they.

hei proud.

hele heal.

helmis helmets.

helys heels.

heme uncle.

hend end.

hende gracious.

hender hinder.

hennis hence.

her here.

her hear.

her their.

herbraine harebrain.

herbred hairbreadth.

herytoure heir, inheritor.

hestes instructions.

hete heat.

hevede head.

hevely gravely.

hey hurry.

hie, hye hasten.

hind end.

hit it.
ho she.
hold old.
hole whole.
hol(l)y wholly.
holydome holy relic.
hom home.
honde hand.
hoo hold, stop.
hore whore.
horkynt hearken.
hostice hostess.
hote give.
houge huge.
hourded hoarded.
hower hour.
howll-flyght twilight.
howrecop time-server.
hucking haggling.
hyder hither.

I, J

I aye (yes).
iacke-a-napes monkey.
iapes, iapys tricks.
japynge jeering.
iavel(l) rascal.
i-bor(r)e born.
ich I.
jelousie suspicion.
ientle gentle.
ieoberd, ieoparde, ieopardi risk.
iet (v.) show off.
jett, iett (n.) fashion.
jewellys testicles.
ifer together.
i-got cast.
Iisse Jesus.
i-kaghte grabbed.
i-korne, i-korre chosen.
i-liche alike.
i-lore lost.
i-mad made.
impertinent irrelevant.
imps fools.
incontinent speedy.

indyfferent, indifferent(ly) impartial(ly).
inow enough.
inquisicion inquiry.
insolence pride, presumption.
insue follow.
interleccyone conference.
ioincte limb.
ioy (v.) rejoice.
irerit raised.
i-sen seen.
isner I never.
ist is it.
i-sworne bound by oath.
i-take met.
iuell jewel.
i-wis, i-wysse indeed.

K

kane can.
kay key.
kele cool, assuage.
kempes champions.
kepte cared for.
kete brave.
keyser caesar, emperor.
keytyfs wretches.
kind(e) (n.) nature, breed, breeding.
kind(e) (adj.) natural.
kindly according to natural affection.
kith quits.
knacking beating.
knele kneel.
kneys knees.
kocko cuckoo.
kokscome coxcomb.
kornin chosen.
kuffe blow.
kye key.
kynyit consider.
kyst threw.
kyste kissed.
kyt quit.
kyxe stalk.

L

lade lad.
lafte left.
lake stream.
largely copiously.
larnid learned.
lat late.
lau(-is) law(s).
lawde laud.
lawhe laugh.
lawryel laurel.
lay strike.
laysyr leisure.
leace leash.
lease pasture.
lease (v.) destroy.
lech(e) physician.
lecuri lechery.
led(e) (n.) lead.
leddys leads.
lede people.
ledinge rule.
le(e)se lose.
leint length.
lemman, lemmon mistress.
lenger longer.
lerit learned.
lese lose.
lest least.
lesing, lesynges (n.) lie(s).
lesyst loses.
let (n.) hindrance, obstacle.
let (v.) omit, hinder, prevent, stop.
let (v.) spare.
leut ignorant.
lev believe.
lev live.
lev love.
lev(e) leave.
lever rather.
levit loved.
levynge living.
lewdly wickedly.
lewdnesse ignorance.
lewyde ignorant.
leyeth adduces.

leyser leisure.
lib live.
liberal of educational value.
licence permission.
lightly, lyghtlye easily.
likinge pleasure.
lim, lym limb.
liments lineaments.
list pleasure.
lisst liest.
lit light.
loden loaded.
lond(e) kingdom.
longeth belongs.
looce loose.
looke expect.
looke how just as.
lor doctrine.
lordlich lordly.
lore lost.
losell vagabond.
loume loin.
lovelich lovely.
lowted flowted.
loytring loitering.
lurche lurk, stay.
luste wish.
lustye pleasant.
lydger ledger.
lyfte left.
lyghtnes triviality.
lyke (v.) liken.
lyke (v.) please.
lynde lime-tree.
lynkes links of chain armour.

M

mac mate.
mace mass.
made mad.
maifay by my faith.
maister (adj.) pre-eminent.
maistri authority.
make (n.) equal, mate.
make-bate make trouble.
mall club.

mallis malice.

maner manor.

maner type.

manerly well-behaved.

manniers manners.

marde spoiled.

margerium marjoram.

marres marsh.

marryde ruined.

mashyp mastership.

mate friend.

maynpris bail.

mayntenaunce illegal support.

meanly moderately.

mecocke coward.

med(e) reward, profit.

medson medicine.

meed reward.

meere entirely.

me(e)te suitable.

mekyll great.

mell interfere.

mende renew.

mene complain.

menge mix.

menys means.

mervayle, mervell, merveyle marvel.

met may.

metall gold.

mete meat, food.

meth power.

metis food.

meve move.

meyne, meyny attendants, company.

mickle great.

mightes powers.

miriest cheer.

mit might.

mitir mitre.

moche much.

made manner.

moder adjust.

moke mock.

molde earth.

mome fool.

mone sorrow.

monyshyd admonished.

moryn plague.

most must.

mot(e) (v.) may be, might be.

mote (n.) speck.

movd urged.

mow many.

mowght (v.) might.

mucil much.

munith has in mind.

mutable changing.

myldams mill-dams.

myndes minds, wishes.

mynding intending.

myserie miserliness.

myster be needed.

myswrought done wrong.

N

nappy foaming.

nas was not.

nast has not.

nawghtie wicked.

ne not, nor.

nedes of necessity.

neere near, nearer.

ner never.

ner(e) near, nearer.

nete ox.

neuar nowhere.

ney nearly.

nie near.

nil, nel will not.

nis is not.

nobles, noblesse nobility.

nocke, noke crevice, corner.

noght not.

nold would not.

nonce, nones the once, the occasion.

nost knowest.

not(e) did not know.

note consider.

nother neither.

nou now.

nyce, nyse foolish, extravagant, elaborate.

nyfuls trivialities.
nynnat will not.

O

obey bow.
obiecte complained about.
o-bowte about.
occacion opportunity.
of off.
off of.
ofīr over.
o-gein against.
ole owl.
orīn them.
ongodely ungodly.
onis, onys once.
onlerit ignorant.
on-one at once.
onredyly with difficulty.
ons once.
openyng revealing.
or before.
or lest.
orels or else.
other or, either.
othermoe others of the same kind.
othir other.
othis oaths.
oughe owe.
oughte anything.
our hour.
overdylew dig over.

P

painted elaborated.
parate parrot.
parel(l) peril.
parnel wanton.
parson person.
pash crush.
passe (v.) care.
passe (v.) pause.
passeth surpasses.
passith leaves.
patcherie clowning.
patted struck.

paynefull careful.
peaching informing.
peake peep.
pees, pes, pesse peace.
pele peal.
percase by chance.
percell part.
perch gallows.
pere equal.
pereles without equal.
perke show off.
permouted advanced.
person parson.
persupetat precipitate.
peryshe destroy.
pestell plague.
petie petty.
petticote undergarment.
pety pity.
petying desiring.
picheree begging.
pick filch.
pie magpie.
pieke pick.
piepe peep.
pipes purses.
plaist playest.
plaste placed.
playster plaster.
plente plenty.
plight bound.
plounge plunge, fall.
ply make best use of.
plyght (v.) promise.
poke beg.
pol pool.
polytyke wise.
poppetes idols.
popt put.
porte style of living.
poste speed.
potycary apothecary.
poure power.
power powder.
powring pouring.
poynt appoint.

practise contriving.
praies preys.
pranck (adj.) adorned.
prancke (v.) dance.
pranketh forces out.
praty skilful.
prece press.
prechistou do you preach?
precit preached.
prentise apprentice.
pre(a)ste ready.
presse crowd.
presyd thronged.
pretence, pretens intention.
prevayle benefit.
prevely secretly.
price esteem.
princelest most princely.
prise value.
privy secret, thorough.
privyte private parts.
probacion proof.
proces action, judgement.
processe plot.
procys proceeding.
proling prowling.
promytt promise.
protestacyon protest, reluctance.
prowe advantage.
prowte proud.
pue pew.
pugging pulling.
purvaide provided.
purveyd sent.
pynne note, pitch.
pytfallys traps in form of a pit.

Q

qualletie fraternity.
quasse drink deeply.
quaynt cunning.
quecke choke.
que(e)ne strumpet.
quere choir.
queynes harlots.
quod said.

quycke (v.) bring to life.
qwher where, whither.
qwher-of of what.
qwho who.
qwyll while.
qwyst hush.
qwyte requite.

R

rahated reproved.
rake gather, drag.
rancke abundant.
rast rest.
rate portion, lot.
rather more quickly.
raught(e) reached.
raunge go free.
ravnyng ravening.
rayde arrayed.
recke care.
recure restore.
red(e), reade (v.) advise, consider.
rede (adj.) red.
rede (n.) advice, opinion.
redowne add.
refel dispel.
refrayne restrain.
rehersall description.
reherse repeat.
reheytynge scolding.
remede remedy.
ren run.
render accomplish.
rennis runs.
renovacion restoration.
reparacyons repairs.
repeale put right.
replication reply.
reportur narration.
repreve prove wrong.
reseyte waiting (for game).
resurging beating.
reuth pity.
reuthyless merciless.
reve deprive.
revell riotous outburst.

revelynge reviling, grumbling.
reverted turned aside.
reyne rain.
reysyth lift.
ridducke gold coin.
rife plentiful.
rift strikes.
rishes rushes.
risseave receive.
ro roe-deer.
rod(e) rood, cross.
roilled ruled.
roisters swaggerers, revellers.
ronde whisper.
ronne run.
ronner upper millstone.
roste roost.
rot root.
rotyde rotted.
rounde whole.
roundely directly.
rowte snore.
roylled ruled.
ruffe rough.
ruffling bullying.

S

sade heavily.
sadnesse seriousness.
salvegarde safeguard.
sauter psalter.
save safe, cured.
savrit savoured.
savy save.
sawe bidding, saying.
scabye scoundrel.
scaeceness poverty.
scanning judgement.
scant (n.) want.
scant (adj.) scarce.
scantely, skantely hardly, scarcely.
schend shining.
schent scolded.
scheude shown.
schreude wicked.

schyte excrete.
screu shrew.
scudde hurried.
se throne.
se sea.
sease cease.
seche seek.
se(e)ns already.
seist sayest.
seistou sayest thou.
selde seldom.
sell moment.
sely dear.
sen seen.
sente scent.
sentence, sentens judgement, decision, opinion.
sew sue.
sewer sure.
sewt(t)ers suitors.
sey tell.
seylys sails.
shambles meat market.
shape (v.) plan.
sharinges shearings.
shatter wave.
shieres shires.
shott reckoning.
shrewd severe.
shriddinges prunings.
sib relative.
sidis sides.
sig, sigge say.
sike sigh.
sikir secure.
sit sight.
sith since.
skamble scramble.
skambling quarrelling.
skerd afraid.
skeymishe squeamish.
skil fitting.
skill, skyll (v.) matter.
skip-iack fop.
skitbraind harebrained.
skowrynge scouring.

skyls (v.) matters.
slake (v.) mitigate.
slake (adj.) slack.
slakker slacker.
sledge strike.
sleye cunning.
slow slew.
smart, smert suffer.
smertli swiftly.
snatche grab.
snuffeth snorts.
so unless, as.
soles souls.
solfe to sing solfa.
solycyter advocate.
sonde message.
sondis sands.
sone soon.
sonlyght sunlight.
sooll, soolly sole, solely, fully.
soondred parted.
soon(n)e son.
sor sorrow.
sore (adj.) vigorously.
sore (n.) trouble.
sort(e) company.
sortly appropriate.
soth(e) truth.
soughte searched.
soule soul's.
sous pickles.
soverens masters.
sowterly vulgar.
soyle answer, resolve.
spaignell spaniel.
spar spare.
sparth spares.
sparye spare.
sparyng frugality.
specialities particulars.
sped (adj.) successful.
sped (v.) support.
spede (v.) thrive, fare.
spelle story.
spiede speedy.
spill(e), spyll destroy.

spittle, spyttell lazar-house.
spounge sponge.
spyndyll spindle.
squatt(ed), sqwatt(ed) squashed.
stabil firm.
staf verse.
staigh support.
stale still and strong (ale).
stale (v.) stolen.
stand delay.
stant, stont stands.
starke (adj. and adv.) utter, complete(ly), vigorous.
starve perish.
state public responsibilities.
states people of rank.
staunched dried up.
steede stead, place.
ster star.
stere stir, move.
sterne rudder, helm.
sterve die, starve.
stet clever.
stif valiant.
stile style, mode.
still continuously.
stockefishe dried cod.
stoke stock.
stones testicles.
storyde stored.
stotey cunning.
stounde time.
stowne stolen.
stowte brave.
straite immediately.
strang strange.
strawed strewn.
streyint, strynth strength.
strussioners destroyers.
stryf content.
strynth strength.
stues stews.
sturres arises.
stutter stutterer.
stynt allotted portion.
suer sure.

sufferaigne sovereign.
sufferent patient, tolerant.
supersidias writ.
sute suit.
swaynis men.
swete (adj.) sweet.
swete (v.) sweat.
swette sweated.
synde assigned.
synes signs.
synguler particular.
syns since.
sythyne since.
sytyca sciatica.

T

take, toke strike, struck.
tal tale, speech.
talente wish, desire.
tary cause to wait.
tast enjoy, use.
tayle bottom.
tayle entail.
tayll tally.
techit taught.
ten(e) vex.
tent probe.
termes clever, technical language.
than then.
thar there.
the thee.
the they.
the(e) (v.) thrive.
thede kingdom.
then than.
thie thy.
thieke that.
thies these.
thing think.
thone the one.
thorow through.
thout thought.
thowt thought.
thrall slave.
thralles troubles.
thrift fortune.

throwhe through.
thuncurable the uncurable.
thutmooste the utmost.
thwart oppose.
thyrlyth pierces.
tide occasion.
to-beten thrashed.
to-draw torn apart.
toe two.
tole toll.
tome tomb.
the ton(e) the one.
tooting prying.
to-pens twopenny pieces.
toritee authority.
tormoyle torment.
the to(o)ther the other.
tottering hanging.
toun town.
toure tower.
tourne reject.
towarde (adj.) promising.
towarde (adj.) impending.
towchyng concerning.
toyes jokes, trifles.
trace dance.
traine time.
travailer traveller.
travelles labours.
travers with cross with.
trecri treachery.
trespas wrong.
treu true.
trindill trindle.
tripth trips over.
trist trust, consolation.
tristili trustworthy.
tro trust.
troll pass.
trone throne.
trought trust.
trowght truth.
trunions, tronnions the Trinity.
trycke smart.
trycke(d) decked out.
try(de) test(ed).

tryppe error.
tryse, trysyde snatch, snatched.
twydlyng concerned with trifles.
twygg youngster.
twygge (v.) pull about.
tyde occasion.
tytyll whisper.

U

uer where.
uer (v.) were.
uey way.
undirstond consider.
universall know-all.
untyll to.

V

vade fade, tarnish.
vane absent.
var-well farewell.
vast face.
vaste fast.
vault fault.
vayleable beneficial.
venery lust.
venter venture, risk.
verai certainly.
veray, very true.
viage journey.
vildely vilely.
vinde find.
vouchesalve vouchsafe.
voyde vacant.
vvage voyage.
vyser visor.

W

wallet pack, scrip.
wan won.
wand when.
wane absent.
wannion vengeance.
war where.

ware careful.
warke work.
warnit warned.
warrant is worth.
warrantyse guarantee.
wase was.
waytes musicians.
weale origin, spring.
we(e)ne think, suppose.
wel comfort.
welde wield.
weldes wields.
wemme blemish.
wend(e) go, gone, turn about.
wende (v.) thought.
wente know, knew, think.
wepyne weapon.
werie weary.
werre war.
wete (n.) flood.
wethere whither.
weye woe.
weye road.
weyke weak.
wheale blow, sore.
whether which of the two.
where whether.
whie why.
whit small piece.
wieslye wisely.
wight person.
wights wits.
wil whim.
wincheth hesitates.
wirch exercise, carry out, do.
wit, wite find out, know,
    understand.
witeth alleges.
wittin know.
without unless.
wnelusty dull.
wode, wood mad.
wol(l) will.
woldistou do you wish?
wo-lo-wo full of sorrow.
woltou will you.

433

GLOSSARY

womanis woman's.
wondur wonderfully.
wone one.
wonschild child of plenty.
wore were.
workes painful task.
wostou you know.
wot(te) know, knows.
wrablinge gabbling.
wrake destroy.
wralling railing.
wreist annoy, accuse.
wrest twist.
wrowte worked.
wry distort.
wul(l) wool.
wyght man.
wyl wild.
wyld willed.
wyll while.
wylth wishes.
wynde go.
wyne win.
wyt learn.

wyttynge knowledge.

X
xall shall.

Y
yar ready.
ye(a)rth earth.
year(e)thlye, yerthly earthly.
yei eye.
yelpe, yilp boast.
ympe child.
ynowe enough.
yournynge journeying.
yren iron.
yrke weary.
yyng ready.

Z
ʒedge say.
ʒelousie mistrust.
ʒo so.
ʒorte group.

More about Penguins

Penguinews, which appears every month, contains details of all the new books issued by Penguins as they are published. From time to time it is supplemented by *Penguins in Print*, which is a complete list of all available books published by Penguins. (There are well over three thousand of these.)

A specimen copy of *Penguinews* will be sent to you free on request, and you can become a subscriber for the price of the postage. For a year's issues (including the complete lists) please send 30p if you live in the United Kingdom, or 60p if you live elsewhere. Just write to Dept EP, Penguin Books Ltd, Harmondsworth, Middlesex, enclosing a cheque or postal order, and your name will be added to the mailing list.

Note: *Penguinews* and *Penguins in Print* are not available in the U.S.A. or Canada

Three Elizabethan Domestic Tragedies

ARDEN OF FAVERSHAM/A YORKSHIRE TRAGEDY
A WOMAN KILLED WITH KINDNESS

EDITED BY KEITH STURGESS

Only some half dozen of the Elizabethan domestic tragedies
survive. Celebrating the unheroic passions of ordinary life, as
opposed to the fortunes of kings and princes, these plays can
be seen as the forerunners of domestic tragedies of the
eighteenth century and even of the 'kitchen-sink' dramas of
today. Their plots were generally based on true stories and
the plays provided topical and sensational entertainment,
whilst purporting to fulfil a moral purpose as 'warning'
literature.

Arden of Faversham (1592) and *A Yorkshire Tragedy*
(1608) were both based on chronicles or pamphlets describing
authentic murders and both, at one time or another, attributed to Shakespeare. *A Woman Killed with Kindness* (1603)
was the work of Thomas Heywood and has claims to be
regarded as his best play. The plot is fictional.

The Penguin English Library